DATA
WAREHOUSING

REEMA THAREJA

Assistant Professor
Department of Computer Science
Shyama Prasad Mukherjee College for Women
University of Delhi

OXFORD
UNIVERSITY PRESS

OXFORD
UNIVERSITY PRESS

Oxford University Press is a department of the University of Oxford.
It furthers the University's objective of excellence in research, scholarship,
and education by publishing worldwide. Oxford is a registered trademark of
Oxford University Press in the UK and in certain other countries.

Published in India by
Oxford University Press
22 Workspace, 2nd Floor, 1/22 Asaf Ali Road, New Delhi 110 002

ISBN-13: 978-0-19-569961-6
ISBN-10: 0-19-569961-0

Typeset in Book Antiqua
by Pee-Gee Graphics, New Delhi
Printed in India by Manipal Technologies Limited, Manipal

For product information and current price, please visit www.india.oup.com

*Dedicated to
my family
and
especially to
my uncle Mr B. L. Thareja
for his inspiration*

PREFACE

Data warehousing is one of the most heavily researched topics in computer science today. Data warehouses were developed to meet the growing demand for information analysis that could not be met by the more traditional operational systems. It is a technology that enables the organization to make use of an enterprise-wide data store to link information from diverse sources and make the information accessible to the users for strategic analysis.

Data warehouse is an architectural construct of information systems that forms the cornerstone of an organization's ability to do effective information processing, thereby enabling the discovery and analysis of trends and dependencies which would have gone unnoticed otherwise.

In principle, data warehouses are designed to satisfy the informational needs of managers and executives of an organization. Once deployed, a data warehouse provides strategic business opportunities by allowing all its users to access the corporate data without violating the security measures.

About the Book

This book has been written keeping in mind the requirements of undergraduate students of computer science and engineering and postgraduate students of computer applications. The chapters covered in this book explain what a data warehouse is all about and why there is an emerging need to adopt this technology. The book may also be useful as a reference and resource to young researchers working on information processing and related applications.

The book contains a running case study which introduces the theme of every chapter. It raises awareness of the prevailing problems in the information processing area and gives an insight into the4 benefits of adopting data warehousing technology.

Several examples have been given with the support of explanatory diagrams so that the students can get a clear picture of the underlying text. The book provides sufficient detail on recent trends and practices of information retrieval for strategic analysis.

The overall objective of this book is to provide a sound understanding of data warehousing systems and to prepare them for taking up challenging tasks in the area. An attempt has been made to acquaint the reader with the tools, techniques, applications, and the challenges existing in the area.

Content and Structure

The book is organized into 14 chapters.

Chapter 1 offers an insight into data warehousing technology and sheds light on factors that have contributed towards the adoption and popularity of this technology.

Chapter 2 defines the basic features of a data warehouse system. It also discusses important terms like data velocity, life cycle of data, and data granularity. This chapter gives a complete overview of the information delivery mechanism that is used to provide strategic information to the end-users. It also describes the vital role of metadata.

Chapter 3 discusses different kinds of architectures along with their advantages and drawbacks. It also explains what data marts are, the approach that should be followed to build them, and other related issues.

Chapter 4 focuses on the needs, importance, and different techniques that are applied to gather requirements for a data warehousing project. It also provides an insight into dimensional analysis.

Chapter 5 discusses various principles of managing a data warehousing project. It explains the importance of planning a big project and the constituents of a good project plan. Finally, the chapter also gives an insight into the selection criteria that must be applied while choosing the server, the hardware, and other tools for the upcoming environment.

Chapter 6 brings out the differences between ER modelling and dimensional modelling. It also discusses different data warehouse schema along with their pros and cons and explains those using suitable examples.

Chapter 7 covers the characteristics of the fact tables, dimension tables, and the factless fact tables. It discusses the technique that is applied to handle slowly changing as well as rapidly changing dimensions. It also explains the different techniques that can tweak the overall performance of a system.

Chapter 8 gives a detailed explanation of the data extraction, transformation and loading (ETL) process. It discusses the challenges encountered in the ETL process and the issues related to quality of data.

Chapter 9 focuses on the review of data warehouse design and testing techniques that must be used to test a new environment. It describes the ways in which a data warehouse must be monitored for growth and fine-tuning.

Chapter 10 provides a deep insight into the various aspects of online analytical processing (OLAP) technology. It describes the process of multidimensional analysis and the different models along with their pros and cons. It gives an insight into the applications and tools that are prevalent in the market.

Chapter 11 summarizes the steps that need to be followed to build a data warehouse system.

Chapters 12 and *13* introduce the data mining technology. While Chapter 12 discusses the different techniques of data mining, Chapter 13 contains a comprehensive discussion on the application areas of the data mining technology. It also discusses web mining, text mining, spatial mining, sequence mining, and temporal mining.

Finally, *Chapter 14* focuses on the trends in data warehousing technology. It covers the details about different data warehousing solutions present in the market along with their benefits and limitations. This chapter covers the intriguing aspect of how to integrate data warehousing with other technologies to gain more than what was bargained for.

Acknowledgement

Writing this textbook was a mammoth task which required a lot of help from all quarters. Fortunately, I have had the fine support of my family, friends, and the fellow members of teaching staff at the Institute of Information Technology and Management (IITM, New Delhi).

First of all, I would like to pay my sincere thanks and regards to my parents, Mr Janak Raj Thareja and Mrs Usha Thareja, who are a source of abiding inspiration and divine blessings for me. My brother, Pallav, and my sisters, Kimi and Rashi, have also been a source of tremendous energy for me. Their love and trust in me provided an exceptional boost to my writing efforts. I am especially thankful to my son, Goransh, who has been very patient and cooperative in letting me realize my dreams.

I am grateful to Dr Anjana Gossain who has taught me this subject. I am particulary indebted to Mr V. A. Eshwar, former Director of IITM; Mr Satish Jain, Dean (IT), IITM; and the wonderful library staff who had always been there to motivate me and offer their warm support in all aspects of this project.

My special thanks go to my uncle, Mr B.L. Theraja, for his inspiration and guidance in writing this book.

Finally, I wish to express my gratitude to the entire team of Oxford University Press for all their support.

Reema Thareja

CONTENTS

PART II

PART I

1

INTRODUCTION TO DATA WAREHOUSING

Learning Objectives

This chapter aims to provide an overview of the fundamental concepts of data warehousing. It endeavours to answer questions regarding the need for a data warehouse, its evolution, characteristics, and applications.

Case Study

We shall introduce a case study of a company that requires a data warehouse to ease the running of its operations. Through the decisions taken by the managers, we shall study construction, operation and management of a data warehouse. This case study shall run throughout the book.

Pallav Raj is the CEO of a large garments retail chain called JRTs. He asks one of his employees to provide him with a status report on the business as he wishes to know if the company was making an overall profit or loss. JRTs has approximately 100 stores spread throughout the country. Although this is not a difficult question to answer, the problem lies in collecting the relevant data that is spread across 100 stores.

With great difficulty, the employee contacts each and every store and asks the store managers to give a summarized figure describing whether the store is running at a profit or loss.

After obtaining 100 such figures, he calculates the cumulative result and gives it to Pallav Raj.

The problem does not end here for the employee! Pallav Raj now wants a detailed product report of the previous year as he wishes to know which products sold well and those that did not even have a marginal sale. Again the employee contacts each and every store and thus the entire process is repeated.

Such situations prevail in a non-data warehouse environment. This is where the concept of data warehouses comes into picture. In a data warehouse environment, the entire data of all the stores is stored at one place, that is, on one single computer system at the main office. In such a situation, the employee's work would have been very easy. Or rather, he would not have been required as the CEO could have himself gained access to all the data while sitting on his chair.

1.1 A SHORT HISTORICAL NOTE

Computers came into existence in 1914 and since then, the field of computer science has witnessed a tremendous growth in hardware as well as software technologies. Computers that were one day meant only for scientific applications became so widespread, that today hardly any business runs without a computer.

Information technology professionals work on computer applications as analysts, programmers, designers, developers, database administrators or project managers. Depending upon the industries in which they work, they are usually involved in applications such as order processing, general ledger inventory, in-patient billing, checking accounts, insurance claims, and so on. These applications are the lifelines of the business as they are used to run the businesses.

These applications process orders, maintain inventory, keep the accounting books, service the clients, receive payments, and process claims. The situation today is that without these computer systems, no modern business can survive. Companies started using these kinds of applications in the 1960s and now they cannot even think of running their businesses without a computer.

However, in the 1990s, businesses grew more complex with corporations spreading globally. As the competition in the market became fiercer, business executives became desperate for information to stay competitive and improve the bottom lines of their business. The operational computer systems were meant to provide information to run the day-to-day business operations, but the business executives and managers needed different kinds of information that could be readily used to make strategic decisions. For example, business executives need to know where to build the next warehouse, which product lines to expand, and which markets should be strengthened. The operational systems could not provide this strategic information to its users. Businesses, therefore, were compelled to turn to new ways of getting strategic information. This new way is called *data warehousing*.

Data warehousing is thus a new paradigm that provides strategic information to its users. In the 1990s, organizations began to achieve competitive advantages by moving into this technology. Basically, data warehousing is a comprehensive term which indicates the various activities involved in the construction, maintenance, and use of the *information oriented architecture*.

Business organizations can achieve considerable competitive advantages by analysing their historical data. This analysis can reveal certain unusual trends in sales that in turn can indicate opportunities for new business. Moreover, the analysis of past customer demands can help to forecast production needs. A data warehouse is thus an integrated collection of *enterprise-wide data*, oriented to decision making that is built to support this activity.

Data warehousing systems facilitate business executives and managers to acquire and integrate information from heterogeneous sources and to query very large databases efficiently. Building and implementing a data warehouse calls for adoption of design and implementation techniques that are strikingly different from those applied in underlying operational information systems.

1.2 INCREASING DEMAND FOR STRATEGIC INFORMATION

Before we look into the need for strategic information, let us first clarify what is meant by strategic information. Strategic information is not required for running day-to-day operations of the business and neither is it required to produce an invoice, make a shipment, settle a claim, or post a withdrawal from a bank account. Yet it is critical for the survival of the corporation in a highly competitive world as critical business decisions depend on the availability of proper strategic information in an enterprise.

Strategic information in an enterprise is meant for the executives and managers who are responsible for keeping the enterprise competitive. They need this information to make the right decisions at the right time, to formulate business strategies, establish goals, set objectives, and monitor results. Here are some examples of business objectives:

- Retain the current customers of the business.
- Add to the customer base by at least 10% over the next 3 years.
- Enhance the market share by 15% in the next 2 years.
- Launch new and better products in the market by the next year.
- Improve product quality of top five selling products.
- Increase sales in the north west region.

For making decisions about business objectives, executives and managers need different kinds of information to:

- Get detailed knowledge of the company's operations.
- Analyse how key business factors affect each other.
- Monitor how the business factors change with time.
- Compare the company's performance with that of their competitor's.

For making effective decisions the executives and managers need to focus on customer's needs and preferences, emerging technologies, sales and marketing results, and quality levels of products and services. The information needed for formulating and executing business strategies and objectives is meant for the entire organization. Such type of information is referred to as *strategic information*. Table 1.1 lists the characteristics of strategic information.

Table 1.1 Characteristics of strategic information

▪ **Integrated**	▪ Must have an overall enterprise-wide view
▪ **Data integrity**	▪ Data in all the tables must be accurate
▪ **Accessible**	▪ Easily accessible by the users with intuitive access paths
▪ **Timely**	▪ Information must be available within the stipulated time

1.2.1 The Information Crisis

The various computer applications in an organization produce a huge amount of data which keeps building up and getting stored over a period of several years. The organizations are thus faced with two astonishing facts:

- Organizations have a huge amount of data.
- Information systems that they have are ineffective at turning this into useful strategic information.

Since the past several years, companies have been accumulating tons and tons of data from their day-to-day operations. Thus, colossal amounts of data already exist and this information is said to double every 18 months. As a result, these companies have witnessed an information crises not because of lack of sufficient data, but due to the unavailability of data that is readily useful for strategic decision making.

The large quantities of data that exist within an organization are very useful for running the business operations but hardly amenable for use in making decisions about business strategies and objectives. Hence, information crises persist because of two main reasons:

- The data in a corporation resides in various disparate systems, multiple platforms, and diverse structures. But, for proper decision making on overall corporate strategies and objectives, we need information integrated from all systems.
- Data needed for making strategic decisions must be available in a format that enables executives and managers to analyse trends in order to lead their companies in the right direction. For this they need to review the data from different business viewpoints. The tremendous amounts of operational systems data cannot be readily used to spot trends.

Operational data is event driven, that is, you record the details of each and every transaction that happens. This data cannot be used to state the prevailing trend in the market. For this purpose you need to provide data from different viewpoints to the managers and executives. For example, they must be able to review sales quantities by product, salesperson, region, and customer demographics. Of course, operational data cannot be directly used for reviewing data from different angles.

1.2.2 Inability of Past Decision-support Systems

To start with the topic, let us first analyse a real time scenario that existed when the concept of a data warehouse was not present. The marketing department in a company has been concerned about the performance of a particular region as the sales numbers from the monthly report of that month are drastically low. The marketing manager wants to get some report from the IT department to analyse the performance over the past two years, product by product and compared to monthly targets. He wants to take quick strategic decisions to rectify the situation. Now, there may not be any regular reports to give to the marketing department on what they want. The IT department has to gather the data from multiple applications and start forming the report from scratch.

Sometimes, they have to get the information required for such ad hoc reports from the databases of not one but several applications, perhaps running on different platforms. What happens next? The marketing department likes the report but now they may like the report to be produced in a different form, containing some more information as illustrated in Fig. 1.1.

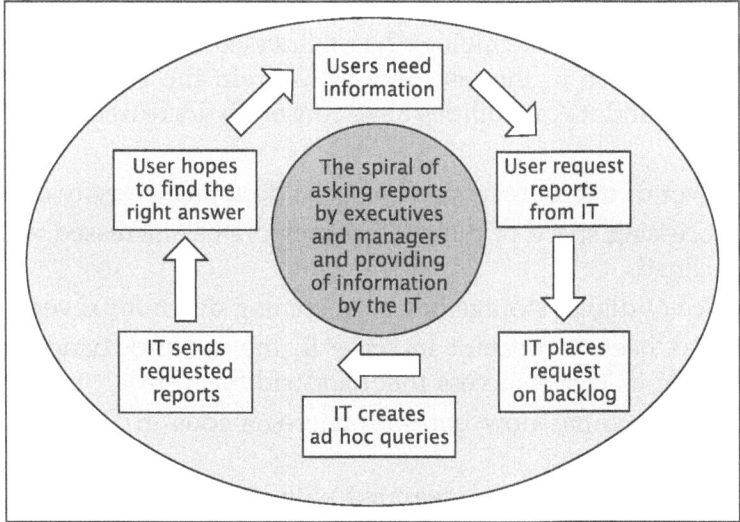

Figure 1.1 Inadequate attempts by IT to provide strategic information

Most of these attempts by IT in the past ended in failure as the users could not clearly define what they wanted in the first place. After seeing the first set of reports, they wanted more data in different formats. The chain continued. The mess was clearly due to the very nature of the process of making strategic decisions.

Information needed for making strategic decisions must be available in an interactive manner so that the users can query online, get results, and query further. The information must be in a format suitable for analysis. Hence, some factors that were responsible for the inability to provide strategic information in the past prior to data warehousing are as follows:

- IT received too many ad hoc requests for a variety of reports. But with limited resources, IT was not able to generate all the reports in the requested manner and within the assigned timeframe.

- Requests were not only numerous, but also kept changing over time with users wanting more reports subsequently to expand and understand earlier reports.

- The users indulged themselves into the spiral of asking for more and more supplementary reports thereby increasing the IT load even further.
- The users depended on IT to provide the information as they could not access the information directly in an interactive manner.
- As a result, IT was unable to provide an environment for flexible and conducive analysis to the managers and executives for making strategic decisions.

1.2.3 Presence of Better Technology

The field of information technology has witnessed the breathtaking changes that have taken place in the last decade wherein the IT infrastructure has changed rapidly and its capabilities have constantly increased as evidenced by the following:

- The power of microprocessors has been doubling every two years.
- The processing speed of the microprocessors has increased while its cost has declined.
- The price of digital storage has been coming down for several years.
- There has been a constant increase in the network bandwidth and a decrease in its cost to access that bandwidth.
- The workplace has now become heterogeneous in terms of hardware and software.
- Legacy systems are now integrated with new applications.

Also hardware economics and miniaturization allow a workstation on every desk and provide increasing power at reducing costs. New software provides user friendly systems. Improved connectivity, networking, and the internet open up interaction with an enormous number of systems and databases. All of these improvements in technology are meritorious as they have made computing faster, cheaper, and widely available.

To provide strategic information a large collection of corporate data stored in suitable formats is required. Technology advances in data storage and reduction in storage costs fulfils the data storage needs for strategic decision-support systems. Executives, managers, and business analysts use strategic information to analyse data and spot prevailing trends. The user does the analysis in an interactive manner by asking a question and getting the results then asking another question, looking at the results to ask yet another question. Tremendous advances in interface software make such *interactive analysis* possible.

Processing huge volumes of data and providing interactive analysis demands massive computing power. The tremendous increase in the computing power and its lower costs has made strategic information feasible and thus we can think of a new system that provides the users with this type of information.

1.2.4 Expectations from the Decision-support System

We need a different type of decision-support system to provide strategic information that is different from available operational systems. We need a new type of system environment for the purpose of providing strategic information for analysis, discerning trends, and monitoring performance. The advantages of this type of system environment designed for strategic information are:

- Database designed for analysing large volumes of data.
- Data extracted from multiple applications.
- User friendliness.
- Intuitive to use for long interactive sessions by users.
- Containing read intensive data usage that is stable in nature.
- Enables easy usage of the system by the users without assistance from IT professionals.
- Periodically updating of data content.
- Contain current as well as historical data.
- Ability for users to formulate and execute queries and get results online.

1.2.5 Operational vs. Decision-support System

Table 1.2 given below summarizes the differences between the two systems–the current operational system and the needed decision-support system.

Table 1.2   Operational versus decision-support system

Attributes	Operational Systems	Decision-support System
Data content	Current values	Archived, summarized, derived
Data structure	Optimized for transactions	Optimized for complex queries
Access frequency	High	Medium to low
Access type	Read, update, delete	Read
Usage	Predictive, repetitive	Ad hoc, random
Response time	Sub-seconds	Several seconds to minutes
User number	Large numbers	Relatively small number
Characteristic	Operational processing	Informational processing
Orientation	Transaction	Analysis
Users	Clerk, DBA, database professional	Executives, managers, business executives
Function	Day-to-day operations	Long-term informational requirements, decision support
Database design	ER based, application oriented	Star/snowflake, subject oriented
Summarization	Primitive, highly detailed	Summarized, consolidated
View	Detailed, flat relational	Summarized, multidimensional
Unit of work	Short, simple transaction	Complex query
Records accessed	Tens	Millions

Table 1.2 Continued

Table 1.2 Continued

Attributes	Operational Systems	Decision-support System
Database size	100 MB to GB	100 GB to TB
Priority	High performance, high availability	High flexibility, end-user autonomy
Indexes	Few	Many
Joins	Many	Some
Duplicated data	Normalized DBMS	Denomalized DBMS
Derived data and aggragates	Rare	Common

In the data warehouse model, operational systems are not accessed directly to perform information processing. But still they play a key role by acting as the source of data for the data warehouse. The users will use this data warehouse which is the information repository and point of access for information processing.

1.3 DATA WAREHOUSE DEFINED

Data warehouses were developed to meet the growing demand for information analysis that could not be met by operational systems for a range of reasons:

- The processing load of reporting affected the response time of the operational systems.
- The database designs of operational systems were not optimized for information analysis and strategic decision making.
- Generally all big organizations had a number of operational systems so enterprise-wide reporting could not be supported from a single system.

As a result, separate databases were built that were specifically designed to support management information and analysis purposes. Data warehouses collected data from a range of different data sources, such as mainframe computers, minicomputers, as well as personal computers and office automation software such as spreadsheet, and integrate this information in a single place. The bottomline of success of such type of databases is its capability, coupled with user-friendly reporting tools and freedom from operational impacts.

The data warehouse enables the organization to make use of an enterprise-wide data store to link information from diverse sources and make the information accessible to the users for strategic analysis. Here the term strategic analysis is a comprehensive term that includes trend analysis, forecasting, competitive analysis, and targeted market research.

The data warehouse is thus an informational environment which does the following:

- provides an integrated view of the enterprise.
- renders the enterprise's current as well as historical data readily available for making strategic decisions.
- makes decision making possible without hindering operational systems.
- makes the organization's information consistent and easily accessible.
- provides a flexible, conducive and interactive source of strategic information.

1.3.1 What Can a Data Warehouse Do?

In this section, we will study about the capabilities of a data warehouse. So let us have a look at what a data warehouse can do.

Immediate information delivery   Data warehouses reduces the time period lapsed between the request for information and the actual delivery of information to the users. For example, the sales report was formed once in every month, usually in the first week of every month. But with data warehouses the same report can be formulated on a daily basis thereby enabling the business analysts to exploit opportunities that could otherwise have been raised.

Integration of data from within and outside the organization   Data warehouses combine data from multiple sources. The data is collected from different departments like sales, marketing, finance, and accounting. Besides this, data is also taken from external sources like business magazines, news reports, survey's etc.

Provides an insight into the future   Data warehouses store large amounts of historical information that enables the decision makers to analyse the prevailing trends in the market and produce goods according to the customers demands.

Enables users to look at the same data in different ways   A data warehouse provides its users with tools for analysing and manipulating data in many different ways. It facilitates the users to drill down into detailed data with the click of a mouse that could have otherwise taken a few days with the traditional approach.

Provides freedom from the dependency on IT   With data warehouses, the users have to no longer depend on the availability of IT professionals to answer their queries. Now, if the manager needs an ad hoc report, he can himself form it without the assistance of any computer guru.

Table 1.3 illustrates how a data warehouse can help its users to analyse sales.

Table 1.3 Sales analysis by a data warehouse

Sales Analysis
▪ Determine sales to take vital decisions regarding price and distribution.
▪ Determine the success and failure attributes by studying the historical sales data.
▪ Determine successful products and learn about their key success factors.
▪ Understand the profits as well as revenue implications of a decision.
▪ Identify the most promising customers.
▪ Identify customers who are no longer loyal to the organization.
▪ Identify the salesperson that have performed extremely well and those who could not work to fulfill their expectations.

1.3.2 What Can a Data Warehouse Not Do?

A data warehouse is not a magical box; it does have some limitations. It acts as an information repository that collects and reports data that already exists. It cannot create additional data on its own. For example, if a manager wants to analyse the sales of a product based on customer's income level, and if the income of the customer is not captured by the source systems, then the data warehouse will not be able to help the users in any way until and unless a mechanism is devised to gather the income data.

Apart from this, if an organization has dirty data in the source systems, the data warehouse will not be able to correct results until and unless the data is first cleaned. In this context, a data warehouse will only be able to identify where the problem exists, but corrections will have to be made in the source systems that capture that data.

1.3.3 Data Warehouse—An Environment or a Product?

A data warehouse is a user centric environment that enables its users to use the data stored in it directly for making strategic decisions. To consider it as a part of either a software or hardware product that can be purchased from the market to provide strategic information is not correct. Rather, it is an overall strategy, or process, for building decision support systems, a knowledge-based applications architecture and an environment that supports long-term decision making.

It is an architectural construct of information systems that provides users with current and historical information to support strategic decisions that are otherwise hard to access or present in traditional operational data stores. In fact, the data warehouse is a cornerstone of the organization's ability to do effective information processing that thereby enables the discovery and analysis of trends and dependencies that otherwise would have gone unnoticed.

In principle, data warehouses are designed to satisfy the informational needs of managers and executives. A data warehouse once deployed is meant to provide strategic business opportunities by allowing all its users to access the corporate data without violating the security measures. The characteristics of this new computing environment called the data warehouse are:

- An ideal environment for data analysis and decision making.
- Flexible, intuitive, and interactive.
- User friendly.
- Conducive and responsive to formulate and execute interactive queries.
- Enables the users to discover answers to complex queries.

1.3.4 A Blend of Many Technologies

The key reason for the implementation of a data warehouse is to bring together information from disparate sources and put the information into a format that is conducive for making business decisions. This calls for a set of activities that are far more complex than just collecting data and reporting against it (Refer Fig. 1.2). Data warehousing requires both business and technical expertise and involves the following activities:

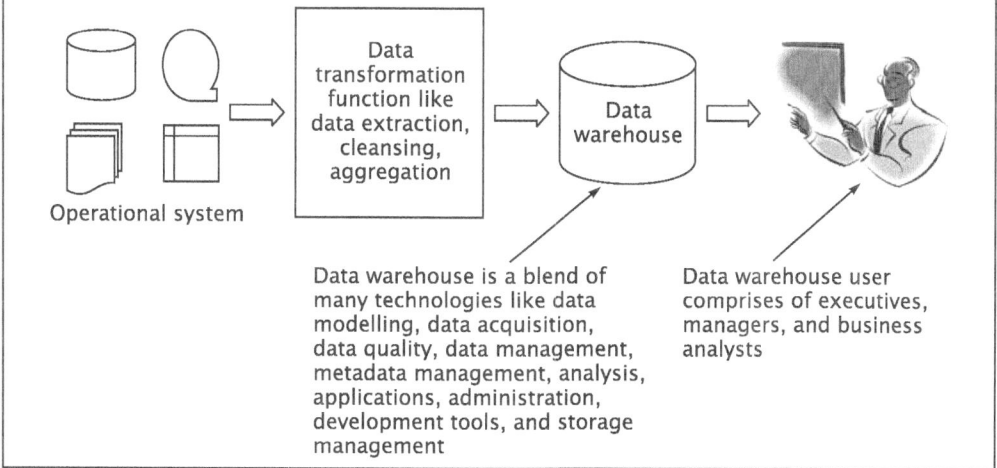

Figure 1.2 Data warehousing is a blend of many technologies

- Accurate identification of business information that must be stored in the warehouse.
- Identification and prioritization of subject areas to be included in it.
- Defining the scope of each subject area.
- Development of a scaleable architecture.
- Selection of the hardware/software/middleware components needed.

- Extracting, cleansing, aggregating, transforming, and validating the data to ensure accuracy and consistency.
- Providing user-friendly, powerful tools to the users with which they can gain access to the data warehouse.
- Giving adequate training to the users.
- Establishing a data warehouse helpdesk to support the users in their day-to-day tasks.
- Establishing procedures for maintenance and enhancement of the data warehouse.

Thus, the basic operations of data warehousing are to:

- Extract data from the operational systems.
- Include relevant data from outside sources like magazines, journals, reports of other organizations in the same industry.
- Remove inconsistencies and transform and clean the data.
- Store the data in such a way so that it is for easy access for decision making.

Although data warehousing seems to be a simple concept, it however involves different functions like data extraction, data loading, transforming, storing the data, and providing user interfaces. Table 1.4 shows various uses of a data warehouse system.

Table 1.4 Applications of a data warehouse system

Industry	Applications
Retail	Customer loyalty, targeted marketing
Financial and banking	Risk management, fraud detection
Airlines	Route profitability, promotional schemes
Manufacturing	Cost reduction, resource management
Government	Manpower planning, development, and cost control

Other application areas include: insurance companies, utilities providers, health care providers, financial services companies, telecommunications service providers, travel, transport and tourism companies, security agencies, logistic, inventory, and purchasing.

1.4 DATA WAREHOUSE USERS

A data warehouse is primarily designed to support executives, senior managers, and business analysts in making complex business decisions. They provide the business users with access to accurate, consolidated information from various internal and external sources.

The ideal data warehouse users are the people who can be described by characteristics as given here.

- People whose job involves analysing data to draw meaningful conclusions and make decisions based on large masses of data without the need to organize the data for this purpose.
- Those who are not supposed to access the database in a highly technical fashion to find the desired information.
- Those whose decisions have enough value in terms of enhanced productivity, increased sales, better quality of products, targeted advertising, etc. to the organization to justify the data warehousing effort.

A data warehouse is a high level solution for making strategic decisions and is not meant to be used by every user in the organization. That is, a data warehouse is not the universal solution to all types of business's information needs. The users of the data warehouse include executives, senior managers, CEOs, business analysts, and some high level computer professionals. Now after having a look at the people who need to access the data warehouse, let us also study which are the people who do not need to have a data warehouse.

- People whose job involves dealing with individual data records (daily transactions).
- Anyone whose job includes updating the organizational database, not just looking at what data is already stored in it. These users may need an operational database for the purpose and not the data warehouse.

Therefore, we see that, anyone who needs strategic information is expected to be a part of the group of users of the data warehouse. The user group includes business analysts, business planners, managers, and senior executives. Every group of users has specific business needs for which they expect to get answers from the data warehouse. It is always better to classify the user groups depending on what information they expect from the warehouse. Every user is supposed to perform a particular business function and needs information to support that function.

In order to make the information delivery mechanism best suited for the data warehouse environment, you need to have a good understanding of the classes of users (Refer Fig. 1.3). We will classify the users based upon two perspectives—their computing proficiency and their job function.

Casual or novice user   Uses the data warehouse occasionally and needs a very intuitive information interface.

Regular user   Uses the data warehouse almost daily. These users are comfortable with computing options but cannot create reports and queries on their own and thus make use of query templates and predefined reports.

Power user   These users are well versed and highly proficient with the technology. They are capable of creating reports and executing queries on their own and can even write macros and scripts for their applications.

Users can also be classified based upon their job functions as below:

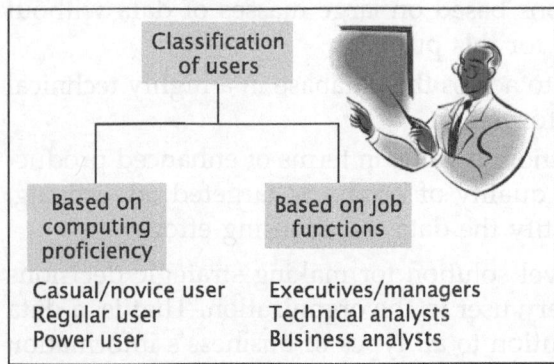

Figure 1.3   Data warehouse users classification

Executives and managers   They need information for making high level strategic decisions. They prefer customized and personalized reports.

Technical analysts   They perform complex analysis and statistical analysis, perform drill-down, roll-up, slice and dice operations on the data.

Business analysts   Although these users are comfortable with the technology, they may not be able to write queries and create reports from scratch. So, they rely on predefined queries and reports to satisfy their information needs.

1.4.1   Why Do They Want Information?

Any organization that has implemented data warehousing can exploit the extensive data stored in it for activities like planning, execution, and assessment of results. The data warehouse can assist in planning for a market expansion and in the assessment of the results of the execution of marketing campaigns for that purpose. We will go through a few general areas of the enterprise where the data warehouse can be useful in the planning and assessment phases of the management loop.

Profitability growth   To increase profits of the business, the managers and executives need to understand the underlying relationship that exists between profit and product categories, markets and services. For this managers must know which products and markets produce greater profits. The information from the data warehouse provides support to plan for profitability, growth, and to assess the results when plans are executed.

Strategic marketing   Strategic marketing guides the process of business growth. The data warehouse offers great information potential for strategic marketing by providing the users with information regarding up-selling and cross-selling to its existing customers and for expanding the customer base.

Customer relationship management   The data warehouse contains all the information about the customers that is extracted from various disparate source systems, transformed and integrated. This provides an opportunity to the executives and managers to learn their customers individually from the information available in the data warehouse and thus create better relations with them.

Corporate purchasing   The data warehouse contains corporate-wide information about the different vendors' and the customers' purchasing patterns. So, the data warehouse can easily empower the corporate management to plan for streamlining purchasing process.

For these purposes, the end-users try to find information in two distinct modes.

Verification mode   In this mode, the data warehouse user proposes a hypothesis and then asks a series of questions to either confirm or repudiate it. Consider, that the marketing department has launched a new product in the market. Now the marketing department wants to assess the sales of the product. So, the marketing department goes to the data warehouse with the hypothesis that the product has a tremendous sale in the market. The information from the data warehouse will help confirm the validity of this hypothesis.

In this mode, the users can retrieve historical as well as current data and perform statistical analysis using query and reporting tools. The results may either be in the form of reports or charts. The users may also use complex operations like roll-up, drill-down slice, dice, and pivot. We will learn about all these operations in the coming chapters.

Discovery mode   In this mode, the user does not use a predefined hypothesis. Rather, he attempts to discover patterns of customer behaviour and relationships among the products that sell together. We will learn more about this mode in Chapter 12. Basically, in this mode the user does not have any preconceived notions of the result sets.

To cater to the needs of different users, the user-information interface must have the following features.

- Be easy to use, intuitive, and enticing to the users thereby being very user friendly.
- Support the ability to express business needs clearly in the form of rules.
- Be linked with metadata (data about data, similar to data dictionary).
- Be capable of formatting and structuring output in a variety of ways, both textual and graphical.

1.5 BENEFITS OF DATA WAREHOUSING

There are many benefits in using a data warehouse, some of which are:

- Data warehouses enable end-users to access a wide variety of data.
- Business analysts and decision makers can analyse the current trends in the market to predict future trends for example the analyst can analyse the products sales to find the item with maximum sales in a particular area for the last two years. This may be helpful for future investments in a particular item.

- Data warehouse provides consistent data.
- It helps to increase productivity and decrease computing costs.
- Data warehouses contain data that has been integrated from a number of different sources.
- The results obtained can be presented in a variety of formats in the form of reports, graphs, etc.
- Data warehouse users can obtain trend reports, for example the products that had maximum sales in the northern region within the last two years and exception reports that show actual performance versus goals.
- Data warehouses enhance the value of operational business applications, notably customer relationship management (CRM) systems.

Data warehouse architecture not only enhances the availability of business intelligence data but also improves the effectiveness and timeliness of the startegic decisions. The benefits of the data warehouse can be further subdivided into two categories–tangible benefits and intangible benefits. They are explained as follows.

1.5.1 Tangible Benefits

Successfully implemented data warehouse can realize some significant tangible benefits. For example, assuming an improvement in out-of-stock conditions in the retailing business that results in a 1% increase in sales can mean a sizable cost benefit to the business. As even for a small retail business with $200 million in annual sales, a 1% improvement in sales can yield additional annual revenue of $2 million. However, this benefit is in addition to retaining customers who might not have stayed loyal to the organization if, because of out-of-stock problems, they had to do business with other retailers. Other examples of tangible benefits of implementing a successful data warehouse includes the following:

- Cost of product introduction comes down with targeted marketing campaigns.
- Better decisions in terms of cost and quality are taken by separating query processing from running on operational systems.
- Data warehouses have lead to enhanced asset and liability management since it provides a clear picture of enterprise wide purchasing and inventory patterns thereby indicating otherwise unseen credit exposure and opportunities for cost savings.

1.5.2 Intangible Benefits

Apart from the tangible benfits, data warehouses also provide a number of intangible benefits. Although difficult to quantify, they must also be considered when planning for the data warehouse.

Examples of intangible benefits are:

- Improved productivity that is achieved by keeping all the data in a single location.
- Enhanced customer relations through improved knowledge of individual customer's requirements and trends in the market.
- The information extracted from the data warehouse enables better customer relationship management by tailored product offerings and improved customization.
- Data warehouses enable reengineering of business processes by providing useful insights into the work processes.

1.6 CONCERNS IN DATA WAREHOUSING

- Extracting, cleaning, and loading data are complex, time consuming activities. But tools available in the market can be used to make them easier.
- It is not uncommon for data warehouse projects to go beyond their scope.
- There can be problems of compatibility with the existing systems like the operational systems.
- Providing training to end-users, who may not otherwise use the warehouse at all.
- Security could be a serious bottleneck especially if the data warehouse is web accessible.
- Data warehouse operating and maintenance costs are very high.
- Data warehouses get outdated very quickly, hence there is a risk of delivering suboptimal information to the organization.

1.6.1 Nothing is for Free

No doubt, data warehousing provides a vast range of benefits to its users, but all this comes at a cost. The cost of designing the data model, implementing the data warehouse, addition of extra hardware and ongoing costs that stem from daily data transfer, cleansing and storage of new data entering the warehouse environment can be substantial. Table 1.5 lists the various cost factors involved in moving into this technolology.

Storing large volumes of data has a severe impact on the following:

Cost   As the amount of data that has to be stored in the data warehouse goes up so does the cost of storage media. Initially, the data warehouse starts with a small budget but with the increase in the size of the data, the budget allocated for the data warehouse also grows. This cost is required for having a disk with higher storage capacity, disk controller, communication lines, robust operating systems, business intelligence software, etc.

Table 1.5 Costs incurred in deploying a data warehouse

	Recurring Costs	**One-time Costs**
Capital expenditures	• Hardware maintenance • Software maintenance • Middleware technology	• Hard Disk • CPU • Network hardware and software • DBMS software • Middleware software
Operational expenditures	• Ongoing data refreshing • Integration of data • Data transformation activities • Maintenance of data model • Data archival	• Integration of data • Data transformation • Database design • Data model definition • Netwrok related issues • Data dictionaries

Usefulness Initially when organizations start with, say 50 GB data, the probability of all the data being used is quite high. But as the data grows up in size, the percentage of data that is actually used goes down.

Data management When a data warehouse is recently deployed, it has small amounts of data, so data management is not a complexity. But as the data grows in size, the data management activities become more and more complex and take much more time to accomplish. For example, refreshing the data with new values might have taken only an hour when there was a meagre 50 GB of data in the database but now when the size of database has grown to 50 TB, the same activity may take several hours to complete.

Recapitulation

The operational computer systems provide information to run the day-to-day operations, but they cannot be readily used to make strategic decisions.

Data warehousing is a new paradigm specifically intended to provide strategic information.

Data warehouses support decision making and presents flexible, conducive, and interactive source of strategic information to the managers and executives.

A data warehouse is not a single software or hardware product. Rather it is a computing environment where users are put directly in touch with the data they need to make better decisions. It is a user-centric environment.

A data warehouse is a blend of many technologies as it takes data from different operational systems and from outside sources like magazines, journals, reports of other organizations in the same industry; removes inconsistencies, transforms the data, and finally stores it in formats suitable for easy access for decision making.

Data warehouses are meant to be used by executives, mangers, and other people at higher managerial levels who may not have much technical expertise in handling the databases.

Advantages of data warehouses include better decisions, increased productivity, lower operational costs, enhanced asset and liability management, and better CRM.

While implementing a data warehouse in your organization, you need to be careful about extracting, cleaning, and loading of data; checking its compatibility with systems already in place; providing training to end-users and paying special attention to the security of the data.

The data warehouse is used in two basic modes. In the verification mode, the user proposes a hypothesis and asks a series of questions to either confirm or repudiate it. In the discovery mode, the user desires to discover patterns of customer behaviour and relationships among the products that sell together.

Objective Questions

1. Choose the right statements

(a) Operational systems are meant to provide information to run the day-to-day business.

(b) Operational systems are used to make strategic decisions.

(c) Data warehouse stores historical as well as current data.

(d) Historical data is used to study unusual trends in sales.

(e) Data warehouse contains integrated information from heterogeneous sources.

(f) Strategic information is required to run day-to-day operations.

(g) Strategic information is needed for the survival of the corporation in a highly competitive world.

(h) Operational staff needs strategic information.

2. Fill in the blanks

(a) A _____ is a user centric environment.

(b) _____ provides the users with access to accurate, consolidated information from various internal and external sources.

(c) The users of the data warehouse include _____, _____, _____ and _____.

(d) Data warehouse provides _____ data.

3. Multiple choice questions

(a) Reasons for moving into data warehousing include

  (i) Processing huge volumes of data

  (ii) Providing interactive analysis

  (iii) Increase in the computing power

  (iv) Lower costs

  (v) None of these

  (vi) All of these

(b) Characteristics of a data warehouse include

  (i) Stores only current data

  (ii) Facilitates analyses of large volumes of data

  (iii) Data extracted from only a single application

  (iv) User friendliness

  (v) Contains read intensive data

  (vi) Can be updated

(c) Choose the characteristics of an operational system.

  (i) Current data

  (ii) Optimized for complex queries

  (iii) Predictive usage

  (iv) 100 MB – 1 GB database size

  (v) High access frequency

4. Match the following

(a)	Integrated	1.	Data in all the tables must be accurate
(b)	Data integrity	2.	Information must be available within the stipulated time
(c)	Accessible	3.	Must have an overall enterprise-wide view
(d)	Timely	4.	Easily accessible by the users with intuitive access paths

5. Categorize as Tangible or Intangible Benefit

(a) Better customer relationship management

(b) Reengineering of business process

(c) Reduction in cost of product introduction

(d) Better decisions in terms of cost and quality

Review Questions

1. What do you understand by strategic information? Give suitable examples. Also write down some of the characteristics of strategic information. For a commercial bank, name five types of strategic objectives.

2. Explain the term Information Crisis.

3. As you have seen, a retail store collects huge amounts of data through its operational systems. Name any four types of transaction data that are likely to be collected by the retail store through its daily operations.

4. Differentiate between operational systems and informational systems.

5. Give reasons why operational systems are not useful for making strategic decisions.

6. Explain the factors which lead to the growth and usage of data warehouses.

7. Data warehouse is an environment, not a product. Comment.

8. Write a short note on benefits of data warehousing.

9. How can you say that data warehousing is a blend of many technologies?

10. Data warehousing is the only viable means to resolve the information crisis and to provide strategic information. Justify the statement.

2

DATA WAREHOUSE: DEFINING FEATURES

Learning Objectives

In this chapter, we will learn about the key features of a data warehouse. Then we will discuss the term 'data granularity' which is a very important aspect of a data warehouse. Finally, we will study the components that form a data warehouse.

Case Study

Imagine that Pallav Raj, the CEO of JRTs, has decided to go for a data warehouse. Now one of the main questions that needs to be answered before going for it is the level of granularity that the data warehouse would contain.

Granularity in other words means the level of detail of data. Higher the grain, more is the level of detail and lower the grain, higher is the amount of detailed data that can be stored.

Now, consider a situation in which the data warehouse will contain high level of granularity (low level detail)—imagine data being stored on a monthly basis. When Pallav Raj asks his employee to get the sales of a particular brand of T-shirts in the second quarter of the previous year, then the data of the 4th, 5th, and 6th month will be added and displayed to the user. In case, Pallav Raj asks for the sales of a particular brand of T-shirts in the last year, then twelve months data would be added to give a cumulative figure. This provides a very quick and efficient way of retrieving the desired information.

But things are not that simple. Once Pallav Raj has decided to keep the granularity of data at monthly level, then only monthly figures will be stored and not daily, weekly or fortnightly.

In case of a requirement to check the sales of a particular brand of T-shirts in the last week of December, they don't have sufficient record to perform analysis. Thus, in a way, the data warehouse would be unable to satisfy its user's demand for information thereby defeating its purpose.

However, if Pallav Raj would have decided to keep data at the lowest level of granularity or the highest level of detail (daily records), then such a problem would not have occurred. This option provides enough flexibility to answer any type of query. The tradeoff here is the enormous amount of space that would be needed to store all the records.

2.1 INTRODUCTION

Data warehouses are special types of databases that are specifically built for the purpose of getting information out rather than putting data in, which is the purpose of operational databases. The data warehouse exists to provide answers to strategic questions and assist the managers of organizations in planning for the future.

Data warehouses are not designed to support operational applications such as inventory management, order processing or stock control. Since the primary reason for their existence is to assist business users in decision making, it is, therefore, vital that the data warehouse contains the right information.

According to Todman, a data warehouse is kept separate from the operational (or application databases) because of the following reasons:

- While Operational Transactional Processing (OLTP) systems (operational databases) are optimized to execute insert- and update-type queries, the data warehouses are optimized to execute select-type queries.
- The data in an operational database keeps changing, whereas data warehouses are nonvolatile (do not change).
- While OLTP systems are characterized with large and complex schemas, the data warehouse schema on the other hand, is simplified and denormalized.
- Data warehouses need historical information and this is often missing in the operational systems.

2.2 FEATURES OF A DATA WAREHOUSE

A data warehouse unlike an operational system is an informational delivery system. In other words, it is meant to provide information to its users so that they can make use of this information to make their businesses better. For this purpose, the data warehouse integrates and transforms the organization's data into information that enables strategic decision making. For building a data warehouse we need to extract the current and historical data from the organization's operational databases and from other external sources; transform this data to resolve any conflicts and finally store it in the data warehouse.

In order to set up this information delivery system, different components or building blocks are needed. These components are arranged in the most optimal fashion. Before we get into the details of the individual components, let us first look at some fundamental features of the data warehouse.

Various stalwarts in this field have described the key features of a data warehouse in their own different ways. For our purposes we shall use the definition provided by W. H. Inmon (1992), considered to be the father of data warehousing. He defines the data warehouse as 'a subject-oriented, integrated, non-volatile, time-variant collection of data in support of management's decisions.' In this section we will discuss each of these characteristics and how they differ from the operational sources.

2.2.1 Subject-oriented Data

The first characteristic of a data warehouse, as described by Inmon, is *subject orientation*. The operational environment focuses its attention on the day to day transactions that are part of the normal operation of the business whereas the data warehouse is concerned with the *things* in the business environment that are driving those transactions.

Every business stores data in operational systems that are organized around individual applications as shown in Fig. 2.1 to support those particular operational systems. However, the data warehouse stores data by subjects and not by applications. These business subjects vary from one business to another. For example, for a retail company, sales, customers, products, etc. may be critical business subjects. Hence, in a data warehouse, there is no semblance to an application flavour as the data in a data warehouse cuts across applications.

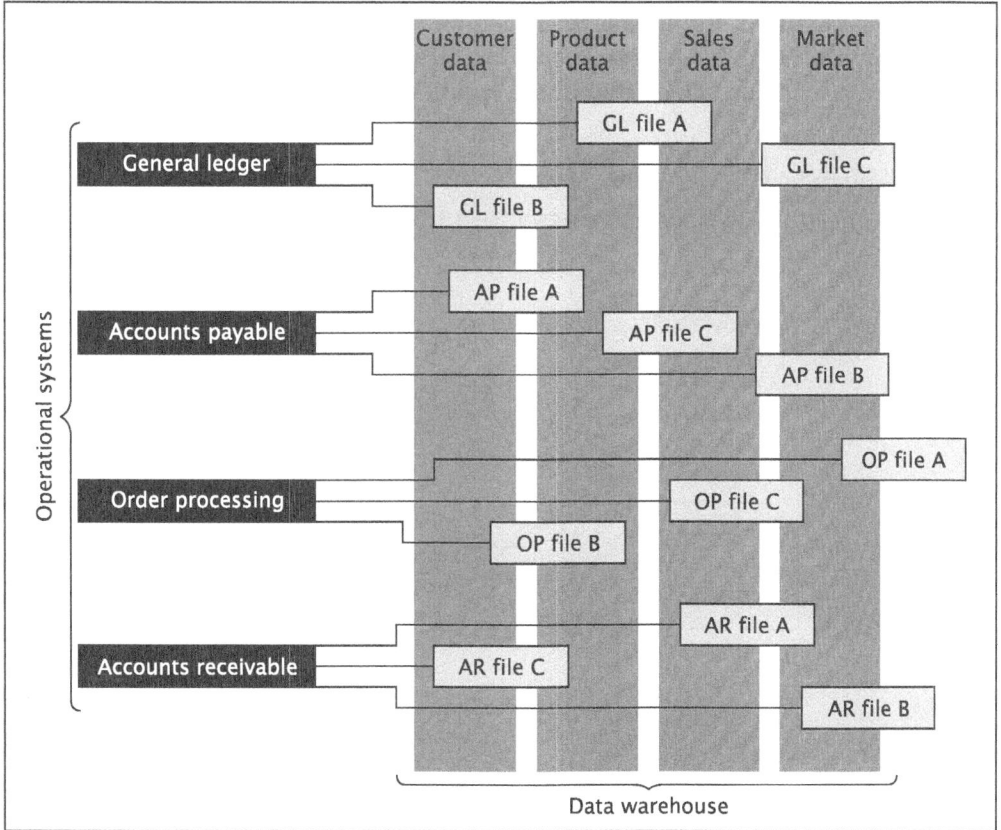

Figure 2.1 In operational systems, we store data by individual applications. The data for these applications is spread among different files.

The transaction-oriented operational system structures data in a way that optimizes the processing of transactions or the operations. These systems typically deal with many users accessing a few records at a time. For example, an employee works in a department that is part of a division. The employee, department, and division information is all related to the subject employee despite the fact that the data will be stored in separate tables.

Operational data is distributed across multiple applications in the source system. A particular subject may be involved in different types of transactions. For example, a customer appearing in the accounts receivable application may also be a supplier appearing in the accounts payable application. Every application has only a part of the customer data. Nowhere is there a single consolidated view of the organization. This structure of data is very cumbersome to access for a decision maker. Firstly, because the decision maker is interested in business subjects, to get a complete picture of any one subject, he will have to access many tables within many applications. Secondly, the strategist is not interested in one occurrence of a subject or an individual customer, but in all occurrences of a subject and all customers.

Since retrieving this data in real time from many disparate systems would be impractical, the warehouse, therefore, gathers all this data into one place. The structure of the data is such that all the data for a particular subject is contained within one table. In this way, the strategist can retrieve all the data pertaining to a particular subject from one location within the data warehouse.

2.2.2 Integrated Data

The data warehouse does more than just gathering the data from multiple sources. The operational data is the basis of the warehouse. The integration process, as shown in Fig. 2.2, forms the data into a single cohesive environment. Data in the data warehouse comes from several diverse applications running in the operational systems. You need to remove all inconsistencies and errors and finally transform this data into a common format before storing it in the data warehouse. The origin/source of the data is invisible to the decision maker in the warehouse environment. The integration process consists of two tasks: *data cleansing* and *data transformation*.

Strategic decision making calls for extracting the relevant data from various applhications running in different operational systems and then storing

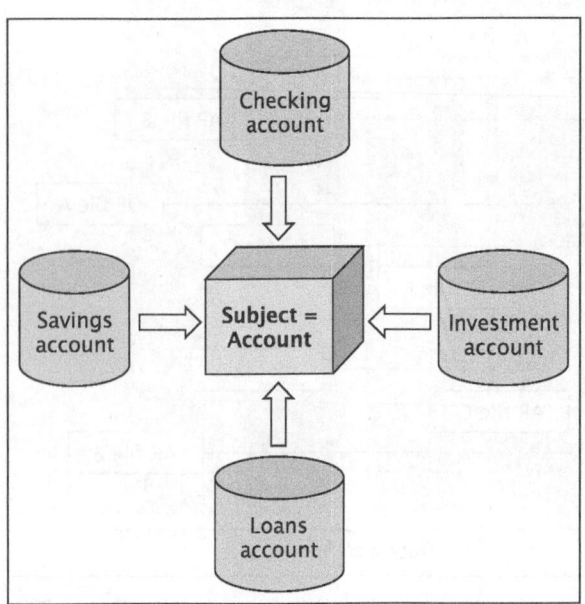

Figure 2.2   Integrated data

them at one big place called the data warehouse. However, this is not a trivial task as the source data may be present on different operational platforms (operating system), stored in different databases, and thus, having different file layouts, character code representations and field naming conventions.

Before the data from various distinct sources can be stored in a data warehouse, all such inconsistencies must be removed. Data elements must be standardized (converted into a common format) and the meanings of data names in each source application must be confirmed. For example, stud-Id in one table may store the student's roll number and in some other table it may be used to store the student's examination roll number as allotted by the university. Thus, some of the items that need standardization are naming conventions, codes, attributes and measurements.

So, now that you have got an idea that integration of data is not an easy task, let us review some of the tasks that have to be performed while integrating the data to finally store it in the data warehouse. Figure 2.3 will help you to gain an insight into the complexity of the data integration process.

Data Cleansing

Data cleansing is the process of removing errors from the input data and is part of the integration process. It is perhaps one of the most crucial steps in the operations of a data warehouse. If the cleansing process is faulty, the decision maker will not trust the data and the purpose of having a warehouse will fail. If the warehouse provides incorrect information and the strategist trusts it, then a wrong strategy could be formulated which could cause irreparable damage to the company.

However, a good cleansing process, can not only improve the quality of the data within the warehouse, but in the operational environment as well. The extraction log, shown in Fig. 2.3, records errors detected in the data cleansing process. The data administrator examines this log to determine the source of the errors. At times, the data administrator will detect errors that have originated in the operational environment. Some of these errors could be due to a problem with the application or may be due to an incorrect data entry. In either case, the data administrator will report these errors to those responsible for operational data quality.

There may be errors in the metadata (that which contains data about data similar to a data dictionary) as well either because the cleansing process did not receive a change to the metadata or because the metadata was incorrect or incomplete. The data administrator

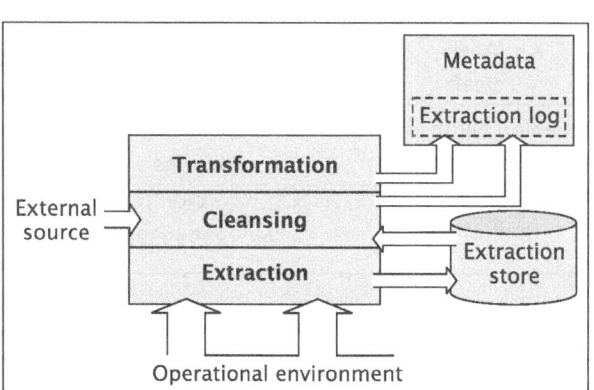

Figure 2.3 Data integration process

must determine the source of this error and take corrective action. In this way, the data warehouse improves the quality of the data throughout the entire organization.

When errors are discovered in the input data, the cleansing process should not incorporate this data in the data warehouse. The errors in this case should be reported to the operational systems where they will be corrected and then resubmitted to the warehouse. It is the responsibility of those maintaining the quality of data in the operational systems to take corrective action. The concern is to make the data in the warehouse reflect what is seen in the operational systems. There should not be any sort of disagreement between the two environments as it could lead to a lack of confidence in the warehouse.

Data Transformation

Rarely does one find operational environments where the data is consistent between applications. In today's world, you will find operational systems have diverse turnkey systems and work in heterogeneous environments. In such situations, data inconsistency is a common problem. Data transformation addresses this issue. The data transformation process receives the input data from the different operational systems and transforms them into one consistent format.

Table 2.1 demonstrates the different types of integration challenges that are being faced by the data warehouse architects. It is observed that as each new source of data is identified, the complexity of the integration process increases. An analysis of every system contributing to the data warehouse must be performed to understand both the data and its format so that an integration process may be defined that will provide consistent data.

Table 2.1 Integration issues

	Sales Voucher	Purchase Order	Inventory
Description	Customer Name IBM	C Name IBM	Customer Name International Business Machines
Encoding	Sex 1 = Male 2 = Female	Sex X = Male Y = Female	Sex M = Male F = Female
Units	Cable Length Centimetres	Cable Length Metres	Cable Length Inches
Coding	Key Character (10)	Key Integer	Key pic '999999999'

2.2.3 Non-volatile Data

We now know that for storing the data in the data warehouse, we extract them from multiple operational systems and from external sources. This data after being extracted has to be transformed, integrated and then stored in the data warehouse.

We move the data from source systems to the data warehouse at specific intervals depending on the requirements of the business. The data movement frequency may vary from twice a day, once a day, once a week, to once in two weeks.

As shown in the Fig. 2.4, business transactions do not update the data in the data warehouse. They update only the operational systems in real time.

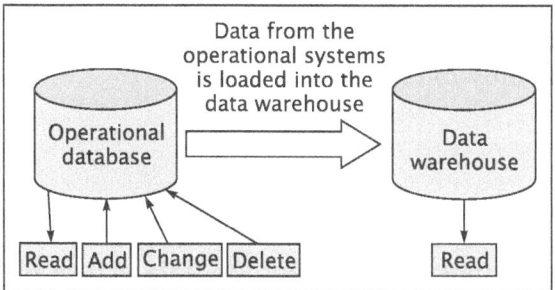

Figure 2.4 Non-volatile data

With each transaction that occurs, the users may add, change or delete data from an operational system but they do not update the data in the warehouse. We do not delete the data in the data warehouse in real-time. Thus, it can be said that the data in data warehouse is not as volatile as the data in an operational database.

Hence, a major difference between the data warehouse and a transaction-oriented operational system is volatility. In the operational environment, data is volatile, that is, it changes. However, in the data warehouse, once the data is written, it remains unchanged. The example given below demonstrates the difference between the two system types as it relates to volatility.

Take the example of a data record on Monday illustrated in Fig. 2.5. The quantity on hand for a product A is 500 units. This is recorded in the inventory system in record under the name PPP. During the Monday extraction, we store the data in the warehouse in record QQQ. Tuesday's transactions reduce the quantity on hand to 200. These updates are carried out against the same record PPP in the inventory system. On Tuesday night, during the extraction

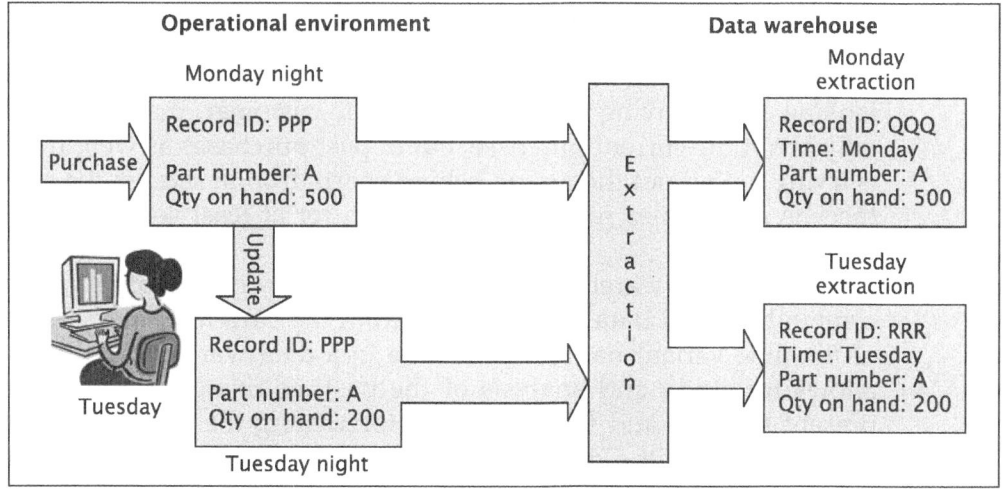

Figure 2.5 Every time the value changes, a new record is entered in the data warehouse, various records are neither selected nor changed.

process, the new quantity is extracted and recorded in a completely separate data warehouse record RRR while the previous QQQ record is not modified. Hence, we can see that data warehouse stores data in bulk. The extraction process adds new records to the database; detailed records already in the database are not modified.

Thus, the non-volatility of the data warehouse creates a *virtual* read-only database system. However, no database can literally be a read-only. Data warehouse fields are also changed but not in the normal course of execution. We will learn more about this in chapter 7, but for the time being we shall think of a data warehouse as a read only database.

2.2.4 Time Variant Data

The non-volatility of the data within the data warehouse adds another *dimension* to the data warehouse, that is, the dimension of time. In a data warehouse environment, the decision makers can view the data across the field of time at whichever level of detail they may wish. This allows the business analysts to view patterns and trends over time. Time has become one variable that the analysts can manipulate. In other words, the data warehouse is time-variant (Refer Fig. 2.6).

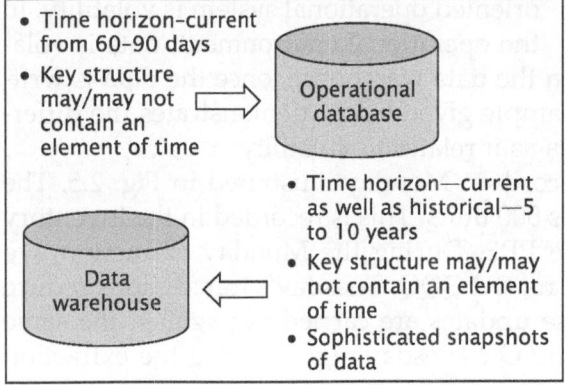

For an operational system, the stored data contains the current values because these systems support day-to-day transactions. For example, in an order entry system, the status of an order is the current status of the order. On the other hand, the data in the data warehouse is meant for strategic analysis and decision making. If a user is looking at the buying pattern of a specific customer, the user needs data not only about the current purchase, but of past purchases as well. If the manager is trying to find out the reason behind sharp drop in sales in the central region then he needs sales record of that region for at least some period extending back in time.

Figure 2.6 Data in a data warehouse is time variant

Thus, a data warehouse, because of the very nature of its purpose, has to contain historical data as well, apart from the current values. The key benefit of the time variant nature of the data in a data warehouse is that such data allows for study and analysis of the past, co-relate the information to the present scenario and finally enables forecasting the future. Therefore, every record stored in the data warehouse has an associated time element which specifies the date/month/year when the sales transaction took place.

The time variant nature of a data warehouse can be easily understood by looking at Fig. 2.6.

2.3 DATA GRANULARITY

The most important aspect that needs to be considered for designing a data warehouse is the issue of granularity. In fact, the issue of granularity strongly influences the entire architecture that surrounds the data warehouse environment. Granularity refers to the level of detail or the level of summarization of data in the data warehouse. In technical terms, data granularity is inversely proportional to the level of detail. More detailed data means lower level of granularity. Similarly, less detail indicates higher levels of granularity. For example, a simple sales transaction would be at a low level of granularity whereas a summary of all the sales transactions for the entire month would be at a high level of granularity.

In an operational system, data is generally stored at the lowest level of detail (highly detailed data). Whenever summary data is needed, individual transactions are summed up to present the results. For example, if the user wants to see how many units of a particular product was sold in the last month then all the orders entered for that month would be read and added. The bottom line is that we usually do not keep summary data in an operational system.

In the course of an analysis session, the user usually starts by looking at summary data. For example, the marketing manager may initially start with total sale units of a product in the previous year. But later on he may want to look at the breakdown by individual quarters. Continuing further with the analysis, he may examine the sales units by the next level of individual months. In a data warehouse environment, it is very common that the analysis begins at a high level and moves down to lower levels of detail.

Generally, in a data warehouse, data is kept at different levels of summarizations. Depending on the query, the user can go to the particular level of detail and satisfy the query. In a data warehouse, if data has to be kept at the lowest level of detail, then a lot of data will have to be stored. Therefore, the choice of granularity is an important design issue because:

- The lower the level of granularity, the larger is the amount of data stored in the warehouse.
- The higher the level of granularity, the lesser is the level of detail for which queries can be answered.

The choice of granularity, calls for a trade-off between volume of data and the level of query detail (See Fig. 2.7). A second trade-off is between the level of granularity and the amount of computing power required. For low levels of granularity, there are large

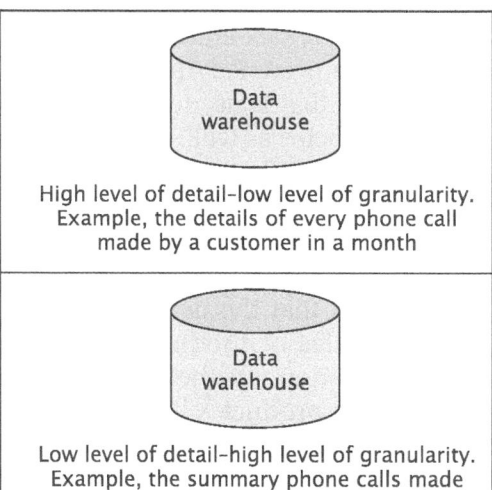

High level of detail-low level of granularity. Example, the details of every phone call made by a customer in a month

Low level of detail-high level of granularity. Example, the summary phone calls made by a customer in a month

Figure 2.7   Granularity of a data warehouse

amounts of detailed data. Therefore, for every query that needs summarized data, computing power is required to aggregate the information on fly (when need arises) so that answers are presented quickly on the screen.

2.3.1 Benefits of Granularity

Data warehousing provides an invaluable foundation for decision support and strategic analysis. Organizations may build a data warehouse to solve one purpose and then later on use it for some other purpose. Thus, a data warehouse provides an extremely flexible and reusable atmosphere. The concept contradicted detailed data found in the data warehouse is the key to reusability because the available data can be used in any way. Within an enterprise, the same data might be used to answer the queries posed by different departments like marketing, sales as well as the accounting department. For example, marketing department may want to see sales of a particular product by region in the last month, human resource department may want to see sales made by a particular salesperson last year and the finance department may want to see revenues generated in the last quarter.

Another advantage of having detailed data is the flexibility with which the data can be viewed by the users. Detailed data allows the users of the data warehouse to view the same data from different angles in different perspectives. The detailed data stored in the warehouse can easily cater to the changing needs and requirements of the data warehouse users.

2.3.2 Data Granularity—Pros and Cons

If storage space is a problem in a data warehouse, storing the data at a higher level of granularity is a much more efficient than storing the data at lower level of granularity. When the data is stored at a lower level of granularity then not only fewer bytes of data are required but also fewer index entries are needed. However, the volume of data and the storage space occupied are not the only factors of concern. The amount of computing power that is needed to process a large volume of data in order to access the data is a factor as well. Thus, the data in the data warehouse must be compacted to realize significant savings in space, number of indexes and the processor resources required to manipulate the data.

On the other side, with the increase in the level of granularity, there is a corresponding loss in the ability to answer queries using the data, as a high level of granularity limits the number of questions that the data can handle. For example, when you have just the quantity sales of product X of every month, then you will not be able to answer the question whether customers in the age group of 40–50 years prefer purchasing the product X or not.

Now also take for example the calculation of average sales of product X during the last quarter. However, certain queries can be answered by both a high level and a low level of granularity. But in answering it, there is a tremendous difference in the resources used, because, a low level of granularity uses much more resources than used by data kept at a higher level of granularity.

2.3.3 Dual Levels of Granularity

Generally, organizations need efficiency in storing, accessing, and analysing the most granular data. When an organization has huge volumes of data in the data warehouse, it becomes crucial to consider two levels of granularity. When the data warehouse is designed to handle dual levels of granularity, the data warehouse will contain two types of data—summarized data and detailed data. The detailed data can include details of even 10 years of history.

By storing the data at dual levels of granularity in the data warehouse, we are actually trying to kill two birds with one stone. A majority of the decision support processing will be performed against the lightly summarized data where the data is compact and efficiently accessed. And whenever detailed data will be required, say 5% of the time, the true archival level of data would be used to satisfy the query.

2.4 THE INFORMATION FLOW MECHANISM

In this section, we will learn how the huge mountains of data that exist in the source system get delivered to the data warehouse users as useful pieces of information. For this, we will have a look at the various stages through which data passes before reaching the end-user's desktop (Fig. 2.8).

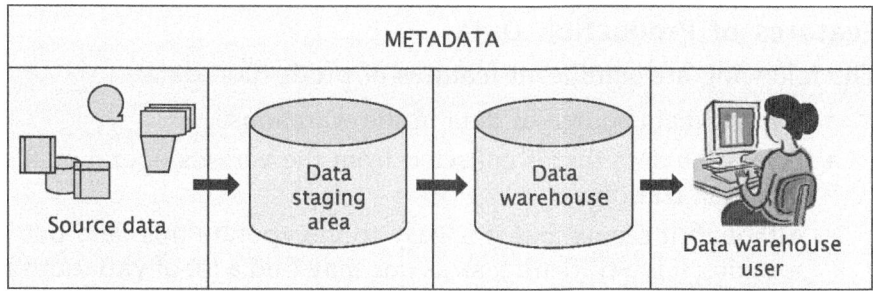

Figure 2.8 The figure shows the information flow from the source systems to the end-users

Before going into the details of each stage, let us first glance at Fig. 2.9 which shows the steps involved in the process of transformation of data into information.

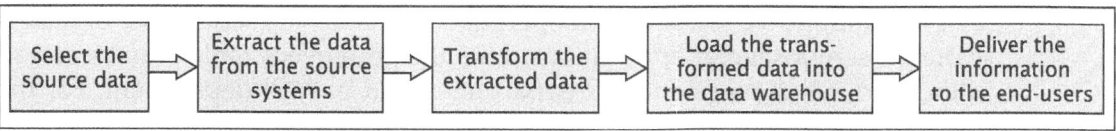

Figure 2.9 The ETL process

2.4.1 Select the Source Data

Source data coming into the data warehouse may be grouped into four broad categories as explained below. The data warehouse project team needs to collect data from all these sources of data.

As shown in Fig. 2.10, there are four categories of source data. Let us study the key features of each of the data.

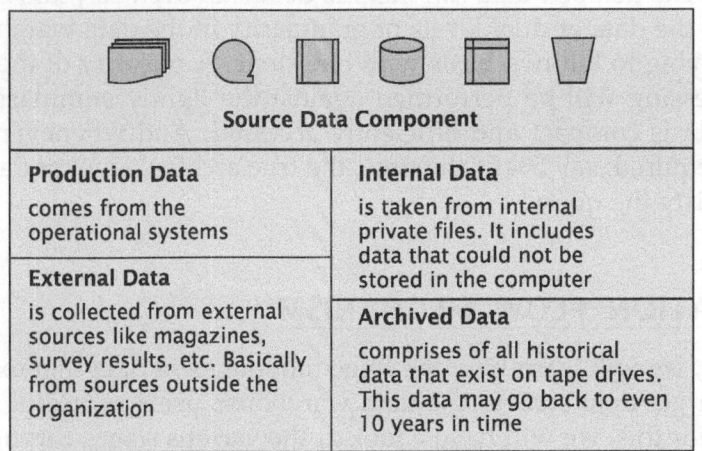

Source Data Component

Production Data	Internal Data
comes from the operational systems	is taken from internal private files. It includes data that could not be stored in the computer
External Data	
is collected from external sources like magazines, survey results, etc. Basically from sources outside the organization	**Archived Data**
	comprises of all historical data that exist on tape drives. This data may go back to even 10 years in time

Figure 2.10 Categories of source data

Features of Production Data

The following are significant features of production data:

- It is the main source of data in the warehouse.
- This is the data that is collected from the various operational systems of the organization.
- Although it seems that it is easy to incorporate this data but practically speaking it is a difficult task as one may find a lot of variations in the data formats as these data reside on different hardware platforms, may possibly be supported by different database systems and operating systems and may have been collected from several vertical applications.
- Disparity is the main issue in using the production data. Thus, the job of standardizing and transforming the disparate data from the various operational systems, and finally integrating it into useful data for storage in the data warehouse becomes challenging.

For example, we know that in operational systems the same piece of data is scattered across several applications. Like the employees table may be stored in the accounts department, HR department, and payroll department. For the data to be stored in the data warehouse, it must be collected from all these operational systems. This is our production data. Now disparity could arise because in one table, employee name may be defined as ENAME and is 20 bytes long, in the other operational system it may be defined as EMP NAME and is 16 bytes long, and in another table it may be represented as NAME. So before the production data is stored in the data warehouse, all the related data must be collected and standardized into one single format.

Features of Internal Data

Internal data is taken from private files and could include data that is not stored on a computer. Its features are as follows:

- The internal data comprises of various personal spreadsheets, documents, customer profiles, etc that the users often keep with themselves especially when they deal with customers on a one to one basis.
- This kind of data can also be useful in a data warehouse when contribution of each customer is significant.
- Although some internal data may be extracted from production systems but a lot more of it has to be extracted from individual's documents and private files.
- Internal data adds additional complexity to the process of transforming and integrating the data, so strategies have to be designed to collect the data from spreadsheets and textual documents, and to tie them into departmental databases.

Features of Archived Data

An operational system is used to run the day-to-day business transactions and for this you need to keep only current information in the database. So, in every operational system, periodically the old data is taken and stored in archived files. For example, if we are using a table that stores historical data of 10 years and is used once every 4–5 years then it makes no sense to keep this table online. Thus, it is shifted from the online disk to a magnetic tape from where it can be accessed whenever the need arises to access the records stored in that table.

Basically, what information is archived and when it will be archived will vary from one organization to the other. Generally, organizations follow staged archival methods as given below.

Stage 1 - recent data is archived to a separate archival database that may still be online.

Stage 2 - the older data is archived to flat files on disk storage.

Stage 3 - the oldest data is archived to tape cartridges and even kept off-site.

A data warehouse keeps current as well as historical data for discerning patterns and analysing trends. So, to serve this purpose, data from the archived datasets also needs to be extracted.

Features of External Data

To learn about the importance of external data, let us first take an example. The marketing manager wants the analyst to formulate a report. The analyst makes a very good report by collecting data that is available in the organization and the data that is present in business magazines. The manager is really impressed. After a few days, the manager again asks the analyst to get some report ready based on the former report. The analyst uses the report to make a new report but the original source of the data is lost. If there be a need to further analyse and reprocess the data from magazines, then it is hard to recall about the original source of data and ensuring its availability.

The external data is mainly collected from business magazines, industry newsletters, technology reports, reports generated by the consultants especially for the enterprise, competitive analysis reports, sales and marketing analysis reports, etc.

- Executives depend on data from external sources as well for making strategic decisions.
- For this they use statistics relating to their industry produced by external agencies, market share data of competitors and standard values of financial indicators for their business to check their performance.
- The insights obtained from the production, internal, and archived data are not sufficient for making strategic decisions. You need to include data from external sources as well to get a broader and a clear view of the data.
- The first issue with storing external data is the frequency of availability. Unlike the internal data there is no fixed pattern of appearance of external data. Constant monitoring must be set to ensure that the right external data is captured.
- The second issue is that usually data from outside sources do not conform to the organization's standards, so this data must be converted into internal formats.
- The third issue is that of data granularity. Suppose an organization stores the sales of its individual products in the database but the external data that is present contains the information about sales of every product category. Then this will be a problem as how to get the detail data.
- The fourth issue is data unpredictability. Since the external data may be available from any source and at any time, it becomes hard to capture.

2.4.2 Extract Data from the Source Systems

The data extraction process has to deal with multiple data sources. In a data warehouse environment one thing is for sure that the source data will be inconsistent, erroneous and stored in multiple formats. So the extracted data is temporarily stored in the data staging area where all data cleansing and transformation functions are performed.

The source data may be from different machines having the data stored in diverse formats. Part of the source data may be in relational database systems whereas some data may be in flat files or in spreadsheets. So data extraction may become complex. These days, many tools are available in the market to extract data from the source systems. Example of these tools include, Abinitio, Actaworks RT, Mapforce, Barracuda Integrator, Benetl, Data Integrator, Clover ETL, Data Exchanger, D2K, Octopus, etc. However, these tools may also be built in house. The data extraction process performs the following functions:

- Identify the sources of data
- Finalize the filters that will be applied to every individual source system to extract the data
- Produce automatic extract files from the operational systems
- Generate intermediary files to store selected data to be merged later
- Render automated job control services for creating extract files
- Reformat input from outside sources or sources external to the enterprise
- Reformat and standardize the input from departmental data files, databases, and spreadsheets
- Produce common application code for data extraction
- Resolve inconsistencies for common data that will be extracted from multiple source systems. For example, if in one source system the marital status of a customer is stored as 'married' and in another if it is 'single', then the inconsistency is removed by finding the true value of the attribute.

Data Staging Area

Data staging area is the place where all the extracted data is temporarily stored and prepared for loading into the data warehouse. It is rightly compared to an assembly plant or construction area where the extracted files are examined, business rules are reviewed, the data transformation functions are performed, data is sorted and merged, inconsistencies are resolved, and the data is cleansed.

Finally, when the data is processed and prepared for an enterprise wide data warehouse, it temporarily resides in the staging area repository waiting to be loaded into the data warehouse repository look at the Fig. 2.11 which shows the functions that takes place in the data staging area. In most of the data warehouses, data in the staging area is kept in sequential or flat files but these days the trend is that more and more staging area data repositories are becoming relational databases.

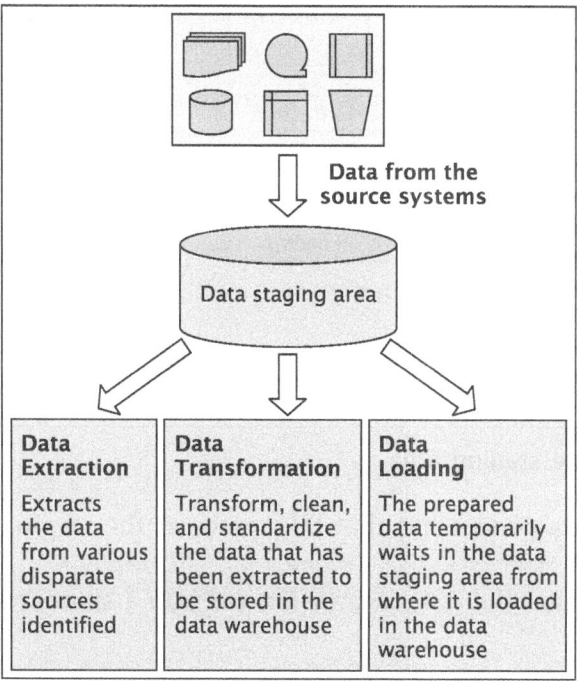

Figure 2.11 Data extraction, transformation, and loading (ETL) process.

Why Do We Need a Separate Staging Area?

The norm that most of the organizations follow is to have the data warehouse staging area implemented in a separate physical server (staging server). No doubt this adds to the, complexity and cost but still this approach has certain advantages like:

- This approach isolates the raw data that has been extracted from a variety of sources from the processed data.
- Since the data warehouse users are not supposed to access the staging area, this offers additional security and process quality.
- This approach helps in sharing load as 'data preparation' tasks and data warehouse querying tasks are handled by separate systems.
- It eases the development of a central metadata repository which maintains documentation for all involved systems: operational systems, ETL process, data warehouse, tools and predefined reports.

The main issue of concern is—in a data warehouse, you pull in the data from many source operational systems as shown in Fig. 2.12 and store it in terms of subjects and not by applications. Data in a data warehouse is subject-oriented and cuts across applications. A separate staging area is thus compulsorily needed for preparing data for the data warehouse.

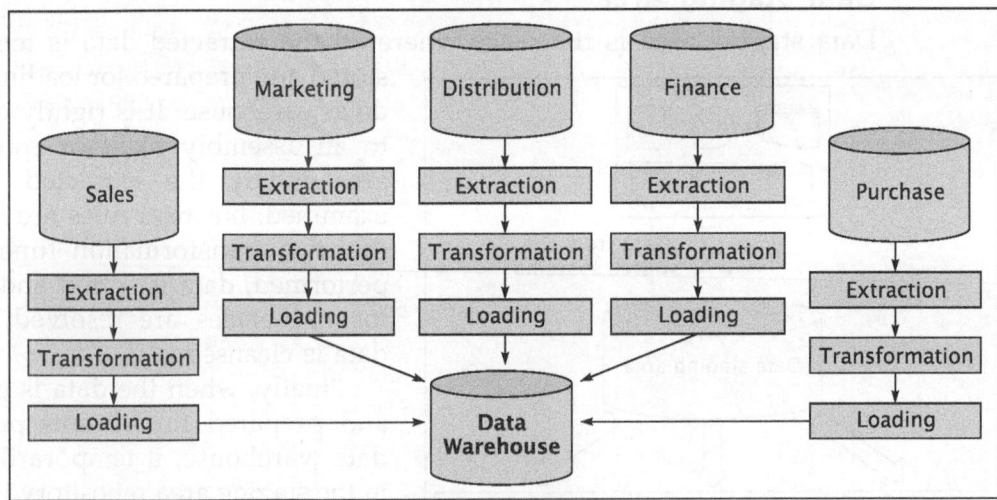

Figure 2.12 Data processing at the staging area

The various types of raw data processing that take place at the staging area are:

- Standardization of data so that the data is transformed into a standard format.
- Sorting of records.

- Comparing and merging of those records that belong to the same object or entity, but are derived from different sources (e.g. order records of the same customer from different order handling systems). Merging is always done after standardization.
- Aggregation and summarizations of data.
- Creation of surrogate keys.
- Filling in the missing values with the default values.
- Converting the data according to the technological platform (DBMS and operating system) used by the data warehouse server.

2.4.3 Transform the Extracted Data

The data extracted from the source system cannot be stored directly in the data warehouse mainly because of two reasons. First, this is raw data that must be processed to be made usable in the data warehouse. The data in the operational systems is not usable for making strategic decisions. Secondly, because operational data is extracted from many old legacy systems, the quality of data in those systems may not be good enough for the data warehouse. So before putting this data in the data warehouse, the data needs to be enriched and its quality must be improved.

Before moving the extracted data into the data warehouse, various kinds of data transformation have to be performed. Since this data come from several dissimilar source systems, there is a need to transform the data according to a standardized format. Also it must be ensured that the data does not violate any business rules.

Good quality data is of great importance in the data warehouse as this data forms the basis of a sound strategic decision. If the data quality is not good, then the effect of strategic decisions based on incorrect information can be devastating for the organization. Thus, improving the quality of data forms a major effort within data transformation process.

The data to be stored in the warehouse comes from several disparate systems. If data extraction for a data warehouse poses great challenges, data transformation goes even a step further as the source data may be in different formats using different encoding and units of measurements. A number of tasks are performed as a part of data transformation. First the extracted data is cleaned. Cleaning of data includes correction of misspellings, resolution of conflicts between data elements, providing default values for missing data and at last elimination of duplicates when data is taken from multiple systems.

The next task which forms a major part of the data transformation process is standardization of data elements. The data types and the field lengths of same data elements received from various sources are standardized. Apart from this, semantic standardization is another task where the synonyms and homonyms are resolved. When two or more terms from different sources mean the same thing, you resolve synonyms. For example, the fields DOB and

Date of Birth in two systems may have different field names but they give the same piece of data, say the date of birth of a customer. Similarly, when a single term means many different things in different source systems, you resolve the homonym. For example the word train has two meanings– to train a student and the other is our railway. You need to resolve all these issues in the source data before finally storing it in the data warehouse.

Then you may need to merge certain fields or split certain fields depending upon the structure of the data warehouse database. You need to build primary and foreign keys for the records that have to be stored in data warehouse tables as you cannot use the keys of operational tables as keys of the data warehouse tables.

Finally, you may not want to keep the data at detailed level in the data warehouse. In such cases, the data transformation function will also create summarizations at the desired level. For example, in a retail data warehouse, there may not be a need to keep the details of each and every transaction that take place every day. Rather the users may wish to keep sales of products that take place every month. Then daily data will not be stored but aggregate or summarized data obtained from all the daily records for that month will be created and stored in the data warehouse.

To summarize the transformation process applies rules or functions to the data extracted from the source systems to make it ready to be stored in the target data warehouse database. Although some data may require very little or even no manipulation but some of it will need the following types of transformations to meet the business and technical needs of the target database:

- Translating coded values. For example, if the source system stores 1 for yes and 2 for no, but the warehouse stores Y for yes and N for no, the source data has to be written in the data warehouse supported format.
- Deriving a new calculated value. For example, storing the value of profit in the data warehouse by caclulating it as SP-CP rather than storing the value of CP and SP as available from the source systems.
- Merging and splitting of fields. For example, it we have a field NAME then it can be split to form two fields namely, FIRST NAME and LAST NAME similarly, if we have three fields DD, MM, YY then these fields can be merged to form one field called DATE.
- Aggregating and summarizing data rows.
- Generating primary and foreign keys.
- Applying data validation rules.
- Resolving synonymns and homonymns.

2.4.4 Load Transformed Data into Data Warehouse

When the data transformation function ends, we have a collection of data that is integrated, cleaned, standardized, and summarized. Now the data is ready to be loaded into the data warehouse (see Fig. 2.13). Two categories of tasks

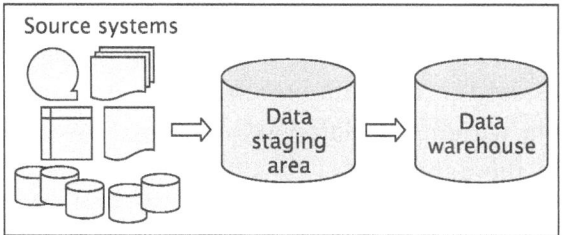

Figure 2.13 Data moves from source systems to the staging area and from there to the data warehouse

form the data loading function. When the design and construction of the data warehouse is completed and the organization decides to go live for the first time, the initial loading of the data into the data warehouse storage is done. The initial load moves large volumes of data thereby consuming a lot of time.

When the data warehouse becomes operational, continuous extraction of the changes to the source data, transformation of the data revisions, and feeding of the incremental data revisions becomes never ending process. Thus, initial loading of data warehouse moves a large amount of data in the warehouse. Once the initial loading is over, the data warehouse is constantly updated to add new records. The refresh cycle of the data warehouse (that is, whether the data warehouse will be daily, weekly, monthly, quarterly or yearly) will be decided by the specific business.

Why Do We Have a Separate Data Warehouse Repository?

The data repositories for the operational systems typically contain only the current data and this data is structured in highly normalized formats for fast and efficient processing. In contrast, the data repository of a data warehouse contains large volumes of historical data for analysis which is structured in a way that is suitable for analysis, and not for quick retrieval of individual pieces of information. Therefore, the data storage for the data warehouse is separate from that of operational systems.

The data in the operational databases could change from moment to moment as a transaction takes place. But data in the data warehouse is stable and represents snapshots at specified periods. Since users are working with the data, the data storage must not be in a state of continual updating. For this reason, the data in the data warehouse is a read-only data repository. Most of the data warehouses employ relational database management systems and others employ multidimensional database management systems where data is stored in multi dimensional cubes in contrast to relations or tables as in case of relational databases.

Functions of Data Warehouse Repository

Following are the important function of a data warehousing repository:

- Load data for full refreshes of the tables in the data warehouse repository.
- Perform periodic incremental loads of the tables in data warehouse.
- Provide support for loading into multiple tables at the detailed as well as summarized levels.
- Ensure optimization of the loading process of data warehouse repository.

- Render automated job control services for loading the data warehouse.
- Provide backup and recovery services for the data warehouse database.
- Provide security for the data stored in the data warehouse.
- Monitor and fine-tune the data warehouse database.
- Periodically archive data from the database.

2.4.5 Deliver Information to End-users

The key objective of building a data warehouse is to provide strategic information to the users. The users visualize the data warehouse and use it with what is made available to them in the information delivery system.

The information delivery area spans a broad spectrum of different techniques that are used to make the information available to the users. The strength of the data warehouse architecture rests on the robustness and flexibility of the information delivery component. In a data warehouse, the data flows from the data warehouse and data marts to the users through queries, reports, and special applications like EIS, OLAP, and data mining. The user interface for information is what determines the ultimate success of the data warehouse. If the interface is intuitive, easy to use, and enticing, the users will keep coming back to the data warehouse. On the other hand, if the interface is difficult to use, cumbersome and convoluted, the project will not be successful.

Before reading about how information is delivered to the end-users in a data warehouse environment, let us first have a look at how Information Delivery in a Data Warehouse differs from that of operational systems (Refer Table 2.2).

The operational systems are built for running the day-to-day business and providing information that enables its users to monitor and control the current business operations. On the contrary, information from the data warehouse provides its users the opportunity to analyse growth patterns in revenue, profit-

Table 2.2 Comparison of information delivery mechanism

Information Delivery Method	Data Warehouse	Operational System
Reports	- User driven reporting - Predefined reports	- Predefined and preformatted reports through applications - User driven reporting is rare
Queries	- User driven queries - Query templates available - Predefined queries	- Limited predefined queries - No ad hoc queries
Analysis	- Complex queries - Long interactive sessions	- No complex queries - No long interactive sessions
Applications	- Data feed to decision-support applications	- Data does not feed to decision-support system

ability, market penetration, and customer base. This analysis forms the ground for making strategic decisions to keep the business sound and competitive.

The underlying difference that exists between the operational system and the data warehouse system makes it impossible to apply the principles of information delivery of operational systems to the data warehouse. Information delivery from the data warehouse is entirely different and thus, different methods are needed. In a data warehouse environment, the users are expected to gather information and perform analysis from the data in the data warehouse interactively on their own without the assistance of IT professionals. So the information from the data warehouse must be made easily and readily available to the users in their own terms.

Information Delivery

The information delivery system is responsible for distributing the data stored in the warehouse to its end-users. Delivery of information may be based on time of day or on the completion of an external event. For example, one user may want the sales of a particular product to be displayed on his screen at 5 PM everyday and another user may want the names of all the products to be displayed on his screen as soon as their number of units become less than minimum units that needs to be in stock at a particular time.

The usability of a data warehouse is maximized when users who need information get the right information where they need it and when they need it the most. The range of users who use the data warehouse for their information needs is very wide. For example, the novice users who generally have no training to use the data warehouse need prefabricated reports and preset queries. The casual users who need information once in a while and not on a regular basis need prepackaged information. Business analysts who use the data warehouse for strategic decision making purposes such as trend identification, forecasting, competitive analysis, and targeted market research perform complex analysis using the information stored in the data warehouse. The power users navigate throughout the data warehouse contents to extract information by formatting their own queries. They drill through data and create customized reports and ad hoc queries.

Thus, to satisfy the informational needs of a wide range of users, the information delivery component includes different methods of information delivery. As shown in Fig. 2.14, predefined reports and queries are primarily meant for novice and casual users. Business analysts and power users are satisfied by the provision for complex queries, multi dimensional analysis and statistical analysis. Information fed into *Executive Information Systems* (EIS) and data mining systems is meant for senior executives and high-level managers.

In a data warehouse, information delivery through queries and reports is the most common mechanism where the users enter their requests online and receive the results online. However, the trend these days is to set up delivery of scheduled reports through e-mail via internet or the organization's intranet.

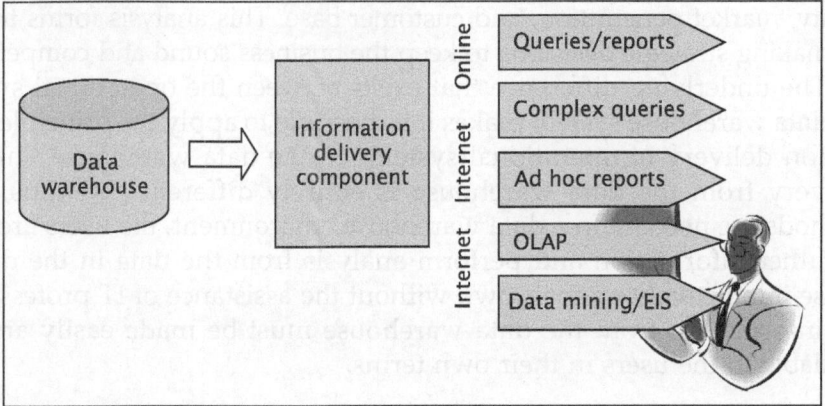

Figure 2.14   Deliver the information to the end-users

The End-user Community

Some authors have categorized the data warehouse users in four types of communities—farmers, explorers, miners and tourists. Each of these individual communities has a different sets of needs. Table 2.3 summarizes the characteristics of these different types of end-user communities.

Generally, there are more of farmers in the data warehouse environment but practically speaking an end-user may change types on fly at any point of

Table 2.3   Characteristics of end-user communities

 Farmer	• Most predominant type of user. • The farmer knows what he or she wants. • A predictable user who performs the same activity on a routine basis. • Executes short queres that have similar access patterns.
• The explorer does not know what he or she wants. • He operates in a mode of unpredictability. • Looks at large volumes of data to discover patterns that may or may not exist in the data. • The operator operates in a heuristic mode.	 Explorer
 Miner	• The miner digs into piles of data. • The miner works on an assertion to determine its validity and strength. • The miner uses statistical tools for analysis. • The miner create queries that operates on large datasets. • The miner operates in a heuristic mode. • While the explorers create assertions and hypotheses, the miners determine its strength and validity.
• The tourist knows where to find things like- data, metadata, indexes. • The tourists have a breadth of knowledge not depth of knowledge. • The tourist can work with structured as well as unstructured data. • Tourists are familiar with the source code and know how to read and interpret it.	 Tourist

time. That is to say, an end-user may use the data warehouse as farmers at one moment and as an explorer the other moment. Therefore, depending on the task in hand, the same user may access the data warehouse as a different type of end-user at different point of time.

Functions of Information Delivery System

In the process of delivering information to the end-users, the information delivery system performs the following functions:

- Provides security to control information access by different users.
- Monitors user access patterns to improve service and for future enhancements.
- Enables the users to browse the contents of the data warehouse intuitively.
- Simplifies data access by hiding complexities of data storage from users
- Performs optimization by reformatting the queries.
- Makes use of aggregate tables (if they exist) for faster query results.
- Provides preformatted and predefined queries and reports.
- Enables the users to perform complex analysis.
- Enables data feeds to downstream applications like OLAP, EIS, and data mining.

Information Delivery Methods

In this section, we will read about different ways in which information can be delivered to the end-users. Look at Fig. 2.15 which shows how a data warehouse user accesses the data warehouse.

Queries Query management ranks high in the provision of information delivery in a data warehouse environment. Features of a managed query environment are:

- The query is formed and the results are displayed on the client site.
- Metadata guides the execution of the query.
- Enables the users to navigate easily through the data.
- Information is deliberately pulled by the users.
- Query environment must be flexible to cater to the needs of different classes of users.

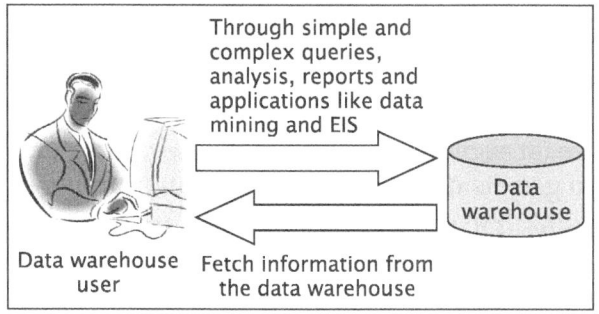

Figure 2.15 Different methods to access the data warehouse

Reports The characteristics of reports as an information delivery mechanism are listed below.

- Reports are generally inflexible when compared with queries.
- Information is pushed to the users through reports and not deliberately pulled by them as in case of queries.
- For every report that is published in the data warehouse environment, the users must subscribe themselves for receiving those reports.
- Reports are rigid as they are generally preformatted.
- As compared to queries, the user has less control over the reports.
- Report generation takes place on the server machine.

Analysis Business strategists, market researchers, business analysts, managers are the people who need information from the data warehouse. Since, the data warehouse contains both the current and historical data, it is well-suited for analysis. It helps the users to search for trends, discern patterns and find correlations.

An analysis session is an interactive session of a series of related queries. The user starts with an initial query—what are the monthly sales for the last year by product categories? The user looks at the numbers and further drills down by individual products in the product category. The next query is for a breakdown by regions. The analysis continues with comparisons of the monthly sales of the last two years.

In analysis, there are no predefined paths rather, the queries are formulated and executed at the speed of thought. One significant difference between query and analysis is that each query in an analysis is linked to the previous one thereby forming a link. Analysis is thus, rightly called an interactive exercise.

Applications In the data warehouse environment, any downstream system that takes data from the data warehouse to enable its users to access the data content of the warehouse directly forms a decision support application. Building a decision support application that takes it data feeds from the data warehouse rather than from operational systems has one major advantage. The data in the data warehouse is already cleaned, consolidated, integrated and transformed. So no such work needs to be redone.

Executive Information System (EIS) is a good example of downstream applications. EIS built with data from a data warehouse performs much better than EIS applications that were based on data from operational systems. However, the latest development in downstream applications is the wide use of data mining applications. Data mining also gets its data feeds from the data warehouse.

OLAP On-line analytical processing (OLAP) tools allow a sophisticated user to analyse the data using elaborate, multidimensional, complex views. Typical business applications for these tools include product performance and profitability, effectiveness of a sales program or a marketing campaign, sales forecasting and capacity planning. We will learn more about OLAP in chapter 10.

Data mining A critical success factor for a business lies in its ability to use information effectively. The strategic use of data can result from opportunities presented by discovering hidden, previously undetected and after extremely valuable facts about customers, retailers, suppliers and business trends. After discovering this information, the organization can formulate effective business strategies, target promotional activity, and discover new markets. A relatively new technology that is targeted towards achieving this strategic advantage is known as data mining.

Many authors have defined data mining as the process of discovering meaningful new correlations, patterns and trends by digging into large amounts of data stored in data warehouses. The scope of data mining extends beyond the scope of OLAP. Although, data mining is still an emerging discipline, it has a huge potential to gain significant benefits in the marketplace and is continuously being adopted by many industries today. Figure 2.16 shows how information passed from OLTP to the data warehouse and from there to he users through the data mining.

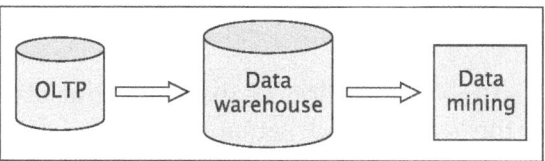

Figure 2.16   Information flow in case of data mining applications

2.5 METADATA

Before going into the details of the metadata component, we will first understand why metadata is important in the data warehouse environment. Imagine that the data warehouse project team has completed the project and everything was done as per to the schedule and within the estimated budget. The results have been tested and the data warehouse is ready for deployment. After deployment, when the first user sits at the machine to execute his queries. We will have a number of questions in his mind like—

- Are there any predefined queries?
- What are the various elements of data in the warehouse?
- Does it contain the data that I need?
- How can I browse the data to find out what data is available?
- From which source systems has the data in the data warehouse been collected?
- How old is the data in the warehouse?
- Is there any summary data?
- To what level has the summarization/aggregation of data been done?
- Is there any pre-calculated data already available in the data warehouse?
- When was the data last refreshed?

It is the metadata in the data warehouse which answers all the questions. Let us take an example of an entity called *customer*, in the data warehouse. If the user wants to know about this entity, he will search for this information in the metadata repository.

Definition A client is a person or an organization that purchases goods or services from your company. **Remarks** Customer entity includes regular, current and past customers. **Source systems** Orders placed, Maintenance contracts, Online sales.	Create date: 26 April 2005 Last update date: 16 November 2006 Update cycle: Weekly Last full refresh: 5 June 2005 Full refresh cycle: Every Quarter Data quality reviewed: 25 September 2006 Last de-duplication: 19 September 2006 Planned archival: 16 January 2007 Responsible user: John Mathew

Figure 2.17 A sample metadata

A metadata does not give you just the description of the entity but also gives you other details explaining the syntax and semantics of the data elements. Metadata describes all the pertinent aspects of the data in the data warehouse fully and precisely to help the users and the developers of the data warehouse. A typical metadata contains information about the following:

- Structure of data from the programmer's perspective
- Structure of data from the end-user's perspective
- Source systems that feed the data warehouse
- Transformation process that was applied before the data from the source systems could pass into the data warehouse
- Data model
- History of data extraction process

A sample look of how the details are stored about an entity is given in the Fig. 2.17.

2.5.1 Role of Metadata

Metadata in the data warehouse is similar to the data dictionary in a database management system. The metadata component stores data about the data in the data warehouse. The metadata is often used for building, maintaining, managing, and using the data warehouse. It is the key to providing users and developers with a road map to the information in the Warehouse. Thus, it forms an essential ingredient in the transformation of raw data into knowledge. The three main functions that metadata performs in a data warehouse environment are that it

- Connects the different parts of the data warehouse thereby acting as a glue that connects all the parts.
- Provides information about the contents of the data and its underlying structure to the data warehouse administrator and other users.
- Enables the end-users to search for the desired data in their own business terms.

Metadata can be looked at as tongs that handle the raw data. Without a proper metadata in place, data stored in the warehouse will be meaningless since the users will not be able to know- what, where, why and how the data exists within the organization. And in the absence of this crucial knowledge they will never be able to query this data.

Table 2.4 illustrates that a data warehouse in the absence of metadata is like simply filling the cabinet with a number of papers with no folder or label. No person will be able to find any valuable piece of information from those pages. Similarly is the case with a data warehouse.

Table 2.4 Role of metadata in a data warehouse

Metadata plays a key role in converting raw data into knowledge as it helps to provide valuable description about the data so that it can be understood and converted into meaningful information.	
Data	
12 233 870	This string of digits could either be sales of a product or population of a city.
06/07/08	This date could either be Date of Birth or date when the sales transaction took place. This date could either mean 6 July 2008 or 7 June 2008.
Metadata contains data about data	
12 233 870	Sale of T-shirts in the western region
07/06/08	Refers to the date of sales transaction stored in the format—dd/mm//yy

2.5.2 Classification of Metadata

Metadata can be classified in three main groups (Refer Fig. 2.18):

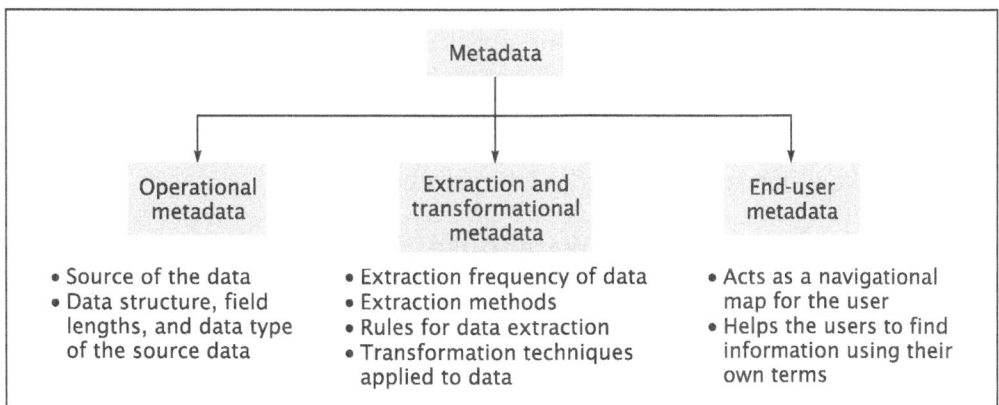

Figure 2.18 Types of metadata

Operational metadata   Data for the data warehouse comes from several operational systems of the organization which contain different data structures, that have varying field lengths and data types. In selecting data from the source systems, you may either have to split certain records or may have to combine parts of records from different files and deal with multiple coding schemes and field lengths. The end-users may ever want to be able to tie back to the original source datasets. The operational metadata solves this purpose by containing all of this information about the operational data sources.

Extraction and transformational metadata As the name suggests, the extraction and transformational metadata contains data about the data extraction from the source systems and the various transformation techniques that were applied to the data before storing it in the data warehouse. Extraction and transformational metadata serves a technical purpose for development and maintenance of the warehouse. The primary reason for this metadata is to map every individual data element from its source system to the data warehouse. This calls for identification of the data element by its source field name, destination field name, transformation rules applied, business rules for usage and derivation and its format, key, size, and index.

End-user metadata The end-user metadata acts as a navigational map of the data warehouse by enabling the end-users to find information from the data warehouse using their own business terminologies. End-user metadata translates a cryptic name code of a data element into a meaningful description of the data element so that end-users can understand and use that data. For example, it is duty of the metadata to clarify that the data element 'CName' represents "Customer Name for the business."

2.5.3 Importance of Metadata

All the processes that are carried out during the building and administering of the data warehouse generate parts of the data warehouse metadata. Metadata generated by one application is used by some other application. In the data warehouse environment, metadata occupies a key position. It is only through metadata that the communication among various applications and processes is made possible. It will not be wrong to say that the metadata acts like a nerve centre in the data warehouse.

For Using the Data Warehouse

In a data warehouse system, the users themselves retrieve the information by creating ad hoc queries and running them against the data warehouse. They format their own reports. So before creating their own reports and queries, the users need to know about the data in the data warehouse. For this they need the metadata.

The users need sophisticated methods for browsing and examining the contents order to derive maximum output from the data warehouse. Users should know the meaning of the data elements so that due to their ignorance about the exact meanings, they may not draw wrong conclusions from their analysis.

For Building the Data Warehouse

A data warehouse developer may be an expert in data extraction and transformation techniques and may know very well how to work with different tools. But, to apply his expertise he first needs to know the data structures and contents of the data warehouse. Only after having a firm understanding of the data, the data warehouse developer can determine the mappings and the transformations that have to be done with the data available. Therefore, to build the data extraction and data transformation components of the data warehouse, metadata about the source systems, source-to-target mappings, and data transformation rules is needed.

Even the database administrator of the data warehouse needs the metadata for creating the physical design of the database, for doing the initial loading of the data and for performing the incremental loads. The metadata in this case, will provide information like—the logical structure of the data warehouse database, the data refresh, and the load cycles.

For Administering the Data Warehouse

The underlying complexities and enormous sizes of the data warehouses make it impossible to administer the data warehouse without substantial metadata. One cannot administer the data warehouse without addressing some barely minimum set of questions which are listed below:

- How to include new data sources?
- How to drop some external data sources?
- How to handle data changes?
- How to audit the applications?
- How to add new summary tables in the data warehouse?
- How to control run away queries?
- How to expand storage?
- When to schedule platform upgrades?
- How to add new information delivery tools for the users?
- How to continue ongoing training?
- How to maintain and enhance user support functions?
- How to monitor and improve query performance?
- When to schedule backups?
- How to perform disaster recovery?
- How to maintain security?
- How to monitor load balancing?

2.5.4 Metadata Management

The metadata forms a vital element in a data warehouse environment, but the seamless integration of all the parts of metadata is a formidable task. There exist a few sets of challenges that force the data warehouse developers to abandon the requirements for proper metadata management. However, once the data warehouse development team has decided to go for metadata, it needs to address these issues or challenges. Some of these challenges are:

- A number of tools are used in the data warehouse environment where each software tool has its own proprietary metadata, so reconciling these formats is not a trivial issue.
- There are no industry-wide accepted standards that exist for the format of metadata.
- There has always been a debate over the advantages of a centralized metadata repository as opposed to a collection of fragmented metadata stores.
- Passing the metadata from one process to the other as data moves from source systems to the staging area and from there to the data warehouse is not easy.
- Since the source systems contain data in different formats, having different standards, naming conventions, definitions, attributes, values, and units of measures, it becomes a cumbersome task to unify the metadata.

2.6 TWO CLASSES OF DATA

In large data warehouses, there are two categories of data– frequently used data and infrequently used data. As time passes, the frequently or actively used data moves to the other state and becomes infrequently used. The data that is used once every 2–3 months is placed under the frequently used category and the data that is used 0.6 times per year is classified as infrequently used.

It is important to classify the data under these categories so that the less frequently used data can be separated from that used frequently. If we place all this data together on the same data warehouse disk storage, then it will call for huge sums of money. Therefore the most viable option is to split the data warehouse data over multiple forms of storage. The frequently used data is stored on high performance disks and the less frequently used data is moved to low cost bulk storage. This bulk storage is sequential in nature and is also known as near-line storage. Segregating the data into two categories and thereby placing them on different storage media enhances the performance of the data warehouse environment.

When we place all the data including the frequently and infrequently used data on the same disk storage, the performance deteriorates. Inmon in his book *Building the Data Warehouse* has given a very good analogy. He says that a disk with mixed data is like that of data being flowed within the arteries that is clogged with cholesterol. But when data is split based on its frequency of usage, the data flows through arteries smoothly as there is less cholesterol.

The near line storage stores huge amounts of data and is relatively less expensive than the disks. Whenever the user needs data that is stored in near line storage, all the records except the first one is fetched in nanoseconds. The first record takes longer to access, because it takes time to reach the first block of data. Once the first block is accessed, the subsequent data is stored sequentially and thus takes only a few nanoseconds to fetch.

2.7 THE LIFECYCLE OF DATA

Every piece of data that enters into the organization goes through a life cycle. Figure 2.19 shows this cycle.

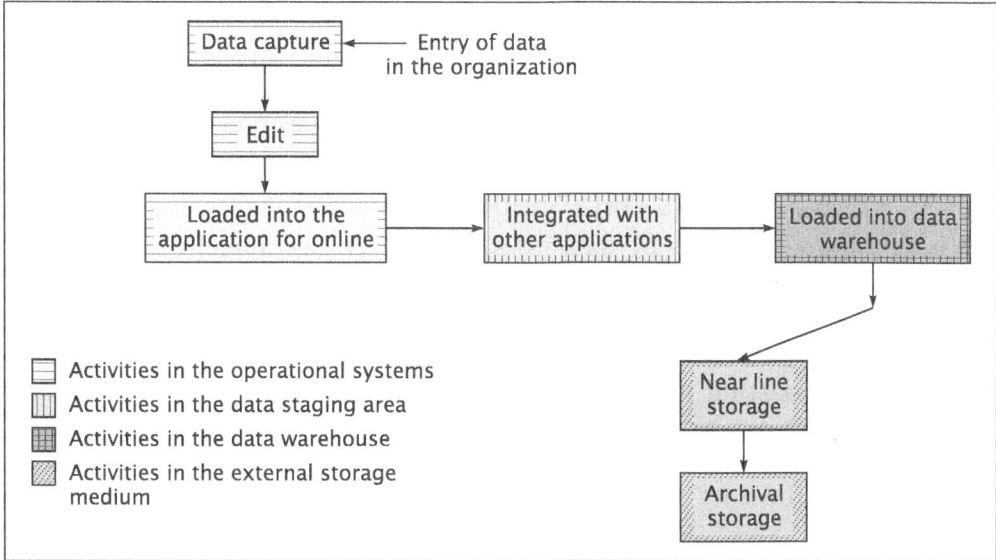

Figure 2.19 Life cycle of data

Data enters an organization as soon as any transaction that captures the data takes place. This captured data is edited and undergoes validity and domain checks. The verified and edited data is then loaded into some application so that it can be accessed online by its users. If the data warehouse has been deployed in the organization then all the data from various operational systems is collected and integrated to be finally stored in the data warehouse.

The data warehouse is then used for strategic purposes. The data is stored there for about 2–3 years and when this data grows old and is being used very infrequently then it is removed from the warehouse and stored in some near line storage and then placed into archives.

Although archival storage is similar to near line storage, the difference is that it stores data which is seldom used, approximately 0.1 times in a decade.

Even when the usage of this data has almost dropped to zero, there is a need to store this data for any future usage.

When the data is stored in the near line storage, the location of the data is said to be transparent to the end-user. By transparent, we mean that the end-user is not aware of the location of the data, that is, whether the data exists on a high speed disk or on a near line storage media. But when the data is stored on archives, the transparency diminishes as the user always knows that the data he wants to fetch is stored offline on some archived media.

To achieve this level of transparency, it is important that the data must be stored in the same format on the near line storage as it is stored in the data warehouse. The near line storage database must be compatible with that of data warehouse and the data warehouse database must be able to fetch the data stored in the near line storage in a matter of few seconds. Of course, these restrictions are not meant for archival storage as there is no transparency in the data access that is made from the data warehouse and the archives. So archival storage may not be compatible with the data warehouse and may not store the data in same format as the data warehouse stores.

2.7.1 What is Data Velocity?

Inmon defines data velocity as the speed with which data passes from initial capture to the point of use by the analyst. It is calculated by finding out the average time elapsed between the entry of data into the system and the usage of the data by the end-user analyst. It includes the time needed for editing the data, passing it to the appropriate application, then for Extraction, Transformation, Loading (ETL) processing so that the data can be stored in the warehouse from where the end-user will finally access it. The main factor that affects the data velocity is the integration process—more the data to be integrated lesser is the velocity.

2.7.2 Moving Data from One Medium to Another

We have seen that data constantly passes from one medium to another. There are three different mechanisms to manage the flow of data from the data warehouse to the near line storage. These are discussed as follows:

Manual Transfer

In manual transfer, the data warehouse administrator himself moves the data from one medium to another. The administrator places a data warehouse monitor that continuously monitors the usage of data. The data that is not being used frequently is moved from the data warehouse environment to the near line storage. This option provides flexibility and uses minimal technology. The advantages of manual transfer include: (a) simplicity, (b) immediate availability, and (c) operability at the row level. On the flip side, this process is error-prone and requires human interaction.

Hierarchical Storage Management (HSM)

This mechanism is fully automated and is free from any human intervention. It moves entire sets of data between the data warehouse and the near line storage. This technique is fairly simple, inexpensive, and fully automated.

On the negative side, HSM operates at the dataset level.

Cross Media Storage Management (CMSM)

It is a fully automated procedure. The main difference between the HSM and CMSM is that, CMSM operates at the row level of granularity so that rows can be migrated to and from the data warehouse and the near line storage. Although this approach is better than the former two approaches it is the most complicated one. The CMSM approach makes the data transfer transparent to the user so that he does not know where the data is actually located.

When the user poses a query that needs data stored in the data warehouse, the system fetches the data and proceeds with the execution of the query. However, if the data is present in any near line storage, then first the system collects the data from the near line storage media and then proceeds with the query.

Although, the user sees no difference between posing the query against the data warehouse or the near line storage, but there does exist a difference in the time required to execute that query.

In the CMSM approach, it is the data warehouse monitor that continuously monitors what data is being used by the queries posed by the end-users. It identifies the data that is not being used frequently by the queries and monitors the usage of data at the row level so that data can be more finely tuned with the warehouse.

The data warehouse monitor is available as part of the DBMS as well as from the third party vendors. Reports say that monitors obtained from vendors perform much better than those provided with the DBMS. The monitors that are a part of the DBMS call for a greater overhead on resources and thus are less preferred. CMSM is fully automated and operates at row level. But it is expensive and complex to implement. Its operation is not easy either.

2.7.3 Inverted Data Warehouse

In a normal data warehouse that we have studied so far, the frequently used data resides on the high performance disks. When the data ages it is moved from the disk to some near line storage. When its usage drops even more, the data is finally transferred to the archives.

An inverted data warehouse is an alternate data warehouse in which the data is first entered into near line storage. When a query is executed, the data is moved from the near line storage to the disk environment from where the data is accessed and analysed. The query makes use of this data as if the data permanently resided in the disk storage. When the query execution is over, the data is again transferred to the near line storage from the disk. Hence, in an inverted environment the current data resides on near line storage as opposed to disks. The key benefit of having an inverted data warehouse is that it can handle and manage any amount of data.

2.8 DATA FLOW FROM WAREHOUSE TO OPERATIONAL SYSTEMS

Till now, we have read that data is moved from the operational systems to the data warehouse. But is it possible to move the data out from the data warehouse to be stored in the operational systems? Even if it is possible, does it really make any sense to do so? In this section, we will have a look at the answers to these questions.

The operational systems can access the data stored in the data warehouse in two different modes—direct and indirect.

2.8.1 Direct Access Mode

In direct access mode, a request for data is made in the operational system. The requested data lies in the data warehouse, so the request for the data is transferred to the data warehouse. When the request is processed, the data is transferred to the operational system. Although this approach seems very simple, it brings forward a number of serious and uncompromising limitations that are listed below:

- The response time must not be bounded as it may take even 24 hours to transfer the requested data.
- The requested data must be of minimal amount that can be measured in bytes and not in mega bytes.
- The underlying technology (in terms of protocols used, capacity) of operational systems must be compatible with that of the data warehouse system.
- There should be minimal formatting required for the data that has to be transferred from the data warehouse to the operational system.

These conditions make the transfer of data from the data warehouse to the operational system minimal as these conditions preclude most data being directly transferred in the backward direction.

2.8.2 Indirect Access Mode

Before seeing how data in the data warehouse is indirectly accessed from the operational systems, let us first see why a data warehouse's data is actually needed by the operational systems users. For this purpose, we will have a look at two different scenarios.

1. A customer contacts a travel agent to get his airline ticket. The travel agent talks to the operator at the airline office to enquire about the availability of seat, cost of seat, and the amount of commission that will

be paid to him. The operator at the airline office needs to provide a brisk response to the agent or else he will lose the customer.

Since the operator has to manipulate a lot of data, as answers to these questions depends on not just one but several factors, it is recommended that offline calculation and analysis be done periodically on the data warehouse data and the result be stored in small, easy to access tables in the operational system. This would help the airline clerk to get instant information and would enable him to provide quick and fast response to the agent.

2. A customer of a retail chain calls a sales representative to place his order. If details about the last time the customer made a purchase, the items he purchased, and other personal information about the customer gets displayed on the sales representative's computer screen, it would help him to personalize his conversation with the customer.

It would enable him to gauge the shopping interests of the customer, and give him information about other new products that he is likely to buy and even tell him about discounted items that may interest him. All this is possible by indirectly using the data warehouse.

In the background, that is, in the data warehouse environment, an analysis program is run that reads and analyses customer historical records and deduces useful information about them. The result of the analysis is stored in a file that is passed to the operational environment. It contains information like last purchased data, items that were bought, and other data demographics data. When the customer calls, the online file is used by the operator to personalize the conversation.

With the help of these two examples, it is clear that certain situations make it a necessity that the data from the warehouse be moved into the operational systems. The mechanism of this data transfer is very simple. The data warehouse is periodically analysed by a program that examines the relevant characteristics. The analysis creates a small file that contains succinct information about the business. This small file is then moved to the operational environment where it is used easily and quickly. The periodic refreshment moves the data from the data warehouse to the operational system.

Recapitulation

Data warehouse is a subject-oriented, integrated, non-volatile, time-variant collection of data.

In the data warehouse, data is stored by subjects and not by applications as in case of operational systems where the data is distributed across multiple applications in the source system.

Data cleansing is the process of removing errors from the input stream and it is part of the integration process.

The data in data warehouse is not as volatile as the data in an operational database is. The data in a data warehouse is for query and analysis. In essence, the non-volatility of the data warehouse creates a *virtual* read-only database system.

Source data component includes four types of data: production data, internal data, archived data, and external data. Production data comes from the various operational systems of the enterprise. Internal data is stored in private spreadsheets, documents, and customer profiles. Archived data consists of historical data. External data includes the statistics relating to industry produced by external agencies, and market share data of competitors.

The ETL process takes place at the data staging area. Data staging provides an area with a set of functions to clean, change, combine, convert, and prepare the source data.

Data transformation includes standardization of the data types and field lengths of same data elements received from various sources, resolving of synonyms and homonyms, merging or splitting of certain fields depending upon the structure of data warehouse database and building of primary and foreign keys for the records that have to be stored in data warehouse tables.

The loading process involves initial loading and incremental feeds. The initial load moves large volumes of data, but as the data warehouse starts functioning, you continue to extract the changes to the source data, transform the data, and feed the incremental data revisions as an ongoing process.

A data warehouse repository can either store the data using tables in relational DBMS or in multidimensional cubes.

Metadata in the data warehouse is similar to the data dictionary. The metadata component stores data about the data in the data warehouse.

The management and control component coordinates the services and activities within the data warehouse.

Granularity refers to the level of detail of data in the data warehouse. The more the detail, lower is the level of granularity.

Business metadata focuses on providing support for the end-users at the workstation. It must make it easy for the end-users to understand what data is available and how they can use it.

Technical metadata is like a support guide for the IT professionals to build, maintain and administer the data warehouse, to understand the data extraction, data transformation, and data cleansing processes.

Objective Questions

1. **Choose the correct answer**
    (i) Standardization must be done to:
    (a) Naming conventions
    (b) Codes
    (c) Attributes
    (d) Measurements
    (e) All of these
    (f) None of these
    (ii) The process of removing errors from the input data that is a part of the integration process
    (a) Data extraction
    (b) Data cleansing
    (c) Data loading
    (d) Information delivery
    (f) None of these
    (iii) Which system is designed to update the data in real time?
    (a) Data warehouse
    (b) Operational system
    (c) Infomational system
    (iv) Arrange the options according to the stages in data archival
    (a) Archival database
    (b) Tape drives
    (c) Disk storage

    (v) Data cleansing is performed in

       (a) Source systems

       (b) Data warehouse repository

       (c) Data staging area

2. Fill in the blanks

    (a) While _____ are optimized to execute insert- and update-type queries, the _____ are optimized to execute select-type queries.

    (b) A _____ is an informational delivery system.

    (c) The _____ must determine the source of this error and take corrective action.

    (d) _____ refers to the level of detail of data in the data warehouse.

    (e) _____ contains information about operational systems, ETL process, data warehouse, tools and predefined reports.

    (f) The _____ is responsible for distributing the data stored in the warehouse to its end-users.

    (g) _____ pull information from the warehouse and _____ push information to the users.

3. Match the following

1.	Higher level	(a)	More storage space
2.	High level of granularity detailed data	(b)	Glue that holds the contents together
3.	Production data	(c)	Fewer index entries

    4. Internal data   (d) Spreadsheets, documents, customer profiles

    5. Novice users   (e) Multidimensional analysis.

    6. Power users   (f) From operational systems.

    7. OLAP   (g) EIS and data mining systems.

    8. Metadata   (h) Prefabricated reports and preset queries

4. State true or false

    (a) The data in an operational system keeps changing, whereas data warehouses are non-volatile.

    (b) While OLTP systems are characterized with large and complex schemas, the data warehouse schema on the other hand, is simplified and denormalized.

    (c) Operational systems do not store historical information.

    (d) Data in data warehouse systems are organized around applications whereas the operational systems stores data by subjects and not by applications.

    (e) More detailed data means lower level of granularity.

    (f) Operational systems and data warehouse systems have the same keys.

    (g) The metadata is often used for building, maintaining, managing and using the data warehouse.

Review Questions

1. Define a data warehouse. Relate this definition to that of an operational system and explain.

2. A data warehouse cuts across several applications in the source systems. Comment.

3. Discuss the issues in integrating from various disparate sources.

4. Why is data cleansing and data transformation functions considered to be a vital task in the integration process. Explain these functions and also mention where these functions take place.

5. Explain the ETL process.

6. Write a short note on the components of a data warehouse.

7. Why is time considered to be an important element while storing the data in the data warehouse?

8. Explain the difference between different types of source data.

9. Why do you need a separate staging area in a data warehouse environment?

10. Write a short note on the importance of metadata in a data warehouse.

11. What do you understand by the term data granularity? Give some advantages and disadvantages of keeping detailed data in the data warehouse. What practical approach is followed in a data warehouse when we talk about data granularity?

12. Name a few operational applications from which data will be extracted and fed into the data warehouse of on airline.

13. List down potential users and the various information delivery methods for a data warehouse supporting a large international retail chain.

3

ARCHITECTURE OF A DATA WAREHOUSE AND DATA MART ISSUES

Learning Objectives

The architecture is the logical and physical foundation on which the data warehouse will be built. In this chapter, we will study the physical architecture of a data warehouse and see how it is different from that of an operational system. Then we will learn some of the architectural goals, challenges, and considerations in deploying two-tier and three-tier architecture.

Apart from this, we will also study about data marts and whether an organization should build it or not. In case it is necessary for an organization to have one or more data marts, then what approach should be followed to build them. Finally, we will draw some key points explaining the comparison between data warehouses and data marts.

Case Study

The second most important question that has to be answered before going for a data warehouse is whether to build a data mart first or a data warehouse first. A data mart is just a departmental version of a data warehouse.

Consider a company ABC Corp which wants to build a data warehouse for its organization. The strategy that they follow is to build a number of data marts first and when they grow enormously large in size they are combined to form a data warehouse. Although this approach is simple it is not workable because

in this a data warehouse is just a combination of data marts and badly lacks its own architecture. After two years of implementation of such a data warehouse, the company finds it difficult to work with it and the success of this decision support system is lost.

In view of the drawbacks of this strategy, another company Westward Lee decides to follow a well defined architecture for a data warehouse as well as for a data mart. They follow a strategy of implementing first a data warehouse and then going for individual data marts. This is a better strategy as it incorporates an enterprise view of data and is inherently architected rather just being a union of disparate data marts. But even this approach has some setbacks, like, it takes longer to build a data warehouse and includes a higher risk of failure.

Now after analysing the pros and cons of Westward Lee's strategy, Pallav Raj, CEO of JRTs, decides to follow a bottom up strategy of building a data warehouse wherein the data marts will be implemented first and then the data warehouse, bearing in need the architecture of data marts and data warehouses. This approach has advantages of providing faster and easier implementation of data marts and less risk of failure but suffers from problems like redundancy of data and thus presence of inconsistent and irreconcilable data.

3.1 INTRODUCTION

Data warehouse architecture can be defined as a description of the elements and services of the warehouse, with details showing how the components will fit together and how the system will grow over time.

The architecture provides the overall framework for developing and deploying the data warehouse. In other words, it is a comprehensive blueprint. An efficient architecture is critical for the success of the data warehouse.

The architecture of a data warehouse includes everything that is needed to prepare the data and store it and finally all the means for delivering information from the data warehouse to the users.

The architecture is further composed of rules, procedures, and functions that enable the data warehouse to operate and cater to business requirements. The architecture is thus made up of technology that empowers the data warehouse.

When all the components perform their predefined functions and render the required services, then the whole architecture supports the data warehouse to achieve its goals and business requirements.

Tools are the means to implement the architecture. That is to say, the architecture comes first and then the tools. Thus you have to select the tools that are most appropriate for your data warehouse.

3.2 CHARACTERISTICS OF DATA WAREHOUSE ARCHITECTURE

We need a sound architecture before actually building any system, be it an operational system or a data warehouse system. The architecture of a data warehouse is very different from that of an operational system. The architecture for an operational system includes the file conversions, initial population of the database, methods for data input, information delivery through online screens. Data warehouse architecture is wide, complex, and expansive. But before discussing the architecture of the data warehouse, let us first review the distinguishing characteristics of data warehouse architecture.

3.2.1 Different Objectives and Scope

The data warehouse architecture enables users to make strategic decisions. The purpose of a data warehouse database is strikingly different from that of an operational system. In the operational system, the user may need data about a product and its related sales, but the queries that are posed against a data warehouse would contain a much larger result set.

When users extract information from an operational application, the information content and quantity per user session is limited. But a data warehouse architecture must have components that enable its users to access large volumes of data in a single session. This requirement calls for a data warehouse that has a different and elaborate architecture.

The scope of operational systems can be defined by having a look at the number of functions that the application will support; the number of users, data repositories, and the output screens. However, the scope of a data warehouse is much wider.

In defining the scope of a data warehouse, first one needs to consider the number and extent of the data sources (internal sources, external sources, archived data, and production data). Second, the extent to which the data transformation and integration functions will be performed. Data granularity, data volumes, and the impact of the data warehouse on the operational systems are also important considerations.

3.2.2 Data Content

Data warehouses contain read-only data. However, before this data is brought into the data warehouse and stored in it, a number of functions are performed on it. As discussed in the previous chapter it is extracted then from multiple sources. Transformed, cleansed, and integrated in the data staging area. Finally it is moved into the data warehouse repository as read-only data. On the contrary, operational data is not read-only data.

Further, the data warehouse architecture must support the storing of data centred around business subjects and not by applications as in the case of operational systems. The data in the data warehouse is time variant in nature and stores current as well as historical data as opposed to operational systems which keep only current data. Data warehouses often store 10 years of historical data. Thus, the data warehouse architecture must support storing of very high volumes of data.

3.2.3 Complex Analysis and Quick Response

The data warehouse architecture must support complex analysis of the data stored in it. Information retrieval processes in an operational system are far behind in complexity when compared to that of a data warehouse. The end-users extract information from the warehouse in an interactive manner. The user usually starts with a high level query, reviews the result set obtained, and based upon the result, again initiates the next query that presents the data in a slightly different way, and so on. This makes the user sessions continuous and long lasting.

The data warehouse architecture must enable the users to perform operations like drill-down, roll-up, slice and dice, and play with what-if scenarios. Since users may not always want the data to be displayed only textually, the architecture must have the provision to convert the result in tabular formats and graphical charts. Thus, it is crucial that the data warehouse architecture has the appropriate components that support quick response to the end-users to enable them to make strategic decisions.

The data warehouse must enable its users to extract information so that they can take quick decisions to handle the critical situation efficiently. For example, if the sales of a particular product are continuously going down for last three weeks then, the marketing manager must take immediate decision to cater to this situation. The data warehouse must provide the users appropriate tools and data to help them make strategic decisions. For this the architecture must contain the components that are placed to provide quick response to its users.

3.2.4 Flexible and Dynamic

In the case of data warehouse development, the project team does not have a comprehensive knowledge base about business requirements well in advance. With the help of the information package diagrams (see chapter 5), the team is able to access most of the requirements and create the dimensional model (see chapter 7) based on the data requirements. But since the requirements were not very clear, the team must ensure that the data warehouse is flexible enough to accommodate additional requirements as and when they surface. The additional requirements will pop up as business conditions keep changing. If the data warehouse architecture is designed to be flexible and dynamic, then the warehouse can easily cater to the additional requirements as and when they arise.

3.2.5 Metadata Driven

In the data warehouse architecture, the data moves from the operational systems to the end-users in the form of strategic information. The entire architecture is surrounded by metadata that holds data about every stage of data movement. In an operational system, there is no component that plays the same role that metadata plays in a data warehouse. The data dictionary that is present in the operational systems is a faint shadow of the metadata in the data warehouse. Metadata component in the data warehouse acts as the glue that connects all the parts of the data warehouse together and provides a navigational map to the end-users to enable them to find relevant information using their own terminologies.

3.3 DATA WAREHOUSE ARCHITECTURE GOALS

Warren Thornthwaite writes "Every data warehouse has an architecture, either ad hoc or planned; implied or documented. Unfortunately, many warehouses are developed without an explicit architectural plan, which severely limits flexibility."

A data warehouse can be built in the absence of a sound architecture, however, without architecture, subject areas don't fit together, connections lead to nowhere, and the warehouse becomes difficult to manage and change.

Besides this, there is a very important saying "Architecture first, then the tools." This means that the architecture of a data warehouse becomes the framework for product selection.

Thornthwaite has very rightly compared the development of a data warehouse to building a real house. He insists on the fact that no one can ever build a $3 million mansion without technical blueprints that specify the drawings, specifications, and standards showing how the house will be constructed, at multiple levels of detail.

Like the house analogy, he lays stress on the data warehouse architecture that in itself is a set of documents, plans, models, drawings, and specifications, with separate sections for each key component area and enough detail to allow their implementation by skilled professionals. According to him, the architecture has to be driven by the business.

Thus, a data warehouse exists to serve its users and it should be designed to satisfy the following requirements:

Gain user acceptance which is the measure of success; Provide a user intuitive and user friendly environment; Allow the users to do query processing without interfering with the operational systems; Provide a central repository of consistent, accurate, cleaned, and integrated data; Respond to complex queries quickly and efficiently; Provide support to run powerful applications like EIS, OLAP, and data mining.

3.4 DATA WAREHOUSE ARCHITECTURE

Data warehouse architecture is a way of representing the overall structure of the data, processing and presentation that exists for end-user computing within the organization. It is the business requirements that drive the entire architecture. So before jumping right into building the data warehouse, the project development team should first consult business managers, analysts, and power users.

The team must also talk to existing data warehouse/DSS (Decision Support System) support staff, OLTP application groups, and DBAs; as well as networking, OS, and desktop support staff regarding architecture documents, IT principles, standards statements, organizational power centres, etc if any.

Although there are not many standards that exist for data warehousing, yes there are standards for a lot of the components.

- For middleware technology, use ODBC, OLE, OLE DB, DCE, ORBs, and JDBC.
- For data base connectivity, use ODBC, JDBC, OLE DB, and others.
- For data management, use ANSI SQL and FTP.
- For network access, use protocols like DCE, DNS, and LDAP.

Regardless of what standards they support, major data warehousing tools are metadata-driven. The architecture is made up of a number of interconnected components as shown in Fig. 3.1.

3.4.1 Operational Database Layer

Operational systems process data to support day to day operational needs. To accomplish this, applications in the operational systems are created to provide an efficient processing structure for a relatively small number of well-defined business transactions. Due to the limited focus of operational systems, the databases designed to support operational systems have difficulty accessing the data for informational purposes. This difficulty in accessing operational data is amplified by the fact that many operational systems are often 10 to 15 years old which means that the data access technology available to obtain operational data is itself dated.

The goal of a data warehouse is to combine the information in the operational databases with information from other, external sources of data for making strategic decisions.

3.4.2 Information Access Layer

The information access layer is the layer that the end-user deals with directly. In particular, it represents the tools that the end-user uses, e.g. Excel, Lotus 1-2-3, Focus, Access, SAS, etc. This layer also includes the hardware and software involved in displaying and printing reports, spreadsheets, graphs and charts for analysis, and presentation. Over the past two decades, the information access layer has expanded enormously with an increase in users demand to view the results in different formats. Today, more and more sophisticated tools exist on the desktop for manipulating, analysing, and presenting data.

3.4.3 Data Access Layer

The data access layer is involved with allowing the information access layer to talk to the operational layer. This is done by using a common language SQL which is considered to be the standard language for data interchange.

One of the key breakthroughs in the last few years has been the development of a series of data access "filters" that make it possible for SQL to access

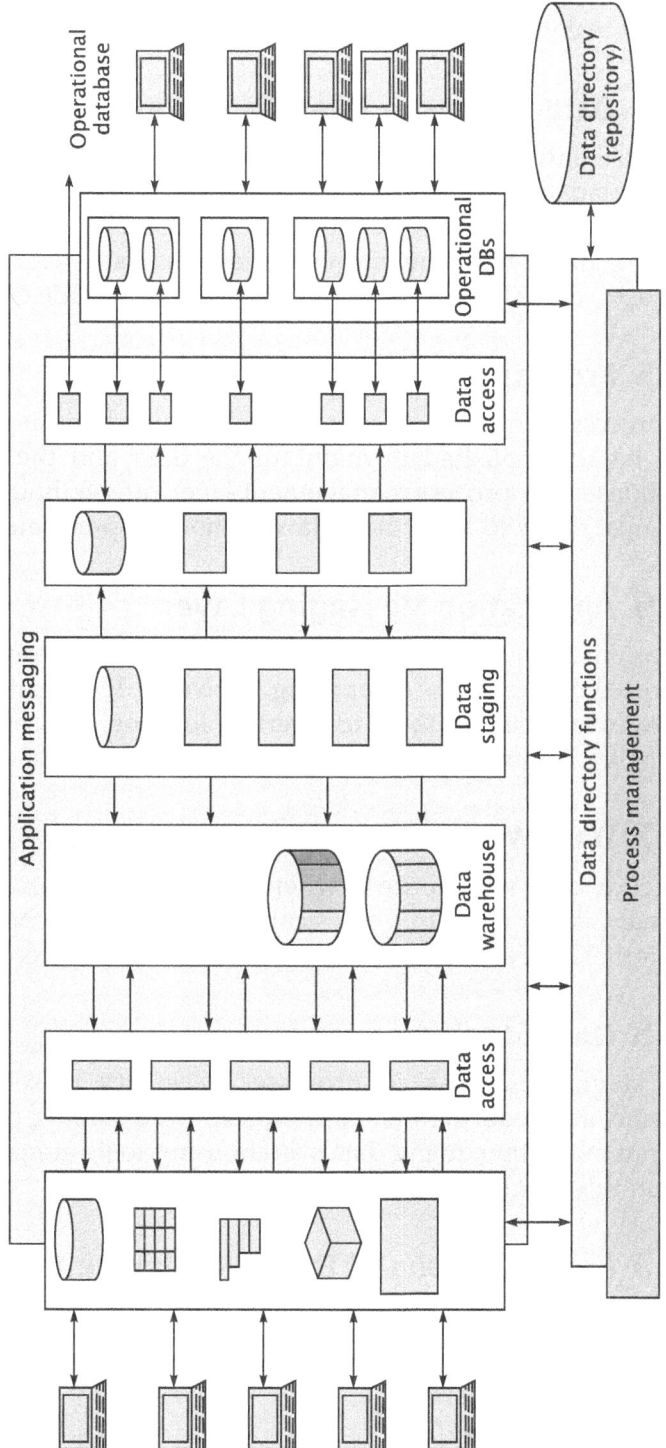

Figure 3.1 Data warehouse architecture

nearly all DBMSs and data file systems, relational or non-relational that may even be twenty years old.

3.4.4 Data Directory (Metadata) Layer

To enable universal data access, it is necessary to maintain some form of metadata. Metadata is the data about data within the organization. In order to have a fully functional data warehouse, it is necessary to have a variety of metadata available data about the end-user views of data, data about the operational databases, etc. All these types of metadata are included in this layer.

3.4.5 Process Management Layer

The process management layer is involved in scheduling the various tasks that must be accomplished to maintain the data and the metadata in the data warehouse. The process management layer can be thought of as the scheduler that must occur to keep the data warehouse up-to-date.

3.4.6 Application Messaging Layer

The application message layer is concerned with transporting information around the enterprise computing network. It can also be used to collect messages and deliver them to a certain location at a certain time. Application messaging is thus the transport system underlying the data warehouse.

3.4.7 Data Warehouse (Physical) Layer

The (core) data warehouse is where the actual data used primarily for strategic analysis is stored. In a physical data warehouse copies of operational and or external data are stored in a form that is easy to access and is highly flexible.

3.4.8 Data Staging Layer

Data staging includes all processes necessary to select, edit, summarize, combine, and load the data warehouse. Data staging often involves complex programming, thus many data warehousing tools are present in the market to help in this process.

3.4.9 Pros and Cons of Data Warehouse Architecture

Data warehouse architecture has some pros and cons. Its advantages are:

- Enables non redundancy of data that rules out any scope of having inconsistent data.
- Keeps secured data.
- Provides user-friendly and intuitive data access.

- Provides consistent data for accurate and reliable results.
- Enables aggregate and summarized data for efficient access.
- Simplifies data collection from multiple sources.
- Minimizes impact on the performance and functioning of operational systems.
- Enables the analysts to manipulate the data easily since they can refer to a high-level representation of data that is easy to understand and interpret.
- Provides interoperability between different systems.
- Is scalable enough to cater to the additional requirements.
- Provides description of the data at the internal level.

However some of its disadvantages include:

- Data is not always current.
- Initial setup and design costs are considerable.
- Higher storage space, bleeding edge technologies call for a lot of cost involved.

3.4.10 Two-tier Architecture

The two-tier architecture focuses on the performance, integrity, and administration of the warehouse in the more traditional way. This architecture consists of a front-end client component and a back end server component that makes use of the existing host computers as database servers (as shown in Fig. 3.2).

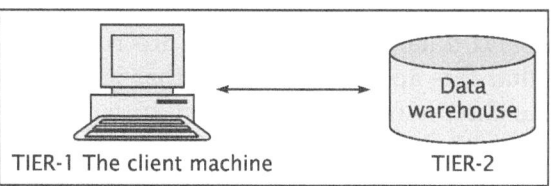

Figure 3.2 Two-tier architecture of data warehouse

The function of the front-end applications is to hide the underlying complexity of the existing mainframe systems. In the two-tier architecture of the data warehouse, SQL statements are hidden beneath the graphical user interface and an application programming interface (API) is required for communication between the client machine and the database server. Thus, in this approach large front-end systems are developed in which the majority of the processing is done on desktop workstations.

At this point of time, the two-tier architecture may seem very attractive. The key benefit of this option is that it utilizes the existing legacy systems as database servers and requires minimal investment in additional hardware and software. However, the downside of this approach prevents it from being used widely. It is not scalable and cannot support a large number of online end-users without additional software modifications. The two tier topology runs into significant performance problems when a large number of users access and query the database at the same time. There are even congestion problems when a large amount of data is moved over the network for client-based analysis network.

In the two-tier topology, the data warehouse resides on a dedicated RDBMS server and both the DSS engine and DSS client reside on the client hardware. This approach provides more scalability and better performance than the one-tier model, but at the cost of a dedicated server. Despite this, two-tier topology is preferable to the single-tier model in which the DSS engine, DSS client, and RDBMS server all need one single machine.

3.4.11 Three-tier Architecture

The three-tier architecture is strikingly different from two-tier architecture as it separates the graphical user interface, business logic, and the data. Figure 3.3 shows the three-tier topology. A typical data warehouse consists of three tiers where the base is a DBMS and a specially designed data warehouse database, in the middle tier are the application logic i.e., the programs and underlying networks that feed the data warehouse from operational systems and other sources. The topmost tier consists of the reports and query tools that are responsible for delivering information to the users.

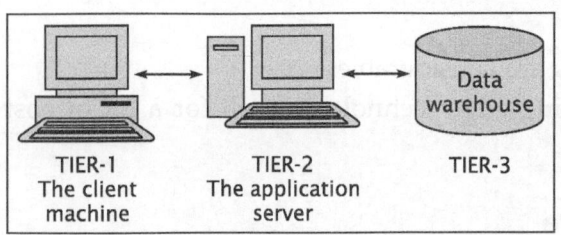

Figure 3.3 Three-tier architecture of data warehouse

In a three-tier architecture, there are three distinct layers of software–presentation, core application logic, and data. All these layers are run on its own processor. The key advantage that this approach offers is that it offloads the processor intensive tasks from the client workstation. This, in turn, enables the organizations to utilize clients with lesser amounts of memory and processing power.

Three-tier topology is far more scalable than two-tier model. But this advantage involves higher costs. In three, tier architecture additional costs are imposed as the warehouse is maintained and data must be replicated to the local servers.

In this approach, the data is put closer to the end-users, which enhances the response time and simplifies security issues. In this approach the users are not required to know where or how the data is stored, or the complexity of the underlying databases. The other plus point here is that it optimizes performance.

However, the three-tier topology has some drawbacks. First, the DSS engine needs to be more complex because for each request it has to determine the location of the data. Second, the three-tier architecture necessitates some local data administration as the data design needs to be controlled and optimized for different queries.

The three-tier architecture eliminates the resource constraint issues that exist in a two-tier architecture. Having the processing done by a separate DSS engine allows the organization to reduce the cost of fat clients (clients that require more intelligence, processing capability, and storage). However, the trade-off involved in this case is the cost of many fat clients versus one relatively expensive server to perform the DSS server functions.

In a three tier architecture, the network traffic consists only of the answers for the query being transmitted back to the client. The client machine has the software installed to improve the presentation of the results received from the DSS server and to manipulate this data as per the users needs. The user may need to further manipulate data to perform additional calculations, graphing, pivoting, and rotation to view the data across different dimensions.

This architecture permits the DSS engine and the databases to be distributed among various departments so that they function as individual data marts. The data relevant to each data mart can be transmitted during off-peak hours without increasing the network traffic.

3.4.12 Four-tier Architecture

The underlying principle of a four-tier architecture is that some data is delivered to the client's desktop, either by replicating from the warehouse or targeting the query to a desktop database. The benefit behind it is that "what if" processing could then be accomplished without polluting the data in the warehouse and the end-users could be made responsible for their own desktop data recovery.

There is no single perfect data warehouse architecture. While some organizations may prefer a two-tier architecture as it minimizes the cost and complexity of building a data warehouse, the others like to go for the three-tier architecture as it offers greater performance and scalability. Organizations generally prefer three-tier architecture as compared to two-tier architecture because in it the data extracted from source systems is cleansed, transformed, and stored in high speed database servers which are used as the target database for front-end data access.

3.4.13 Three-tier vs. Two-tier Architecture

The data warehouse gets its data loaded from multiple heterogeneous operational systems. This data however must be first standardized, cleaned, and transformed before being actually stored in the warehouse. At the receiving end, the data warehouses use various indexing and table partitioning schemes to store the relevant data.

Generally, a relational DBMS is used as the underlying component of the data warehouse. While the data warehouse may start out small, it grows exponentially in a very short span of time. To reduce the response time from such a massive store of data, where justifiable, the underlying hardware architecture of the data warehouse may use parallel computing to improve performance and scalability.

In a three-tier architecture, the DSS engine retrieves large amounts of data from the data warehouse in response to user queries. The time window to retrieve this data must be bounded since the very idea of online analytical processing is defeated if data is not available when needed. For this purpose the DSS engine should be placed close to the data warehouse database because otherwise transmitting large quantities of data would cause traffic congestion.

In a two-tier architecture, the DSS engine and the data warehouse both reside on the same platform. This arrangement at times causes hardware and processing resource constraints since both the loading and storing of warehouse data, and the analysis functions call for intensive use of resources.

In this architecture, the DSS server functions are performed on the client machine. This further worsens the situation by causing network traffic bottlenecks. However, one solution to the traffic congestion problem can be that the most frequently used data be loaded onto the client during off-peak times. The user can use this pre-loaded data for analysis at a later time.

The other solution can be to pre-compute the most frequently asked queries. But if the user's requirements are not consistent, this solution will not be feasible and in that case adding more hardware resources to the warehouse platform will be the only solution left. Hence, there is a trade-off in increased network traffic versus the need for hardware resources when designing a two-tier architecture.

These design considerations raise the question of whether a two tier or a three-tier architecture would be preferable to implement the data warehouse.

3.4.14 Interfacing

A data warehouse is designed to receive and then pass the data to other technologies. For example, the data comes into the data warehouse from several diverse operational systems and then it passes to data marts and several other decision support applications like OLAP, data mining, EIS. When the data becomes old it is passed from the data warehouse to the archival storage. It is very crucial that the passing of data from one technology to the other be extremely smooth and easy. A data warehouse that does not support this feature is worthless to use.

Besides being easy and efficient, the interface must also be able to work in batch mode. Although the idea of operating in online mode is interesting but this mode is rarely used to transfer data to and from the data warehouse. The transfer usually takes place in batch mode because we know that when data arrives in the operational systems, it is not extracted and directly transferred to the data warehouse in real time. There is a latency time involved which occurs due to the processing that is done to the data.

Next, the interface to different technologies requires resolving certain issues, such as:

- Can the data be easily passed from one DBMS to the other?
- Can the data be easily passed from one operating system to the other?

- Is there a need to change the underlying format of the data (ASCII, EBCDIC, etc.)?
- Can data be easily passed for multidimensional processing?
- Is it necessary to pass entire tables or incremental passage of data can be done that captures only the changes in the source data?

In addition to easy and efficient interfaces between the different technologies in the data warehouse, the data warehouse must also support a rich language specification. The language used by the programmers and the end-users must be easy to use, efficient, and robust in nature. A robust language interface eases the entering and accessing of data in the warehouse.

The language interface in the data warehouse environment does the following:

- Enables data access record by record.
- Ensures the application of one or more indexes to satisfy a given query.
- Enables an SQL interface.
- Provides ability to insert, delete or update data.

There is not just one but many languages that are used in the data warehouse environment. A different language is used for performing statistical analysis on data to run data mining and exploration functions, a different language for simple data access, another language for handling pre-fabricated queries, and finally a different set of languages is used to optimize on the graphic nature of the interface. Each of these languages have their own strengths and weaknesses.

Since the end-users may not be well versed in IT technologies, they may find it difficult to formulate the SQL queries on their own. So a language is needed that can create and manage the SQL queries so that the end-users are free from this burden of writing and executing queries. For the users a language interface that is much simpler than SQL and is easy to use is highly desirable.

3.5 DATA WAREHOUSE AND DATA MART

A data mart is a decision support system that stores a number of subject areas based on the needs of the users in that department. A data mart can thus be thought of as a subset of the enterprise wide data warehouse. The finance department of the organization has their own data mart, marketing has their separate data mart, likewise the sales department has their own and so on. The data mart of every individual department hardly resembles that of any other department.

Every individual department owns the hardware, software, data, and programs that are needed for that data mart. Each department wants customization of data that will be stored in their data mart. The database design for a data mart is done using a star-join structure that is optimal for the needs of the users within that department. Obviously, before formulating the star join structure, requirements are gathered from its users.

The data mart unlike a data warehouse does not contain detailed data. Rather, the data in a data mart is granular only to the level that the users of a department find appropriate for analysis. The other striking contrast that data marts have with data warehouses is that a data mart contains only a modicum of historical information. The data mart is typically centred on multidimensional technology which is flexible enough for analysis but is not optimal for large amounts of data. Data found in data marts is highly indexed.

There are two kinds of data marts—dependent and independent. A dependent data mart is one that takes the data feed from data warehouse whereas an independent data mart is one that depends upon the legacy applications environment for its data source (Refer Fig. 3.4 a&b). In other words, all dependent data marts are fed by the same source which is the data warehouse. The data warehouse gathers all the information from the various operational systems and other external sources. The dependent data marts are created with a subset of the information in the data warehouse. These data marts are easier to use because they have only the information that the specific user group within that particular department needs and are architecturally more sound and stable than the independent data marts. However, each independent data mart is fed separately by the operational systems applications.

Although, the independent data marts may seem lucrative to some organizations but in the long run when the number of data marts increases, the architecture becomes nothing but a mesh of databases. This makes the structure very complex and thereby increases the total cost of the independent data mart solution. The independent data mart architecture presents major challenges to integrating the data. The disadvantages in adopting this approach are:

- Several source systems need to be handled to get the data content.
- Additional effort and time is needed to clean, transform, and integrate the data.
- It is difficult to acquire data from external sources.
- There are additional complexities involved for flexibility, reliability, and maintenance of data.
- There are problems in maintaining data consistency.

3.6 ISSUES IN BUILDING DATA MARTS

According to Bill Inmon, the single most important issue facing the data warehouse team is whether to build the data warehouse first or the data mart first. The data mart vendors are of the view that data warehouses are difficult and expensive to build, because they take a long time to design and develop, require a lot of thought and investment, and involve issues such as integration of legacy data, managing massive volumes of data, and cost justifying the entire data warehouse effort to the management committee. Therefore, for their own selfish reasons the data marts vendors had painted a gloomy picture for building the data warehouse.

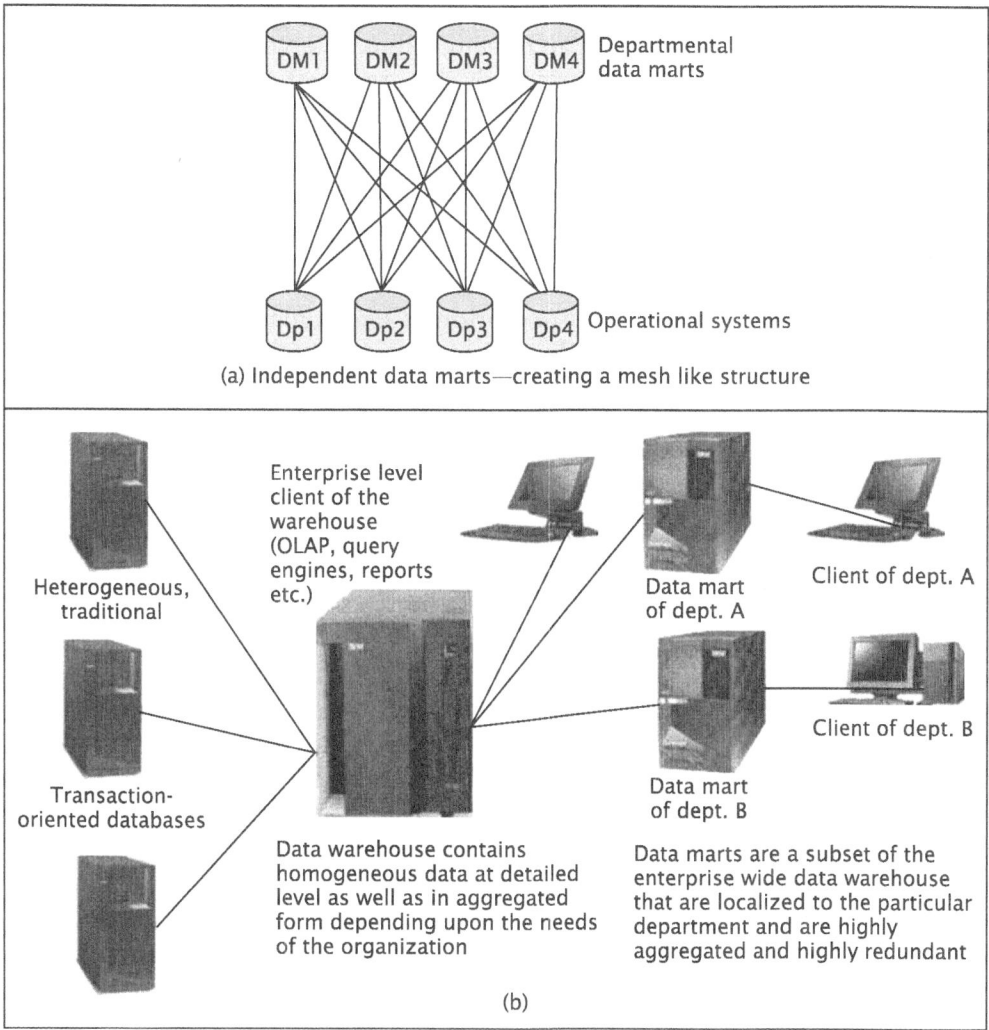

(a) Independent data marts—creating a mesh like structure

(b)

Figure 3.4 The relationship between a data warehouse and a data mart (dependent). Operational systems feed the enterprise-wide data warehouse which in turn feeds the individual data marts

They generally do not prefer data warehouses as they see it as an obstacle in fetching the revenue that comes from the sale of a couple of data marts. Hence the need to avoid the use of data warehouses. The main reason behind this approach of data mart vendors is that data warehouse lengthens the sales cycle.

There was a popular notion that there may be alternate paths to strategic success than building a data warehouse. One of those paths was to build several data marts and when they grew big enough, call them a data warehouse. According to this strategy there was no need to build the actual data warehouse. It was argued that this approach would also help the organizations to build a decision support system quickly and cheaply and that there was no need for a long-term architecture.

Unfortunately, these data mart vendors failed to realize the concept of data warehousing. An architecture that is devoid of any data warehouse and consist only of data marts leads the organization into an even larger mess. As of now, instead of messy operational systems, there were now messy data marts as well. The data warehouses are meant to provide a long term benefit but the data mart vendors have been selling a short-term solution at the expense of long-term architectural success.

With this approach of data warehousing, there was no integration when all that was built was data marts. According to Bill Inmon, a decision support environment without integration is like a man without a skeletal system—hardly a useful entity.

It has after all been assumed that a data warehouse is merely a collection of integrated data marts. However this notion and the absence of an actual data warehouse leads to the following:

- Redundancy of detailed and historical data within different data marts.
- Inconsistent results from different data marts due to high redundancy.
- Redundancy and inconsistency of data led to irreconcilable results.
- An unmanageable interface between the data marts and the operational systems.

Thus, it became clear that a data warehouse forms the backbone of a DSS environment and building data marts is not the proper way to proceed in DSS.

Putting it in simple words, one cannot build data marts, watch them grow, and finally turn them into a data warehouse when they reach a certain size. Apart from this, integrating data across data marts is impossible as the definition of data marts itself states that each department that owns its data mart has its own unique specifications. The other reasons that support this statement include:

- The data mart is designed to meet the requirements of the users of a particular department. In general, an organization will have several data marts, each of which will be built with different objectives and with its own distinctive look and feel. On the other hand, the data warehouse is designed to meet the collective requirements of the users of the entire organization. A given design can be optimal for a single department or the enterprise, but not both as the design objectives of the two are entirely different from each other.
- The granularity of data stored in the data mart is very strikingly different from that of the data warehouse. While the data mart contains aggregated/summarized data, the data warehouse contains the most detailed data. One can always summarize detailed units of data into summarizations but cannot easily go the other way as the data mart granularity is much higher than that found in the data warehouse.
- The amount of historical data stored in a data mart is very different from that of a data warehouse. While data warehouses are designed to contain robust amounts of history, the data marts contain only modest amounts of history.

- The subject areas found in the data mart may or may not be related to the subject areas found in the data warehouse.
- The types of queries that are executed in the data mart are different from those executed in the data warehouse.
- The kinds of users who use the data marts are different from those of data warehouse, for example, a data mart may be accessed by a departmental manager but business executives, high level managers, CEOs, board of directors will use the data warehouse.

Therefore, in order to understand why one or more data marts cannot be transformed into a data warehouse, you must first understand why a data mart is different from a data warehouse. A data mart and a data warehouse are diverse architectural structures, even though when viewed from afar they appear to be very similar.

3.6.1 How are Data Warehouses and Data Marts Different?

Data warehouses are markedly different from data marts. Data warehouses are arranged around the business subject areas and are owned by centrally coordinated organizations. The data warehouse represents a truly corporate effort.

It contains the most granular detailed data while a data mart contains less granular data. The data in the data warehouse represent the business needs for the users. Data warehouse contains a greater volume of data as compared to a data mart and hence warehouses are generally indexed lightly. The data warehouse contains an enormous amount of historical data as well as current data. The data that is stored in the data warehouse is integrated from the many legacy sources and is cleansed, standardized, and transformed before being stored.

Table 3.1 shows some of the differences between a data mart and a data warehouse.

Table 3.1 Differences between a data mart and a data warehouse

Data Warehouse	Data Mart
• Corporate/Enterprise wide scope	• Departmental scope
• Low level of granularity	• High level of granularity
• Normalized structure robust amount of historical data	• Star join structure
	• Modest amount of historical data
• Technology optimal for holding and managing massive amounts of data	• Technology optimal for data access and analysis
• Lightly indexed	• Highly indexed
• Combination of more than one business processes	• A single business process
• Structure for corporate view of data	• Structure to suit the department
• Takes months to years for implementation	• Takes months for implementation
• Data warehouse size varies from 100 GB to a few TB	• Data mart size is less than 100 GB
• Flexible query and analysis	• Restrictive query and analysis

Due to its enormous size, it is recommended that the data warehouse must be built iteratively. If you do not build the warehouse iteratively, you will spend years building the warehouse. In order to avoid lengthy efforts involved in building a data warehouse, and to enable the end-user to reap its benefits as quickly as possible, the warehouse must be built in an iterative manner. Figure 3.5 shows the recommended construction path for data warehouses.

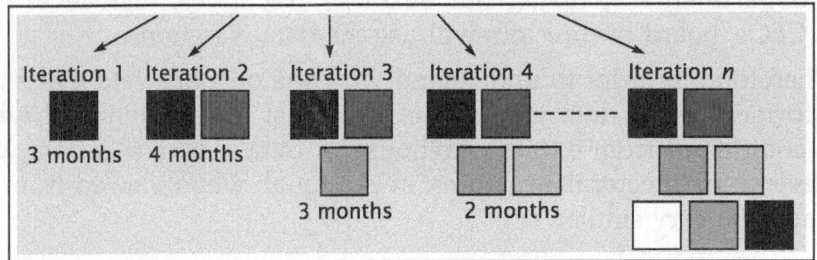

Figure 3.5 Iterative development of a data warehouse

3.6.2 Reasons for Creating Data Marts

Data marts are erected for the following reasons:

- To enable access to the data that the department needs to analyse most often
- To provide data in a form that matches the collective view of the data by a group of users in a department or a business function
- To improve end-user response time, which is enabled by the reduction in the volume of data to be accessed
- To provide appropriately structured data as dictated by the requirements of end-user access tools
- Data marts use less data, so tasks such as data cleansing, loading, transformation, and integration are much easier and hence implementing and setting up a data mart is simpler than establishing a corporate data
- The potential users of a data mart are more clearly defined and can be more easily targeted to obtain support for a data mart project rather than a corporate data warehouse project.

3.6.3 Advantages of a Data Mart

Data marts have a number of advantages over data warehouses:

- The cost is low.
- The lead time to implementation is short, often under 90 days.
- They are controlled locally rather than centrally, conferring power on the user's group.

- They contain less information than the data warehouse and hence have more rapid response and are more easily understood and navigated than an enterprise-wide data warehouse.
- They allow a business unit to build its own decision support systems without relying on anyone else.
- The use of several data marts also allows the querying load to be spread among several different computers. This can reduce network traffic.

3.6.4 Limitations of a Data Mart

A multiple data mart environment harbours a number of limitations:

- Performance degradation occurs as the size of the data mart increases.
- Administration of multiple data marts becomes difficult.
- The problems in building and implementing multiple data marts arise.
- Issues in accessing remote data marts also surface over time.

3.7 BUILDING DATA MARTS

The father of data warehousing, Bill Inmon has rightly stated in one of his books that, "The single most important issue facing the IT manager this year is whether to build the data warehouse first or the data mart first."

There are two main approaches of building the data marts. In the first approach, that is the top-down approach, the data warehouse project team looks at the larger picture of the organization, and builds a huge data warehouse first that will feed the individual data marts.

In the second approach, that is the bottom-up approach, the data warehouse project team caters to the requirements of individual departments and builds data marts first that will feed data to the corporate wide data warehouse. In this approach, the departmental data marts are created first. They are built one by one and a priority scheme is used to determine which data marts must be built first. The major drawback of this approach is data fragmentation. Also every independent data mart will be blind to the overall requirements of the organization as a whole. Table 3.2 make a comparison between these two approaches. Figure 3.6 shows the two approaches.

Although both the top-down and bottom-up approaches have their own advantages and drawbacks, an approach accommodating both views appears to be practical. The chief proponent of this practical approach, Ralph Kimball has suggested the following steps:

- Gather requirements from the users.
- Define these requirements at the enterprise level.
- Establish the scope of the data warehouse and its intended use.

Table 3.2 Differences between the top-down and bottom-up approach

Top-down Approach	Bottom-up Approach
• Data is extracted from the operational systems, transformed, cleaned, and integrated to finally store it in the data warehouse.	• Data is extracted from the operational systems, transformed, cleaned, and integrated to finally store it in the data mart
• Presents an enterprise view of data	• Presents data only at the departmental level
• Inherently architected as it is not just a union of disparate data marts	• Inherently incremental as the team can schedule important data marts first
• Single, central storage of data	• Data dispersed in different data marts
• Implementation of centralized rules and control	• Implementation of departmental rules
• Takes longer time to build the overall data warehouse	• Faster and easier implementation of individual data marts
• High risk to failure	• Less exposure to failure
• No proof of concept	• Proof of concept
• Return on investment takes longer	• Early return on investment

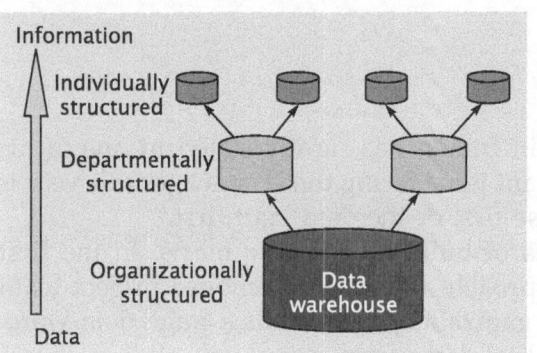 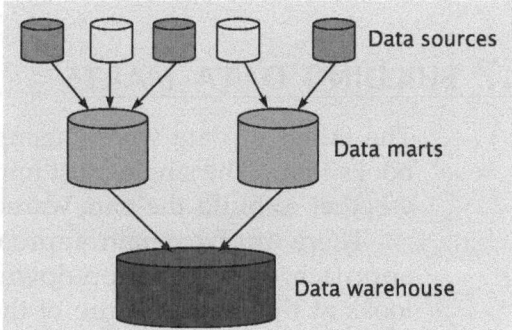

Figure 3.6 Top-down and bottom-up approches

- Define and prioritize the business requirements and the information needs of the users that the upcoming data warehouse will address.
- Design the architecture for an overall data warehouse.
- Make a list of the subject areas needed; prioritize it and then define the sequence of implementation projects accordingly.
- Form a logical data model that will direct the physical implementation model.
- Conform and standardize the data that would be stored in the warehouse.
- Implement the data warehouse as a series of super marts, one by one.

In this practical approach, the data warehouse team first determines what exactly the organization wants in the long term. Requirements are gathered at the overall level and the architecture is established for the complete warehouse. Then the data content for each super mart is defined. Super marts are carefully designed and architected data marts. Then these super marts are implemented, one at a time. However, before implementation, the team must make sure that the data content among the various super marts are conformed in terms of data types, field lengths, precision, and semantics.

In the practical approach, a data mart is considered to be a logical subset of the complete data warehouse. A data warehouse, therefore, is a conformed union of all data marts where every individual data mart is targeted to a particular business department within the enterprise.

3.8 OTHER DATA MART ISSUES

This section briefs us on other issues regarding data marts, which are discussed at length in the chapters to come.

3.8.1 Types of Data Marts based on Underlying DBMS

The data marts can be classified into two groups: multidimensional (MDDB) or relational (RDBM) data marts. Aggregated data can be stored in multidimensional cubes whereas in case of relational data marts, data is stored in a table. While MDDB provides faster query execution, RDBMs are helpful when complex analysis and multiple query executions have to the performed.

3.8.2 Loading a Data Mart

The data mart is loaded using a load program. This program needs to consider the frequency of loads, schedule of data loading activity, refreshing of data, selection of data (from the warehouse in case it is a dependent data mart or from the operational systems if it is an independent data mart), creation of aggregations and summarizations, loading time optimization, integrity of data, maintaining relationships, and keys and updating of metadata so that it contains information about the new data as well.

The Types of Data Marts to Load

If the data warehouse is being developed using a top-down approach then, after building the data warehouse the next job is to build the data marts. It is important to note here that there are two distinct types of data marts that will affect the loading strategy deploy:

Temporal data marts   In this category of data marts, all the history is displayed, that is, every dimension reflects a number of historical hierarchies and the facts are stored against the hierarchies defined. Facts and hierarchies will be discussed in chapter 4. For example, if the organizational hierarchy has changed over time, the facts would have been reported against hierarchy at the time when the event took place rather than the hierarchy's current shape.

These data marts are advantageous for the users who need in-depth trend analysis. But the downside is that these data marts provide slow response to the users who want to view the current position of the business.

Current or non-temporal data marts In this category of data marts, all the history is not retained and every dimension reflects the current hierarchy only. The data in these data mart would reflect the current data. This provides a benefit for the managers who want to perform current analysis as it reduces the size and simplifies the data. Storing only the current data also reduces the size of the fact table.

Loading a Temporal Data Mart

The loading of a temporal data mart can take one of the following two routes:

Complete refresh These data marts are loaded by reloading the entire tables every time. This is done by truncating the tables and then loading the data again. The key benefit with this technique is that it captures every thing that is in the transaction repository and reduces the backup requirements. But when the data mart grows to a very large size, then the performance of the execution of load programs will deteriorate. In that case, a cumulative refresh may be more appropriate.

Cumulative refresh In this technique, you just need to append to the data mart all facts from transaction repository that has appeared since the last load program was executed. This technique, if followed, speeds up the load process considerably for large data marts. However it is more complicated to perform backups in case of cumulative refreshes.

Loading a Non-temporal Data Mart

For loading non-temporal data marts, complete refresh is the technique that is most widely followed. This is because the load will become difficult due to the updates required on facts and particularly on dimensions. Non-temporal data marts can be loaded either from operational system or from the temporal data marts. Although it is better if non-temporal data marts are fed by temporal marts, let us analyse each of these approaches.

Loading from the transaction repository When the data is loaded from the transaction repositories then we are actually going directly to the source systems. In this case, we build the current data mart without relying on the temporal data mart having been loaded first. This technique has the advantage of making the data available to the users on time. One point to be noted here is that this technique takes longer time than using the temporal data mart as it will have to repeat denormalizations already carried out in the temporal data mart.

Loading from the temporal data mart This method seems to be most attractive as it takes full advantage of the work already done by the load of the other data mart. As long as the dependency on the load time for the temporal data mart is not an issue, this technique is always recommended for best performance.

3.8.3 Metadata for a Data Mart

Metadata describes data about data in the data mart. It contains information about the data, its source, the form in which the data element was originally present in its source system, transformation rules that were applied on the data, the procedure used to perform summarizations and aggregations, etc. For example, the field price may be stored in dollars in the data mart, but in one of its sources it may have been stored in rupees.

The metadata of a data mart is created and updated from the load programs. The metadata must be simple, understandable, and well established so that the end-users can use it to find the information that they want. The metadata must also be easily interpreted by the data warehouse administrator for maintenance of the warehouse.

3.8.4 Maintenance of a Data Mart

The maintenance activities of a data mart include activities like loading, refreshing, and purging of data. In a data mart environment, data is refreshed on a regular basis as per the nature and frequency of data updates. For example, stock exchange prices data may be refreshed on a daily basis, whereas stock of the products may be refreshed weekly. Thus in a data mart, the data may be refreshed daily, weekly, monthly, quarterly, or yearly depending on the nature of the data.

Purging of data involves periodically monitoring the data in the data mart and archiving the old data on some other storage medium. The criteria for purging the data in a data mart would in turn depend on date, time, and periodicity based on the requirements of the application.

3.8.5 Nature of Data in a Data Mart

The data in a data mart is cleaned, transformed, and standardized before being stored. In addition to this, the data is aggregated and summarized to the level as specified by its users.

3.8.6 Software Components of a Data Mart

The software components of a data mart include the underlying DBMS, data access and analysis tools, software for purging and archival of data, and metadata management tools. In a data mart environment, the data access and analysis tools enable the end-users to navigate the data contents to extract relevant information and manipulate the data to present it in the form of graphical charts before displaying it on the screen. As discussed earlier, the DBMS for a data mart can either be relational or multidimensional.

3.8.7 Performance Issues

The performance considerations in a data mart environment are strikingly different from that of operational systems. Even the complex queries executed in the operational systems should not take longer than some few seconds.

But in a data mart environment, query processing time is slightly relaxed as data has to be analysed thoroughly to derive the specific information from it. However, techniques like star schema, star-index, and star joins can be used to improve performance. These concepts are discussed in Chapter 6.

In addition to this, the data mart performance will also depend upon whether multidimensional databases or relational databases are used as the underlying technology to store the data. Obviously, multidimensional databases are preferable in comparison to relational databases as discussed above.

3.8.8 Monitoring Requirements for a Data Mart

Data marts need to be monitored periodically for activities such as data usage and data content tracking on the following lines:

- What data is being accessed?
- What is the frequency of data access?
- Who are the users and which user is accessing what data?
- Whether detailed or summarized data is needed by the users?
- What are peak periods of usage?
- What other data needs to be stored in the data mart?
- Is there any corrupted data in the data mart?

With the increase is the size of the data marts, the complexity of the monitoring activities also grows.

3.8.9 Security in a Data Mart

A data mart stores highly secured data and thus, it needs to be protected from unauthorized access. It is the responsibility of the database administrator to cater to security needs through firewalls, log-in identification, application based security, DBMS security, encryption, and decryption.

3.8.10 Structure of a Data Mart

Every organziation has multiple data marts where each data mart is relevant to a particular business unit for which it was designed. Every department is considered to be the owner of their data mart which includes its data and hardware and software components.

Data marts enable the users of every department to use, manipulate, and develop their data according to their own needs and aspirations. Since the basic purpose of a data mart is to provide easy access to relevant information, the star join schema is used to enable the same.

3.9 INCREASED POPULARITY OF DATA MARTS

There are multiple reasons for the increased popularity of more narrowly defined data marts over enterprise data warehouse systems.

- Data marts have dramatically lowered the cost of DSS and have put the deployment of decision support technology within an affordable range of a large number of organizations. While the implementation budgets for data warehouses typically are in the range of 2–5 million dollars, data marts on the other hand, cost between $100K–$1 million for the total project.

- Data marts are preferred by autonomous departments and small business units as a way to have their separate decision-support systems.

- Data marts have become the preferred way for IT to build large, central data warehouses. They build one data mart at a time, thereby supporting business analysts to see concrete benefits every 3–6 months.

- As compared to enterprise data warehouses, data marts have limited scope and are more focused on a group set of user needs which in turn leads to a focused challenge and a focused team.

- Data marts allow for faster prototyping for capturing decision-support system requirements.

Thus, it is more appealing to start a decision-support system with a modest plan and then grow, if necessary, after learning more about the source data and the end-users' needs.

3.10 CAN DATA WAREHOUSE AND DATA MART CO-EXIST?

One may think that it is judicious to build the data warehouse and the data mart on the same processor. Though practically possible, it is not advisable due to the reasons enlisted below:

- Having a large processor calls for huge sums of money. Thus, putting data marts on separate machines will bring down the cost of processing by substantial amount.

- Processing of data becomes easily manageable when the data marts workload is separated from that of the data warehouse.

- Placing the data warehouse and the data mart on separate processors helps in accurately planning for the capacity.

- The most important benefit of having the data warehouse and data marts deployed on separate processors is that different departments can take ownership of their data marts.

3.11 PUSHING AND PULLING DATA

When data is moved into the data warehouse we are pushing the data. On the other hand, when we move the data from the data warehouse to the data marts, we are pulling data from the data warehouse.

While in the push process, data is moved as soon as it is available, in the pull process data is moved only when the need arises. This means that the data velocity will vary for the data that comes in the data warehouse and the data that goes out of the warehouse to the end-users.

Consider an example, if the requirements of a data mart A dictate that the data must be moved to the data mart as soon as it is available in the warehouse, then the data velocity will be higher. But, in case the requirement of the data mart B is such that it needs the new data only at the month ends, then there is no urgency in transferring the data. Thus, data velocity is very slow as the time elapsed between the entry of data in the system and its availability to the end-users will be more.

From the above example, we learn that although a higher data velocity is better, it is not always desirable.

Recapitulation

The architecture of a data warehouse is composed of rules, procedures, and functions that enable your data warehouse to work and fulfill the business requirements.

The data warehouse architecture differs from that of operational systems because it has to support the requirements for providing strategic information to its users.

Data warehouse architecture also provides controlled non-redundant data copies and security but at the same time calls for more storage space, technologies, and cost.

Data warehouse architecture includes operational database layer, information access layer, data access layer, metadata layer, process management layer, application messaging layer, data warehouse layer, and the data staging layer.

Information access layer includes the hardware and software involved in displaying and printing reports, spreadsheets, graphs, and charts for analysis and presentation.

The data access layer is involved in allowing the information access layer to talk to the operational layer through SQL queries.

The process management layer is involved in scheduling the various tasks that must be accomplished to build and maintain the data warehouse and data directory information.

The application message layer has to do with transporting information and messages around the enterprise computing network.

Two-tier architecture incorporates a front-end client component and a back-end server component that utilizes existing host computers as database servers.

The three-tier architecture enforces a separation of the GUI (presentation layer), business logic (application layer), and the data. However, the advantage achieved in scalability must be weighed against the greater cost and complexity of the solution.

In the four-tier architecture, some data is delivered to the desktop, either by replicating from the warehouse or targeting the query to a desktop database in addition to the screen.

A data mart is a collection of subject areas organized for decision support based on the needs of a given department. The data mart is typically housed in multidimensional technology.

There are two kinds of data marts: dependent and independent. A dependent data mart is one whose source is a data warehouse. An independent data mart is one whose source is the legacy applications environment.

Depending on the underlying DBMS, the data marts can be classified into two groups: multi-dimensional (MDDB) or relational data mart.

Objective Questions

1. **Choose the correct answer.**

   (i) In which architecture are large front-end systems developed where in a majority of the processing is done on the desktop workstations.

   (a) Two-tier

   (b) Three-tier

   (c) Four-tier

   (ii) Which apprach implements centralized rules and control?

   (a) Top-down

   (b) Bottom-up

   (c) Practical approach

   (iii) In which apprach does the team have proof of concept and less risk of failure?

   (a) Top-down

   (b) Bottom-up

   (c) Practical approach

   (iv) In which data mart does every dimension reflect a number of historical hierarchies?

   (a) Temporal

   (b) Non-temporal

   (c) Dependent

   (v) In which approach, the data marts are loaded by reloading the entire tables

   (a) Complete refresh

   (b) Cumulative refresh

   (c) None of these

   (vi) In a data warehouse environment, security is implemented using

   (a) Firewalls

   (b) Log ins

   (c) Encrytion

   (d) Decryption

   (e) All these

   (f) None of these

2. **Fill in the blanks**

   (a) The _____ provides the overall framework for developing and deploying the data warehouse.

   (b) _____ are the means to implement the architecture.

   (c) Information access layer to talk to the _____ layer.

   (d) _____ is the transport system underlying the data warehouse.

   (e) The three-tier architecture consists of layers for _____, _____ and _____.

   (f) A _____ is a decision support system that stores data based on the needs of the users in a department.

   (g) Database design for a data mart is done using a _____ structure

   (h) While a _____ data mart takes the data fed from data warehouse, an _____ data mart is depends upon the legacy applications environment for its data source

   (i) For loading non-temporal data marts, _____ refresh is most widely followed.

3. **Match the following**

(a)	Data warehouse architecture	1.	Carefully designed and architected data marts
(b)	Metadata	2.	Provides a navigational map to the end-users

(c) Middleware technology

(d) Data management

(e) Network access

(f) Process management layer

(g) Data mart

(h) Super mart

3. Subset of data warehouse

4. DCE, DNS, and LDAP

5. Scheduler

6. Comprehensive blueprint

7. ODBC, OLE, OLE DB, DCE, ORBs, and JDBC

8. ANSI, SQL, and FTP

4. State true or false

(a) It is mandatory to have an implied architecture before building the data warehouse.

(b) Business requirements drive the entire architecture.

(c) Data staging includes all of the processes necessary to select, edit, summarize, combine, and load data warehouse.

(d) Data warehouse architecture has minimal impact on the performance and functioning of operational systems.

(e) In the two-tier topology, the DSS engine and DSS client do not reside on the client hardware.

(f) Two-tier architecture is more scalable than the three-tier architecture.

(g) Data warehouse contain modicum of historical data.

(h) Independent data marts are architecturally more sound and stable than the dependent data marts.

Review Questions

1. Discuss some of the distnguishing characteristics and goals of data warehouse architecture.

2. Explain the architecture of a data warehouse.

3. Compare two-tier and three-tier architecture of a data warehouse.

4. Explain how a data warehouse differs from a data mart.

5. What do you understand by dependent and independent data marts? Explain the issues involved in building data marts.

6. Write a short note describing advantages, disadvantages, and reasons for creating data marts.

7. Compare top-down approach with bottom-up approach of building data marts. Explain the practical approach.

8. How can you categorize the data marts depending on the underlying DBMS? Which strategy will you follow to load them?

9. Data marts are becoming popular day-by-day. Comment.

PART II

4

GATHERING THE BUSINESS REQUIREMENTS

Learning Objectives

In this chapter, we will learn about the importance of gathering business requirements and the techniques that can be applied to gather useful pieces of information from the end-users. We will also try to find out how gathering requirements differ for data warehouse projects when compared with operational systems.

Case Study

The first stage in any software development life cycle is requirements gathering. This holds for a data warehouse project as well. Once it has been decided that JRTs would go for a data warehousing solution, a project team must be formed under the supervision of a project manager.

In our case, David is appointed as the project manager of the JRTs. But before he can actually begin to build something he must first know what exactly do the users expect from their data warehouse. That is, what information they want to fetch and how do they think, the data warehouse can help them in their day-to-day business.

There are various techniques of requirements elicitation but the bottom line of every technique is that information related to a data warehouse has to be collected from its users group. Collecting information from users for a data warehouse project is not a trivial task as most users are absolutely unaware of the new technology.

When David and his team members need to make clarifications with, the users they are unable to help them simply because they are not familiar with the technology. It is difficult for them to anticipate the screens they can view, the information that can be displayed, the data that can be stored, and even old data that can be stored, the applications that can be run, etc.

So, the team finds it difficult to pen down what has to be made and without knowing what has to be made they are unable to proceed.

4.1 INTRODUCTION

A data warehouse is an information delivery system as it is meant to provide strategic information to its users. Thus, a data warehousing solution is not about technology but about solving user's problems and providing them useful information. In the requirements definition phase, the data warehouse project team needs to concentrate on the information that the users expect from the warehouse.

Most of the developers of data warehouses are considerably experienced in developing operational systems that are primarily data capture systems. But a data warehouse is an information delivery system. So, when they begin to collect information for the data warehouse, the developers need to shift their paradigm from a data capture model to an information delivery model.

When the data warehouse project team designs and develops a data warehouse, it should reflect precisely what the users need to aid their business processes. The decision support system must provide the users well designed GUI screens and must have the correct logic to perform the functions. Last, but not the least the data warehouse project will be successful only when the users receive the required output screens and reports and are satisfied with it. Therefore, the requirements definition phase guides the entire process of system design and development. The accuracy of this phase is thus, critical for the success of the system.

Data warehouses are used by the users independently without any help from IT professionals to search for strategic information, execute queries, get results, manipulate it to view the results along several dimensions in graphical format, and then perform analysis. It is therefore extremely important that the data warehouse contain all the needed elements of information in the most optimal formats.

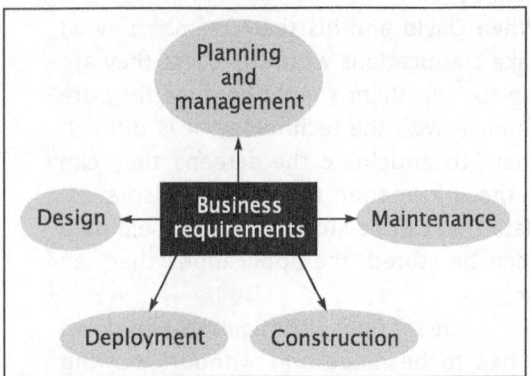

Figure 4.1 Business requirements as the driving force of all the phases of the project development

In a data warehouse environment, the requirements of the users form the single most powerful driving force (see Fig. 4.1). Every task that is performed in every phase in the development of the data warehouse is guided by the requirements of the users. Be it data design, architectural design, infrastructure planning or planning of information delivery mechanisms—every decision is based on user requirements. Thus, the data warehouse project must ensure that the requirements definition document, which will be discussed later in this chapter; contains adequate details to support each phase.

4.2 DETERMINING THE END-USER REQUIREMENTS

During the requirement-gathering process, the requirements gathering team has to collect and then document the end-user requirements. For this task, they need to study how end-users are involved in business processes and information analysis activities.

Since the end-users hardly know about the data warehousing technology, the team should ask questions that allow them to gain an understanding of specific business problems. For this purpose, the team may interview end-users, study existing documents and monitor ongoing information analysis activities. End-user requirements can be collected in terms of business objectives and business queries.

4.2.1 Business Objectives

In a data warehouse environment, business objectives are nothing but the goals of information analysis. There may be one or more business objectives. For example, a business objective could be: "The data warehouse has to support the analysis of sale of products in a particular region." The cumulative set of business objectives helps to determine the scope of a data warehouse project, the subjects of interests, and the measures of the business processes that the end-user wants to analyse.

4.2.2 Business Queries

Business queries like business objectives are expressed in business terms. These queries relate to either analysis of data or proving of some hypothesis. Business queries can be broadly classified into the following categories:

- Existence checking queries like "Whether a customer has withdrawn any money from the ATM in the last week?"
- Trend-analysis queries, like "What is the sales growth for John Players shirts when they were put on a 40% discount?"
- Queries to analyse ratios, rankings, and clusters, such as "Rank the top five customers in the last financial year."
- Statistical analysis queries, such as "Calculate the average shirts sales per sales region."
- Item comparison queries like "Compare the sales of John Players shirts in New Delhi with the sales of Peter England shirts."

4.2.3 Functional Requirements

While the end-user requirements are collected to understand the current business processes, the functional requirements help the project team to get an insight into the services that the customer expects from a data warehouse.

Such information is generally collected from key business managers, IT professionals, and the potential end-users. The functional requirements are needed to set the overall project goals. So, in order to collect these requirements from the users the team should collect information about the following aspects:

- Information analysis capabilities that users need to improve their business. A detailed definition of the reports that are expected to be built from the data warehouse must be collected.
- The problems that the users are facing in the existing data analysis process.
- The potential users of the data warehouse and the location from which they will be accessing the data warehouse.
- The users who will be participating with the project team to develop the data warehouse solution. The roles and the responsibilities of these users.
- The budget allotted for the project.
- The time allocated for the completion of the project.
- The security mechanisms that must be implemented for the data warehouse.

4.2.4 Information Infrastructure Environment

The customer's network environment can be simple or complex. The project team must document all the details related to the data warehouse production environment in order to design and configure the data warehouse. Some information that must be documented includes:

- The network connectivity and protocols used in the production environment.
- The average and peak throughput of the network traffic.
- The number of end-users that the data warehouse must need to support.
- The operating systems and reporting applications that will be used by the users.
- The technology through which information will be delivered to the end-users—whether it will be through LAN, the public Internet or a WAN, a VPN, or some combination of these.

4.2.5 The Data Quality Levels

Data quality is one of the important issues in identifying data sources. Before starting the data warehouse project, the project team should not only be aware of the availability of the data but also about the quality of data of all data sources (if it is high enough to support the business requirements). If there are any data quality problems, it must be taken seriously.

The project team should know:

- The data sources that will be used for the project.
- The location of these data sources.
- The accessibility of these data sources.
- The frequency with which new data will be generated every day in all the data sources.
- The frequency of the data updates in the data warehouse.
- The quality of data in the source systems.
- The extent of presence of missing data or dirty data.
- The people responsible for the data cleaning and the business rules that will be used to clean the data.

4.3 REQUIREMENTS GATHERING METHODS

This section discusses the methods for gathering requirements. These techniques will be used to collect information from the users so that the data warehouse project team can strive to build a data warehouse that meets the expectations of its end-users.

First of all let us classify the users of the data warehouse as follows:

- Senior executives who will give the data warehouse project team a direction and scope for the upcoming data warehouse.
- Key departmental managers who are supposed to report to the executives.
- Business analysts are the people who prepare reports and analyses for the executives and the managers.
- People from IT like Data Base Administrator (DBA) will give you information about the data sources for the data warehouse.

The data warehouse project team will have to go to different groups of users in the various departments to gather the requirements. The basic techniques of requirements elicitation are elaborated in this section.

4.3.1 Interviews

Interviewing is an information gathering technique that is used to collect information from key stakeholders in a software project. It can either be conducted in small/large groups or in a formal/informal manner. To be successful, interviews must be conducted only by experienced persons that follow a structured process in gathering requirements from stakeholders. The key components of this technique include planning and scheduling, preparing, opening, conducting, closing, and follow up.

Planning and scheduling is performed so that interviews can be conducted in a top to down fashion. For example, managers should be interviewed before their subordinates.

It is always advantageous if the person who would be conducting the interview is conversant with the key ideas and terminology within the interviewee's domain. Interview preparation includes doing background domain research and for this the person must review the organization's reports to gain a sense of the projects scope, objectives, and setting. Thus we see that pre-interview research is crucial to the success of the interviews, some key research topics on which the project team member must be well versed include:

- History of the business.
- The current structure of the business.
- Number of employees, their roles, and responsibilities.
- Location of users.
- Primary and secondary purpose of the business unit.
- Relationship of the organization with other organizations.
- The organization's marketplace and its competitors.

The structured interview is very formal and may be considered as an oral presentation of a written questionnaire. The interviewer would ask a few questions that the person being interviewed will answer; other interaction is kept to a minimum.

Structured interviews generally have a fixed number of questions that usually have a restricted set of responses. This also means that the questions used in structured interviews are closed questions although this is not always the case. Some people argue that structured interviews are more efficient in terms of the time taken to collect the data, the degree of reliability, and validity.

The main disadvantage with a structured approach is that the data gathered will lack the richness obtained by open-ended interviews. Also, since closed questions have a limited number of responses, participants may be forced into giving responses which do not reflect their true feelings about an issue.

In an unstructured interview, the interviewer does not ask prepared questions or have fixed interview schedules, instead they have a number of issues which they aim to explore. The questions asked will be unstructured so that the participants can provide more knowledge to them. In this type of interview the interviewees have more control over the interview as they are free to discuss any issue that arise and not necessarily in an order predetermined by the interviewer.

The key advantage of asking open-ended questions is the richness of data which is unbiased by any interpretation which the interviewer may have placed on it. However unstructured interviews are time consuming, and the data collected from different respondents are at times conflicting. Therefore, this raises issues of reliability and validity for data collected in this way.

Since the interview sessions consume a fair amount of the project time. The requirements gathering team must prepare very well for it. Before the project team starts the interview process, the following major tasks are completed:

- Select and provide formal training to the project team members who will be conducting the interviews.
- Assign specific roles for each team member.
- Prepare list of users who will be interviewed.
- Prepare a schedule for the interview.
- List the expectations from the interview, list out what information you want from the users.
- Conduct a pre-interview research.

Finalize the interview questionnaire. Characteristics of a good interview include:

- Two or three users at a time.
- Ease of scheduling.
- Good approach when details are difficult to obtain.
- Some users are comfortable to talk only with one-on-one interviews.
- Needs good preparation to be successful in gathering requirements.
- Pre-interview research helps to conduct an effective interview.
- Encourage users also to prepare themselves for the interview.

Another technique of gathering requirements from users that is similar to interviews is group session. Some of the basic characteristics of group sessions include:

- For an effective group session interview there must be less that users at a time.
- Must be used only after getting a baseline understanding of the requirements.
- May not be effective for initial data gathering.
- Very useful for finalizing requirements by confirming them with the users.
- Need to be well organized.

4.3.2 Joint Application Development (JAD)

JAD, as the name implies is a joint process, with all the concerned groups getting together for a well-defined purpose. Since client is involved throughout the development process, the JAD approach lead to faster development process (development of data mart or data warehouse). In addition to this, JAD is also responsible for improving the quality of the final product by focusing on the initial stages of the development lifecycle, which in turn leads to drastic reduction in the likelihood of errors that are expensive to correct later on.

JAD is widely used to develop computer applications jointly by the users and the IT professionals in a well structured manner. JAD works by conducting well structured discussion workshops that last a couple of days under the direction of a facilitator. JAD workshops are conducted in a room where everyone sits and talks so that everyone hears what others have to say. In this way, there is no delay between question and answer.

JAD methodology overcomes the problems associated with traditional meetings which are not considered to be a productive form of work. JAD turns meetings into workshops which are less frequent, more structured, and more productive. The JAD process is based on four principles:

- People who actually perform the job have the best underdstanding about that job.
- IT professionals have the best understanding of the technology.
- Information systems and business processes work hand in hand.
- The best information sytems are designed when all of these groups work together for the project.

Under suitable conditions, the JAD approach may be adapted for building a data warehouse. JAD consists of a five-phased approach:

- Project Definition: Completing interviews.
- Research: Becoming familiar with business areas and documenting user requirements.
- Preparation: Prepare a checklist of objectives.
- JAD Sessions: Review agenda, data requirements, business metrics and dimensions, and resolve all other issues.
- Final Document: Convert the working document, list all gathered information, data sources, business metrics, dimensions, and hierarchies.

The success of a project following the JAD approach depends on the composition of the team. The nature and purpose of the data warehouse will determine the size and mix of the JAD team. The typical composition of the JAD team must have the following pertinent roles present where one or more persons are assigned for every individual role.

- Executive sponsor who will control the funding, provide direction, and empower other team members.
- Facilitator who will guide the team throughout the JAD process.
- Scribe who is designated to record all decisions.
- Full-time participants who are involved in making decisions about the data warehouse.
- On-call participants are those persons who will be affected by the project, but only in specific areas.
- Observers who would like to sit in on specific sessions without participating in the decision making process.

JAD approach allows key users to participate in the requirements defini- tion process. This gives them a feeling of a sense of ownership in the results, and the support for the new system. Thus, JAD results in a more accurate statement of system requirements, a better understanding of common goals, and a stronger commitment to the success of the new system. But when compared with traditional methods, JAD is more expensive and can be cumbersome if the group is large in proprtion to the size of the project.

4.3.3 Review of Existing Documentation

Apart from the requirements gathering through interviews, group sessions, JAD or any other technique, the data warehouse team will be able to gather useful information from the review of existing documentation. The best part of this technique is that it can be done by the project team members without too much involvement from the users of the business units.

Documentation from User Departments   The requirements gathering team need to look at user documentation to get information about all the operational systems used and know what is important to the users. User documentation helps to know how the users perform their functions by getting a review of various processes and procedures that users have to perform. The documentation also give an insight to the team about the types of analyses the users in these business units are likely to be interested in.

Documentation from IT   The documentation from the IT will help the team to know what data is stored in the operational systems. The operational system DBAs and application experts from IT needs to play a key role in gathering the data for the requirements gathering team. It is they who provide the team with all the data structures, individual data elements, attributes, value domains, and relationships among fields and data structures. All this data needs to be well understood by the team because they will need this information while populating the data warehouse from these source systems.

Apart from this, the application experts could help the requirements gathering team to learn about business rules, data ownership rights, people responsible for data quality, mechanism by which data is gathered and processed in source systems, so on and so forth.

4.3.4 Brainstorming

Brainstorming involves both idea generation and idea reduction. The goal of the former is to identify as many ideas as possible, while the latter ranks the ideas into those considered most useful by the group. Brainstorming is a powerful technique because the most creative or effective ideas often result from combining seemingly unrelated ideas. Also, this technique encourages innovative thinking and unusual ideas.

4.3.5 Questionnaires

This approach is much more informal and can have a limited value. However, questionnaires are good tools to use with persons in remote locations or with those who will contribute only minor input into the overall requirements of the system. A questionnaire can also be used to obtain quick statistics, such as the number of people who would use certain features, or to get a sense of the relative priority of requirements. Apply the rules of a user-centred design for formulating a questionnaire. There are two types of questionnaires: closed-ended and open-ended.

Closed-ended Questionnaires

Closed-ended questionnaiers are those in which the partcipants have a limited set of answers. This type of questionnaires include closed-ended questions that include:

- Yes/no questions – The partcipants just have to answer with a "yes" or a "no".
- Multiple choice – The interviewee is given a set of options from which to choose.
- Scaled questions – In this type of questions the interviewee has to give response that are graded on a continuum (example : rate the quality of the product on a scale from 1 to 10, with 10 being the best qulaity).

Advantages of closed-ended questionnaires are:
- Easy and quick to answer.
- Easy for the user to understand.
- Easy to form.
- Does not consider the difference that exist between articulate and inarticulate respondents.

Disadvantages of closed-ended questionnaires include:
- Might give misleading results due to limited range of options.
- It is difficult for the researcher/interviewer to understand the concept that participant has to explain especially in cases when the participant has to say "yes... but". That is, not every question can be answered by a straightforward yes or no.

Open-ended Questionnaires

Open-ended questionnaires have no predefined set of answers exist. Rather, the participants supply their own answer without restricting themselves to a fixed set of possible responses. Examples of open-ended questions include:

- Completely unstructured – In which the participant is asked to write his opinion on the subject of discussion.
- Word association – In this, the participants are given certain words and they are expected to mention the first word that comes to mind.
- Sentence completion – In this type of questions, the paticipants are asked to complete an incomplete sentence. For example, "The most important issue in buying this product is . . ."
- Story completion – In this, the participants have to complete an incomplete story.

- Picture completion – These type of questions call for filling in an empty conversation balloon.
- Thematic apperception test – In this type of questions, the participants have to explain a picture or make up a story telling about what they think is happening in the picture.

Advantages of open-ended questions include:

- It provides the freedom of expression to the participants.
- The interviewer can understand and interpret the participants viewpoint more clearly without any bias that exist due to limited response ranges.
- Respondents can qualify their answers.

Disadvantages of open-ended questions include:

- It takes a lot of time to code.
- Researcher/interviewer may misunderstand a response.

The sequence of questions in a good questionnaire includes:

- Questions should follow a logical sequence.
- The answer to a question must not be influenced by previous questions.
- Questions should be included in a sequence that flows from the more general to the more specific.
- Questions should follow the least sensitive to the most sensitive sequence.
- Questionnaire should start from questions that are more factual and behavioural questions to attitudinal and opinion questions.
- Questions should begin with unaided and then go to aided questions later on.
- The best sequence of questions may include screening and rapport questions followed by all the product specific questions and demographic questions.

4.3.6 Where to Stop?

The collection of end-user requirements cover many areas which bring out many factors that could have an effect on the final data warehouse. These factors include the end-user's business knowledge, how well the users can express themselves, and how much time they can take out to give the interview.

The key question is that how does the data warehouse team know when they have successfully identified the user's requirements? There is no definitive test for it. However, whenever the team has collected information in the following areas, the team probably has enough information to begin the next phase of the project:

- The subject areas that are most valuable for analysis.
- The operational systems which generate data about important business subject area.
- The types of the source systems that support these subject areas.
- The level of details present in the existing information delivery systems.

- The business dimensions along with different hierarchies and categories present.
- The way in which the performance of the business unit is currently measured.
- The critical success factors that influence the business and the manner in which these factors are monitored.
- The key metrics (discussed later in the chapter).
- The frequency of data updates.
- The amount of historical data needed for the data warehouse.

4.4 REQUIREMENTS ANALYSIS

The data warehouse project team will generate reports describing business subject areas, key dimensions, and performance measures. Using the requirements analysis techniques, the team can build a warehouse data model, which will represent the end-user requirements. Thus, the results of the requirements analysis will be the primary input for data warehouse modelling.

Also on the basis of requirements analysis, the team will determine the resource gap that exist in the organization and finally prepare a project proposal. Determining the resource gap includes evaluating personnel, skills, domain knowledge, schedules, and budgets. For this, the following areas call for special attention:

- Will the client organization be able to provide the kind of skills and personnel hours that will be needed to support the project?
- Is the budget allocated for the project sufficient to cover the complete set of business requirements? If the answer is no then determine which subject areas are most important to cover under the current budget.
- What kind of data management and data analytic tools are already available within the client organization and what service do these tools provide?

4.4.1 Requirements Definition Document

Formal documentation in a data warehouse project cannot be neglected as the project team goes through the requirements definition phase. In this phase, the team gathers the necessary information to support the subsequent phases in the system development life cycle. In case the detailed documentation of the requirements definition is skipped, then many problems can creep in.

First of all, the requirements definition document is the cornerstone for the next phases in the development life cycle. If project team members who played an active role while collecting requirements have obtained a very good understanding of the project have to leave the project for any reason, the project will not suffer from people walking away with the knowledge they have gathered.

Finally, the formal documentation will also validate the findings when reviewed with the users. Hence, we come up with what is known as the requirements definition document which contains the following elements:

- Introduction stating the purpose and scope of the project.
- General requirements description that includes interview summaries thereby broadly stating what types of information requirements are needed by the users.
- Specific requirements including the details of source data needed. It also includes the data transformation and storage requirements and a description of the types of information delivery methods needed by the users.
- Information packages provide details of user requirements in the form of information package diagrams. We will discuss them in the next section.
- User expectations stating how the users expect to use the data warehouse.
- User participation and sign-off listing the tasks and activities which would involve active user participation throughout the development life cycle.
- General implementation plan providing a detailed plan for implementation.

4.5 DIMENSIONAL ANALYSIS

For a data warehouse project, the techniques discussed in the previous section will be used to collect requirements from the end-users. Data will be collected in terms of dimensions, hierarchies, and facts or measures. We will discuss all these three terms in this section. Another term for collecting information for a data warehouse project is 'dimensional analysis', because in a data warehouse environment, all users think in terms of dimensions. This will be clearer after reading further.

Building a data warehouse is very different from building an operational system. This difference pops up from the very first phase of the requirements gathering. The traditional methods of collecting requirements for building operational systems cannot be applied for building data warehouses.

While gathering requirements for an operational system, the users are able to give enough details of the required functions, information content, and usage patterns. Since an operational system is application oriented, the users can inform the requirements gathering team about the various tasks they wish to accomplish with the system and the order in which certain activities need to be performed to complete that task. On the other hand, for a data warehousing system, the users are unable to define their requirements clearly. They may not necessarily be able to define what information they want from the data warehouse, nor can they express how they would like to use the information.

This is basically because users have always worked with one or the other operational system but had never used a data warehouse as they do not know and cannot visualize the scope and benifits of it.

In dimensional analysis, the data warehouse project team will collect information about three things—business dimensions, facts and the categories/hierarchies within the business dimensions. In this section, we will have a look at all these concepts.

Business Dimensions

Data warehouse users may not be able to fully describe what they want in a data warehouse but they can definitely provide the team with very important insights into how they think about the business. They can at least visualize and tell what measurement units are important for them by describing how they measure success in their particular department and how they combine the various pieces of information for strategic decision making.

To put it in simple words, the executives and managers think of business in terms of business dimensions. For example, the marketing manager is interested in the revenue generated by the new product in different regions, every month, by customer demographics, by product brand, so on and so forth. These are his business dimensions along which he wants to analyse his numbers. For example, the manager may like to know how many shirts of John Players were sold in January 2008 in Delhi and the income level of the customers who bought those shirts.

Now once the team knows that users think in terms of business dimensions, they can also go about gathering requirements for the business in terms of these dimensions.

Thus, we see that business dimensions are nothing but syntactical categories that allow the users to specify multiple ways to look at the same information, according to natural business perspectives under which its analysis can be performed. The concept of business dimensions is a key to the requirements definition of a data warehouse. Table 4.1 provides examples of business dimensions in various industries.

Table 4.1 Business dimensions in various industries

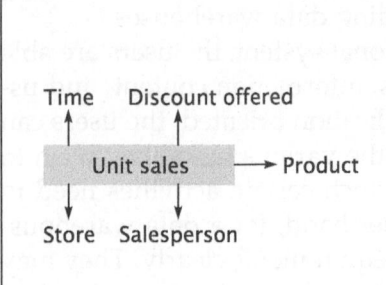	**Retail chain:** In a retail chain, the business analysts view the sales of a product according to time dimension. For example, the monthly sales of a product; discount offered to see how many units of the product were sold when a discount was offered on it; product dimension to view the sales of different products that are sold in the shop like sale of shirts, T-shirts, jeans, trousers, etc.; salesperson dimension to see how much efficient a particular sales person is by analysing how much he sales. Finally, the store dimension to analyse the sales of a product in different stores as one store may report a higher sale than the other.
	Here the **student's performance** is analysed with respect to time, semester, subject, course and professor dimensions. Time

Table 4.1 Continued

Table 4.1 Continued

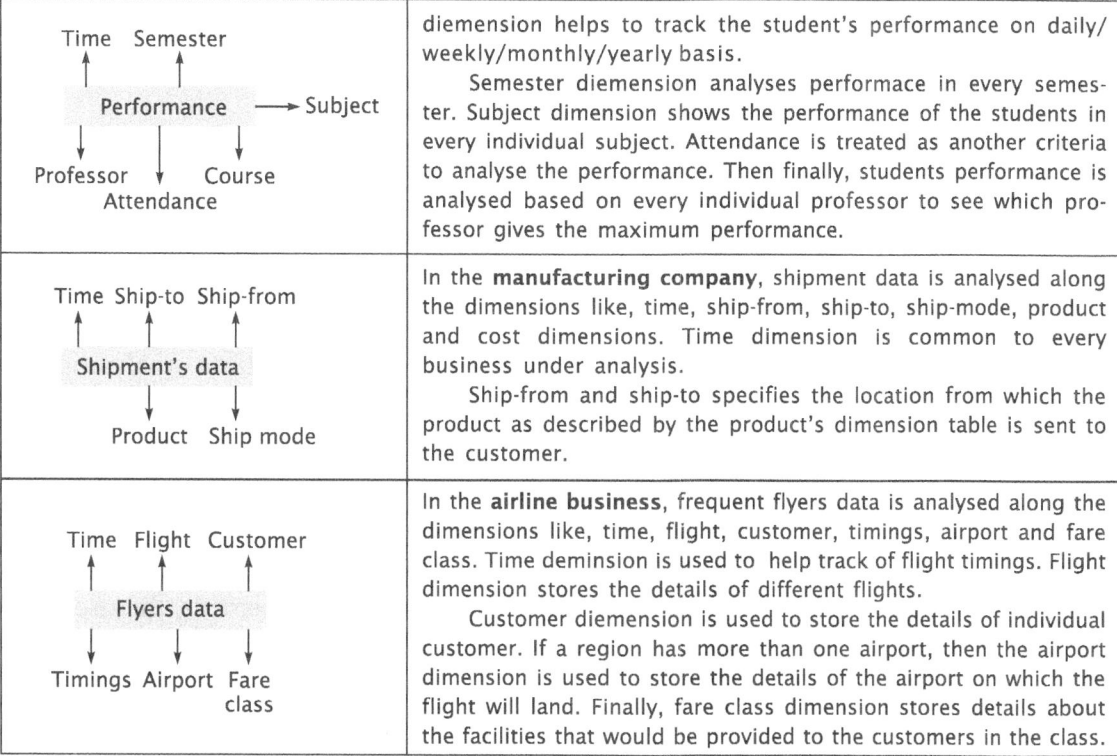

Time Semester Performance ⟶ Subject Professor Course Attendance	diemension helps to track the student's performance on daily/weekly/monthly/yearly basis. Semester diemension analyses performace in every semester. Subject dimension shows the performance of the students in every individual subject. Attendance is treated as another criteria to analyse the performance. Then finally, students performance is analysed based on every individual professor to see which professor gives the maximum performance.
Time Ship-to Ship-from Shipment's data Product Ship mode	In the **manufacturing company**, shipment data is analysed along the dimensions like, time, ship-from, ship-to, ship-mode, product and cost dimensions. Time dimension is common to every business under analysis. Ship-from and ship-to specifies the location from which the product as described by the product's dimension table is sent to the customer.
Time Flight Customer Flyers data Timings Airport Fare class	In the **airline business**, frequent flyers data is analysed along the dimensions like, time, flight, customer, timings, airport and fare class. Time deminsion is used to help track of flight timings. Flight dimension stores the details of different flights. Customer diemension is used to store the details of individual customer. If a region has more than one airport, then the airport dimension is used to store the details of the airport on which the flight will land. Finally, fare class dimension stores details about the facilities that would be provided to the customers in the class.

From the examples given above we conclude that the business dimensions vary from one industry to another and these dimensions depend on the subject for analysis. We notice that the time dimension is a common dimension in all examples, the reason being that all business analyses are performed over time.

Now we know that business dimensions form the underlying basis of the new methodology for requirements definition for a data warehouse. Data must be stored to provide information with respect to the business dimensions. The business dimensions and their hierarchical levels form the basis for all the phases of design.

Let us examine the business dimensions for a retail chain whose goal is to analyse sales in a number of ways. The first dimension would, of course, be the product dimension. The second obvious dimension would be the time dimension. Now, since the retail chain owner may want to analyse sales made at every single store, store therefore can be taken as the third dimension.

The owner may also like to know the sales breakdown along customer demographics like—how do the customers like to pay, which income group customers like to buy which range of products, which brand of products, what effect does putting discounts have on sales? The method of payment will act as the fourth dimension for analysis. So finally, we have come up with the following dimensions for the subject of sales for an automaker: product, store, customer demographics, method of payment, and time.

Let us take another example of a hotel chain. When we talk about hotel occupancy, the dimensions that we can talk of could be hotel room, facilities, and time. We will discuss more about it in the following section.

4.5.1 Dimension Hierarchies

Every business dimension is organized in a hierarchy of levels, corresponding to data domains at different granularity. For example, the time dimension has the hierarchy starting from a single day going up to the entire year. However, in this hierarchy a level can also have descriptions associated with it. Within a dimension, values of different levels are related through a family of roll-up functions.

In a data warehouse environment, when a user starts analysing the metrics along a business dimension, he may start by looking at summary data and then may like to see the same data at different levels of detail. This is what is called traversing the hierarchical levels of a business dimension for getting the details at various levels. For example, the marketing manager may first like to see the sales of John Players shirts in Delhi in the previous year, then in the course of his analysis session, he may move down to the level of quarters and look at the sales broken down by individual quarters. After this, the user may proceed to view even more detailed data by viewing the sales in every individual month of the year. Thus, we see that the hierarchy of the time dimension consists of the levels of year, quarter, and month (Refer Fig. 4.2).

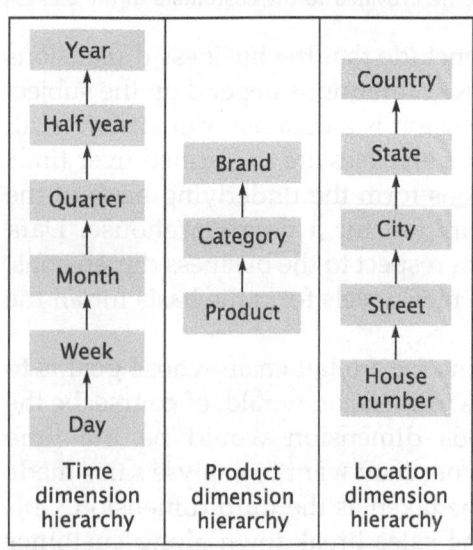

Figure 4.2 Dimensional hierarchy

Business dimension hierarchies are nothing but the paths for drilling down or rolling up while analysing the data at different levels of detail. Within each major business dimension there are hierarchies and categories of data elements that can also be useful for analysis.

Thus, every dimension is organized into a hierarchy of levels, corresponding to data at different levels of granularity. When level $l_1 < l_2$ in the hierarchy, we say that l_1 rolls up to l_2. It is important to note that a level may have descriptions associated with it. Within every individual dimension, values at different levels are related through a family of roll up functions. If a roll up function associates a value v_1 of a certain level to a value v_2 of an upper level of hierarchy, we say that v_1 rolls up to v_2.

4.5.2 Metrics or Facts

We now know what business dimensions mean. By using these business dimensions, what exactly are the users trying to analyse? The numbers that the users analyse are the measurements, facts or metrics that measure the success of the business.

A user typically needs to evaluate or analyse some aspect of the organization's business. The requirements that have been collected must represent the two key elements of this analysis: what is being analysed, and the evaluation criteria for what is being analysed. The evaluation criteria are referred to as measures (a numeric attribute of a fact), and what is being analysed is referred to as dimensions (a description attribute of a fact). Together, one set of dimensions and its associated measures make up what is called a fact.

In case of the retail chain, these metrics relate to the sales as the numbers that the owner is analysing tells him about the performance in sales of each individual product. Other useful metrics for analysing sales can be: actual sales, forecast sales, price, and discount.

For the hotel occupancy, these metrics will be different as the nature of the metrics depends on what is being analysed. Therefore, the metrics in this case would relate to occupancy of rooms in each branch of the hotel chain. Some meaningful and useful metrics for analysing hotel occupancy are: occupied rooms, vacant rooms, unavailable rooms, number of occupants, and cost.

4.6 INFORMATION PACKAGE DIAGRAMS (IPD)

In order to record information requirements for a data warehouse project and present the various insights, thoughts and opinions expressed during the process of collecting requirements in terms of business dimensions and facts, IPDs are used. The IPD, are very useful for taking the development of data warehouse to the subsequent stages.

4.6.1 What Information does an IPD Contain?

The primary concern of the requirements definition phase of IPD is to compile information packages for all the subjects that are relevant for the data warehouse. The IPD enables the data warehouse project team to define the subject areas, key business metrics, the way in which the users will aggregate or roll up data, the data granularity, and the size of the data warehouse size.

As we have already discussed that the traditional methods of gathering requirements for operational systems are not applicable for a data warehouse project, we need a new technique for determining requirements for a data warehouse system that is based on the metrics and the business dimensions along which the facts are analysed. This new technique is known as IPD. For every specific subject, we form an IPD.

To sum up, the subject goes on the top most position of the IPD, the metrics forms the next section, the business dimensions will be the row headings and in each row you will include the hierarchies and categories for the business dimensions.

4.6.2 Example

Let us first consider a simple example of our student monitoring system and form its IPD as shown in Fig. 4.3. Once the concept is clear, we will take two more examples that will discuss the features of IPD in more detail.

This IPD is very simple. Here we are analysing two facts—student's aggregate marks and his attendance. These facts are measured along different dimensions. The first obvious dimension is time that is used to monitor daily/weekly, monthly/yearly, and attendance of the student in the entire semester. A student can perform much better in the same subject if it is taught by a different professor. Professor dimension is therefore the next important dimension that we have. Here we analyse every professor's name, his professional qualification, experience, grade, and number of subjects that he is teaching.

Subject: Student's performance					
Facts: Attendance, aggregate					
Time dimension	Day	Week	Month	Semester	Year
Professor dimension	Name	Professional qualification	Experience	Grade	No. of subjects
Subject dimension	Name	Semester	Theory/ practical		
Student dimension	Name	Grad/PG	Family income	Division in class XII	Grade
Course dimension	Name	Duration	Type	University	

Figure 4.3 IPD for a student monitoring system

It is not surprising that a student may perform poorly in one subject and outstandingly in the another, our next dimension is the subject dimension. Here we will analyse the student's attendance and aggregate based on the name of the subject, whether it is theory or practical and the semester in which the subject is taken (some students perform better in semester in which there are less activities).

The most obvious dimension is the student dimension. This dimension contains all the details of every individual student. The course dimension incorporates the details of the course that the student is pursuing.

Figure 4.4 shows the information package diagram for analysing sales for a retail chain. The subject is sales. The measured facts that are of interest for analyses are shown in the bottom section of the information package diagram. In this case, the metrics to be analysed are actual sales, forecast sales, price, and discount.

Subject: Sales					
Facts: Actual sales, forecast sales, price, discount					
Time dimension	Day	Week	Month	Quarter	Year
Product dimension	Name	Brand	Category	Colour	Price
Customer dimension	Name	Age	Income	Gender	Marital status
Store dimension	Name	City	State	Country	Operational from year
Payment method dimension	Payment type	Interest rate			

Figure 4.4 IPD for sales analysis

The business dimensions along which these facts/metrics are to be analysed are shown as row headings. In our example, these dimensions are time, product, customer, store, and payment method. Each business dimension contains a hierarchy or levels. For example, the time dimension has the hierarchy going from the year down to the level of a single day. The other intermediary levels in the time dimension could be year, quarter, month, and week. These levels or hierarchical components are shown as attributes within their particular column headings in the IPD.

Similarly, the IPD of the hotel business can be formed as given in Fig. 4.5. Here the dimensions are time, hotel, the type of room, and finally the facilities that are provided to the customers. The facts are number of occupied rooms, number of vacant rooms, number of unavailable rooms, number of occupants, and revenue generated.

Subject: Hotel occupancy					
Facts: Occupied rooms, vacant rooms, unavailable rooms, occupants, revenue					
Time dimension	Day	Week	Month	Quarter	Year	Holiday flag
Hotel dimension	Branch name	Branch code	Region	City	Construction year	Renovation year
Room dimension	Room type	Room size	No. of beds	Bed size	Max No. of occupants	Price
Facilities dimension	Gym	Side view	Swimming pool	Cultural activities	Out door games	SPA

Figure 4.5 IPD of the hotel business

One thing to note is that, it is not necessary that all the IPDs of the hotel business will be the same. It will vary depending upon the requirements of the users—what they want to measure and along what dimensions they want to measure.

4.6.3 Reason for Forming the IPD

Once the facts, dimensions and the hierarchies/categories within the dimensions are finalized, we will see how dimension tables and fact tables are formed from a given IPD. To build the logical design of the data warehouse, we will form two types of tables– the fact table and the dimension table.

For a given IPD, there will be *n* number of dimension tables where *n* is the number of dimensions. The name of the dimension table will come from the name of the dimension itself, that is, the row heading of the IPD will become the name of the dimension table. The hierarchies/categories shown in the IPD will become the attributes of the dimension table. Figure 4.6 shows the dimension tables that are formed from the retail chain IPD.

Note that apart from other attributes of the dimensions, there is one more attribute– the Key. It represents the primary key of every individual record that will be stored in the dimension table. Its value will be used to uniquely identify one entity from the other. Most preferably, the value of the key is a system generated sequence number. We will learn more about this in the next chapter.

The metrics or facts from the IPD will form the fact table. Figure 4.6 shows the fact table that is formed. The fact table gets its name from the subject for analysis. In this case, it is sales. Each fact item or measurement goes into the fact table as an attribute for sales. Note that the fact table contains the fact plus the primary keys of all the dimension tables.

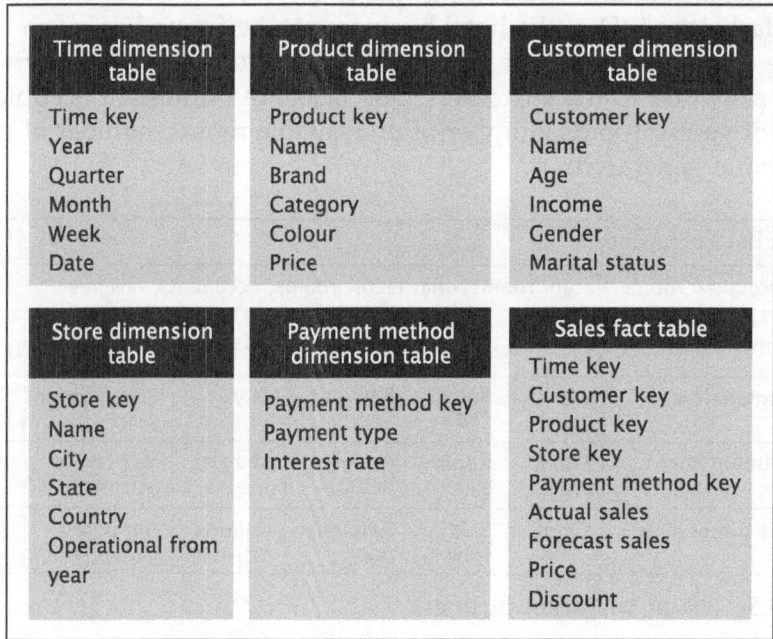

Figure 4.6 Fact tables and dimension tables formed from the given IPD

Recapitulation

Requirements definition guides the whole process of system design and development.

Business data is dimensional in nature and the users of the data warehouse think in terms of business dimensions like product, customer, time, region, etc.

Information package diagrams (IPD) are the backbone of the requirements definition. An information package records the critical measurements or facts and business dimensions along which the facts are normally analysed.

Business objectives in a data warehouse project can help to determine the project scope, identify information subject areas and measures of the business processes that the end-user is analysing.

Data quality is one of the important issues in identifying data sources. It determines not only whether there is business data available, but also whether the data quality of all data sources is high enough to support the business requirements.

Joint application development (JAD) leads to faster development times and greater client satisfaction as the client is involved throughout the development process.

Brainstorming involves both idea generation and idea reduction. Questionnaires are good tools to use with stakeholders in remote locations or with those who will have only minor input into the overall requirements.

The complete project proposal forms the basis for the final project contract with the customer. It must include details about customer's information infrastructure and data environment, scope, subject areas, and the definition of the project's final deliverables.

Content of the requirements definition document include introduction, data sources, data transformation, data storage, and information package diagrams.

Objective Questions

1. **Multiple choice questions**

    (i) Which type of questionnaire has no pre-defined set of answers

    (a) Close-ended

    (b) Open-ended

    (c) Structured

    (d) Unstructured

    (ii) For a data warehouse project, data will be collected in terms of

    (a) Dimensions

    (b) Hierarchies

    (c) Facts

    (d) All of these

    (iii) An operational system is

    (a) Application oriented

    (b) Information oriented

    (c) Analysis oriented

    (iv) The numbers that the users analyse are called

    (a) Dimensions

    (b) Hierarchies

    (c) Facts

    (d) All of these

2. **Fill in the blanks**

    (a) While the _____ requirements are collected to understand the current business processes.

    (b) The _____ requirements help the project team to get an insight into the services that the customer expects from a data warehouse.

    (c) Structured interviews usually contain _____ questions.

(d) _____ is used to gather detailed requirements.

(e) _____ is used for finalizing requirements by confirming them with the users.

(f) _____ leads to faster development times and greater client satisfaction.

(g) For every specific subject, we form _____ IPD.

(h) _____ involves both idea generation and idea reduction.

(i) _____ questionnaires contain yes/no, multiple choice and scaled questions.

(j) The other name of collecting information for a data warehouse project is _____.

(k) Managers think of business in terms of _____.

(l) _____ are the paths for drilling down or rolling up while analysing the data at different levels of detail.

(m) _____ are used to visualize multidimensional cubes.

3. Match the following

(a) Whether a customer has withdrawn any money from the ATM in the last week   1. Existence checking queries

(b) Gives information about the data sources for the data warehouse   2. Statistical analysis queries

(c) Calculate the average sales per sales region   3. Senior executives

(d) Directs the project team   4. Structured interview

(e) Limited responses   5. IT staff

(f) Efficient but lacks the richness of information   6. Closed questions

(g) Open-ended questions   7. Unstructured interview

4. State true or false

(a) While a data warehouse is a data capture system, the operational systems are information delivery systems.

(b) The requirements definition phase guides the whole process of system design and development.

(c) It is important to document all the details related to the data warehouse production environment in order to design and configure the data warehouse.

(d) It is not important that the interviewee be conversant with the interviewer's terms and terminology.

(e) The structured interview is an oral presentation of a written questionnaire.

(f) Structured interviews have a fixed number of questions that usually have a restricted set of responses.

(g) Unstructured interviews are time consuming and less reliable.

(h) The interviewer must ask more of open-ended questions, as closed questions limit the input by the interviewee.

(i) JAD turns meetings into workshops which are infrequent, unstructured, and unproductive.

(j) User documentation helps to know how the users perform their functions.

(k) Every business is analysed along the same dimension.

Review Questions

1. What are the essential differences between defining requirements for operational systems and data warehouses?

2. What does an information package diagram contain?

3. Write a short note on dimensional analysis.

4. As a member of requirements gathering team for your upcoming data warehouse project, list some of the end-user requirements that you will be interested to gather.

5. List the types of users who must be interviewed for collecting requirements. What information can you expect from them?

6. Why are reviews of documents important? What can you expect to get out of such reviews?

7. Explain different methods of gathering requirements from the users. Which one method do you think will prove to be the most effective one?

8. When can you say that you have successfully gathered the requirements?

9. Explain the requirement definition document and project proposal.

10. You are the vice-president for a nation-wide appliance manufacture company. Describe any three different ways you will tend to analyse sales. What will be your business dimensions?

11. You are on the data warehouse project of Auctions.com, an internet auction company selling upscale works of art. Your responsibility is to gather requirements for sales analysis. Find out the key metrics, business dimensions, hierarchies and categories. Draw the IPD.

12. GlobalBook Inc. is a large distributor with domestic and international distribution channels. The company orders from publishers and distributes publications to all the leading booksellers. You want to build a data warehouse to analyse shipments that are made from the company's warehouse. Prepare an IPD showing all the facts, dimensions and the hierarchies within each dimension.

5

PLANNING AND PROJECT MANAGEMENT

Learning Objectives

It is worth noticing that more than 50 per cent of the data warehouse projects end in a failure. In most of the cases, the project is not completed and the system is not delivered. In a few cases, although the project is completed, the end-users categorize the data warehouse just as a data basement. The key reason behind such a situation is common—the project was improperly sized and architected, the data warehouse project is not in line with the business.

So, in this chapter, we will learn the issues related to planning and project management that arise when we are headed towards building a data warehouse.

Case Study

This chapter covers the details of the project plan that we have already discussed in the last chapter. Issues like infrastructure planning, project team, and the roles and responsibilities of the team members are all a part of the project plan.

David, the new project leader is supposed to make the final conclusion regarding the operating system platform, database platform, server hardware, DBMS, and the tools. Obviously, David cannot simply make the decision in isolation. He can not simply choose the best and the latest technology for the data warehouse without client's permission because it is they who have to bear the cost.

Hence, it is crucial that the data warehouse project leader must be well informed about the latest trends and updates in the market. Then, the leader must pen down all the hardware options available along with their advantages and limitations, so that the client can have a better understanding, can analyse them in breadth and finally take an appropriate decision.

5.1 PROJECT MANAGEMENT PRINCIPLES

Effective project management is a key to the success of a data warehouse project. In this section, we will consider project management issues that are vibrant in data warehouse projects, study the basic guiding principles that the project team must follow and enumerate the success factors.

While project management is critical for developing operational systems, it is even more critical for a data warehouse project, as there is little expertise available in this rapidly growing discipline. The data warehouse project manager is expected to embrace new tasks and deliverables, develop an entirely different strategy to work with the end-users and work in an environment that is far less defined than traditional operational systems.

Data warehouse project management deals with project plans, scope agreements, resources, schedules, configuration and change management, contingency plans, and the application of project management tools and methodology.

The difference between a successful data warehouse and a disastrous data warehouse depends on the application of sound project management techniques were applied. It is wrong to believe that since data warehouses are different from operational systems, the project team may ignore the importance of project plans, schedules, resources, risk, scope agreements, and management control.

A paramount determining factor in the success of data warehousing is the input of the stakeholders of the project. Project management for a data warehousing project allows for large amounts of user input in all phases of the project. There are many commercial software products available in the market tailored for data warehouse project management. A good project plan should list the critical tasks that must be performed and when each of these tasks should start and by what time it should end. The plan identifies who is to perform the tasks, describes deliverables to be created, and identifies milestones for measuring progress.

5.1.1 Key Considerations

We must consider some guiding principles that pertain to data warehouse projects. At every stage of the project, the guiding principles must be kept as a backdrop to condition each project management decision and action. The major guiding principles are:

- *Sponsorship* No data warehouse project can be successful in the absence of a strong and committed upper level management support.
- *Project manager* For the success of the project it is necessary that the project manager is not only technology oriented but should be user-oriented and business-oriented.

- *New paradigm*   Data warehousing is a new technology, so innovative project management techniques are crucial to deal with unexpected challenges.
- *Team roles*   The team roles should not be assigned arbitrarily, but must vary from one project to the other depending upon the need.
- *Data quality*   The most important principle of a data warehouse is the quality of data.
- *User requirements*   User's requirements form the driving force of every task scheduled to complete the project.
- *Building for growth*   Once the data warehouse is deployed, the number of users, the number, and complexity of queries will always go up. A data warehouse that is not built to cater to the growing needs cannot succeed.
- *Realistic expectations*   Setting right and attainable expectations are also critical for the success of the data warehouse.
- *Dimensional data modelling*   A well-designed dimensional data model is the basic requisite to lay the foundation and form the blueprint of the upcoming data warehouse.
- *External data*   A data warehouse does not survive by internal data alone. It needs data from relevant external sources as well.
- *Training*   Since data warehousing is a new technology, the end-user tools are also different and new. So adequate training must be given to the user staff or else if the users do not know how to use the tools, they will not use the data warehouse and hence the project will result in a failure.
- *Security*   The organization will have to face a tough problem with security, especially if it wants to make the data warehouse web-accessible. More the accessibility of the warehouse, greater is its security risk.

5.1.2 The Ideal Approach

As a data warehouse designer, you should not be bogged down in the strictness of the principles, rules, and methods. A practical approach must be followed to manage the project. A practical approach is simply a common-sense approach that has an excellent blend of practical wisdom and hard-core theory and is result-oriented. You simply have to balance significant activities against the less important ones and adjust the priorities. You need to be driven by business requirements and not by technology. For a data warehouse project a few tips on adopting a practical approach are given below:

- Running a project in a pragmatic way means constantly monitoring any kind of deviations and slippages, if any. In case such deviations exist, then taking corrective actions to stay on course. Rearrangement of the priorities must be done as and when necessary.
- Make use of the project schedule for a smooth workflow to achieve results and not just to control the project.

- Continuously review project task dependencies and minimize the wait time for department tasks.
- It has been that in some cases, too much planning is done which thereby bogs down the success of the project. At times, a ready-fire-aim methodology may prove to be a better option.
- Avoid using bleeding edge technologies.
- It is always recommended to produce early deliverables as part of the project since these deliverables will be helpful in sustaining the interest of the users and also serve as proof-of-concept systems.
- Paulraj Ponniah in his book *Data Warehousing Fundamentals* (2001) said that "Architecture first, and then only the tools". It will prove disastrous to choose the tools first and then build the data warehouse around the selected tools. Rather an efficient architecture, centered on business requirements must be created first, and then the tools to support the architecture must be selected.

Review the suggestions for the data warehouse project, especially if this is the first data warehouse project. The users of the data warehouse are not attracted by fancy screens, but are concerned with how user friendly and useful the warehouse is.

5.2 DATA WAREHOUSE READINESS ASSESSMENT

The data warehouse readiness assessment is done using five factors. If these five factors are not showing positive indications, then it is always better to take a break and resolve certain issues. These key factors include:

- *Strong management sponsorship* Having a strong management sponsorship is critical for the success of a data warehouse project. These sponsors have a clear vision of the data warehouse's impact on the organization and thus hold a strong conviction for their vision.
- *Compelling business motivation* By itself, data warehouse will do nothing. It simply enables the user to perform strategic analysis. The data warehouse will be readily accepted by the end-users when there is clear and easily articulated motivation for the data warehouse project.
- *Level and quality of IT and end-users liaison* IT is just one department of any business like marketing and finance. No organization can build a data warehouse without an IT department and the IT cannot build a successful data warehouse without the help of the user department. A successful data warehouse project brings together all the users and the IT department together to form a cohesive culture.
- *Analytic culture of the organization* A data warehouse can enable the users to get the information but they cannot make the users analyse. If an organization does not lay much stress on information and analysis then

the readiness for its data warehouse become questionable. The most successful data warehouse exists in those organizations where facts are analysed to make decisions. That is, if the work culture of the organization is heuristic rather than holistic then the purpose of the data warehouse is defeated.

- *Feasibility for the data warehouse* This factor is concerned with the feasibility of converting the existing system into a data warehouse system. If the existing model shows signs of inconsistent, redundant or inaccurate data and there is a strong need to implement certain business rules then the organization must think about a data warehousing solution.

Kimball has suggested a data warehouse litmus test which tests how well the organization is capable of handling the challenges listed above. Table 5.1 lists the readiness factors and their description.

Table 5.1 Data warehouse readiness factors

Readiness Factor	Low-level Readiness	High-level Readiness
Strong management sponsorship	• Hard to gain access • Not respected • Not interested • Don't even know what a data warehouse is	• Easily accessible • Widely respected • Determined for a data warehousing solution • Have realistic expectations • Active participation
Compelling business motivation	• Vision is not clear • Project viewed as a tactical rather than strategic solution • Project is viewed for cost savings • Inaccurate measurements of payback value	• Project is viewed as a necessity—Clear vision • Project viewed as a strategic solution rather than a tactical one • Project viewed for generating revenue • Articulated payback value
Level and quality of IT and end-users liaison	• Organization depends on external IT consultants • Not getting along well with IT	• End-users and IT works as a team • It effectively involved in the business activities
Analytic culture of the organization	• Decision still made without analysing data • Users not asking for more data • Users are not using all the predefined reports	• Fact based decision making • Users asking for more and more data • All the reports are extensively used • Information is shared widely within the organization
Data warehouse feasibility	• Data warehouse project calls for a lot of purchases for the new • Experienced IT personnel are committed to other	• Availability of skilled personnel in the project technology • Availability of high quality data strategic solutions

Table 5.2 Warning sings for a data warehouse project

Bad Indications	Action to be Taken
▪ The requirement definition phase is well past the target date.	▪ Stop capturing unwanted information. Conduct meetings with users and set firm final date.
▪ Need to write too many in-house programs.	▪ If there is time and budget, get different tools else increase programming staff.
▪ Users not cooperating to provide details of data.	▪ It's a delicate issue so the team needs to talk to the project sponsors to resolve the issues.
▪ Computing problems with data brought over to the staging area.	▪ Revisit all data transformation and integration routines. Ensure that no data is missing. Include all warehouse users in the verification process.
▪ Users not comfortable with query tools.	▪ First ensure whether appropriate query tools are being used and then provide extra training to the users.

5.2.1 Bad Performance Indicators

As the data warehouse project team proceeds with the data warehouse project following the phases of development life cycle, it must keep a close watch for any warning signs that may lead to disaster.

Some of these warning signs may be pointing to certain inconveniences calling for minor action. Some of them need corrective action to ensure success, while some of the warning signs may portend serious drawbacks that require immediate remedial action. Irrespective of the nature of these warning signs, the team needs to be vigilant and keep a strict eye on them. As soon as a potential problem is recognized, corrective action must be taken immediately.

Table 5.2 illustrates some of the warning sign and corresponding action that could be taken. However, in the real data warehouse project, there can be many more warning signs and the nature of these signs will vary from project to project and company to company.

5.2.2 Indications of a Successful Project

Once you have applied all the techniques of effective project management and completed the development of your data warehouse, you finally need to know whether your data warehouse has succeeded in its mission or not.

You cannot wait for three–four years to calculate the return on investment (ROI) and then compare past performance of the company with the new metrics obtained. For this reason, there exist some success factors that can be observed within a short time after implementation.

The following happening indicates a success data warehouse project:

- Tremendous growth in the number of queries and reports requested by the users.
- The nature of queries gets complicated and more sophisticated.
- Increase in the number of users.

- The users spend more time in the data warehouse looking for information.
- Reduction of turnaround time needed to draw strategic information from the data warehouse.

5.3 DATA WAREHOUSE PROJECT TEAM

Organizing the project team means putting the right person on the right job. As a good starting point, the project manager must list all the project challenges and specialized skills needed for activities like planning, requirements elicitation, defining queries, data modelling, tools selection, database design, quality control, setting up metadata, etc.

You also need to assign individual persons to the team. The data warehouse project team must have the skills, knowledge and experience, attitude, team spirit and a strong commitment towards the project.

5.3.1 Key Roles

The project manager specifies the team roles that are designated to perform one or more related tasks. In data warehouse projects, the team roles are often used for allotting the job titles given to the team members.

Data warehousing practitioners classify the roles or job titles in various ways. Some of the classifications are: staffing for initial development, testing, ongoing maintenance, management, front-office users, end-users, staffing for development, support, administration, data acquisition, data storage, information delivery. Once you have classified the roles, then you need to assign individuals to accomplish each role.

5.3.2 Users Involvement

In a typical OLTP application, the users interact with the system through GUI screens to receive information from the system. If they need special reports, they take the help of IT to write programs that are not a part of a regular application.

In striking contrast, user interaction with a data warehouse is direct without any mediation from IT. There is no predictability in the types of queries that will be executed and the reports or analysis that will be done. The usage of an OLTP system is entirely different from that of a data warehouse system. So, the users must have a strong voice in the development of the data warehouse.

A data warehouse project has to apply joint application development techniques. The project can be a success only if users are made a part of the development team and if their knowledge and experience about the business is intelligently tapped. The support that active user participation can provide to the development team can be given as below:

- The project sponsors can support the development team in all their efforts.
- User representatives can help to coordinate meetings with all other users and ensure their active participation throughout the life cycle of the project.
- The subject area experts from the user organization can provide sufficient details regarding the user requirements in their specific area and clarify the semantic meanings of the business terminology that they use.
- Users can review and confirm the data elements and relationships that exist between them.
- Users can examine and test information delivery tools and can also assist in the selection of the tools.

5.4 PLANNING FOR THE DATA WAREHOUSE

Data warehouse projects that are initiated in the absence of a project plan may suffer from lack of resources. They are usually late, exceed the budget, not of the desired quality and most importantly, they do not give the users what they expect.

The main reason behind it is the lack of proper planning and application project management principles. The first question that must be asked is whether the company really needs a data warehouse. We must first assess expectations from the data warehouse and then decide which type of data warehouse is needed. We must have a clear view of where the data is going to come from, who will use the data warehouse, the manner in which they will use it, and the times at which the data warehouse will be used.

Figure 5.1 Key issues to be considered while planning the data warehouse

Planning the data warehouse begins with a thorough consideration of the key issues that are vital for the proper planning and the successful completion of the project. Some of these key issues are illustrated in Fig. 5.1.

Values and expectations Before jumping into data warehousing, the company must first assess the value to be derived from the proposed system and then enumerate the benefits and values propositions.

It must be determined well in advance as to whether the data warehouse will help the executives and managers to make better decisions or will it be used to improve the bottom line of the business, if yes then by how much—these are certain questions that need to be answered. As part of the overall planning, the starting point is to make a list of the realistic benefits and expectations.

Assessment of the risk factor involved In every project, there are two main terms—project risks and the cost of the project. Often project planners misunderstand these terms and treat them as one. But the cost of the project is not equivalent to the risk associated with the project.

The risk faced by the company in case the project fails is much more than simply the loss from the project costs. What are these risks and what losses are likely to be incurred if the project fails are certain issues that will be resolved by a proper mechanism of risk assessment. Risk assessment is broad and relevant to each business. It is vital that risk assessment be included as a part of the planning document.

Selection of an approach The top-down approach implies starting at the enterprise-wide data warehouse, although it can be build iteratively. The data from the overall, large enterprise-wide data warehouse flows into departmental and subject data marts.

On the contrary, the bottom-up approach focuses on building individual data marts first. The conglomerate of these data marts will make up the enterprise data warehouse. Then there is a practical approach of going bottom-up and simultaneously ensuring that all the data marts are conformed to one another so that they can be viewed as a whole.

The data warehouse project team has to weigh these options as to other they apply to the particular company. The implication of the choice is documented in the planning document.

Build or buy decision This is a major issue. No organization can build the entire data warehouse from scratch by in-house programming. The question is how much work is to be done in-house and how much work needs to be outsourced. How many data marts must be built in-house, how many data marts may be built by external organizations.

A data warehouse, offers a large range of functionality for which a number of functions have to be written. The decisions that need to be taken are—whether the project team wants to write more in-house programs for data extraction, data transformation, data loading, data storage or whether the users want to use vendor tools for information delivery. These questions need to be answered in the planning stage itself.

Single vendor or best-of-breed tools There are different categories of vendors who offer multiple products that cater to the services and functions rendered by the data warehouse. Basically, any organization has two main options—first, to use the products of a single vendor or to use the products from more than one vendor. The advantages and disadvantages of both the options are listed in Table 5.3.

Table 5.3 Pros and cons of single-vendor and multi-vendor approaches

Advantages	Disadvantages
Single-vendor Products	
<ul><li>Fine and high level integration among the different tools.</li><li>Consistent look and feel.</li><li>Seamless cooperation among components.</li><li>Centrally controlled information exchange.</li><li>Final price can be negotiated.</li><li>Enables the data warehouse to be well integrated and function coherently.</li></ul>	<ul><li>The organization may have to compromise for one tool because of the other.</li><li>Lack of customization.</li><li>Inability to select the product which is best suited for the specific function.</li></ul>
Multi-vendor Products	
<ul><li>Could build an environment to fit every individual organization.</li><li>No need to compromise for one tool because of the other one.</li><li>Option to select products best suited for the function.</li></ul>	<ul><li>Compatibility among the tools from the different vendors could become a serious problem.</li><li>The organization has less negotiation power with regard to individual products and may incur higher overall expense.</li></ul>

5.4.1 Gathering the Business Requirements

Data warehouse practitioners say "Let business requirements drive the data warehouse, not technology." It has been observed that many data warehouse projects violate this fact and thereby end up in failure. Some data warehouse designers prefer to put beautiful pictures on user's screen, but they either forget to concentrate on the actual requirements of the users or try to build systems that exploit the depths of the technology.

It should always be kept in mind that data warehousing is not about technology but only about solving user's need for strategic information. There should be a clear understanding of user's requirements. The data warehouse project team should start by concentrating on what information is needed and not on how the needed information will be delivered.

There are no hard and fast rules regarding the usage of specific tools, infact such decision can be taken at a later stage. The data warehouse architecture that is centered on user requirements is more important. So, before finalizing the overall plan, a preliminary survey of user requirements must be conducted. The outcome of this survey will help the team to formulate the overall plan. It will be crucial to set the scope of the project.

5.4.2 Gaining Support for the Project

No major initiative in an organization can succeed without support from the sponsors or the senior management. This is even more critical in the case of data warehouse projects. The data warehouse project must have full support of the top management right from day one.

The enterprise-wide data warehouse system provides an opportunity to unify the information view of the entire organization for purposes of strategic advantage. A department or a user cannot sponsor such a big undertaking within the organization. Hence the data warehouse must satisfy various conflicting requirements in the company and must gain focus of sponsors from the highest level of management.

5.5 DATA WAREHOUSE PROJECT PLAN

A good project plan enumerates the tasks that have to be performed, the sequence in which they have to be performed, the persons who will perform the task, describes the deliverables that have to be created and identifies the milestones for measuring progress of the project.

The decision to build a data warehouse may be made either to stay competitive or to provide a solution to the existing information problems persisting within the organization. Whatever may be the reason to go for data warehousing, the real initiative begins with a well-designed project plan. This plan lays the direction and goals of the project (Refer Fig. 5.2).

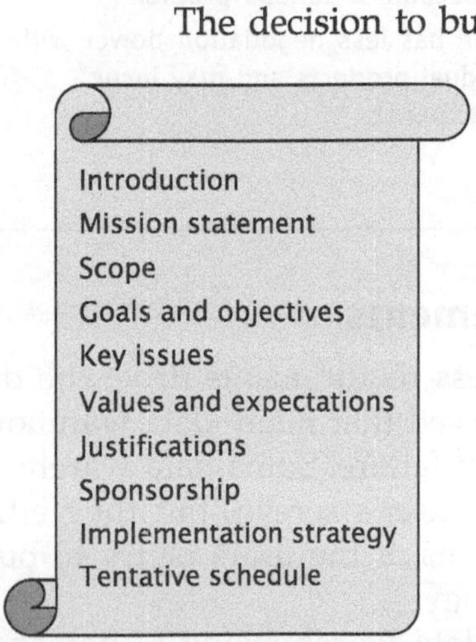

Introduction
Mission statement
Scope
Goals and objectives
Key issues
Values and expectations
Justifications
Sponsorship
Implementation strategy
Tentative schedule

Figure 5.2 The overall plan for data warehousing initiative

The plan describes the type of data warehouse solution needed and clearly states the end-user's expectations. This plan creates the basis of recognizing the need and authorizing a formal project. The contents of the formal plan is constituted by: introduction, mission statement, scope, goals and objectives, key issues, values and expectations, justifications, sponsorship, implementation strategy and tentative schedule.

The data warehouse project plan is the primary document of understanding between IT and the user. It makes a clear boundary by stating which functions will be delivered and which will not be delivered. This plan forms the basis of a scope agreement that is a signed document by the IT department and the end-users. Without a well-stated scope agreement, the user might expect more than IT is planning to deliver. In the absence of such an agreement, there will be no yardstick to measure the success or failure of the project.

The scope agreement should be periodically reviewed with the end-users to inform them that the team is working towards the specific deliverables listed in the document. The most challenging job for the data warehouse project manager is getting the internal skilled personnel involved with the project, because competent workers have their hands full with one or the other project. The manager must also have consultants to seek advice and direction.

Another important resource is budget. In the absence of sufficient funds, there will be no scope of hiring skilled personnel, choosing the best products and tools, acquiring the right hardware and hiring quality consultants and contractors. The following factors give us an idea of how much money is required for a data warehouse project:

- Size of the database.
- Complexity of the applications.
- Rigorousness of the data cleansing functions.
- Number and types of source systems.
- Number of users.
- Choice of tools.
- Network connections, networking software, and hardware.
- Extent of training sessions.
- Gap between the required and the available skills.

Data warehouse schedules are usually set before a project plan has been developed. The project plan states the durations, assignments, predecessor tasks and is the only valid and accurate means of determining the actual duration of the data warehouse project. In the absence of a detailed plan, promising a delivery date is wishful thinking at best.

The users will always want that the data warehouse be delivered to them in a very short span of time. In fact, vendors misguide users by promising a quick delivery of the warehouse without taking into amount the following factors:

- Understanding and documentation of requirements.
- Cleaning of data.
- Integration of data from multiple sources.
- Time required to resolve performance related issues.
- Time required to train the data warehouse end-users to enhance and maintain the data warehouse.

Failing to understand these issues, the data warehouse vendors often deliver small warehouses that are not robust enough to be enhanced much use to anyone. Data warehouses must be scalable and built in phases so that increments can be developed and delivered in pieces. Although every individual phase will have its own schedule, but there should be an overall schedule that incorporates each of the phases.

For any data warehouse project, a new set of requirements can always be expected. These requests may call for new data to be stored in the warehouse, formation of new pre-formatted reports, a new information delivery tool, the integration of more external data or access by more users. Many a times, these small changes accumulate to the point where the existing schedule can no longer handle the additional requirements. This situation is called scope creep. However, when the users either request for large and complex changes, new and complex source data or some new technology implementation, that situation is called scope gallop. With a realistic project schedule, a major change cannot be adjusted with an existing schedule.

Every project is prone to a degree of risk. The project manager needs to recognize these impending risks and take appropriate actions to mitigate them. Since data warehousing is a relatively new technology, the risks are not as apparent as in operational systems. For example, losing the support of a sponsor is an ever-present risk which can be mitigated by having not just one but multiple sponsors.

Another risk could be that the users may deny using the system. This problem can be prevented by having the user involved right from the beginning of the project including source data selection, data validation, query tool selection, and user training. The other possible risk could be poor performance of the system. However, this problem can be overcome by a good database design with a clear understanding of the query tools that access the database. Apart from this, constant monitoring can provide early insight into what is going wrong.

Generally, the most neglected aspect of a data warehouse project is to keep everyone informed. Important people like project sponsors, end-user representatives and IT representatives must be well informed about every decision made in context of the project. For this, periodic formal communications should be made an integral part of every data warehouse project plan, especially large data warehouse projects.

The project plan should include monthly presentations to sponsors and end-user representatives that include:

- Review of project scope, deliverables, and project time line.
- Discussion of issues that are difficult to resolve or are behind schedule.
- Review of the coming month's activities.
- Discussion for formulating a contingency plan either to make for slip of schedule or to address problems.
- A question-and-answer round followed by a summary.

Data warehouse projects cost a lot of money, involve a lot of manpower, and include many activities that are usually not familiar to the project sponsors and the end-users. This being the case, the data warehouse project plan needs a lot of goodwill from within the entire organization.

5.6 ECONOMIC FEASIBILITY ANALYSIS

For every project, an economic feasibility analysis is done which studies the economic impact on the organization. This activity is similar to performing a cost benefit analysis. For best results, there should be a comprehensive analysis that will identify all types of benefits expected from the new system and all types of costs that have to be incurred to design and implement the system. If the proposed system passes the economic feasibility test only then can it be treated as ready for the next step.

5.6.1 Costs and Benefits of the System

The term benefit means something that directly or indirectly either increases the profit or decreases the cost. The team's best effort must be to maximize benefits and minimize costs.

There are two types of benefits—tangible and intangible. Tangible benefits are those benefits that can be identified with certainty and easily expressed in terms of money value, whereas intangible benefits, on the other hand, are those benefits that cannot be identified by certainty or expressed in terms of money. Although difficult to quantify, the intangible benefits contribute to the overall economic analysis of the system. Intangible benefits are like icing on the cake. The data warehouse is not designed to realize intangible benefits, but they come as an additional benefit to the system.

Like benefits, there are two types of costs—tangible and intangible. Tangible costs can be identified with certainty and easily expressed in terms of money value. The intangible costs are those costs that cannot be identified by certainty or expressed in terms of money. Failing to quantify the intangible tasks can be disastrous for the system. There is however, another category of costs—development costs and operating costs. While development costs occur once during the development of the project, the operating costs are incurred after the data warehouse is implemented and thus, an ongoing cost. Table 5.4 lists the various tangible and intangible costs and benefits.

Table 5.4 Tangible and intangible costs and benefits

Tangible benefits	Intangible benefits
▪ Reduction in employees	▪ Improved employee morale
▪ Elimination of overtime	▪ Improved goodwill of the organization
▪ Less paperwork	▪ Improved customer services
▪ Smaller inventory needs	▪ More timely information
▪ Less need for travel	▪ Improves decision making
▪ Enhanced product quality	▪ Decrease in time to market
▪ Increased throughput	▪ Increased process flexibility
▪ Launching of new products	▪ Better allocation of resources
▪ Increased sales	▪ Decrease in employee turnover
▪ Products enhancement	▪ Better output of employees
▪ Target marketing	▪ Competitive advantage
▪ New markets	

Table 5.4 Continued

Table 5.4 Continued

Tangible costs	Intangible costs
• Consultation fee for data warehouse designers and developers • Additional training given to users • Materials required • Costs for acquiring new operating personnel • Costs for acquiring hardware and software components • Data conversion costs • Preparing documents • Maintenance and upgrades of the system • Network connectivity charges	• Reduction in employee's morale • Decrease in productivity

5.6.2 Economic Feasibility Measures

There are numerous methods to assess the economic feasibility of the data warehouse project. In this section, we will discuss three such methods.

Payback period   It refers to the period of time required for the return on an investment to "repay" the sum of the original investment. For example, if we have invested Rs 1,00,000 from which we get a return of Rs 25,000 every year. Then, that measn it will take four years for us to get our money back. This method measures how long something takes to "pay for itself". Obviously, shorter payback periods are desriable as compared to longer payback periods. Payback period is widely used due to its simplicity.

The basic formula is: Payback period = Investment ÷ Cash flow. Here, cash flows are assumed to be constant every year.

However, the payback period method suffers from serious limitations as it does not account for the time value of money. Alternative measures of "return" preferred by economists are break even analysis and net present value.

Net present value (NPV)   It is a standard method for the financial appraisal of long-term projects. This method overcomes the shortfall of the payback period method.

In this method, each cash inflow/outflow is discounted back to its present value (PV) and then these values are summed. Therefore,

$$\text{NPV} = \sum_{t=0}^{n} \frac{C_t}{(1+r)^t}$$

where t - time of the cash flow, n - total duration of the project, r - discount rate, and C_t - net cash flow

Note The discount rate is the rate of return that could be earned on an investment in the financial markets with similar risk.

NPV indicates how much value a project will add to its firm. If C_t positive, the project is said to have discounted cash inflow at time t and if C_t is negative then the project is said to have discounted cash outflow at time t. obviously a project with a positive NPV is desirable. Table 5.5 summarizes what effect the NPV has on continuation of the project.

Table 5.5 Effect of NPV on a data warehousing project

NPV	Interpretation	Conclusion
NPV > 0	Project would add value to the firm.	Accept the project.
NPV < 0	Project would reduce the value from the firm.	Reject the project.
NPV = 0	Project would neither add nor reduce any value for the firm.	Depends on organization. Must accept if strategic and competitive advantage is needed or any other factor that cannot be mathematically calculated.

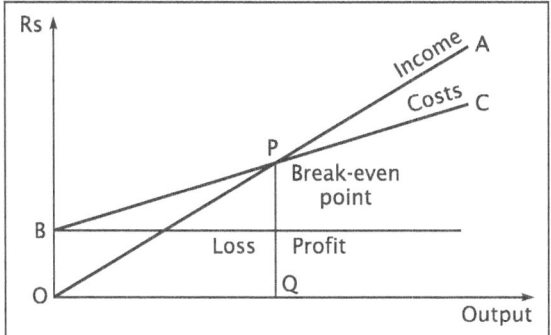

Figure 5.3 Break-even analysis

Break-even analysis This method is used to determine at what point of time the benefits realized from the project will be equal to the costs associated with implementing it. The point where costs and benefits from the project become equal is called the break-even point. To calculate the break-even point, simply plot the expected costs against the expected benefits on a graph as in Fig. 5.3. The point at which the two lines meet, mark it as the break-even point.

5.6.3 Justifying the New System

It has been seen that even for a medium-sized company, the total investment in the data warehouse could be around a few million dollars. A rough breakdown of the costs can be given as in Fig. 5.4.

Before building a data warehouse, the project team must first justify the total costs by balancing the risks against the benefits, both tangible and intangible. However, this is not easy. Real benefits may not be known until the data warehouse is finally built and becomes operational. The users of the data warehouse will use it in any *ad hoc* manner by running queries to make strategic decisions. The number of ways in which the users can pose a query is not limited. So it is not possible to say well in advance what queries and

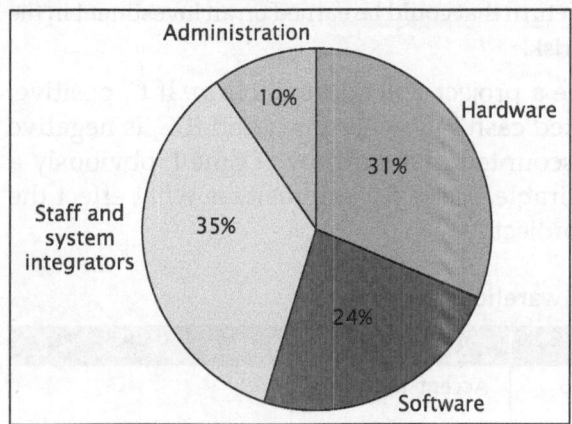

Figure 5.4 Cost breakdown of a data warehouse

analysis will be done, what significant decisions the users will be able to make, and how beneficial these decisions would be to improve the bottom-line of the business.

Many companies join the race of introducing data warehousing without even having a full cost-justification analysis. They justify the new system to be introduced based upon their intuition and potential competitive pressure. In that case only good luck of the company can help it.

5.7 PLANNING FOR THE DATA WAREHOUSE SERVER

Selecting the hardware for the server machine is one of the most important tasks for the data warehouse project team. For selecting the hardware, scalability, and query performance are the main key issues that have to be considered. The data warehouse exists mainly to provide strategic information to the users with the means of ad hoc, unpredicatble, complex queries, and reports. So, if the server hardware fails to support faster query processing, then the entire project will fail.

With the passage of time, as the data warehouse grows with the increase in the number of users and increase in the number of queries, the load on the server hardware will shoot up like anything. So at this point of time, there is a need to scale up the data warehouse. It has been observed that the number of active users doubles in six months. Besides this, as the data warehouse matures, the content stored in the data warehouse will increase due to the increasing the number of subject areas stored in the data warehouse. Corporate data warehouses start at approximately 200 GB and shoot up to terabytes in 1.5–2 years of deployemnt.

The hardware options to provide a scalable architecture and for providing complex query processing capabilities include four types of parallel architecture. Parallel architecture is preferred in order to make the query execution faster by increasing the number of processors, and each processor works on different parts of the query simultaneously. Each of these four types of parallel architectures offers a broad range of benefits, but no single architecture does everything right. The following section reviews these architectures, their features, benefits, and limitations.

5.7.1 Symmetric Multiprocessing

In symmetric multiprocessing (SMP) system, which is basically a multiprocessor computer architecture, two or more identical processors are connected to a single, shared main memory. Today, most of the multiprocessor systems use an SMP architecture. SMP systems enable any processor to work on any task irrespective of where the data for that task is located in the memory. With proper operating system support, SMP systems can easily migrate tasks from one processor to another to balance the workload efficiently.

However, the most prominent downside of this appraoch is that the memory is much slower than the processors accessing them. Even in single-processor machines, we see that the machine spends a considerable amount of time waiting for data to arrive from memory. This situation becomes even more worse in the SMP architecture because in this approach, only one processor can access the memory at a time, thereby causing the other processors to starve.

The operating system must be designed to provide sufficient support for SMP or else, the additional processors remain idle and the system ends up working as a uniprocessor system. SMP costs relatively less and provides greater scalability as compared to its counter-parts. It offers a scalable architecture because with the growth in business needs, additional CPUs can easily be added to cope up with the increased transaction volume. SMP systems range from two to as many as 32 or more processors. The block diagram for SMP is shown in Fig. 5.5.

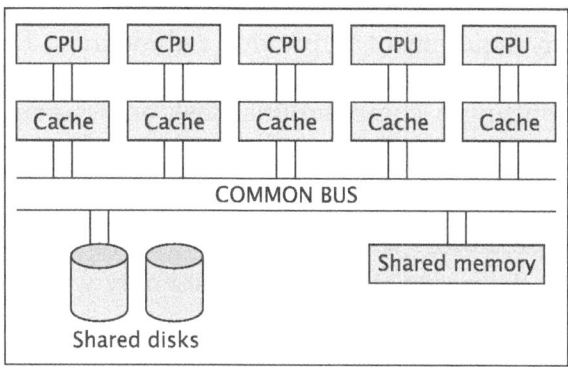

Figure 5.5 Symmetric multiprocessing system

Features   The features of a symmetric multiprocessing system are:

- This is the simplest architecture.
- This is a shared-everything architecture.
- With the help of a common bus every processor has full access to the shared memory.
- The processors communicate with each other using a common memory.

Benefits   Its benefits are as follows:

- It is a proven technology that has been used since last few decades.
- Many concurrent queries can be run.
- It balances the workload very efficiently.
- It provides for scalability in performance by allowing the addition of more processors to the system bus.
- Server administration is easy.

Limitations However, the drawbacks of an SMP are that:

- The available memory may not be always sufficient.
- It is inherently slow as memory is much slower than the processors accessing them, so a considerable amount of time is spent waiting for data to arrive from memory.

This option can be considered if the size of the data warehouse is expected to be a few gigabytes and concurrency requirements are reasonable.

5.7.2 Clusters

A computer cluster is a group of loosely coupled computers that work together closely so that they can be viewed as though they are a single computer. Fast local area networks are used to connect the components of a cluster. Clusters are implemented to improve performance, while typically being much more cost-effective than single computers of comparable speed.

Clusters are implemented primarily for improving the availability of services. They operate by having redundant nodes that are used to provide service when system components fail. The most common size for a cluster is two nodes, which is the minimum requirement to provide redundancy. The second reason for using clusters is for load balancing purposes to improve the performance of the system by splitting a computational task across many different nodes in the cluster.

Features Clusters have the following features:

- Every node has one or more processors with its associated memory.
- Memory is not shared among the nodes rather it is shared only within a node.
- A high speed bus is used for communication.
- This architecture is nothing but a cluster of individual nodes.

Benefits The advantages of using clusters are:

- Provides high availability as data will still be accessible even if one node fails.
- Allows incremental growth of the system.
- There is a single database.

Limitations They have the following limitations:

- Scalability of the system can be limited by the bandwidth of the bus.
- Increase overhead of the operating system.
- Each node has a data cache so cache consistency needs to be maintained for internode synchronization.

This option can be considered if the data warehouse is expected to grow in well-defined increments. The block diagram of a cluster is given in Fig. 5.6.

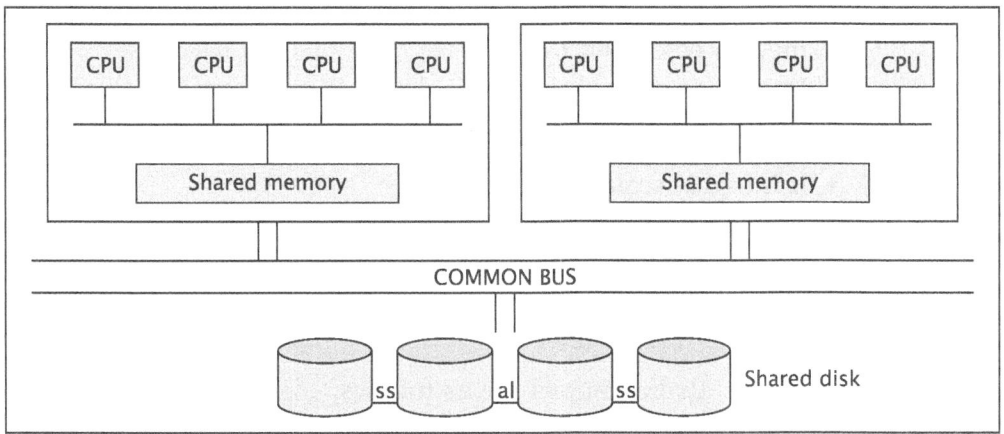

Figure 5.6 Cluster systems

5.7.3 Massively Parallel Processing

Massively parallel processing systems are the epitome of high performance computing systems. The architecture of massively parallel processing systems is illustrated in Fig. 5.7. The key distinction between massively parallel processing (MPP) and symmetric multiprocessing (SMP) systems is the former's use of fully distributed memory; each processor is self-contained with its own cache and associated memory. However, many MPP systems allow users to run on individual processor nodes as if they were entirely stand-alone computers.

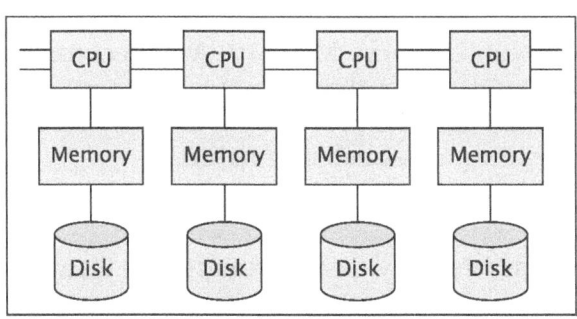

Figure 5.7 Massively parallel processing system

The loose coupling of the MPP architecture allows more processors to be connected together than the SMP model; MPP platforms range from modest systems of 32–64 processors up to 512–1024 or even more.

Since the memory is distributed to each processor, connecting large numbers of processors together is more straightforward than in the SMP model, because there is no need to design a complex bus architecture to allow processors to access the same memory area. However, it is much harder to exploit the parallel nature of the machine in the operating system.

Features MPP architecture has the following features:

- It is a shared-nothing architecture.
- Each processor has its own cache memory, main memory and secondary memory that is disk.
- The architecture is more biased towards disk access rather than memory access.

- The access to a database located on a particular disk, depends entirely on the processor that owns it.
- Inter node communication is done via processor-to-processor connection.

Benefits Its benefits are:

- It is highly scalable.
- Provides fast access between nodes.
- Improves the availability of the system, because any failure is local to the failed node and not to the entire system.
- Cost per node is low.

Limitations Its limitations are as follows:

- Data access is limited rather restricted.
- The architecture calls for partitioning of the data.
- Offers limited workload balancing capabilities.
- Cache consistency must be maintained within the entire system.

This option is good for building a medium-to large-sized data warehouse of size ranging from 400–500 GB, but it is not suitable for building a data warehouse in the terabyte range.

5.7.4 ccNUMA or NUMA

Under ccNUMA (Cache-coherent Non-Uniform Memory Architecture), a processor can access its own local memory faster than non-local memory. The non-local memory is the memory local to another processor or memory shared between processors. NUMA architectures are scalable in nature.

Basic Concept

CPUs operate much faster than the main memory that is connected to them. As a result CPUs *starve for data*, while they wait for memory accesses to complete the processing. Many supercomputer designs of the 1980s and 1990s focused on providing high-speed memory access as opposed to faster processors, thereby allowing PCs to operate on large datasets at an enormous speed. NUMA provides separate memory for each processor thereby avoiding the performance hit when several processors attempt to address the same memory.

Every CPU architecture today consists of a very fast non-shared memory known as cache to make use of the locality of reference in memory accesses. With NUMA, maintaining cache coherence across shared memory calls for a significant overhead.

Although simpler to design and build, non-cache-coherent NUMA systems are quite complex to program. Therefore, all CPUs designed on NUMA architecture use special-purpose hardware to maintain cache coherence, and thus this class of NUMA computers are better known as "cache-coherent NUMA" or ccNUMA.

Inter-processor communication between cache is used to maintain cache coherence. This is done by keeping a consistent memory image when more than one cache stores the same memory location. However, this causes a drop in performance of the ccNUMA architecture when multiple processors attempt to access the same memory area in rapid succession. The operating system is designed to support the NUMA architecture by reducing the frequency of this kind of access. The operating system allocates processors and memory in NUMA-friendly ways and avoids scheduling and locking algorithms that make NUMA-unfriendly accesses necessary.

Features   Its features are as follows:

- The architecture is relatively new. It was developed in the 1990s.
- It is similar to a big SMP broken into smaller ones that are easier to build.
- The hardware considers memory units as one big piece of memory. The system has one big memory address space over the entire machine. The memory addresses start with 1 on the first node and continue on the nodes that follow. Every node in this architecture maintains a list of memory address within that node.
- The time consumed to access a memory value varies. For example, the first node may need to access a value that resides in the memory of the fourth node. Hence, this architecture is called non-uniform memory access architecture.

Benefits   ccNUMA has the following advantages:

- Offers maximum flexibility.
- Overcomes memory limitations as in case of SMP.
- Provides better scalability features than SMP.
- If there is a need to partition the data warehouse, this is a good option.

Limitations   Its disadvantages are:

- More complex to program.
- Availability of software support is limited for this architecture.
- Technology is still maturing.

It is a very good approach to follow for the data warehouse, but it is to be used only if the data warehouse project team has a fairly good experience in hardware technology. The block diagram of NUMA architecture is shown in Fig. 5.8.

5.8 CAPACITY PLANNING

The capacity plan for a data warehouse is defined with the help of business requirements that we collected during the requirements definition stage. To determine the capacity required by the hardware is one of the most difficult

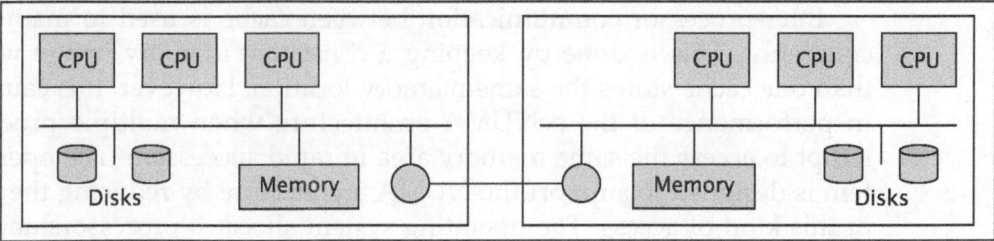

Figure 5.8 NUMA architecture

decisions. For this, a clear understanding of the usage profiles of all the users of the data warehouse is needed. To have this understanding you need to have answers for the following issues:

- Maximum number of users.
- Whether the users pose more of ad hoc queries or simple repetitive queries.
- The frequency of execution of ad hoc queries.
- The average size of a query.
- The maximum size of a query.
- The peak hours of usage.
- The number of queries that run during the peak hour of the day and during other times of the day.

However, these usage profiles will keep changing over time, but they are useful for growth predictions and capacity planning (See Fig. 5.9).

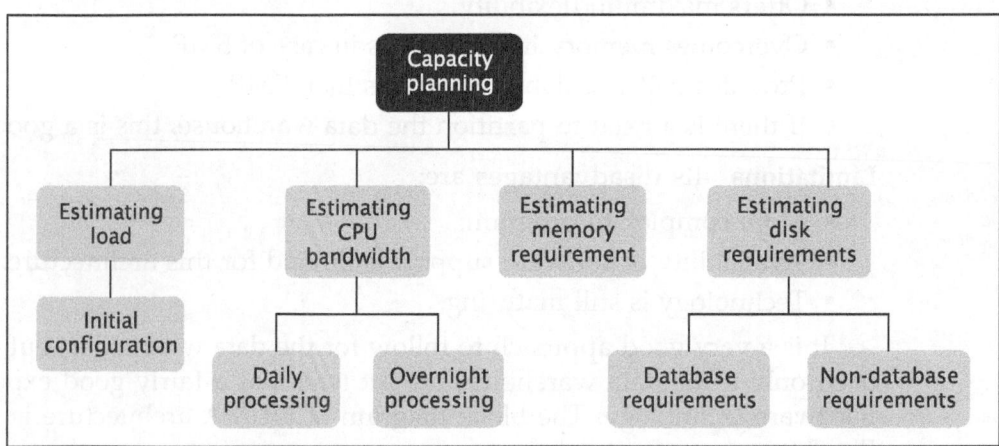

Figure 5.9 Capacity planning

5.8.1 Estimating the Load

When choosing the hardware for the data warehouse, several issues need consideration. One thing that should always be taken for granted is that the data warehouse will grow rapidly from its initial configuration. It is therefore, not sufficient to consider just the initial size of the data warehouse. The data warehouse project team must take into consideration the ultimate size of the data warehouse, otherwise they will have to face a messy situation where the hardware does not scale up to the users requirements. Changing the hardware configuration in midstream proves to be very expensive.

There are various elements that need to be considered, but the main factors influencing the decision includes how much CPU capacity, how much memory and how much disk space will be needed. Project sponsors often complain about the costs incurred in hardware decisions. Costs do affect the choice of hardware architecture, they may affect the choice of vendor, but they should never be allowed to affect the capacity planning.

For a large project like that of a data warehouse, small changes mean large changes in reality. A small growth in requirements in a data warehouse environment can result in adding of significant amount of hardware. For example, adding even a single byte to the fact table may result in adding 4 GB of storage for every year.

Initial Configuration

When sizing the initial configuration of the data warehouse the project team will have no information or statistics to work with. In such a situation the team will have base the sizing on the predicted load. However, predicting the load in itself is not a trivial task because of the ad hoc nature of the data warehouse. Therefore, a phased approach is adopted in which the ad hoc element will be small to start off with, and as the functionality is phased in, the system can be grown to meet the demand.

In an ad hoc environment, the best thing that can be done is to estimate the configuration based on the known requirements. This makes the business requirements phase even more important. The requirements definition document along with the knowledge of the business is sufficient enough to allow a reasonable sizing to be carried out. If, in course of time, the requirements change, the sizing can be adjusted accordingly.

When deciding on the initial configuration for the data warehouse, you will have to plan for contingencies as well, because the exact requirements are difficult to enumerate and the load can be far from what it was expected.

5.8.2 How Much CPU Bandwidth

To start with, the project team must take into account the distinct loads that will be placed on the system, like query load, data load, backup load, etc. In order to estimate the load on the CPU that occurs because of these tasks, let us divide these activities into two phases—daily processing and overnight processing.

Daily Processing

Daily processing is primarily centered on the user queries. To estimate the CPU bandwidth required for daily processing, the team must therefore estimate the time that each query will take to execute. However, it is very difficult to estimate the requirement of ad hoc queries. The first thing that can be done is to estimate the size of the largest likely query which may take pieces of data from a number of tables in the data warehouse.

Overnight Processing

During the night, the CPU is required for data transformation tasks. How much CPU bandwidth will be needed will depend on the amount of data processing that has to be done. Similarly, the CPU bandwidth required for backing up data will depend on the amount of data that has to be backed up.

Backing up large quantities of data in a short period of time will cause a major kickback onto the CPU. At night, the CPU's bandwidth is also used for creation of aggregation and index tables and then finally to load the data in the data warehouse database. Data loading requires massive parallelism to speed up its operation. But if you use fewer parallel streams it will use less CPU bandwidth and will take longer to run.

Besides estimating the CPU bandwidth that will be required, you must also estimate the time that will be taken to accomplish the overnight processing. It is not a good practice to assume that you will have more than 10 hours overnight to complete all the processing, even if the user day is only 8–9 hours long. Ensure that the overnight processing is completed on time without running over into the business day.

As every data warehouse is different, it is impossible to give explicit estimates for the tasks that have to be completed overnight. It is even impossible to lay firm guidelines as each aggregation is a different complex query.

5.8.3 How Much Memory

Memory is a commodity that you will always fall short of, but still the team has to estimate the minimum requirement. First, there are database requirements for caching data blocks as they are used. But how much memory you need for this purpose will vary from DBMS to DBMS. Sorting also requires space. Any process that is performing a sort operation will require an amount of sort area from the main memory. Again one has to specify how much space you want for the sorting programs.

Every user connected to the system will require some amount of memory. How much memory every user needs will vary depending on how they are connected to the system and what software they are running. Finally, the operating system needs some memory. Again the amount of memory needed by the operating system will depend on the features and tools the users are using. In the context of operating systems, the hardware vendor may help the team to estimate the amount of memory the system will require.

5.8.4 How Much Disk

The largest calculation for estimation is done to calculate the amount of disk space that will be required. This can be a very tricky thing to do, but it can be done successfully if the analysis has captured all the requirements accurately. The disk requirements can be broadly classified into two categories: database requirements and non-database requirements.

Database requirements include administration functions, fact tables and dimension tables, and aggregate/summary tables.

Non-database requirements include operating system requirements, software requirements, data warehouse database requirements, and user specific requirements.

A majority of the disk space will be occupied by the data warehouse database. There are a number of aspects to the database sizing that need to be considered. First, there are system administration requirements of the database. You need disk space for storing the data dictionary and a temporary storage area for performing sort operations. It is quite obvious that in a data warehouse system large data sorts are going to be required especially for performing aggregations and summarizations. Sizing the sort space is almost an impossible task. The team needs to allot a large space to sort the entire fact and dimension tables data to ensure that it will always be large enough to support the system.

Then memory space is needed for storing the fact tables and the dimension tables. This is can be easily estimated by having answers to questions like—the correct level of fact table, whether to denormalize tables or not and the size of the fact table record. Even a small change in any of these factors will have an enormous effect on the sizing. Clearly, when performing an initial investigation, a lot of information will be missing, so you have to base your estimates purely on the size of the base data. For each table, determine the following parameters:

- Number of rows.
- Average size of a row.
- Anticipated monthly increase in the number of rows.
- Initial size of the table in megabytes.
- Calculated table sizes in 6 months and in 12 months.
- Space needed for storing indexes.
- Calculated space for indexes in 6 months and in 12 months.

Also you need to estimate the temporary work space for processing. The following sub-section will cover more details of estimating the physical storage medium for the data warehouse.

When estimating the size of the fact or dimension tables, you will have to consider the record definitions, with each field type and size specified. It is important to keep in mind that the average length of a data field can be very different from the maximum length. Even a few bytes of difference between them can lead to many gigabytes difference in the size estimate. Therefore, the average field size should be estimated by using real data.

In the next step, the size of the index space required for the fact and dimension tables needs to be estimated. For performance enhancements, fact tables should be lightly indexed as otherwise the cost in terms of index maintenance would become extremely heavy. The final determinant of the fact table size is the amount of data that you intend to keep online. Once this is known, the next step is to decide on the partitioning strategy. Finally you need to estimate the size of aggregate fact tables.

For estimating the size of non database requirements, you need to know how much space the operating system will occupy. You may install the operating system on an individual node or may install it on the server node and make its features available through facilities such as the network file system (NFS). The problem with this approach is that if the node that has the actual software is lost then all access to that software will also be lost. In a data warehouse environment, you cannot afford to have even a single point of failure into the system.

The operating system will require its own space varying approximately from 500 MB to 1 GB. Then there will be other software and third party tools that have their own disk requirements for storing their code. Make sure that space is also reserved for log files and trace files that these tools will produce, this is particularly important for monitoring purposes.

5.9 SELECTING THE OPERATING SYSTEM

The computing environment of a data warehouse includes the hardware and the operating system. All the jobs involved in data extraction, transformation, and integration run on the selected hardware under the chosen operating system.

When we move the data from the staging area to the data warehouse repository, the server hardware and the operating system are involved in the entire process of data movement. Similarly, when users initiate queries from their client machine, the server hardware, in conjunction with the database software, executes the queries and produces the results. Some general principles for hardware selection are:

Scalability When the data warehouse grows in terms of number of users, the number of queries, and the complexity of queries, then the hardware should be easily scalable to cater to the growing needs.

Support Make sure to get vendor support which is very crucial for maintenance of the hardware.

Vendor reference and vendor stability The team must cross check the vendor references with other organizations that are using hardware from the same vendor. Also check for the stability and staying power of the vendor in the market.

The operating system that is chosen must be compatible with the selected hardware. Once the hardware is selected, the appropriate operating system must be selected. Some general guidelines for selecting the operating system are:

Scalability   Data warehouses keep on growing fast after they are deployed, so the first criteria is always that the selected hardware and the operating system must be able to support the increase in the number of users and their applications.

Security   In a multi user environment where multiple clients simultaneously access the server, the operating system must provide a secure environment by protecting each user and associated resources.

Reliability   The operating system must provide protection against applications malfunctions.

Availability   The operating system must be available even after abnormal termination of the application.

Pre-emptive multi-tasking   The operating system must be able to equally share its resources among the multiple tasks and also be able to execute a higher priority task to preempt another task when required.

Multi-threading   The operating system must support a multi-threaded environment so that in a multi-processor hardware configuration, multiple requests can be handled concurrently by distributing threads to multiple processors.

Memory protection   Since there are multiple users having multiple queries in a data warehouse environment, an operating system having this capability is required to prevent one task from violating the memory space of another.

For data warehouse projects, the development team basically has three options—use mainframes, UNIX or NT servers. Refer Fig. 5.10 which highlights the key points of these operating systems.

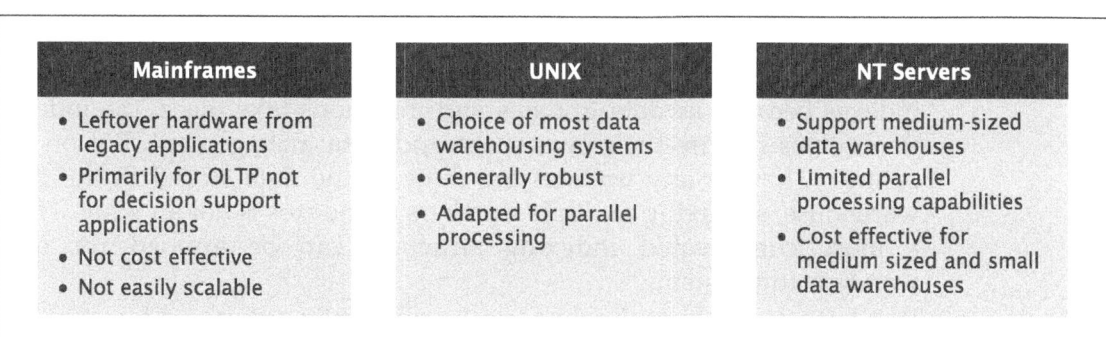

Mainframes	UNIX	NT Servers
• Leftover hardware from legacy applications • Primarily for OLTP not for decision support applications • Not cost effective • Not easily scalable	• Choice of most data warehousing systems • Generally robust • Adapted for parallel processing	• Support medium-sized data warehouses • Limited parallel processing capabilities • Cost effective for medium sized and small data warehouses

Figure 5.10 Key features of different operating systems

5.10 SELECTING THE DATABASE SOFTWARE

With the advent of data warehousing, decision support technology has become an integral part of the enterprise. To support this technology, a new kind of DBMS is required that is specifically optimized for data warehousing and DSS processing.

5.10.1 General DBMS and Data Warehouse-specific DBMS

There is a tremendous difference between the DBMS that is needed for operational systems and data warehouse systems. These are listed as follows:

(i) The operational system DBMS is efficient for transaction processing. But a data warehouse is much more complex than a transaction oriented operational system. A data warehouse takes its data feed from several operational systems, but before storing the data in its database, the data is thoroughly processed. The data warehouse DBMS must support all these activities.

(ii) The data warehouse DBMS must provide efficient storage of a large amount of data.

(iii) The third difference in the DBMS required for operational systems and the DBMS required for a data warehouse system lies in the mechanism to update the database. The general purpose DBMS must be able to accommodate record-level, transaction based updates. For this purpose, it needs to provide facilities for locking the dataset, COMMITS, creating check points, processing log tapes and handling deadlocks. No doubt, providing all these facilities is not free as a lot of overhead is involved in it. However, no such overhead of update is required in a data warehouse specific DBMS.

(iv) A general purpose DBMS requires data management at the block level. It includes reserving space for future block expansion in case of data inserts and updates. It is not uncommon for the free space to be as high as 50 per cent. On the other hand, for a data warehouse free space is equal to 0 because there is no scope for future expansion in the physical block once it has been loaded.

(v) A general purpose DBMS is restricted to work with a finite number of indexes because as data updates and insertions take place, the indexes themselves require their own space and data management. But on the contrary, hardly any updates are done to the data stored in the data warehouse, so having multiple numbers of indexes is not an issue. Thus, a more complicated indexing structure can be applied for data warehousing systems.

(vi) Last but not the least the data can be physically optimized for only one purpose, either for decision support analysis or for transaction processing but not for both at the same time. So there has to be an entirely different kind of DBMS for both of these areas.

As data warehousing technology is maturing, the data warehouse features are being included in the software products. Even the data warehousing related add-ons are today being made a part of the database offerings. The database software that was once developed for operational systems is now being enhanced to cater to the needs of a decision support system also. In order to support large databases, the DBMS have been scaled up.

Some RDBMS products now include support functions for data acquisition, mass loading and retrieval of data from other database systems, data transformation functions and functions for incremental loading and bulk refreshes.

Besides these enhancements, the more prominent features include load balancing and query performance, as these issues are critical in a data warehouse environment. Since data warehouse provides a query centric environment, everything that can be done to improve query performance is highly desirable. In this section, we will study the parallel processing options within the DBMS that can take full advantage of parallel server hardware.

5.10.2 How to Choose?

DBMS is the most vital component of a data warehouse. The server hardware must be chosen with appropriate parallel architecture and the choice of the DBMS must match with the selected server hardware. These are crucial decisions for the data warehouse. Besides the load balancing and parallel processing options, the other key features of a DBMS that must be considered for selection for the upcoming data warehouse are:

- Ability to abort runaway queries.
- Ability to optimize the queries.
- Ability to balance the execution of all the queries.
- Ability for high performance of data loading, recovery and restart functions.
- An active data dictionary.
- Scalability in terms of both number of users and data volumes.
- Provision of extensibility to OLAP databases.
- Portability across platforms.
- Provision of administrative support for all DBA functions.

In the requirements definition phase, when the users were interviewed, the that has to be selected was not discussed. The user requirements will definitely influence the selection of the proper DBMS. The relational DBMS that are widely available in the market are usually bundled with a set of tools for processing queries, writing reports, and interfacing with other products.

Broadly speaking, the business requirements that affect the choice of the DBMS include:

Level of user experience If the users of the data warehouse do not have much experience with the database systems, the DBMS must have features to monitor and control queries. On the other hand, if there are more number of power users who would be executing their own queries then the DBMS must support an easy SQL type language interface.

Types of queries For a data warehouse environment in which most of the queries executed would be complex in nature and would produce a large result set, the DBMS must have an efficient query optimizer. Even if the data warehouse users pose an even mix of simple and complex queries, there must be some sort of query management in the database software to balance the query execution.

Data loads The data volumes and load frequencies are factors that influence the robustness of the data loading, recovery, and restart functions.

Data repository locations Depending on whether the upcoming data warehouse will reside at a central location or in a distributed environment will determine whether the selected DBMS must support distributed databases.

Data warehouse growth While collecting business requirements, a rough estimate of the growth in the number of users, and in the number and complexity of queries must be gained. These estimates will have a direct effect on the how the selected DBMS supports scalability.

5.11 SELECTING THE TOOLS

In this step, the project team identifies the required tools for developing and implementing the data warehouse architectures. The tools that best meet the business and technical requirements of data warehouse architecture must be selected.

A good data warehouse designer designs the architecture first and then choose the tools to match the functions and services stipulated for the architectural components. Having dwelt on the architectural concerns, let us move on to review the types of software tools appropriate for a data warehouse. Subsequently, we will learn about the different categories of tools that are needed. Table 5.6 summarizes the different types of tools that are required in the data warehouse environment.

5.11.1 Information Delivery Tools

The success of the data warehouse rests on the strength of the information delivery tools. If the tools are effective and user friendly, the users will repeatedly use the data warehouse to fetch the information they want. In reverse circumstances, the users will resist using the data warehouse and the project will fail. So, the information delivery tools need to be selected with great care and thoroughness.

Table 5.6 Tools for data warehouse

Tool	Purpose
Data modelling	<ul><li>Enables the data warehouse development team to create and maintain data models for the source system as well as data warehouse databases.</li><li>Allows forward engineering facility to generate database schema.</li><li>Provision for reverse engineering to generate the data model from the data dictionary entries of existing source databases.</li><li>Provide dimensional data modelling capabilities for creating STAR schema.</li></ul>
Data extraction	<ul><li>Provides capabilities for full refreshes and incremental loads.</li><li>Choice of tools depends upon source system platforms and databases.</li></ul>
Data transformation	<ul><li>Transforms extracted data into standard formats.</li><li>Fills in the missing values with the specified default values.</li><li>Provides functions like field-splitting, consolidation, standardization, de-duplication.</li></ul>
Data loading	<ul><li>Loads transformed and consolidated data into the data warehouse repository.</li><li>Creates indexes for the tables being loaded.</li></ul>
Data quality	<ul><li>Performs functions of locating and correcting errors.</li><li>Can either be applied on the source systems or in the staging area.</li><li>Provides the capability of resolving data inconsistencies.</li></ul>
Queries and reports	<ul><li>Allows users to create sophisticated reports that may even include some sort of graphics.</li><li>Enables the users to formulate and execute their queries.</li></ul>
Online analytical processing	<ul><li>Enables the execution of complex multidimensional queries.</li><li>OLAP has two main categories: ROLAP and MOLAP. While MOLAP works with proprietary multidimensional databases that receive data feeds from the main data warehouse, ROLAP provides online analytical processing capabilities from the relational databases of the data warehouse itself.</li></ul>
Alert systems	<ul><li>Captures user's attention when the specified conditions take place.</li><li>Generates alerts from data warehouse database for making the right decisions at the right time.</li><li>Alerts can be generated from data warehouse database, data marts or from the individual source systems.</li></ul>
Middleware and connectivity	<ul><li>Provides transparent access to individual source systems running in heterogeneous environments.</li><li>Provides transparent access to different types of databases stored on different platforms.</li><li>Provides interoperability among the different components of the data warehouse.</li></ul>
Data warehouse management	<ul><li>Provides support to assist data warehouse administrators in day-to-day management.</li><li>Focuses on tracking data loading process.</li><li>Provides capabilities to track types and number of queries and users.</li></ul>

Information delivery tools come in different formats to serve different purposes of data warehouse users. The principal class of tools comprises query or data access tools which enables the users to define, formulate and execute queries and obtain results. An other class of tools includes report writers or reporting tools for formatting, scheduling and running reports. Other tools specialize in complex analysis.

When the information delivery tools receive user's requests of queries and reports, they first translate their requests into SQL statements and send them to the DBMS. Then after receiving the results from the data warehouse, they format those results in suitable formats and present the result set to the users. The requests sent to the DBMS, retrieve and manipulate large volumes of data that are stored in the data warehouse and it is quite obvious that compared to the volumes of data retrieved, the result sets contain much lesser data.

Tool Selection Technique

The enormous importance of information delivery tools in a data warehouse environment, forces the data warehouse project team to have a well thought, formalized methodology for selecting the appropriate tools. A set of tools may be the best for a given data warehouse environment but may be a total disaster in another data warehouse environment. There is no specific tool for information delivery, but since they are meant for the end-users it always recommended that the user representatives be a part of the information delivery tools selection team. The methodology that needs to be followed to select the information delivery tools can be understood by looking Fig. 5.11.

To select the appropriate information delivery tool, first nominate an experienced member of the team or the data warehouse administrator to lead the team and drive the process. You also have to keep the users involved throughout the selection process. To choose the most appropriate tool, it is very important that you are not just satisfied with vendor demonstrations but also have hands-on evaluation. These considerations help to choose the best information delivery tool for the data warehouse.

Criteria for Selecting the Tool

As stated in the previous section, we need to apply some selection criteria to shortlist the tools available in the market as per the data warehouse environment. The following are some of the selection criteria that can act as guide to choose the most appropriate information delivery tool for your data warehouse environment. The information delivery tool should have the following features:

- Easy to use for even the casual users.
- Provide acceptable performance.
- Compatible with requirements of users of all the classes.
- Have utility functions to configure and control the information delivery environment.
- Able to publish web pages over the internet or intranet.

Select the team which includes about 4–5 persons including the executive sponsor, user representative and data warehouse administrator.

Re-assess user requirements in relation to information delivery and document them to describe the expectations of users belonging to different classes.

Specify the selection criteria for every broad group of tools such as query tools or reporting tools.

Conduct a preliminary research on different tools and vendors available in the market and prepare a document containing the features and functions of each tool to see whether these functions and features matches the users requirements.

Select three or a maximum of five candidate tools.

Attend product demonstrations of the candidate tools. During demonstrations, constantly try to match the functions of the tools with the user requirements.

Complete the evaluation by IT to check for technical compatibility with the data warehouse environment, and a complete evaluation by users for user acceptance testing.

Re-evaluate the tools that are very close to the requirements to ensure post-implementation technical support, vendor stability and his reputation in the market. And finally select the most appropriate tool for your data warehouse environment.

Figure 5.11   Steps to be performed while selecting information delivery tools

- Have security features to safeguard critical data.
- Provide easy navigation features to help the users to browse the data and metadata. The GUI must be very clear so that even the novice users find the desired information easily by clicking on icons and menu items.
- Able to connect to any of the leading database products.
- Able to present the result sets in a variety of formats including text, tables, charts, graphs, maps, etc.
- Scalable enough to handle a large number of users, thus a larger volume of data and extra complexity of requests.

5.11.2 Query Tools

Query tool is one of the most significant tools for a successful data warehouse. The last few decades have witnessed a tremendous improvement in the performance of query tools. The vendors have enhanced their query tools to provide:

- Ease of use.
- Ability to present results online and in different formats.
- Ability to recognize the existence of summary or aggregate tables and in case these tables exist, automatically route queries to them when summarized results are desired.

- Ability to query against multiple subjects.
- Ability to access heterogeneous data sources on different platforms.
- SQL extensions to execute queries that can not be handled through standard SQL.

5.11.3 Browser Tools

Before using the data warehouse, the end-users must first know what information is available there. For this, the users need an efficient browser tool to browse through the metadata and locate the information they want. Some of the recent trends in browser tools are:

- Tools are extensible to define any type of data.
- Provide new powerful browsing functions to navigate through hierarchical groupings.
- Allow the users to browse the data dictionary to find information of interest.
- Application of web browsing features and search engines to browse through the metadata.

5.11.4 Metadata Tools

One major challenge that the data warehouse project team faces in implementing the metadata management environment is the actual extraction, merging, and storage of metadata. The end-users who will use the data warehouse are systems integrators and not application developers; so it is desired that minimum coding be done. For this the team depends on the tool vendors to implement this aspect of the metadata management environment. Unfortunately, they have very few alternatives.

The team should look for tools that support an industry standard. At this point, CASE Data Interchange Format (CDIF) is the only standard for which vendors provide any level of support. Even if better standards are available in the market they are futile if vendors do not implement them in their products. The CDIF standard provides a neutral format that allows translation of metadata between products. By translating to and from this neutral format, vendors can ensure that their products are able to interface with others.

With a group of data warehouse vendors founding the Metadata Coalition to enable the sharing of metadata within the data warehouse environment, a new metadata interchange standard will emerge. Most of the leading vendors in data warehouse extraction, OLAP, DBMS, and repositories are a part of this coalition. The Coalition's interface specification, known as the Metadata Interchange Format (MIF), has been ratified and stresses on supporting metadata that is used to map source data to the data warehouse database, both from the physical perspective and the end-user's perspective. The plus point of MIF includes its simplicity to understand and implement, and its support to nearly all the metadata requirements of the end-users.

If the vendors do not support either of these standards, the team should look for tools that interface with one another by translating one tool's metadata into another tool's metadata into a format that it can import.

Extensibility, query, and versioning facilities necessary to manage the metadata were the key attributes of traditional repository products, such as MSP's DataManager, R&O Inc.'s Rochade, and Platinum Technology's Repository. With the growing importance of metadata in a data warehouse environment, data warehouse vendors (such as Prism Solutions Inc., Carleton Corp., Apertus Technologies Inc., and ETI Solutions Inc.) are beginning to incorporate more metadata management capabilities into their products.

However, a new class of tools specifically designed to manage a data warehouse's metadata is also becoming available in the market now-a-days. Intellidex Systems Inc.'s Metadata Control Center is an example of this new genre of metadata management tools which is specifically designed to capture and integrate metadata from various source tools so that it can be accessed by the end-users.

Configuring metadata management environment is rightly compared with building an airplane with bubble gum and rubber bands, but sooner there will be tools to properly manage it. With an increasing demand for data warehouse business users to access their metadata, vendors are cooperating to provide the integrated environment that facilitates capturing and delivery of the metadata.

5.11.5 Data Quality Tools

The data quality tools can be applied to the source systems or in the staging area before loading the data in the data warehouse. The data quality tools are made to assist the project team in two ways. First, the data error discovery tools work on the source data to identify inaccuracies and inconsistencies. Second, the data correction tools help to fix the corrupted data.

The data correction tools use different algorithms to parse, transform, match, consolidate and correct the data. Although these two categories of tools are distinct parts of the data cleansing process, most of the tools can do both of these tasks. Figure 5.12 shows the list of functions that a data quality tool is expected to perform.

In many ways the DBMS in itself is used as a data quality control tool. Relational database systems provide much more functionality than simply providing a database engine to its users.

RDBMS takes care to prohibit the entry of errors in the data warehouse in the following manner:

- Prevents entry of data if the entered value is outside the defined range of domain.

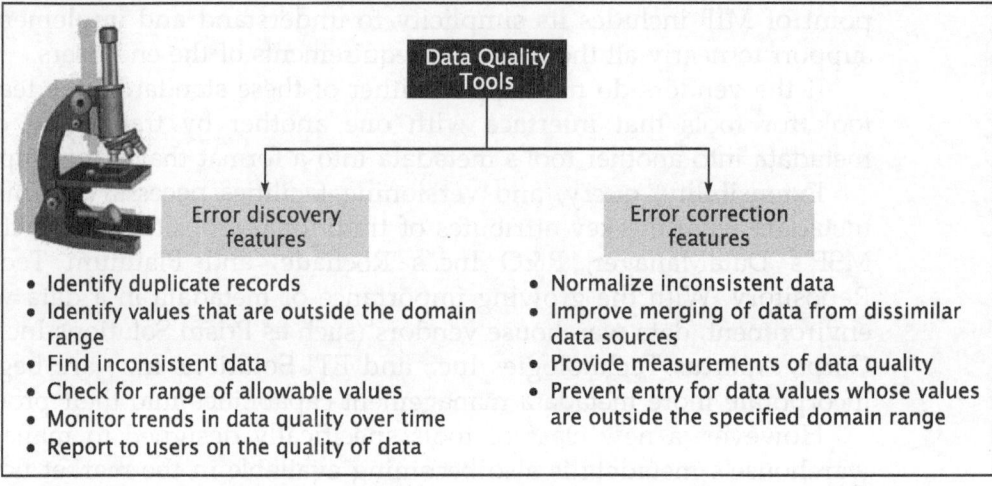

Figure 5.12 Data quality tools

- Prevents unauthorized updates to the database. Some users may intentionally or unintentionally update the data with incorrect values.
- Prevents the entry of duplicate records that have the same primary key.
- Checks for referential integrity before entering the data in the data warehouse.
- Use trigger programs and stored procedures to enforce business rules. These are special scripts compiled and stored in the database itself. The trigger programs are written to execute automatically when the designated data items are about to be updated or deleted. Stored procedures are called from application programs to ensure that the entered data conforms to specific business rules.

Recapitulation

The data warehouse infrastructure may be classified into two categories: operational and physical infrastructure.

Operational infrastructure supports the management of the data warehouse and maintains its efficiency. It includes people, procedures, training, and the management software.

The physical infrastructure consists of the hardware components, the operating system along with utility software, the network and the network software, and all the required set of tools.

In the single platform option, all functions from the back-end data extraction to the front-end query processing are performed on a single computing platform.

In hybrid option, there is a separate platform for the source data and a separate platform for the staging area.

To move data across platforms, several options that are available include shared disks, mass data transmission through data ports, using real time connections with the help of TCP/IP protocols and manual methods with the help of using external medium like magnetic disks.

Data warehouses are built using client server architecture where the DBMS runs on the server machine. The client workstations handle the presentation logic and provide the presentation services. We choose parallel architecture for the server machine.

SMP is a multiprocessor computer architecture where two or more processors are connected to a single shared main memory.

A computer cluster is a group of loosely coupled computers that work together closely, so that they can be viewed as though they are a single computer. The components of a cluster are connected to each other through fast LANs.

NUMA attempts to provide separate memory for each processor, avoiding the performance hit when several processors attempt to address the same memory.

The query dispatcher software is responsible for splitting the work, distributing the units to be performed among the available query server processes and balancing the load.

In interquery parallelization, several server processes handle multiple queries simultaneously, thereby increasing the throughput and supporting more users.

Using the intraquery parallelization, the DBMS splits the query into the lower level operations and then each one of these operations is executed in parallel on a single processor.

For horizontal parallelization, the data is partitioned across multiple disks. Parallel processing occurs within each single task in the query. After the first task is completed from all of the relevant parts of the partitioned data, the next task of that query is carried out.

Vertical parallelism occurs among different tasks, not just a single task in a query as in the case of horizontal parallelism.

In the hybrid method, the query decomposer partitions the query both horizontally and vertically.

Data warehouse tools include the tools for data modelling, data extraction, transformation, loading, cleaning, queries and reports, performing OLAP, middleware and connectivity, and management of the data warehouse.

The major guiding principles for data warehouse project management include committed upper level management support, a dedicated project manager, appropriate assignment of team roles, good quality of data, user requirements, working as a driving force of every task, building for growth, realistic expectations, well-designed dimensional data model, external data, user training, and security.

Objective Questions

1. Fill in the blanks

1. The _____ list the tasks, the schedule, the people who will perform the deliverables and milestones.

2. The project manager should not only be technology oriented but also be ____ oriented.

3. _____ first then the tools.

4. _____ drive the data warehouse, not technology.

5. _____ vendor tools provide seamless integration among the components.

6. The _____ forms the basis of a scope agreement that is a signed document by the ____ and the _____.

7. _____ are those benefits that can be identified with certainty and easily expressed in terms of money value

8. A _____ is a group of loosely coupled computers that work together closely.

9. Under _____, a processor can access its own local memory faster than non-local memory.

10. _____ is used to maintain cache coherency.

11. _____ tools work on the source data to identify inaccuracies and inconsistencies

12. The ____ standard provides a neutral format that allows translation of metadata between products.

2. Match the following

1. Data warehouse project management
2. Organizing the project team
3. Scope gallop
4. Break-even point
5. Daily processing
6. Data correction tools

(a) Costs and benefits from the project become equal
(b) Put the right person in the right job
(c) Centred on the user queries.
(d) Users either request for large and complex changes
(e) Fix the corrupted data
(f) Project plans, scope agreements, resources, schedules, configuration and change management, contingency plans

3. Multiple choice questions

(i) Money needed for a data warehouse project depends on
   (a) Size of the database
   (b) Complexity of the applications
   (c) Number of users
   (d) Choice of tools
   (e) Number and types of source systems
   (f) All of these

(ii) The cost that is incurred after the data warehouse is implemented is called
   (a) Tangible cost
   (b) Intangible cost
   (c) Developing cost
   (d) Ongoing cost
   (e) None of these
   (f) All of these

(iii) Identify the features of SMP architecture
   (a) Simplest
   (b) Shared everything
   (c) Shared nothing
   (d) Scalable
   (e) None of these
   (f) All of these

(iv) In which architecture, the hardware considers memory units as one big piece of memory.
   (a) SMP
   (b) MMP
   (c) NUMA
   (d) Clusters
   (e) None of these
   (f) All of these

(v) Overnight processing includes activities like
   (a) Data transformation
   (b) Creation of aggregation
   (c) Backing up data
   (d) Index creation
   (e) None of these
   (f) All of these

(vi) Database requirements comprises of
   (a) Data transformation
   (b) Software
   (c) Aggregate/summary tables
   (d) Operating system
   (e) Administration functions
   (f) All of these

4. **State true or false**

   1. Tremendous growth in the number of queries and reports requested by the users indicates a successful data warehouse.
   2. User interaction with a data warehouse is direct without any mediation from IT.
   3. The plan plays no role in laying the direction and goals of the project.
   4. Scope creep occurs when small changes accumulate to the point where the existing schedule can no longer handle the additional requirements.
   5. Longer payback periods are desriable.
   6. A project with a negative NPV is desirable.
   7. In clusters, every node has one or more processors with its associated memory.
   8. The computing environment of a data warehouse includes the hardware and the operating system.
   9. Data warehouse DBMS requires facilities for locking the dataset, creating check points, processing log tapes and handling deadlocks.
   10. MMP platforms range from modest systems of 32–64 processors up to 512, 1024 or even more.

Review Questions

1. Explain the key issues to be considered while planning for a data warehouse.
2. Compare single-vendor solution with multi-vendor solution. Which one do you prefer? Justify your answer.
3. Write a short note on the overall project plan.
4. List some warning signs in a data warehouse project and the corrective actions that need to be taken to resolve these potential problems.
5. Explain the success factors in a data warehouse project.
6. Why is user participation essential for the success of a data warehouse project? For a data warehouse project of a renowned bank, write a report on how the user departments can participate in the development. Mention the roles and responsibilities of these users.
7. Compare physical and operational infrastructure. List the composition of both of these infrastructures of the data warehouse.
8. What criteria will you follow for selecting an appropriate operating system for your data warehouse?
9. Explain the different options available for the staging area. Write the merits and demerits of each option.
10. Explain the methods for data movement within the data warehouse.
11. List the features, benefits and limitations of the different parallel server hardware options.
12. Describe the different types of software tools used in the data warehouse.
13. Consider a case in your company where all source systems reside on a single UNIX based platform except one legacy system which resides on a mainframe. Analyse the different platform options that can be used for your data warehouse and state which one of them you find most appropriate and why?
14. For a data warehouse having initial size of 500 GB, examine the options for server hardware, suggest which one you would choose for this data warehouse and justify your answer.
15. Describe the criteria that you will use to select the RDBMS for your data warehouse.

16. Discuss the client server architecture of a data warehouse.

17. Why is parallel processing important in a data warehouse environment? Discuss the various options available for query parallelization.

18. You are the senior analyst responsible for selecting the tools in your data warehouse.

Make a list of the tools you will provide for use by the developers and the end-users of your data warehouse. Describe the features of these tools.

19. State the guiding principles for any data warehouse project.

6

DATA WAREHOUSE SCHEMA

Learning Objectives

In this chapter, we will learn about the different schemas that can be used to organize the fact and dimension tables. We will also learn about the pros and cons of each schema so that the reader can make out the most efficient and optimized schema that should actually be used to build the data warehouse.

Case Study

Once the requirements gathering phase is over, the next stage is that of dimension modelling in which the data tables are designed, physically created and linked with each other.

The data warehouse project team of JRTs decides to use the same principles for dimension modelling that we generally use to design operational system's databases. So while designing the tables, the team does its best to normalize each and every table in the best possible manner.

However after the data warehouse gets deployed, it is observed that query processing takes a long time, the structure gets very complicated and thus it becomes very difficult for the actual data warehouse users to understand it and therefore use it. Again the data warehouse success lies in vain as a successful data warehouse is that which is easy for the end-users to understand, interpret and use it.

6.1 INTRODUCTION

The requirements definition completely lays the ground for the data design for the data warehouse. Data design consists of putting together various data structures. Logical data design for a data warehouse project includes determination of the data elements that are needed, the combination of the data elements into structures of data, and finally establishing the relationships among these data structures.

As shown in Fig. 6.1, the results of the requirements gathering phase are documented in the requirements definition document. The most crucial part of this document is the set of information package diagrams, which shows the metrics, business dimensions and the hierarchies within individual business dimensions. The information package diagram acts as a cornerstone for the logical data design for the data warehouse. The result of the data design process is a dimensional data model.

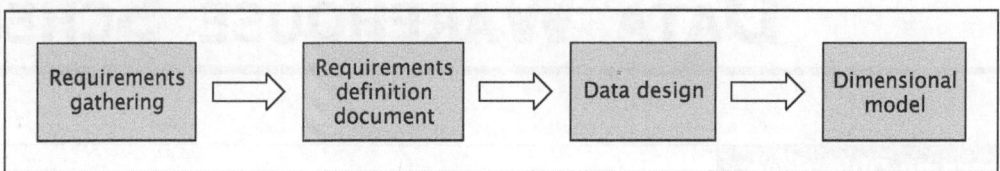

Figure 6.1 From requirements to data design

6.2 DIMENSIONAL MODELLING

In Chapter 4, we have discussed the terms—fact, dimension table, and fact table. In this section, we will use the fact and dimension tables to prepare the logical design of the data warehouse.

Dimensional modelling gets its name from the business dimensions that we incorporate into the logical data model. It is a design technique to structure the business dimensions and the metrics.

This modelling technique is intuitive enough for analyzing the metrics along with the business dimensions. The dimension provides high performance for queries and analysis. Before going into the details of dimensional modelling let us first find out the difference between data warehouse modelling and operational system modelling.

6.2.1 Data Warehouse Modelling and Operational Database Modelling

"Entity relation data models [...] cannot be understood by users and they cannot be navigated usefully by DBMS software. Entity relation models cannot be used as the basis for enterprise data warehouses."

- A data warehouse is an end-user-oriented product which will be directly accessed by its users. Thus, the data model for a data warehouse must allow easy data access. In an operational database, the user does not directly interact with the database, they do it using applications which have predefined queries.
- A data warehouse is designed for data analysis. The users execute queries that test and verify hypotheses with information present in the data warehouse, look for trends and make projections for the future.

- Since requirements for the data warehouse are quite vague, this calls for a flexible modelling process.
- A data warehouse is an integrated collection of databases that will cater to all kinds of informational needs of the users throughout the organization. This huge collection of data will always grow in size.
- A data warehouse contains data structured around different information subject areas.
- A data warehouse would be designed to contain both current as well as historical data.

6.2.2 Dimensional Model and ER Model

As discussed before, dimensional modelling is used for designing tables for a data warehouse and ER modelling is used for designing the tables for operational systems. Let us understand how the two modelling techniques differ from each other and why ER modelling cannot replace the role of dimension modelling:

- ER diagram is a complex diagram that is used to represent multiple processes. A single ER diagram can be broken down into multiple DM diagrams.
- In a dimension model, we prefer keeping the tables denormalized whereas in an ER diagram, the main aim is to remove redundancy by normalizing the tables.
- ER model is designed to express microscopic relationships between the data elements, whereas the key idea behind a DM model is to capture business measures.
- A dimension model is designed to answer queries on the overall business process to reveal trends. They are based on how managers think of their business. But, an ER model on the other hand is well suited to answer queries at transaction level.

6.2.3 Need for a Dimensional Model

In data warehouse environment, a dimensional model is created so that it can provide the following pieces of information to the data warehouse developers.

- The process which includes the set of all subject areas that are actually the logical structures which have to be designed.
- The level of detail of data.
- The business dimensions to be included in the logical structure and making sure that each particular data element in every business dimension is conformed to one another.
- The facts to be included in the logical structure.

- The time the database should span. This is done by determining how much of archived data must be stored in the data warehouse.

6.2.4 Features of a Good Dimensional Model

Once the fact and dimension tables have been formed, how should these tables be arranged in the dimensional model? What are the relationships and how should we depict them in the model? The dimensional model should primarily facilitate queries and analyses in which the metrics inside the fact table are analysed across one or more dimensions using the dimension table attributes.

Consider a query in our retail chain example-how much sales was recorded last year from store XYZ that sold the product A to customers having income level 50–60K per month who paid through credit cards. Now this query will have to fetch data from all the tables. Every attribute value will act as a filter to constraint the records that have to be accessed. For example, from the store dimension table, you will access only those records which pertain to the store XYZ. From the customers dimension table, you will be needing the data of only those customers who have their income level in the range of 50K to 60K per month.

So our dimensional model must be such that it facilitates the users to easily access data from all the related tables. Thus, we can conclude that our ideal dimension table must exhibit the following features:

- Best data access.
- Query centric.
- Optimized for query and analysis.
- Depict the way in which the fact table interacts with the dimension table.
- Allow equal interaction of every dimension table with the fact table.
- Enable the users to perform roll up and drill down operations along dimension hierarchies.

In a data warehouse environment, we can form the dimensional model using three types of schema. The choice of schema that will be used to form the dimensional model of the data warehouse will vary from organization to organization. The three types of data warehouse schema are:

- Star schema.
- Snowflake schema.
- Fact constellation schema (also known as family of stars).

6.3 THE STAR SCHEMA

Just imagine a dimensional model with the fact table in the middle and dimension tables arranged around the fact table. This model represents a star formation with the fact table at the core and the dimension tables along the spikes of the star. This particular arrangement is thus called a star schema.

In this arrangement, every dimension table has a direct relationship with the fact table in the middle thereby allowing every dimension table with its attributes to have an equal chance of participating in a query to analyse the attributes in the fact table. Thus, the star schema satisfies all the aforesaid conditions. Hence, it is the most widely accepted logical schema for data warehouses.

The star schema is perhaps the simplest data warehouse schema. It is called a star schema because its diagram resembles a star, with points radiating from a central table. The centre of the star consists of a large fact table and the points of the star are the dimension tables.

The fact table contains primary information in the data warehouse, and the dimension tables contain information about the entries for a particular attribute in the fact table. The schema graph resembles a starburst, with the dimension tables displayed in a radial pattern around the central fact table.

Each dimension table is joined to the fact table using a primary key to foreign key join, but the dimension tables are not joined to each other. Figure 6.2 shows a simple star schema. It shows order fact table in the middle and four dimension tables of customers, salesperson, time, and product.

The users in the marketing department will analyse the orders using order dollars, order quantity, and profit dollars. This information is found in the fact table of the structure. The users will analyse these measurements by breaking down the numbers in combination by customer, salesperson, date, and product. The star schema structure is a structure that can be easily understood by the users and with which they can work comfortably and intuitively. The structure clearly reflects how the users normally view their critical measures along the business dimensions.

Any table that references or is referenced by another table must have a primary key, which is a column or group of columns whose contents uniquely identify each row. In a simple star schema, the primary key for the fact table consists of one or more foreign keys. A foreign key is a column or group of columns in one table whose values are defined by the primary key in another table.

As we see in Fig. 6.2, every dimension table contains the hierarchies and categories within that dimension plus a primary key which uniquely identifies every row or more specifically every record in that table. Recall that in SQL, to create relationship between two tables we use primary and foreign keys. The same we do here in a star schema to join the fact table with various dimension tables. By keeping the primary key of the dimension table as a foreign key in the fact table a link is created between the two tables.

6.3.1 How Does a Query Execute?

When a query is executed against the star schema, the results of the query are produced by combining or joining one or more dimension tables with the fact table.

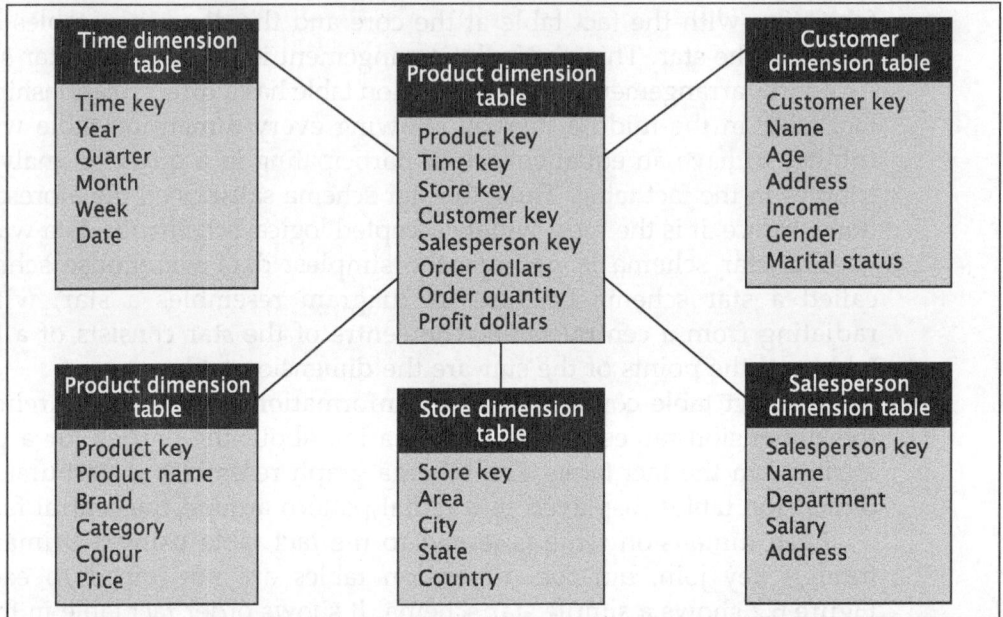

Figure 6.2 A star schema

Take a simple query against the star schema. Let us say that the marketing department wants the quantity sold and order dollars for product A, relating to all female customers, obtained by salesperson John, during the month of May in the Delhi store. Figure 6.3 shows how this query is formulated from the star schema.

6.3.2 Example

Let us now see how query processing takes place in case of a star schema. Till now we have seen how the logical design of the data warehouse is made by placing the fact table in the middle and all the dimension tables around it. Now we will see how this logical design is used to make the physical tables and process queries against it.

Consider our sample star schema; we will create tables using it as shown in Tables 6.1 (a)–(g) below and execute the query to find– "How much profit in dollars did the salesperson David make on 2 January 2006 by selling trousers to Jenny at the Delhi store?"

Look at Fig. 6.3 According to the star schema, we have five dimension tables namely—time, customer, product, store, and salesperson. Each of these table will store data related to its name. Also there is a fact table which stores certain facts and keys of the dimension tables.

For the sake of understanding the concept these tables have been filled with arbitrary values.

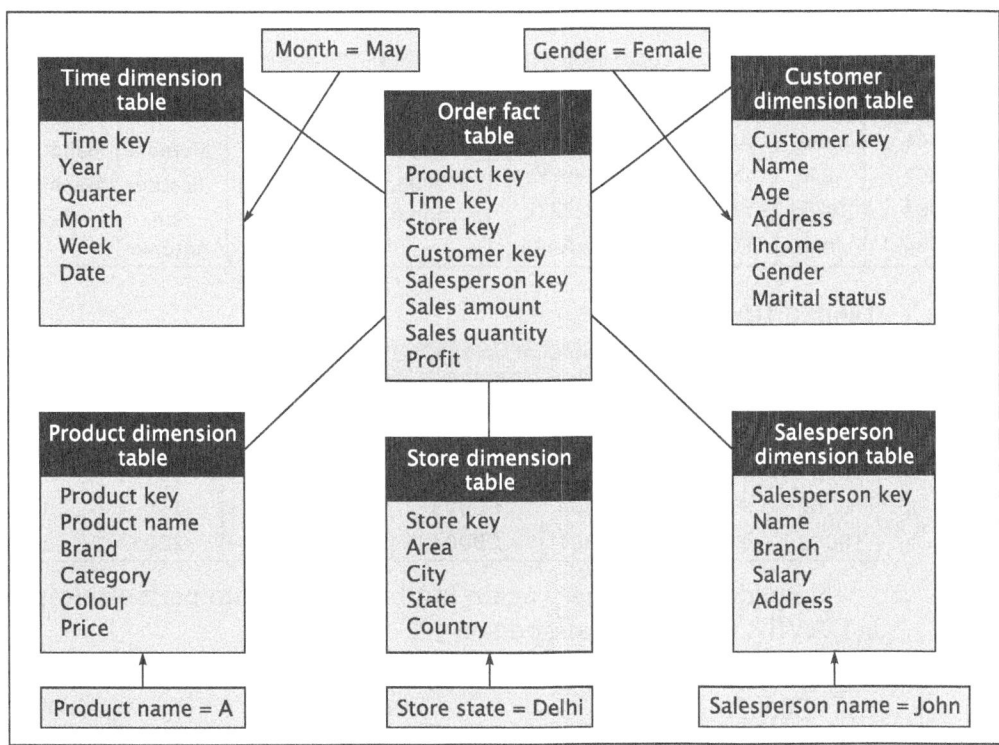

Figure 6.3 Representation of a star schema

Table 6.1(a) Customer dimension

Customer Key	Name	Age	Address	Income	Gender	Marital Status
C0001	Mary	25	XXXXXX	35K	Female	Single
C0002	Joe	32	YYYYYY	40K	Male	Married
C0003	Ken	30	ZZZZZZ	27K	Male	Single
C0004	Jenny	43	AAAAAA	43K	Female	Married

Table 6.1(b) Time dimension

Time Key	Year	Quarter	Month	Week	Date
T0001	2006	First	January	First	01
T0002	2006	First	January	First	02
T0003	2006	First	January	First	03
T0004	2006	First	January	First	04

Table 6.1(c) Product dimension

Product Key	Product Name	Brand	Category	Colour
P0001	Shirts	John Player	Formals	White
P0002	T-Shirts	Lee	Casuals	Maroon
P0003	Trousers	Peter England	Formals	Black
P0004	Jeans	Levis	Casuals	Blue

Table 6.1(d) Salesperson dimension

Salesperson Key	Name	Branch	Salary	Address
S0001	James	ABC	10K	XXXXXX
S0002	Bill	DEF	8K	YYYYYY
S0003	David	ABC	10K	ZZZZZZ
S0004	John	PQR	9K	AAAAAA

Table 6.1(e) Store dimension

Store Key	Area	City	State	Country
ST0001	Karol Bagh	Delhi	New Delhi	India
ST0002	Thane	Mumbai	Maharashtra	India
ST0003	Kondael Mall	Seattle	Washington	USA
ST0004	Bronchure Mall	San Antonio	Texas	USA

Table 6.1(f) Order fact

Time Key	Product Key	Store Key	Customer Key	Salesperson Key	Sales Amount	Sales Quantity	Profit
T0001	P0001	ST0003	C0001	S0001	200	20	30
T0001	P0002	ST0001	C0002	S0002	180	17	35
T0002	P0002	ST0004	C0003	S0004	150	15	27
T0002	P0003	ST0001	C0004	S0003	220	18	20

Now look at the query again but breaking it into parts—salesperson name is DAVID, the key of salesperson

- Salesperson David will be taken from the dimension table. His key is S0003.
- Time is 2 January 2006, time key will be fetched of course, from the time dimension table. The time key for the given date is T0002.
- Product is trousers. The key for this product is present in the product dimension table. The product key of trousers is P0003.
- Jenny is the name of the customer. Jennys key will be present in the customer dimension table. Jenny's key is C0004.
- Store is in Delhi, so its corresponding key will be taken from the store dimension table the key of Delhi store is ST0001.

Once we have the keys of all the dimension tables, the fact table record will be that has C0004, T0002, P0003, ST0001, and S0003 in its customer key, time key, product key, store key and salesperson key fields respectively and hence the result.

Table 6.1(g) Resultant row from the fact table

T0002	P0003	ST0001	C0004	S0003	220	18	20

From each dimension table, we take the corresponding primary keys and then search for the measures in the fact table by concatenating the dimension table keys.

6.3.3 Pros and Cons of Star Schema

Star schema is simply a relational model with a one-to-many relationship between the fact table and every dimension table. It has a special arrangement of the fact and dimension tables which makes it eminently suitable for the data warehouse. In this section, we will discuss the reasons for its wide use and success in providing optimization for query processing.

Star schema is a denormalized relational model. However, a strict adherence to this arrangement is not always the best option. For example, if the product is one of the dimensions and if the company has a very large number of products, a denormalized product dimension table may not be desirable as it would increase the size of the fact table. Besides this, the advantages far outweigh any shortcomings.

A star schema is *easy to understand*. We all know that, operational systems users interact with the applications using predefined screens or preset query templates. The users need not know the data structures behind the scenes. All the issues related to data structures and the database schema is meant to be handled by the IT professionals.

However, users of a data warehouse will themselves formulate queries. So, they need to be familiar with the available data, understand the data structures and know how the various pieces are associated with one another in the overall scheme. In short, the users must be able to comprehend the connections without difficulty.

The star schema reflects how users think of their data and how they need to query and analyse. Users think business in terms of facts or measures which are present in the fact table. They analyse these facts in terms of business dimensions which are present in the dimension tables. Apart from this, the star schema defines the join paths in exactly the same way users normally visualize the relationships. For example, if the user needs to find the sales_unit of product A on 2 February, 2008, then as the users are thinking, the product information will be taken from the product dimension table, date information will come from time dimension and the sales units is a fact that will be picked up from the sales fact table.

The facts will be obtained from the fact table and the dimensional attributes will be available in the respective dimension tables. Thus, the star schema is intuitively understood by the users.

The second major advantage is that a star schema *optimizes navigation*. In a data warehouse database schema, the relationships between the fact table and dimension tables exist to fetch information that users want. In other words, the relationships enable navigation through the database.

If the database schema contains multiple convoluted join paths, then navigation through the database gets difficult and slow. On the contrary, if the join paths are simple and straightforward, navigation becomes efficient and faster. The star schema optimizes navigation through the database. Even for a complex query the navigation is still simple and straightforward.

The third main reason for the widespread use of a star schema is that it *enhances query execution*. Star schema is a query centric structure as it is most suitable for query processing. Whatever may be the number of dimensions that participate in the query and whatever the level of complexity of the query, every query will be executed in the same fashion. Every query first selects rows from the dimension tables using filters based on the query parameters and then extracts the corresponding fact table rows.

The arrangement of the fact table and dimension tables in a star schema offers simple and straightforward join paths. No intermediary tables need to be navigated to reach the fact table from the dimension tables.

Another important aspect of data warehouse queries is the ability to drill down or roll up. Drill down is a process of going into further details by selecting additional rows from the fact table and rolling up is a process of looking at aggregate data rather than detail data.

To summarize we can say that the star schema is optimized for access. Thus the core benefits include:

Simplicity Star schema architecture is the simplest data warehouse design.

Analytic flexibility The facts can be accessed and analysed across multiple dimensions. The users can even perform drill down or roll up operations to gain meaningful insights into the data

Easy to reconfigure Dimensional attributes and fact elements can be added easily without affecting the other tables.

Best for ad hoc Star schema provides interactive data access to its users.

Enable summarization The star schema's flexibility and efficiency make it a better choice for creating aggregations and summarizations. We will read more about in the next chapter.

The star schema deficits are a result of the compromises that make it work.

- A star schema has a narrow scope in terms of the facts and dimensions represented as compared to a relational model.
- A star schema is good to store current data. Although it can store historical data but maintenance and addition of more of historical data can lead to some problems.
- Star schema offers moderate performance.
- Not suitable for storing detailed data.

6.4 THE SNOWFLAKE SCHEMA

The snowflake schema is a variation of the star schema model, in which some or all the dimension tables are normalized, thereby further splitting the data into additional tables. The resulting schema graph forms a shape similar to a snowflake. Thus, snowflaking is a method of normalizing the dimension tables in a star schema. The snowflake schema is a more complex data warehouse model than a star schema. It is called a snowflake schema because the diagram of the schema resembles a snowflake.

Snowflake schema normalizes its dimension tables to eliminate redundancy. That is, the dimension data is grouped into multiple tables instead of one large table. Snowflake schemas are generally used when a dimensional table becomes very big and when a star schema can't represent the complexity of a data structure. If the concept of normalization is not known to the reader then refer Section 7.8.3.

For example, a product dimension table in a star schema might be normalized into a products table, a product_category table, and a product_brand table in a snowflake schema. While this saves space, but it increases the number of dimension tables and requires more foreign key joins thereby resulting in complex queries and reduced query performance.

Assume that there are 1,00,000 product dimension rows. These products fall under 100 brands and these brands fall under 10 product categories. If the users run a query constraining just on product category and if the product dimension table is not indexed on product category, the query will have to search through 1,00,000 rows. On the contrary, if the product dimension is normalized by separating out brand and product category into separate tables, the query will have to scan only 10 rows in the product category table.

6.4.1 The Technique

Many ways of snowflaking or normalization of the dimension tables exists as you can fully/partially normalize all/some of the dimension tables.

In the snowflake schema, the attributes with low cardinality in each original dimension table are removed to form separate tables. These new tables are linked back to the original dimension table through artificial keys. Observe Fig. 6.4 to see how a snowflake schema is formed.

The main difference between snowflake schema and star schema is that the dimension tables of the snowflake model are normalized to reduce data redundancies. Such tables are easy to maintain and saves storage space when the dimension table becomes very large. But on the downside, the snowflake schema reduces the effectiveness of browsing since more joins will be needed to execute a query. Therefore, the decision to use a star schema or snowflake schema involves evaluating tradeoffs between ease of use and ease of maintenance.

6.4.2 Example

Let us take an example of a query that needs to fetch data of quantity ordered of blue shirts that belongs to John Players brand, in a sales transaction made on 2 January 2006, by a salesperson who is from Chennai to Indian customers. The tables from 6.2(a)–(j) are formed based on the snowflake schema given in Fig. 6.4.

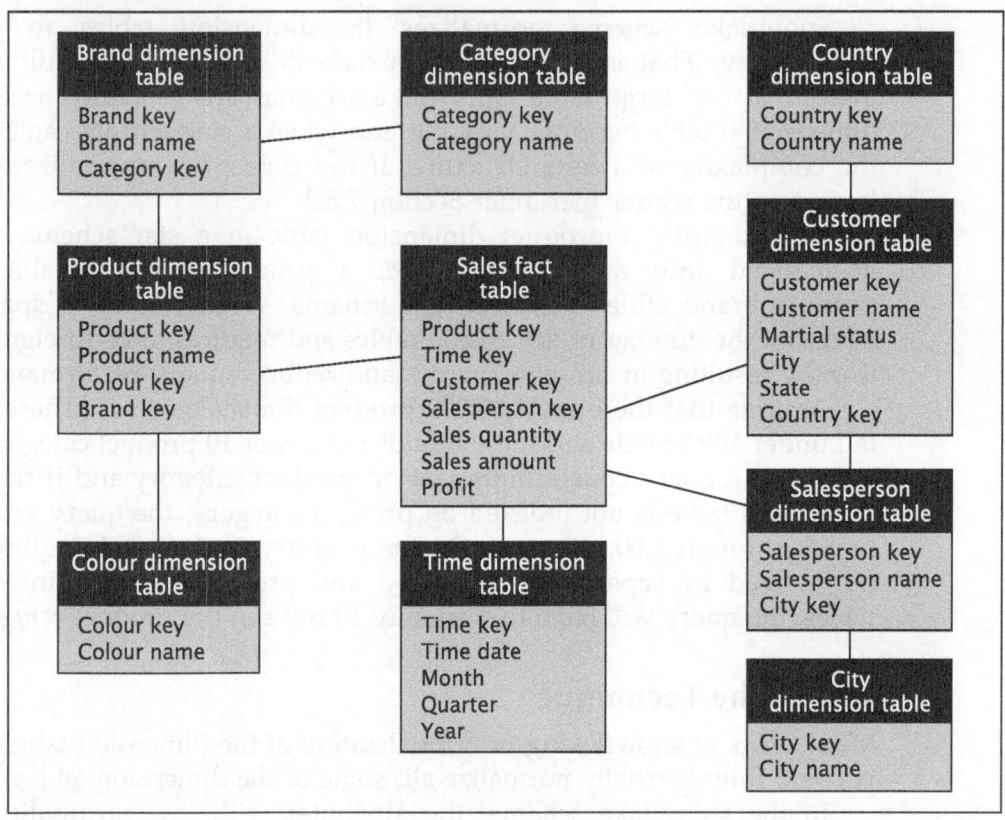

Figure 6.4 Representation of a snowflake schema

Table 6.2(a)
Brand dimension

Brand Key	Brand Name	Category Key
B01	John Players	CK01
B02	Peter England	CK02
B03	Allen Solly	CK01

Table 6.2(b)
Colour dimension

Colour Key	Colour Name
C001	Blue
C002	Black
C003	White
C004	Gray

Table 6.2(c)
Category dimension

Category Key	Category Name
CK01	Men's Formal
Ck02	Men's Casual

Table 6.2(d)
Product dimension

Product Key	Product Name Key	Brand Key	Colour Key
P001	Shirts	B01	C001
P002	Trousers	B01	C002
P003	T-shirts	B02	C003
P004	Shirts	B03	C00

Table 6.2(e)
Time dimension

Time Key	Year	Quarter	Month	Week	Date
T0001	2006	First	January	First	01
T0002	2006	First	January	First	02
T0003	2006	First	January	First	03
T0004	2006	First	January	First	04

Table 6.2(f)
Customer dimension

Customer Key	Name	Age	City	State	Country Key	Marital Status
C0001	Mary	25	XXXXXX	Delhi	CT01	Single
C0002	Joe	32	YYYYYY	Texas	CT02	Married
C0003	Ken	30	ZZZZZZ	Washington	CT02	Single
C0004	Jenny	43	AAAAAA	Punjab	CT01	Married

Table 6.2(g)
Country dimension

Country Key	Country Name
CT01	India
CT02	USA

Table 6.2(h)
Salesperson dimension

Sales Person Key	Salesperson Name	City Key
SP001	Neelam	CI01
SP002	Ram	CI02
SP003	Ishaan	CI03

Table 6.2(i)
City dimension

City Key	City Name
CI01	Chandigarh
CI02	Mumbai
CI03	Chennai

Now to understand query execution in case of a snowflake schema, break down the query into its individual components.

(i) *Blue shirts is the product*
See the products dimension table. There are two rows for shirts. Which one to choose? Note that we have to look for a blue shirt where blue is the colour. Product dimension table stores colour key. So jump to the colour dimension table to obtain the key for blue. Blue has key C001. This means from the products dimension table we will select the key where product name = "shirt" and colour key = C001.

(ii) *John Players brand*
In product dimension table brand name is not mentioned. We only have brand keys. So to get the brand key for JOHN PLAYERS we will have to jump to the BRAND dimension table. We find that the key for JOHN PLAYERS is B01. Hence, from the product's dimension table we will select the key of the row where product name = "shirt", colour key C001 and brand key = B01.

(iii) *2nd Jan 06*
2nd Jan 06 specifies that the time key will be fetched from the time dimension table. The key is T0002.

(iv) *Salesperson from Chennai*
See in the salesperson dimension table. We observe that the name of city is not present. Rather city key is present. Now we will find the city key corresponding to Chennai. The answer is to jump to the city dimension table. Chennai's key is CT03. Now come back to the salesperson table

and find the key of the salesperson where city key = C103. So the corresponding salesperson key that we get is P003.

(v) Indian customers

See the customers dimension table. We have to fetch customer key of all the customers whose country is "India". Observe that we do not have country name in the customer dimension table. We have only country key. So now jump to the country dimension table, to obtain the country key of India. The country key is CT01 so now select all the rows from customer dimension table where country key = CT01.

Table 6.2(j)
Sales fact table

Time Key	Product Key	Customer Key	Salesperson Key	Sales Amount	Sales Qunatity	Profit
T0001	P001	C0001	S0002	200	20	30
T0002	P003	C0002	S0003	180	17	35
T0003	P002	C0003	SP004	150	15	27
T0002	P001	C0004	SP001	220	18	20
T0002	P001	C0001	SP003	300	10	50

Once we have all the necessary primary keys of the dimension tables, we will row fetch the desired rows from the fact table. Now we have: Time key = T0002, Product key = P0001, Customer key = C001 and C0002, Salesperson key = SP003.

6.4.3 Is Snowflaking Really Helpful?

You may want to snowflake by eliminating all the long text fields from the dimension tables to save storage space. For example, if you have men's wear as one of the category names, that text will be repeated in every product row in that category. At the first go, removing such redundancies might appear to save significant storage space when the dimensions are large.

Let us assume that the product dimension table has 1,00,000 rows and by snowflaking you are able to remove 1,00,000–20 byte category names. But at the same time, you have to add a 4-byte category key to the dimension table. Thus, the net savings comes out to be 1,00,000 times 16, that is, about 1.6 MB.

If the product dimension table occupies about 40 MB of storage space and the corresponding fact table another 10 GB. The savings are just 4%. Therefore, we see that the small savings in space does not compensate for the other disadvantages of snowflaking.

6.4.4 Pros and Cons of Snowflake Schema

The key benefits of the snowflake schema include:

- Small savings in storage space.
- Easy to update and maintain a normalized structure.

- If a dimension is very sparse (most of the dimension rows have no data) and/or a dimension has a very long list of attributes, the dimension table may occupy a significant proportion of the database and snowflaking may be appropriate.

However, the downside of this schema are:

- It is less intuitive for the end-users.
- End-users are put off by the complex structure.
- Navigation of the data warehouse contents is difficult.
- Query performance degrades due to additional joins in the table.

Snowflake schema is generally not used in a data warehouse environment because normalization affects the query performance and that is something which is of utmost priority in a data warehouse environment.

6.5 AGGREGATE TABLES

Aggregate fact tables contain pre-calculated summaries derived from the most granular (detailed) fact table. Aggregate fact tables are created as a specific summarization across any number of dimensions. They are mainly designed to reduce runtime processing. Other reasons for implementing aggregate fact tables can be listed as below:

- Aggregate tables store data needed for multiple executions of the same query or execution of multiple similar queries using the same data subset.
- They give high performance for specific tasks.
- Aggregate tables are good for repetitive action such as reporting.
- They act as a good source for summaries based on the defined subset of elements.

6.5.1 Need for Building Aggregate Fact Tables

This section explains why we should build aggregate tables in addition to the base fact tables.

Large size of the fact table   Study the calculations in Table 6.3. We will take examples from different business to get an estimate of how large a fact table is in the real world.

Table 6.3   Size of fact tables in different business areas

Retail industry	- If we keep at least 5 years of data in the fact table, then there will be at least (5 years = 1825 days) 1825 rows - If there are at least 300 stores all over the world, then the fact table size becomes 1825 × 300 - If we assume that in every store at least 400 products sell daily, then we now have the fact table size = 1825 × 300 × 400 - Total = 2 billion

Table 6.3 Continued

Table 6.3 Continued

Telecommunication industry	• If we keep at least 3 years of data in the fact table, then there will be at least (3 years = 1095 days) 1095 rows • If the company tracks at least 150 million calls every day, all over the world, then we have fact tables rows to be 1095 × 150 million Total = 164 billion
Tracking credit Transaction	• If we keep at least 4 years of data in the fact table, then there will be at least (4 years = 1460 days) 1460 rows • If we assume that there are at least 150 million customers, then the fact table rows becomes at least 1460 × 150 million • If every customer makes at least 20 transactions per month then, the fact table contains as many rows as, 1460 × 150 × 20 million • Total = 144 billion

The above examples show the typical enormity of the fact tables that are at the lowest level of granularity. Rarely will the users use individual fact table rows during the session of his analysis. But a decision to ignore detailed data may result in the inability to answer certain queries that require data at the lowest level of granularity.

To speed up query execution Let us begin our study of aggregate tables by examining a sample star schema in which the fact table is at the lowest granularity as shown in the Fig. 6.5. Table 6.4 reviews a few typical queries against the sample star schema.

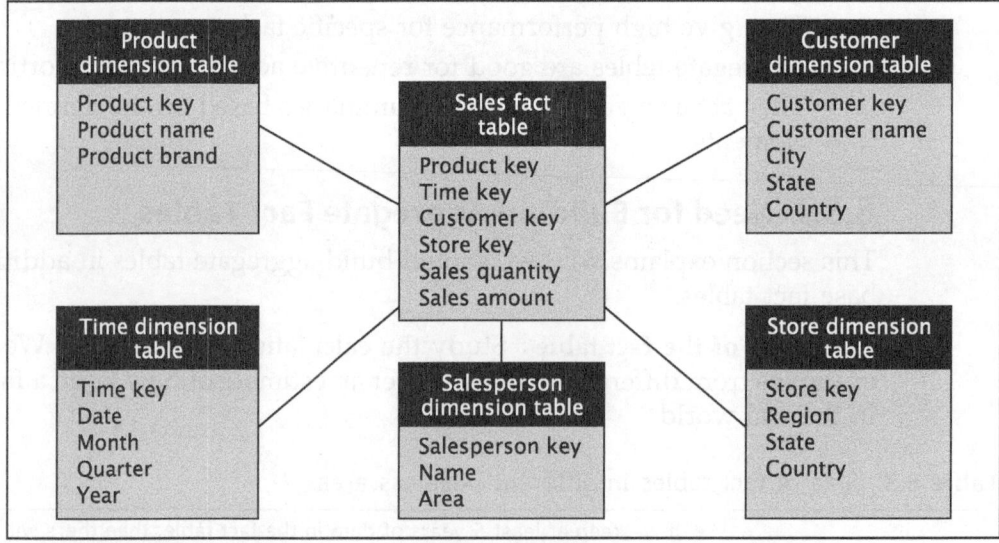

Figure 6.5 Star schema with the most granular fact table

Table 6.4 Queries against star schema shown in Fig. 6.9

Query	Result Set	Max No. of Rows
• Display the total sales for customer Meera during the first week of December 2007 for product A	• All fact table rows where the customer name is Meera, the product key relates to product A and the time key relates to the first seven days in the week of December 2007.	• 7 rows
• Display the total sales for customer Arpan during the first quarter of 2007 for product A	• All fact table rows where the customer name is Arpan, the product key relates to product A and the time key relates to about 90 days.	• 90 rows
• Display the total sales for all customers in the Southern region for the first two quarters of 2007 for product brand ABC	• All fact table rows where the customer key relates to all customers in the Southern region, the product key relates to all products in the product category ABC, and the time key relates to about 180 days.	• A large number of rows

Assumption   A customer makes at most one purchase of a single product in a single day.

In the last query of Table 6.4, the execution time will be very high as a large number of rows need to be accessed. But had we created an aggregate table, the process would have got speeded up.

So, now the question is that if you need to store detailed data in the base fact tables, then how will you deal with summarizations of fact table rows to produce query results? Consider the following queries related to a retail chain data warehouse:

- How did the four new stores in Delhi perform during the last quarter compared to the national average?
- What is the effect of the latest holiday sales campaign on men's wear?
- How do the 24 December sales by product categories compare to that of last year's?

Each of these queries requires selections and summations from the rows of the base fact table. To summarize the fact table rows, detailed data based on one or more dimensions and summary totals based on other dimensions is needed. For example the last query needs detailed daily data based on the time dimension, but summary totals by product categories. In case you had pre-calculated aggregates readily available, the queries would run faster thereby improving the performance of the queries.

To understand the need of aggregate fact tables, let us take another example of a star schema of a retail chain as shown Fig. 6.6. In its 100 stores, there are 1000 products and 40 products per brand. Besides, there are 5,000 salesperson working, 1,00,000 customers and 30 brands.

Note   We assume that there is at least one sale per product per store per week.

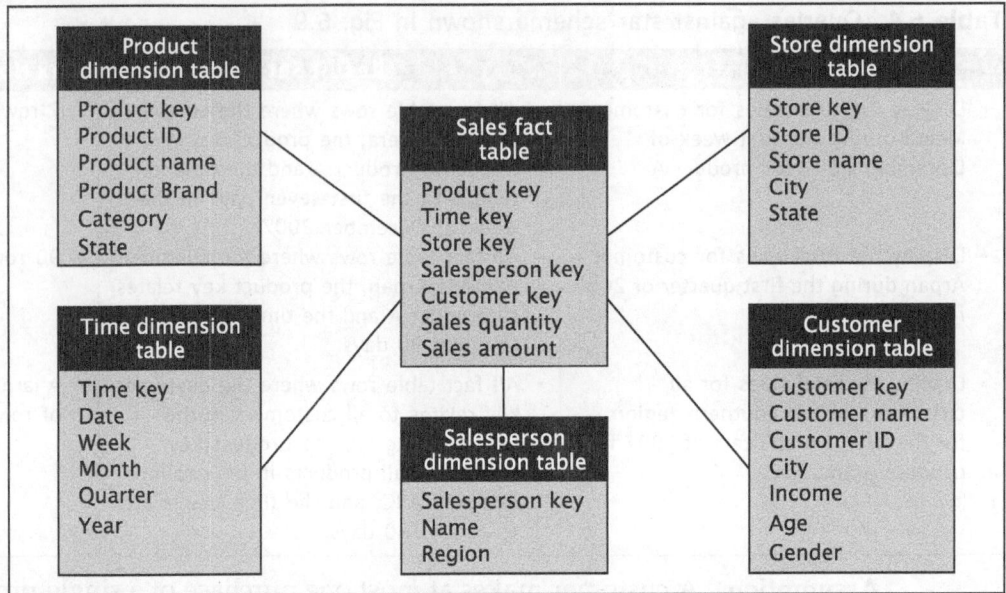

Figure 6.6 Star schema of a retail chain

Using Fig. 6.6, let us estimate the number of fact table rows to be retrieved and summarized for the following queries:

Display data against 1 product, 1 store, 1 week– this query will fetch 7 rows if the data is not summarized and kept at the daily level. In case the fact table is summarized to store weekly data then the query would have to fetch only 1 row.

Display data against 1 store, 1 day, all brands– this query will fetch 1000 rows if the data is not summarized and stored with respect to individual product. In case the fact table is summarized to store data according to different brands, then the query would have to fetch only 30 rows.

Thus, aggregate fact tables have much fewer rows than the base fact tables. Therefore, when the queries are executed against the aggregate fact tables instead of the base fact table, query execution becomes faster and efficient.

6.5.2 Limitations of Aggregate Fact Tables

However, it is not always beneficial to create and maintain aggregate fact tables because of the following bottlenecks.

- Aggregate fact tables must be re-aggregated every time there is a change in the source data to reflect those changes in the data warehouse.
- Aggregate fact tables do not support exploratory analysis and hence have a narrow applicability.
- Narrow capability also leads to a limited interactive use.

6.6 FACT CONSTELLATION SCHEMA

For each star schema or snowflake schema, it is possible to construct a fact constellation schema (families of stars). Almost all data warehouses contain multiple star schema structures where each star serves its specific purpose. This collection of related star schemas is called a fact constellation schema or simply a family of stars. The main disadvantage of the fact constellation schema is that it has a more complicated design, as many variants of aggregation must be considered.

Families of stars are formed for various reasons. First, a family of stars may be formed by just adding aggregate fact tables and the derived dimension tables to support the aggregates, as we had seen in the previous section. Second, a family of stars may be created to support a core fact table containing facts useful to most users and customized fact tables for specific user groups. Third, a family of stars is formed when we have transaction and snapshot tables in the data warehouse. Fourth, a family of stars is formed to support the value chain of the enterprise. We will discuss all these cases in detail in this section.

Aggregate Fact Tables and Derived Dimension Tables

The first example of a family of stars comes into picture when we create aggregate fact tables sharing the dimension tables with the base fact table. Usually, the time dimension is shared by most of the fact tables in the group. In the above example (see Fig. 6.7), two fact tables are likely to share the time dimension, thereby forming a family of stars.

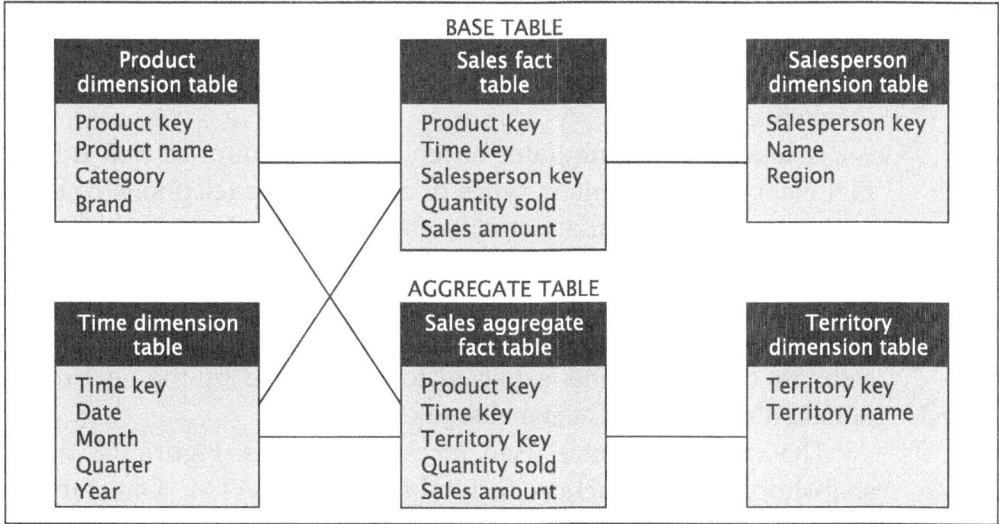

Figure 6.7 Aggregate fact table and derived dimension tables

The aggregate fact tables are derived (either by summarizations or aggregations) from a single base fact table. These derived aggregate fact tables are then joined to the derived dimension tables. Figure 6.7 illustrates this concept.

Snapshot and Transaction Tables

The second area where a family of stars is formed is in the case of snapshot and transaction tables. At times the users want a snapshot-like summary of a business at some intermediate point in time. In such cases, it makes sense to start with the immediately preceding snapshot and add the effect of the incremental transactions between the beginning of that period and the desired date.

This task will be easy if the measure in which the user is interested exists within the snapshot table. However, if the measure is not part of the snapshot, then the user may have no choice but to crawl the transaction table. For example, if the user wants to know how many times a customer has been denied credit then if this data is present in the snapshot table then it would be very straight forward to answer but otherwise the user would have to search the entire transaction history from the beginning.

Transaction tables and snapshot tables are thus the yin and yang of a data warehouse. Whereas transaction tables give us the fullest possible view of detailed behaviour, the snapshots allow the users to measure the status of the enterprise quickly. We need both the tables as used together, transactions and snapshots provide a quick and complete view of the business.

Let us take an example of a telephone company. A number of individual transactions make up a telephone customer's account. A usual pattern of telephone usage is that more transactions happen during the holidays and weekends for residential customers. However corporate organizations and institutions use the phones on weekdays rather than over the weekends.

A telephone accumulates an enormous amount of rich transaction data that can be used for many types of analysis. The telephone company needs a schema capturing transaction data that supports strategic decision making for expansions and service improvements. It also needs a schema capturing snapshot data to answer questions from the customers related to their account balances. Snapshot tables also help the accounting department to have an estimate of the amounts expected to be received by the next month and the outstanding balances of the customers.

The same concept is used in case of ATMs. Figure 6.8 that shows the snapshot and transaction fact tables for an ATM. One table tracks the individual transaction amounts for customer accounts. The other table holds a snapshot view of the balance of each account at the end of each day. The two tables serve two distinct functions. Notice how dimension tables are shared between the two fact tables.

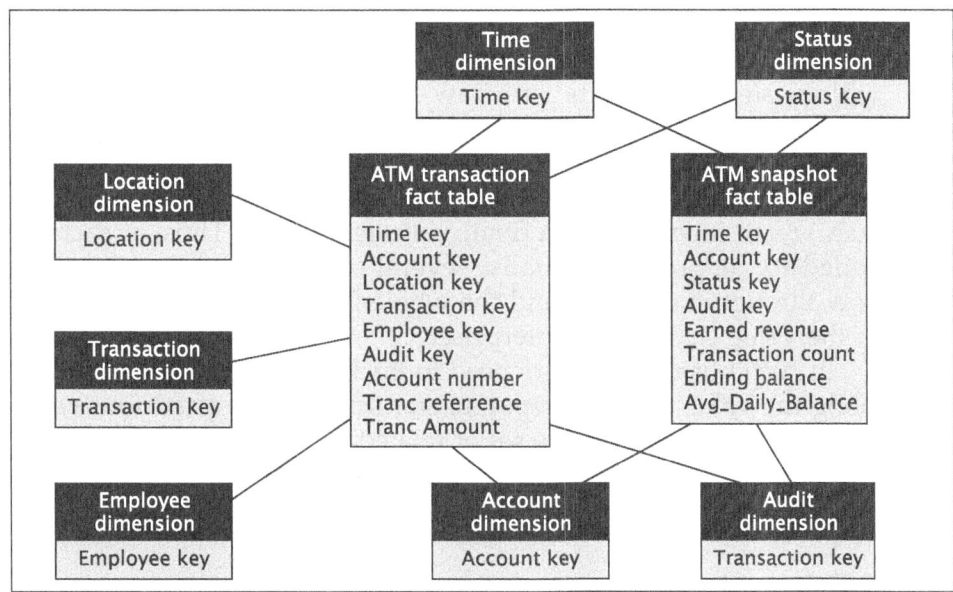

Figure 6.8 Transaction and snapshot tables for an ATM

Core and Custom Table

Consider two types of businesses that are apparently dissimilar. Take an example of a bank that offers a large variety of services, all related to finance in some or the other way. Most of these services are different from each another. For example, the checking account service and the savings account service are similar in most ways, but the savings account service does not resemble the credit card service in any way. The question now is, how will the data warehouse track these dissimilar services?

For such types of business, a different variety of family of stars is needed in which all products and services connect to a core fact table and each product or service relates to individual custom tables. Figure 6.9 shows the core and custom tables for a bank. The core fact table holds the metrics that are common to all types of accounts and each custom fact table contains the metrics specific to that line of service. Note how the core tables and custom tables share dimension tables thereby forming a family of stars.

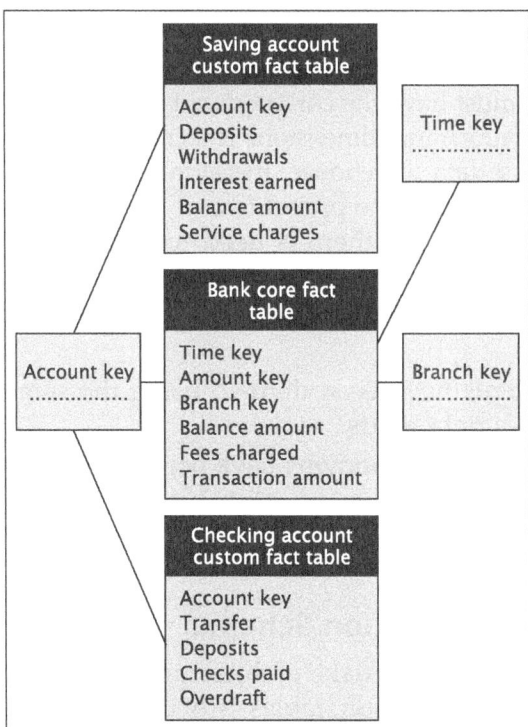

Figure 6.9 Core and custom table

Supporting Enterprise Value Chain or Value Circle

In a manufacturing business, the product development life cycle consists of various steps that starts with raw materials and ends with finished goods. Every step includes addition of ingredients, assembly of materials, process control, packaging, and shipping to the warehouse. From the warehouse the product moves into shipment, then to distributor inventory, distributor shipment, retail inventory, and finally into retail sales. Thus, at each step value is added to the product. Usually, several operational systems will support the flow through these steps and the whole flow together forms the supply chain or the value chain of an enterprise.

In such businesses, users need to track important metrics at different steps along the value chain. A separate star schema is created for every significant step and thus, the complete set of related star schemas forms a family of stars. The family of stars contains multiple fact tables and a set of corresponding conformed dimensions for each important step in the value chain.

6.6.1 Prerequisite for a Fact Constellation Schema

In families of stars, dimensions are shared among the fact tables. For dimensions to be conformed, you have to deliberately make sure that common dimensions are used between two or more stars. So the attributes of the shared dimension must have the same meaning in every fact table.

Paulraj Pooniah, in his book *Data Warehousing Fundamentals* (2001), writes that "A conformed dimension is defined as a comprehensive combination of attributes from the source systems after resolving all discrepancies and conflicts." In a conformed dimension, each attribute must have the correct data type and must have proper lengths and constraints. Conforming dimensions is a crucial ingredient for consistent and accurate data in a data warehouse, therefore, conforming dimensions is one of the major responsibilities of the project team.

Besides the task of conforming dimensions there is need to standardize facts. As you already know that the fact tables work across star schemas, they should be designed very carefully. Let us review the issues in the standardization of fact table attributes:

- Ensure that the same data elements have been defined using the same definition and terminology across data marts.
- Ensure that all types of homonyms and synonyms have been resolved.
- Ensure that the same algorithms are used to derive data in each fact table.
- Ensure that every fact/measure uses the right unit of measurement.

6.6.2 Pros and Cons of Fact Constellation Schema

This schema is more complex than star or snowflake architecture, because it contains multiple fact tables and the dimension tables are to be shared amongst many fact tables.

This is a flexible solution, however it is difficult to manage and support. The main disadvantage of the fact constellation schema is its complicated design because many variants of aggregation have to be considered.

6.7 THE STRENGTHS OF DIMENSIONAL MODELLING

The dimensional model offers certain features that the ER model lacks. A dimension model has a standard framework. End-user tools, like report writers and query tools, all use the dimension model to make the user interfaces simple and query processing more efficient.

It has predictable framework of the star schema in which every dimension is equal. All dimensions are symmetrical and have a direct relation with the fact table. Apart from the dimensions, the user interfaces, query strategies and the SQL queries generated against the dimensional model are all symmetrical.

It is gracefully extensible to accommodate new data and design decisions. The term 'gracefully extensible' implies three things—first, all existing tables can be altered to add new data rows in the table, second no query or reporting tool needs to be reprogrammed to accommodate the change, and third all old applications continue to run without creating any problem.

It has standard approaches for handling common modelling situations that can be specifically programmed in report writers, query tools, and other user interfaces.

A final strength of the dimensional model is the use of aggregates, which are nothing but summary records that are logically redundant with base data already in the data warehouse, but they are required to enhance query performance.

6.8 DATA WAREHOUSE AND THE DATA MODEL

Thus, we see that the data warehouse is designed using a data model that has three different levels—high level data model, middle level data model, and the low level data model.

The high level data model depicts the different subjects around which the data will be organized. The example of these subjects includes sales, customers, products, etc.

The middle level data model contains the details of the data warehouse. These details include identifying the keys, relationships, attributes etc.

Finally, the low level data model contains details about the physical database design like the partitioning scheme to be applied, definition of foreign keys, indexes and other physical aspects of the design.

Recapitulation

Dimensional modelling is a design technique to structure the business dimensions and the metrics that are analysed along these dimensions.

The metrics or facts from the IPD will form the fact table; similarly all the dimensions from the IPD will form the dimension tables.

In a simple star schema, the primary key for the fact table consists of one or more foreign keys. These foreign keys are nothing but primary keys of individual dimension tables with which you have to link the fact table.

We use dimensional modelling for designing tables for data warehouse and ER modelling for designing tables for OLTP systems.

The strength of dimensional modelling includes—a predictable framework, symmetrical dimension tables with the fact table, graceful extensibility to accommodate unexpected new design decisions and existence of standard approaches for handling common modelling situations.

Typically, a dimension table has many columns or attributes. So it is considered to be wide, has textual attributes where some of the attributes may not be related with other attributes in the same table, is not normalized and provides the facility to perform drill-down and roll-up operations.

Fact tables are often very large, containing millions of rows storing numeric measures. The primary key of the fact table must be the concatenation of the primary keys of all the dimension tables.

Some fact tables don't have any facts at all. They may consist of nothing but keys. These are called factless fact tables. The factless fact table is a table that records an event.

Snowflaking is a method of normalizing the dimension tables in a star schema. While this saves space, it increases the number of dimension tables and requires more foreign key joins.

Aggregate fact tables contain pre-calculated summaries derived from the most granular fact table. They are mainly designed to reduce runtime processing.

Almost all data warehouse contain multiple star schema structures where each star serves a specific purpose to track the measures stored in the fact table. A collection of related star schemas is called a family of stars.

Transaction tables give the fullest possible view of detailed behaviour, and snapshot tables give you a summary of a business at some intermediate point in time to measure the status of the enterprise quickly.

The core fact table holds the metrics that are common to all types of services in the company (example in banks) and each custom fact table contains the metrics specific to that line of service.

Objective Questions

1. Multiple choice questions

(i) Which is the key that is defined as a column or group of columns in one table whose values are defined by the primary key in another table?

(a) Primary key

(b) Secondary key

(c) Foreign key

(d) None of these

(ii) What does a dimension table contain?

(a) Primary key

(b) Hierarchies/categories

(c) Foreign key

(d) All of these

(iii) Which type of relationship does a star schema contain between the fact table and every dimension table?

(a) One-to-one

(b) One-to-many

(c) Many-to-one

(d) Many-to-many

(iv) Which process helps the users to go in further details by selecting additional rows from the fact table?

(a) Drill-down

(b) Roll-up

(c) Slice

(d) Dice

(v) Which table is used to allow the users to measure the status of the enterprise quickly?

(a) Transaction

(b) Core

(c) Custom

(d) Snapshot

(vi) Which level data model identifies the keys, relationships, attributes, etc.?

(a) High level

(b) Low level

(c) Middle level

(d) None of these

2. Fill in the blanks

1. The _____ lays the ground for the data design for the data warehouse.

2. The result of the data design process is a _____ model.

3. _____ is a design technique to structure the business dimensions and the metrics.

4. A single ER diagram can be broken down into _____ number of DM diagrams.

5. In a dimension model, we prefer keeping the tables _____ whereas in an ER diagram the main aim is to remove redundancy by _____ the tables.

6. Star schema has the _____ table in the middle and _____ tables arranged around it.

7. _____ table contains the primary information in the data warehouse.

8. The _____ tables are not joined to each other.

9. Star schema is _____ query execution.

10. In a snowflake schema, dimension tables are _____, thereby further splitting the data into additional tables.

11. In the snowflake schema, the attributes with _____ cardinality in each original dimension table are removed to form separate tables.

12. _____ table contains pre-calculated summaries derived from the most granular fact table.

13. Query executed against the aggregate fact tables instead of the base fact table are _____ and _____.

14. The collection of related star schemas is called a _____ schema.

15. _____ dimension is shared by most of the fact tables in the group.

16. The aggregate fact tables are derived using _____ from a single base fact table.

17. High level data model depicts different _____.

3. State true or false

1. The IPD acts as a cornerstone for the logical data design for the data warehouse.

2. ER diagram is a complex diagram that is used to represent a single business process.

3. ER model is designed to express macroscopic relationships between the data elements, whereas the key idea behind a DM model is to capture business measures.

4. Star schema is optimized for query and analysis.

5. Star schema allows every dimension table with its attributes to have an equal chance of participating in a query to analyse the attributes in the fact table.

6. Fact table contains information about the entries for a particular attribute in the fact table.

7. Star schema does not optimize navigation.

8. The star schema is a more complex data warehouse model than a snowflake schema.

9. Aggregates fact tables have much fewer rows than the base fact tables.

10. Aggregate fact tables must be re-aggregated every time there is a change in the source data to reflect those changes in the data warehouse.

11. Aggregate fact tables leads to a fact constellation schema.

Review Questions

1. Explain dimensional modelling.

2. Write a short note on star schema. Explain it with a relevant example. Mention some of its advantages and shortcomings.

3. How is data warehouse modelling different from that of operation systems? Differentiate between ER modelling and dimensional modelling.

4. List down the features of a fact table and a dimension table.

5. A fact table is deep and narrow, while a dimension table is wide. Justify.

6. Write a short note on factless fact table. Draw a star schema representing a factless fact table of a patient visiting a hospital.

7. Differentiate between fully-additive measures, semi-additive measures, and non-additive measures with example.

8. Can a fact table contain sparse data? If yes, how and if no, why?

9. What do you understand by surrogate keys? Why are they important in a data warehouse environment?

10. Draw a star schema using the hotel occupancy IPD discussed in the last chapter.

11. Draw star schemas of GlobalBook Inc. and Auctions.com. You have already designed IPDs for them as an exercise in the previous chapter.

Appendix 6.1

THE TRADITIONAL APPROACH

In the traditional approach, we will be forming the dimensional model using the ER diagram. For this purpose, let us take a sample ER diagram to see how an ER diagram can be used to design multidimensional databases.

But before going further with this approach, we will make some assumptions. First, we assume that the ER diagram does not contain generalization hierarchies. Second, we have only simple attributes. No attribute is composite or multi-valued. Third, the ER diagram represents a complete knowledge about the operational systems. Fourth, we assume that the ER diagram is fully normalized.

The ER diagram describes an integrated view of operational databases. The methodology to build an MD database from a pre-existing ER scheme consists of the following steps.

1. Identify the facts and dimensions.
2. Restructure the ER scheme.
3. Derive the dimensional graph.
4. Translate the dimensional graph into the MD model.

Although, the fist two steps may be performed sequentially or in parallel but the third and the fourth steps need to be performed in a sequential manner. In the process of restructuring of the ER scheme, selected facts and dimensions can be refined and modified.

Figure A6.1 describes the ER diagram of a retail database. The retail company has a chain of stores in which several products are sold. The database contains information about its frequent customers also.

Identify Facts and Dimensions

The ER diagram is carefully analysed to select the facts and the dimensions of interest. In the ER scheme, facts are considered to be the entities, attributes or relationships that are needed for making decisions. A measure, in turn is an atomic property of a fact that the user intends to analyse. In other words, a measure is a numeric attribute of a fact.

On the one hand, the end-user may be interested in analysing trends in the volume of sales and in the corresponding incomes and, on the other hand, he may wish to see the analysis of the variation of production costs on product's sale. Thus, the identified facts are- the attribute **price** of the entity product and the entity **sales**. Thus, the measures that we get for the sales

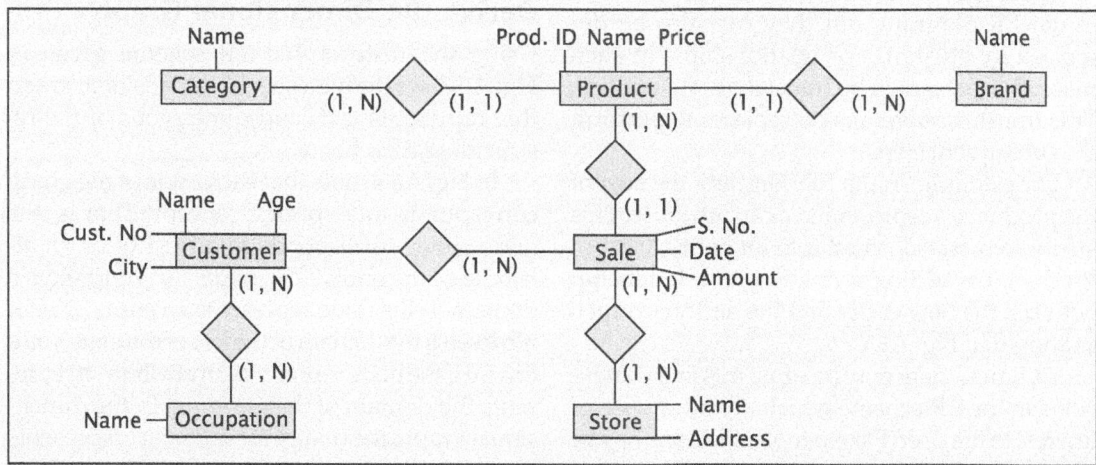

Figure A6.1 ER diagram of a retail database

entity are-number of sales (total count of the instances of the entity) and the amount of the sales (as represented by the attribute amount). However, there is only one measure for the former fact- the value of the price.

When we consider the fact entity sale, we see that each sale is related to the corresponding product sold and each product is in turn related to the corresponding category and brand. This means that the sales can be analysed according to the types of product sold at different levels of aggregation (single product, category of products, brand). Thus, the product dimension is an obvious dimension for analysing the sales. This dimension includes the entities product, brand, and category.

In our database since we already have information about the related customer; customers can be grouped by age, city of residence and occupation. Hence, the other dimension for the analysis is customer. According to the ER diagram, the customer dimension includes the entities customer and occupation.

Restructure the ER Scheme

This step reorganizes the original ER scheme in order to describe facts and dimensions in a better, more explicit way. The basic motive of this step is to generate a new ER scheme that can be directly mapped to the MD model.

Although, facts correspond to entities of the initial ER diagram, but they can also be described by attributes or relationships. In such cases, the facts must be translated into entities. This transformation makes it easier to perform the subsequent steps.

For example, in the ER diagram, the cost of the products is represented as an attribute. This attribute is transformed into an entity, Cost of Product, by adding a one-to-one relationship between the new entity and the entity product, as shown in Fig. A6.2.

At times, there may be some missing dimensions in the ER scheme which are otherwise of interest to the user. For example, the user may be interested in temporal validity of a fact or in the geographical origin of the fact. These types of dimensions must be included for analysis.

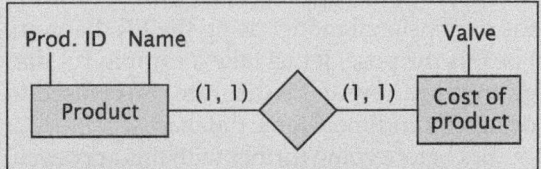

Figure A6.2

On similar grounds, the location of the sales is another possible dimension for analysis. Thus, the store entity will be made another dimension which will describe the location using the attributes name and address.

Within each dimension we have various levels of aggregations that are of interest for analysis. We need to represent even these levels within the dimensions explicitly. For example, let us consider the time dimension. The user may like to aggregate the sales in the entire month, quarter or year. In the diagram, this can be done by adding entities and one-to-many relationships as shown in Fig. A6.3. Same is the case with the store dimension. We will make new entities for city and area. When all the dimensions are analysed in this way, we get the ER scheme as given in Fig. A6.3.

Derive the Dimensional Graph

Using the restructured ER scheme given in Fig. A6.3, we derive a special dimensional graph that represents facts and dimensions of the restructured ER scheme.

In Fig. A6.4, note that each node of the graph corresponds to a specific concept. That is, the node either corresponds to an entity or an attribute of the entity. The node also represents a domain. If the node represents an entity, then it represents the domain of the key of the entity, otherwise if the node represents an attribute, it represents the domain of the attribute. In the dimensional graph, the node *Cost of Product* represents

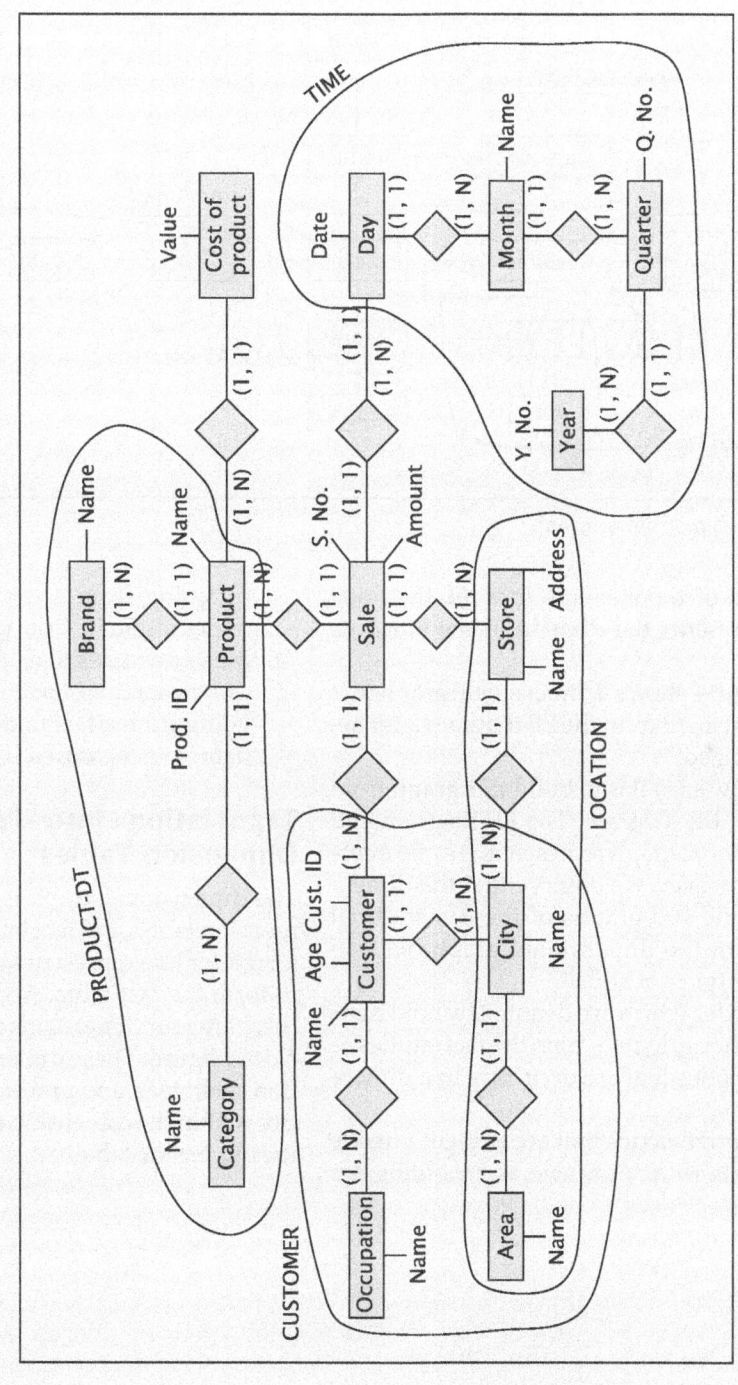

Figure A6.3 Restructured ER scheme

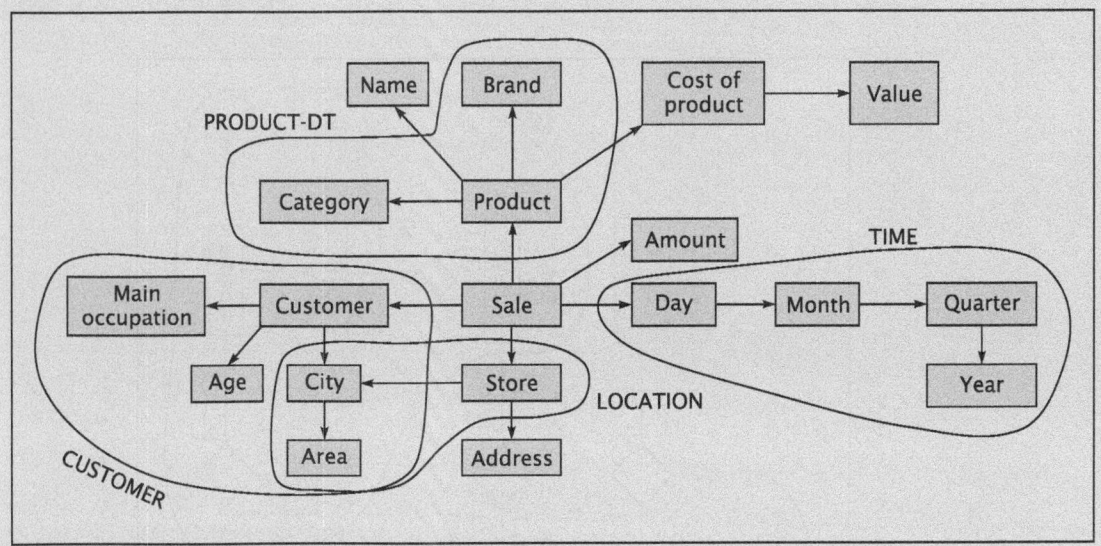

Figure A6.4 Dimensional graph

the domain of the attribute *Prod_Id*, the node *Month* represents the domain of the attribute *Name*

Figure A6.4 shows a dimensional graph that has been obtained from the ER diagram after being reorganized.

Note how easy it is to build this graph from the original ER diagram. The ER diagram and the dimensional graph represent the same information. However, we observe that the dimensions become sub-graphs of the dimensional graph. From the dimensional graph, we can obtain four types of nodes:

1. Fact nodes which are denoted by bold margins. They originate from the fact entities.
2. Level nodes that are occurring in a dimension
3. Descriptive nodes that are present outside the dimension and have an incoming arc outgoing from a level node. Descriptive nodes originate from descriptive attributes
4. Measure nodes that are present outside the dimension and have an incoming arc outgoing from a fact node. These nodes originate from measures.

Translation into Fact Tables and Dimension Tables

The dimensional graph is used to form the dimension tables and fact tables. The entities with a broader line represent facts. So it will be used to form the fact table. According to the figure, there are four dimensions represented by an enclosed figure. These dimensions are time, location, customer, and product. The individual entity within the dimension forms the attribute of the dimension table.

7

DIMENSIONAL MODELLING

Learning Objectives

The study of dimensional modelling would be incomplete until we go into further details to discuss some advanced topics. In the star schema, the dimension tables allow the data warehouse users to analyse the data in many different ways. So, it is important to have an in-depth knowledge of these dimension tables.

In this chapter, we will differentiate rapidly changing and slowly changing dimension tables. How do we handle these dimension tables? What are the different types of fact tables and dimension tables? Let us explore dimensional modelling to find out the answers.

Case Study

In Chapter 2, we have discussed about data granularity. If we keep data at a high level of details in the data warehouse, then any query can be answered from it. Hence, detailed level data gives maximum flexibility of executing data warehouse queries.

Bearing this in mind, Pallav Raj, the CEO of JRTs decides to keep a detailed level of data in the data warehouse. But when the data warehouse was deployed, it was observed that query performance had degraded and it was taking a long time to execute those queries that demanded data at lower levels of detail.

For example, if Pallav Raj wanted to see the daily sales of T-shirts of a particular brand, then answering this query becomes very simple and straight forward as all the data that

is needed is present in the database. But when he tries to look at the sales of the same T-shirt in the first quarter of the previous year, then imagine first the data of approximately 90 rows has to be fetched, added together to produce a cumulative result, and then displayed on screen. This process takes time and thus, increases the query response time.

Now, if Pallav Raj, wants to see just one figure describing the total sales of that T-shirt in the previous year, then 365 rows have to be fetched to produce the results. Imagine the delay in response that would then be created. If the database contains millions of rows, fetching 365 rows, then manipulating them to produce the desired result set takes a huge amount of time.

Therefore, to solve this problem, aggregate fact tables are used in which we store aggregate/summarized data. In the data warehouse database, we store two types of tables—base fact table and aggregate fact table, where the base table will store detailed data (daily records). This provides maximum efficiency and flexibility in executing queries, as all the queries demanding detailed data would be switched to the base fact table and queries demanding less detailed data would be switched over to the aggregate fact table.

7.1 CHARACTERISTICS OF A DIMENSION TABLE

Dimension tables contain descriptions that data analysts use as they query the database. For example, the store dimension table contains store names and addresses; the product table contains product, its brand, colour, and packaging information; and the time dimension table contains month, quarter, and year values. Every row in the dimension table is uniquely identified by a primary key which is composed of one or more columns. In this section we will see some features of a dimension table.

Dimension table key The primary key of the dimension table is used to uniquely identify each row in the table.

Table is wide Generally, a dimension table has many columns or attributes. Some dimension tables may have more than 50 attributes. Therefore, the dimension table is said to be wide as if you lay it out as a table with columns and rows, the table is spread out horizontally.

Textual attributes A dimension table will hardly contain any numerical value. The attributes in a dimension table are of textual format that represent the textual descriptions of the components within the business dimensions. These descriptors will be used by the users to compose their queries.

Attributes not directly related Many a times, some of the attributes in a dimension table are not directly related to the other attributes in the table. For example, package colour is not directly related to product exterior colour, but still both these attributes could be a part of the product dimension table.

Not normalized The attributes in a dimension table are used to constrain queries. For efficient query performance, it is best if the query picks up the value of an attribute from the dimension table and then takes the corresponding data directly from the fact table and not through other intermediary tables. By normalizing the dimension tables, there will be a number of such intermediary tables created which will make query processing thereby inefficient. Therefore, a dimension table is not normalized.

Drilling-down, rolling-up The attributes in a dimension table enables the users to get to the details from higher levels of aggregation to lower levels of details. For example, the three attributes month, quarter, and year form a hierarchy. The business analyst may get the total sales by year, then drill-down to total sales by quarter and then by every individual month. Going the other way, the analyst may first get the totals by month, and then roll-up totals by quarter and year.

Multiple hierarchies   As in the example given above, there is a hierarchy going up from month, quarter, and finally to year. Practically speaking, dimension tables often provide for multiple hierarchies, so that drilling-down may be performed along any of the multiple hierarchies. For example, the other hierarchy could be day, week, month, quarter, and country. Now you may perform analysis along any hierarchy.

Fewer number of records   Generally, a dimension table has fewer number of records or rows when compared with fact tables. For example, a product dimension table may have just 500 rows, but the fact table which represents its daily sales may contain millions of rows.

7.2 CHARACTERISTICS OF A FACT TABLE

Fact tables contain the factual details of business events. They are often very large and contain hundreds of millions of rows thereby consuming hundreds of gigabytes or multiple terabytes of storage. While dimension tables contain records that describe facts, the fact table contains foreign keys (primary keys of the dimension table), and numeric fact values.

The measures that a fact table contains are quantitative or factual data about the subject. These are numeric measures that correspond to the *how much* or *how many* aspects of a question. Examples of measures are product cost in dollars, product sales units, product profit margin, and so forth. In this section we will see some features of a fact table.

Concatenated key   Every row in the fact table is directly related to the rows in all the dimension tables. For example, you find unit sales as an attribute of the fact table, which is measured along the dimensions product, time, customer, and store. If the lowest levels in the dimension hierarchies are individual product, a calendar date, a specific customer, and a single store, then a single row in the fact table contains data about a particular product, a specific calendar date, a specific customer, and an individual sales representative. Thus, every row in the fact table must be identified by the primary keys of all the dimension tables. Hence, the primary key of the fact table is nothing but a concatenation of the primary keys of all the dimension tables.

Data grain   Data grain means the level of detail for the measurements or metrics. In our example, the metrics are stored at the detailed level as the sales unit is a number related to the quantity of a particular product on a single order, on a certain date, for a specific customer and sold in a specific store. However, if we keep the sales units as the quantity of a specific product for each quarter, then the data grain is said to be at a higher level.

Fully additive measures Let us look at the attributes sales_dollars, and sales_units. Both these facts represent the data about a particular product on a certain date for a specific customer sold in an individual store. But if the user poses a query that wants the total sales for the particular product on a certain date, not for a specific customer, but for customers of a particular store, then we need to find all the rows in the fact table relating to all the customers of that store and add the sales_dollars, and sales_units to come up with the totals. The values of these attributes are obtained by simple addition. Such measures are known as fully additive measures. Thus, fully additive facts are facts that can be summed up through all of the dimensions in the fact table.

Semi-additive measures and non-additive measures Let us take an example of a fact table having attributes, cost_price_dollars, selling_price_dollars, and profit_dollars. Here profit_dollars can be derived or calculated from the first two attributes. That is, profit_dollars = selling_price_dollars – cost_price_dollars. Such attributes that can be derived from other attributes are called semi additive measures. Finally, measures which are neither fully additive nor semi-additive can be classified as non-additive measures.

Table deep, not wide Generally a fact table contains fewer attributes than a dimension table. The fact table will have only primary keys of the dimension tables and the facts as its columns. For example, if there are 3 facts to be analysed and 4 dimension tables, then the fact table will have 4 columns—one for every dimension table's key (4) and three columns for every fact (3). It is not uncommon for fact tables to have 10 attributes or less. But the number of records in it is very large.

Take a very simple example of 20 products, 500 customers, 30 days, and 3 stores represented as rows in the dimension table. Even in this example, the number of rows in the fact table will be 9,00,000 which is very large in comparison to the number of rows in a dimension table. Thus, the structure of a fact is narrow with a small number of columns but very large number of rows.

Sparse data When the data is stored at the lowest level of granularity, then every single row in the fact table relates to a particular product, a specific calendar date, a specific customer and an individual store. In other words, there is a corresponding row in the fact table for every product, date, customer and store.

Just imagine, what will happen when the date represents a closed holiday and no orders are received and processed. The fact table rows for such dates will not have any value for the facts. There is no need for such data to be kept in the fact table. Therefore, it is important to realize this type of sparse data and understand that the fact table could have gaps.

7.3 THE FACTLESS FACT TABLE

A fact table is said to be *empty* if it has no measures. It is designed to only record the occurrence of events.

In the previous section, we have said that the fact table contains numeric values or facts stored in them but some fact tables do not have any facts at all and they may consist of nothing but keys. These are called factless fact tables. Such fact tables are used to record events. Thus, many event-tracking tables in data warehouses are rather factless fact tables. An example is given below. Imagine that you have a modern student tracking system that detects each student attendance event each day. The dimensions for tracking the attendance include the following:

- Date: one record per calendar date.
- Student: one record per student.
- Course: one record per course taught in each semester.
- Teacher: one record per teacher.
- Facility: one record per every room, laboratory, or athletic field.

As shown in Fig. 7.1, the grain of the fact table represents the attendance of every individual student. It is assumed that when the student walks through the door into the lecture, a record is generated. In this example, the fact table records would contain only five keys (primary keys of the five dimensional tables). The dimension tables contain all the necessary details of the student attendance event.

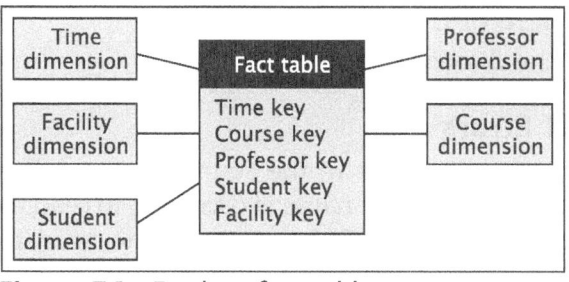

Figure 7.1 Factless fact table

The factless fact table has no obvious fact to record each time a student attends a lecture. This may give the feeling of some missing data because the table contains no data but keys. The importance of a factless table can not be under estimated. Such a table can be used to answer many interesting questions like the classes which were most heavily attended, most consistently attended, the teachers who taught the most students, etc.

7.4 UPDATES TO THE DIMENSION TABLES

We all know that over time, the fact table will keep growing with every new transaction that takes place. For example, every day with the occurrence of every individual sales transaction, new rows will get added to the fact table. However, fact table rows are generally not updated with changes. In case there are some adjustments to be made to the prior data stored, these are also processed as additional adjustment rows and added to the fact table.

Let us now consider dimension tables. When compared with the fact table, dimension tables tend to be more stable and less volatile. The fact table changes through the increase in the number of rows. A dimension table on the other hand, not only changes just through the increase in number of rows, but also through changes to the attributes themselves. In this section, we will study how the dimension tables change and what method is applied to handle such changes in the data warehouse.

7.4.1 Slowly Changing Dimensions

As stated earlier, a characteristic of dimensions is that data in dimension tables is relatively more stable because data may be added as new products (in product's dimension table) are released or customers are acquired, but data, such as the names of existing products and customers, changes infrequently. However, in real world scenario, business events do occur that causes changes in dimension attributes, and the effects of these changes on the data warehouse must be managed.

"Slowly changing dimensions" is the customary term used for managing issues associated with the impact of changes to attributes of a dimension table. Design approaches that deal with the issues of slowly changing dimensions are commonly categorized into the following three change types:

- Type 1: Overwrite the dimension record.
- Type 2: Add a new dimension record.
- Type 3: Create new fields in the dimension record.

Type 1 Changes: Correction of Errors

Type 1 changes relate to the correction of errors in the source systems. For example, suppose a spelling error in the customer name is corrected to read as July Michael from the erroneous entry of July Michel. There is no need to preserve the old values. Since the old name is erroneous, it must be discarded. When the users need to find all the orders from July Michael, the users will use the correct name. To summarize:

- These changes relate to correction of errors in source systems.
- These changes do not have any significance in the source systems.
- The old value needs to be discarded.
- New value overwrites the old value in the source systems.
- Such changes in the source system need not be preserved in the data warehouse.

Figure 7.2 illustrates the method for applying Type 1 changes. Now let us see how Type 1 changes are applied to the data stored in the warehouse.

- Overwrite the value of the attribute with the new value in the dimension table row.
- The old value of the attribute is discarded, that is, not preserved.

- No other changes are made in the dimension table row.
- The key of this dimension table row is not affected.

These type of changes are the easiest to implement.

Customer key	Customer ID	Customer name	Marital status	Address
–	–	–	–	–
22522134	C12345	July Michael	Single	AAAAAAA
–	–	–	–	–

Incremental load

Customer ID: C12345
Customer name: July Michael

Customer key	Customer ID	Customer name	Marital status	Address
–	–	–	–	–
22522134	C12345	July Michel	Single	AAAAAAA
–	–	–	–	–

Figure 7.2 Method for applying Type 1 change

Type 2 Changes: Preservation of History

Type 2 changes cause history to be partitioned at the event that triggered the change. Data prior to the event continues to be summarized and analysed as before; new data is summarized and analysed in accordance with the new value of the data.

Take the example of a customer, Jenny David, whose marital status has changed, this cannot be handled as a Type 1 change because in the data warehouse one of the essential requirements may be to track orders by marital status in addition to tracking by other attributes. If the change to marital status happened on 16 January 2006, all orders from Jenny David before that date must be included under marital status: single, and all orders on or after 16 January 2006, should be included under marital status: married. Hence, in the data warehouse, there must be a way of separating the orders for the customer so that the orders before and after that date can be added separately. The type of change for marital status and customer address are Type 2 changes. To summarize:

- These changes relate to true changes in source system.
- The history must be preserved in the data warehouse.
- These changes cause the history to be partitioned in the data warehouse.
- Every change that occurs in the attribute value must be preserved.

Now let us see how Type 2 changes are applied to the data stored in the warehouse.

- A new dimension table row with the new value of the changed attribute is added.
- A new column called the effective date is added in the dimension table.
- The original row in the dimension table is not changed.

- The key of the original row remains the same.
- The new row is inserted with a new surrogate key in the dimension table.

Figure 7.3 illustrates the method for applying Type 2 changes.

Customer key	Customer ID	Customer name	Marital status	Address
-	-	-	-	-
22522134	C12345	Jenny David	Single	AAAAAAA
-	-	-	-	-

Incremental load

Customer ID: C12345
Martial status: Married

Customer key	Customer ID	Customer name	Marital status	Address	Effective date
-	-	-	-	-	-
22522134	C12345	Jenny David	Single	AAAAAAA	1/Mar/03
-	-	-	-	-	-
11231234	C12345	Jenny David	Married	AAAAAAA	16/Jan/06
-	-	-	-	-	-

Figure 7.3 Method for applying Type 2 change

Type 3 changes: Tentative Soft Revisions

Type 3 solutions track changes horizontally in the dimension table by adding fields to contain the old data as well as the new data. In Type 2 changes, we have seen that only the original and current values are retained and intermediate values are discarded. Type 3 changes are applied when the intermediary values are also required. The advantage of Type 3 solutions is the avoidance of multiple dimension records for a single entity. However, the disadvantage is complexity of queries.

Generally, most of the changes to dimension values are either Type 1 or Type 2 changes where Type 1 changes are even more common. We have studied that Type 2 changes preserve the history. When a Type 2 change is applied on a certain date, then that date is treated as the cut-off point. The queries will either take older data or new data but not both. For example, if the marital status of Jenny David changed on 16 January 2006, then any orders placed by the customers before 16 January will fall into older data group and any after this date will fall into the newer dataset. That is, either the order will belong to older data or new data, but not both.

Can you imagine, how will you count the orders on or after the cut-off date in both groups during a certain period after the cut-off date? No, this change can not be treated as a Type 2 change because here you have to keep track of both the old and new values of changed attributes for a certain period. These types of changes are Type 3 changes.

Type 3 changes are tentative or soft changes. Let us take an example to understand it better. Assume that the manager is trying to reset the price value of a book. But before making a permanent change in the price, he may want to count the sales of the book according to the current price and also according to the proposed price. This type of provisional or tentative change is a Type 3 change. To summarize:

- There is a need to track history with both old and new values of the same attribute.
- Type 3 changes are used to compare performance across the transition.
- They enable the users to track data in both forward and backward directions.

Now let us see how Type 3 changes are applied to the data stored in the warehouse.

- An "old" field is added in the dimension table for the affected attribute.
- The existing value of the attribute is pushed down from the "current" field to the "old" field.
- The new value of the attribute is kept in the "current" field.
- A "current" effective date field is also added for the changed attribute.
- The key of the row is not affected.
- No new dimension row is added in the dimension table.
- The existing queries will automatically switch to the "current" value.
- Revision must be done to queries that need to use the "old" value.
- This technique works well with one soft change at a time and if there are a succession of changes, more sophisticated techniques must be devised.

Figure 7.4 describes the method for applying Type 3.

Salesperson key	Salesperson ID	Salesperson name	Old location	Current location	Effective date
–	–	–	–	–	–
22522134	S001	Jenny David	–	Delhi	1/Mar/03
–	–	–	–	–	–

After applying Type 3 change, we have:

Salesperson key	Salesperson ID	Salesperson name	Old location	Current location	Effective date
–	–	–	–	–	–
22522134	S001	Jenny David	Delhi	Mumbai	16/Jan/06
–	–	–	–	–	–

Figure 7.4 Method for applying type 3 changes

7.4.2 Example

Table 7.1(a) is a product dimension table that contains four attributes namely, Product ID which is the primary key, launch year in which the product was brought into the market, name which specifies the name of the product and finally product price which tells the price of the product. As shown in Table 7.1(a), in the year 2005, the price of Product 1 was Rs 350 which later on changed to Rs 450. With this information, let us consider the three types of Slowly Changing Dimensions.

Table 7.1(a) Product price in 2005

Product ID (PK)	Launch Year	Product Name	Product Price
P01	2005	Product 1	Rs 350

Type 1: Overwriting the Old Values

Let us assume that in the year 2006, the price of the product changed from Rs 350 to Rs 450, then the old values of the columns "Year" and "Product Price" must be updated to contain the new values. If we consider it as a Type 1 change then there we cannot find out the old value of the product "Product 1" in year 2005 as the table now stores only the new values for these attributes. The updated table is given in Table 7.1(b).

Table 7.1(b) Type 1 change applied to the original table

Product ID (PK)	Launch Year	Product Name	Product Price
P01	2006	Product 1	Rs 450

Type 2: Creating Another Additional Record

However, if we treat it as a Type 2 change, then the old values will not be discarded. Rather, an additional row containing the new values of the changed attributes will be added to the product dimension table. So the old values and new values can be retrieved and compared any time the user wants. This could be useful for reporting, querying and analysis purposes. The updated table is given as Table 7.1(c).

Table 7.1(c) contains as error because the field product ID is the primary key of the product dimension table, and thus, it cannot store duplicate values. Also, this table does not specify the effective date of Product 1, so how will the users know when the change took place. Therefore, Table 7.1(c) must be changed to avoid primary key violation.

Table 7.1(c) Type 2 change applied to the original table

Product ID (PK)	Launch Year	Product Name	Product Price
P01	2005	Product 1	Rs 350
P01	2006	Product 1	Rs 450

In Table 7.1(d), the primary key is a combination of two fields: Product ID and Effective Date, thereby forming a composite primary key. Now there is no violation of primary key constraint. Also, the addition of the Effective Date column will provide the information about the product's effective date that denotes the date from which changes have been applied. Type 2 changes occupy more space in the data warehouse, since for every changed record an additional row has to be created.

Table 7.1(d) Rectified table

Product ID (PK)	Effective Date (PK)	Launch Year	Product Name	Product Price
P01	01-01-2005 12.00 AM	2005	Product 1	Rs 350
P01	01-01-2006 12.00 AM	2006	Product 1	Rs 450

Note that in Table 7.1(d), we have not used any surrogate key. Rather, we have made the combination of Product-ID and Effective-Date as the primary key of the product dimension table. This is an alternative to using surrogate keys. However, this option is rarely used.

Type 3: Creating New Fields

However, if we treat this change as a Type 3 change then the latest update to the changed values will also be stored. Table 7.1(e) shows the way in which we manage to keep track of changes. Look carefully, the table stores both the current price and the older price of the product, Product 1.

Table 7.1(e) Tpye 3 change applied to the original table

Product ID(PK)	Current Year	Product Name	Current Price	Old Price	Old Year
P01	2006	Product 1	Rs 450	Rs 350	2005

The problem with the Type 3 approach is that if the product price changes several times, then the complete history may not be stored and only the latest change will be visible to the users. For example, Table 7.1(f) shows that in year 2007, if Product 1's price changes to Rs 550, then we would not be able to see the complete history from 2005, since the old values would have been updated with 2006 product information of 2006.

Table 7.1(f) Type 3 change applied to Table 7.1(e)

Product ID(PK)	Year	Product Name	Current Price	Old Price	Old Year
P01	2007	Product 1	Rs 550	Rs 450	2006

7.5 CYCLICITY OF DATA—THE WRINKLE OF TIME

The cyclicity of data means the time elapsed between a change of data in the operational system and reflection of that change in the data warehouse. For example, if the customer name was edited in the operational system on 5 June 2008 at 12 PM and this change was reflected in the data warehouse on 6 June 8 AM, then cyclicity of data is 20 hours.

Once there is a change in data stored in the operational system, it must be reflected in the data warehouse as well. As a rule, at least 24 hours can pass between the reflection of change in the data warehouse and occurrence of change in the operational system. We should never rush to apply the change in the data warehouse database. This wrinkle of time is necessary due to several reasons.

First, tight coupling between the data warehouse and operational systems calls for the application of expensive and complex technology. A 24 hour wrinkle time can easily be provided with the conventional technology. Although a 12 hour and 6 hour wrinkle time is not difficult to achieve but then it calls for a greater cost in technology. Second, the wrinkle of time provides sufficient time for the data to settle before it is moved in the data warehouse. Any necessary adjustments that have to be made, transformations that have to be done can be done before the data is moved to the data warehouse.

7.6 OTHER TYPES OF DIMENSION TABLES

After considering the types of changes to the dimension attributes and the procedure to handle them, we will now discuss other issues. Previously, we have stated that dimensional attributes do not change frequently. But in practicality, some dimensional attributes change many times. In case these attributes are handled as Type 2 changes, then for every change an additional row will be created in the dimension table and that dimension will no longer be a slowly changing dimension table. In this section, we will take up these issues in detail.

7.6.1 Large Dimensions

A dimension table is said to be large based on two factors. A large dimension may either be deep or wide. A deep dimension table has a very large number of rows and a wide dimension may have a large number of attributes. In either case, the dimension table is said to be large. There are special considerations for large dimensions. You need to handle populating large dimension tables in a special way by separating out some mini-dimensions from a large dimension.

When a data warehouse is designed for a company that deals with general public, the customer and product dimensions are likely to be very large. The customer dimension table may even approach the size of the number of households in the country and may have as many as 100 million rows. The number of dimension table rows of companies in telecommunications, retail and travel industries may also run in millions.

A large dimension is a serious consideration issue. Due to its sheer size, query processing that involves large dimensions would become slow and inefficient. Therefore, effective design methods involving building of indexes and applying other optimizing techniques must be used.

7.6.2 Rapidly Changing Dimensions

A rapidly changing dimension is the dimension in which one or more of its attributes changes frequently in many rows. When a series of Type 2 changes are applied to a rapidly changing dimension, the dimension table can grow very large. Thus, it can be concluded that the terms "rapid" and "large" are relative. For example, a customer table with 1,00,000 rows and an average of 3 changes per customer per year will grow to about million rows in 10 years (provided the number of customers does not grow).

The solution for a dimension with rapidly changing attributes is to break the frequently changing attributes out of the dimension and create one or more new dimension. For example, an important attribute for customers might be their loan payment status (good, late, very late), and the history of their loan status. Over a period of time, many customers will move from one of these status to another.

Therefore, if this attribute is a part of the customer dimension table and a Type 2 change is applied each time the loan status of a customer changes, then new row will be added every time. The solution here is to create a separate loan_status dimension with four members to represent the different states.

Take another example. Let us assume that the product dimension changes once or twice a year. If the number of rows in dimension table is less, say about 10,000 or so, applying a Type 2 change by creating additional rows with new values of the attributes is easily manageable. But in a customer dimension, there are large number of rows, may be in some millions. When significant attributes of the dimension table change several times in a year; rapidly changing large dimensions become very problematic for the Type 2 approach.

The most effective approach to handle rapidly changing large dimension tables is to break the large dimension table into one or more dimension tables. The dimension table is broken by storing the rapidly changing attributes into another dimension table, leaving the slowly changing attributes behind in the original table. Figure 7.5 illustrates how a customer dimension table may be separated into two dimension tables.

7.6.3 Junk Dimensions

When we design for a data warehouse and review the individual fields in source data structures for customer, product, order, sales territories, promotional campaigns, etc., we include most of these fields in the dimension tables. However, some fields like miscellaneous flags and textual fields are left in the source data. These include yes/no flags, textual codes, and free form texts.

Some of these flags and textual data may be too obscure to be of real value. Nevertheless, many of these data elements could be of value once in a while in queries. On one hand, they cannot be included as significant fields in the major dimension tables and on the other hand, these flags and texts cannot be discarded.

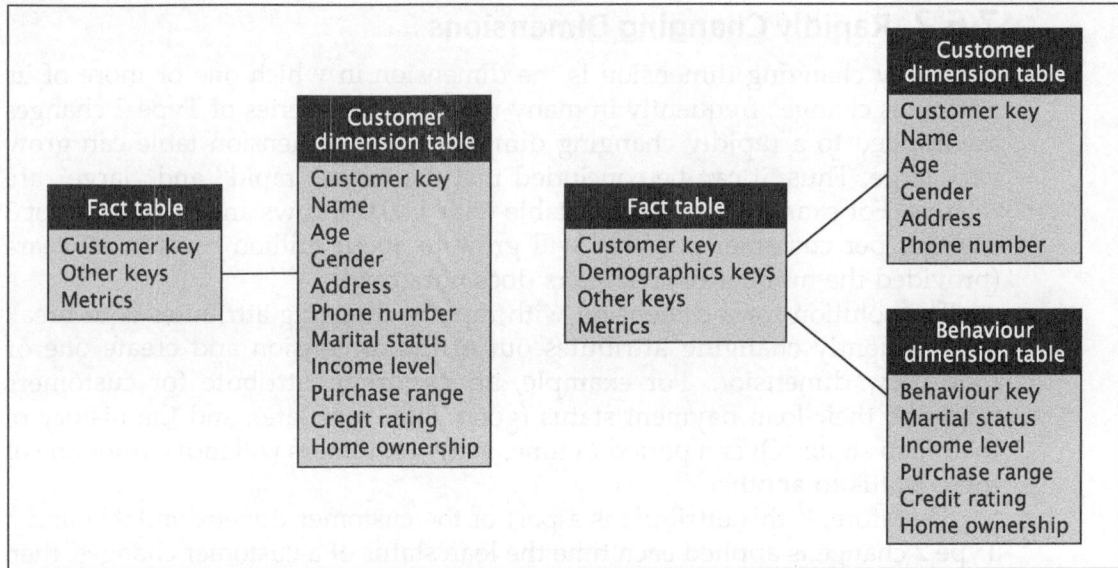

Figure 7.5 Dividing a rapidly changing dimension table

You are left with the following design choices to handle individual data items:

- The first option is to exclude and discard all flags and texts. But as discussed above, it is not a good option as you may throw away some useful information.
- The second option is to store the flags and texts in the fact table. But it is also not a good one, as it will increase the size of the fact table.
- The third option is to make each flag and text a separate dimension table on its own. Again this is not a good one either, as it would increase the number of dimension tables.
- Thus, the best viable option is to keep only those flags and texts that are meaningful, group all the useful flags into a single "junk" dimension. Junk dimension attributes will be useful for constraining queries based on flag/text values.

7.7 KEYS IN THE DATA WAREHOUSE (STAR) SCHEMA

Keys play a crucial role of providing an identity to the data contained in the table or maintaining relationships among tables.

7.7.1 Primary Keys

Each row in a dimension table is uniquely identified by an attribute designated as the primary key of the dimension. For example, in a customer dimension table, the primary key (customer_id) identifies each individual customer uniquely. In the product dimension table, the product_key identifies every product uniquely. Similarly, in the sales representative dimension table, the employee_id or the salesperson_key or the social security number of the sales representative can be used to identify every sales representative.

7.7.2 Surrogate Keys

Before discussing surrogate keys, let us first try to find out whether we can use production system keys as primary keys of dimension tables and if not, what are other candidate keys? Answering these questions will help you to choose appropriate primary keys for dimension tables.

We know that the primary key has in-built meanings in the operational system. For example, consider Fig. 7.6 which shows the individual components that join together to form the primary key of a product dimension table.

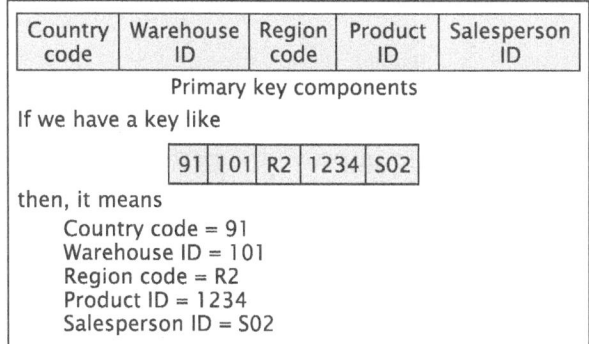

Figure 7.6 Primary key of operation table

Thus, we see that operational system's primary keys have built in meanings.

Now, in future if you change the warehouse of the product for some or the other reason, the primary key will change as warehouse ID is a part of the primary key.

We cannot keep the primary key of the operational system as the primary key of the data warehouse system as it may change every now and then.

Consider a second scenario. In companies, customers may not be loyal to one particular company, as they may keep changing their company of choice. It is not uncommon that the customer numbers of discontinued customers are reassigned to other new customers of the company. Now, in case we had stored the operational system customer key as the primary key for the customer dimension table in the data warehouse, a major problem could occur as the same customer number would relate to data of the new as well as the old customer. This will give erroneous results in analysis. Therefore, the second principle is: do not use production system keys as primary keys for dimension tables.

It is now very clear that we cannot use the primary keys of the operational system as the primary key of the dimension table. Then, what should we use as primary keys for dimension tables? The answer to this question is surrogate keys. Surrogate keys are system generated sequence numbers that do not have any built-in meanings. They will be mapped to the operational system keys. For mapping the keys, the operational system primary keys will also be stored as attributes in the dimension tables. To summarize:

- Creation and usage of surrogate keys in the dimension tables is one of the most crucial aspect of data warehouse design.
- A surrogate key is the primary key for a dimension table.

- A surrogate key is independent of operational system keys.
- Surrogate keys do not have built-in meanings.
- The operational system primary key is also stored in the dimension table but is not used as the primary key of the data warehouse dimension tables.
- Every join between dimension tables and fact tables should be made using surrogate keys.

7.7.3 Foreign Keys

As already discussed in the star schema, every dimension table has one-to-many relationship with the central fact table. To maintain the relationship, the primary key of each dimension table is stored as a foreign key in the fact table. We will discuss this in detail later in this chapter.

7.8 ENHANCING THE DATA WAREHOUSE PERFORMANCE

In this section, we will study some techniques to improve the performance of a data warehouse. For example, compaction of the data while writing to the storage space allows more data to be loaded into a single block. That also means more data can be read in a single read operation. Another technique of improving performance is the merging of tables so that more data can be read within a single read operation. Regular purging of unwanted and unnecessary data from the data warehouse also enhances performance. So let us study additional methods of boosting performance in a data warehouse environment.

7.8.1 Table Compression

Data warehouse systems usually involve large amounts of data stored in a few very large tables. As these systems evolve, there can be an escalating demand on the disk space required. In today's environment, data warehouses of hundreds of terabytes have become the norm.

For disk capacity management, the table compression feature introduced in Oracle 9i Release 2 can significantly reduce the amount of disk space used by database tables and thereby improve query performance in some cases.

The table compression feature that operates at the database block levels works by eliminating duplicate data values found in database tables. When a table is defined to be compressed, the database reserves space in each database block to store single copies of data that appear in multiple places within that block. This reserved space is known as the symbol table. Data tagged for compression is stored only in the symbol table and not in the database rows. When the data tagged for compression appears in a database row, the row stores a pointer to the relevant data in the symbol table, instead of the data record itself. The space of the disk block is saved by eliminating redundant copies of data values in the table.

The process of table compression is made transparent to the user or the application developer. Developers access a table the same way irrespective of whether a table is compressed or not. Therefore, the SQL queries do not have to change once you decide to compress a table. Table compression settings are usually configured and managed by database administrators with little intervention of the application developers or the users.

To create a compressed table, use the COMPRESS keyword in the CREATE TABLE statement. The COMPRESS keyword directs the database to store rows in the table in a compressed format wherever possible. Given below is an example of the CREATE TABLE COMPRESS statement:

```
CREATE TABLE SALES_TRANSACTION_HISTORY_COMP(
    PRODUCT_ID VARCHAR2(50) NOT NULL,
    STORE_ID VARCHAR2(50) NOT NULL,
    SALES_DATE DATE NOT NULL,
    QUANTITY_SOLD NUMBER(10,2) NOT NULL
)
COMPRESS;
```

You may also use the ALTER TABLE statement to change the compression attribute of an existing table, as in the following:

```
ALTER TABLE SALES_HISTORY_COMP COMPRESS;
```

In operational systems, data is usually inserted using regular inserts. As a result, these tables generally cannot draw much benefit from using table compression. Table compression works best on read-only tables that are loaded once but read many times. Thus, the tables stored in data warehouse database are good candidates for table compression. However, the main issue with this technique is that updating data in a compressed table requires rows to be uncompressed, thereby defeating the purpose of compression. Therefore, tables that require frequent updates are not suitable candidates for table compression.

7.8.2 Parallel Execution

Consider a query that accesses huge volumes of data, performs summations, and then makes a selection based on multiple constraints. To enhance performance, the processing can be split into components and then these components are executed in parallel. The simultaneous concurrent executions produce faster results. Parallel processing features are transparent to the users. As a query designer, the user need not know the details of breaking down his query for parallel processing. The chosen DBMS must enable the user to avail the benefits of this feature.

Parallel processing techniques work in conjunction with the data partitioning scheme and are extensively applied in data loading and data reorganization. The server hardware has a parallel architecture that strongly influences the way parallel processing options must be invoked.

Parallel Processing Options

The database software offers parallel processing options only for machines with multiple processors. A majority of the database software present in the market today can parallelize a large number of operations like mass loading of data, query execution, aggregation, sorting, creating indexes, inserting rows from other tables, and so on.

Let us try to learn what happens when a user initiates a query sitting at his workstation. Every query session uses a server process to access the database. The query is first sent to the DBMS, then the data is retrieved from the database and the results are sent back, all under the control of the dedicated server process. In this whole procedure, the query dispatcher software does the job of splitting the work, distributing the units to be performed among the available query server processes and balancing the load. Finally, the result sets obtained by executing the query are assembled and returned as one single, consolidated result.

Interquery parallelization   In this method, several server processes handle multiple queries simultaneously thereby increasing the throughput and supporting more concurrent users. However, interquery parallelization is very limited. Although, multiple queries are processed concurrently in this approach, each query is actually being processed serially by a single server process. Suppose a query consists of index read, data read, sort and join operations; these operations are carried out in the same sequence where each operation must finish before the next one can begin. In this approach, parts of the same query do not execute in parallel.

Intraquery parallelization   In this technique, the DBMS performs two main functions. It first splits the query into the lower level operations of index read, data read, data join, and data sort and then executes each one of these basic operations parallely on a single processor. The final result set is obtained by consolidating the intermediary results. The basic approach is parallelization of parts of the operations within the same query itself.

Horizontal parallelization   Horizontal parallelization is best suited for the systems where the data is partitioned across multiple disks. In this approach, parallel processing happens within each single task in the query. Take the example of data read operation that is performed on multiple processors concurrently on different datasets that have to be read from multiple disks. On the completion of the first task from all of the relevant parts of the partitioned data, the next task of that query is accomplished, and then the next one is completed. The main pitfall of this approach is the wait time involved until all the needed data is read.

Vertical parallelism   Unlike horizontal parallelism in which parallelism occurs on a single task in vertical parallelism, it is practiced among different tasks. All the query operations are executed in parallel, but in a pipelined manner. This technique can be practiced only if the RDBMS has the built in capability to decompose the query into subtasks where each subtask has all the operations of index read, join, and sort. Then each subtask is executed serially on the dataset.

In this approach, once the database records are ideally processed by one step then they are immediately given to the next step for processing thereby avoiding the wait times. Thus, to implement this approach, the DBMS must posses a very high level of sophistication in decomposing tasks.

Hybrid method   In this method, the query decomposer partitions the query both horizontally and vertically thereby producing the best results. Greatest utilization of resources, optimal performance, and high scalability are the advantages of this approach.

7.8.3 Table Partitioning

Assume that the data warehouse contains five dimension tables with approximately 100 rows in each table. Although the number of rows in a dimension table will be limited, the potential number of records in the fact table may be in some millions. Fact tables contain a very large number of records as compared to dimension tables. The problem with large tables is that they are not easy to manage and the entire table has to be closed for the users during the loading process. Apart from this, backup and recovery of large tables pose difficulties because of their sheer size.

Typically, a data warehouse contains large tables and some of them may contain millions of rows. Many problems exist with handling of large tables. First, loading of large tables becomes a very time consuming process. Second, creating indexes for such large tables is another time consuming task. Third, queries take longer time to run when attempting to process large volumes of data to obtain the result sets. Fourth, backing up and recovery of huge tables takes longer. Fifth, purging and archival of historical data also takes unexpectedly long time. So, it is always better to divide large tables into manageable chunks (Refer Fig. 7.7).

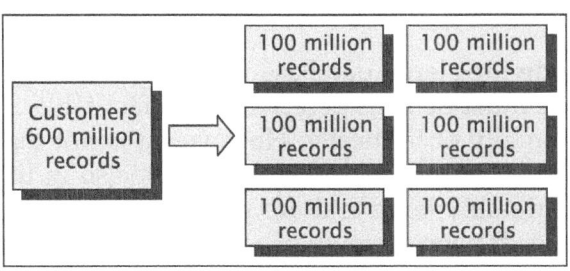

Figure 7.7   A large dimension table is partitioned into six smaller tables

Partitioning is a crucial decision and must be planned up front before the data warehouse is deployed. Partitioning is a technique that deliberately splits a table and its corresponding index data into manageable parts. The DBMS provides support for partitioning. Every partition of a table is treated as a separate table and is spread across multiple disks to gain optimum performance. Partitioning minimizes the volume of data scanned that too without the overhead of having to using indexes. This leads to improved query performance at the cost of minimal additional operational overhead.

It is recommended not to partition the tables to a degree with a large number of physical tables. A good check is to ensure that the data warehouse does not contain more than 500 tables at any time as it is quite impossible for a database administrator to manage more number of tables than this. Reasons to partition tables are as follows:

For ease of management The key reason to partition a table is to assist the management of data. A data warehouse may grow to a few terabytes in size. This is quite a huge size and hence needs to be partitioned. Also creating and maintaining indexes on a table of that size would simply be a nightmare. It would be impossible to drop and re-calculate indexes for a data load. And if you go for loading while maintaining the indexes, it would become a very slow process.

To assist backup and recovery Backing up and recovery of fact tables is an important task that has to be done in a data warehouse environment. The reason of backing up in the data warehouse environment is to cut down on the amount that has to be backed up on a regular basis. If you have not partitioned, you have to back up the whole fact table (exception in case of incremental backup). To reduce the backup size, all partitions other than the current partition can be marked as read-only. Then once backed up that can be forgotten and only the current partition needs to be backed up.

To boost performance Star schema forms the best way to minimize the set of data that needs to be scanned to respond to a query. Query performance can still be enhanced by separating large parts of the fact table from the data that has to be scanned. This is done by splitting the fact table into partitions and then requiring the query to scan the relevant partitions.

The Partitioning Technique

Partitioning is a technique which divides large database tables into manageable parts. The partitioning options must be considered for each fact table. A fact table can be partitioned horizontally or vertically. However, it is not that only the fact tables have to be partitioned, some dimension tables also in the data warehouse database are considerably large and are good candidates for partitioning. For example, customer dimension table of a telecommunication company may contain millions of records. Every dimension table must be examined to determine which of them needs to be partitioned. In this step, we come up with a definite partitioning plan which may include:

- The selected fact tables and dimension tables suitable for partitioning.
- The partitioning to be applied in each table whether horizontal or vertical.
- The number of partitions that have to be created for every individual fact table.
- The criteria that will be used to divide the fact table (for example, sales by every quarter).

- Description regarding how the queries posed by the users will be made aware of partitions that exist in the data warehouse environment.

Now let us study two ways of creating partitions—one by horizontal partitioning and second by vertical partitioning. In vertical partitioning, the partitions are created by grouping selected columns together. Each partitioned table contains the same number of rows as the original table. Usually, wide dimension tables are the best candidates for performing vertical partitioning. In striking contrast, horizontal partitioning divides the table by grouping selected rows together. For example you can horizontally partition a table into partitions of recent events and past history.

Horizontal partitioning   A large table can be horizontally partitioned into smaller tables using different techniques as discussed in this section.

Partitioning by time into equal segments   This is the most widely used and the standard form of partitioning in which the fact table is partitioned on a time period basis. Each time period is a significant retention period within the business. For example, if a large number of users pose their queries against monthly data values then a good option is to partition the entire fact table data into monthly segments. Similarly, if majority of the users need to query on fortnight data values then consider partitioning into fortnightly segments. Make sure that the total number of tables does not exceed 500.

But with this approach, one partition may contain small number of rows and the other may be heavily loaded with data records. For example, higher sales volumes will be recorded during festivals like Diwali and Christmas as compared with the rest of the year. Thus, the partitions containing data of the festive season months will have much more data than the partitions storing other month's data.

Therefore, to ensure completeness while minimizing the redundancy, horizontal partitioning must satisfy two properties: completeness and disjointness. A partition is said to be *complete* if each tuple of the original table belongs to one of the fragments, and it is *disjoint* if each tuple belongs to one and only one partition.

Partitioning by time into different-sized segments   Some of the organizations may use the historical data infrequently, for such organizations it is good to partition the fact table into different-sized segments. This means that we can create small partitions for relatively current data, larger partitions for less active data and even larger partitions for inactive data. For example, in a data warehouse where the analysis is usually done on monthly data, we could consider having three monthly partitions (for the recent three months), one quarterly partition (for the previous quarter), one half-yearly partition (for the remainder of the year) (See Fig. 7.8).

Similar partitions would be created for every year. The advantage of this technique is that detailed information remains available online. The number of tables is also relatively less which thereby reduces operating costs. However,

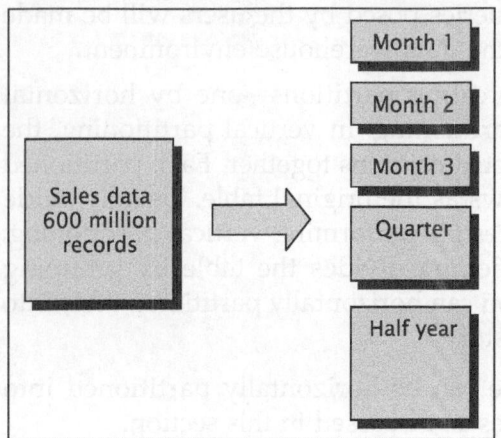

Sales data
600 million
records

Month 1

Month 2

Month 3

Quarter

Half year

Figure 7.8 Similar partitions would be created for every year

the disadvantage of this technique is that data must be physically re-partitioned at the start of the every month which leads to moving large portions of the database on a regular basis thereby increasing the operational costs of the data warehouse.

Partitioning on a different dimension Time-based partitioning is the best method for partitioning fact tables since the grouping of calendar periods is highly unlikely to change within the life of the data warehouse. But partitioning the fact tables by other dimensions like product category, region, supplier, etc are also good alternatives to partition the table.

For example, if we know that the query is frequently posed on a state-by-state basis, then it is effective to partition the fact table into regional partitions. This improves the query execution, as all the queries for a particular region collect the data from its own partition without having to scan information that is not relevant.

When using a form of dimensional partitioning, it is vital that the basis for partitioning is unlikely to change in the future. It is very important to avoid situations that call for reconstruction of the entire fact table to reflect a change in the grouping of the partitioning dimension. For example, if the definition of what constitute a region changes then the fact table would have to be restructured again to represent the new regional groupings.

So, unless you are sure that the suggested dimensional grouping is not going to change throughout the life of the data warehouse, partitioning on time dimension is highly recommended.

Partitioning by size of table In certain situations, there may not be a clear basis for partitioning the fact table on any dimension. In such situations, consider partitioning the fact table on size basis, that is, when the table is about to exceed a predetermined size, a new table partition is created.

If we consider a customer-event data warehouse which tracks all the calls made by the customer, we would find that a customer can make a call during any time of the day, and can make any number of calls during the day. In this case, partitioning on the basis of time is not a good option.

If no other dimension seems to be appropriate for partitioning then consider partitioning by size of the table. This means while transactions are being loaded into the data warehouse, new table partitions are created when a predetermined size is reached. However, this partitioning scheme is very complicated as it requires metadata to identify what data is stored in each partition and it is even difficult to manage.

Using round-robin partitions If the data warehouse is holding the complete historical information then whenever a new partition is required, the oldest partition is selected and archived so that the partition can then be reused to hold the latest data. This technique requires metadata to allow user access tools to refer to the correct table partition.

This technique, due to its simplicity, is widely used to automate many of the table management facilities within the data warehouse. Round robin partitioning strategy allows the system to refer to the same physical table partitions. Although the information that a partition contains may change but this is handled by using appropriate metadata.

Partitioning dimensions Large dimensions are usually partitioned in the same way as a fact table because a large dimension table may affect query response time. For example, customers of a bank may be in some millions. Storing such a huge amount of data in a table in not advisable due to performance reasons, so partitioning dimension tables is a common practice.

Vertical partitioning In vertical partitioning, as the name says, splits the data in a vertical fashion. This process has two variations- row splitting and normalization. Generally, in data warehouses, large tables are not normalized even if the table is consuming a lot of storage space because in a data warehouse environment, query performance takes the highest priority and when the table is normalized, data needs to be joined from more than one table which will lead to an increase in query response time thereby degrading the performance. In Fig. 7.9, the Employee_Dept table has been normalized to from the Employee and Department tables.

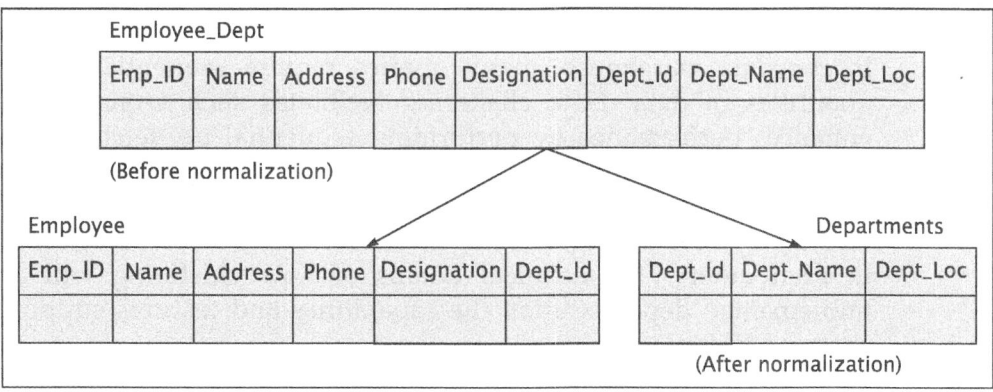

Figure 7.9 Vertical partitioning through normalization

Many a times, vertical partitioning is used in a data warehouse to split less used columns out from a frequently accessed fact table. Don't confuse row splitting with normalization as row splitting tends to leave a one-to-one map between the partitions, whereas normalization will leave a one-to-many mapping. Figure 7.10 illustrates the difference. The primary goal of row splitting is to speed up access to the large table by reducing its size.

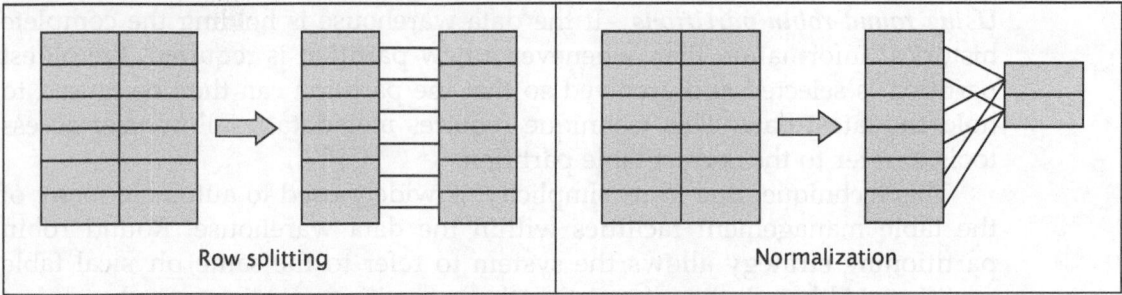

Figure 7.10 Row splitting and normalization

Advantages of Partitioning

Partitioning provides the following benefits:

- A query needs to access only the necessary partitions and thus run faster when accessing smaller amounts of data.
- An entire partition may be taken offline for maintenance as you can separately schedule maintenance of partitions. Thus, partitions promote concurrent maintenance operations.
- Index creation becomes faster.
- Loading data becomes easy and manageable.
- Backup and recovery of small partitions reduces downtime.
- The input-output loads gets balanced by mapping different partitions to various disk drives.

7.8.4 Data Clustering

In the data warehouse, many queries require sequential access of large quantities of data. Data clustering facilitates such sequential access and enhances performance by performing sequential pre-fetch of related data. Data clustering is achieved by physically placing related tables close to each other in storage. If you declare a cluster of tables to the DBMS, then these tables are placed in neighbouring areas on the disk so that they are stored close to each other. The technical details of how clustering will actually be implemented depends upon the capabilities and features supported by the chosen DBMS.

When large quantities of data are accessed in a sequential manner, clustering is used to gain improvement in performance. Clustering involves placing and managing related units of data in the same physical block of storage so that the related units of data can be retrieved together in a single input operation.

The task of clustering must be done before completing the physical model. Examine each and every table and find pairs that are related. These related pairs are often accessed together for processing so it is a good option to store these pairs close together on the medium. Clustering is generally used when a table is partitioned, so that the rows from the related tables are usually accessed together for processing.

7.8.5 Data Summarization

As discussed earlier, the data warehouse stores both detailed and summary data. You need to select the levels of granularity for the purpose of optimizing the input/output operations. Let us say that you have kept the sales data at the levels of daily detail. If the users frequently request monthly sales information, then to improve the query performance keep summary data at the monthly level. The drawback here is that if you keep only summary information and not detailed information then every query for details cannot be satisfied.

You need to choose summary and detail levels carefully based on user requirements. Also, rolling summaries are especially useful in a data warehouse. Suppose in your data warehouse, you have kept daily data, weekly data, monthly data, quarterly, and finally yearly data, then you need to create mechanisms to roll the data into next higher levels automatically with the passage of time; like daily data automatically gets rolled up to weekly data, weekly data to monthly data, so on and so forth.

7.8.6 Bypassing the Referential Integrity Checks

Referential integrity constraints ensure the validity between two related tables by governing the values of the foreign key in the child table and the primary key in the parent table. Every time a row is created, deleted or updated, the DBMS checks that the referential integrity is preserved. This is done to ensure that parent rows are not deleted until even a single child row exists and child rows are not added without the presence of parent rows in the table.

Turning off the referential integrity verification produces significant gains. Switching this option will not cause any harm in the data warehouse environment because by the time load images are created in the staging area, the data structures have already gone through the phases of extraction, cleansing and transformation. In the staging area, when the data is being prepared for storage in the data warehouse, this check has already been made at that time for correctness as far as parent and child rows are concerned. Therefore, there is no need to repeat referential integrity checks in the data warehouse. Thus, turning off this feature will in turn produce significant performance gains.

7.8.7 Indexing the Data Warehouse

Indexing is one of the most effective techniques for improving performance and results in enormous benefits. We need to develop an indexing plan for each table indicating the columns selected for indexing, the sequence of the attributes in each index, the attributes qualifying for bit-mapped indexes and the sequence in which the indexes will be created.

In a query-centric environment like that of a data warehouse, the need for efficient and faster query execution dominates. If the users are not satisfied with the response time of the queries, they may never like to use the data warehouse because they would always prefer a proper match between the speed of query results and their speed-of-thought. Indexing is the most widely used technique to improve query performance.

In a data warehouse database, most of the indexing is done on dimension tables. When a table grows in size, the indexes also grow thereby requiring more space for storage. The maximum number of indexes varies inversely with size of the table. Large number of indexes affects the data loading process. Therefore, a balance must be created between several factors before deciding on the number of indexes per table.

In order to select the columns in a table which are most suitable for indexing, the project team needs to examine the common queries and make a note of the columns that are frequently used to constrain the queries. These columns form the best candidates for indexing and will thereby boost the performance of the data warehouse environment. Generally, it is better to start with indexes on just the primary and foreign keys of each table. Then monitor the performance of the system carefully and make a note of queries that run for a long time. To cater to this situation, the team needs to add even more indexes to boost the performance of the data warehouse environment.

However, when there are a large number of indexes, the data loading process slows down considerably because every time a record is added to the table, the corresponding index entry must be created. The problem is more severe during the initial loading process. However, this problem can be addressed by dropping the indexes before running the load jobs. Now, the loading process will not create the index entries and thus you have to run separate jobs to construct the index files after the loading process completes. Construction of the index files is very time-consuming but not as much as creating index entries during the loading process.

Large tables containing million records cannot support many indexes, because if you build more than one index for such a large table, it will always add to difficulties and complexities. If there are many indexes for a table, then it is better to split the table before defining more indexes.

In order to retrieve the data, the index record is read first and then the corresponding data read takes place. It is the job of the DBMS to select the best index from the many indexes available. For example, if a table has indexes based on four columns, then the DBMS first selects the best index, reads the index record, and then reads the corresponding data record. You need at least two input/output operations to retrieve the data.

Building the B-Tree Index

Majority of the DBMS today use the B-Tree (balanced tree) index technique as the default indexing method. RDBMSs create B-Tree indexes automatically on primary key values when the programmer codes statements using Data Definition Language (DDL) to create an index. This technique supercedes other techniques of creating indexes mainly due to its data retrieval speed, ease of maintenance, and simplicity. Figure 7.11 shows a B-Tree index.

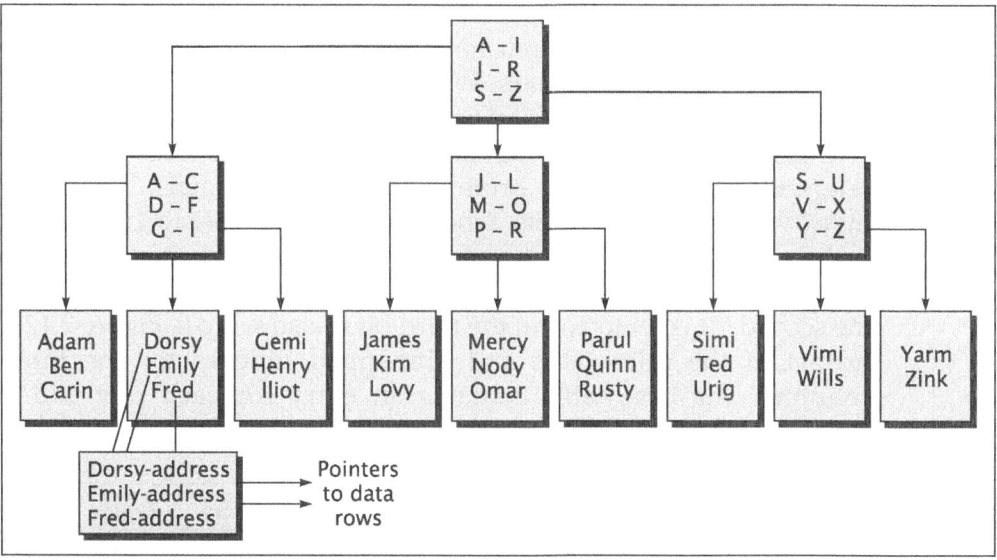

Figure 7.11 B-Tree index

It forms a tree structure with the root at the top. The index consists of a B-Tree structure based on the values of the indexed column. In this example, the indexed column is "name" and the B-Tree is created using all the existing names that are the values of the indexed column. The upper blocks of the tree contain index data pointing to the next lower block and so on, thus forming a hierarchical structure. The lowest level blocks also known as the *leaf blocks* contain pointers to the data rows stored in the table.

If a table has a column that has many unique values, then the selectivity of the column is said to be high. B-Tree indexes are most suitable for highly selective columns. For example, the column colour (say of shirt in product dimension table) contains many unique values and is thus suitable for indexing. In case the column is not highly selective, you can still improve its selectivity by concatenating two fields in such a way that the combination becomes much more selective and then create a B-Tree index on both the columns together. But the disadvantage here is that, it causes a sharp increase in size when the indexes contain concatenation of multiple columns. Now let us study another indexing technique.

Building the Bitmapped Index

A bitmap index is a special kind of index that stores the data as bit arrays (commonly called "bitmaps"). B-Trees are suitable for high selectivity data, while bitmapped indexes are highly suitable for low selectivity data. A bitmap is an ordered sequence of bits where one bit is used for each distinct value of the indexed column. The bitmap index are known for having a significant space and performance advantage over the commonly used trees. Bitmap indexes are used in the data warehousing environment for joining a large fact table to several small dimension tables.

Assume that the column for category has three distinct values, namely formals, casuals, party wears. We can construct a bitmap using these distinct values. Each entry in the bitmap contains three bits. Say the first bit indicates formals, the second bit when set indicates casuals, and finally the third bit refers to party wear. If a product category is formals, then the bitmapped index will contain three bits, where the first bit is set to 1, the second bit to 0, and the third bit is also set to 0. However, if the product category is casuals, then the bitmapped index will contain three bits, where the first bit is set to 0, the second bit is set to 1, and the third bit is also set to 0. Figure 7.12 presents an extract of the sales table and bitmapped indexes for the three different columns. The base table contains an entry for each row and each entry contains the address of the base table row.

Row ID	Date	Product	Category	Region	Units
0001ABC.0011.0111	1-Dec-06	Shirts	Formals	East	250
0001ABC.0012.0111	1-Dec-06	T-shirts	Casuals	West	400
0001ABC.0013.0111	2-Dec-06	Shirts	Formals	West	300
0001ABC.0011.0111	2-Dec-06	Jeans	Casuals	North	500
0001ABC.0012.0111	2-Dec-06	Trousers	Formals	South	350
0001ABC.0013.0111	3-Dec-06	Evening Gown	Party wears	East	450
0001ABC.0011.0111	3-Dec-06	T-shirts	Casuals	South	525

Bitmapped for product

Row ID	BITMAP
0001ABC.0011.0111	10000
0001ABC.0012.0111	01000
0001ABC.0013.0111	10000
0001ABC.0011.0111	00100
0001ABC.0012.0111	00010
0001ABC.0013.0111	00001
0001ABC.0011.0111	01000

Bitmapped for category

Row ID	BITMAP
0001ABC.0011.0111	100
0001ABC.0012.0111	010
0001ABC.0013.0111	100
0001ABC.0011.0111	010
0001ABC.0012.0111	100
0001ABC.0013.0111	001
0001ABC.0011.0111	010

Bitmapped for region

Row ID	BITMAP
0001ABC.0011.0111	1000
0001ABC.0012.0111	0100
0001ABC.0013.0111	0100
0001ABC.0011.0111	0010
0001ABC.0012.0111	0001
0001ABC.0013.0111	1000
0001ABC.0011.0111	0001

Figure 7.12 Extract of sales data

Product	Region	Row ID
⟶ 10000	⟶ 1000	0001ABC.0011.0111
01000	0100	0001ABC.0012.0111
⟶ 10000	0100	0001ABC.0013.0111
00100	0010	0001ABC.0011.0111
00010	⟶ 0001	0001ABC.0012.0111
00001	⟶ 1000	0001ABC.0013.0111
01000	⟶ 0001	0001ABC.0011.0111
Hence, we see the first row satisfies the query.		

Figure 7.13 Bitmapped index data retrieval

Figure 7.13 explains how the bitmapped indexes work to retrieve the requested rows. Consider a query against the sales table in the above example.

```
Select the rows from Sales table
Where product is "Shirts" and
Region is "east" or "South"
```

It is very clear from the above example that bitmapped indexes not only support queries using low-selectivity columns but also takes less space than B-Tree indexes for low selectivity columns. Bitmapped indexes perform well in what-if analysis which includes more than one column for analysis. This is the reason why bitmapped indexes are more suitable for a data warehouse environment than for an OLTP system. Advantages of bitmap indexing include:

- Ad hoc queries take less time to execute.
- Less space needed to store data.
- Enhanced hardware performance with even a small number of CPUs or a small amount of memory.
- Efficient maintenance of data loading process.

However, this indexing technique also has some disadvantages. First, whenever new values are introduced for the indexed columns, the bitmapped indexes have to be reconstructed. Second, the necessity to access the data tables even after the bitmapped indexes are accessed. This is not the case in B-Tree indexes, as they do not require table access if the required information is already contained in the index.

Indexing the Fact and Dimension Tables

We have already seen that the primary key of the fact table is nothing but a concatenation of keys of its dimension tables. If you have five dimension tables of store, time, product, salesperson, and customer, then the primary key of the fact table is the combination of the primary keys of store, time, product, salesperson, and customer. Apart from the primary key, the other columns in the fact table are sale units, sale dollars, margin, discount, etc. These are the columns that have to be considered while indexing. Now let us study some points that need to be considered while creating indexes for a fact table.

- A B-Tree index is deliberately created on the primary key if the chosen DBMS does not create an index on the primary key.
- While designing the index, take care of the order of individual key elements in the full concatenated key. Make sure that the keys of dimension tables that are referred frequently while querying are placed in the higher order of the concatenated key.

- If the DBMS supports combinations of indexes for access, then indexes are created on each individual component of the concatenated key.
- You may also create index on the columns containing the metrics. For example, if many queries look for sales_units, then this column is a good candidate for indexing.
- Bitmapped indexes do not apply to fact tables as there are hardly any low selectivity columns.

The dimension table columns are used as predicates in queries to constrain them. Take an example of a query like: How much are the sales of shirts in the last quarter in the southern region? Here the columns product, month, and region from three different dimension tables are candidates for indexing. Inspect the columns in each dimension table before creating an index plan. It has been observed that indexing the columns in the dimension table gives a tremendous boost in performance as compared with the hike in performance level achieved after indexing a fact table. Let us now study some points that need to be considered while creating indexes for a dimension table.

- Create a unique B-Tree index on the primary key.
- Examine the columns that are frequently used to constrain the queries as these columns are candidates for bitmapped indexes.
- Observe the columns that are frequently accessed together in large dimension tables to create multi-column indexes. Also carefully design the arrangement of the columns so that columns that are more frequently accessed are placed in the high order of multi-column indexes.

7.9 TECHNOLOGY REQUIREMENTS

Table 7.2 lists the technologies that are needed for a successful data warehouse.

Table 7.2 Requirements for a successful data warehsoue

Manage large volumes of data	The data warehouse technology must support terabytes and petabytes of data. To be effective, the data warehouse technology must be able to store large volumes of data in a very efficient manner.
Manage multiple media	The data warehouse must be able to work with different storage media like main memory, cache, DASD, magnetic tapes, and optical disk because large amounts of data cannot be stored on a single media.
Indexing the data	A data warehouse is designed for unpredictable access of the data warehouse. The dat must be accessed quickly and easily by its users. For this, the data warehouse must be efficiently indexed.
Monitoring the data warehouse	The data warehouse must be constantly monitored to see what data is being used, what activities are being performed, and the free space available.

Table 7.2 Continued

Table 7.2 Continued

Interfaces to many technologies	A data warehouse is designed to receive data from several operational systems. The data stored in the data warehouse is further passed to several other datamarts and DSS applications like EIS, OLAP, and data mining. This calls for a well-defined interface between all the technologies involved.
Flexibility of data placement	The technology that enables the programmer to arrange for the physical placement of the data to coincide with its usage is highly desirable.
Parallel storage of data	Significant boost in performance can be observed when the data is managed in parallel in the data warehouse environment. Further, more parallel storage of data increases the amount of data that can be managed. As a rule of thumb, the boost in performance is inversely proportional to the number of physical devices over which the data is physically distributed. This rule holds true when there is an even probability of data access.
Metadata management	For effective use of data warehouse, the user must be able to access the metadata that is accurate and up-to-date. In the absence of an efficient metadata, it becomes difficult for the end user to work with a huge amount of data that is available to them.
Language interface	The complexity of SQL inhibits the end-users to formulate their own queries. So, a language interface is highly desirable that can create and manage the SQL queries.
Efficient data loading	Data loading is done faster using a utility program. To reduce the burden on the loading process, the load process is often parallelized.
Data compaction	A data warehouse is meant to store huge volumes of data. To store such enormous amounts of data efficiently, the data must be compacted.
Variable length data	The data warehouse must be able to store and manage variable length data efficiently.
Lock management	The data warehouse DBMS must ensure that the same record is not being updated by two or more processes at the same time.
Quick restore	The data warehouse must ensure quick restore in case of failure.

Recapitulation

Type 1 changes relate to correction of errors in source systems which may or may not have any significance. To handle it, the old value needs to be discarded and the new value simply overwrites the old one. The key of this dimension table is not changed.

Type 2 changes cause history to be partitioned at the event that triggered the change, that is, there is a need to preserve the history in the data warehouse. To handle such a change, add a new dimension table row with the new value of the changed attribute and a new surrogate key. An effective date field may be included in the dimension table and no changes are done to the original row.

Type 3 solutions attempt to track changes horizontally in the dimension table by adding fields to contain the old data. The advantage of Type 3 solutions is the avoidance of multiple dimension records for a single entity. They also provide the ability to track forward and backward.

A dimension table is said to be large if it has a very large number of rows or if it has a large number of attributes.

A dimension is considered to be a rapidly changing dimension if one or more of its attributes change frequently. To handle such rapidly changing dimensions, you need to break off the rapidly changing attributes into another dimension table, leaving the slowly changing attributes behind in the original table.

Objective Questions

1. **Multiple choice questions**

   (i) Which table contains foreign keys and numeric fact values?

   (a) Fact table

   (b) Dimension table

   (c) Factless fact table

   (d) None of these

   (ii) Which facts can be derived from other attributes?

   (a) Additive measures

   (b) Semi additive measures

   (c) None of these

   (iii) Which table is more stable and less volatile?

   (a) Fact table

   (b) Dimension table

   (c) Factless fact table

   (d) None of these

   (iv) Which changes are called soft changes

   (a) Type 1

   (b) Type 2

   (c) Type 3

   (d) Type 4

   (v) Which technique allows more data to be loaded into a single block?

   (a) Compaction

   (b) Indexing

   (c) Partitioning

   (d) Clustering

2. **Fill in the blanks**

   1. _____ tables contain the details of business events.

   2. _____ tables contain gigabytes or multiple terabytes of data.

   3. _____ tables contain records that describe facts.

   4. Primary key of the fact table is the concatenation of the primary keys of all the _____ tables.

   5. Data grain means the level of detail for the _____.

   6. A fact table is said to be empty if it has no _____.

   7. _____ changes relate to the correction of errors in the source systems.

   8. _____ means the time elapsed between a change of data in the operational system and reflection of that change in the data warehouse.

   9. _____ are system generated sequence numbers that do not have any built-in meanings.

   10. The _____ keyword directs the database to store rows in the table in a compressed format wherever possible.

   11. _____ is a technique which divides large database tables into manageable parts.

   12. A partition is said to be _____ if each tuple of the original table belongs to one of the fragments.

   13. _____. Technique physically places related tables close to each other in storage.

   14. B-Tree indexes are most suitable for _____ columns.

3. Match the following

1.	Inter-query parallelization	(a)	Parallelization of parts of the operations within the same query itself.
2.	Intra-query parallelization	(b)	Greatest utilization of resources, optimal performance, and high scalability.
3.	Horizontal parallelization	(c)	The systems where data is partitioned across multiple disks.
4.	Vertical parallelization	(d)	Query operations executed in a pipelined manner.
5.	Hybrid parallelization	(e)	Server processes handle multiple queries simultaneously.

4. State true or false

1. The fact table is wide.
2. A fact table hardly contains any numerical value records.
3. Fact table contains fewer attributes than a dimension table.
4. Type 3 changes cause history to be partitioned at the event that triggered the change.
5. We must make primary keys with built-in meanings in the dimension tables of the data warehouse.
6. A surrogate key is independent of operational system keys.
7. Table compression works best on read write tables.
8. Tables that require frequent updates are best candidates for table compression.
9. The maximum number of indexes is directly proportional to the size of the table.
10. Wide dimension tables are the best candidates for performing vertical partitioning.
11. Row splitting tends to leave a one-to-one map between the partitions, whereas normalization will leave a one-to-many mapping.
12. DBMS today use the B-tree index technique as the default indexing method.

Review Questions

1. What do you understand by slowly changing dimensions? Explain the three types of changes that are applicable to such dimension tables with relevant examples.

2. How do you handle large dimensions or rapidly changing dimensions in the data warehouse environment?

3. Write a short note on junk dimensions.

4. Explain the snowflake schema with its advantages and disadvantages. Also make a comparison between the star schema and snowflake schema. Which of the two schemas will you prefer using for your data warehouse?

5. What are aggregate fact tables? Why are they necessary? Justify your answer with the help of an example.

6. Explain the four cases in which a family of stars is formed.

7. Write a short note on snapshot and transaction tables.

8. For an insurance business, identify at least two examples of slowly changing dimensions and also specify what strategy you will apply to handle these changes.

9. For a retail chain, design a star schema to track the sales units and sales amount with a set of minimum three dimensions.

Remember that the schema should include a base fact table and a two-way aggregate fact table as well.

10. For a manufacturing company, design a family of stars to support the entire value chain.

8

THE ETL PROCESS

Learning Objectives

In this chapter, we will study the ETL (extraction, transformation, and loading) process in detail. The ETL process is one of the most crucial and time-consuming process in a data warehouse environment. Thus, knowing the subtleties of this process is of great importance for any user.

Case Study

Now, before the data warehouse is actually built, a few more important decisions have to be taken by Pallav Raj, the CEO of JRTs.

The first issue that needs to be resolved is whether the data that would be stored in the data warehouse will come only from systems within the organization or from sources outside the organization also. These external sources may include market surveys, business magazines, statistics related to the competitor's market, etc.

The second issue is whether to extract data in real time or not. If Pallav Raj has decided to extract data in real-time, then which approach will be followed—database triggers, log files, or source applications. In case it is decided that data would be extracted in a non-real time mode then whether it would be done using timestamps or by comparisons of files. All these approaches have advantages and disadvantages. All the pros and cons have

to be analysed before making the final decision.

The third issue is the range of information delivery mechanisms the data warehouse will provide to its end-users. These different mechanisms can be simple queries and reports, ad hoc and complex queries, OLAP, EIS, and data mining.

Other issues that Pallav Raj has to resolve before the project team can start working building the data warehouse includes decisions related to the transformation tasks that would have to be performed, when to go for data warehouse refresh and when to go for an update and finally the underlying data warehouse technology, that is whether it would be based on relational databases or multidimensional databases.

Once all these questions are answered, the team can go ahead and implement the data warehouse for the users.

8.1 INTRODUCTION

ETL functions (extraction, transformation, and loading) that take place in the data staging area reshape the relevant data from the source systems into useful information to be stored in the data warehouse (Refer Fig. 8.1). Without these functions, there would be no strategic information in the data warehouse.

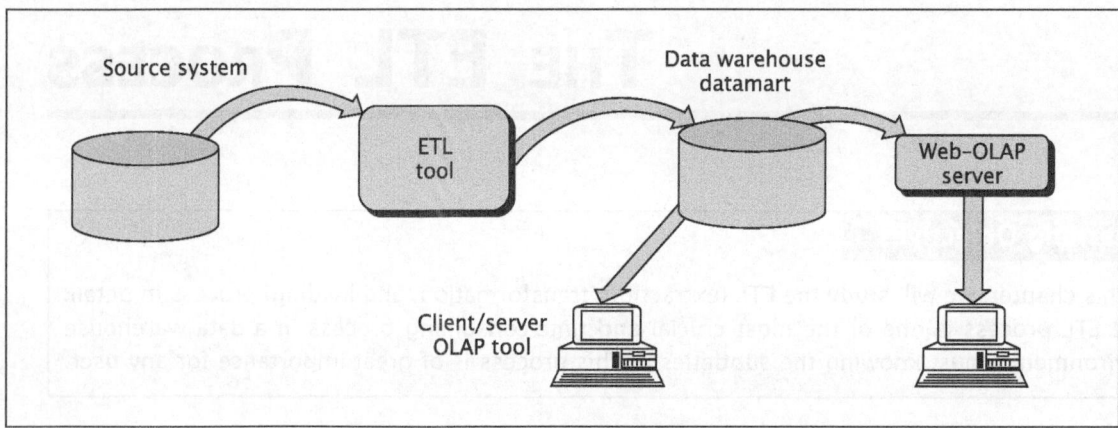

Figure 8.1 Data transfer from source systems to the data warehouse

If the source data is not extracted correctly, cleansed, and integrated in the proper formats, query processing—the backbone of the data warehouse—will not take place. Design and implementation of the automated ETL process, often represents a major part of the effort to develop a data warehouse (international statistics estimate that it exceeds 70% of total effort to build a data warehouse).

8.1.1 Challenges in ETL Process

ETL functions are challenging because of the nature of the source systems. A lot of disparities in the source systems make the ETL functions a challenging task to accomplish. Given below is a list of reasons for the types of difficulties in the ETL functions:

- Source systems are diverse and disparate.
- Source systems run on different platforms and have different operating systems installed.
- Most of the operational systems do not preserve historical data which is critical for a data warehouse.
- Quality of data cannot be guaranteed in the older operational source systems.
- Structures of the source systems keep changing over time with the advent of new technology.

- The prevalence of data inconsistency in the source system, (i.e. same data element represented differently in different source systems) is a major challenge in the ETL functions.
- Lack of consistency is one problem and the lack of means for resolving the inconsistencies is another problem.
- Data in the source system may be ambiguous, or stored in a cryptic form which hardly provides any help to the users.
- The data type, format, and naming convention may be different in different source systems.

Refer Fig. 8.2 which shows the major steps that are performed during the ETL process.

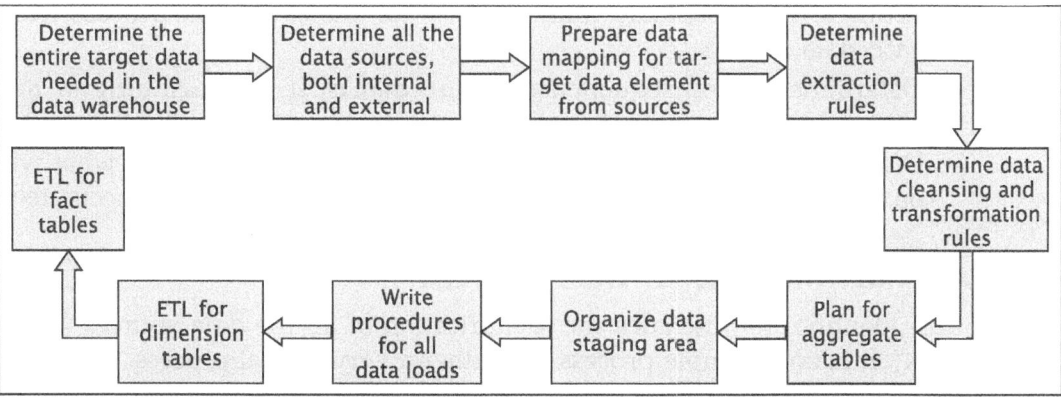

Figure 8.2   Major steps in the ETL process

8.2 DATA EXTRACTION

In this stage, the data flows from the data sources and pauses at the staging area as shown in Fig. 8.3. After transformation and integration, the data is made ready for loading into the data warehouse repository. For majority of the data warehouses, the primary data source consists of the enterprise's operational systems.

Many of the operational systems are sill legacy systems, while some of the operational systems run on the client/server architecture and some have ERP data sources, so extracting data from such disparate systems is not a trivial issue.

Apart from extracting the data from these production systems, data from out-

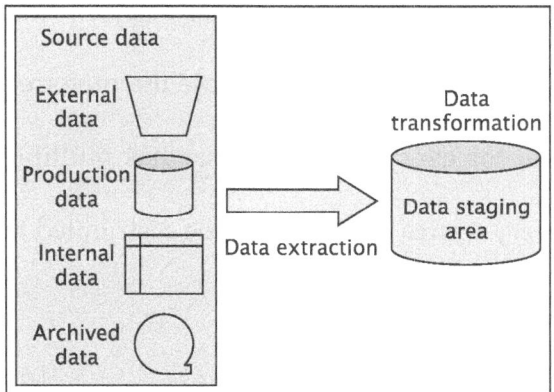

Figure 8.3   Technical architecture for data extraction

side sources as well needs to be extracted and for that; temporary files are used to hold the data from these external sources.

Effective data extraction is a key to the success of data warehouses. Therefore, you need to consider the following issues and formulate a data extraction strategy for the success of the data warehouse.

- Identify the applications and systems from which the data will be extracted.
- For each identified data source, determine the method for data extraction, i.e. whether it will be done manually or by using the tools.
- For each data source, determine the extraction frequency, i.e. decide whether the data will be extracted daily, weekly or monthly from the source systems.
- Estimate the acceptable time window for the extraction process from each data source.
- Determine the job sequencing feature that is, if the beginning of one extraction job has to wait until the previous one has completed or not.
- Determine how the exceptional conditions will be handled like what will be done to handle the input records that could not be extracted accurately.

8.2.1 Identification of Data Sources

Source identification includes the identification of all the data sources (Refer Fig. 8.4). It is not a simple process but rather a very critical process. For every piece of information that has to be stored in the data warehouse, first its source has to be identified.

The process of source identification needs thoroughness, time, and exhaustive analysis. This process can be better understood by taking a look at the sequence of steps performed in the source identification.

- List every fact needed for analysis in fact tables.
- For every dimension table, list each and every attribute.
- For each target data item, find the source system and the appropriate source data item.
- If there are multiple sources for the same data then choose the preferred source.
- Formulate a consolidation rule for every data item that has multiple sources.
- Formulate splitting rules for every source field that will be distributed to multiple fields.
- Determine the default values.
- Search the source data for the missing values.

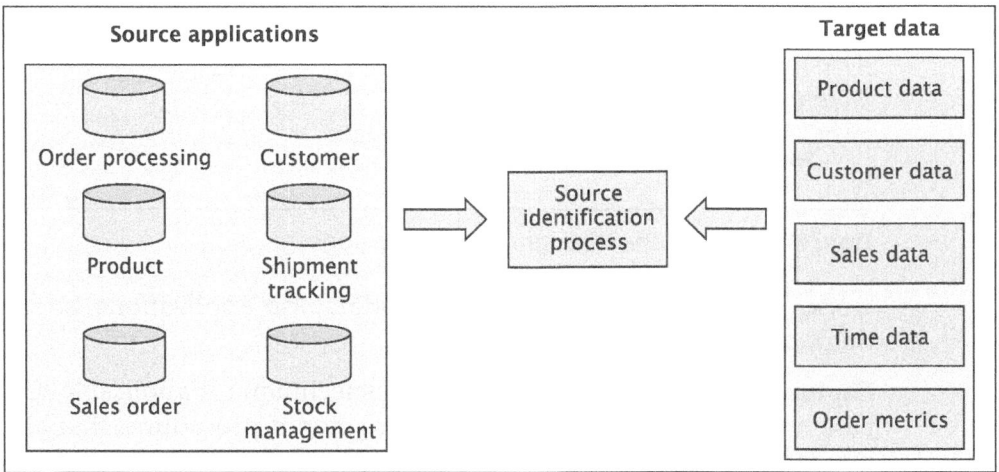

Figure 8.4 Identification of source systems

8.2.2 Extracting Data for Refreshing

In this section, we will discuss various data extraction techniques. These techniques can be broadly classified into two categories—immediate data extraction and deferred data extraction—and these categories further have sub-categories.

Immediate Data Extraction Technique

In this technique, the data extraction is real-time. It occurs as the transactions happen at the source databases and files. The three options for immediate data extraction are given below.

Capture through transaction logs This technique makes use of the transaction logs of the DBMSs. The transaction logs are maintained for recovery from possible failures. As each business transaction adds, updates, or deletes a row from a database table, the DBMS immediately updates the log file as well by writing every entry in it.

Capture through transaction logs technique reads the transaction log and selects all the committed transactions. Since logging is already done as a part of the transaction processing in all the modern DBMS today, there is no extra overhead incurred in the operational systems. But one caution that needs to be taken is that the transactions are extracted before the log file gets refreshed. As these log files on disk gets filled-up, the contents are backed up on some other media. So, one must ensure that all the transactions are extracted for data warehouse updates. The technique of capture through transaction logs is shown in Fig. 8.5.

This technique is the best one if all the source systems are database applications. But in case some of the source systems for the data warehouse are on flat files or on other non-database applications then this option will not

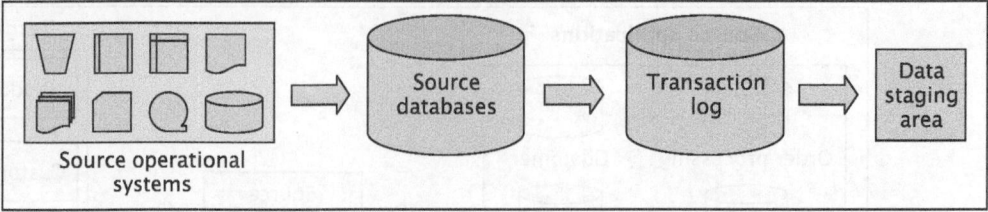

Figure 8.5 Capture through transaction logs

work. There are no log files for non-database applications, so you have to think of another technique.

Capture through database triggers This technique is applicable only for database applications. Basically, triggers are stored procedures that are stored on the database and fired when certain predefined events occur. Triggers can be created for all events for which data needs to be captured. The output of the trigger program is written on a separate file that will be used to extract data. The extracted data will then be stored in the data warehouse as shown in Fig. 8.6. For example, if you need to capture all updates, deletes, and additions in the orders table, you can write a trigger program to capture all changes in that table.

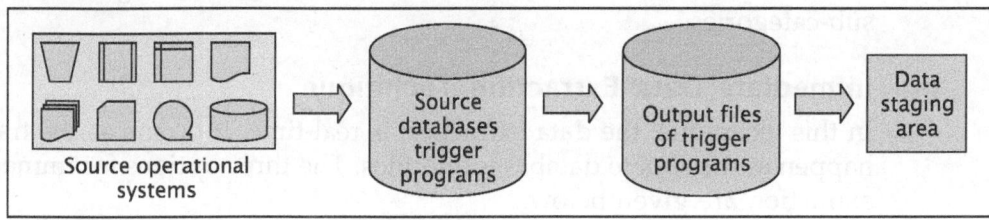

Figure 8.6 Capture through database triggers

Data capture through triggers occurs at the source system. This feature makes this technique more reliable. Another advantage of using trigger programs is that both the before and after images of data can be captured. However, creating and maintaining trigger programs and executing them during transaction processing is an extra overhead for the data warehouse project team.

Capture in source applications In this technique, the source application is used to capture the data for the data warehouse. All the relevant applications that write to the source files are modified to write all adds, updates, and deletes to both, the source files and database tables (Refer Fig. 8.7).

Unlike the previous two techniques, this technique works well for all types of source data. This technique is equally suited for databases, indexed files, flat files, and all other types of files. In this technique, the relevant programs in the source systems need to be revised. However, this task can become complex if the number of source systems is very large. The main pitfall of this technique is

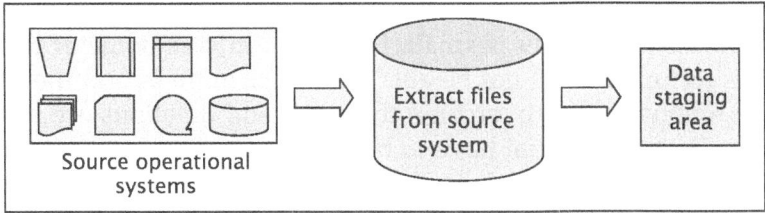

Figure 8.7 Capture in source applications

that it leads to performance degradation of the source applications which occurs due to the additional processing needed to capture the changes on separate files.

Deferred Data Extraction

In the data extraction techniques discussed above, data capture takes place while the transactions occur in the source operational systems, whereas in the deferred data extraction technique, the data capture does not take place in real-time. The capture is done at a later point of time.

Capture based on date and timestamp   Every time a record in the source system is created or updated, it is marked with a timestamp that will be used for selecting the records for data extraction. The timestamp shows the date and time at which the source record was created or updated. Unlike the immediate data extraction technique the data will be captured at a later point of time and not while each source record is created or updated. The data is usually extracted during the midnight. Everyday the records with timestamp later than the midnight of the previous day are selected for extraction as shown in Fig. 8.8.

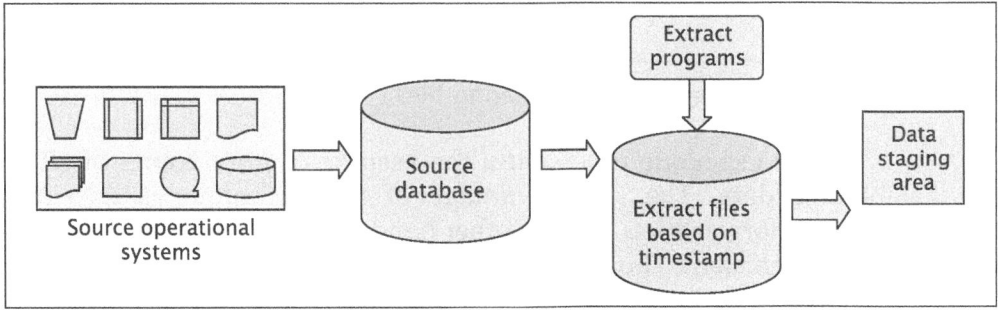

Figure 8.8 Capture based on data and timestamps

Provided that the date and timestamp are also stored with the records, this technique will work with every type of source system, be it database tables, indexed files or flat files. This technique captures the latest state of the source data.

Deferred data extraction technique gives good performance if the number of records revised everyday is small. However, in case some of the rows are deleted, this technique will not be able to recognize them and thereby update the data warehouse. So to overcome this problem, deletions are handled in a special way. The records that have to be deleted are just marked and after the extraction process is run and completed successfully then the records are actually deleted from the source systems.

Capture by comparing files   If none of the technique discussed above suits the data warehouse environment or are not feasible for some or the other reason, then this technique can be taken as the last option. This technique is also known as snapshot differential technique because, it compares two snapshots of the source data.

For example, if you want to apply this technique to capture the changes in the sales data, then while performing today's data extraction for changes to sales data, a full file comparison between today's copy and previous day's copy of the sales data is done to capture any changes between the two copies (Refer Fig. 8.9).

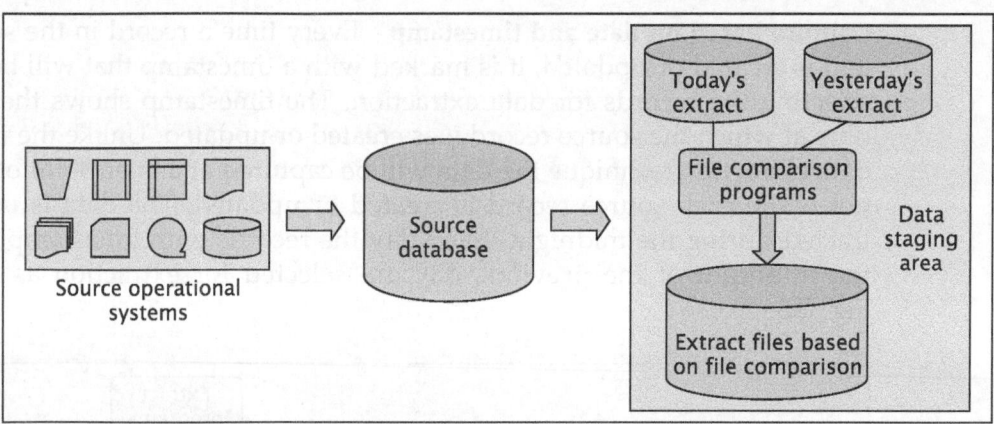

Figure 8.9   Capture by comparing files

This technique necessitates the keeping of prior copies of all the relevant source data. The key advantage of this technique is its simplicity and straightforwardness. On the other hand, a full comparison of large files can be very inefficient. Thus, this technique must be considered only for some legacy systems that do not have transaction logs or date and time stamps recorded in the source data files.

Evaluation of Extraction Techniques

Before concluding which technique is best for your environment, let us first take a quick glance at the features of these techniques (Refer Table 8.1).

Table 8.1 Evaluation of extraction techiques

Capture through transaction logs	• Does not provide much flexibility for capturing specifications. • Does not affect the performance of source systems. • Does not require any revisions to the existing source applications. • Cannot be used on file-oriented system.
Capture through database triggers	• Does not provide much flexibility for capturing specifications. • Does not affect the performance of source systems. • Does not require any revisions to the existing source applications. • Cannot be used on legacy systems. • Cannot be used on file oriented systems.
Capture in source applications	• Provides flexibility for capturing specifications. • Does not affect the performance of source systems. • Requires the existing source applications to be revised. • Can be used on file-oriented system. • Can be used on legacy systems.
Capture based on date and timestamp	• Provides flexibility for capturing specifications. • Does not affect the performance of source systems. • Requires the existing source applications to be revised. • Can be used on file-oriented system. • Cannot be used on legacy systems.
Capture by comparing files	• Provides flexibility for capturing specifications. • Does not affect the performance of source systems. • Does not require the existing source applications to be revised. • May be used on file-oriented system. • May be used on legacy systems.

After having discussed the advantages and disadvantages of different techniques, let us try to conclude which technique will fit better for which environment. If there are old legacy systems, then one may consider file comparison method a better option. Capture through transaction logs and database trigger techniques are comparatively cheap and easy to implement. There is no overhead on the source operational systems. In the case of database triggers, there is a need to create and maintain trigger programs, but still the overhead and maintenance effort is much less compared to other techniques.

Data capture in source systems calls for a lot of development and maintenance work as it requires substantial revisions to existing source systems. The deferred data extraction techniques have minimal impact on the operational systems.

Data capture in source systems is not preferred much as a lot of development and maintenance cost is involved. Capture through database triggers and transaction logs are the most preferred options. Also, these techniques are not applicable to non-relational databases. The file comparison method is the most time-consuming for data extraction. This technique should always be applied as the last option.

8.2.3 Managing Reference Tables

When we talk of the source systems feeding the data warehouse, the first thought that comes to our mind is that the source system tables comprises of the sales data, inventory data, product data, customer data, etc. Here we usually miss one thing that is called reference data. Every organization has some reference tables. These reference tables are often taken for granted and create problems later when they are needed. So care must be taken to store the reference tables also in the data warehouse.

In order to bring the reference tables in the data warehouse, there are two techniques. The first technique captures the snapshot of the reference tables every six months. Although this approach is simple but it lacks practicality. For example, if snapshots of the reference tables are taken on the 1 January and 1 July every year, and if a record that was added on 10 January was deleted somehow on 15 April, then the data that was recorded will be lost as it was never captured in the data warehouse (Refer Fig. 8.10).

On 2 January				On 7 June				On 30 June			
CustId	Name	Address	Rating	CustId	Name	Address	Rating	CustId	Name	Address	Rating
C001	James	123AAA	A	C001	James	123AAA	A	C001	James	123AAA	A
C002	John	234BBB	B	C002	John	234BBB	B	C002	John	234BBB	B
C003	Mary	345CCC	A	C003	Mary	345CCC	A	C003	Mary	345CCC	A
				C004	Adam	456DDD	C	C004	Adam	456DDD	C
				C005	Noah	567EEE	B	C006	Mathew	678FFF	A
				C006	Mathew	678FFF	A	The data about customer having ID 'C005' will never be entered in the data warehouse.			

Figure 8.10 Managing reference tables (1st approach)

In the second technique, a snapshot of the reference table is created. Then all the activities that take place against that reference table throughout the year are collected. So, any addition, deletion, and updation can be captured. Although this approach is widely used and more sensible than the first one, but implementing it is not a trivial task (Refer Fig. 8.11).

On 2 January				

CustId	Name	Address	Rating	3 February- add
				        C004, Adam, 456DDD, C
				7 March- add
				        C005, Noah, 567EEE, B
				27 May- add
				        C006, Mathew, 678FFF, A
				5 June- delete
				        C005, Noah, 567EEE, B

C001	James	123AAA	A	
C002	John	234BBB	B	
C003	Mary	345CCC	A	
The changes that are made to the reference table throughout the year are written in a separate file so that the table can be reconstructed at any time using this file.				

Figure 8.11 Managing reference tables (2nd approach)

8.3 DATA TRANSFORMATION

The data extracted from the source system cannot be stored directly in the data warehouse mainly because of two reasons. First, this is raw data that must be processed to be made usable in the data warehouse. The data in the operational systems is not usable for making strategic decisions. Second, because operational data is extracted from many old legacy systems, the quality of data in those systems may not be good enough for the data warehouse. So before putting this data in the data warehouse, the data needs to be enriched and its quality improved.

Before moving the extracted data into the data warehouse, various kinds of data transformation have to be performed. Since this data come from several dissimilar source systems, there is a need to transform the data according to a standardized format. Also, it must be ensured that the data does not violate any business rules.

Good quality data is of great importance in the data warehouse as this data forms the basis of a sound strategic decision. If the data quality is not good, then the effect of strategic decisions based on incorrect information can be devastating for the organization. Thus, improving the quality of data forms a major task within data transformation process.

8.3.1 Tasks Involved in Data Transformation

Now in this section, we will consider specific types of transformation tasks which are most commonly performed on the extracted data before being moved in the data warehouse.

Format revision These revisions include changes to the data types and lengths of individual data fields. For example, in the source systems, the customer's income level may be identified by codes and ranges in which the fields may be text or numeric. Again the length of the customer's name field may vary from one source system to the other.

Decoding of fields When the data comes from multiple source systems, the same data items may have been described by different field values. The most common example is the coding for gender, with one system using 0 and 1 for male and female, another using M and F, and the other using male, female. Data with cryptic codes must also be decoded before being moved in the data warehouse.

Splitting of fields Earlier legacy systems stored names and addresses in large text fields. For example all the components of name—first name, middle name, and last name were all stored in one large field called 'Name'. Similarly, city, state, and zip code were stored as a single field address. But the need today is to separate out or split these individual components of the name and address fields into separate fields. This gives two benefits. First, the operating performance can be improved by indexing on the individual components. Second, the users may want to perform analysis using individual components, e.g. analyse the buying pattern of customers in the same city.

Merging of information This type of data transformation is neither the opposite of the previous task nor it means merging a number of fields to form a single field; instead, it means bringing together the relevant information from different data sources. For example, the details of the customers could be collected from a number of data sources. Like customer name and code can be fetched from one table, his income level and age from the other table and his address and living style from yet another table.

Character set conversion This type of data transformation is done to the textual data to convert its character set to an agreed standard character set. Some of the legacy systems on the mainframes may have the source data in EBCDIC characters while in other source systems the data may be stored using the ASCII character set. So you need to convert the data from one character set to the other.

Conversions of units Many companies have global branches. So the sales amount may be represented in different currencies in different source systems. But before moving the data in the data warehouse, you need to convert the figures into a common unit of measurement.

Date and time conversion The date and time values also need to be represented in a standard format. For example, the American and the British date formats may be standardized to an international format. The date of 1 October 2006 is written as 10/01/2006 in the US format and as 01/10/2006 in the British format. This data needs to be standardized and written in a common format.

Summarization This type of transformation is done to derive summarized/aggregate data from the most granular data. The summarized data will then be loaded in the data warehouse instead of loading the most granular level of data. For example, instead of keeping the details of each and every sales transaction in individual stores, you can summarize this data and keep the summary data storing the total sales in each store on every individual date.

Key restructuring While extracting data from the data sources, you have to form the primary keys for the fact tables and the dimensions tables. You cannot keep the primary keys of the source data tables as the primary keys for the fact and dimension tables because the primary keys of the source data have built-in meaning. For example, in Fig. 8.12, the product code has a built-in meaning. If you use the product code as the primary key, then if you place

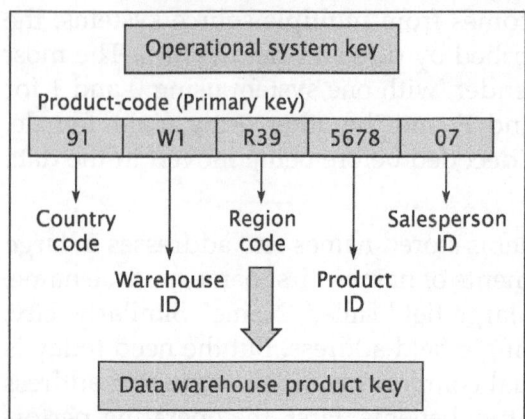

Figure 8.12 Key structuring

the product in the new department, then the code of the product will change and hence its primary key. You cannot keep such changing keys as the primary keys of the fact and dimension tables in the data warehouse. So, for dimension tables, you have to use system generated keys with no inherent meanings as the primary key. The primary key of the fact table will be a concatenated key, that is combination of primary keys of all the participating dimension tables.

De-duplication In many companies, the records for the same customer may be stored in many files. When you extract data from the source systems, you have to pay special attention to find such duplicate records and remove the duplicates while storing the record in the data warehouse, ensuring that the information about the customers is stored only once forming a single record.

When the data warehousing technology had just emerged in the market, transformation programs were written by programmers using languages like COBOL and C, but soon it was realized that these programs were tedious to write, repetitive and required ongoing maintenance. So, ETL software were developed that could automate the process of integrating the data from the operational systems, i.e. extract the data, transform it, and finally load it in the data warehouse.

Generally, ETL software is of two types—one that produces code and the other that produces a parameterized run time module. The code producing ETL software is much more powerful than the one producing run-time modules as it can easily access legacy data in its own format. On the other hand, the ETL software that generates run time module requires the legacy data to be flattened before it can be accessed. In any case, the function of ETL software is to convert, reformat, and integrate data from multiple source systems.

8.3.2 Role of Data Transformation Process

The data transformation process takes the following course.

- Map the input data from the source systems to data for data warehouse repository.
- Clean the data, fill all the missing values by some default value.
- Remove duplicate the records so that they may be stored only once in the data warehouse.
- Perform splitting and merging of fields.
- Sort the records.
- De-normalize the extracted data according to the dimensional model of the data warehouse.
- Convert to appropriate data types.
- Perform aggregations and summarizations.
- Inspect the data for referential integrity.
- Consolidation and integration of data from multiple source systems.

8.4 DATA LOADING

Once the extraction and transformation of data has been done, the next major set of functions consists of taking the prepared data, applying it to the data warehouse, and storing it in the data warehouse repository. Generally, we use three phrases in context of loading the data into the data warehouse. The first is 'Initial Load' in which we populate all the data warehouse tables for the first time. The second is 'Incremental Load' in which we apply ongoing changes periodically and the third is 'Full Refresh' in which the contents of one or more tables are erased completely and then reloaded with fresh data.

During the data loads, the data warehouse has to be offline for the duration of the loading process. So you need to find a time window when the loads may be scheduled without affecting the warehouse users. Therefore, it is better to divide the load process into smaller chunks and populate only a few tables at a time. This technique will render two main benefits—you can run smaller loads in parallel and keep some parts of the data warehouse online while loading the other parts. It is difficult to estimate the time that the loading process will take to complete, especially in the case of initial load and complete refresh.

After the loading process is over, you need to test the loads to verify the correctness of the loads. Procedures need to be provided to handle the data that could not be loaded as a part of the loading process. And also have a plan for quality assurance of the loaded records.

Let us now review the steps involved in completing the initial loading process.

- Drop any indexes built on the data warehouse tables. Index building during the loading process consumes a lot of time. Initial loading may involve large volumes of data containing millions of rows and anything slowing down the load process cannot be afforded.
- In some cases, the initial loading process may take several days to complete. If the initial loading process gets aborted midway, due to some failure in the system or because of any other reason, you will have to redo the entire process. Therefore, it is better to have proper checkpoints so that you can pick up from the latest checkpoint and continue from there.
- Load the dimension tables first and then the fact tables. This is done because the key of the fact table is nothing but a combination of the keys of the dimension tables. Until the parent row is available, you cannot insert the child rows.
- Once the dimension tables and fact tables have been loaded, create the aggregate tables.
- After the loading of fact tables, dimension tables, and aggregate tables, now it is the time to create indexes on these tables.

8.4.1 Techniques of Data Loading

Before we discover the various techniques of loading data into the data warehouse repository from the data staging area, let us consider the different modes in which the data can be applied to the warehouse.

Load If the target table to be loaded already exists and contains some data records, then the load process will wipe out the existing data and store the data from the incoming file. This is illustrated in Fig. 8.13. However if the table is empty, the load process simply applies the data from the incoming file.

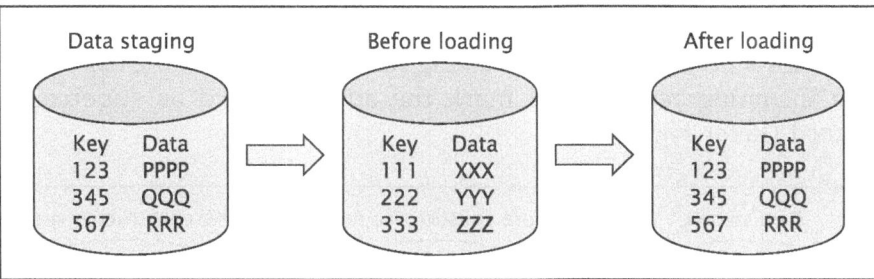

Figure 8.13 Load mode of data loading

Append This mode is an extension to the previous one. If data already exists in the table, the append process adds the incoming data, thereby preserving the existing data in the target table. This is shown in Fig. 8.14. When the incoming record is a duplicate of an already existing record, then this situation may be handled in any one way. First, you may either allow the incoming data to be added as a duplicate or may be rejected during the append process.

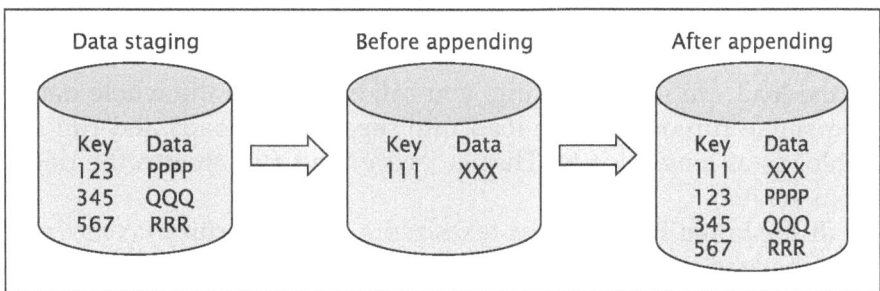

Figure 8.14 Append mode of data loading

Destructive merge In this mode, the incoming data is applied to the target data. If the primary key of the incoming record matches with the key of an existing record, then the existing record is updated. And in case the incoming record is a new record without a match with an existing record, the incoming record is added to the target table. Figure 8.15 explains this process.

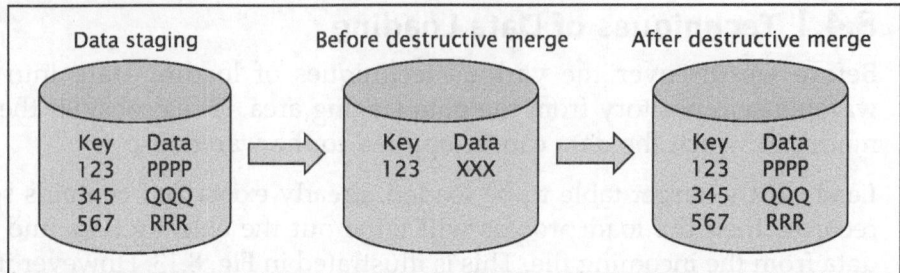

Figure 8.15 Destructive merge

Constructive merge In this mode, if the primary key of an incoming record matches with the key on an existing record, then leave the existing record, add the incoming record, and mark the added record as superceding the old record (Refer Fig. 8.16).

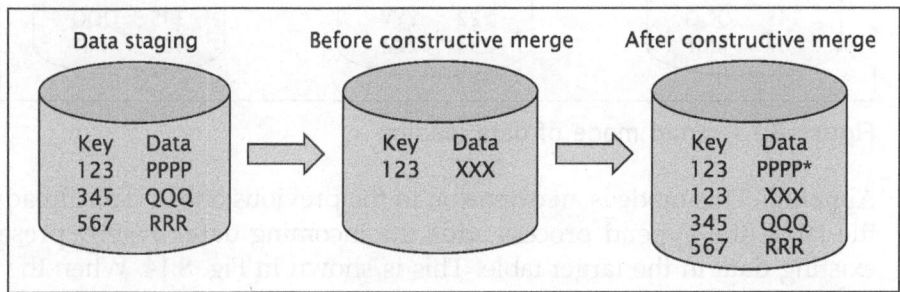

Figure 8.16 Constructive merge

After getting a basic understanding of different modes, now let us discuss how these modes of applying data to the data warehouse fit into the three types of loads.

Initial load In initial loading, you can either load the whole data warehouse in a single run or split the load into separate subloads and run each of these subloads as single loads. That is, every load run creates the database tables from scratch.

If the initial load process takes more than one run to create a single table, then the load process has to be scheduled to run several days. In this scenario, for the first run of the initial load of a particular table, the load table command is used and in all other subsequent runs the incoming data will be applied using the append mode.

Creation of indexes on initial loads or full refreshes needs special attention. Index creation on mass loads can be too time-consuming, so it is recommended to drop the indexes prior to the loads to make the loading process fast. Then these indexes are regenerated after the loading process is complete.

Incremental load Incremental loading process is actually the application of ongoing changes from the source systems. If you follow the constructive merge mode, then if the primary key of a new incoming record matches with the key of an existing record, then the existing record is not changed and the incoming record is added and marked as superceding the old record. Even if you are considering the timestamp field, the constructive merge is used to preserve the periodic nature of the changes.

Now consider the destructive merge mode. If you are applying Type 1 changes in the slowly changing dimension, then the change to a dimension table record is meant to correct an error in the existing record. The existing record must be replaced by the corrected incoming record. Here the destructive mode will be applied rather than constructive merge mode. This mode is applied in cases where historical perspective is not important.

Full refresh Full refresh process involves rewriting the entire data warehouse. Although, at times you can do partial refreshes also, but doing a partial refresh is quite rare as every dimension table is tied to the fact table.

Full refreshes may be considered similar to the initial load. The only difference lies in the case if records already exist in the data warehouse table, they will be completely erased and the table will be populated by the incoming records.

8.4.2 When to Go for Data Update Rather than Data Refresh

After the initial load, the data warehouse is updated using two methods:

- **Update** Application of incremental changes in the data sources.
- **Refresh** Complete reload at specified intervals.

Refresh is much simpler than update. To apply the update technique, first you need to extract the changes from each data source and then apply the changes or the extracted records to the data warehouse. But in the case of refresh, complete replacement of the data warehouse tables takes place. Refresh jobs take long time to complete. For refreshing the data warehouse, you have to keep it offline for a long time and the case worsens if the database has large tables.

The cost of refresh remains the same irrespective of the number of changes in the source systems whereas the cost of updates varies depending upon the number of changes in the source system. If the number of changes increases, the cost of updates also increases, but the cost of refresh remains the same. As general guidance, if the number of records to be updated falls between 15%–25% as shown in Fig 8.17, then the update option is preferred but if 25% of the records change daily, then it is better to refresh the data warehouse.

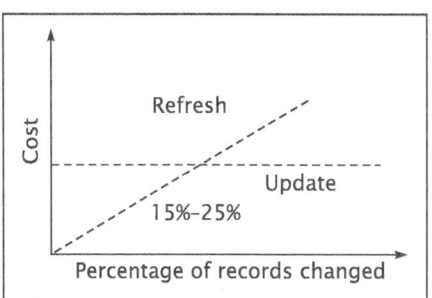

Figure 8.17 Application of refresh and update process

8.4.3 Loading the Fact Tables and the Dimension Tables

In a data warehouse, dimension tables contain attributes that are used to analyse basic measurements such as sales, costs, profits, etc. Customers, salesperson, time, region, product are some common examples of business dimensions. The procedure of maintenance of dimension tables includes initial loading of the tables, thereafter, applying the changes on an ongoing basis.

The keys of records in the source systems are different from the keys of the data warehouse. Therefore, before source data can be applied to the dimension tables, whether during initial loading or during updating, the production keys must be converted to system generated keys in the data warehouse. These key conversions must be done as a part of transformation process. The next issue is how to handle Type 1, Type 2, and Type 3 changes in the data warehouse. Figure 8.18 shows how we deal with this issue in the data warehouse.

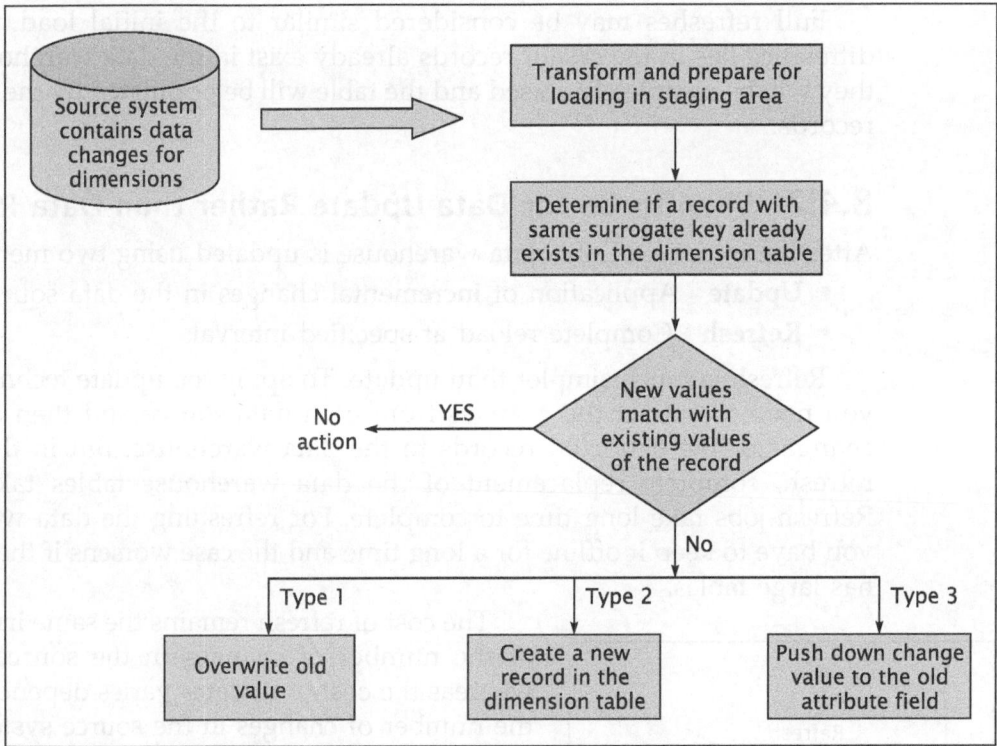

Figure 8.18 Handling Type 1, Type 2, and Type 3 changes

As discussed earlier, the key of the fact tables is a concatenation of the keys of the dimension tables. This is the reason why dimension tables are loaded before the fact tables. First the keys of the dimension tables are formed, they are surrogate keys or system generated sequence numbers. After these surrogate keys have been formed, then the fact table keys are formed and the corresponding record is entered.

8.5 DATA QUALITY

Can you imagine that a small error that may be irrelevant in the operational system may cause huge distortion in the results obtained from the data warehouse. Poor data quality in the source systems results in poor decisions by the users of the data warehouse. Dirty data is one of the most common reasons for the failure of a data warehouse.

The moment the users realize that the data is of unacceptable quality, they lose their confidence in the data warehouse. Hence all the efforts made by the users, sponsors, and members of the project team are lost. Once the users lose their trust in the warehouse, they will never be willing to come back to it for making strategic decisions.

8.5.1 The Need for Data Quality

To understand the criticality of data quality in a data warehouse system, let us first examine the benefits of data quality.

Boosts confidence in decision-making and enhances strategic decision-making If the data in the data warehouse is reliable and of high quality, then decisions based on the information will be sound and effective. No data warehouse can add value to a business until the data is clean and of a high quality.

Enables better customer service Different types of customers need different types of services. Quality information helps the executives and managers to cater to the needs of different groups of users as per their aspirations and expectations.

Increases opportunity to add better value to the services Good quality data in a data warehouse opens the doors to immense opportunities to cross-sell across product lines and departments. The marketing managers can form a list of buyers of one product and then use this information to determine all other products that every individual buyer may be interested in. So after getting this information, the marketing department can conduct well targeted campaigns.

Reduces costs and risks The topmost risk behind lack of quality data in the data warehouse is that poor data would lead to poor decisions and can some-times also lead to disastrous consequences. Other risks include wastage of time and resources and malfunctioning of the entire system. For example, if the data about the customers is incorrect or incomplete in the data warehouse, sending mails for letting them know about promotional coupons will be futile.

Improves productivity The primary goal of a data warehouse is to provide enterprise-wide information to the users for streamlining processes and operations. It is the accurate, timely, and business wide information which in turn leads to effective decision making thereby increasing the productivity of the business as a whole.

Figure 8.19 reveals the importance of maintaining the quality of data in a warehouse.

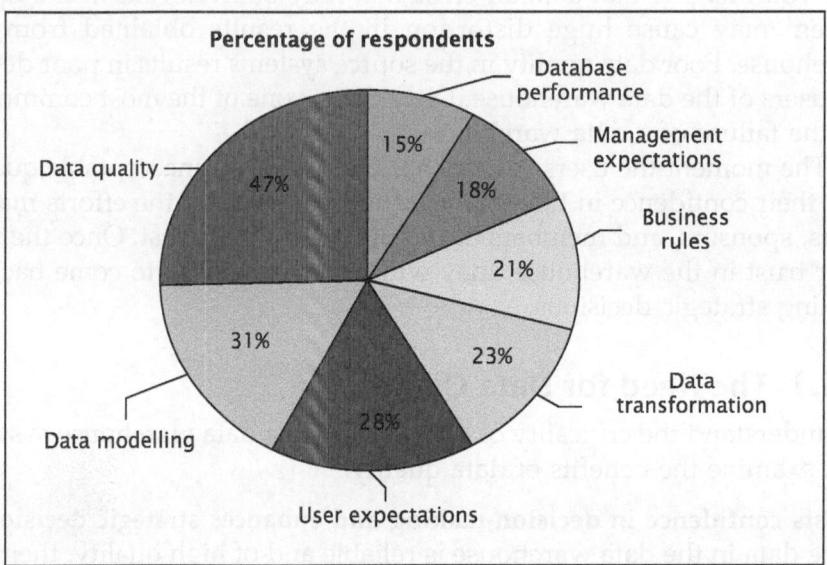

Figure 8.19 Data quality is the top-most challenge in a data warehouse environment

After analysing the benefits of data quality, let us talk about the costs of poor data quality. Cleansing the data and improving the quality of data requires both money and effort, but these expenditures are justifiable in a data warehouse environment. The cost of not having good quality data can be viewed as below:

- Bad decisions.
- Lost business opportunities.
- Wastage of resources.
- Inconsistent data reports.
- Time and effort needed to correct the data.

8.5.2 Categories of Errors

The categories of errors which affect the data quality can be divided into four categories: (a) incomple errors, (b) incorrect errors, (c) incomprehensibility errors, and (d) inconsistency errors.

Incomplete Errors

Missing records This means a record that should be in a source system is not present. It is not possible to spot this type of error unless there is another system or old reports to tally with.

Missing fields   These are fields that should be there but are absent.

Records or fields that, by design, are not being recorded   That is, by intelligent or careless design, data that is needed in the data warehouse are not being recorded anywhere. This situation can arise because of any of the two factors–first, there may be dimension table attributes that needs to be recorded but which are not in any system feeding the data warehouse. For example, the marketing manager may have a personal classification scheme for products indicating the degree to which items are being promoted. Second, if the data is being fed from multiple systems and one of the source systems does not record a field that will be needed by the data warehouse users.

Incorrect Errors

Wrong codes   This generally takes place when an old transaction processing system has assigned a code that the new transaction processing system does not use. Now if the code is not valid, the system is going to fall into problems.

Wrong calculations, aggregations   This situation can occur when the data that has to be loaded has already been calculated or aggregated outside the data warehouse environment. Before loading the data a check has to be made on it.

Duplicate records   This problem occurs when there are duplicate records in the source systems that are feeding the data warehouse.

Wrong information entered into the source system   A source system may contain data that was incorrectly entered into the system. For instance, someone may have keypunched 6/9/07 as 9/6/07.

Incomprehensibility Errors

These are the types of conditions that make source data difficult to read.

Multiple fields within one field   This situation occurs when the source system has one field that in turn contains information for multiple fields in the data warehouse database. By far the most common occurrence of this problem is when the field name is broken into multiple fields like first name, middle name, and last name, e.g. "Tim E. Burnard", is kept in one field in the source system and it is necessary to parse this into three fields in the warehouse.

Unknown codes   There may be certain codes whose meanings are not possible to interpret, may be due to lack of documentation.

Inconsistency Errors

The inconsistency errors form the biggest category of errors as similar data from different systems can easily be inconsistent.

Inconsistent use of different codes   The most common example of this error is that one system uses M and F and another system that uses 0 or 1 to distinguish gender.

Table 8.2 Various sources of pollution of data

System conversion	System conversions and migrations are prominent reasons for data pollution.	For example, conversion from flat file to hierarchical database and finally to relational database.
Data aging	Older values lose their significance with the passage of time.	For example, the product code as a part of product table's primary key may not be relevant and newer applications thus want to remove it.
Heterogeneous system integration	Heterogeneous and disparate source systems may lead to corrupt or inconsistent data.	For example, if the sources for one table involve several heterogeneous systems like flat files, network databases, relational databases, and hierarchical databases.
Poor database design	DBMS not providing support for verification of the conformance of business rules can pollute the data.	Adhering to entity and referential integrity prevents some kind of data pollution.
Incomplete information at data entry	Some fields may either have no values for the data items or the have N/A or other generic values that may be of no use.	For example, the users may not have filled the data about their telephone number or may have filled 2's in all the ten digits.
Fraud	Deliberate attempts to enter incorrect data.	For example, fields containing the units of product sold may represent an incorrect value.
Lack of policies	If there are no prevention rules followed by a company to cater for incorrect and corrupted data, then it would lead to creeping of data quality problems.	For example, if there are no checks to see if the user is filling the value within the specified domain range, then the user may intentionally or unintentionally fill incorrect values.

Inconsistent meaning of a code   This problem arises when the definition of an organizational entity changes over time. For example, in 2003, the organization's customers are A, B, C, and D. Later on in the year 2006, Customer A buys Customer B, followed by Customer A buying Customer C in 2007 and finally in the year 2008, Customer A sells of a part of what was A and C to Customer D. If suppose the data warehouse is built in 2008, the data warehouse project team may face the problem of identifying the sales to customers A, B, C, and D in previous years.

Inconsistent aggregating   Due to inconsistent business rules multiple sets of aggregated data will contain different results in different source systems.

Lack of referential integrity   This error occurs when the source systems have been built without this basic check.

Table 8.2 lists the various sources which can pollute the data.

8.5.3 Issues in Data Cleansing

Before beginning to take an initiative to improve the quality of the data, the users and the members of the project team have to take a number of decisions. Data cleansing is not a simple task. Besides, having absolute data quality is unrealistic in the real world.

When it comes to data cleansing, you are faced with a few fundamental questions and answering them is a must. In this section, we will study what these questions are and what sort of decisions need to be taken.

Which Data to Cleanse

It is a root decision on which both the users and the project team must jointly work. It must primarily be the user's decision. IT professionals alone can help them decide. But it is the users who know better what type of data they need from the data warehouse. The team must determine how the data has to be cleaned and weigh the benefits of data cleansing with the aftermaths of leaving the dirty data to study how it will affect any analysis made by the users in the data warehouse.

Where to Cleanse

It is worth noting that the operational systems are not only the sources of data that has to be stored in the data warehouse but they are a the source of corrupted data. It is from these source systems that the corrupted data moves into the staging area and finally from the staging area, to the data warehouse. This leaves the members of the data warehouse project team with three options while deciding where to cleanse the data. Figure 8.20 shows where to cleanse the data.

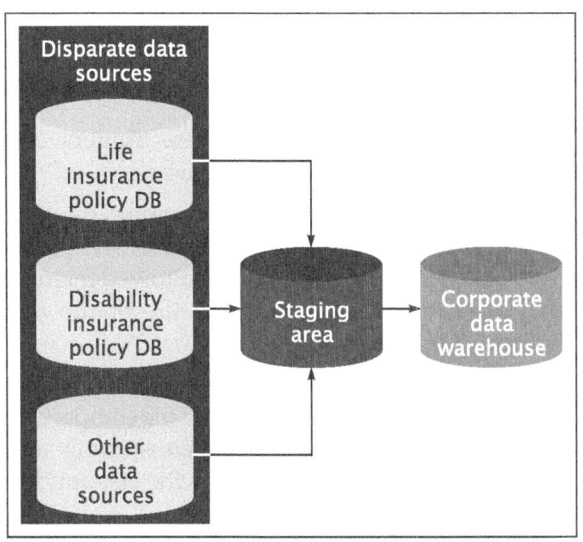

Figure 8.20 Issues in data cleansing

Practically speaking, cleansing the data after it has arrived in the data warehouse repository is not feasible, as it may result in undoing the effects of many of the processes for moving and loading the data. So, the data is cleansed before loading it into the data warehouse. Thus, now the project team is left with only two options where they can cleanse the data.

Cleansing the data in the staging area is easy and sounds practical. In the data staging area you have already solved extraction problems and you are well aware of the structure, content and nature of the data. But even this approach has some limitations. Polluted data will continue flowing into the staging area from the source systems. The cost of dirty data in the source systems does not get reduced and the source systems will be suffering from the consequences of data corruption. The same reports produced from the source system and the data warehouse may be inconsistent or may be contradictory at the worst. On the other hand, if the data is cleansed in the source systems, it would be similar to undertaking a complex, expensive and a difficult task in hand.

How to Cleanse

If the teams decide to cleanse the data in the source systems, then it will have to find the appropriate tools that can be applied to source system files and formats. This may not be easy if most of the organization's source systems are fairly old. In that case, the team will have no option but to fall back on in-house programs.

8.5.4 Conclusion

- A lot of tedious work needs to be done for keeping good quality data.
- The data warehouse project team may spend much more time checking for errors than cleaning up errors.
- The errors of inconsistency are the most difficult to tackle.
- The complexity of a data warehouse increases geometrically with the number of sources of data fed into it.
- The complexity of a data warehouse increases geometrically with the span of time of data to be fed into it.

Recapitulation

ETL functions are challenging because the source systems are disparate and run on different platforms. They do not preserve historical data and the quality of data cannot be guaranteed. Also the data type, format, and naming convention may be different in different source systems.

Various types of raw data processing that take place at the staging area include–data standardization, transformation, sorting and merging of records, management of surrogate keys, and production of aggregate data.

Data extraction issues involve source identification, method of extraction, extraction frequency, time window, job sequencing, and exception handling.

Data extraction techniques can be broadly classified into two categories–immediate data extraction and deferred data extraction.

In immediate data extraction the data extraction is real-time. The techniques that can be followed include – capture through transaction log, capture through database triggers, and capture through source applications.

In deferred data extraction technique, the data capture does not capture the data in real-time. The techniques that can be followed include: capture based on date and timestamp and capture by comparing files.

Data extraction based on timestamp is the most preferred technique while the file comparison method is the most time-consuming and should always be applied as the last option.

Data can be loaded in four different ways: initial load, incremental load, full refresh, and update.

During the data loads, the data warehouse has to be offline for the duration of the loading process. So you need to find a time window when the loads may be scheduled without affecting the warehouse users.

In destructive merge of data loading, the incoming data is applied to the target data. If the primary key of the incoming record matches with the key of an existing record, then update the matching target record.

In constructive merge, if the primary key of an incoming record matches with the key on an existing record, then leave the existing record, add the incoming record, and mark the added record as superceding the old record.

Management and control component has two major functions– to constantly monitor all the ongoing operations, and to recover from problems when things go wrong. Management services include monitoring the growth and periodically archiving data from the data warehouse and governing the data security.

Poor data quality in the source systems results in poor decisions by the users and hence becomes the most common reason for failure of a data warehouse. On the other hand, good quality data enhances strategic decision making, enables better customer service, increases opportunity to add better value to the services, and improves productivity.

Categories of data quality errors include incomplete errors, incorrect errors, incomprehensibility errors, and inconsistency errors.

Incomplete errors are those errors where some fields may have missing values; incorrect errors occur because of wrong values in the fields; incomprehensibility errors arise due to multiple fields within one field; and inconsistency errors occur as a result of inconsistent use of codes and attributes.

The data quality tools can be applied to the source systems or in the staging area before loading the data in the data warehouse.

Generally, the data quality tools assist the project team in two ways. Data error discovery tools work on the source data to identify inaccuracies and inconsistencies. Data correction tools help to fix the corrupt data.

Objective Questions

1. **Multiple choice questions**
    (i) Where do ETL functions take place?
        (a) Source systems
        (b) Data warehouse
        (c) Data staging area
        (d) None of these
    (ii) Which technique cannot be used on file-oriented system?
        (a) Capture through transaction log
        (b) Capture by date and time
        (c) Capture by comparing files
        (d) Capture through database trigger
    (iii) Which technique is the most time consuming?
        (a) Capture through transaction log
        (b) Capture by date and time
        (c) Capture by comparing files
        (d) Capture through database trigger

    (iv) If 25% of the records change daily, then which option is preferred?
        (a) Update
        (b) Refresh
        (c) Initial load
        (d) Noe of these

2. **Fill in the blanks**
    1. ETL stands for _____, _____, and _____ process.
    2. Capture through transaction logs reads all _____ transactions.
    3. Capture through database triggers is applicable only for _____ applications.
    4. _____ are stored procedures that are stored on the database.
    5. Capture through database triggers cannot be used on legacy systems.

6. If there are old legacy systems, then _____ technique is a better option.

7. In _____ the contents of tables are erased completely and then reloaded with fresh data.

8. Load the _____ tables first and then the _____ tables.

9. Type 1 changes uses destructive mode.

10. The cost of _____ remains the same irrespective of the number of changes in the source systems whereas cost of _____ varies.

3. State true or false

1. For a data warehouse, the primary data source consists of its operational systems.

2. Capture through transaction logs is applicable to non-database applications also.

3. Data capture through triggers does not occur at the source system.

4. Capture through transaction logs affect the performance of source systems.

5. Capture in source applications can be used on legacy systems.

6. Capture based on date and timestamp cannot be used on file-oriented system.

7. The deferred data extraction techniques have maximum impact on the operational systems.

8. Primary keys of the source tables can be taken as the primary keys for the fact and dimension tables.

9. During initial data loading, ongoing changes are periodically applied.

10. During the data loads, the data warehouse has to be offline for the duration of the loading process.

Review Questions

1. In a data warehouse, business requirements of the users form the single most powerful driving force. Justify.

2. For information delivery, what is the flow of data in case top-down and bottom-up approaches are followed for implementing the data warehouse?

3. List the major functions and services for information delivery. Describe each briefly.

4. Write a short note on the importance of metadata in a data warehouse environment.

5. Why is metadata important for IT and for the end-users?

6. How does metadata play a vital role in automation of tasks in data warehouses?

7. Why is metadata used for data acquisition, data storage, and information delivery?

8. Explain business metadata and technical metadata.

9. List some of the requirements that a metadata repository must satisfy.

10. As a data storage specialist, what type of metadata can help you? Choose one of the data storage processes and explain the role of metadata in that process.

11. ETL functions are most challenging in a data warehouse environment. Why?

12. List some activities that are a part of the ETL process. List the steps followed in the ETL process.

13. The diversity of source systems poses a great challenge in the ETL process. Justify.

14. List the functions that form a part of data transformation process.

15. Why do you need a separate staging area? Explain how the raw data is processed in the staging area.

16. List some of the functions of data extraction. Discuss the issues involved in data extraction and in source identification.

17. Write a short note on the different data extraction techniques.

18. Compare the data extraction techniques and state which technique you will prefer the most for your data warehouse environment. Give reasons to justify your answer.

19. Why is key structuring important before loading the data in the data warehouse?

20. Define the terms: initial load, incremental load, full refresh, and update.

21. Differentiate destructive merge and constructive merge.

22. Compare data refresh with updates in case of a data warehouse environment.

23. Give reasons why data quality is critical in a data warehouse environment.

24. Explain the merits of having quality data in your data warehouse. Discuss some of the side effects of having poor quality data.

25. Explain the role of different participants in the data quality team.

26. As a data quality expert for a large bank having many branches, list the major considerations and produce an outline for a document describing the initiative, policies, and the procedures.

27. How does the data warehouse differ from an operational system in usage and values?

28. Explain the procedure for loading dimension tables and fact tables. Of these two tables, which table will be loaded first?

29. Write a short note on the data storage component.

30. Explain the potential of information in a data warehouse environment.

31. Discuss the information usage modes and approaches in a data warehouse environment.

32. How will you classify the users of the data warehouse?

33. How does the process of information delivery differ in a data warehouse from that of an operational system?

34. Write a short note on the methods of information delivery.

35. What criteria will you follow to select an appropriate tool for delivering information in your data warehouse environment? List the steps that would be taken to make the final selection.

36. List and categorize the errors which affect the quality of data in a data warehouse.

37. Write a short note on data quality tools. How will you categorize these tools? Explain.

38. Explain the data quality framework and the data purification process. State the role that the steering committee plays in the data quality framework.

9

TESTING, GROWTH, AND MAINTENANCE

Learning Objectives

This chapter concentrates on the testing, growth, and maintenance aspects of the data warehouse. Once the data warehouse design is ready, it has to be tested and reviewed to weed out problems and issues that have not been solved and could be problematic in the future.

Thereafter, we will analyse how a data warehouse should be tested for robustness and various other parameters that are important for the end-user. Last but not the least, we will see why and how the data warehouse should be continuously monitored for future enhancements.

Case Study

Once the project team is through with building the data warehouse, David who was very excited about the project made a big mistake of deploying it in the client's organization soon after the data warehouse was ready. David had taken the best decisions and utmost care to see that everything works according to what was planned, yet this does not guarantee that the data warehouse will be able to satisfy its user groups as well. After all, the best shoes made in this world may not fit your feet well.

When the data warehouse was implemented in the client's environment, the users seemed to be unhappy as the front-end was not very user-friendly and they found it difficult to work with. Moreover, some users complained that the information drawn from the warehouse was erroneous. The whole thing upset the client and the software company and gradually no user was ready to use the data warehouse.

Hence, it is very crucial that the data warehouse be tested before it is finally deployed in the client's organization. There are different levels of testing about which we will read in this chapter.

Even after testing the data warehouse, David's job is not over as it is his team's duty to see that the users are given appropriate training and support to learn how to use the new system, see that it is working well with time, and upgrade it to the changing needs of the users.

9.1 DATA WAREHOUSE DESIGN REVIEW

Data design review is one of the most effective techniques to ensure quality in the OLTP systems. With an effective design review, a majority of the errors can be detected even before coding actually starts. No doubt, earlier the error is detected the easier and cheaper it is to correct. The concept of reviewing the design also applies to the data warehouse.

A data warehouse is built iteratively so that it is developed around one subject at a time. Thus, it is recommended to review the design whenever a subject area is designed and is ready to be added in the data warehouse environment.

All the people who are at stake in the data warehouse project must be a part of the whole process of design review. These people include: the data warehouse administrator, programmers, the analysts, end-users, and other staff from the operations, system support, and management departments. When all these people are present together at the same place to review the design, there is no scope of miscommunication and misinterpretation and hence, it can lead to a better design.

During the design review, all issues regarding the design, development, project management or usage of the data that may prevent success are discussed. Thus, any aspect of the system that is seen as a hindrance to the success of the project forms a crucial part of the review process. The result of the design review is an appraisal to the management regarding the issues and recommendations for further action, the complete documentation of current status of the project, and a list of actions that have to be taken.

One thing that must be taken care of during design review is that the facilitator of the review process must never be the project leader. As a matter of fact, it is best that the facilitator be a person who has nothing to do with the project. This would in turn help to provide a useful insight with an external perspective and a fresh look. The facilitator will feel free to criticize the project and this criticism will make the design review even more powerful.

9.1.1 Contents of a Typical Design Review

Issue 1 Are all the concerned parties attending the review process? This is very important as the attendance of all the people involved is vital for the success of the project.

Issue 2 Have the end-user requirements been anticipated and are these requirements represented in the design? If end-user's requirements have not been anticipated and are thus not a part of the design, then the success of the project lies in jeopardy.

Issue 3 What part of the data warehouse has already been built. Which are the subjects that have been added, in what detail, and how much processing has already been done, are important questions to answer.

Issue 4 How many major subjects have to be built in the data warehouse and how many have already been implemented? Since a data warehouse is built iteratively one subject at a time, these questions are vital to answer.

Issue 5 Is there any decision support system other than the data warehouse that has been implemented in the organization? Because if two DSS systems will work in parallel, then there may arise some conflicts or overlapping.

Issue 6 Before the data warehouse can be built, is the high level data model which identifies the entities and relationships complete?

Issue 7 Have the source systems been identified, have the attributes for the records been identified, how will the missing values be filled, how will data be standardized, to what level the data will be summarized, are other questions to be answered.

Issue 8 How frequently will the data be extracted from the source systems to be stored in the data warehouse? Which extraction technique will be followed: based on timestamps, comparison between before and after images of data, using log files, or through applications? It is an issue because answers to these questions will have a direct impact on the resources that are required for refreshing the data warehouse.

Issue 9 What is the amount of data that will be stored in the data warehouse?

Issue 10 Which ETL tool will be used to feed the data warehouse, what are its bottlenecks, to what extent does it require technical support?

Issue 11 Is the data warehouse that is being built easily scalable so that at later point of time, more storage, more data, and more subjects can be added to it.

Issue 12 How frequently will the data in the data warehouse need to be restructured? That is, how frequently will there be a need to add columns, modify keys, etc. The extent to which these activities may impact other ongoing processes is also estimated.

Issue 13 What is the expected level of performance? Has the DSS service level agreement been signed that clearly specifies the average performance during peak hours and non-peak hours, worst performance during peak hours, and non-peak hours, etc?

Issue 14 What indexing technique will be used and how will the data be partitioned?

Issue 15 At what level of granularity is the data stored in the data warehouse: high level, low level, or at multiple levels of granularity? Choosing the right level of granularity is one of the most important design decisions that have to be taken.

Issue 16 In case of a system failure, how long will it take for the system to recover? The time it takes for recovery, the frequency of failures, and the effect that the failure has on the system are important issues to be considered.

Issue 17   What is the security mechanism that has been implemented for the data in the data warehouse?

Issue 18   What are the audit requirements in the data warehouse environment?

Issue 19   What are the overheads involved in compaction and de-compaction of data and encoding and de-coding of data when encoding of data is done to save storage space?

Issue 20   What external data will be stored in the data warehouse, how frequently, how will it be entered in the data warehouse, and what techniques will be used to test the accuracy of the data?

Issue 21   What will be the partitioning technique that will be followed to segregate the data into multiple partitions?

Issue 22   Will any sparse indexes be created to save huge amounts of processing? Since sparse indexes call for a lot of overhead, it is a significant design issue.

Issue 23   What techniques will be used to monitor the performance of the data warehouse at row level, column level, and the table level?

Issue 24   What are the resources required for loading the data into the data warehouse? Can the loading process get completed during overnight processing or does parallel loading have to be done to accomplish it?

Issue 25   Will the data warehouse collect clickstream data? If yes, then to what extent will the granularity manager filter the web generated data? We will learn more about it in the last chapter.

Issue 26   Will the data warehouse store unstructured data also? Although unstructured data is very useful but integrating this data into the data warehouse calls for a lot of editing and organization of the data to suit the formats of the data warehouse. If unstructured data will be stored, then what will be the techniques applied to reduce the amount of space that is needed to store them?

Issue 27   At what rate is the data warehouse data expected to grow? Early anticipation is always good as it will help in capacity planning.

Issue 28   Will the data warehouse database be designed using relational technology or multidimensional technology?

Issue 29   What kind of training will the end-users be given before they can actually start using the data warehouse?

Issue 30   How will the users be made aware of any changes that are made in the data warehouse like whenever new data is added, a new subject is added, or other changes are made to benefit the users?

9.2 DEVELOPING THE DATA WAREHOUSE ITERATIVELY

Building a data warehouse is a very big project. The entire data warehouse is never built in one go, rather it is built iteratively. The data warehouse is built in parts. The second part follows the first the third part is built once the second one is complete, so on and so forth. There are many reasons why iterative development is preferred for a data warehouse project.

- The companies that have opted for iterative development of a data warehouse have done it successfully. Considering the track record of success, iterative development is always recommended.
- The end-users find it difficult to articulate the requirements in the absence of first iteration.
- The project can get a good support of management when the first iteration yields tangible benefits.
- Results can be visualized earlier.

For iterative development, the data warehouse design model should support such a kind of development effort so that the future iterations do not clash with the first iteration. With a sound data design model, this will not be the case because all the iterations will be based on the common data model. Building the iterations under a unifying data model produces a cohesive and tightly orchestrated system.

9.3 TESTING

In the traditional operational systems, organizations put everything that was newly developed through the "test" environment. Only after the developed code was tested, it was put into the production system. However, with a shift towards decision support system (DSS) like that of data warehouse environment, the "test" environment seems to have dropped by the wayside.

Usually the data warehouses do not have a mirror test environment. The first reason behind it is the cost. Data warehouses cost huge sums of money with terabytes of data and the processors and software needed to control and manage that data. It is not possible to spend the same amount of money just to have a place to test. No organization can afford the double expenses.

The second reason for not having a test data warehouses is that there are no programs to be tested. The data warehouse environment is strikingly different from the operational systems. In the operational systems, when a new system goes live, there are programs and databases that need to be tested but a data warehouse is initially empty and the data is simply added.

The third reason behind not having any test place is that the data warehouses are built in small iterations. When initial data loading is done the data becomes a part of the data warehouse. In this case testing can be done only on the new data being added incrementally.

However, the fact that there is no separate test environment for the data warehouse does not mean that testing does not need to be done at all. In fact, the data warehouse needs to be tested thoroughly and there has to be a quality assurance for the data warehouse environment.

The first and foremost place that needs to be tested is the ETL process. ETL processing is done with the data being passed from the operational systems to the data warehouse environment. Under ETL processing, the data undergoes a complex set of transformations. Thus, it is this place where the code that incorporates the complexity needs to be tested. It is during ETL processing that the data is checked for its quality. The second place that needs extensive testing is the data warehouse environment where the extracted, integrated and transformed data is loaded.

9.3.1 Testing the Data Warehouse

Like every other operational system, data warehouse also needs testing. The complexity and the large size of the warehouse systems make extensive testing even more difficult and crucial. The fact that queries may take several minutes to hours to execute means that small-scale testing is not sufficient. The queries scale with the data thereby making comprehensive testing take more time to complete. There are different levels of testing:

- Unit testing.
- Integration testing.
- System testing.
- Acceptance testing.
- Performance testing.

Unit testing   In unit testing, also called *white box testing*, each development unit is tested on its own by the developer of that particular module. It is vital that before any test plan is enacted, the unit testing should be complete. During the course of its life cycle, every module undergoes frequent testing, as each change made to the module will require the unit to be re-tested.

Integration testing   In integration testing, different modules that make up a component of the data warehouse application are tested to ensure that they work together. Integration testing takes place quite late in the development cycle.

System and acceptance testing   In system testing, the entire data warehouse application is tested as a single unit. Each component of the warehouse is tested to ensure that when put together, they work properly and that they do not cause system resource bottlenecks. However, system testing should not be confused with user acceptance testing. Acceptance testing also tests the complete data warehouse application but the basic difference is that during acceptance tests the users will conduct their own tests on the system.

The bought-in products such as management and query tools are tested in the full system environment during the system testing. This will often indicate the usefulness and overhead of the tools, as isolated testing of these tools gives no real indication of their effect on the system. However, to carry out this activity, the testing team should have a firm understanding of the functionality of the business and must validate the amount of data that is transferred from the source systems to the target data warehouse.

System and acceptance testing are two different activities. In system testing, the system is tested with full functionality and is expected to function as in the production environment. After system testing is over, the system should be acceptable to the client for use in terms of ETL process integrity and business functionality. This is ensured in user acceptance testing. Table 9.1 summarizes different types of testing in case of a data warehouse environment.

Performance testing It is the most important aspect after data validation as many data warehouse systems might satisfy all the tests above and may fail at the performance level test at the end. Performance testing should:

- Test whether the ETL process completes within the load window. Also check the ETL process for the time taken for updating and processing of reject records.
- Test the time taken to refresh standard reports.
- Test the time taken for refreshing complex reports.

Table 9.1 Testing the data warehouse

Unit testing	<ul><li>Check whether extraction routines access all the required data accurately.</li><li>Check if all computations done as per the business rules are accurate.</li><li>Check whether the correct value for the data is entered.</li><li>Check if the slowly changing dimensions are handled correctly.</li><li>Check for the correctness of surrogate keys.</li><li>Test whether the data from the schema is reflected correctly in the report.</li><li>Test if the data has been drawn from the correct table as per the database design.</li><li>Test if the OLAP tools that make cubes on fly show the correct data.</li><li>Test if the displayed results are in the specified units.</li><li>Test the graphical results against correct type, labels, legends, font, and colour.</li></ul>
Integration testing	<ul><li>Test for the sequence of jobs followed to compute the result.</li><li>Study the dependency on how error in one job affects the other subsequent jobs.</li><li>Test the generation of error logs.</li><li>Test the restarting of jobs after failure.</li></ul>
System testing	<ul><li>Test if the fields present in the reports are as per the specifications.</li><li>Test the roll-up and drill-down features.</li><li>Test whether column headings are as per the specifications.</li><li>Test whether the displayed data is in correct units.</li><li>Test the validity of the graphs.</li><li>Test other special features like alert in exception reports.</li></ul>

For performing such tests in the data warehouse environment, at least one year's data should be present in the data warehouse. Besides this, data loads for single days or batch windows should be done to test whether they complete within the specified time window. For this there are a number of tools available in the market to simulate the number of concurrent users accessing the system.

9.3.2 Developing the Test Plan

The first and foremost task in developing a test plan is to come up with a test schedule. A majority of the product development methodologies include metrics for producing time estimates for testing as well as development. But it has been observed that due to its enormous size and complexity, these metrics fall well short of the requirements for testing a data warehouse application.

The data warehouse environment is a new system and rapid testing to a rigid schedule is simply not possible. For example, hardware failure like losing a disk or human error such as accidentally deleting or overwriting a large table can cause unwanted delays.

Therefore, a rule of thumb is to apply normal metrics for estimating the time required for testing and then simply double it. However, this doubling should be done after making adjustments for contingency factors and other normal factors. So in case of everything being normal, if the metrics predicts that it may take 60 days to test the data warehouse application then the team must add at least 50% contingency, bringing the total to 90 days and then double this figure making 180 days.

As a reader, you may think that the team has a lot more time than actually required and that this time may be close to or even exceed the development times allocated, but it is vital to allow enough testing time if the data warehouse has to run as a successful decision support system.

9.3.3 Testing Backup and Recovery Processes

One of the key tests will be performed while testing the backup and recovery strategy. This testing needs to cater for the following aspects:

- Failure of the media.
- Any loss or damage of the log files.
- Any kind of loss or damage of the archive files.
- Failure that occurs during data movement.
- Other miscellaneous scenarios.

It is important that complete testing is carried out in a data warehouse environment. Simply backing up a file does not ensure that it can be easily recovered at any later point of time. Rather any backup management software should be fully tested. For example, to test the recovery process of a lost data file, a data file is first deliberately deleted and then recovered from its backup copy.

9.3.4 Testing the Data Warehouse Environment

Testing of the data warehouse is another important test that will have to be performed. There are a number of aspects that need to be tested:

- Security of data.
- Configuration of disks.
- Job scheduler.
- Management tools.
- Database management software.

In a data warehouse environment, security is difficult to test unless there is a clear document specifying what operations are allowed by which group of users. Thus, testing should be done by extracting the list of all disallowed operations and devising a test for each. These tests should be run multiple times during system testing to ensure that newly added data and aggregations do not cause security breaches.

The disk configuration should be tested thoroughly to identify any potential I/O bottlenecks during system testing. In order to control the daily operations of the data warehouse, some sort of scheduling software will be needed that would have to be thoroughly tested during the system testing.

Since there is a possibility for many of the processes in the data warehouse to swamp the system resources, if allowed to run at the wrong time, scheduling control of these processes is essential for the success of the data warehouse.

Then, it is important to control the sequencing of certain processes. For example, until and unless the daily data loading is complete, the overnight aggregation maintenance processes cannot be run. In case it is allowed to run before the data loading gets completed then some data would be missing from the aggregations. Unwinding this type of problem may consume a lot of time and in certain cases may be effectively impossible.

System testing entails verification of all the management tools that are going to be used to operate the data warehouse. The aim of the system test is to test all of the following areas:

- Data warehouse application code.
- Day-to-day operational procedure.
- Overnight processing.
- Backup and recovery strategy.
- Query performance.
- Scheduling software.
- Management and monitoring tools.

9.3.5 Testing the Database

Data warehouse testing is categorized by three types of tests:

- Testing the database manager and the monitoring tools.
- Testing features of the data warehouse.
- Testing performance of the data warehouse database.

In order to test the database manager and monitoring tools, it is recommended to use them in creating, running, and managing of the test database. To test the database software, first make a list of the features that have to be tested.

The main features that must be tested are:

- Parallel query execution.
- Parallel building of the indexes.
- Parallel data loading.

Next, you need to test the performance of the queries. The fixed queries that are run regularly can conveniently be tested thoroughly. But, to test the performance of the ad hoc queries is not a trivial task. For that the team must use the documented user requirements along with their knowledge of the business to generate some queries that are meaningful to the business and then thoroughly test those queries.

You must try to test the most complex and awkward queries that one can ever think could be run. Any simpler queries that the user may run should also be tested. Then, these queries should also be run with different aggregations, different indexing strategies, with different degrees of parallelism and against different sized-datasets. As the amount of data grows, it is likely that the query execution plans will change. Therefore, make a note of the resource usage implications posed during the testing process.

Finally for testing aggregations, they can be classified into two categories: *ad hoc* and *identified*. Identified aggregations are those that have already been specified in the requirements whereas ad hoc aggregations are those that are created to solve particular performance problems and they will be created and deleted as required.

Each identified aggregation must be tested thoroughly. Generally, there are different ways in which a given aggregation table can be created and maintained. Therefore, each method should be checked to find the best compromise in terms of performance and resource usage. You may also try to build aggregations from other aggregations rather than from the base data as it would be much faster and efficient. All such options should be explored during the testing process.

9.3.6 Logging of Test Results

The team must strictly adhere to the logging and analysis of test results and the corresponding documentation of the test results. One example of such analysis is given in Table 9.2.

Table 9.2 Error category area characteristics

Error Category	Area	Characteristics
Minor	ETL	- Incorrect naming conventions followed in ETL.
Major	ETL	- Wrong transformation, target table record count not tallying with source tables and rejects.
Cosmetic	OLAP reports	- Positioning of data items, colour font, and order of columns in report.
Minor	OLAP reports	- Incorrrect heading, data formats. - Incorrect transformation. - Incorrect unit conversions.
Major	OLAP reports	- Data items absent, incorrect drills.
Fatal	System	- Incorrect data.

- For verification of the report data with the operational system, log the query results along with screenshots of the reports and then later on compare with results obtained from the operational systems.
- Before starting the testing process, fix the grain of measuring testing activities. This would help in designing the test cases.
- Testing process does not end with executing the test cases. Thus, maintain the count of the number of conditions that were executed, number of conditions which failed and number of conditions which could not be executed with reasons.
- Finally, maintain proper traceability between all the testing documents.

9.4 MONITORING THE DATA WAREHOUSE

Once you have successfully completed the user acceptance testing and have deployed the initial version of the data warehouse, you find the users are very happy. They are fully trained and now they make use of the data warehouse without any kind of assistance from the IT. But this is just the beginning. The data warehouse project team needs to ensure that the data warehouse is poised for growth. The team also needs to make sure that the monitoring functions are all in place, the training and support functions are consolidated and streamlined properly, and the database administration and tuning functions are ready and working appropriately.

When you as a part of the project team implement an OLTP system, you do not stop your work after the deployment of the system. The database administrator regularly inspects the performance of the system. Same is the case with a data warehouse. You cannot stop your work after the deployment of the system, but you need to continuously monitor the system performance.

The scope of monitoring the data warehouse environment is much wider than that of monitoring an OLTP system because it extends over many features and functions. In the absence of a formalized manner to monitor the data warehouse, desired results cannot be achieved.

Only a sound monitoring process can give a direction as well as provide the appropriate data that is needed to plan for growth and to improve the performance of the warehouse.

Figure 9.1 shows the data warehousing monitoring activity. The monitoring statistics serve as the life-blood of the monitoring activity that leads into growth planning and fine-tuning of the data warehouse.

The information about data warehouse functioning is collected using monitoring statistics that are indicators of the warehouse perpormance. These values provide information on the utilization of the hardware and software resources and help you to determine how the data warehouse is performing.

The DBA monitors the data warehouse by viewing statistics, such as disk storage utilization, memory buffer activities, usage of buffer cache, perfor-

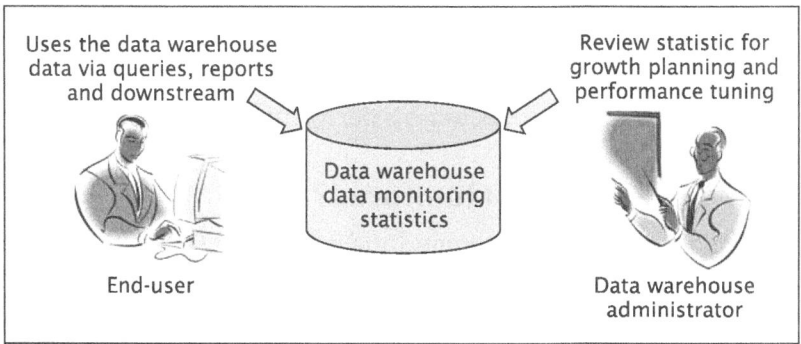

Figure 9.1 Monitoring activities

mance of input-output devices, memory management, number of customers, tables size, number of accesses to the fact tables, usage of subject areas, number of completed queries during the day, minimum time for which each user stays online with the data warehouse, total number of daily users, maximum number of users during different time slots within a day, total length of the daily incremental data loading process, number of valid and invalid users, response time of queries, number of reports formulated in a day, number of active tables in the data warehouse, and the like. These indicators present the growth trends and give insights into the utility of the end-user tools.

The main issue is how to collect these statistics from the data warehouse. Two methods generally used for this purpose are: the *sampling method* and the *event-driven method*. Table 9.3 makes a comparison of the methods that are used to collect the monitoring statistics in a data warehouse environment.

Table 9.3 Sampling and event-driven method

Features	Sampling Method	Event-driven Method
Technique	It measures specific aspects of the system activities at regular intervals.	Statistics are not recorded at the specified intervals, but only when a specified event takes place.
Recording of statistics	When interval expires. This interval will be set by the DBA and will vary from one organization to another.	When an event as specified by the DBA takes place.
Impact on system overhead	Minimal.	Increased overhead.
Example	If this value is set to 30 minutes for monitoring processor utilization, then utilization statistics are recorded every 30 minutes.	If you want to monitor the product dimension table, you can set the monitoring mechanism to record the statistics when an update takes place to the dimension table.

There are a number of tools available for collecting monitoring statistics. Such types of tools are available with the database server and the host operating systems are turned on by default to collect the monitoring statistics. The third party vendor tools not only gather the values for such indicators but also interpret the results. These tools have two components: the *data collector* components as the name suggests collect the statistics and the *analyser* component analyses the statistics thus collected by performing the interpretation part.

9.4.1 Why are Statistics Monitored?

It is not unusual to observe a tremendous growth in the number of users and the complexity of the queries posed by them, even after one month of the deployment of the data warehouse. If the data warehouse is web-enabled, then this increase will be all the more. So, planning must be done for the obvious growth of the data warehouse. For doing this, you need to answer some of the crucial questions such as where is the expansion actually needed and what is the reason behind the increase in query response time.

The monitoring provides sufficient details about what is happening in the data warehouse and how the data warehouse can be prepared for growth. Table 9.4 lists the various monitoring statistics and the actions that can be taken to handle the growth problems in a data warehouse environment.

Table 9.4 Monitoring statistics and remedial actions

Monitoring Statistics	Remedial Actions
<ul><li>Disk storage utilization.</li><li>Memory buffer activities.</li><li>Usage of buffer cache.</li><li>Performance of input-output devices.</li><li>Memory management.</li><li>Number of customers.</li><li>Table size.</li><li>Number of accesses to the fact tables.</li><li>Usage of subject areas.</li><li>Number of completed queries during the day.</li><li>Minimum time for which each user stays online with the data warehouse.</li><li>Total number of daily users.</li><li>Maximum number of users during different time slots within a day.</li><li>Total length of the daily incremental data loading process.</li><li>Number of valid and invalid users.</li><li>Response time of queries.</li><li>Number of reports formulated in a day.</li><li>Number of active tables in the data warehouse.</li></ul>	<ul><li>Allocate more disk space to the data warehouse database.</li><li>Reserve some space for additional tables.</li><li>Try to minimize fragmentation by modifying file block management parameters.</li><li>Create more summary tables to quickly respond to queries that ask for summarization information.</li><li>Increase the number of memory buffers.</li><li>Try to offload report generation to some middle tier.</li><li>Plan for workload during the peak period.</li><li>Partition tables for parallel execution of the data loading process.</li><li>Manage data backups.</li></ul>

Monitoring statistics also helps in managing the performance of the system by providing key information that is useful for fine tuning the data warehouse process like query performance, incremental loads, OLAP tools, data warehouse content browsing, and report generation.

9.5 TUNING THE DATA WAREHOUSE

The *ad hoc* and entirely unpredictable nature of the data warehouse makes the tuning process even more difficult than tuning an operational database. A data warehouse usage will keep evolving over time as the user profile changes. The change in user profiles and data access patterns has a direct impact on the queries that are being run. These changes will thereby affect the aggregation tables that need to be created.

Before going live with the data warehouse, the team must have some basic measures of performance to work with. These measures include:

- Average query response time.
- Throughput rates for performing I/O operations.
- Time needed by every individual query.
- Memory requirements for every process.

The team must be clear with the target values of these measures that should be achieved in the ideal case. For example, it is useless trying to tune average response time if they are already better than those required. In fact, tuning beyond requirements can prove counterproductive. Also, it is very important that when assessing performance, the team as well as the end-users must have realistic expectations. However, in a data warehouse environment, the size and complexity of the warehouse and the ad hoc nature of the queries make expectations difficult to set.

In a data warehouse environment, it is unreasonable to expect all queries to complete in less than 3 minutes or in fact in any given time-scale. The *ad hoc* nature of the data warehouse makes it impossible to tune the system for every possible query that can be run. Thus, a reasonable expectation and thereby a reasonable goal would be that 90% of all queries against recent data to complete in under 5 minutes. Therefore, with the ad hoc nature of the data warehouse, only limited tuning can actually be done.

9.5.1 Tuning the Data Load

Data loading being the entry point into the system provides the first opportunity to improve performance. Data loading is done during overnight processing, because it is likely that nothing else can run until the data load is complete. Any problem that takes place while transferring the data, or delays in data arrival, has a direct impact on overnight processing. Therefore, anything that can be done to improve the data load performance will be beneficial.

Creation and maintenance of indexes is a crucial part of the data loading process. This activity can consume a lot of time, especially if the data is being loaded into a table that already contains some data. Here, the team has two options, either to maintain the indexes while data loading or to drop the indexes and re-create them once the loading process gets completed. Generally, the latter option is likely to be more efficient.

However, the answer to this question very much depends on how much data is already loaded, and how many indexes and constraints need to be built. For example, if we have the fact table partitioned into monthly data, then at the beginning of every month, the current monthly table will be empty, and there will be no indexes. In this case, the team may go for loading the data first and then creating the indexes.

This decision is actually a trade-off between the cost of index creation and index re-builds. Which one is better will depend on the size of the data already in the partition and the number of indexes in that partition.

Further, referential integrity checks have to be made on the data. This activity again has a direct impact on the performance of overnight processing. As already discussed, it is better to ignore such checks on the data warehouse system. However, it does not mean that integrity issues should be ignored, but rather it means that they need to be addressed in the source systems.

If all the data transformation or integrity checks occur before the data arrives at the data warehouse system, all you need to know is the expected time of arrival; otherwise the whole process will affect the capacity and performance of the data warehouse.

The data loading process can be accelerated by keeping the aforesaid points in mind. Apart from these, the process can be further improved by using parallelism. Multiple processors can be used to speed the load by sharing the workload of a single CPU. However, when using multiple processors, care must be taken to avoid I/O bottlenecks. Then the source data can also be spread over multiple disks to avoid contention on a single disk or I/O controller.

Finally, care must be taken to see that the load destination does not become a bottleneck, especially when a large number of load processes are being used. This can be done by spreading the database files across multiple disks, or by spreading the table to be loaded over multiple database files.

9.5.2 Tuning the Queries

Every data warehouse has two types of queries to execute. There are *fixed* queries that are clearly defined and well understood. Example of fixed queries include regular reports, canned queries, and common aggregations. Then there are *ad hoc* queries that are unpredictable, both in quantity and frequency. In order to tune the data warehouse, both types of queries need to be tuned, but obviously with a different technique for dealing with each one of them.

Fixed Queries

Tuning the fixed queries is generally done in the same manner as the operational databases are tuned. These queries have predictable resource requirements. Since the team knows about the query, it can perform various tests to find the best execution plan. The only real parameter with these queries is the size of the data being queried. Even this is not an issue as such because the query can be tested as often as desired.

When testing fixed queries, the team records and stores the most successful execution plan for each query. However, care must be taken to ensure that any tuning done does not adversely affect the performance of *ad hoc* queries.

Ad Hoc Queries

The number of users of the data warehouse has a direct effect on the performance of the system, especially when more of these users are *ad hoc* users. The team must have a firm understanding of the usage profiles of all the users. The more unpredictable the usage, the larger is the query size and hence more complicated is the task of tuning. Since usage profiles may keep changing, it has to be tracked over time. Besides tuning the warehouse, usage profiles are also essential for growth predictions and capacity planning.

Thus, it is clear that more the *ad hoc* nature of the query, the more difficult it is to tune the data warehouse. The team must ensure that any tuning performed on the regular run queries does not affect the performance of other important tasks taking place in the data warehouse environment. Therefore, it is best to move the query mix from *ad hoc* to predictable. To accomplish this, first the team needs to identify any similar *ad hoc* queries that are frequently run and then initiate changes to make their running more efficient. These changes include adding of indexes and aggregations especially for those queries.

Every query posed against the data warehouse database must be controlled via the query manager or some front-end tool that limits what the users can see. When a user submits a query, the query manager will place it on a query queue, and the query will be executed only when it reaches the top of the queue. Now a good question to answer here is, how many queues to create? The answer will depend on the number of concurrent queries that must be running during the day, and on the number of queries that can be left running during the night. Obviously, any query running during the night will clash with the overnight processing.

In a data warehouse environment, query management takes priority, as otherwise, the system may rapidly descend into chaos. Any query can monopolize the entire set of resources. If two such queries are run simultaneously, then problems will easily creep into the system. Thus, no query should be allowed to monopolize the system and such queries once detected should be instantly killed. These queries should then be modified by the users so that it runs in a meaningful time-frame using reasonable resources.

The other job of the query manager is to collect and maintain the following data:

- Syntax of the query.
- Execution plan of the query.
- Processor used.
- Usage of memory.
- Usage of I/O devices.
- Query elapsed time.
- Frequency of execution of the query.

Another important function that the query manager must perform is to transform any queries submitted through it. The query manager needs to be aware of the aggregate tables.

If there is a mix of small and large queries to be run, then the small queries should be executed first. But this may lead to starvation. So, multiple queues can be used, with a separate queue for smaller queries. Apart from small and large queues, there are priority queues. If there are queries with higher priority, then queue prioritization has to be done. The system may even have a separate priority queue that requires privilege to access. For this approach to become feasible, any running query should be pre-empted to allow the priority query to run immediately. The query that was halted can be restarted later. Restarting the query is not an issue, as query details are captured by the query manager when the query is submitted.

9.6 THE FEEDBACK LOOP

The success of a long-term project like that of development of a data warehouse depends on the feedback loop that exists between the data architect and the business analysts. For getting the feedback, the data warehouse is first populated with data from the source systems. The business analyst is then asked to use the data from the data warehouse for carrying out strategic analysis. On discovering new opportunities, the business analyst informs the data architect about some additional adjustments that are required. These adjustments may include: adding data, deleting data, altering data, etc.

No doubt, a shorter feedback loop cycle results in a higher success rate of the data warehouse. Whenever the data analyst informs the data architect about the changes that must be made in the data, those changes must be implemented as early as possible. However, the duration of the feedback loop also depends on the amount of data that has to be changed. Obviously, it is easier to change 100 MB of data rather than changing 100 GB.

As a final note, failing to implement the feedback loop can hamper the success of the data warehouse development effort.

Recapitulation

In unit testing, also called *white box testing*, each development unit is tested on its own.

In integration testing, the separate development units that make up a component of the data warehouse application are tested to ensure that they work together.

In system testing, the whole data warehouse application can be tested together.

In user acceptance testing, the users conduct their own tests on the system.

Performance testing should check for: ETL process completing within the load window and the refresh times for standard and complex reports.

To test the recovery process of a lost data file, a data file should actually be deleted and recovered from backup. It is not sufficient to check that a particular data file has been backed up, and to therefore assume that it can be recovered. Any backup management software to be used should also be fully tested.

For a data warehouse you need to test the security, disk configuration, scheduler, management tools, and the database management.

To test the database software, you need to perform test cases to test features like querying in parallel, creation of indexes and data loading in parallel and the performance of the fixed and ad hoc queries.

Monitoring statistics are indicators whose values provide information about the performance of data warehouse functions. They may be collected using two different techniques: the sampling method which measures specific aspects of the system activities at regular intervals, and the event-driven method which records statistics only when a specified event takes place.

The first step in formulating a schedule for user training is to determine the areas where the users need to be trained, and then you need to match the content of the training with anticipated usage of the warehouse as well as the levels of skills and knowledge of different users.

The success of a training program depends on the joint participation of user representatives and the IT, coverage of all the topics about data content, applications and tools, matching of the training program with the requirements of your organization, catering to all the group of users and simple course documentation.

You must establish a proper support structure and make clear to every user the support path to be taken. Include support on how to find and execute predefined queries and preformatted reports.

To fine-tune the data warehouse, one needs to set a reasonable goal, e.g. 90% of all queries against recent data to complete within 5 minutes, improve the data load performance, maintain the indexes on that data, and limit referential integrity checking as much as possible on the data warehouse system.

The more *ad hoc* the nature of the query, the more difficult the job of tuning the data warehouse is. The trick with tuning this sort of enviroment is to move the query mix from *ad hoc* to predictable.

Objective Questions

1. **Multiple choice questions**

    (i) The people who must be a part of design review team includes

    (a) Data warehouse administrator

    (b) Programmers

    (c) Analysts

    (d) End-users

    (e) All of these

    (f) None of these

    (ii) Which is the testing technique that tests the different modules of the data warehouse?

    (a) Unit testing

    (b) Integration testing

    (c) Performance testing

    (d) Acceptance testing

    (e) All of these

    (f) None of these

  (iii) Which is the testing technique that tests for the refresh times for standard reports?

    (a) Unit testing

    (b) Integration testing

    (c) Performance testing

    (d) Acceptance testing

    (e) All of these

    (f) None of these

2. Fill in the blanks

  (i) The data warehouse is developed around one _____ at a time.

  (ii) In _____ testing, the entire data warehouse application is tested as a single unit.

  (iii) _____ are indicators that present the growth trends and provide insights into the utility of the end-user tools.

  (iv) _____ components collect the monitoring statistics.

  (v) Data loading is done during _____ processing.

  (vi) The more unpredictable the usage, the _____ is the query size.

  (vii) Queries posed against the data warehouse database must be controlled via the _____.

  (viii) Feedback loop exists between the _____ and the _____.

3. Match the following

1. Design review	(a)	Users conduct their own tests on the system
2. Unit testing	(b)	White box testing
3. Acceptance testing	(c)	Test for the refresh times for complex reports
4. Performance testing	(d)	Manages the performance of the system
5. Monitoring statistics	(e)	Issues regarding design, development, project management, or usage of the data that may prevent success

4. State true or false

  (i) Earlier the error is detected, the easier and cheaper it is to correct.

  (ii) The data warehouse should be built iteratively.

  (iii) The design must be reviewed after the subject is added in the data warehouse.

  (iv) The facilitator of the review process must be the project leader.

  (v) The data warehouses do not have a mirror test environment.

  (vi) The disk configuration should be tested to identify any potential I/O bottlenecks.

  (vii) Logging and analysis of test results is hardly of any use in the data warehouse environment.

  (viii) *Ad hoc* queries are clearly defined and well-understood.

  (ix) Longer feedback loop cycle results in a more successful data warehouse.

Review Questions

1. Explain the different types of testing that must be performed before and after the deployment of the data warehouse. State how much time will you give the testing team to test the new system.

2. Explain all the features of a data warehouse that you would like to test.

3. Describe the significance of monitoring statistics. How are they collected? Give examples of some important statistics that you would like to collect for your data warehouse.

4. How can the monitoring statistics help for growth planning, fine-tuning the system, and publishing trends of a data warehouse?

5. Explain the content of the user training material? Why is it helpful?

6. As the person responsible for improving the query performance of your data warehouse, list the types of statistics that you would need and also state the activities that you will undertake to accomplish your task.

7. For a data warehouse that works with a MOLAP based system, establish a training program.

8. Write a short note on multi-tier support structure of a data warehouse.

9. As a data warehouse administrator, how will you manage the system? What aspects do you think need to be managed and why?

10. Why is tuning of a data warehouse so important? List the activities that you will perform to tune the data loading process and the execution of both fixed and *ad hoc* queries.

10

OLAP IN THE DATA WAREHOUSE

Learning Objectives

In this chapter, we will explore the Online Analytical Processing (OLAP) technology in detail. We will learn how OLAP is used to perform multidimensional analysis. We will also discuss the functions, applications, and different models of OLAP. Thereafter, we will read about the design considerations and the tools present in the market.

Case Study

Till now, Pallav Raj, has decided the level of granularity of data that would be stored in the data warehouse, and the project team has already completed requirements gathering and dimensional modelling.

What has to be decided next is how will the functions that the users need to perform be provided to them. When the project team started extracting the functions that the users needed to perform, they found that the users of JRTs needed the data warehouse to help them measure the metrics along several dimensions, support multidimensional analysis, enable the application of complex mathematical formulas and calculations, improve the pre-sentation of results through visual presentations using graphs and charts.

Just imagine how good it would be if a single tool can enable the users to perform all these functions efficiently. This is where OLAP tools come into picture. OLAP tools, if incorporated, would help the JRTs users to perform all the desired tasks efficiently on the data warehouse.

Note, a data warehouse is just an integrated, non-volatile, time-variant, and subject oriented collection of data. It is the OLAP tools which enable the data warehouse users to carry out their functions in an easy, efficient, faster, and effective manner.

10.1 NEED FOR OLAP

We have come across the term OLAP in Chapter 2. There, we enumerated OLAP as an information delivery method. It is very clear from the name itself that OLAP has to do with analytical processing. It is well said that the data warehouse provides the best ground for analysis and OLAP is the vehicle for carrying out the involved analysis.

With the availability of advanced OLAP tools in the market from multiple vendors, a data warehouse without an OLAP tool is something beyond imagination. So, in this chapter, we will explore OLAP in depth.

A data warehouse is designed to perform strategic analysis using the data that is stored in it. The key reason to perform strategic analysis against the data warehouse is to make strategic decisions which in turn are used to set business goals and to formulate business strategies.

The cornerstone for performing strategic analysis is that the data must be stored and presented in a way to facilitate analysis of key indicators over time along business dimensions. Any data structure designed using the dimensional modelling technique fits the framework of carrying out such analysis.

10.1.1 Multidimensional Analysis

Every business model can be represented with a multidimensional view. Let us discuss it with a few examples.

Query   How many units of Product X were sold?
Type   One-dimensional query
Reason It is because a fact called unit_sales is being analysed along the product dimension.

Query   How many units of Product X were sold on 17 February 2008?
Type   Two-dimensional query
Reason It is because two dimensions, viz. time and product are required to get the answer.

Query   How many units of Product X were sold on 17 February 2008 in New Delhi?
Type   Three-dimensional query
Reason This query involves three dimensions, viz. time, product, and place.

As the complexity of the queries increase, the number of dimensions adds up. Multidimensional analysis means analysing the facts across multiple dimensions. These days, none of the existing business models are limited to three dimensions or less.

For planning and making strategic decisions, it is important for the managers and executives to probe into business data through scenarios. For example, they compare actual sales against targets and against sales in prior periods. As explained above, they analyse the same fact by considering multiple dimensions. Data warehouse end-users are no longer satisfied with one-dimensional queries and simple analysis.

For effective strategic analysis, the data warehouse users must be empowered with tools that enable them to perform complex analysis very easily along several business dimensions. The users need an environment that offers a multidimensional view of data.

Multidimensional analysis lays the foundation for analytical processing. Apart from multidimensional analysis, the users must be able to analyse the data at any level of aggregation/summarization and finally be able to view the results in a variety of formats. Without a solid system for true multidimensional analysis, the success of a data warehouse is beyond imagination.

10.1.2 Fast Access and Powerful Calculations

The query and analysis system must have consistent response times. Users must not be aware of the underlying complexity of their analysis. Irrespective of the query whether it is simple or complex, whether it is single dimensional or multidimensional, the amount of time to receive the result sets must be consistent.

Figure 10.1 shows the steps through a single analysis session. Every single analysis session is a train of thoughts and each step in turn constitutes a query. The managers and executives formulate a query, execute it and wait for the result set. When they get the result on their screens, they study it and based upon their understanding, again formulate another query. This process is repeated until the users find the information that they wanted from the data warehouse.

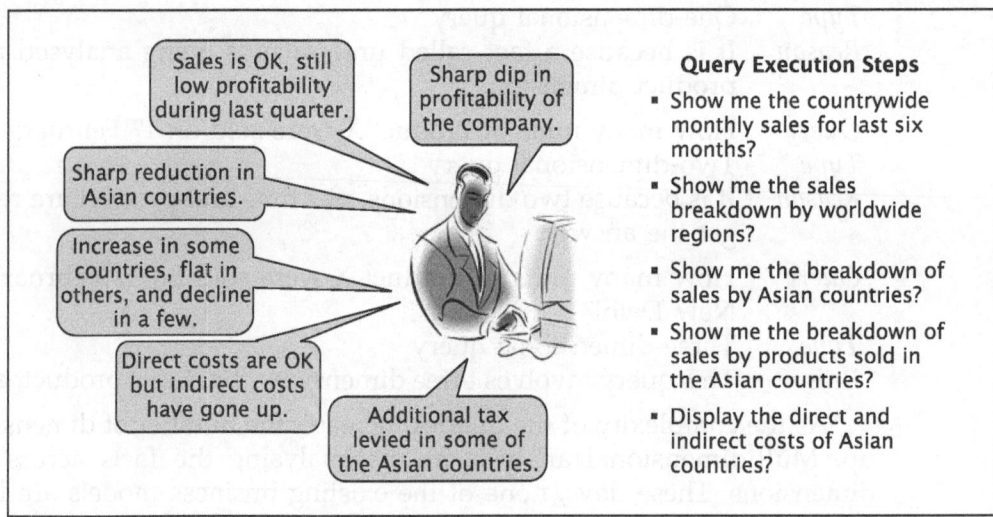

Figure 10.1 A typical analysis session

No user can maintain his train of thoughts unless the momentum is preserved. Thus, to provide an effective analytical processing environment, fast access of data is a necessary ingredient. Last but not the least, the environment must also support complex and powerful calculations.

10.2 OLAP

Data warehouse users perform complex multidimensional analysis that involves enormous amount of calculations. The traditional report writers, query tools, spreadsheets, and language interfaces are not sufficient for this purpose. Obviously, the tools that are used in the operational databases do not match the set of tools and products that are specifically meant for serious analysis in a data warehouse environment. We need OLAP in the data warehouse. The basic virtues of OLAP are as follows:

- Enables the analysts, executives, and managers to gain useful insights in business.
- Enables the analysts to measure metrics along several dimensions.
- Allows data to be viewed from different perspectives.
- Supports multidimensional analysis.
- Enables the analysts to drill-down or roll-up within each dimension.
- Enables the application of complex mathematical formulae and calculations to measures for analysis.
- Provides fast response, thereby encouraging speed-of-thought analysis.
- Complements the use of other information delivery techniques such as data mining and EIS.
- Improves the presentation of results through visual presentations using graphs and charts.
- Can be implemented on the web.
- Supports highly interactive analysis.

Table 10.1 Illustrates the differences between OLTP and OLAP systems.

Table 10.1 OLTP and OLAP systems

Characteristics	OLTP Systems	OLAP Systems
• Analytical capabilities	• Low	• Moderate
• Data access in a single session	• Limited	• Medium to large size
• Resultant set size	• Limited	• Large
• Response time	• Fast	• Fast to moderate
• Level of detail of data	• Detailed data	• Detail and summary data both
• Data content	• Recent	• Recent and historical
• Usage	• Predefined and repetitive	• Predefined and ad hoc
• Basic motivation	• Collect and input data	• Provide information
• Data model	• Design for data update	• Design for executing queries
• Data structure	• For transaction	• For analysis
• Frequency of update	• Very frequent	• Read-only data
• User interaction	• Single transactions	• Throughout data content

10.2.1 OLAP Defined

The term OLAP or as defined by the OLAP council states that – "Online Analytical Processing (OLAP) is a category of software technology that enables analyst managers, and executives to gain an insight into the data through fast, consistent, interactive access in a wide variety of possible views of information that has been transformed from raw data to reflect the real dimensionality of the enterprise as understood by the user."

The main aim of OLAP tools is to provide multidimensional analysis to the underlying data. For this, the OLAP tools employ multidimensional models for data storage and presentation.

Dr E.F. Codd has given twelve basic guidelines that are used to measure the effectiveness of OLAP tools and products available in the market. A good OLAP system must conform to these guidelines. When an organization wants to purchase an OLAP tool, it can prioritize these guidelines and select tools that meet the highest priority features. These guidelines for an OLAP system are discussed below.

Multidimensional conceptual view *Data should be presented to the user in a multidimensional paradigm.* Provide a multidimensional data model that is intuitively analytical and easy to use. Since business analysts need a multidimensional view of their enterprise, therefore, a multidimensional data model conforms to how the users view business problems. OLAP databases support a multidimensional view of the data, allowing for the classic "slice and dice" operations or pivoting and rotation of the conceptual cube of data.

Transparency *Users need not know that they are using an OLAP database.* The users neither need to know that they are looking at an OLAP database nor should they know the source of the data. As far as they are concerned, they are using tools with which they are familiar to get the data they require in order to make the decisions they have been charged with making.

Accessibility *Tools should choose the best source of data to support a query.* The tools in use should have a map of data sources within it, which point to the most appropriate source of data to support a specific query and perform any conversions of data or semantic meaning in order to give the correct interpretation of the enterprise business model.

Consistent reporting performance *Performance should be the same regardless of the number of dimensions in use.* As the number of dimensions or the number of levels of aggregation changes, there should be no change in the way calculations are performed. The data model should be robust enough to cater to the changes made to the enterprise model. This is essential if the figures presented in the OLAP tool are to be believed and its analysis or predictions are to be trusted. Also, ensure that the users do not experience any significant degradation in reporting performance as the number of dimensions or the size of the database increases. Users must perceive consistent run-time, response time, or machine utilization every time a given query is run.

Client–server architecture *Tools should be deployed in a client-server architecture.* The OLAP tools should be capable of being deployed in a client-server environment, implying that the multidimensional database server should be accessible from a range of other applications and tools. The system must be conformed to the principles of client-server architecture for optimum performance, flexibility, adaptability, and interoperability. The server component must enable various clients to be attached with a minimum of effort and integration programming.

Generic dimensionality *Dimensions are all equal; there should be no bias towards any one dimension.* Every data dimension must be equivalent in both its structure and operational capabilities. The basic data structure, formulae, and reporting formats should not be biased towards any one data dimension.

Dynamic sparse matrix handling *Null values should be stored in an efficient way.* Typical multidimensional models can easily run into millions of cell references, many of which will have no data at any one point in time. These null values should be stored in an efficient way and these values should not have an adverse affect on the accuracy or speed of information retrieval.

Multi-user support *Tools should support more than one user.* OLAP tools should support and indeed encourage group working and the interchange of ideas and analyses between users. To achieve this, multi-user access to the data and thus data security and data integrity is essential.

Unrestricted cross-dimensional operations *Aggregation rules should be applied consistently across all dimensions.* The rules which govern the progress of data "roll-ups" through levels of a hierarchy should be defined and available so that no matter which slice of data is taken, the rules will be applied consistently. The system must recognize the presence of multiple hierarchies in the system and should provide the ability to manipulate the data and perform complex calculations across any number of dimensions.

Intuitive data manipulation The user views of data should contain everything required without being bogged down into complex menus or multiple trips across the user interface. The analyst's view of the data should at all times contain all information necessary to effect the navigations (the slicing and dicing) which are appropriate.

Flexible reporting *Users should be able to present data in any way they like.* The data warehouse users should be able to retrieve any view of the data required and present it in any format of their choice. The OLAP system should also provide capabilities to the business user to arrange columns, rows and cells in a manner that facilitates easy manipulation, analysis, and synthesis of information.

Unlimited dimensions and aggregation levels *There should be no limit to the number of dimensions and levels in a model.* There should be no limit imposed by the OLAP tool to the number of dimensions which can be built into a model.

Each of these dimensions must allow an unlimited number of user-defined aggregation levels.

10.2.2 OLAP is a Data Warehouse Tool

OLAP is a technology that provides superior performance in executing business queries that perform complex strategic analysis. It is designed to operate efficiently with data that is organized according to the dimensional model used in data warehouses.

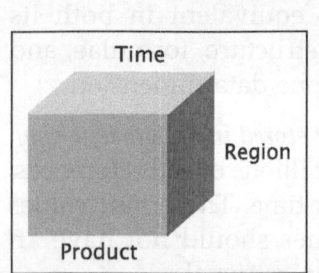

A data warehouse provides a multidimensional view of data in an intuitive manner to match the types of queries that can be posed by business analysts and decision makers. OLAP organizes data in the form of multidimensional cubes based on this dimensional model, and then preprocesses these cubes to provide maximum performance for queries.

Figure 10.2 OLAP cube with time, region and product dimensions

OLAP cubes summarize the data available in the data warehouse in a number of ways. For example, a query that requests the sales_amount and quantity_sold for a range of products in a specific geographical region for a specific time period can typically be answered in a few seconds regardless of the millions of rows of data that are stored in the data warehouse database. Figure 10.2 shows such a multidimensional cube that stores data along three dimensions: product, region, and time.

To summarize, the most fundamental characteristics of OLAP are:

- It allows the users to have a multidimensional and logical view of the data in the data warehouse.
- It provides the ability for interactive query and complex analysis for the users.
- It enables the data warehouse users to perform drill down operations for greater details and roll up operations for summarizations of facts along single or multiple business dimensions.
- It enables the users to perform complex calculations and comparisons.
- It displays results in a variety of formats including charts and graphs.

10.3 OLAP AND MULTIDIMENSIONAL ANALYSIS

According to Chaudhari and Dayal, multidimensional databases are large collections of data, used for statistical analysis oriented to decision making, in which factual data is described according to different dimensions. These characteristics enables its users to summarize and view the data but pose some difficulties in constructing and maintaining complex analytical models of the organization data. So to ease their work, OLAP systems are designed with several query languages that can be executed at different levels of abstraction.

In the data warehousing technology, the terms OLAP and multidimensional analysis are often used interchangeably to describe both databases and tools.

10.3.1 Multidimensional Logical Data Model

In a logical relational data model, data is stored in the form of a two-dimensional table containing n number of rows and columns. But in a multidimensional model, data is visualized as a multidimensional cube. In a cube, the dimensions are displayed along each axis, and measures are stored in individual cells as shown in Fig. 10.3.

Any multidimensional model must allow the users to slice and dice the cube in any way across any of the dimensions, to answer queries such as:

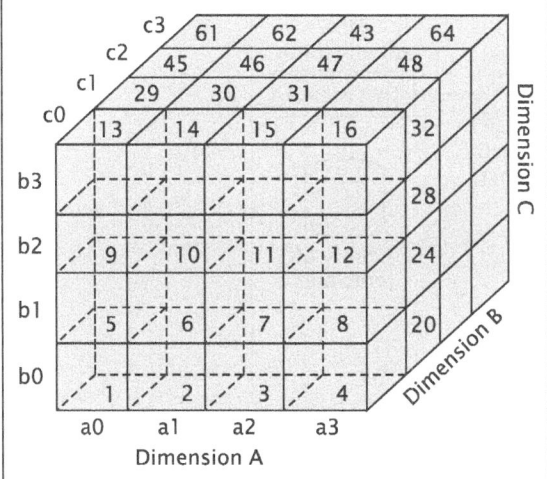

Figure 10.3 Multidimensional data cube

- Display the total sales in every individual store of north region for the month of May.

- Show the average sales of products in individual months for each store in the last year.

- Analyse in the last quarter, the largest selling product in every store.

The users must be able to summarize the data stored in individual cells across any dimensions and be able to manipulate the data as a cube.

10.3.2 Users of Multidimensional Model

Prior to examining the main components of a multidimensional structure, we will discuss the different classes of users involved with the various activities.

The main user of a multidimensional structure is a traditional analyst (or end-user) who executes analytical queries on the data warehouse data. The software component used to extract data from the data warehouse is called the Data Warehouse Interfaces (DWI). The multidimensional structure administrator is the person who is responsible for the construction and maintenance of data warehouse interfaces. The DWI Wizard allows the creation and modification of a DWI.

The data warehouse administrator is responsible for building and maintaining a data warehouse accessed which is accessed by the multidimensional structure. This person must communicate any change in the data warehouse organization to the MDS administrator. However, the different tasks and thus the various user classes can overlap in multidimensional structure model.

10.3.3 Multidimensional Structure

The overall framework of a multidimensional structure is shown in Fig. 10.4. In the figure rectangles represent software modules; cylinders represent repositories of data, and lines denote the direction of flow of information.

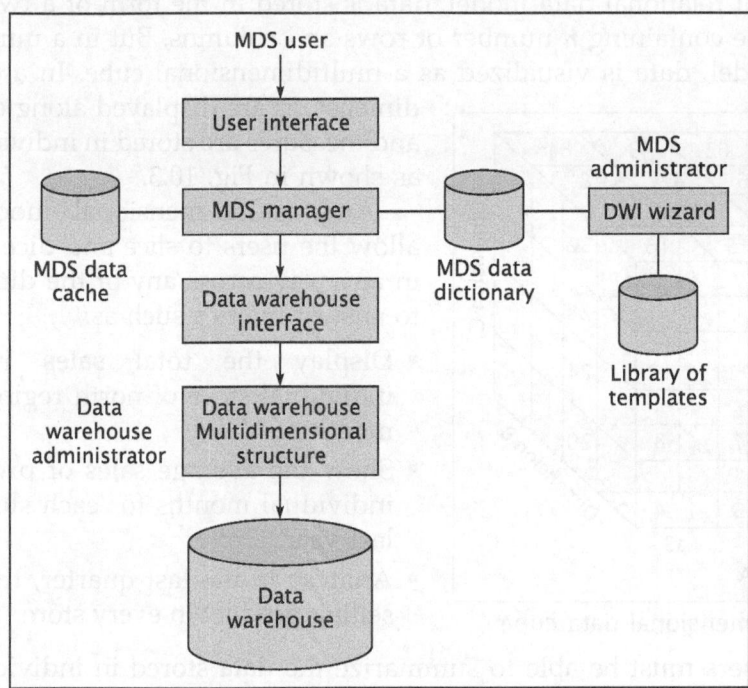

Figure 10.4 Multidimensional structure

The whole environment is loosely coupled with the data warehouse repository. These systems can either be OLAP servers (relational or multidimensional) or, a generic data storage system that allows the multidimensional aspects of data analysis.

The DWI performs two important functions:

- It performs mapping between an multidimensional database schema and the actual organization of a data warehouse.
- It converts multidimensional queries into operations that can be executed on the underlying data warehouse management system.

The DWI Wizard helps the MDS Manager to construct a DWI. Although this tool is separated from the MDS Manager, it is integrated with it. The DWI Wizard uses a special library of DWI templates which contain a specific data model used in a data warehouse management system. The DWI Wizard generates a DWI from a DWI template based on the actual data warehouse schema, as specified by the MDS Manager.

The main responsibility of MDS Manager is to perform the following tasks:

(i) It imports the underlying data warehouse schema from a data storage system through the corresponding DWI and stores it into a local multidimensional data dictionary.

(ii) It receives multidimensional queries from the users against a stored multidimensional schema, converts it into a format that can be executed by the DWIs.

(iii) It receives the result of query execution from one or more DWIs, combines them, and then displays the final result to the user.

(iv) It receives the request for a creation of a view and stores its definition in the multidimensional data dictionary.

The local cache of multidimensional data helps to enhance the efficiency of query evaluation. The cache is used to store pre-computed aggregations of basic fact tables. When a query is executed that needs aggregated data, the system checks whether there is any fact table in the cache that can be used to answer the query efficiently.

The User Interface as the name suggests allows efficient interaction between the user and the system through both textual and graphical tools that includes menus and forms. To conclude, the multidimensional structure allows:

- Visualization of the data warehouse schema in terms of the multidimensional model so that it can be used as reference for querying.
- Execution of textual and graphical queries against available multidimensional schemas and views.
- Specification of views.
- Visualization of the result set of query execution.

10.3.4 Multidimensional Operations

Besides the slice and dice operations for data retrieval, multidimensional systems also offer a rich set of analytical functions for processing measure values, like ranking (top 10, bottom 10), percentage change (growth on same period last year), rolling averages and cumulative totals.

10.3.5 The Business Need

The competitiveness of today's business environment has lead to a drastic increase in the need for up-to-date, accurate information about all aspects of an organization. Besides responding to the user's queries for satisfying their operational needs, the users need information to improve their business, improve the efficiency and quality of the products, exploit new markets, identify wasted effort, detect prevailing sales trend, and analyse where costs can be cut.

With the increase in the volume of data captured in corporate databases, the dependence of business on that data also increases. This in turn leads to an increasingly urgent need for more access and analysis of the data by a large number of users across the organization. This requires a great deal of functionality in information analysis tools, of which multidimensional analysis is just one part.

10.4 OLAP FUNCTIONS

OLAP is more than just an information delivery system for the data warehouse. A data warehouse is designed to store data and provide easy access to that data. In a data warehouse environment, the OLAP system has lifted the information delivery capabilities to new heights. Figure 10.5 shows some of the basic and advanced features of an OLAP system.

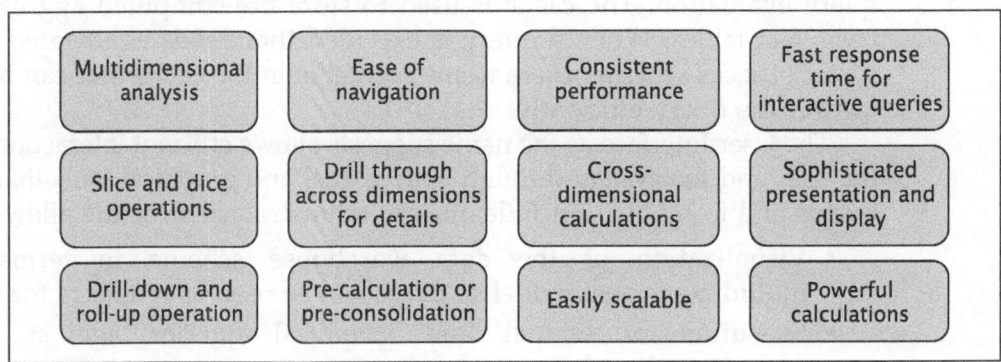

Figure 10.5 Features of OLAP

10.4.1 Dimensional Analysis

Dimensional analysis is such a strong suit in the arsenal of OLAP that any OLAP system that does not support multidimensional analysis is hardly of any use. Take an example of a simple star schema having three business dimensions, namely product, time, and store. The fact table contains sales.

Figure 10.6 exhibits a three-dimensional data model as a cube, with products on the X-axis, time on the Y-axis, and stores on the Z-axis. Now, the question that arises is, what are the values represented along each axis? For example, in the Star schema, time is one of the dimensions and month is one of the attributes. So naturally, values of this attribute month are represented on the Y-axis. Similarly, values of the attributes product name and store name are represented on the X and Y axes respectively.

Figure 10.6 shows a star schema. From the dimension tables, we will extract the relevant attributes. Like we will pick the attribute product name from the product dimension, month from the time dimension and store name from the store dimension. The cube representing the values of all the three attributes along the primary edges of the physical cube are shown in the figure here.

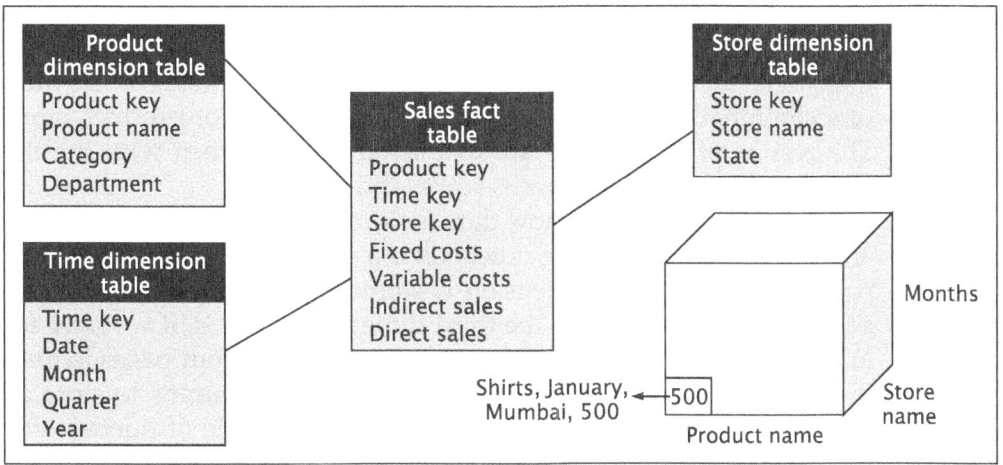

Figure 10.6 Star schema with its corresponding data cube

If you are displaying the data for sales along these three business dimensions using a two-dimensional table, the columns (Y) may display the product names, the rows (X) the months, and pages (Z) will display the names of the stores. Figure 10.7 shows a screen display of a page of this three-dimensional data. The page displayed on the screen shows a slice of the cube.

Pages:
Store dimension, ex-Delhi

Columns:
Product dimension

	Shirts	T-shirts	Jackets	Trousers
Jan	200	550	350	500
Feb	210	480	390	510
Mar	190	480	380	480
Apr	190	430	350	490
May	160	530	320	530
Jun	150	450	310	540
Jul	130	480	270	550
Aug	140	570	250	650
Sep	160	470	240	630
Oct	170	480	260	610
Nov	180	520	280	680
Dec	200	560	320	750

Rows: Time dimension

Chennai, jackets, Dec = 185

	Shirts	T-shirts	Jackets	Trousers
Dec	200	550	350	500
Nov	210	480	390	510
Oct	190	480	380	480
Sep	190	430	550	490
Aug	160	530	320	530
Jul	150	450	310	540
Jun	130	480	210	550
May	140	570	250	650
Apr	160	470	240	630
Mar	110	480	260	610
Feb	130	520	280	680
Jan	200	560	320	750

Kolkata 220 330 285 290
Chennai 250 490 185 400
Mumbai 300 400 290 380
Delhi ? ? ? ?

Products

Figure 10.7 Table storing data along three dimensions of the star schema given in Fig. 10.6

In the cube and the table given in Fig. 10.7, we have seen how we can display three business dimensions and a single fact on a two dimensional page and also on a three-dimensional cube. The numbers in each cell on the page of the 3-D cube are the sales numbers on which the users can perform multidimensional analysis. The users can view the sale numbers along the hierarchies of a combination of the three business dimensions of product, store and time. The results of the queries are displayed on the screen with the three dimensions represented in columns, rows, and pages.

To easily understand how data is stored in a three dimensional cube, take an analogy of a notebook. The notebook is a cube which has several pages. On each page, data along two dimension is stored, time and product in our case. Each page act as an attribute of the third dimension. That is, if we have four stores—in Delhi, Mumbai, Chennai, Kolkata, then there are four pages in the noteobook. Every page in the notebook has 12 rows and 4 columns to store data of four products in 12 months. Table 10.2 displays a sample of queries and the result sets obtained during a multidimensional analysis session.

Table 10.2 Some general queries

Query	Display of Results
Display the total sales of all products for past five years in all stores.	Rows: Year numbers 2006, 2005, 2004, 2003, 2002 Columns: Total sales for all products Page: One store per page
Compare total sales of all stores, products by products, between years 2006 and 2005.	Rows: Year numbers 2006, 2005; difference; percentage increase or decrease Columns: One column per product, showing all products Page: All stores
Show comparison of total sales for all stores, product by product, between years 2006 and 2005 only for those with reduced sales.	Rows: Year numbers 2006, 2005; difference; percentage decrease Columns: One column per product, showing only the qualifying products Page: All stores
Show comparison of total sales by individual stores, product by product, between years 2006 and 2005 only for those with reduced sales.	Rows: Year numbers 2006, 2005; difference; percentage decrease Columns: One column per product, showing only the qualifying products Page: All stores
Show results of the previous query, but rotating and switching the columns with rows.	Rows: One row per product, showing only the qualifying products Columns: Year numbers 2006, 2005; difference; percentage decrease Page: One store per page Rows: One row per store
Show results of the previous query, but rotating and switching the pages with rows.	Columns: Year numbers between 2006, 2005; difference percentage decrease Page: One product per page, displaying only the qualifying products

In the above examples, we had only three business dimensions and all the three dimensions could be represented along the edges of the cube or the results could be displayed as columns, rows and pages of a relation. What if we add a fourth dimension also? How will the results be displayed then as a 3-D cube is not sufficient enough to display four business dimensions? This leads us to a discussion of hypercubes.

10.4.2 Hypercubes

The hypercube is a generalization of a 3-cube to n-dimensions, also called an

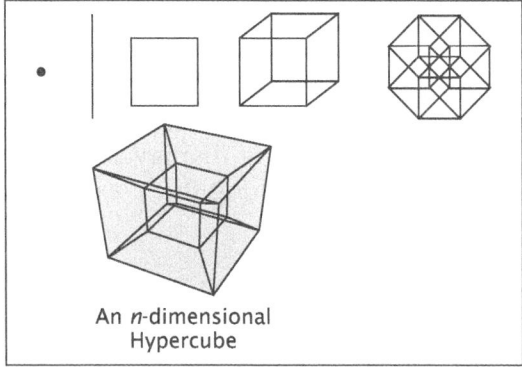

An n-dimensional Hypercube

Figure 10.8 An n-dimensional hypercube

n-cube. Figure 10.8 represents a hypercube. The first figure shows a point in the zero dimensional space, a line in the one dimensional space, a square in a two-dimensional space and finally a hypercube.

Let us say, we have four business dimensions along which we want to analyse the measure "sales". Consider the star schema in Fig. 10.9. See how we represent these four business dimensions on a 2-D table and 4-D hypercube.

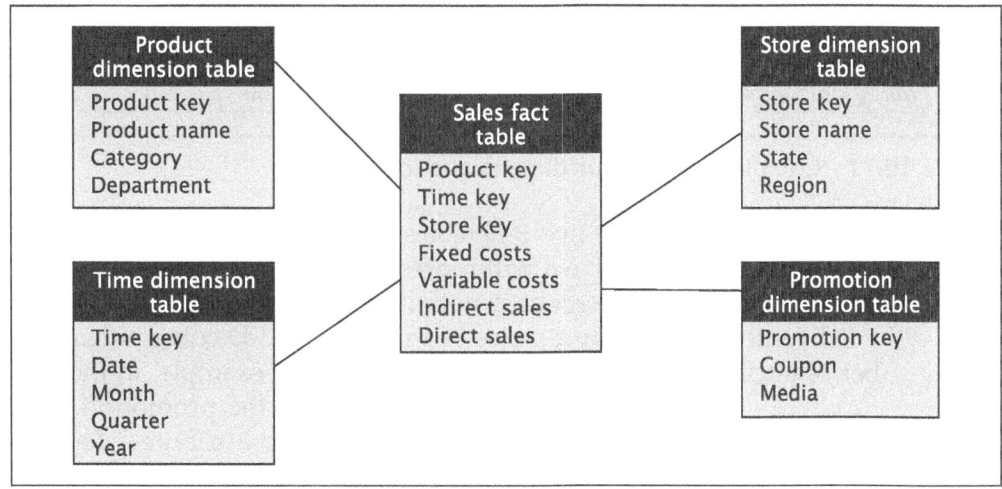

Figure 10.9 Star schema having four dimensions

Now since you have to display four dimensions along three axes, obviously you will have to combine two dimensions to be displayed on a single axis. Displaying the entire two-dimensional table is not possible here, as it will take a lot of space. So, we will show only a portion of the entire table. In the table, instead of taking all the attributes, we will take only a few attributes, just to give you an idea about how the original table would be. Figure 10.10 exhibits the attributes which we have chosen to display in the table.

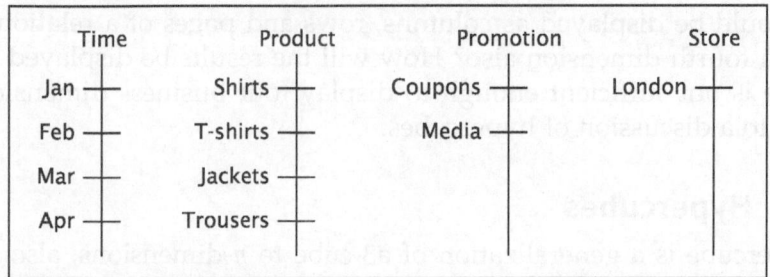

Figure 10.10 Attributes of the dimensions given in the star schema of Fig. 10.9

Thus, in the table given below, store and promotion dimensions are combined on the Z-axis or pages, the time dimension is displayed on the X-axis or rows and the product dimension is displayed along the Y-axis or in the columns.

Pages: Store and promotion dimension combined
London: Coupon
Columns: Product dimension

Rows: Time dimension		Shirts	T- shirts	Jackets	Trousers
	Jan	200	550	350	500
	Feb	210	480	390	510
	Mar	190	480	380	480
	Apr	190	430	350	490

Pages: Store and promotion dimension combined
London: Media
Columns: Product dimension

Rows: Time dimension		Shirts	T- shirts	Jackets	Trousers
	Jan	150	450	310	540
	Feb	130	480	270	550
	Mar	140	570	250	650
	Apr	160	470	240	630

Figure 10.11 Combination of four dimensions in a table

Figure 10.11 shows two 2-D tables or two pages/slices of a single cube. The next figure shows how we will represent the same data in a hypercube. Mathematically, an n-D hypercube is nothing but a series of $(n-1)$-D cubes. That is, a 4-D hypercube is simply a series of x number of 3-D cubes, where x is the number of attributes in the fourth dimension. In our example, in the fourth dimension, i.e. the promotion dimension, we have two attributes. Therefore, in this case, we will make two 3-D cubes to form a 4-D hypercube, as illustrated in Fig. 10.12.

After you have gained a clear understanding of how we represent four dimensions on a table and a cube, you can easily extend the concept to display any number of dimensions. Likewise if you have six dimensions,

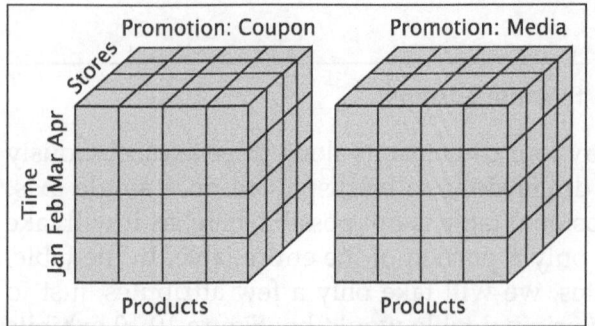

Figure 10.12 Data represented in a hypercube

then you will have to create a series of 5-D cubes. And you will have to combine two dimensions on every axis. Figure 10.13 is a relation representing five business dimensions. Again, assume we are considering only a portion of the entire table by taking only a few attributes from each dimension.

Pages: Store and promotion dimensions combined, London: Media
Columns: Product dimension

	Shirts	T- shirts	Jackets	Trousers
Jan: High-income	150	450	310	540
Jan: Low-income	150	450	310	540
Feb: High-income	130	480	270	550
Feb: Low-income	130	480	270	550
Mar: High-income	140	570	250	650
Mar: Low-income	140	570	250	650
Apr: High-income	160	470	240	630
Apr: Low-income	160	470	240	630

(Rows: Time customer demographics dimension)

Figure 10.13 Table storing data along five business dimensions. The five dimensions are store, promotion, production, time, and demography

10.4.3 OLAP Operations in Multidimensional Data Model

In the multidimensional model, data is organized into multiple dimensions, and each dimension contains multiple levels of abstraction. This organization provides users with the flexibility to view data from different perspectives.

A number of OLAP data cube operations exist to materialize these different views, allowing interactive querying and analysis of the data at hand. Hence, OLAP provides a user-friendly environment for interactive data analysis. Given below are some of the operations that a user can perform using OLAP.

Roll-up

The roll-up operations, also known as drill-up operation, performs aggregation on a data cube by climbing up a dimensional hierarchy. For example, if the time dimension is defined by a hierarchy: Week < Month < Quarter < Year, then the roll-up operation when performed will create and aggregates move up in the dimension hierarchy, i.e. if you were viewing the sales data of a particular product in particular week of a store, then performing a roll-up operation means you want to see the data at higher levels of details, say for the entire month rather than of individual weeks as deputed in Fig. 10.14.

Drill-down

Drill-down is the reverse of roll-up, as it navigates from less detailed data to more detailed data. Drill-down can be realized by stepping down the dimensional hierarchy. The diagram given in Fig. 10.14 can be used to

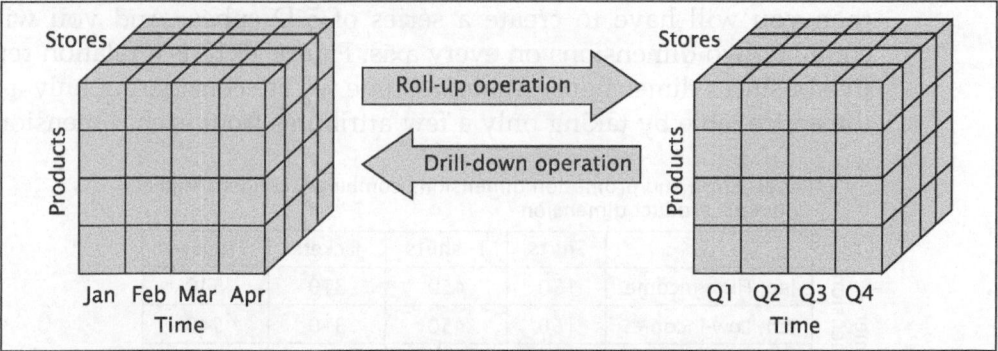

Figure 10.14 Roll-up and drill-down operation

understand the drill-down operation as well. For example, if the time dimension is defined by a hierarchy: week < month < quarter < year, then the roll-up operation when performed will move down in the dimension hierarchy, i.e. if you were viewing the sales data of a particular product in particular month of a store, then performing a drill-down operation means you want to see the data at lower levels of details, say for the individual weeks. In Fig. 10.15, we have seen how the data is shown in case of a cube, now let us see how the data changes in case of table.

Pages: Store dimension, ex-Delhi
Columns: Product dimension

Rows: Time dimension	Shirts	T-shirts	Jackets	Trousers
Jan	200	550	350	500
Feb	210	480	390	510
Mar	190	480	380	480
Apr	190	430	350	490
May	160	530	320	530
Jun	150	450	310	540
Jul	130	480	270	550
Aug	140	570	250	650
Sep	160	470	240	630
Oct	170	480	260	610
Nov	180	520	280	680
Dec	200	560	320	750

Pages: Store dimension, ex-Delhi
Columns: Product dimension

Rows: Time dimension	Shirts	T-shirts	Jackets	Trousers
Quarter 1 Jan + Feb + Mar	600	1510	1120	1490
Quarter 2 Apr + May + Jun	500	1410	980	1560
Quarter 3 Jul + Aug + Sep	430	1520	760	1830
Quarter 4 Oct + Nov + Dec	550	1560	860	2040

Figure 10.15 The first table is the base which stores data of individual month. The second table stores summarized data of every quarter.

Slice and Dice Operations

The slice operation performs a selection on one dimension of the given cube, resulting in a subcube. Figure 10.16 depicts an operation where the sales data are selected from the central cube for the store dimension New Delhi. The dice operation on the other hand defines a subcube by performing a selection on two or more dimensions. The figure given below also shows a dice operation on the central cube based on the selection criteria that involve three dimensions: store = 'London', time = 'March' and product = 'Jackets'.

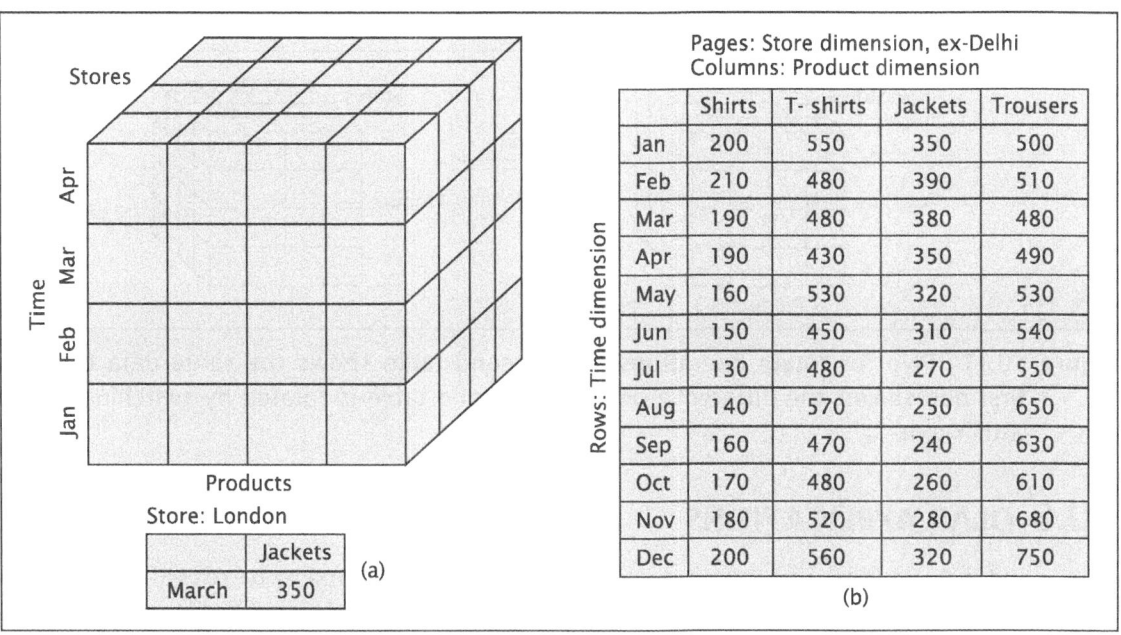

Figure 10.16 The (a) table shows the result of a slice operation and the second table (b) shows the result of a dice operation

Pivot or Rotate

Pivot is a visualization operation that rotates the data axes in view in order to provide an alternative presentation of the data. You can rotate the data stored either in the form of a table or in the form of a cube. Figure 10.17 shows how the presentation of data changes when a pivot operation is applied to a table and a cube.

Other OLAP Operations

Some OLAP systems offer additional drilling operations. For example, drill-across queries involving more than one fact table or across fact tables. The drill-through operation makes use of relational SQL facilities to drill through the bottom level of a data cube down to its backend relational tables. Other OLAP operations may include ranking the top N or bottom N items in lists, as well as computing moving averages, growth rates, interests, internal rates of return, depreciation, currency conversions and statistical functions.

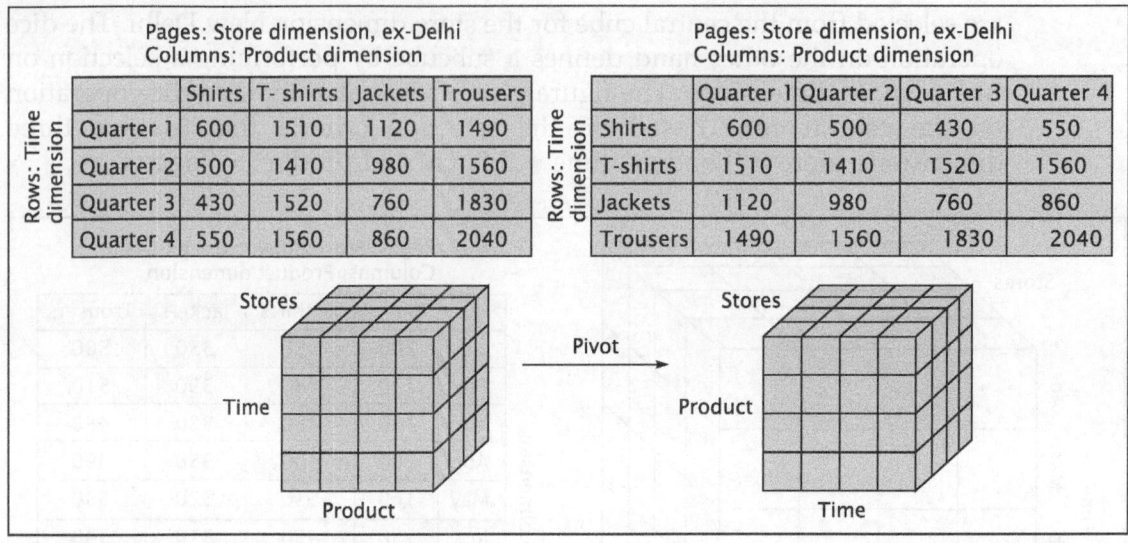

	Shirts	T- shirts	Jackets	Trousers
Quarter 1	600	1510	1120	1490
Quarter 2	500	1410	980	1560
Quarter 3	430	1520	760	1830
Quarter 4	550	1560	860	2040

Pages: Store dimension, ex-Delhi
Columns: Product dimension
Rows: Time dimension

	Quarter 1	Quarter 2	Quarter 3	Quarter 4
Shirts	600	500	430	550
T-shirts	1510	1410	1520	1560
Jackets	1120	980	760	860
Trousers	1490	1560	1830	2040

Pages: Store dimension, ex-Delhi
Columns: Product dimension
Rows: Time dimension

Figure 10.17 Pivot or rotate operations. The second table shows the same data that the first one shows, the difference being the second table is rotated by switching X-axis with Y-axis

10.5 OLAP APPLICATIONS

OLAP cubes, like other data mining tools, allow users to reveal trends and structures in datasets. Similar to other data mining tools, OLAP cubes are not application based. The list of OLAP applications is very extensive. Probably, the most common use of OLAP cubes is in marketing, including database marketing and Web marketing. Other typical applications are retail sales and profitability analysis, quality control analysis, financial and budgeting applications, and management reporting.

OLAP technology is a vital part of management and decision making in numerous banks (including the World Bank), airlines (British Airways), media and entertainment (Time Warner), information technology (Hewlett-Packard, Sun Microsystems), insurance (Thomas Cook), auto industry (Subaru), etc.

10.5.1 Integrating OLAP with GIS

Spatial data represent an essential part of analysis and provide solutions in many applications. It is interesting to know that many other non-spatial attributes can be aggregated geographically and then these additional statistics can be computed allowing the user to analyse every variable (dimension) in a geographical context.

So far, the integration of OLAP technology and geographical analysis has been limited to the building and using of so-called spatial warehouses for visualization of results. The methodology based on similarities between OLAP cubes and map cubes is very promising. Whereas non-spatial warehouses utilize OLAP cubes mostly as summary tables, the spatial warehouses provide map cubes which are nothing but collections of maps.

The striking contrast between OLAP cubes and map cubes calls for different types of aggregation operations. Aggregation functions like arithmetic mean, median, mode, standard deviation, minimum, maximum, count, or sum have their equivalents in map algebra for raster data types. Spatial queries utilizing geometric operators (like area, perimeter, and centroid) and topological operators (inside, within, intersect, contains, connects, and borders), supplement non-spatial SQL queries.

In today's scenario, a bridge needs to be established between OLAP and GIS to allow the OLAP users, who deal with spatial data to display OLAP cubes as maps using GIS. Similarly, a foundation for going from GIS to OLAP must also be designed to enable GIS users to create SQL queries with geometric and topological operators and then pass this information to OLAP cubes.

Thus, the final step of the integration that would render a smooth blending of the technologies would be to allow the user to interactively browse OLAP cubes and to simultaneously view the results on maps. Likewise, the user should also be able to query a map and view corresponding data using OLAP cubes.

10.6 OLAP MODELS

In the OLAP world, there are mainly two different types of models: Multidimensional OLAP model (MOLAP) and Relational OLAP model (ROLAP). Hybrid OLAP (HOLAP) model refers to technologies that combine MOLAP and ROLAP and then there is DOLAP or Desktop Online Analytical Processing. The analytical processing however will remain online, only the storage methodology is different.

10.6.1 MOLAP

Multidimensional Online Analytical Processing (MOLAP) tools utilize a pre-calculated dataset commonly referred to as a data cube or optimized multidimensional array storage that contains summarized data. In MOLAP, data is stored in a multidimensional cube. The storage is not in the relational database, but in proprietary formats. MOLAP tools feature very fast response, and the ability to quickly write back data into the dataset. Primary downsides of MOLAP tools are:

- **Limited scalability** as the cubes get very big when you start to add dimensions and more detailed data.
- **Inability to contain detailed data** as you are forced to use summary data unless your dataset is very small, and high load time of the cubes.

The most common examples of MOLAP tools are: Hyperion (Arbor) Essbase and Oracle (IRI) Express. Examples of commercial products that use MOLAP are: Microsoft Analysis Services, Essbase, and TM1. There is also an open source MOLAP server: Palo. MOLAP tools are best used for users who have "bounded" problem sets, as they need to ask the same range of questions every day/week/month on an updated cube, e.g. finance.

The MOLAP engine takes the data from the warehouse and then stores the data in proprietary data structures, summaries, and pre-calculates as many outcomes as possible.

Figure 10.18 shows the MOLAP model. There are three layers in this model: Presentation layer (desktop client), Application layer (holds the MDBMS server), and Data layer (RDBMS server). The MOLAP engine installed in the MDBMS server creates and stores summary data cubes.

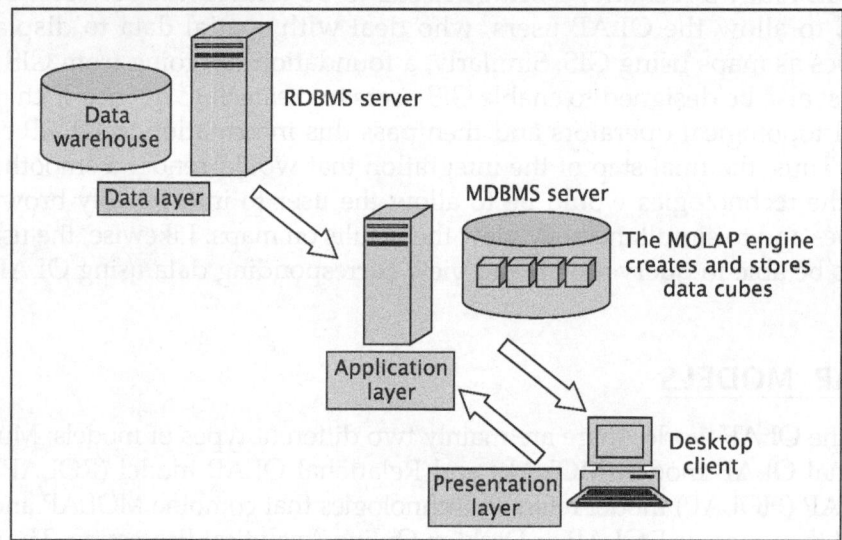

Figure 10.18 The MOLAP model

The characteristics of this model are as follows:

- Data is stored as pre-calculated array.
- The data resides in a propriety multidimensional database. Both the data and index are held in arrays.
- The database is organized to allow rapid retrieval of related data across multiple dimensions.
- Data can be off-loaded from the server onto the client for local access, reducing network traffic. However, it can take time to form the cubes on the client workstation.
- MOLAP typically assumes non-volatile data but whenever the data changes again the cubes have to be created.
- The MOLAP tools store and process multidimensional data efficiently.
- The calculation engine creates new information from existing data through formulae and transformations.
- The complexity of the underlying data is transparent to the user.
- The tools can exploit the complexity of the analysis involved.

- The complex analytical querying capabilities enable a business to respond to change faster.
- Pre-aggregated summary data and pre-calculated measures enable quick and easy analysis of complex data relationships.

Advantages   MOLAP has the following advantages:

- Excellent performance. MOLAP cubes are built for fast data retrieval and are optimal for slicing and dicing operations.
- Can perform complex calculations. All calculations have been pre-generated when the cube is created. Hence, complex calculations are not only doable, but they return quickly.
- Fast query performance due to optimized storage, multidimensional indexing, and caching.
- Smaller on-disk size of data compared to data stored in a relational database due to use of compression techniques.
- Automated computation of higher level aggregates of the data.
- It is very compact for low dimension datasets.
- Array model provides natural indexing.
- Effective data extract achieved through the pre-structuring of aggregated data.

Disadvantages   MOLAP proves disadvantageous in the following ways:

- Limited in the amount of data it can handle. Because all calculations are performed when the cube is built, it is not possible to include a large amount of data in the cube itself. In cubes only summary-level information will be included.
- Requires additional investment. Cube technology is often proprietary and does not already exist in the organization. Therefore, to adopt MOLAP technology, chances are additional investments in human and capital resources are needed.
- The data loading and processing can be quite lengthy, especially on large data volumes. This is usually remedied by doing only incremental processing, i.e. processing only the data which has changed instead of reprocessing the entire dataset.
- Certain MOLAP tools have difficulty updating and querying models with more than ten dimensions.

10.6.2 ROLAP

Relational Online Analytical Processing (ROLAP) tools do not use pre-calculated data cubes. Instead, they intercept the query and pose the question to the standard relational database and bring back the data required to answer the question.

ROLAP tools feature the ability to ask any question (you are not limited to the contents of a cube) and the ability to drill down to the lowest level of detail in the database. This methodology relies on manipulating the data stored in the relational database to give the appearance of traditional OLAP's slicing and dicing functionality. In essence, each action of slicing and dicing is equivalent to adding a "WHERE" clause in the SQL statement. ROLAP tools are best suited for users who deal with "unbounded" problems.

With ROLAP, it is possible to create additional database tables—*summary tables* or *aggregations* which summarize the data at any desired combination of dimensions.

Primary downsides of ROLAP tools are slow response and some limitations on scalability. The most common examples of ROLAP tools are MicroStrategy and Sterling (Information Advantage). Examples of commercial products using ROLAP include Microsoft Analysis Services, Microstrategy and Business Objects. There is also an open source ROLAP server called Mondrian.

Figure 10.19 shows the ROLAP model. It has three layers as in the MOLAP model (Fig. 10.18). The ROLAP engine installed in the analytical server creates data cubes dynamically. When the user requests for data, the request goes to the analytical server where SQL queries are formed. These complex SQL queries are executed against the data warehouse to fetch the desired data. The result is then sent back to the user through the analytical server. In case, the user wants to have a multidimensional view of the result set, the data cubes will be formed dynamically and sent to the client.

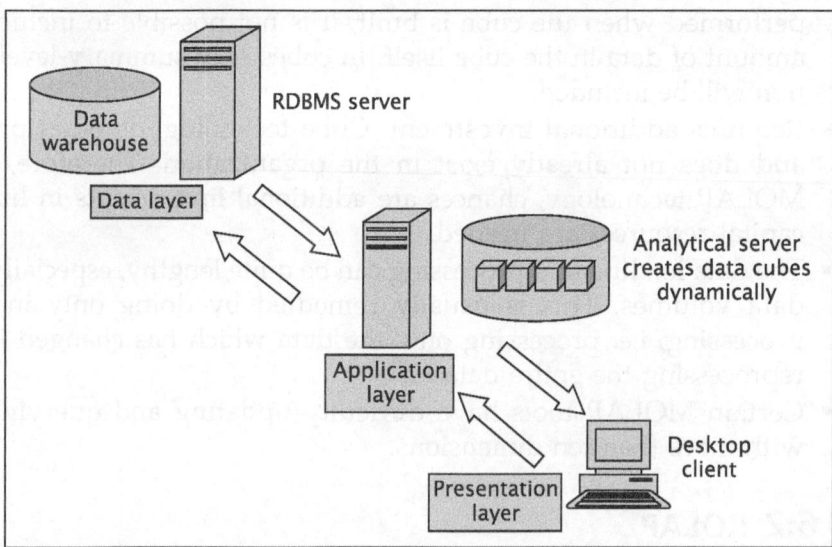

Figure 10.19 The ROLAP model

The ROLAP engine takes data from the data warehouse stored in a two-dimensional atomic or aggregated form. The engine uses its built-in SQL functionality to create a three-dimensional representation of the data and presents that to the user as a multidimensional view. There are no specialized data structures between the engine and the user.

The characteristics of this model are as follows:

- Data and meta data is stored as records in the relational database.
- End-users are supplied with a multidimensional viewing tool, to view the relational data.
- There is high capacity connectivity to powerful servers.
- There are no limitations to the size of the database or the kind of analysis that may be performed. However, if the server is SQL driven, some engines may severely affect performance if the user joins several tables, or performs complex computations.
- Complex SQL code is generated by the ROLAP tool.

Advantages   The advantages of ROLAP are:

- Can handle large amounts of data. ROLAP itself places no limitation on data amount but it can get limited because of the data size of the underlying relational database.
- Can leverage functionalities inherent in the relational database. Relational database already comes with a host of functionalities and since ROLAP sits on top of the relational database, it can therefore leverage these functionalities.
- ROLAP is considered to be more scalable in handling large data volumes, especially the dimension models with dimensions having very high cardinality.
- With a variety of data loading tools available, the load times are generally much shorter than with the automated MOLAP loads.
- ROLAP tools are better at handling *non-aggregatable facts* or (e.g. textual descriptions). MOLAP tools tend to suffer from slow performance when querying these elements.

Disadvantages

- Performance can be slow. Because each ROLAP report is a combination of one or more SQL queries in the relational database, the query time can be long if the underlying data size is large.
- Limited by SQL functionalities. Because ROLAP technology mainly relies on generating SQL statements to query the relational database and SQL statements may not be able to fit all needs of the data warehouse users (for example, it is difficult to perform complex calculations using SQL), ROLAP technologies are traditionally limited by what SQL can do. To overcome this problem, ROLAP vendors are trying to build into the ROLAP tool out-of-the-box complex functions as well as the ability to allow users to define their own functions.

- The loading of *aggregate tables* must be managed by the custom ETL code, as the ROLAP tools are not designed to carry out this task. This means additional development time and more code is needed to support this feature.
- Downside of flexibility. Some companies select ROLAP because they intend to re-use existing relational database tables which may not not be optimally designed for OLAP use. The superior flexibility of ROLAP tools allows this less than optimal design to work, but performance suffers. MOLAP tools in contrast would force the data to be re-loaded into an optimal OLAP design.

Table 10.3 Difference between ROLAP and MOLAP

ROLAP	MOLAP
• Detailed and light summary data available.	• Various summary data kept in proprietary databases (MDDBs).
• Very large data volumes.	• Moderate data volumes.
• All data access from the warehouse storage.	• Summary data access from MDDB, detailed data access from warehouse.
• ROLAP engine in analytical server creates data cubes on the fly.	• Creation of pre-fabricated data cubes by MOLAP engine.
• Data is stored in tables.	• Data is stored in multidimensional arrays.
• Slower access.	• Faster access.
• Limitations on complex analysis functions.	• Large library of functions for complex calculations.
• Drill-through to lowest level easier.	• Extensive drill-down and slice and dice capabilities.
• Drill-across not always easy.	
Query Processing Mechanism	
• User uses his own language to fetch data from the data warehouse that stores data in the form of relations.	• The analytical server creates and stores data cubes.
• The analytical server converts user's language into complex SQL queries to fetch data from the data warehouse	• User uses his own language to fetch data from the data warehouse that stores data in the form of relations.
• The query is executed on the data warehouse server and the desired data is sent to the analytical server.	• The analytical server checks whether summary data is requested in multidimensional format or detailed data is required. Based upon the condition, either of the two things is done:
• The analytical server checks the form in which the data is required by the user and based upon that, it does either of the two things:	• If summary data is required in the form of data cubes, then the analytical server simply sends the data cubes to user since it already has summary data available in the form of cubes.
• If the user wants to see the result set in the form of relation, then the analytical server simply passes it to the client	• However, if detailed data is required, that data is not present in the data cube as it has only summary data available. So the analytical server forms a complex SQL query to fetch the data from the warehouse and then forward it to the user.
• however, if the user wants the result set to be presented in multidimensional format, then the analytical server creates dynamic cubes on fly from the result set and then forward it to the client	

10.6.3 HOLAP

Hybrid OLAP (HOLAP) addresses the shortcomings of ROLAP and MOLAP by combining the capabilities of both approaches. HOLAP tools can utilize both pre-calculated cubes and relational data sources. Thus, in a way, HOLAP technologies combine the advantages of MOLAP and ROLAP.

When summary information is required, HOLAP leverages cube technology for faster performance and when detail information is needed, HOLAP can "drill through" from the cube into the underlying relational data to satisfy the users need for information. The OLAP server has the task of figuring out where to access the data. In case of aggregated data requests, the information is sought from the MDDB cube while granular queries are redirected to the relational database.

The most common example of HOLAP architecture is OLAP services in Microsoft SQL Server 7.0. OLAP vendors of all stripes are working to make their products marketable as "hybrid" as quickly as possible. It is critically important to closely examine the architectures of these "repackaged/repositioned" offerings, as their "HOLAP" claims may be more marketing hype than architectural reality.

10.6.4 DOLAP

In this technology, multidimensional cubes are formed and downloaded on the users desktop. Here, datasets are limited to the boundaries defined by the user with no access to granular data. Depending on the tool selected for the data warehouse users, either ROLAP, MOLAP or a combination of both can be implemented. However, it is always best to start with ROLAP architecture for large voluminous data and then later on move in to MOLAP cubes when aggregate data is needed.

With Web-based access on the increase to encompass as many users as possible, Desktop OLAP (DOLAP) is becoming increasingly popular. DOLAP server just performs the task of sending a cube of the requested data to the client like that of a Java applet which resides on the client machine and enables viewing, analysis and computation of this data. Such client analysis applets download MOLAP cubes on the user's desktop so that reports can be generated. Linking cubes to related cubes or sharing them with users across the network can be easily achieved with DOLAP servers.

In addition to this, Web-based architectures can be further enhanced to include OLAP caching servers to improve query performance in a data warehousing environment. Then, parallel processing can also be implemented to improve query performance even to a greater extent.

10.6.5 OLAP Survey

In the OLAP industry, ROLAP is usually perceived as being able to scale for large data volumes, but suffers from slower query performance as comapred to MOLAP. The OLAP Survey, the largest independent survey across all major OLAP products, conducted from the year 2001 to 2005 have consistently found that companies using ROLAP report slower performance than those using MOLAP.

However, as with any survey, there are a number of subtle issues that must be taken into account when interpreting the results.

- ROLAP tools are selected by companies with larger volumes of data (high cardinality dimensions), due to ROLAPs superior scalability. According to the OLAP Survey, ROLAP tools can easily handle data volumes of 312 GB compared to 4 GB for MOLAP tools, but on the other hand, larger data volumes lead to longer query times.
- The survey also shows that ROLAP tools have seven times more users than MOLAP tools within each company. Systems with more users will tend to suffer more performance problems at peak usage times.
- There is also a question about complexity of the model, measured both in number of dimensions and richness of calculations. The survey does not offer a good way to control for these variations in the data being analysed.

10.6.6 OLAP Trends

The undesirable trade-off between additional ETL cost and slow query performance has ensured that most commercial OLAP tools now use a HOLAP approach, which allows the model designer to decide which portion of the data will be stored in MOLAP and which portion in ROLAP. The difference between the two design approaches is given in Table 10.4.

Table 10.4 ROLAP and MOLAP design approaches

ROLAP	MOLAP	ROLAP	MOLAP
Database	Database	Table	Cube
View	Formula	Primary key(s)	Dimension(s)
Row	An instance of several variables	Referential Integrity	Implied by singular definition of dimensions
Triggers	N/A	Indices	N/A
System catalog definition	Metadata/data	JOIN clause	N/A
WHERE clause	LIMIT command	GROUP BY clause	GROUP command
ORDER BY clause	SORT command	GRANT	PERMIT
Stored procedures/ scripts/stored SQL	Programs and user-defined functions	Null columns	Null values
Control of Flow Language (PL/SQL, Transact-SQL and others)	Express stored procedure language	Aggregations (SUM, AVG, COUNT, MIN, MAX)	Express functions and formulas
Computations include mathematical operations and operations performed on strings and date/time	Computations include formulae of math, statistical, financial, forecasting, modelling, date/time and string functions	SELECT	REPORT
INSERT	MAINTAIN ADD	DELETE	MAINTAIN DELETE
UPDATE	SET	COMMIT	UPDATE

10.7 OLAP DESIGN CONSIDERATIONS

The underlying DBMS of most of the large data warehouses comprises of relational databases. Data warehouse design is one of the most critical aspects linked directly to OLAP deliverables. Some OLAP tools that are widely used today give specific guidelines about the design structure of the data warehouse.

There should be an OLAP tool expert as a part of the design formulation who has a thorough understanding of the tool features and is able to map the database design to the front end. The tool expert should have a good knowledge of the features discussed below and its impact on design.

OLAP input to the design structure of the data warehouse would not only help to meet the user's requirements gracefully but will also influence its performance. Therefore, utmost care needs to be given on the limitations of various tools that would be used.

Cross-functional requirements need to be designed. Often, functional areas are kept aloof from the security point of view. If the data warehouse users intend to access cross-functional data, then there must be a design that would cater to the data security issues as well. Thus, data warehouse design must incorporate the behaviour of the OLAP tool in the following aspects:

- Aggregation. There should be a clear understanding of how the OLAP tool behaves with aggregation. Drilling features of the OLAP tool must also be considered along with aggregation.
- Security handling. When users create complex reports on the fly, it becomes necessary to secure sensitive data. Thus, most OLAP tools provide for scoping of data on the basis of certain attributes or dimension values.
- Report-level calculations. Tools provide various functions to do calculations at the report levels, so it is important to understand properly the calculations, which can be done at the reporting levels so that these capabilities of the tools does not left unutilized.
- OLAP performance is always measured along with other sub-processes of the data warehousing implementation such as design and ETL.

10.8 OLAP TOOLS AND PRODUCTS

The OLAP market is constantly growing and many OLAP products have come out that are highly flexible and provide quality results. The OLAP tool that you select for your organization must satisfy the following requirements:

- Must be scalable, as the OLAP system will always grow in terms of the number and complexity of the queries and the number of users.
- Easy to administer.
- Give good performance.

- Flexible.
- Cater to the analytical needs of the users.
- Exhibit multidimensional representation of data.
- Have an extensive library of formulae and complex calculations.
- Provide the facility for cross-dimensional calculations.
- Support operations like- pivoting, drill down, roll up, drill through, drill across, etc.
- Provide an interface of OLAP with other applications and software.

Before using any tool, first finalize the OLAP strategy. For this, first classify the reports based on complexity: complex, medium, or simple, and assign time frames for them.

Generally, the OLAP tools provide an abstract layer which contains business names that are mapped to the database layer. Therefore, it is always preferable to choose appropriate business names for the objects which will be visible to the user, so that it becomes easy for them to generate reports.

Before these business names are finalized, they must be reviewed by the end-users for their approval. Last but not the least, the reports should be tested after development for functional fit and cosmetics:

- Create reports in accordance with the organization's existing applications.
- The colours and the fonts used for display of data must be consistent with that of other applications.
- The tool must provide support for eye-catching graphical features.
- Data verification. The data displayed in the reports must be verified for its accuracy.
- Data scenario testing. Special data scenarios like conversion of measures into different units must also be tested, e.g. conversion of value shown in rupees to dollars.

10.8.1 Report Scheduling and Sharing

OLAP tools provide the capability to schedule and share reports. They contain in-built user management features. Depending on the security of data configuration, the users can share documents across their group. Report scheduling is generally used for data intensive reports, which takes more time for refresh and thus, can be scheduled to run during off peak load periods.

10.8.2 Ad Hoc Reporting

The OLAP implementation team must ensure that all documented requirements of the users are met. In a data warehouse environment, it is the efficiency of executing *ad hoc* queries that will bring accolades or brickbats.

The OLAP tool must be thoroughly tested for various combinations of facts and dimensions, as some tools allow selection of dimensions or measures, which is functionally nonsensical. The tools should therefore be able to recognize such combinations and advise them to select functionally compatible facts and dimensions. *Ad hoc* analysis must also be able to highlight the limitations of the existing application so that new valid business requirements can be identified.

10.8.3 OLAP Customization

The OLAP tools these days support advance customization features using which the front-end can be made similar to existing applications. This would in turn provide a single interface to the user along with other applications.

Customization requirements of the users must be properly documented, as these would involve data warehousing as well as programming skills. However, customization issues also involve configuration of third party software and specialized authentication setup. The third party software includes ASP/JSP programming and Active X plug-ins that can be combined with OLAP APIs to establish compatible front-ends.

10.8.4 The Human Angle

Concentrate on automation, as in every project, there would be OLAP aspects that can be automated. Attempts should be made to simplify or reduce documentation, as with rapid development tools, teams generally spend up more time on writing documents rather than putting more effort on the actual development.

Usually, when there are changes in the developed reports, they need to be cascaded back to the entire set of associated documents which thereby increases the overhead. The project team also gets frustrated if the rework that needs to be done is very high. Thus, efforts should be made to avoid any kind of rework without affecting the quality of the final deliverable.

10.9 EXISTING OLAP TOOLS

In this section, we will discuss different OLAP tools that exist in the market.

10.9.1 Spreadsheet OLAP Clients

Traditional OLAP tools used dedicated, proprietary client tools. Even today, most OLAP products available in the market can still work this way. However, in the early 1990s, vendors began to provide add-ins to present multidimensional data via Lotus 1-2-3 and Microsoft Excel, although the more recent implementations work only with Excel (See Table 10.5).

Table 10.5 Compatibility of OLAP products

OLAP Product	LOTUS 1-2-3	Microsoft Excel	Type of Access
Applix TM1	Yes	Yes	Read/write
Arbor Essbase	Yes	Yes	Read/write
Gentia OLAP Database	–	Yes	Read/write
Hyperion Pillar	–	Yes	Read/write
IBM DB2 OLAP Server	Yes	Yes	Read/write
Informix MetaCube	–	Yes	Read-only
Microsoft OLAP Server	–	Yes	Read-only
MicroStrategy DSS Server	–	Yes	Read-only
Oracle Express	–	Yes	Read/write
Pilot Analysis Server	–	Yes	Read-only
Seagate Holos	–	Yes	Read/write

The basic advantage of this approach lies in the combination of flexible display, formatting strengths, and *ad hoc* calculations of spreadsheets with the data management, calculations, and performance of multidimensional database technology. The other advantage that the spreadsheet approach offers is that, no data is stored in the spreadsheet, no macros are required, and the spreadsheet's notorious maintenance hole is eliminated.

Since many OLAP applications are designed in a way that allows the users to enter plans, budgets, and comments, so an increasing number of OLAP servers now allow read/write spreadsheet access. This feature makes the OLAP tool even more attractive. The spreadsheet approach allows the end-users to use their familiar spreadsheet data entry without having to manage or upload the data that thereby resides in a properly secure multi-user database. Thus, it is the OLAP engine and not the spreadsheet package that manages access controls and multi-write concurrency.

Since in most organizations a large group of users are spreadsheet-literate, financial OLAP applications and sales and marketing OLAP applications use the spreadsheet approach. Moreover, spreadsheet add-ins are often free. With licensing based on concurrent server connections, buyers usually do not have to pay for each desktop installation of the add-in. Therefore, the economics of this approach outshines the Web deployment because the hardware and software costs are much lower in this approach.

10.9.2 Other OLAP Clients

Although very good, spreadsheets are not the only means of OLAP clients. The other three options that are available are: standard desktop OLAP products, specialized applications, and Web browsers.

Several vendors produce desktop OLAP tools that many other application providers resell by adding value to these tools by integrating data from their own application into the OLAP data structure. These application vendors implement functions to generate the desktop cubes nearly automatically using the application's metadata. The most common examples of such vendors are Cognos, Business Objects, Brio Technology, and AppSource.

10.9.3 Embedded OLAP

Another form of OLAP embedding comes when specialized applications include licensed off-the-shelf OLAP servers. The most common examples are Comshare and Hyperion. Both have a history of building their own multidimensional engines, but they now licence third-party OLAP servers for some of their applications.

In this approach, it is necessary to add two extra layers: one layer that exists between the application server component and the standard OLAP server, and a second layer that exists on the "output" side of the generic server that handles post-OLAP processing such as exception scanning or data mining.

Thus, although it may look simple to use this approach, but in practice, a significant amount of development effort is required on the server, the client, and even the client/server communications. But the good news is that, despite these complexities, the Microsoft OLAP Server has made this a popular architecture for many applications that can use multidimensional processing.

10.10 DATA DESIGN

Till now, we have studied that the data warehouse feeds the OLAP system. Thus, the flow of system has been from the operational source systems to the data warehouse, and from there to the OLAP system.

However, you may also wonder to build the OLAP systems on top of the operational source systems themselves without the need to move the data into the data warehouse and from there to the OLAP system. Given below are a few reasons why this approach is flawed.

- An OLAP system needs transformed and integrated data. The data warehouse contains this data but if you go directly to the operational systems, you have to clean the data, remove all the disparities, do all transformations, etc. all over again.
- The operational systems keep limited amount of historical data, but OLAP system requires extensive historical data.
- An OLAP system requires data in multidimensional representations, so you need to do summarizations in different ways. Since the data has to be collected from a number of source systems before summarizing it, the whole job of creating summaries in the operational system is quite untenable.
- It is not easy to create different interfaces of the OLAP systems for different departments, e.g. a separate interface for marketing department, separate for finance department, etc.

OLAP systems rarely use data at lowest level of detail, rather they use summarized data for executing the queries, thereby making the analysis more fast and flexible. Every instance of the OLAP system in the data warehouse environment is customized for the purpose that instance serves. In other words, OLAP data tends to be more departmentalized. Given below are a set of techniques required for preparing OLAP data for a specific group of users or a particular department.

- Select the subset of detailed data the particular department is interested in.
- Summarize and prepare aggregate data structures depending upon the needs of the departments.
- Combine the relational tables and see that they are not normalized for efficient query processing.
- Build the index tables.

The implementation steps involved in building the OLAP system can be summarized as in Fig. 10.20.

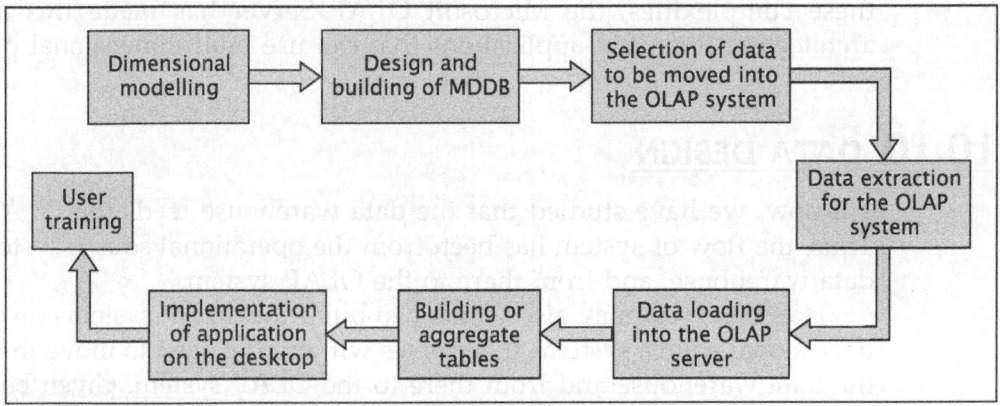

Figure 10.20 The process of building an OLAP system

10.11 ADMINISTRATION AND PERFORMANCE

The OLAP system is part of the overall data warehouse and therefore administration of the OLAP system forms an essential part of the data warehouse administration. Let us discuss some of the key considerations for administering and managing the OLAP system.

- Expectations of what data will be accessed and how it will be accessed.
- Selection of relevant business dimensions.
- Selection of appropriate filters that will be used for loading the data from the data warehouse.
- Techniques that would be used for moving the data into the OLAP system, especially the MOLAP system.

- Choosing the right level of aggregations, summarizations, and pre-calculations required.
- Size of the multidimensional database.
- Drill down to the lowest level of detail, drill through to the data warehouse or operational systems and drill across among OLAP system instances.
- Access and security privileges.
- Backup and recovery functions.

When you install the OLAP system, the queries that once used to execute against the data warehouse are now shifted to the OLAP system. Thus, when long and complex analysis session gets directed to the OLAP, the overall performance of the data warehouse improves. Apart from this, multidimensional databases provide a reasonably predictable, fast, and consistent response to every complex query by creating summarized data well in advance.

But this speed and performance comes with a cost, as you have to compromise with the load performance. OLAP systems are not refreshed daily for the simple reason that it takes a lot of time to pre-calculate the data and load it in the hypercubes. Most OLAP systems are refreshed once in a month.

10.12 OLAP PLATFORMS

Initially, the data warehouse and the OLAP system are very small in size, so both start out on the same platform, as this approach is cost justifiable. However, when the data in the data warehouse starts growing at a tremendous speed, in order to avoid congestion problems, it would be better to separate the OLAP system to another platform. But when should you proceed for this separation?

Given below are some guidelines that indicate when you should shift the OLAP system to a platform other than that of a data warehouse.

- When the size and the usage of the data warehouse grows tremendously and requires all the resources of the common platform, then there is a need to separate the platforms.
- If many departments need the OLAP system, then the OLAP requires additional platform to run.
- Users expect stability and good performance from the OLAP system. Therefore, if the daily transactions of the data warehouse begin to disrupt the stability and performance of the OLAP system, then move the OLAP system to another platform.
- If the chosen OLAP tools need a different configuration from that of the data warehouse, then the OLAP systems need to be put on a separate platform having the desired configuration.

Recapitulation

OLAP is a category of software technology that enables analysts, managers, and executives to gain insight into data through fast, consistent, interactive access; supports multidimensional analysis and improves the comprehension of result sets through visual presentations using graphs and charts.

The roll-up operation or drill-up operation performs aggregation on a data cube by climbing up a dimensional hierarchy.

Drill-down is the reverse of roll-up, as it navigates from less detailed data to more detailed data. Drill-down can be realized by stepping down the dimensional hierarchy.

The slice operation performs a selection on one dimension of the given cube, resulting in a sub-cube.

The dice operation defines a subcube by performing a selection on two or more dimensions.

Pivot is a visualization operation that rotates the data axes in view in order to provide an alternative presentation of the data.

Applications of OLAP include retail sales and profitability analysis, quality control analysis, financial and budgeting applications, and management reporting. OLAP is widely used in banks, airlines, media and entertainment, information technology, insurance, and auto industry.

In MOLAP, data is stored in a multidimensional cube. It gives very fast response, provides excellent performance and can perform complex calculations. It is constrained by the limited amount of data it can handle and the requirement of additional investment.

ROLAP intercepts the query and poses the question to the standard relational database and its tables to select the data required to answer that question. There are no limitations to the size of the database or the kind of analysis that may be performed.

HOLAP tools can utilize both pre-calculated cubes and relational data sources. They attempt to combine the advantages of MOLAP and ROLAP. For summary-type information, HOLAP leverages cube technology for faster performance; and when detailed information is needed, HOLAP utilizes the underlying relational data.

DOLAP is meant to provide portability to users of online analytical processing. In this, multidimensional datasets are created and transferred to the desktop machine, requiring only the DOLAP software to exist on that machine. DOLAP is a variation of ROLAP.

OLAP systems can also be built on top of the operational source systems without the need to move the data into the data warehouse and from there to the OLAP system.

Objective Questions

1. **Multiple choice questions**

   (i) Mathematically speaking, an n-D hypercube is nothing but a series of
   - (a) $(n-1)$-D cubes
   - (b) n-D cubes
   - (c) $(n+1)$-D cubes
   - (d) None of these

   (ii) Which operation performs data aggregation by climbing up a dimensional hierarchy?
   - (a) Slice
   - (b) Dice
   - (c) Roll-up
   - (d) Drill-down

(iii) Which OLAP is best for bounded problems?

(a) ROLAP

(b) MOLAP

(c) DOLAP

(d) HOLAP

(iv) Which OLAP can utilize pre-calculated cubes as well as relational data?

(a) ROLAP

(b) MOLAP

(c) DOLAP

(d) HOLAP

2. Fill in the blanks

(i) A data warehouse is designed to perform _____ analysis.

(ii) The data warehouse data is _____ in nature.

(iii) OLAP tools must be deployed in _____ architecture.

(iv) _____ means that all the dimensions are equal.

(v) Measures are stored in the _____.

(vi) _____ is the software component that is used to extract data from the data warehouse.

(vii) _____ is used to store pre computed aggregations of basic fact tables.

(viii) _____ is a generalization of a 3-cube to n-dimensions.

(ix) _____ is a visualization operation that rotates the data axes in view.

(x) In MOLAP, data is stored in a _____.

3. Match the following

1. OLAP	(a) Factual data is described according to different dimensions
2. Multi dimensional databases	(b) Responsible for the construction and maintenance of data warehouse interfaces
3. Multidimen-sional cube	(c) Performs a selection on one dimension
4. MDS administrator	(d) Dimensions displayedalong each axis
5. MDS Manager	(e) Receives multidimen-sional queries from the users
6. Slice operation	(f) Enables speed-of-thought analysis

4. State true or false

(i) Multidimensional analysis calls for the ability to analyse the data at any level of aggregation.

(ii) The query and analysis system must have consistent response times.

(iii) MDS administrator performs mapping between an MD database schema and the actual organization of a data warehouse.

(iv) Facts contain multiple levels of abstraction.

(v) Drill-down navigates from less detailed data to more detailed data.

(vi) The slice operation defines a subcube by performing a selection on two or more dimensions.

(vii) In HOLAP, multidimensional cubes are formed and downloaded on the users desktop.

(viii) OLAP systems are refreshed daily.

Review Questions

1. Write a short note on multidimensional analysis.

2. Define an OLAP system. Also write down some of its essential characteristics.

3. List and briefly explain different operations of an OLAP system.

4. Describe the 12 guidelines given by Dr Codd for an OLAP system.

5. What are hypercubes? What purpose do they solve in an OLAP environment?

6. Briefly explain the different models of OLAP. Differentiate ROLAP and MOLAP.

7. How will you accommodate three or more dimensions in a relation and in a cube? Explain by using relevant examples.

8. Give reasons why feeding data into the OLAP system directly from the source systems is not preferred.

9. Write a short note on applications of OLAP in the real world.

10. Write a short note on OLAP tools and products.

11. Explain the issues in OLAP administration.

12. As a member of a data warehouse project team for a publishing company, prepare a report on the implementation of OLAP describing how OLAP can be used to facilitate the end-users.

13. If you have been asked to implement OLAP system for a heavy chemicals company, which option will you prefer—ROLAP or MOLAP? Justify your answer. Explain which platform you will use for implementing the OLAP system.

PART
III

11

BUILDING A DATA WAREHOUSE

Learning Objectives

After having read the technicalities of forming a data warehouse, in this chapter, we will club all the principles and steps together to see how to proceed step-by-step while building the data warehouse.

Case Study

The previous chapters have thrown light on all the trivial aspects of building a data warehouse. In this chapter, we will see the sequence of steps that are performed for implementing the data warehouse.

Rohit, the project leader of the JRTs data warehouse team, who has all the knowledge regarding the technical issues involved, decides to leave the organization. But before leaving, he signed the contract with JRTs specifying that the team would deliver the complete functional data warehouse in the next two years and within a particular budget.

Ten days after Rohit left, a new project leader joined the team. He finds that nothing had been documented regarding what has been discovered after gathering user's require-

ments and how the team has to proceed further.

With zero knowledge of the current scenario, he has to start everything from the scratch and finds that either the deadline would be difficult to meet or the project will have to be over-budgeted. But this is not acceptable both to the client (JRTs) and to the vendor (the data warehouse building team's organization).

Hence, had everything been clearly documented and had activities been performed in a proper sequence, no such problems would have occurred. Thus, even for a data warehouse, requirements that are gathered have to be documented, a well-defined project plan has to be formulated followed by a sound design, testing, and implementation.

11.1 INTRODUCTION

Once the decision to build the data warehouse has been taken, the next step is to organize for what is usually a very large project. All the principles of project management that we apply in an operational system project will be applied to the data warehouse project as well. Tasks like determining the critical success factors, selecting a project leader, formulating a project plan that includes allocation of funds, schedules, deliverables, and more as well as assigning of staff has to be done.

Managing the design, development, implementation, and operation of an enterprise-wide data warehouse is a difficult and time-consuming task. In this chapter, we will have a look at the primary steps to ensure a successful data warehouse development effort.

11.2 PROBLEM DEFINITION

The definition and recording of the problem to be solved is one of the first tasks that need to be done for any development effort. The project team must not jump right into the problem to solve it. Although for small, negligible cost efforts, this can be done; but for the data warehouse design, ignoring the problem definition step can lead to disaster. In this step, the data warehouse project team must write down and widely publish the answers to the following questions, targeted to defining the problem and not solving it.

Is there any need of a data warehouse? This is an obvious question, but it should be taken seriously. For some businesses, the answer could be yes, but for others, there may be better solutions. It is recommended to seek professional advice when answering this question. This may cost some money upfront, but they are far less costly early on in the development.

What problems will be resolved by the data warehouse? The team should write down all the problems that the data warehouse will solve. The problems should be clearly specified and have testable criteria for success and they should be publicized to get user and management feedback.

What are the resources available in the organization? These resources include time, money, and personnel. Knowing what resources are already present in the organization at the beginning of the project is critical for defining the development path. If the budget allocated to the project is low, the team should consider down-scaling the effort; if time is short, the team can better use off-the-shelf products, and in case personnel resources are scarce, then outsourcing can be done to overcome the problem. Being realistic about the actual resources present will help the data warehouse project team to prevent overruns and project disappointments.

If the organization has resources for a normal database and is trying to jump into building a data warehouse, that situation will always doom a project. In case the organization lacks a lot of resources, the upper management must be informed about it and only then the team should proceed with any other efforts to start the project.

What criteria will be used to measure success? This question is very often ignored in the problem definition but in the idealistic situation for every problem stated, a means for determining the success of the project must also be defined. Until and unless the success criteria are specified clearly, the problem definition step could not be considered complete.

The team should avoid giving vague statements like "The data warehouse will be storing the accounts data." Rather it should be restated in quantifiable terms as "The data warehouse must handle the current 25GB of accounts data including all metadata with an expected 2% growth per year."

11.3 CRITICAL SUCCESS FACTORS

Jack F. Rockart uses the term "critical success factor" to refer to those things that must go right if an undertaking is to become successful. For a data warehouse project, these critical success factors include:

Set specific, achievable, and measurable goals A data warehouse project is a very large project and often tends to suffer from "scope creep" in spite of putting in large sums of money. Scope creep generally happens when the users define new requirements as the project progresses, thereby adding to the initial set of requirements.

Although every individual request for increasing scope may be valid, the combination of these requests result in late and over budget projects. Thus, for a big project of building a data warehouse, the expectations should be managed and the goals should be kept specific and achievable.

Involve everyone throughout the project The stakeholders in a data warehouse project are the internal people of the organization. This group comprises of the business analysts, managers, executives, sponsors, and other IT users. All of these people are important for the success of the project and so must be a part of the project right from the beginning.

They should be kept abreast of the developments as the project proceeds. The project team must keep all these people in the loop well-informed and involved and must take utmost care to keep everyone contented, as in certain situations, there may be collision in thinking among these people.

Keep an eye on the big picture The primary motive of a data warehouse is to provide answers to business problems. So, utmost care should be taken to avoid moving on with other, more local agendas.

Examples of such agendas may include:

- Using bleeding edge technology (new technology that can be risky to use in terms of stability and productivity) rather than simple solutions already available.
- Using best of breed tools without understanding the problems that have to be solved.
- Trying to establish a perfect data model when the company's business is continually changing.

Pay attention to the details and do not depend on assumptions A data warehouse have an enormous amount of data that is being used by a number of users, so attention to details must be given. However, these details can be affected by the assumptions made in creating the warehouse. Here are some of the pitfalls that can be encountered:

- Assuming that the sources of data are clean, consistent, and have an acceptable quality.
- Assuming that the summary data that is present in the organization is adequate.
- Assuming that the detailed data will not be needed at a later point of time.
- Assuming that development of the project is on track.
- Assuming that users have all the skills needed and are capable enough to use the warehouse and its tools.
- Assuming that the data warehouse experts will be available on short notice to solve last minute problems.
- Assuming that the IT department has all the skills that are required to manage the project.

Consider long-term strategy A long-term strategy for the data warehouse should be developed which must include a lot of detail but should also be flexible enough so that the warehouse can accommodate changes that may have to be done in due course of time. Tactical decisions like those given below often solve immediate problems but create long-term difficulties.

- Building individual data marts without focusing on the long-term warehouse plan.
- Establishing individual data marts without considering enterprise-wide data definitions and standards.
- Not assigning roles to people who should be responsible for maintaining data quality throughout the organization.
- Using a platform that does not scale up as the business grows and the need for data increases.
- Not establishing metadata standards that will be used.

Learn from others Data warehousing is a relatively new concept and firms just beginning to create a data warehouse have to struggle with the learning curve. The best approach is to learn from those firms that have already built a warehouse and are using it. Links could be made at many data warehousing conferences that are conducted every year to bring together vendors, academics, and the most important people who have practical experience about the subject.

11.4 REQUIREMENT ANALYSIS

Requirement analysis is the most crucial factor for the success of any project. In the absence of a clear goal, success rates are low. The steps in the requirement analysis phase that have been found to work can be listed as below:

- Clearly state the problems that have to be solved.
- Identify all data sources and the formats in which the data is stored in them.
- Identify the users of the data warehouse system.
- Clearly specify the budget in terms of time, money, and personnel.
- Ask the users to specify their expectations from the new system.
- Ask the management to specify the success criteria.
- Filter requirements from their desires. Initially start with designing the system as per the requirements, and then later on in the enhancement phase, address the desires.
- Formulate a prioritized requirements document, listing the requirement, its source, the success criteria, and its priority.
- Get a sign-off of the requirements, resource allocation, and schedule from the top management before the team can proceed with later stages.

To begin with requirement analysis, the first and foremost thing that has to be done is to identify the sponsors of the data warehouse project and ensure that these sponsors understand and support the project.

The second thing that needs to be done is to thoroughly understand the business before starting any discussions with the users. Then interview the users and work with them to learn their needs and then, turn these requirements into project requirements.

Identify the information that is needed to make the data warehouse successful. For this, do not go by users and do not try to put what data the users think should be in the data warehouse; rather provide the information that is necessary for the business. And in order to provide this information in the data warehouse, the project team must learn about users' objectives and challenges and how they go about making business decisions. Business users and the team should be closely tied to each other during the logical design process, as the users can tell the meaning of existing data much better.

After understanding the business needs, the team must interview the database administrator of the operational systems as well to know what data exists and where it resides. The team should make sure that all the intended users are thoroughly interviewed and that the users should participate equally in the progress of the requirements definition.

11.5 PLANNING FOR THE DATA WAREHOUSE

A data warehouse is planned in terms of business requirements, personnel, finances, and feasibility. We shall discuss these aspects of planning in the following sub-sections.

11.5.1 Project Staff

The data warehouse team should include:

- Technical staff that includes the project leader, a data analyst, a business analyst, a database administrator, and programmers who are familiar with business problems to be solved.
- An *ad hoc* technical staff who will be called to join the project as and when needed for specific project tasks like for technical support, technical writing, training, and helpdesk.
- An end-user staff that comprises subject matter experts.
- Corporate level sponsors such as executives from the end-user and IT community.

11.5.2 Project Plan

To be successful, a big project like that of a data warehouse calls for good and careful planning. Two kinds of planning are involved:

- An overall plan for creating the data warehouse and its infrastructure.
- Detailed plans for every individual application that would be run in the data warehouse environment.

Overall planning

The overall plan for creating a data warehouse includes two broad aspects: (a) Vision and (b) Validation and estimation.

Vision   Vision of the project states what has to be built. Different people in the organization may have different objectives: the sponsor may want an improved EIS application; the business analyst may want a better source for strategic analysis; and the marketing managers may want to work with data mining applications. All the objectives of the various groups involved cannot be satisfied simultaneously, so the conflicting viewpoints of different individuals must be resolved.

The output of the vision phase is a document that describes why the warehouse is being built, what should be included in the data warehouse and what should not (scope of the project).

Validation and estimation   Along with defining the vision of the data warehouse project, the anticipated costs, schedule, and resources that will be required are estimated during the planning phase. The technical feasibility which is also a validation step is completed. Validation involves cross-checking the requirements and identifying the risks associated with the development.

Estimation and technical feasibility are interlinked with each other. Many trade-offs will have to be made to complete the data warehouse project within a reasonable timeframe and a reasonable budget.

Detailed Planning

Detailed planning moves the project from a conceptual entity to a specific one. The main aim here is to define the budget, schedule, and intermediate and final deliverables for the data warehouse project. Project planning tools are used to allow managers to visualize the time sequence in which the events must occur, the kind of personnel that will have to be assigned, and the hardware and software components that will have to be acquired and integrated.

A well-formulated and a structured plan includes details on every step of the project, from the source of data to how the data is to be cleaned, stored, and used by the end-users, to the end-user training programme. The training part of the plan considers teaching end-users the mechanics of how to obtain information from the warehouse, and how to go on with their need to extract strategic information from the data warehouse.

Infrastructure planning The infrastructure for a data warehouse includes all the hardware and software components that will be needed for the data warehouse to go live. The hardware components include computers, networks, terminals or PCs; and the software components comprises of database, extraction tools, cleaning tools, and query handling. Proper infrastructure planning is critical for a large project like a data warehouse project that often has to be built up from scratch.

11.5.3 Outsourcing vs. Custom Building

The data warehouse, like all other operational systems may be created in-house, outsourced in part, or outsourced completely. In other words, the outsourcing decision is a classic make-versus-buy decision which is a fairly complex one.

Factors like improving the in-house skills, knowledge of how the organization works, and using full knowledge about what data is available, where it is stored and how it is stored are considerations that push the decision towards in-house development. On the contrary, considerations that push decisions towards outsourcing the project include lack of personnel with the appropriate skills, non-availability of data warehouse expertise, and lack of faith that the project can be accomplished in-house.

Since a data warehouse is usually used for strategic analysis and is often considered a decision-support application, the favoured approach is to keep the warehouse project in-house, seeking the help of outside consultants in the design stage and other areas that are beyond existing expertise within the firm.

11.5.4 Detailed Project Plan

A project plan as a whole contains a description about three main issues:

- What will be done? This includes description of the tasks that will make up the overall project.
- When it will be done? This includes the deadlines when a particular task has to be completed.
- What resources will be used for it? This contains a description about the resources that will be needed to accomplish the tasks at hand.

Tasks

In project planning, tasks or activities are considered to be the basic units of work. Every schedule and resource allocation is made as per the activities that have to be performed. The description of every individual task must state what is being done, how it will be done and what will be the end product or the deliverable after that task is completed. It is always recommended that if a task is expected to take a few weeks to complete, then it is good to plan intermediate milestones so that any deviations from the planned schedule at an early date can easily be detected.

The description of each task should also specify the dependencies of the task. Some of these dependencies will be within the project, for example, the testing process cannot start until there is something to test, whereas other dependencies may be external to the project, e.g. the coding phase can start only after the delivery of a server from a hardware vendor. These dependencies will help the project managers to focus their attention on tasks, which if not completed within the expected time frame will delay the completion of the entire data warehouse.

Schedule

Schedule can either be stated in absolute terms like 1 January 2007, or in relative terms like one month after the task T1 is completed. Generally, managers must create a relative schedule. However, some managers may prefer to use calendar dates, as they consider them to be more meaningful to most people and create a vision of when the entire project should be completed. It should be noted that these dates are mere estimates, as the completion of any given task depends on everything that must be done before the task.

Resources

Creating a data warehouse mainly calls for three types of resources that include people, hardware, and software. All these resources must be arranged for and scheduled to be available for the completion of the project. People having a varied level of expertise would be required to complete the project.

The list of people includes the following:

- Business analysts, executives, managers for defining the warehouse, which is also called the scope of the project. They would help the team to identify users of the data warehouse.
- Data architects for defining the data models, identifying and collecting the data needed, performing transformation, and loading the data in the data warehouse.
- IT staff for testing the tools.
- End-user support staff for user training and support activities.
- Sponsors of the warehouse who will support the project team in every possible way.

Resource requirements are translated into financial terms when planning a project so that the cost of a project can be estimated. Expressing resource requirements in financial terms by time period creates a project budget, which in turn, is used to monitor project expenditures and take preventive measures if it is getting out of hands.

11.6 THE DATA WAREHOUSE DESIGN STAGE

The design stage of a data warehosue comprises of the following sequence:

11.6.1 Design the Dimensional Model

User requirements guide dimensional modelling (explained in Chapter 7) which is done as a part of the design phase. The dimensional model must address business needs, grain of detail, the dimensions and the facts to include, (The terms, facts, and dimensions are explained in Chapter 5). The dimensional model must be in tune with the requirements of the end-users so that they easily use it for direct access. The model must also be designed so that it is easy to maintain and is flexible enough to adapt to future changes.

An operational system is based on a normalized structure to minimize data redundancy, allow validation of input data, and support a large number of transactions that occur repeatedly. In these systems, a transaction may just involve a single business event, such as placing an order. Thus, an operational system model often looks like a spider web of hundreds and thousands of related tables. In contrast, in a data warehouse environment, the dimensional model uses a star schema or a fact constellation schema (Chapter 7) that is easy to understand and relate to business needs, supports complex business queries, and provides higher query performance by minimizing table joins.

11.6.2 Develop the Architecture

The data warehouse architecture reflects the dimensional model developed to meet the business requirements. The dimension model specifies the dimension table design and fact definitions, thereby specifying the fact table design and finally the relationship between these fact tables and the dimension tables.

Whether to create a star or snowflake schema is not a trivial issue, and it depends more on implementation and maintenance considerations than on business needs. Generally, data warehouse schemas are quite simple and straightforward, in contrast to that of operational database schemas that have hundreds or thousands of tables and relationships. The primary goal of the data warehouse schema is to handle a large quantity of data which can affect the performance and efficiency of the queries. A star schema is good enough for this purpose.

11.6.3 Design for Update and Expansion

Data warehouse architectures must be designed to absorb the ongoing data updates, and cater for future growth with minimum impact on the existing design. The dimensional model and the star schema simplify these activities with records being entered in the fact table with little effect on most dimensions.

For example, a sale made of an existing product, by an existing salesperson, at an existing store, to an existing customer will not call for any changes to be made on the product, customer, salesperson, or store dimension tables. But in case, the product was to be sold to a new customer, then a new record had to be added to the customer dimension table when the record is added to the fact table.

The historical nature of data warehouses implies that records are not deleted from the tables; only updates and additions are done to the existing data in the warehouse.

The dimensional model helps for easy expansion, as new dimension attributes and new dimensions can be added without affecting existing dimensions, its attributes, and other historical data stored in it previously. With due course of time, no doubt, the data warehouse applications will need to be extended, but the existing applications should remain intact. Although some applications may be updated to make use of the new information, their functionality should remain the same. An entirely new business subject area including new fact table and dimension tables and thus a new schema can be added to a data warehouse without affecting the existing functionality.

11.6.4 Design the Relational Database and OLAP Cubes

In this phase, the star schema that is made up of a number of dimensions and fact tables is created, surrogate keys are defined, and primary and foreign key relationships are established. Then, any sort of views, indexes, and fact table partitions are created followed by the design of OLAP cubes to support the strategic needs of the users.

Tables are implemented in the relational database after surrogate keys for dimension tables have been defined and primary and foreign keys have been established.

Views must be created for those end-users who need direct access to the data stored in the warehouse. Appropriate access must be granted to the users so that they can access the underlying data. Generally, the indexed views are designed to improve query performance. OLAP cube design requirements will be designed to support the way the users want to query the data.

11.6.5 Decisions in Design

Critical decisions have to be taken at various levels of design. Discussed below are the details of the issues which are to be resolved at various stages of design.

Design decisions: Organization of the warehouse
- How much data the data warehouse must handle?
- What is the number of tiers that will be present in the architecture of the warehouse?
- What structure of the warehouse is desired: a centralized warehouse or a distributed warehouse?

Design decisions: Back-end
- What will be the source of data (external, internal, production, and archived)?
- Which relational DBMS will be used? What will be the extraction tools that will be needed for extraction and transformation of data?
- Determine the interval between data loads. The more frequently the data is loaded, the more up-to-date it is.

Design decisions: Data warehouse
- The subjects to be included in the warehouse.
- For decision support system which technology to use: ROLAP or MOLAP.
- Deciding the level of granularity at which the data must be stored. Granularity involves a trade-off between increased detail and speed of computation.
- Data can be summarized in a variety of ways so choose the summaries that must be provided.
- To minimize the response time of the queries, some warehouses pre-compute the answers to frequently asked queries. The trade-off is extra storage for speed of response. So the question is how much pre-computation must be done and till what levels.
- Data in the warehouse is moved from one level of storage medium to another, depending on its age. We have discussed it in archived data in Chapter 2 so the design decision involves the time when data must be moved from one medium to another.
- Decisions to create, update, and maintain the metadata.

- Decision involving the computing capability of the data warehouse—whether it should have parallel or serial computing capability.

Design decisions: Front-end

- In data warehousing environment, the users want to access the data at various levels of details. So, decisions have to be made regarding the arrangement of data according to various levels of detail.
- Which users will have access to the data, and which services will be provided to different categories of data warehouse users.
- Decision regarding the front end of the project as the front-end is the user's prime point of contact with the warehouse. Hence, it needs to be designed carefully.

Design decisions: Maintaining the system

- Provisions for monitoring the warehouse need to be designed so that improvements, updates, and changes can be done easily.
- Decisions must be made regarding the subject areas. For example, it should be clear much before time that if it is required to incorporate more subject areas in future, how the situation will be handled.
- Decisions regarding the security of the data warehouse system are crucial as well.

11.6.6 Detail Design

In this stage, the database schema is developed, the metadata is defined, and the source data is expanded to include all the necessary information needed for the subject area, and is validated by the users. In this phase, detailed designing of all procedures that will be implemented for the data warehouse is completed and documented. These procedures are designed to accomplish the following activities:

- Data warehouse capacity expansion.
- Data extraction, transformation, loading and cleansing functions.
- Security of the data warehouse.
- Data refresh.
- Data access.
- Data backup and recovery.
- Disaster recovery.
- Purging and archival of historical data.
- Configuration management.
- Testing of every individual module and the entire system as a whole.
- Transition to production.
- User training and user support.
- Change management.

11.6.7 Other Design Considerations

Since the data warehouse is a very large project with a wide scope, it calls for some key considerations such as:

- Complexity of the project.
- Coordination among the IT and the end-users.
- Costs and benefits of the project.

The huge size of the project and use of many bleeding edge technologies make a data warehouse project quite complex. A tremendous amount of coordination is required to deal with the complex issues. But care must be taken that the team does not spend more time in coordinating and resolving issues rather than spending time for data warehouse design. Several steps can be taken to cope with these kinds of complexity and coordination problems.

- Break the big size project into smaller and manageable modules with each module having a clearly defined set of deliverables.
- The people involved in the project understand their responsibility and are able to deliver the output as per the schedule within the specified time frame.
- Assign fiscal and managerial responsibility for each and every module.

Since the data warehouse project involves a large number of people, there will be a great number of ideas coming from them. Although all these ideas must be encouraged, but then there has to be a common vision of the overall project.

To make a project feasible, an infrastructure must be put in place to develop and implement applications. Basically, applications are implemented one at a time, so there must be a plan for the sequence in which these applications will be applied within the organization.

11.7 BUILDING AND IMPLEMENTING DATA MARTS

We have already studied about data marts, their advantages and limitations in Chapter 3. Once all the design decisions of the data warehouse are made, we move further to build and implement the individual data marts.

Although a data mart is smaller in size as compared to a data warehouse and hence easier to install, some issues like data loading, vendor performance, and software integration can make this task a bit more difficult. To minimize such problems, some vendors offer "data mart in a box" that provides all the required components through one-stop shopping. However, such data marts may not be able to solve all the problems.

An organization may contain *n* number of data marts, so access to the remote data marts is made through the web browser.

11.8 BUILDING DATA WAREHOUSES

After completing the work of building and implementing various data marts at the department level, the next stage is to build a complete data warehouse from these data marts following a bottom-up approach. In case you want to follow a top-down approach of building a data warehouse, you first have to build the complete enterprise-wide warehouse and then make individual data marts from it. Thus, the design decision varies from organization to organization.

The required hardware, software, and middleware components are acquired and installed, establishment of the development and test environment is done, and the configuration management processes are implemented. Software programs to extract, clean, transform, load the source data, and periodically refresh the existing data in the data warehouse are written. These programs must be unit tested against a test database with a sample source data.

Technical and business metadata are loaded in the metadata repository. Canned production reports are produced and sample *ad hoc* queries are run against the test database to measure the validity of the output. Users are provided access to the data warehouse. Once all the components are in place, system functionality and user acceptance testing is conducted for the complete integrated data warehouse system. All system support processes like that of database security, backup and recovery, disaster recovery, data purging, and archival are implemented and tested as the system is prepared for deployment.

11.8.1 Test and Deploy the System

The end-users must be a part of the testing process. After the initial testing is conducted by the development and test teams, users should use the system to execute their queries, form their reports, and do any kind of analysis they wish to do. User involvement in the testing phase provides a significant number of benefits, such as:

- Errors and discrepancies can be found and corrected.
- Users can familiarize themselves with the system.
- Tuning of indexes can be done.

When the users exercise the system during the test phase, with all kinds of queries that they will be generally executing, a considerable amount of empirical index tuning can be done even before the system comes online. Although additional tuning will have to be done after the deployment, the system starts with a satisfactory performance.

Generally, testing and reviews of the data warehouse will be done throughout the development of the system. It is crucial to appoint a single individual in charge of the testing and review process. The person in charge should be empowered with the appropriate authority and must identify most of the problems before they become too big to handle. We will study more about testing the data warehouse in later chapters.

After testing the data warehouse, training sessions are scheduled concurrently with the installation to make effective use of time. The best way to ensure success is to effectively train the users so that they will actually use the system and possibly sing its praises. These training sessions are however ongoing sessions, because new employees or employees being moved or promoted will need to be trained. Also whenever there will be some enhancements made to the system, new training sessions must be scheduled.

11.8.2 Transition to Production

This phase transfers the data warehouse project into the production environment. The production database is created, the extraction, and transformation routines are run on the operations system source data. The project team now works with the operational system staff to perform the initial loading of the data warehouse and execute the first refresh cycle.

The staff is given appropriate training and the programs and applications are moved into the production libraries and catalogs. Good explanatory presentations and tool demonstrations are given to the end-users. The help desk is established and made operational. A Service Level Agreement is signed by the organization. Finally, a Change Management Board is established for ongoing maintenance and the implementation of change control procedures for future development cycles.

11.8.3 User Training and Support

The importance of training and orientation for the users cannot be neglected. From an IT department's perspective, the end-users must be trained mainly in three areas: data, applications, and tools. But, on the other hand, the end-users see the training sessions as one. It is very important that the training program be designed from the user's point of view.

The data warehouse offers many more capabilities and has a lot more potential than that of an operational system. In a data warehouse environment, users are not aware of how much they can really do with the tools in the data warehouse. You need to train the warehouse users in the following areas:

- Database and data storage concepts.
- Features of the data warehouse.
- Contents of the data warehouse.
- Browsing through the warehouse contents of data and metadata.
- Making efficient use of the data access and retrieval tools.
- Usage of the Web for information delivery.
- Predefined queries and reports.
- Analysis that can be performed on the stored data.
- Scheduling and delivery of data reports.
- Usage of query templates.
- Data loading schedules and the currency of data stored in the warehouse.

The first step in formulating a schedule for user training is to determine the areas where the users need to be trained. Try to match the content of the training with anticipated usage of the warehouse. If users use only predefined queries and reports, then the job of training is easier, but this cannot be true in case of a data warehouse. The data warehouse end-users will formulate their own *ad hoc* queries and perform complex analysis. Thus, the content of the training program needs to be more intense. The training program must be both deep and wide to cater to the needs of all user groups.

The other consideration for preparing the contents of the training program is that the different users of the data warehouse have different levels of skills and knowledge. Hence, the training program must cater to the needs of every individual user.

Among other things, there are three basic components that must be included as a part of the training program: (i) the users must be well aware of what data is available for them in the data warehouse. They must be able to navigate through the contents to find the data that they need; (ii) the users must be aware of the different applications that they can perform. They must be informed about the predefined queries and reports and pre-constructed applications; and (iii) train the users on the tools that they would be using to access the information.

In the early days of post-deployment of the data warehouse, every member of the support staff is busy with solving user's wide range of questions, from basic sign-on to performing complex analysis to other hardware issues. The users need a lot of spoon-feeding, at least during the initial stages. Figure 11.1 shows the initial user support structure.

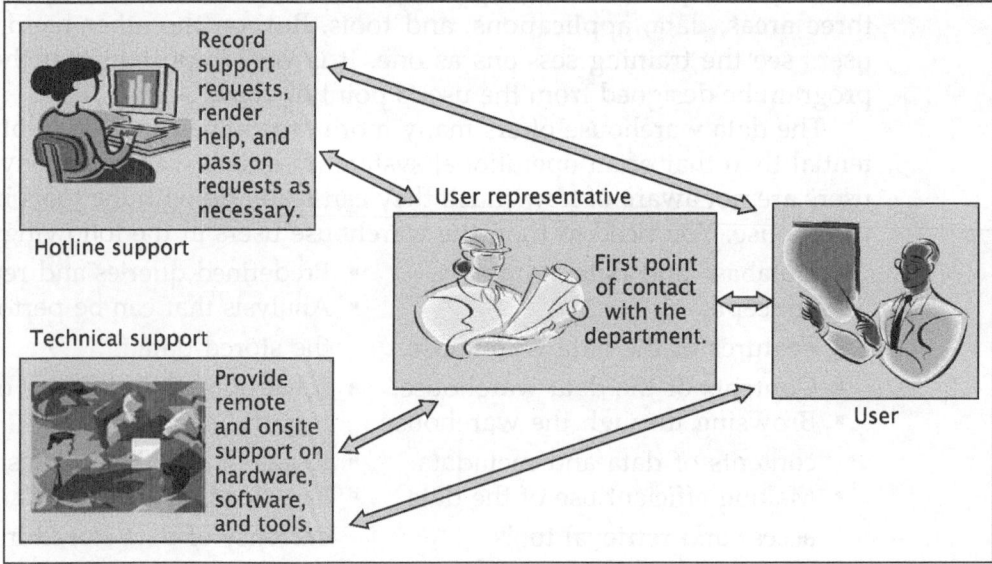

Figure 11.1 Initial user support structure

As seen in the figure, the user representative is the first point of contact within the department. This person must be trained well enough to answer most of the questions on applications, data content of the warehouse, and the end-user tools. The hotline support comes into picture when the user representative is unable to solve user problems.

Apart from user training, emphasis should also be given to user support because user frustration tends to increase in the absence of a sound support structure. Support structure must be in place before the deployment of the data warehouse.

11.8.4 Success Factors of a Training Program

Once you have decided the topics on which the users have to be trained, the next step is to determine who should be given the responsibility of preparing the relevant content/course material. It is only after you have the course material ready with you, you can proceed with training the users. Preparing good course material calls for a lot of effort and this activity cannot be underestimated.

Let us now look at the various tasks needed to prepare a good training program. The training program will of course vary based on the requirements of the organization. Given below are a few general points that must be considered to form a solid user training program.

- The success of a training program depends on the joint participation of user representatives and the IT. User representatives on the project team and the subject area experts in the user departments must work jointly with IT. Let both of them prepare the contents of the course material.

- Do not forget to include all the topics of data content, applications, and tools in the training program.

- Divide the users who need to be trained into different groups based on their level of skills and knowledge. Determine the topics on which each group needs to be trained so that the training program can be tailor made to match the requirements of the organization.

- Determine how many different training courses would actually be needed to train the entire group of users. The set of courses will include an introductory course, an in-depth course, and a specialized course on tool usage. Make sure that the introductory course runs for one day and every user of the data warehouse attends it.

- Design the in-depth course in several tracks in such a way that each track caters to a specific group of users and covers one or two subject areas.

- Make the course documentation simple so that it is easy for the users to understand it. Include enough graphics and pictures. For example, if the course is covering dimensional modelling, then make a sample star schema so that the users can visualize how the relationships are formed between the tables.

- The introductory course material can just be a demo or a theory lecture, but the in-depth course and the end-user tool usage course must provide hands-on experience to the users.

It is always better to complete the training session even before the deployment of the first version of the data warehouse. What the users learn during the initial training sessions will remain fresh in their minds when they start working with the data warehouse. However, ongoing training sessions will continue for additional sets of users. With the implementation of the next versions of the data warehouse, modification of the training materials must be done.

There are always some users who would ask for refresher courses. The users who could not be trained during the initial training session also have to be trained as a part of the ongoing training. Users have their own responsibilities to run the business, and they need to find time to fit into the training slots.

In a data warehouse environment, special consideration needs to be given to train the executives and sponsors, as they would also be using the data warehouse to run queries and produce the desired reports. Some of them may not even know how to look for the information they are interested in. Employees at higher level of the organization may not be interested in attending the training sessions along with user staff. So, separate training sessions need to be arranged for them.

It is not uncommon to find that even after training sessions are completed, there may still be some users who have not been trained, as some of them may be too busy to be able to get away from their business responsibilities or some of them may think that they need not attend any formal course and that they can learn by themselves. The organization must have a strict well-defined policy to cater to such a situation.

When the users access the data warehouse without any formal training, then two things may happen. Either they will disrupt the support structure by asking for too much attention or if they are unable to perform any function, they will blame the system without attributing it to the lack of training. However, the best policy to be followed in this scenario is "No training means no data warehouse access."

11.8.5 Issues in User Support

Let us review some of the general issues that are important in context of the data warehouse.

- Let every user be clear about the support path to be taken. Every user must know whom to contact first if they have any problem regarding software, hardware, applications, or the tool.
- In a multi-tiered support architecture, the roles and responsibilities of every tier must be clearly specified.
- While using the data warehouse, many users will try to match the results obtained from the data warehouse with results obtained from the operational systems, so the support structure must also be able to address such data reconciliation issues.

- Include support on how to find and execute predefined queries and preformatted reports and finally how to navigate through the contents of the warehouse.

- The user support structure will provide you an open channel for communicating with the users and getting their feedback.

11.9 BACKUP AND RECOVERY

A data warehouse stores huge amounts of data that may have taken years to collect. The historical data in the data warehouse may be as old as 10 or even 20 years. Before storing the data in the data warehouse, the data goes through a rigorous process of cleansing and transformation. So, the users cannot afford to lose this data and it is highly desirable that you are able to recreate the data as and when required.

Within a short time after the deployment, the number of users, the complexity of their queries, and the duration of their analysis sessions reach great heights. In this situation, backing up the data content and the ability to recover quickly from malfunctions becomes even more sophisticated. In operational systems, the data is backed up regularly. Whenever a disaster occurs, the recovery process proceeds from the last backup and recovers to the point where the system stopped working.

Some people argue that data backup is not required in a data warehouse environment, as the data warehouse does not represent an accumulation of data directly through data entry. It has been taken from the source systems, so whenever any disaster occurs, data will be recreated from the source systems. Convenient it may sound, but it is rather impractical as recreation would consume a lot of time and the data warehouse users cannot tolerate such long periods of downtime.

Therefore, you need to develop a clear and well-defined backup and recovery strategy. Let us review some of the crucial factors that comprise to form a sound backup strategy.

- Determine what exactly has to be backed up. For this, make a list of the user tables, system tables, and the database logs that have to be backed up.

- Try to make different procedures for backing up the historical and the current data. You may decide to back up the historical data less frequently as compared to backing up of the current data.

- Choose the appropriate medium for backing up the databases.

- Many RDBMS today make use of the container concept to hold individual files. A container is nothing but a larger storage area that can hold many files. Technically speaking, containers are also known as table spaces, file groups, etc. RDBMS adopts special methods to efficiently back up the entire container, so you must use such features provided by the RDBMS.

- You may choose third party tools for a high-speed backup and recovery process.
- You must periodically archive very old data from the data warehouse. A good archival plan helps by reducing the time for backup and restore.
- You must back up even the system databases.

Data warehouse will be used by many users for a constant flow of information. But the huge size of the data warehouse is a serious factor that affects all decisions about backup and recovery. At the time of a disaster, re-extracting data from the source systems and reloading the data warehouse is not viable. So, we need to set up a practical schedule for performing backups.

However, there are a number of issues affecting this practical schedule. First, we must think of scheduling the backups during the night because in a data warehouse environment, the night slots are usually allocated for the daily incremental loads. Second, in case the data warehouse end-users are located in different time zones, then finding a time slot becomes even more difficult. Thus, finally setting up a backup schedule comes down to a question like "How much downtime the users can tolerate before the recover process gets completed?" Hence, a practical schedule will incorporate the following elements:

- Bifurcate the data warehouse into active and static data.
- Assign different time schedules for active and static data.
- Arrange for more frequent backups for active data and less frequent backups for static data.
- As a part of the backup scheme, differential backups and log file backups must also be included.
- Synchronize the backups with the daily incremental data loads.

11.9.1 Recovery Process

Figure 11.2 explains the recovery process in a warehouse environment. Backup files play an important role in the recovery process.

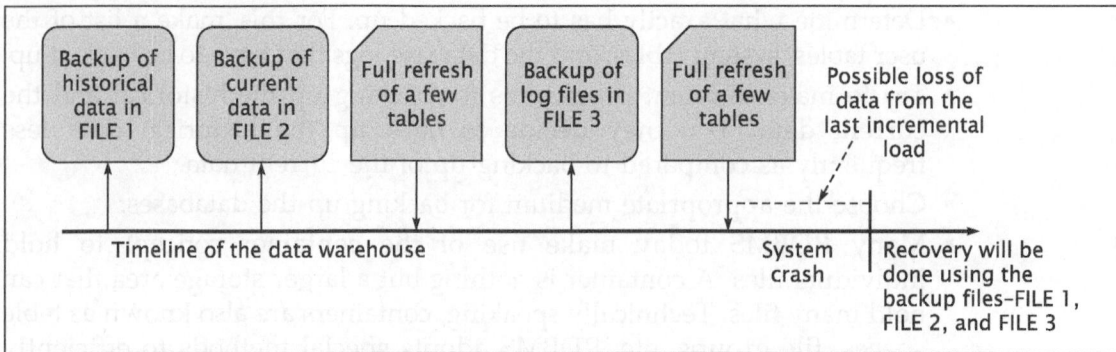

Figure 11.2 Recovery process using backup files

To execute the recovery process, the data warehouse project team must first form a recovery plan. The recovery plan should be such that it lists all the possible disaster scenarios and specify how the recovery will be done in each case. Simply formulating a recovery plan is not sufficient. It must also be thoroughly tested.

Depending upon the conditions prevailing in the organization and the established recovery procedure, the data warehouse project team must estimate an average downtime to be expected for recovery and then get a general agreement from the users about the downtime, so that it should be acceptable for them in case a system crash happens.

The backup strategy lays the ground for a well-defined recovery process. If recovery has to be done from the daily incremental load files, then the backups of these files must be kept handy and in case the recovery has to be done using the source systems, then it must be ensured that the data sources will still be available.

11.10 ESTABLISH THE DATA QUALITY FRAMEWORK

As discussed in Chapter 2, one has to make a number of decisions before actually cleansing the data. For this, you need to go to the sources of possible data corruption and determine the pollution.

Most companies today establish a data quality framework which provides a basis for launching data quality initiatives. It embodies a systematic plan for action and identifies the players, their roles, and responsibilities, thereby guiding the entire data quality improvement effort. Major functions carried out within this framework are as follows:

- Establish a data quality steering committee.
- Identify the business functions affected most by incorrect/corrupt data.
- Select high impact data elements and determine priorities.
- Plan and execute data cleansing for high-impact data elements.
- Institute data quality policy and standards.
- Define quality measurement parameters and benchmarks.
- Plan and execute data cleansing for less-severe data elements.

The steering committee is formed to establish the data quality framework. We will learn about it later. All key players identified must get involved in the steering committee. The data owners of the source systems as well of the data warehouse committee must also be a part of the committee.

The steering committee performs assignment of roles and responsibilities, allocation of resources, and arranging data quality audits. Table 11.1 lists the various roles and responsibilities of people from the IT and user departments who serve as a member of the data quality team.

Table 11.1 Roles and responsibilities with the data quality framework

Roles	Responsibilities
Data consumer	They are the users who use the data warehouse for queries, reports, and analysis and thereby establish the acceptable levels of data quality.
Data producer	These people are charged with maintaining the quality of data input from the source systems.
Data expert	Data experts in the subject matter and data of the source systems are responsible for identifying pollution in the source system.
Data policy administrator	These people are charged with the responsibility of resolving data corruption as data is transformed and moved into the data warehouse.
Data integrity specialist	They are the people who are responsible for ensuring that the data in the source systems conform to the business rules.
Data correction authority	The people comprising the data correction authority are responsible for applying the data cleansing techniques.
Data consistency expert	The expert is responsible for synchronizing the data within the data warehouse repository.

11.10.1 Data Purification

To proceed with the purification process, divide the data elements into priorities with the help of users. You may simply categorize all the data elements into three levels of priority: high, medium, and low. Achieving 100% data quality is critical for the high-priority data elements.

The medium-priority data requires as much cleansing as possible and some errors may be ignored to make a balance between the cost of correction and the potential effect of bad data.

The low priority data may be cleansed if you have any time and resources left. Begin the data cleansing efforts with the high-priority data and then move on to the medium-priority data, and so on.

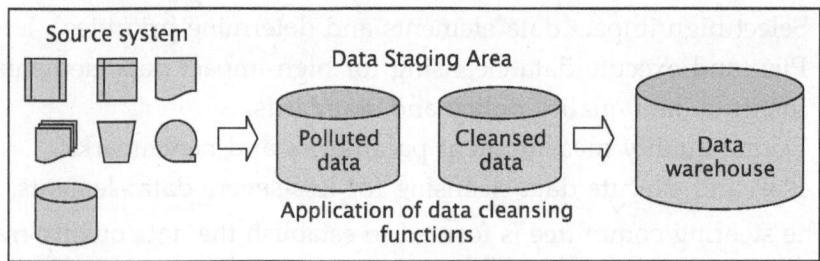

Figure 11.3 Data purification process

A universal data corruption problem relates to duplicate records, so make sure that the overall data purification process includes techniques for correcting the duplication problem. However, pollution of data can also be introduced in the data warehouse from the erroneous external data. If the company has paid for the external data then you have the right to demand a warranty on data quality. But in case you have utilized the external data that is freely available on some public domain, then you need to have some kind of data quality check.

11.12 OPERATING THE WAREHOUSE

Until now, we have concentrated on the design aspects of the data warehouse. However, when the warehouse is built and the initial loading is completed, it is time to make the data warehouse operational.

11.12.1 Day-to-day Operations

The main usage of the data warehouse during the daytime is to service the user's queries. Other operations that can occur during the day are:

- Query management.
- Backup and recovery management.
- Performance management.
- Running of housekeeping scripts.

Query management is a vital part of the daily operations. Some of the monitoring and control can be automated, but a DBA is still needed to solve any problem. If there is any job that is exceeding its quota of resources, then that job needs to be killed immediately. Also there are certain housekeeping scripts that need to be run repeatedly to log-off idle connections. Generally, backup activities are performed during the night to avoid contentions with the user queries during the day.

11.12.2 Warehouse Administration

Continuous monitoring and administering activities in the data warehouse have to be done simultaneously. The basic principles here are:

- The data warehouse will change over time, so hardware and software requires maintenance and updating.
- Automated procedures for routine operations should be present.

The responsibility for administering the data warehouse and data marts lies in the hands of the IT department. One approach, proposed by Inmon and Hackathorn in their book *Using the Data Warehouse* (1994), is to form a data architecture group which would interface with all the concerned parties (management, IT, and end-user) and be responsible for the data warehouse. Its duties include:

- Monitoring the warehouse operations.
- Platform upgrades.
- Supporting end-users.
- Maintaining the metadata.
- Upgrading the warehouse.

- Addition and deletion of enhancements.
- Maintaining security.
- Managing data growth.
- ETL management.

- Storage management.
- Capacity planning.
- Information delivery enhancements.

Monitoring the Warehouse Operations

Monitoring the data warehouse involves activities that track the growth and usage of the data warehouse. It is not uncommon for the growth pattern to be different from what was predicted and designed. Reviewing the end-user activity gives an indication of which data is useful and which is not. The warehouse is also continuously monitored to see that the user queries perform well and do not take more time to execute.

Platform Upgrades

The data warehouse platform comprises of the data transport component, end-user information delivery, data storage, metadata, the database component, and the OLAP components. Thus, a data warehouse is basically a cross-platform environment. The hierarchy of these components can be seen as shown in Fig. 11.4. Over time, upgrades to these components are brought into the market by its vendors.

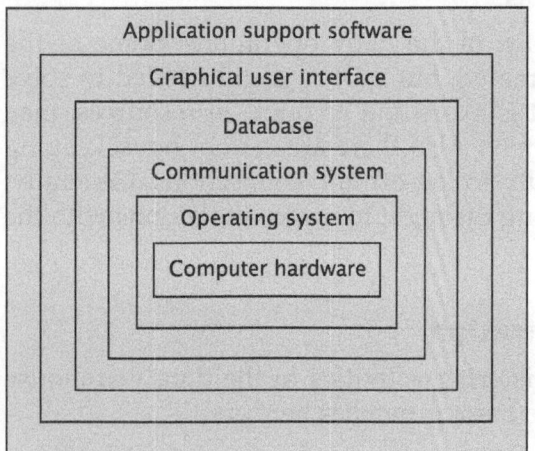

Figure 11.4 Hierarchy of components in a warehouse

After deploying the first version of the data warehouse, make a proper plan for applying the new releases of the platform components. Technically speaking, upgrades must be properly managed, lest they cause potentially serious interruption to the normal work. Good planning minimizes this disruption. Therefore, it is always better to schedule the upgrades at some convenience based on when users can tolerate interruptions.

Addition and Deletion of Subject Areas

As the business of a firm changes, its interests also change. Since the data warehouse is organized around subject areas, major changes will typically involve the subject areas covered by the warehouse.

Managing Data Growth

In the data warehouse environment, managing data growth calls for special attention. Until and unless you are vigilant about data growth, it could get out of hand very soon. Data warehouses already contain large volumes of data and even a small increase can result in substantial additional data.

In the first place, a data warehouse contains too much historical data which may even go beyond 10 years. End-users also tend to keep the data at the detailed level and want some aggregate or summary tables in addition to the detailed data which adds to the data stored in the data warehouse. In the course of usage of the data warehouse, this data will always become more in volume. So, follow some practical approach to manage data growth, e.g. you may archive the old data promptly.

ETL Management

ETL management is an ongoing function, so it must be automated as much as possible. Given below are some useful suggestions on data extraction, transformation, and loading management.

- Run daily extraction jobs on schedule and if for some reasons, source systems are not available, then reschedule the extraction jobs.
- Make sure that all rules for data transformation and cleansing are strictly followed.
- Resolve exceptions detected by the transformation and cleansing functions.
- Verify the data before loading it in the warehouse. Cross-check if the referential integrity constraint is properly followed.
- Ensure completion of daily incremental loads as per the schedule.

Supporting End-users

The end-users need a formal training before they could actually start working with the warehouse. Once they become familiar with the warehouse, their requests for help become more sophisticated. Whenever the data warehouse system produces unexpected results or no results at all, the users need a helpdesk to get their problems solved. Users also need help for executing complex queries.

In case the users want to execute the same set of queries repeatedly, then the IT people can build pre-formatted reports to make that query simple. In order to assist the users, the warehouse design team builds a metadata so that the users can use it to know exactly what data is present in the warehouse. Finally, the warehouse design team will also support changes in user's requirements by addition and deletion of the subject areas in the warehouse.

Maintaining the Metadata

Since the contents of the warehouse keep changing with time, the metadata will also change to reflect the current status of information in the warehouse. Even though, tools for automatic maintenance of metadata are available, manual support for editing the metadata is still needed.

Upgrading the Warehouse

With time, it is often necessary to upgrade the data warehouse contents or performance. Successful data warehouse systems will cause increasing demands from the users and thus, additional data may be needed. Furthermore, if the system is successful, its usage and may be the users will increase, thereby making the response time longer. At this stage, the need to upgrade data warehouse hardware and software arises.

In order to make such upgrades possible, the system may have to be shut down for that duration. But finding the time window when this can be done is not a trivial task, especially when the warehouse is being heavily used by its users. Finally, changes in the warehouse may give a way for errors to creep in the warehouse environment, so it is always recommended to test the upgrades on a separate test system before applying them to the actual warehouse. Generally, overnights and weekends are the most preferred timings to upgrade the data warehouse.

Storage Management

With the increase in the volume of data, the utilization of storage area also increases. Since data warehouses are designed to store a large amount of data, the storage costs tend to be very high. It is not misleading to say that the storage costs are almost four or five times the software costs. So, you cannot overlook the issues involved in storage management. Given below are some tips that are used as guidelines for managing the storage space.

- Plan for the increase in storage amount needed in the near future.
- Ensure that the storage configuration is easily scalable so that more storage can be added with minimum problems.
- Try to use modular storage systems.
- If the data warehouse is deployed in a distributed environment with multiple servers having their own storage pools, consider connecting the servers to a single storage pool that can be intelligently accessed.
- Ensure that it is easy to shift data from bad storage sectors.

Capacity Planning

With the growth of data warehouses, the amount of data stored in it as well as the subject areas that the warehouses cover also grows. With increasing demand of data posed on the data warehouses, the data warehouse that seems to be big enough at the time of implementation now seems too small to handle the user's demands. Capacity planning is needed so that additional hardware, software, and other resources are added and the contents of the warehouse are modified to fit within the existing capabilities.

Maintaining Security

Data warehouse contains enormous amount of data. Utmost care should be taken to see that only authorized people are able to access and modify the content stored in the warehouse. The warehouse is more sensitive from a security point of view than any other operational database because it contains all the data that will be highly desirable by the organization's competitors.

Log-in control is the most common routine security operation. Because people are given access privileges when they log in, care must be taken to make certain that individuals are not given too much or too little access for their needs and responsibilities. Care must be taken that users with special privileges do not cause inadvertent changes to the data in the warehouse. Only limited people should be given special privileges.

The next security operation is to maintain logging information in a separate file. Although logging and tracing consume a large amount of memory, they are necessary to be maintained for the security of the data warehouse. Hence, the optimal solution to this problem is to move all the data related to logging of users to a separate location.

Security of data also refers to maintaining data backups and provisions for recovery if the data is lost. Backups are generally taken overnight. The backup of the data will help in case of data losses that occur as a result of computer crashes and natural disasters like fires and earthquakes.

Security issues in a warehouse   A warehouse is like a gold mine of information, as all of the organization's critical information is readily available in a format that makes it easy to retrieve and use. Besides, the security provisions must cover all the information that is extracted from the data warehouse and stored in applications such as OLAP.

Access may be granted to the individual tables. But in a data warehouse environment, access restrictions are difficult to set up. For example, an analyst may start an analysis session by getting information from one or two tables and then fetch information from other tables. The entire query process is query centric and *ad hoc* in nature. So, which tables are to be restricted and which one should be opened for the analyst, is not a trivial question to answer.

It is critical for the data warehouse project team to establish a sound security policy for the data warehouse. This policy must first recognize the immense value of the data stored in the data warehouse and then design a few guidelines for granting privileges and instituting user roles. Given below are the usual provisions found in the security policy of a data warehouse.

- Physical security of the data . stored in the data warehouse.
- Security of the workstation.
- Security over network connections.
- Tables access privileges.
- User roles and privileges.
- Security at different levels of summarizations.
- Security of the OLAP tools.
- Web access security.
- Resolution of security breaches and security violations.

In a data warehouse environment, security is provided using three mechanisms: managing user privileges, through passwords, and using specific security tools. In this section, we will learn all three of them.

User privileges   For a data warehouse, the project team prefers a role based security. This feature is supported by most of the RDBMS today. A role is noth-

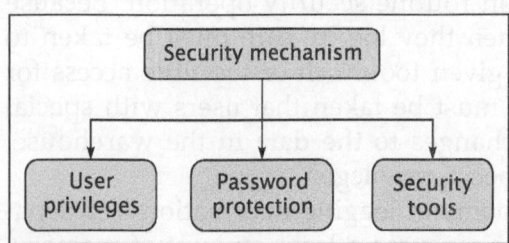

Figure 11.5 Security mechanisms

ing but a grouping of users with common requirements for accessing the database. After creating the roles, users can be assigned appropriate roles. Access privileges may be granted at the level of a role or at the level of an individual. When this is done, all the users assigned to that role will receive the same access privileges that are granted at the level of that particular role.

For example, let us say the user Paul is an end-user. You have granted certain privileges to the users under this role. All the privileges granted to the end-users will be availed by Paul too. However, if some extra privilege to access a dimension table is also given to Paul, then only he can access that one extra dimension table and rest of the end-users cannot. Given below is a list of roles, responsibilities, and privileges that are applied in a data warehouse environment.

- End-users who execute queries and formulate reports against the data warehouse database are given access privileges only for certain tables.
- System analysts and power user who run ad hoc complex queries and themselves formulate their reports are given access privileges for all the tables.
- Support staff that help the users to run their queries and reports and resolve the problems encountered by the users are given access privileges for all the tables.
- Query tool specialists who are responsible for installing and troubleshooting end-user tools and OLAP tools are given access privileges for all the tables.
- Security administrators who are responsible for granting and revoking privileges and monitoring the data warehouse usage are given access rights for the entire data warehouse system including the database administration rights and access to all the tables stored in the data warehouse.
- System and network administrators who are responsible for installing and looking after the maintenance of operating systems and networks are given access rights for the entire data warehouse system but not for database administration rights. No rights are given to access the tables stored in the data warehouse.
- Data warehouse administrators who install and maintain DBMS, provide back up and recovery features are given access rights for the entire data warehouse system including the database administration rights and access to all the tables stored in the data warehouse.

Password protection Security in a data warehouse using passwords follows the same old way; we do it in operational systems. Since the data warehouse is updated only during the loading process, user passwords are relevant to the load jobs. Delete operation also is generally not used in a data warehouse environment. So, the main issue with passwords is to authorize the users for read-only data access.

Users need passwords to get into the data warehouse. It is the duty of the security administrator to set up acceptable patterns and the expiry period for the passwords. The security system of the data warehouse automatically expires the password on its expiry date. A user may change his/her initial password after receiving it from the security administrator.

The users must make sure that the passwords that they use are arbitrary and not easily recognizable by anyone. Users should not use their name, their spouse name, or their pet names as their passwords. Every user has to follow the pattern set by the administrator. Generally, passwords include text and numeric data.

The data warehouse security mechanism must make a record of unauthorized attempts to gain access using invalid passwords so that after a prescribed number of such attempts the user must be suspended temporarily from the data warehouse, that is, until the data warehouse administrator reinstates the user. Following a successful log-in, the number of attempts to deliberately access the system must be reported as it could mean that someone is trying to work at a user workstation in the absence of the authorized user.

Security tools   In the data warehouse environment, the security provided by the chosen DBMS provides the primary security tool. One way of providing security by DBMS is role based security that we have already discussed. Some organizations also have third-party security systems installed to govern the security of the data warehouse system. Using third-party tools brings the data warehouse under the larger security umbrella. However, some of the end-user tools like the OLAP tools come with their own security system. But the drawback here is that the tool based security systems does not offer as much flexibility as the DBMS offers.

If you have provided the security systems in the tool set, there is absolutely no need to repeat it at the DBMS level, but some data warehouse teams go for double protection by invoking the security features of the DBMS as well. Similarly, if you are planning to use the DBMS itself for security protection, then tool-based security may be considered redundant. To implement the security features, you may use security mechanisms at any of the three levels: third party tools, end-user tools, and DBMS.

Information Delivery Enhancements

With the passage of time, the users become more dependent on the data warehouse to get the desired information. They will become more efficient in finding the data themselves and using the data warehouse without any assistance from the IT. They will start posing even more complex queries. Even in the market, you will find that new information delivery tools keep coming, so the users must be provided with the latest tools available. But to do this, keep the following points in mind.

- Ensure compatibility of the new toolset with other components of the data warehouse.
- Ensure integration of the new tool set with the end-user metadata.
- Training on the new toolset must be scheduled.
- If there are any data stores attached to the previous toolset used, then plan for migration of that data to the new toolset.

Other Activities

The other operational issues that can affect the operation of the system that needs to be considered are as follows:

- Startup and shutdown of data warehouse applications, database, and data warehouse server.
- Problem management.

All these operations may have a passive effect on the system and thus require proper management. All these tasks and services must be designed and developed by the data warehouse design team.

Starting up and shutting down functions are executed for the data warehouse server, its database, and the applications. They are, however, critical tasks because shutting down the machine or database incorrectly can cause problems on restart. The data warehouse applications should be shut down gracefully, allowing them to complete whatever work they are currently doing, not just aborted.

Similar is the case with the data warehouse database. Unless necessary, it must not be forced down because this will cause it to perform recovery operations on startup to clean up any jobs that were running when the database was shut down. The other area of concern in shutting down a database is getting all the users connections logged off as it is not uncommon for users to leave connections running and forget about them. Scripts would be needed to find these connecting processes and kill them.

Problem management is an important area that needs to be clearly defined and documented. The administration staff must clearly know whom to approach, where to approach and when to approach if any problem creeps in the system. It is not uncommon to have several groups inside an organization responsible for different parts of the data warehouse where one such group may be a central helpdesk for applications running in the system.

11.12.3 Overnight Processing

Overnight processing is one of the key challenges that any data warehouse designer has to face. There are certain major issues that if not addressed, will become a stumbling block to the success of the data warehouse. The main bottleneck is keeping to the time window so that the overnight processes do not eat into the next business day. The serial nature of the tasks that have to be performed and its sheer volume make this job even more difficult. The tasks that must be completed overnight are:

- Data rollup operations.
- Gathering the data.
- Data transformation functions.
- Data cleansing functions.
- Daily loading and data refreshing.
- Creation of indexes.
- Building of aggregate and summarized tables.
- Taking backups.
- Archival of old data.

In data roll-up, older data is rolled up into aggregated form to reduce the space needed to store the entire data. However, the first step in the overnight processing is that of collecting the data from the source systems. Any delay in the data transfer process from the source systems to the staging area causes a serious risk to the data warehouse. If a key piece of daily data does not make it to the staging area and finally to the data warehouse until the next day, then handling such an instance becomes a difficult task.

Another critical issue that needs to be resolved is that if data is missing, should the available data be made visible to the users? These questions are important as well as difficult to answer. One single answer cannot be applied to every situation, as the effect of missing data will vary from business to business and depend up on the purpose of the data warehouse.

Once the data has been acquired, the next step is data transformation and data cleanup. We already know that the data has to be transformed and cleaned before being loaded in the data warehouse. All the tasks involved in data transformation and data cleanup must be completed during the overnight processing. The next steps, index build and aggregation creation and maintenance will be accomplished once the data has arrived, and has been transformed, loaded and cleaned.

The last overnight operation that has to be done at the end is the backup process. If data has to be archived, then it would be archived as a part of the backup process. However, this process can become an overhead if the frequency of the data archiving is very high. For example, if data is loaded daily, but is archived monthly, then the whole month's data would have to be archived; this extra overhead may not be completed within the overnight window. It is therefore recommended to schedule archiving activities to run outside the overnight window and during periods of low user activity, may be on the weekends.

If data marts also exist in the organization, then even they may have to be refreshed on a regular basis and if the archiving and data mart refresh are part of the overnight process, they need to be very tightly controlled, and their effect on the capacity of the server and the network needs to be well understood. If allowed to take unlimited time, these tasks will rapidly become a resource bottleneck and will drive overnight processing into the business day.

11.13 RECIPE FOR A SUCCESSFUL WAREHOUSE

The following guidelines are to be adhered to build and maintain a successful warehouse.

- Make a list of the sponsors for the data warehouse. It must contain many sponsors so that even if a single sponsor leaves, the system will not get orphaned.
- From the very first day itself, consider data warehousing to be a joint user/builder project.
- Clarify that maintaining data quality will be an ongoing joint user/builder responsibility.
- Train the users step by step.
- Try to build a high level data model in not more than three weeks.
- Monitor the accuracy of the data extracting, cleaning, and loading tools.
- Design the metadata in such a way that it is easy and efficient for the end-users who will use it.
- Formulate a well-designed plan to test the integrity of the data in the data warehouse.
- Encourage the end-users to test the complex queries themselves.
- Before initiating the construction of the warehouse, learn from the experiences of the companies who have already gone for data warehousing.
- Be on the lookout for small but strategic projects.

11.14 DATA WAREHOUSE PITFALLS

The following list summarizes the limitations of a warehouse.

- Much time is wasted in data extracting, cleaning, and loading of data.
- One thing that should always be taken as default is that the scope of the data warehouse will always go beyond expectations.
- There will be a number of problems that the team will have to face because of the disparate source systems that feed the data in the data warehouse.
- Often there will be a need to store data not being captured by the existing systems.
- In continuation with the previous problem, there would also be a need to validate the data that is currently not being validated by the transaction processing systems.
- Some operational systems that act as a source of data for the data warehouse may not be capturing the data at the lowest level of detail.
- Despite the best efforts made by the project team to train the users, many users will never apply their training to solve their problems.

- Many a times, the time needed for data loading will over-run the amount of time in the available window.
- A data warehouse is a high-maintenance system. The data warehouse project team will fail if it will concentrate more on resource optimization and neglect, data and customer management issues and an understanding of what adds value to the customer.

Recapitulation

Before starting a data warehouse project in your organization, you must answer questions like: Do I need a data warehouse? What specific problems will it solve? What are my available resources (time, money, and personnel)? What criteria will I use to measure success?

After the requirements gathering phase, you as a member of data warehouse project team must clearly state the problem(s) you wish to solve, identify all data sources and formats, identify the users, formulate a specific budget, state the success criteria, and generate a prioritized requirements table.

The data warehouse project team must include technical staff comprising of project leader, data analyst, business analyst, systems administrator, and staff for technical support, technical writing, training and help desk; end-users and the project sponsors.

The overall plan includes four components: vision refers to defining what is to be built; validation and estimation; and infrastructure planning.

A project plan describes three things what tasks will be done, how they will be done and what deliverable is obtained after that task is completed; when it will be done; and what resources will be used for it.

While designing the data warehouse you need to break the project into smaller modules, make sure that people involved in the project understand their responsibility and that they are able to deliver the output as per the schedule.

After the data marts and data warehouses are implemented, you need to test them before the final deployment. User involvement in testing provides benefits like tracing and correcting discrepancies if any and the users become familiar with the system.

Administering the warehouse includes activities, such as monitoring the data warehouse operations, adding and deleting subject areas, supporting end-users, maintaining the metadata, updating the warehouse content, upgrading the warehouse, capacity planning, maintaining security and taking backups.

The overnight processing in a data warehouse includes activities, such as data rollup, loading of data, data transformation, data cleanup, index creation, backup, and data archiving.

Objective Questions

1. **Multiple choice questions**
    (i) Technical staff includes
      (a) Project leader
      (b) Data analyst
      (c) Business analyst
      (d) Database administrator
      (e) Programmers
      (f) All of these
      (g) None of these

(ii) Project planning tools are used to allow

   (a) Managers to visualize the time sequence in which the events must occur

   (b) The kind of personnel that will have to be assigned

   (c) Selection of the software components that will have to be acquired and integrated.

   (d) All of these

   (e) None of these

(iii) The hardware components include

   (a) Database

   (b) Extraction tools

   (c) Cleansing tools

   (d) Network connections

   (e) All of these

   (f) None of these

(iv) The dimensional model must address

   (a) Business needs

   (b) Grain of detail

   (c) Facts

   (d) Dimensions

   (e) All of these

   (f) None of these

(v) The end-users must be trained mainly in three areas: data, applications, and tools.

   (a) Data

   (b) Applications

   (c) Tools

   (d) All of these

   (e) None of these

2. Fill in the blanks

(i) Resources of a data warehouse project include ____, ____, and ____.

(ii) ____ refers to those things that must go right if an undertaking is to become successful.

(iii) ____ happens when the users define new requirements as the project progresses.

(iv) An end-user staff that comprises of ____.

(v) ____ of the project states what has to be built.

(vi) ____ or activities are the basic units of work used in project planning

(vii) ____ provides all needed components through one-stop shopping.

(viii) ____ support helps when the user representative is unable to solve user problems.

(ix) A ____ is nothing but a larger storage area that can hold many files.

(x) In a data warehouse environment, security is provided using three mechanisms ____, ____ and ____.

(xi) The last overnight operation that has to be done at the end is the ____.

(xii) ____ and ____ are the most preferred timings to upgrade the data warehouse

3. Match the following

1. System analysts and power   (a) Helps the users to run their queries

2. Support staff   (b) Run *ad hoc* complex queries

3. Query tool specialists   (c) Responsible for installing and troubleshooting end-user tools

4. Security administrator   (d) Responsible for granting and revoking privileges and monitoring the warehouse usage

5. System and network administrator   (e) Responsible for installing and looking after the maintenance of operating systems and networks

4. **State True or False**

(i) Project management principles that are applied to an operational system project are also applicable to the data warehouse project.

(ii) The definition and recording of the problem to be solved is one of the first tasks that need to be done for any development effort.

(iii) Bleeding edge technology must be used for building the data warehouse.

(iv) Verification involves cross checking the requirements and identifying the risks associated with the development.

(v) In a data warehouse environment, the dimensional model uses a star schema or a fact constellation schema.

(vi) The indexed views are designed to improve query performance.

(vii) In house development of the project includes lack of personnel with the appropriate skills and non-availability of data warehouse expertise.

(viii) User involvement in the testing phase eases the process of tuning the indexes.

(ix) Whenever a disaster occurs, the recovery process proceeds from the last backup and recovers to the point where the system stopped working.

(x) Data quality framework provides a basis for launching data quality initiatives.

(xi) Archiving activities must be run outside the overnight window.

(xii) Tool based security systems offer more flexibility than that provided by the DBMS.

Review Questions

1. Explain the critical success factors of a data warehouse environment.

2. Why is requirement analysis crucial in case of a data warehouse project?

3. Write a short note on planning for a data warehouse project.

4. Give an outline of a project plan made for a data warehouse project.

5. For a data warehouse project, discuss the issues in outsourcing and in-house development.

6. Explain the sequence of steps involved in the data warehouse design stage. Discuss some decisions that you have to make in this stage.

7. Give an account of the activities that must be accomplished to administer a data warehouse. Why is administering of a data warehouse environment important?

8. Explain the importance of overnight processing.

9. Suggest at least five tips of building a successful data warehouse. Mention a few pitfalls which if not taken care of can result in a failure of the whole project.

12

DATA MINING BASICS

Learning Objectives

This chapter introduces an entirely new and an emerging technology called data mining. We will see how data mining can be used with data warehouses to achieve efficient results, and how it differs from OLAP technology and from general purpose DBMS. We will also learn about the different algorithms of data mining.

Case Study

Once the data warehouse is operational at the client's site, the CEO, the managers, the sponsors, the board of directors, and whosoever having an access search the warehouse to extract information. But this search can often be time consuming.

Consider searching for a topic in an encyclopedia or a book. What do we generally do? We will either look up the Index or the Contents. Similarly, when we search the Internet for a certain topic, we punch the keyword in the search box and the Web browser displays all the pages containing that keyword. Our next step is to go through each and every link, search for the information, and then extract it from the contents written on those pages.

Same is the case with data warehouses. When the users want a piece of information,

they have to search the contents of the warehouse using the metadata that acts as an index to its contents. The process of finding the relevant information can take a few minutes to several hours. This is where the technique of data mining fits in.

Imagine how good our life will be if we just type the keyword in the search bar and the Web browser not only displays the useful links but comes up with the desired information as well so that we do not have to go through each and every link. Data mining helps the users of any decision-support system by reducing the time required for searching the relevant data. Users need not have to apply their minds and spend several hours browsing through the contents of the warehouse; rather data mining does this task on their behalf.

12.1 INTRODUCTION

Data mining refers to the technique of searching useful and relevant information from the data warehouse. It is very clear that the technology has something to do with discovering knowledge. Data mining is used in applications, such as marketing, sales, credit analysis, and fraud detection. Data mining is somehow connected to data warehousing. Although a workable data warehouse is not a prerequisite for data mining, but it gives a practical boost to the data mining process.

Figure 12.1 shows the flow of data from operational systems into data warehousing systems.

Now let us study, "Why is data mining being put to use in more and more businesses?" Here are some basic reasons:

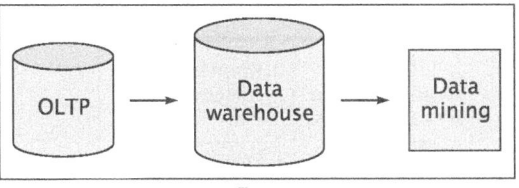

Figure 12.1 Data flow

- These days an organization produces more information in a week than most people can read in a lifetime. Thus, it is impossible for humans to study, decipher, and interpret all that data to find useful information.
- A data warehouse is a collection of integrated, transformed, and cleansed data, formatted into well-organized data structures. But even then, the sheer volume of data makes it practically impossible for anyone to use analysis and query tools to discern useful pattern.
- Recently, many data mining tools that support a wide range of applications have appeared in the market.
- Data mining needs substantial computing power. Parallel hardware, databases, and other powerful components are now available in the market at affordable prices.
- These days organizations are placing great emphasis on building sound customer relationships. Companies want to know how they can sell more to existing customers and determine which of their customers will prove to be of long-term value to them. So, data mining enables companies to find answers and discover patterns in their customer data.
- Finally, it is the fierce competitive considerations that weigh heavily on every company to get into data mining.

12.1.1 What is Data Mining?

Like all decision-support systems, the primary goal of data mining is to deliver information. Figure 12.2 shows the progression of decision-support. In the 1990s, data warehouses with query and report tools assisted users in retrieving the strategic information, they became the primary and valuable source of decision-support information. For more sophisticated analysis, OLAP tools became available.

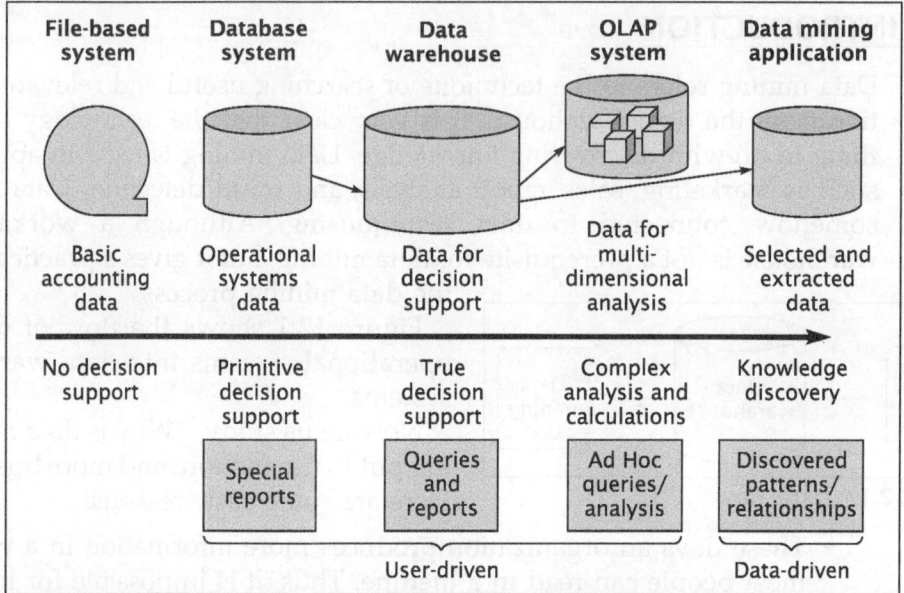

Figure 12.2 Progression of decision-support system

Till now, the approach for obtaining information was driven by the users. But the sheer volume of data renders it impossible to discern useful patterns, so a technology was needed that could learn from past associations and results, and predict customer behaviour. This technology should be a data-driven approach and not a user-driven one. This is where data mining steps in and takes over from the users.

Different authors have given different definitions of data mining. Let us see some of them in this section.

- Data mining involves the extraction of the hidden, predictive information from large databases.
- Data mining is a powerful technology with great potential to analyse important information in the data warehouse.
- Data mining scours databases for hidden patterns, finding predictive information that the experts may miss.

When implemented in a client/server environment or using a parallel processing option, data mining tools can analyse large size databases to provide information like which clients are most likely to respond to the next promotional mailing. The trend these days is towards using this new technology in new application domains so that large passive databases can be made into useful actionable information.

12.1.2 Foundation of Data Mining

Data mining techniques are the outcome of rigorous research and product development. The evolution of data mining process began when business data was first stored on computers, continued with improvements in data access, and generated technologies that allow users to navigate through their data in real time. Data mining takes this evolutionary process beyond data access and data navigation to information delivery. Data mining is applied in the business community because it is supported by three technologies that are now sufficiently mature:

- Techniques to collect massive amounts of data.
- Availability of powerful multiprocessor computers.
- Application of data mining algorithms.

Commercial databases are growing at alarming rates. A recent survey of data warehouse projects found that more than 70% of respondents are beyond the 50 gigabyte level. In some industries, such as retail and telecommunications, these numbers can be much larger. The need for improved computational engines can now be met in a cost-effective manner with parallel multiprocessor computer technology. Data mining algorithms make use of the techniques that have existed for several years but have only recently been implemented and widely accepted as a mature and reliable tool that rank higher than older statistical methods.

The evolution from data to information encompasses multiple steps where every new step is built upon the previous one. For example, while dynamic data access is critical for data navigation applications, the ability to store large databases is critical to data mining. From the user's point of view, Table 12.1 shows the revolutionary steps as they enabled new business questions to be answered accurately and quickly.

For decades, the core components of data mining technology have been under research but today, the maturity of data mining techniques coupled

Table 12.1 Steps in the evolution of data mining

Evolutionary Step	Business Question	Enabling Technologies	Product Providers	Characteristics
Data Collection (1960s)	What were the total sales in the last five years?	Computers, tapes, disks	IBM, CDC	Static data delivery
Data Access (1980s)	What were unit sales in India last month?	RDBMS, SQL, ODBC	Oracle, Sybase, Informix, IBM	Dynamic data delivery at record Microsoft level
Data Warehousing and Decision Support (1990s)	What were unit sales in India last month? Drill down to Delhi	OLAP, multi-dimensional databases, data warehouses	Pilot, Comshare, Arbor, Cognos, Microstrategy	Dynamic data delivery at multiple levels
Data Mining (Still maturing)	What's likely to happen to Delhi unit sales next month? Why?	Advanced algorithms, multiprocessor computers, massive databases	Pilot, Lockheed, IBM, SGI, numerous startups (nascent industry)	Proactive information delivery

with high-performance relational database engines and broad data integration efforts make these technologies practical for current data warehouse environments.

12.1.3 An Analogy

"Data mining refers to using a variety of techniques to identify nuggets of information or decision-making knowledge in the databases and extracting these in such a way that they can be put to use in areas, such as decision-support, prediction, forecasting, and estimation." The data that an organization has collected is often voluminous, but it has low value and no direct use can be made of it. It is the hidden information that is useful.

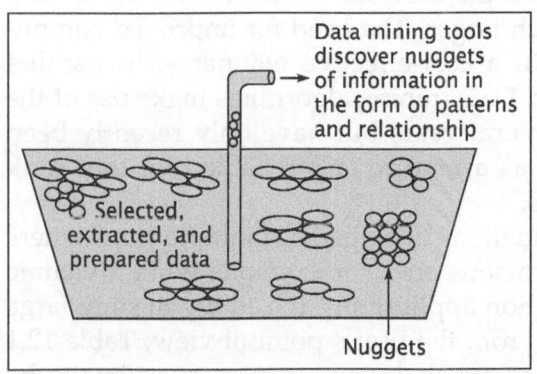

Data mining tools discover nuggets of information in the form of patterns and relationship

Selected, extracted, and prepared data

Nuggets

Figure 12.3 Application of data mining tools to discover useful information from a large source of data

As an analogy, imagine a very wide and very deep mine densely packed with some important material. The miner uses a set of sophisticated drilling tools to dig and unravel the contents. At the time of drilling, the miner does not know what exactly he is hoping to get from his effort. Nothing may turn up, or he may be able to find some real gold nuggets. He may discover this valuable treasure that he never knew existed. He was not specifically looking for nuggets, but he never knew they were there (Refer Fig. 12.3).

Now, replace the wide and deep mine with a data warehouse, replace the material in the mine with the massive data content stored in the data warehouse, and replace the drilling tools by data mining tools. The gold nuggets are the valuable pieces of information, such as patterns or relationships, which you never knew existed in the data. In fact, the data mining tools are applied to find information that the user did not know existed. This is one aspect of data mining. Thus, data mining is synonymous with knowledge discovery that involves discovering knowledge that the user suspected to exist.

The second aspect of data mining is prediction in which the users look for a specific association with regard to an event or condition. For example, if you put a discount on colour printers, then some customers would like to buy the colour printer as well while they are purchasing the computer.

Hence, data mining is a knowledge discovery process that helps you understand the substance of the data in a special unsuspected way, as it unearths patterns and trends in the raw data you never knew existed. According to Joseph P. Bigus, "Data mining centers on the automated discovery of new facts and relationships in data."

12.1.4 What Can be Discovered?

By and large, the patterns that can be discovered depend upon the data mining tasks employed. Basically, there are two types of data mining tasks: *descriptive data mining tasks* that describe the general properties of the existing data, and *predictive data mining tasks* that attempt to do predictions based on inference from available data.

The data mining functionalities and the knowledge that they discover are briefly summarized below:

Characterization

Data characterization is a summarization of general features of objects in a target class. The data relevant to a user-specified class are normally retrieved by a database query and run through a summarization module to extract the basic features of the data. For example, one may want to characterize the garments store customers who regularly make a purchase of at least Rs 1000 every month.

Discrimination

Data discrimination generates discriminant rules that are basically a comparison of the general features of objects between two classes referred to as the *target class* and the *contrasting class*. For example, a marketing manager may want to compare the general characteristics of the customers who made a purchase of more than Rs 1 lakh in the last year with those who made a purchase of even less than Rs 5000.

Even though the techniques used for data discrimination are very similar to the techniques used for data characterization, data discrimination results include comparative measures.

Association Analysis

Association analysis discovers association rules from the data. It does this by studying the frequency of items occurring together in transactional databases, and based on a threshold called *support*, it identifies the frequent item sets. Another threshold called *confidence* is the conditional probability that an item appears in a transaction when another item appears, is used to depict association rules between different items.

Association analysis is commonly used for market basket analysis. For example, it could be useful for the manager to know which printer is often purchased with an HP computer so that a promotional discount can be offered to its customers.

Classification

Classification analysis is the organization of data in given classes. It is also known as *supervised classification* because the classification uses given class labels to classify other objects in the data whose class labels are not known. Classification approaches make use of a *training set* in which all objects are already associated with certain known class labels.

The classification algorithm learns from the training set and builds a model that is used to classify new objects. For example, a loan company may analyse its customers' behaviour with respect to their credit, and label them with any of the three possible labels: safe, risky, and very risky.

The classification analysis when used will first generate a model that could accurately classify a new customer in any of the three labels and then accept or reject credit requests depending upon their probability to return the money.

Prediction

Prediction approach is used for successful forecasting in a business context. There are two major types of predictions: it can either be used to predict some unavailable data values or trends, or predict a class label for some data. The latter is tied to classification. Once a classification model has been developed based on a training set, the class label of an object can be foreseen based on the attribute values of the object.

Prediction is frequently referred to as the forecasting of missing numerical values, or predicting trends in time-related data. The underlying principle of this approach is to use a large number of past values to consider probable future values.

Clustering

The clustering approach, like classification, organizes the data in classes. The only difference here is that in clustering, class labels are unknown. Therefore, clustering is often known as *unsupervised classification*, because the classification is not dictated by/given class labels. The clustering approach works on the principle of maximizing the intra-similarity (similarity between objects in a same class) and minimizing the inter-cluster similarity (similarity between objects of different classes).

Outlier analysis

Outliers are data elements that cannot be grouped in any class or cluster. They are exceptions or surprises that are often very important to identify. Some applications consider these outliers as *noise* and discard them, but they can reveal important knowledge in certain domains and thus, can prove to be very significant for analysis.

For example, if a customer makes purchases through his credit card in the range of 20K–30K and if in a month, he suddenly makes a purchase of Rs 2 lakh, then it is considered to be a noise or an outlier or rather an exceptional case. This behaviour can be studied to detect any fraud that the customer makes against the banking institution.

Evolution and Deviation Analysis

Evolution and deviation analysis is concerned with the studying of time-related data that change in time. While evolution analysis models evolutionary trends in data, deviation analysis considers differences between measured values and expected values and attempts to find the cause of the deviations from the anticipated values.

12.1.5 What Kind of Data Can be Mined?

The strength of data mining process lies in the variety of data that it can mine. Data mining algorithms are applicable to any kind of information repository storing any kind of data. However, the algorithm and the approach to be applied will vary when applied to different data types. Data mining is applied to a variety of databases including relational databases, object-relational databases and object-oriented databases, data warehouses, transactional databases, unstructured and semi-structured repositories like the World Wide Web, advanced databases that include spatial databases, multimedia databases, time-series databases and textual databases, and even flat files.

Flat files   These are the most common data source for data mining algorithms. They consist of files stored either in text or binary format that contain data related to transactions, time-series data, scientific measurements, etc.

Relational databases   A relational database includes a set of tables containing values of attributes. A table is a combination of rows and columns where columns represent attributes and rows represent tuples or records of the entity. A tuple in a relational table can either be a record of an object or a relationship between two or more objects. Every record in a relation is identified by a unique primary key.

SQL is the language used for retrieval and manipulation of the data stored in the tables. It also allows calculation of aggregate functions, such as average, sum, min, max, and count.

Data warehouse   It is a repository of data collected from multiple data sources, thereby giving the privilege to analyse data from different sources under the same roof. We have already discussed a lot about data warehouses in the previous chapters.

Transaction database   A transaction database is a set of records representing transactions, each with a time stamp, an identifier and a set of items involved in the transaction. Along with the transaction files you could also store a separate file containing descriptive data for the items

Transaction tables are usually stored in flat files. Transaction data is analysed for market basket analysis or association rules in which associations between items occurring together or in a sequence are studied.

Multimedia database It includes audio, video, images, and text media. They are usually stored in object-oriented databases. Multimedia data makes data mining even more challenging. Data mining from multimedia repositories requires the application of many other techniques like computer vision, computer graphics, image interpretation, and natural language processing methodologies.

Spatial database These are databases that store geographical information like maps and global or regional positioning, in addition to usual data. Spatial data presents new challenges to data mining algorithms.

Time-series database It stores time-related data such as stock market data. These databases have a continuous flow of data coming in that may need to be analysed in real time. Data mining techniques are applied to such databases to study correlations between different variables, and predict the trends and movements of the variables in time.

World wide web It is a heterogeneous and dynamic data repository. It is dynamic because a large number of publishers are continuously contributing to its growth and a huge number of users are accessing it daily all around the globe. Data in the World Wide Web is organized using hyperlinked documents that can include text, audio, video, raw data, and even applications.

12.2 ARCHITECTURE OF A DATA MINING SYSTEM

Data mining is the process of discovering interesting and useful knowledge from large amounts of data stored in databases. Data mining is usually applied to data warehouses. The architecture of a typical data mining system, as given by Jiawci Han and Micheline Kamber in their book *Data Mining Concepts and Techniques* (2001), consists of the following components as shown in Fig. 12.4.

Database or data warehouse or other information repository This includes one or more databases, a data warehouse, or any other information repository. Data cleaning and data integration techniques have to be applied to the data before the data mining algorithm can be applied on it. However, in case the data mining algorithms are applied directly on the data warehouses, then cleansing and integration functions may be skipped because a data warehouse already contains integrated and cleansed data.

Database or data warehouse server The database or data warehouse server is used to fetch the relevant data, based on the user's data mining request.

Knowledge base It contains the domain knowledge that is used to guide the search or used for evaluation of the interestingness of resulting patterns. Such knowledge can include concept hierarchies, user beliefs, interestingness thresholds and the metadata.

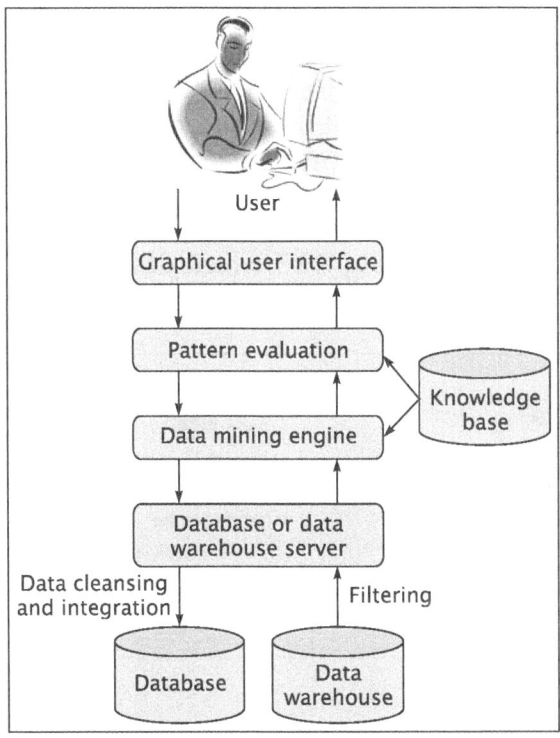

Figure 12.4 Architecture of a data mining system

Data mining engine It consists of a set of functionalities for tasks such as characterization, association, classification, cluster analysis, and evolution analysis.

Pattern evaluation module This component employs interestingness measures and other threshold values and interacts with the data mining engine so as to retrieve only the interesting results. For enhanced efficiency in the performance of data mining algorithms, the evaluation of pattern interestingness must be incorporated deeply into the mining process so that the search can be confined to search only the interesting patterns discovered.

Graphical user interface (GUI) This module interacts with the users and the data mining system thereby allowing the user to use the data mining system either by specifying a query or a task like that of characterization, association, classification, cluster analysis, and evolution analysis.

With GUI, users can also provide extra information to guide the search process. In addition, the GUI component enables the end-users to browse the database, evaluate the mined patterns, and visualize the discovered patterns in different formats.

12.3 THE KNOWLEDGE DISCOVERY PROCESS

Data mining is often described as the process of knowledge discovery as it discovers knowledge or information that you never knew existed in the data. Usually, this uncovered hidden knowledge is encapsulated as relationships or patterns in the data.

Relationships

Let us suppose you are at the super market. While you fetch the bread, you happen to see a pack of butter close by. Yes, you want that. You pause to look at the next five customers behind you. To your amazement, three of those customers also reach for the butter pack. Within a space of few minutes, bread and butter are bought together. Hence, data mining discovers relationships that exist between two or more different objects along with the time dimension.

Patterns

Pattern discovery is another outcome of data mining operations. Consider a credit card company that is always fussy about discovering the pattern of usage that usually warrants an increase in the credit limit or a card upgrade. They want to keep a check on their customers who must be lured with a card upgrade. The data mining algorithms are applied to mine the usage patterns of a number of card holders and discover the potential pattern of usage that will produce meaningful information. Look at Fig. 12.5 which describes the major steps in the knowledge discovery (KDD) process.

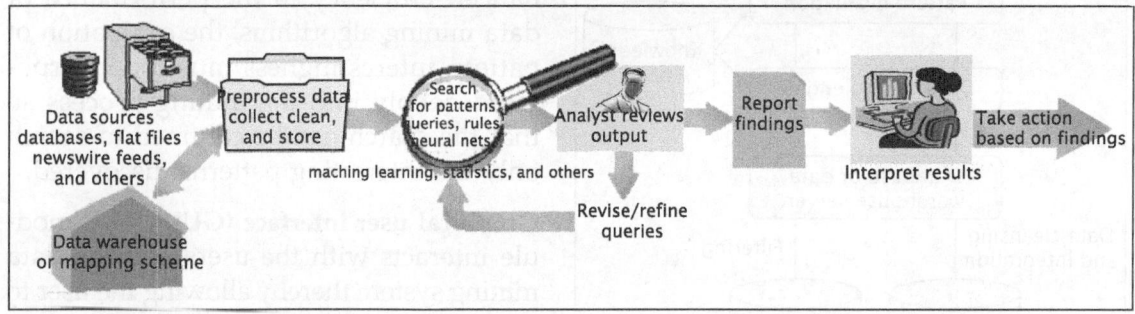

Figure 12.5 KDD process

Step 1 Define business objectives This step is same as we perform in an operational systems project. The first and foremost question to be answered is whether the need for a data mining solution really exists. Then define the objectives clearly like: Are you looking for marketing campaigns or detecting fraud in credit card usage? Are you looking for associations between products that sell together?" In this step, define expectations. Finally, express how the final results will be presented to the users.

Step 2 Prepare data This step consists of data selection, processing, and data transformation. First of all, select the data to be extracted from the data warehouse. For this, use the business objectives to determine what data has to be selected. Then the appropriate metadata is selected that describes data about the selected data. The type of mining algorithm should have been selected at this time, as the mining algorithm has a bearing on data selection.

The selected data is then processed to improve its quality. In case the data is selected from the warehouse, this step can be bypassed as the data warehouse data is already cleansed. Processing of data however involves enriching the selected data with external data. While processing the selected data, the inconsistencies have to be removed and all the missing values have to be filled. However, if the data for mining is selected from the data warehouse, it is again assumed that all necessary data transformations have already been completed.

Step 3 Perform data mining The knowledge discovery engine applies the previously selected data mining algorithm to the prepared data. The output from this step is a set of relationships or patterns. This step and the next step of evaluation may be performed iteratively. After an initial evaluation, the data is adjusted to redo this step. However, the depth of this step depends upon the type of data mining application. For example, if you are creating a predictive model, the models are repeatedly set up and tested with sample data before testing with real database.

Step 4 Evaluate results With the help of knowledge discovery engine, we are actually trying to seek interesting patterns or relationships. These help in understanding the customers, products, markets, and the business. In the selected data, there may be a number of patterns or relationships and in this step all the resulting patterns have to be examined as each one of them may not be interesting for the business at all. So, you need to apply some filtering mechanism and select only the promising patterns to be presented and applied.

Step 5 Present discoveries Presentation of knowledge, discovered by applying data mining algorithm, may be in the form of visual navigation, charts, graphs, or free-form texts. Presentation also includes storing of interesting discoveries in the knowledge base for future use.

Step 6 Incorporate usage of discoveries The goal of application of data mining algorithm is to understand the business well, discern new patterns and relationships, and also turn this understanding into actions. Hence, in this step, the results of the knowledge discovery are assembled in the best way so that they can be exploited to improve the business.

Look at Fig. 12.6 which shows the percentage of total effort in the KDD process.

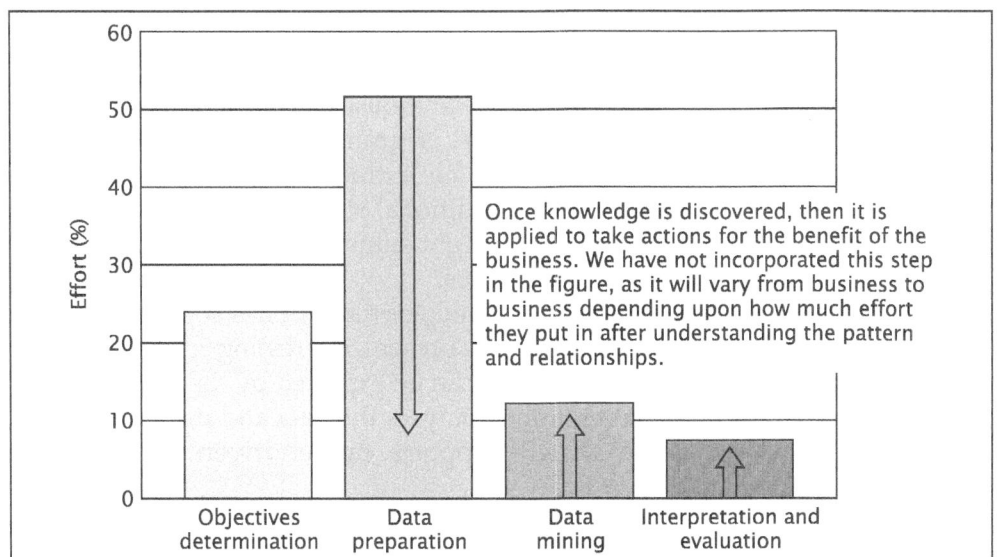

Figure 12.6 Percentage of total effort in the KDD process

12.4 INTEGRATING DATA MINING WITH DATA WAREHOUSE

Data mining fits well in the data warehouse environment, and both the technologies when combined play a significant role for the benefit of any kind of business. It has been aptly stated, "Data warehouse forms the bedrock for data mining." Data warehouse offers a platform on which the data mining algorithms can be operated. The two technologies support each other in the following manner.

- Data mining algorithms need large amounts of data at the detailed level, and data warehouses contain data at the lowest level of granularity.
- Data mining flourishes on integrated and cleansed data, and data warehouses contain such data that is very suitable for data mining.
- The infrastructure for data warehouses is already robust, with parallel processing technology and powerful relational database systems. Since a scalable hardware is already in place, no new investment is needed to support data mining.

There is however one difference between the way data from the data warehouse is used for traditional analysis and data mining. During the analysis of data, say with an OLAP tool, the analyst begins with summary data and then continues through the lower levels of detail by means of drill-down techniques. But sometimes, the analyst need not go down to the detail levels because the data that he wants may be present at the higher levels. Data mining is slightly different in this context, as the data mining algorithm is searching for trends and patterns, so it needs to deal with a lot of detailed data. For example, if the data mining algorithm is looking for buying patterns of customers, then it needs detailed data at the level of the individual customer.

We need to find a compromise approach to determine the most suitable level of granularity in the data warehouse. The best option is to keep the most detailed data at the lowest level of granularity. Otherwise, for data mining, detailed data would have to be extracted directly from the operational systems, that would call for additional steps of data consolidation, cleansing, and transformation. However, light summaries may also be stored in the data warehouse for traditional queries.

Thus, data mining is a technology that applies sophisticated and complex algorithms to analyse data and present interesting information to the users. OLAP organizes data so that it can be explored by the analyst using a suitable model, wherease data mining analyses the data and provides the results to the users. Thus, while OLAP supports model-driven analysis, data mining supports data-driven analysis.

Traditionally, data mining was applied to raw data in the data warehouse database or, more commonly, text files of data extracted from the data warehouse database. In SQL Server 2000, Analysis Services provide data mining technology that can analyse data available either in the form of OLAP cubes or in the relational data warehouse database. In addition to this, data mining results can also be incorporated in the form of OLAP cubes to further enhance model-driven analysis. For example, data mining can be used to first analyse the sales of a product against customer demographics and then create a cube dimension to assist the analyst in the discovery of the information using a data cube.

12.4.1 KDD vs. Data Mining

Knowledge discovery was formalized in 1989 in the pursuit of seeking knowledge from data. The term *data mining* is a high level application technique which is used to present and analyse data for decision-makers.

If you look at the steps given above, you will find that data mining is just one of the many steps involved in knowledge discovery in databases. The other steps include data selection, data cleaning and pre-processing, application of data mining algorithm, and finally the interpretation of the discovered knowledge.

The KDD process is highly iterative and interactive. Data mining deals with detailed data to arrive at reliable conclusions and decisions, by developing an optimal representation of the structure of data during which knowledge is acquired.

Arun K. Pujari and Fayyad *et al.* distinguish between KDD and data mining by giving the following definitions.

- *Knowledge discovery in databases* is the process of identifying a valid, potentially useful, and ultimately understandable structure in data. This process involves selecting or sampling data from a data warehouse, cleaning or preprocessing it, transforming or reducing it, applying a data mining component to produce a structure, and then evaluating the derived structure.

- *Data mining* is a step in the KDD process concerned with the algorithmic means by which patterns or structures are enumerated from the data under acceptable computational efficiency limitations.

Thus, the structures that are obtained as a result of applying the data mining process must meet certain conditions so that these can be considered as knowledge. These conditions include validity, understandability, utility, novelty, and interestingness.

12.4.2 DBMS vs. Data Mining

While DBMS supports query languages which are useful for query-triggered data exploration, data mining supports automatic data exploration. In case the data analyst knows exactly what information he is trying to seek through analysis, a DBMS query can be executed, but if he vaguely knows the possible correlations and patterns that exist in the underlying data, then data mining techniques are useful.

One of the tasks of data mining is testing of hypothesis wherein the analyst formulates a hypothesis and tests it with the help of data in the database. Since this task can even be performed by a DBMS query, we can conclude that DBMS supports some primitive data mining tasks.

From the architectural perspective, there are three different ways in which data mining makes use of a relational DBMS: data mining applications may not use the relational DBMS at all, be loosely coupled, or be tightly coupled.

Data Mining without RDBMS

Most of the data mining systems does not use any DBMS, as they have their own memory and storage management. Such types of systems consider the database to be just a data repository from which the data is extracted into their own memory structures, before the data mining algorithm can be applied. The advantage of this approach is that the memory management can be optimized as per the data mining algorithm.

Loosely-coupled Approach

The second approach is to have a loosely-coupled DBMS in which the DBMS is used only for storing and retrieving data. In this approach, the DBMS uses a loosely-coupled SQL to fetch data records that are required by the mining algorithm. A host programming language that has embedded SQL statements in it is used to implement the front-end of the application.

Like other applications, data mining applications use a SQL select statement to retrieve the records from the database. Generally, a loop is executed from within the application program that copies records from the database address space to the application address space, where computation is performed on them. The loosely-coupled approach makes no use of the querying capability provided by the DBMS.

Tightly-coupled Approach

In the tightly-coupled approach, to perform computations on the datasets, the portions of the application program are selectively pushed to the database system. Thus, in this approach, all processing is done at the back-end. This approach differs from the loosely-coupled approach, as the data is brought from the database to the data mining area.

Recall that in the tightly-coupled approach, the data mining application goes where the data actually resides. The key benefit here is that it avoids performance degradation and takes full advantage of the database technology.

The performance of tightly-coupled approach depends on how the data mining process is optimized while mapping it to a query. There are two ways in which it can be done: to have a built-in query optimizer of the DBMS or to have an external optimizer.

12.4.3 OLAP vs. Data Mining

OLAP reports on the past events, while data mining predicts the future. Table 12.2 provides a sample list of questions which the OLAP and the data mining systems can answer.

Table 12.2 A sample list of questions

OLAP	Data Mining
• Who are our top 100 best customers for the last two years?	• Which 100 customers offer the best profit?
• Which customers defaulted on their loan payments in the last two years?	• Which customers are likely to be bad credit risks?
• What were the sales of each store last year compared to the targets?	• What are the anticipated sales of each store next year?
• Which salesperson sold more than their quota during the last year?	• Which salespersons are expected to sell more than their quota in the next year?
• Last year, which stores exceeded the previous year's sales?	• For the next year, which stores are likely to exceed the previous year's sales?
• Last year, which were the promotions that did well?	• What are the expected returns from next year's promotions?

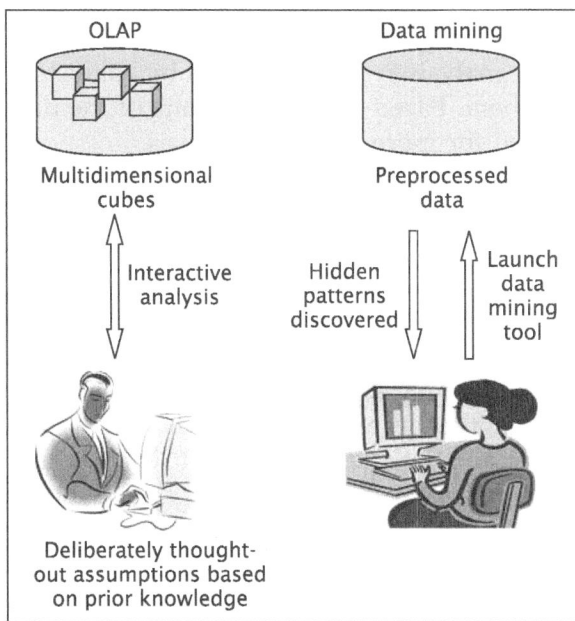

Figure 12.7 OLAP and data mining

With OLAP queries, users are able to obtain interesting patterns using complex queries. Data mining also supports to derive patterns from a huge amount of data. Yet, there is an essential difference between the two. Figure 12.7 shows how OLAP differs from data mining in the way the results are obtained.

As we have stated earlier, OLAP is used to analyse the past, while data mining is used to predict the future. Apart from this broad statement, there are other aspects as well that differentiate OLAP and data mining. Table 12.3 provides a comprehensive list of differences between OLAP and data mining.

Table 12.3 Comparison between OLAP and data mining

Features	OLAP	Data Mining
• Motivation for information request	• What is happening in the organization?	• Predict the future based on why this is happening
• Data granularity	• Summarized data	• Detailed data
• Number of business dimensions	• Small number of dimensions	• Large number of dimensions
• Number of attributes	• Small number of attributes	• Large number of attributes
• Sizes of dimensions	• Not large	• Very large
• Approach for analysis	• User-driven and interactive	• Data driven and automatic knowledge discovery
• Operations	• Multidimensional, drill-down, slice, dice, roll-up, pivot	• Prepare data. Launch mining tool and sit back
• State of the technology	• Mature and widely used	• Becoming more mature day by day

12.5 RELATED AREAS OF DATA MINING

Data mining refers to the finding of relevant and useful information from the databases. Data mining and knowledge discovery in the databases is a new interdisciplinary field that merges ideas from statistics, machine learning, databases, and parallel computing.

Statistics

Statistics is a theory rich approach for data analysis that generates results which can be difficult to interpret. The result sets require user guidance as to how to analyse the data. Statistics analysis is the foundation on which data mining technology rests and statistical analysis systems are used by analysts to detect unusual patterns and explain them. Based upon the results of the data mining algorithm, statistics can be used for more directed analysis.

Machine Learning

Machine learning is the automation of a learning process which includes not only learning from examples, but also reinforcement learning, learning with a teacher, etc. In machine learning, the learning algorithm takes the dataset and its accompanying information as the input and returns a statement, like a concept representing the results of the learning as output.

Inductive learning through which the system infers knowledge from observing its environment, has two main strategies: supervised learning and unsupervised learning. The future situations can be predicted by the model produced by inductive learning methods. It can be used not only for predicting about the states already encountered but also for unseen states that could occur. Multiple models can be formed from a given set of examples. In such situations, the principle of *Occam's Razor* must be applied which states that if there are multiple explanations for a particular phenomenon, then the best way is to choose the simplest one because it is more likely to capture the nature of the phenomenon.

Supervised learning Supervised learning involves learning from examples where a training set is given which acts as examples for the classes. The system finds a description of each class and once such description has been formulated, it is used to predict the class of previously unseen objects. We will learn more about how classification and description problems are handled later in this chapter.

Unsupervised learning Unsupervised learning includes learning from observation and discovery. In this approach there is no training set or prior knowledge of the classes. The system analyses the given dataset to find out the similarities that exist between the subsets of data. The result of this process includes a subset of class descriptions, one for each class, discovered in the environment. This mode of learning is similar to cluster analysis.

While data mining finds hidden knowledge in the data, machine learning on the other hand is concerned with improving the performance of an intelligent system. When database systems are integrated with machine learning techniques, the databases will need more efficient learning algorithms because realistic databases are normally very large and noisy.

Mathematical Programming

The relationship between mathematical programming and data mining was brought into study by O L Mangasarian. Majority of the data mining tasks can be equivalently formulated as problems in mathematical programming for which efficient algorithms are already available. Mathematical programming provides a new insight into the problems of data mining.

12.6 DATA MINING TECHNIQUES

Before learning about the applications of data mining, let us first have a close look at the various data mining techniques that are applicable to each type of application. These techniques (listed in Table 12.4) consist of the specific algorithms/functions that can be used for each application.

12.6.1 Association Rule Mining

Association rule mining finds interesting association relationships among a large set of data items. With massive amounts of data continuously being collected and stored, many industries are becoming interested in mining association rules from their databases.

Table 12.4 Application of data mining

Application Areas	Mining Functions	Mining Processes	Mining Techniques
Detection of fraudulent cases	• Credit card frauds • Internal audits • Warehouse pilferage	• Determination of variations from norms	• Outlier analysis • Memory based reasoning
Risk detection and assessment	• Credit card upgrades • Mortgage loans • Customer retention • Credit ratings	• Detection and analysis of link between different items	• Decision trees • Memory based reasoning
Market analysis	• Market basket analysis • Target marketing • Cross selling • CRM	• Predictive modelling	• Cluster analysis • Decision trees • Neural networks • Genetic algorithm • Association rule mining

A typical example of association rule mining is market basket analysis. This process analyses customer buying patterns by finding associations between the different items that customers place in their shopping baskets. The discovery of such associations can help retailers to develop their marketing strategies by gaining insight into which items are frequently purchased together by customers. For instance, if customers are buying milk, how likely are they going to buy bread on the same trip to the super market? Such information can lead to increased sales by helping retailers do selective marketing and plan their shelf space. For example, placing milk and bread within close proximity may further encourage the sale of these items together within single visits to the store. Associations are affinities between items.

Association discovery algorithms are applied to discover the combinations of items where the presence of one item strongly suggests the presence of another. When association discovery algorithms are applied to the shopping transactions, they will uncover affinities among products that are likely to be purchased together.

Association discovery algorithm generates association rules that represent such affinities. Figure 12.8 illustrates an association rule. The two parts—support factor and confidence factor—indicate the strength of the association that exists between the items. Rules that have a higher support and confidence factors are considered to be more valid, relevant, and useful.

Association discovery algorithms are very simple, as they involve only two factors to be interpreted that in itself are very intuitive for the purpose.

Whenever a customer buys milk, he also buys bread for 25% of all the purchases.	Confidence factor based on transactions that are likely to happen with a probability of 65%.
Support factor based on transactions that have already happened and are currently under study.	A customer in a super market who buys milk will also buy bread in 65% of the cases.

Figure 12.8 Association rule mining

Transaction data file

Sale Date	Customer Name	Products Purchased
15 Nov 2004	John	Computer, Colour printer
15 Nov 2004	Camy	Computer, Colour printer, Scanner
15 Nov 2004	Robert	Laptop
19 Dec 2004	Tom	Laptop
19 Dec 2004	John	Scanner
19 Dec 2004	Tom	Scanner
19 Dec 2004	Robert	Scanner
20 Dec 2004	Camy	Pen drive
20 Dec 2004	Richard	Computer, Colour printer

Sequential patterns—customer sequence

Customer Name	Products Purchased
John	Computer, Colour printer, Scanner
Camy	Computer, Colour printer, Scanner, Pen drive
Robert	Laptop, Scanner
Tom	Laptop, Scanner
Richard	Computer, Colour printer

Sequential pattern discovery with support factors

Sequential Patterns	Support Factor	Supporting Customers
Computer, Colour printer	> 60%	John, Camy, Richard
Computer, Colour printer, Scanner	> 40%	John, Cindy
Laptop, Scanner	> 40%	Robert, Tom

Figure 12.9 Discovery of sequential patterns using association rule mining

Association mining algorithm also discovers patterns where one set of items follows another specific set. Let us take an example in which the algorithm is being used to discover the buying sequence of products. The sale transactions form the dataset for the data mining algorithm. The data elements in the sale transaction consist of date and time of transaction, products bought during how these transactions are stored and how the results are obtained using the association mining algorithm. Notice the discovery of sequential patterns and the support factor that the transaction, and the customer who bought these items. The tables in Fig. 12.9 gives an indication of the relevance of the association.

Association Rule

For any transaction database, an association rule is given as X=>Y, where X and Y are subsets of A. The rule X=>Y is specified with two factors: support factor and confidence factor. The rule X=>Y has a confidence factor, τ, which means that τ% of transactions in the database that support X also support Y. Similarly, the rule X=>Y has a support σ which means that σ% of transactions in the transaction database supports $X \cup Y$.

We use association rules to find transactions that contain X tends to Y as well. Given a set of transactions, T, the problem of mining association rules is to discover the rules that have support and confidence factors greater than or equal to the user-specified threshold, i.e. minimum support and minimum confidence.

12.6.2 Decision Trees

The classification of large datasets is a classical problem in data mining. It is generally applied in databases with a large number of records and for a set of classes such that each record belongs to one of the given classes. The problem of classification is to determine the class of a given record.

Besides this, the problem of classification also generates a description for each class. Decision trees are more concerned with supervised classification in which we have a training dataset of records and for each record of this set, the class to which it belongs is known. Using the training dataset, description of classes is produced by the classification process which in turn is used to classify the unknown records. Apart from the training set, there is also a test dataset which is used to determine the effectiveness of the classification.

There are several algorithms to perform supervised classifications, but decision trees seem to be most attractive because they represent rules. Given below are a set of considerations that must be kept in mind while designing any decision tree construction algorithms for data mining:

- The method should efficiently handle a very large database.
- The method should be capable of handling categorical attributes.

Let us consider the following datasets given in Table 12.5—the training dataset and the test dataset—to have a clear idea of a decision tree.

Table 12.5 Sample dataset

Aggregate	Preference	Class	Aggregate	Preference	Class
55	Commerce	Allot Humanities	72	Science	Allot Commerce
86	Science	Allot Science	40	Commerce	Allot Humanities
73	Science	Allot Commerce	78	Humanities	Allot Humanities
76	Commerce	Allot Commerce	87	Commerce	Allot Commerce
90	Science	Allot Science	75	Science	Allot Science

According to Table 12.5, there are three data attributes. Note that there is a special attribute *class* which serves as the class label. The attribute *aggregate* is numerical, while the attribute *preference* is categorical. The decision tree is used to find a set of rules to specify—for what values of aggregate and preference can the student be allotted a particular subject. Figure 12.10 shows the decision tree.

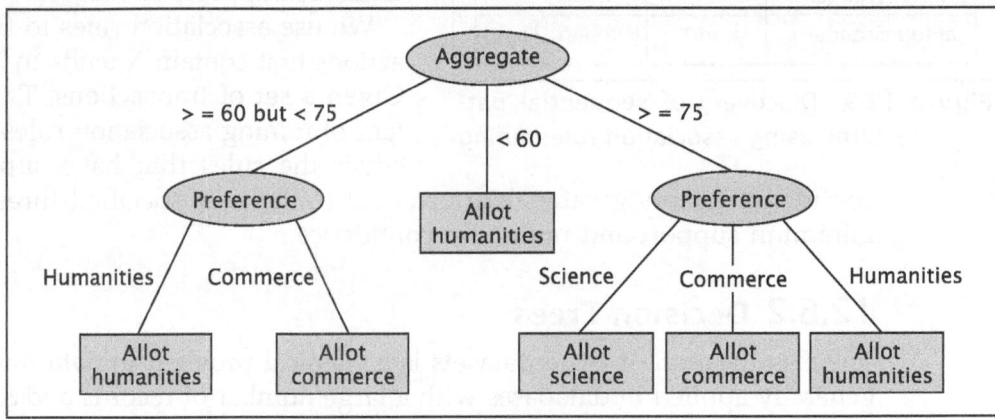

Figure 12.10 Decision tree of data given in Table 12.5

The classification of an unknown input data is done by traversing the tree from the root node to the leaf node (shown as rectangles in Fig. 12.10). When a record enters at the root node, a test is applied to determine which child node will be traversed next. The whole process is repeated until a leaf node is encountered.

In a decision tree, there is a unique path from the root to each leaf and every path represents a rule. The different leaf nodes of the tree may or may not refer to the same class label. However, every leaf node will be used to form a different rule. Table 12.6 lists the rules corresponding to the tree given in Fig. 12.10.

Table 12.6 Rules corresponding to the decision tree

Rule 1	If aggregate is less than 60, then allot Humanities.
Rule 2	If aggregate is greater than or equal to 60 but less than 75 and preference is Commerce, then allot Commerce.
Rule 3	If aggregate is greater than or equal to 60 but less than 75 and preference is Humanities, then allot Humanities.
Rule 4	If aggregate is greater than 75 and preference is Commerce, then allot Commerce.
Rule 5	If aggregate is greater than 75 and preference is Science, then allot Science.

The accuracy of the classifier (decision tree) is determined by the percentage of the test dataset that is correctly classified. For example, in the above tree, we can carry out the classification for an unknown record as follows. Let us assume, for the record, that we know the values of the first four attributes as:

Aggregate = 80, Preference = Commerce

We start from the root node to check the value of the attribute associated at the root node which is the splitting attribute at this node. For a decision tree, at every node, there is a splitting attribute. In the given data record, aggregate (80) is the splitting attribute at the root. Since the value is 80, we have to move to the rightmost child where the splitting attribute is: preference = Commerce. Hence, we move to the middle child to conclude that the class label is "Allot Commerce.

Now, let us have a look at the advantages and shortcomings of decision tree classification. Table 12.7 lists the differences.

Table 12.7 Merits and demerits of decision tree classification

Merits	Demerits
• Decision trees generate understandable rules.	• Some decision trees can work with only binary-valued target classes.
• They are capable of handling both numerical and the categorical attributes.	• When the number of training examples per class is small, the decision trees may tend to produce erroneous results.
• They can identify the fields that are most important for classification.	• It becomes computationally expensive when a decision tree grown to a very large size.

How to Construct a Decision Tree

After having an overview of the basic features of decision trees, we shall now have a bird's eye view of certain principles that you apply to actually construct a decision tree from a given training dataset.

Selection of the splitting attribute At every node of the decision tree, there is an associated splitting attribute whose value partitions the dataset when the node is expanded.

Selection of the splitting criterion The condition on the splitting attribute for splitting the data at every node is called the *splitting criterion* at that node. For a numeric attribute, the criterion can simply be an equation and for a categorical attribute, it can specify a membership condition on a subset of values.

Decision tree construction methods recursively partitions the dataset till homogeneity is achieved. The process of construction of the decision trees is a combination of three main phases.

Construction phase In this phase, the initial decision tree is constructed based on the training dataset. This phase requires recursive partitioning of the training set into two or more sub-partitions depending on the splitting criteria. The whole process is repeated until a stopping criteria is met.

Pruning phase Due to over-fitting, the tree constructed in the previous phase may not give the best possible set of rules. Therefore, the pruning phase is applied to remove some of the lower branches and nodes to improve its performance.

Processing phase In this phase, the pruned tree is processed. During the construction of the decision tree, the splitting criterion must be considered while determining the splitting attribute. For example, some algorithms generate only binary decision trees, therefore they carry out only binary splits. In case of a binary split, there is not much of a problem because the attribute itself takes two distinct values only. But in case the selected attribute takes more than two values, or takes continuous values, or is a categorical attribute, a binary split calls for selecting the splitting criterion. Thus, one thing is for sure that the strategies for binary splits for categorical attributes and numerical attributes are strikingly different from each other.

As discussed earlier, numerical attributes are split using binary split of the form $A \leq v$, where v is a real number. In the set A, the values $A_1, A_2 ..., A_n$ are the sorted values since any value between A_i and A_{i+1} can be taken as the split point.

The splitting point for categorical attributes is strikingly different from that of numerical attributes. Since it is not possible to have any ordering of the values of a categorical attribute, we cannot have value n such that it splits the attribute into two. If $S(A)$ is the set of possible values of the categorical attribute A, then the split test is of the form $A \in S'$ where S' is a subset of S. This means, for an attribute having n values, there exits 2^n possible splits. In case n is small, it will be easy to find the best split, but if n is large, then the split is made by some heuristics and the best spilt among them is taken.

Best split

For a good and optimal decision tree, it is very important that the best attribute is chosen for splitting at every node and the best splitting criterion is applied to it. The main operations that have to be performed during the construction are:

- Evaluate splits for every attribute and select the best split. That is, first determine the splitting attribute.
- Determine the splitting condition on the selected attribute.
- Partition the data based on the best split.

The complexity of the construction of decision trees lies in selecting the best split at every node. The first task is to choose the attribute that makes the best splitter. Here, the best split is defined as one that does the best job of separating the records into groups, where a single class predominates. In order to determine the best splitter at a node, all the independent attributes must be considered.

If an attribute can have multiple values, then first these values are sorted and then using some evaluation function as the measure of goodness, each split is evaluated. The effectiveness of the split provided by the best splitter is compared with that of each attribute. The winner is then chosen to be the splitter for the root node. To know which split is better than the other, we use different evaluation functions to determine the splitting attributes and the splitting criteria. The discussion of these evaluation functions is out of the scope of this book.

Tree pruning

During the construction of decision trees, many of the branches will reflect anomalies in the training data due to the presence of noise or outliers. Tree pruning methods address this problem of overfitting the data. The tree pruning methods use statistical measures to remove the least reliable branches, thereby resulting in faster classification and in the improvement of the classification process.

There are two common approaches to tree pruning: *pre-pruning* and *post-pruning*. In pre-pruning approach, a tree is pruned by halting its construction early in the construction phase by deciding not to further partition the subset of training samples at a given node. When the construction of decision trees halts, the node becomes a leaf. Generally, statistical measures are used to measure goodness of a split. In case the partitioning of the samples at a node results in a split that falls below a pre-specified threshold, then further partitioning of the given subset is halted. Therefore, choosing an appropriate threshold is a critical task, as high thresholds can result in over-simplified trees, while low thresholds could result in very little simplification.

The second approach of tree pruning is post-pruning which removes branches from a fully grown tree. Thus, the lowest unpruned node becomes the leaf node. In the tree, for every non-leaf node, the pruning algorithm first calculates the expected error rate that would occur if the sub-tree at that node were pruned. In the next step, the algorithm will calculate the expected error rate that would occur if the sub-tree at that node were not pruned. If a greater error rate is expected in case the node is pruned, then the sub-tree is kept, else it is pruned.

After a pruned tree is constructed using the training dataset, an independent test set is used to estimate the accuracy of each tree. Obviously, the decision tree with minimum expected error rate is preferred. While post-pruning requires more computation than pre-pruning, it leads to a more reliable tree. But generally, pre-pruning and post-pruning approaches are interleaved for a combined approach.

12.6.3 Clustering Analysis

Data clustering is a technique that makes clusters of objects that are somehow similar in characteristics. Clustering is often intermixed with classification, but there is a difference between the two. In classification, the objects are assigned to predefined classes, whereas in clustering, the classes are also to be defined. The class labels are unknown and there is no prior training set.

Clustering techniques are used for combining observed datasets into clusters or groups which satisfy two main criteria:

- Each group or cluster is homogeneous, that is, data that belongs to the same cluster is similar to each other. The principle here is that there should be maximum intra-cluster similarity between the datasets that lie within the same cluster.

- Each group or cluster should be different from other clusters, that is, data that belongs to one cluster should be different from the examples of other clusters. The principle here is that there should be minimum inter-cluster similarity between the datasets that lie within the same cluster.

Basic Definitions

Let us define some basic terms in cluster analysis as given by different authors.

- *Cluster* – A cluster is an ordered list of objects, which have some common characteristics.

- *Distance between two clusters* – The distance between two clusters involves some or all elements of the two clusters. The clustering method determines how the distance should be computed.

- *Similarity* – A similarity measure SIMILAR(D_i, D_j) can be used to represent the similarity between the documents.

- *Threshold* – The lowest possible input value of similarity required to join two objects in one cluster.

- *Similarity matrix* – Similarity between objects is calculated by the function SIMILAR(D_i, D_j), represented in the form of a matrix is called a similarity matrix.
- *Dissimilarity coefficient* – The dissimilarity coefficient of two clusters is defined to be the distance between them. Smaller the value of dissimilarity coefficient, greater the similarity between the two clusters.
- *Cluster seed* – The first object of a cluster is defined as the initiator of that cluster, i.e. every incoming object's similarity is compared with the initiator, also called the cluster seed.

Clustering Approaches

Clustering is a data mining technique that is generally used for the discovery of data distribution and patterns in the underlying data. The technique aims at discovering both the dense and the sparse regions in the dataset. We will discuss two main approaches to clustering: hierarchical clustering and partitioning clustering. Apart from this, clustering algorithms also differ based on the ability to deal with different types of attributes, numeric and categorical and in accuracy of clustering.

Partitioning clustering These algorithms partition the database into a predefined number of clusters (k clusters) that optimizes a certain criterion function. The partition clustering algorithms are of two types:

- k-means algorithm, using which each cluster is represented by the centre of gravity of that cluster.
- k-medoid algorithm, using which each cluster is represented by one of the objects of the cluster that is located near the centre.

Hierarchical clustering These algorithms create partitions in such a way that each partition is nested into the next partition in the sequence. In this manner, it creates a hierarchy of clusters from small to big or big to small. The hierarchical techniques are of two types:

- *Agglomerative hierarchical clustering* – This clustering technique follows a bottom-up strategy that starts by placing each object in its own cluster and then merges these clusters into larger clusters, until all the objects are placed in a single cluster or until a certain termination condition is encountered. Agglomerative hierarchical clustering methods are the most common clustering technique.
- *Divisive hierarchical clustering* – This clustering technique follows a top-down strategy by starting with all objects in one cluster. At every subsequent step, the algorithm sub-divides the cluster into smaller clusters, until each object forms a cluster on its own or until a certain termination condition is encountered. For example, the termination condition could be—the desired number of clusters or the distance between the two closest clusters is above a certain threshold distance.

K-means Algorithm

The *k*-means algorithm takes as an input a predefined number of clusters *k*. *Means* or *averages* relate to the average location of all the members of a particular cluster. When dealing with clustering techniques, one has to adopt a notion of a high-dimensional space in which the value of each attribute of a data record represents a distance of the record from the origin along the attribute axes. However, the values in the dataset must all be numeric (in case the data is categorical, it must be transformed into numeric) and should be normalized. This allows fair computation of the overall distances in a multi-attribute space.

K-means algorithm is a simple, iterative procedure, in which the centroid plays a crucial role. Many authors have defined the *centroid* as an artificial point in the space of records which represents an average location of the particular cluster. The coordinates of this point are averages of attribute values of all datasets that belong to the cluster. Figure 12.11 illustrates how clusters are formed. The steps of the *k*-means algorithm are given below:

1. Select randomly *k* points or data records to be the seeds for the centroids of *k* clusters.

2. Assign each data record to the centroid closest to the data record, thereby forming *k* clusters of data records.

3. Calculate new centroids of the clusters by calculating the average of all attribute values of the data records belonging to the same cluster (centroid).

4. Check if there is a change in the centroid of the clusters. If yes, start again from Step 2. If no, cluster detection is finished and all records are placed in their respective clusters.

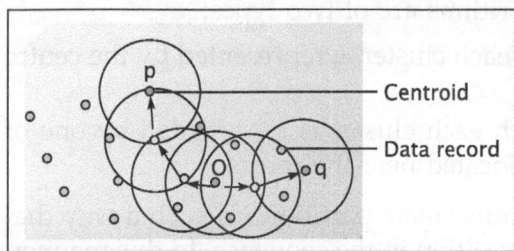

Figure 12.11 Clustering technique

Automatic Cluster Detection

Most of the issues related to automatic cluster detection are connected to the kinds of queries that the user wants to be answered from the data mining system.

- *Distance measure* – Most clustering techniques use the Euclidean distance formula (square root of the sum of the squares of distances along each attribute axes) to calculate the distance between two data records. For this technique to be applied, the non-numeric variables must be transformed and scaled before applying the clustering algorithm.

- *Choice of the right number of clusters* – If the number of clusters *k* in the *k*-means method is not chosen appropriately, then the results will not be good. Thus, you need to keep experimenting with different values for *k*. Technically speaking, the best *k*-value will result in smallest intra-cluster distances and largest inter-cluster distances. However, there are sophisticated techniques available to measure these qualities automatically.

Applications of Cluster Analysis

Clustering techniques are used when there exists a natural grouping in data records. As stated earlier, clusters should represent groups of items (products, events, customers) that have a lot in common or are similar to each other. Cluster mining algorithms are generally used as the baseline for the application of other data mining algorithms, because creating clusters prior to the application of other data mining techniques like decision trees and neural networks helps to reduce the complexity of the problem by dividing the problem space of data records. Every cluster can be mined separately, thereby exhibiting improved results.

Data clustering is widely used in a number of applications pertaining to every field of life. In our day-to-day life, we form clusters of several things based on some sort of similarity. Similarly the use of data clustering plays a key role in the field of information retrieval. Some of the applications are listed below.

Medical image database

Similarity searching in medical image database is a major application of the clustering technique. In medical field, many diseases are detected, e.g. tumor, cancer, and other diseases caused due to genetic disorder. The scanned pictures or the X-rays are compared with the existing ones and the dissimilarities are recognized.

To assist the diagnosis of the patient, clusters of images of different parts of the body are taken. For example, the images of the CT scan of brain are kept in one cluster. To further enhance the clarity, the images in which the right side of the brain is damaged are kept in one cluster.

The application uses a pre-stored medical image database that contains images that have already been analysed and a record is associated with each image. Now when a query image is posed, first it tries to recognize the particular cluster this image belongs to, and then by similarity matching with a healthy image of that specific cluster, the main damaged portion or the diseased portion is identified, thereby detecting the exact location and cause of the disease. Thus, with the clustering technique, the time needed to find the exact match from the database gets reduced.

Data mining

Another important application of clustering is in the field of data mining. Clustering is usually performed as one of the first steps in data mining analysis. It identifies groups of related records that can be used as a starting point for exploring further relationships. One example of such clustering is demographic-based customer segmentation. Further analyses that make use of the other data mining techniques can be used to determine the characteristics of these clusters with respect to some desired outcome. For example, the buying habits of multiple population clusters can be compared to deduce which particular customer segment should be targeted for an upcoming promotional campaign.

Let us consider another example where clustering is applied as the initial point to start a data mining application. A company that sells a large number of products may need to know about the sale of all of their products to keep a check as to which product is giving extensive sales and which is not. This is done by data mining techniques. But, if the system clusters the products that are giving fewer sales, then only the cluster of such products would have to be analysed rather than analysing the sales of all the products. Thus, the clustering technique facilitates the mining process.

Windows NT

Another major application of clustering is in Windows NT. It applies the clustering algorithm to determine the nodes that are using similar resources and accumulate them into one cluster so that the new cluster can be controlled as one node.

World Wide Web

Clustering techniques are used by a number of intelligent software agents to retrieve, filter, and categorize documents available on the World Wide Web commonly known as the Internet. Clustering is also applied to extract salient features of related Web documents to automatically formulate queries and search for other similar documents on the Web.

The traditional clustering algorithms either use a priori knowledge of document structures or use probabilistic techniques like Bayesian classification to define the similarities that exist among the Web documents. However, many of these traditional clustering techniques fail when the dimensionality of the feature space becomes high relative to the size of the document space.

These days, new and far better clustering algorithms that are based on generalizations of graph partitioning are used to effectively cluster documents even in a very high-dimensional feature space. These algorithms do not require pre-specified *ad hoc* distance functions, and are capable of automatically discovering document similarities or associations.

12.6.4 Case-based Reasoning

We as humans solve problems based on our prior experiences that we recall from memory. It is just that experts of a particular field have successful experiences doing that type of task in the past. When the expert encounters a new problem (task), he considers past situations where similar tasks were accomplished successfully.

The similarity is dependent on certain main features of the problem. However, some differences may exist between the new problem and the ones that were successfully done in the past, but the ones remembered as being most similar are usually solved in the same manner. However, more than one task may be drawn from memory because different parts of the new problem have similarities to different experiences. The same principle applies in memory-based or case-based reasoning.

Steps in Case-based Reasoning

The following list describes the steps involved in case-based reasoning. Figure 12.12 illustrates the process.

- A new problem arrives as an input.
- The features of this problem are extracted.
- A case-based search is done to retrieve cases with features that are similar to those of the new problem.
- The cases thus retrieved may be further fine-matched to the given problem, and one or more best matches are identified.
- The features that clearly define the differences between the new and the best matching case problems are extracted.
- For each difference, an adjustment is made to the case solution.
- The proposed solution is checked and tested to ensure that it works successfully.
- If the proposed solution is sufficiently good, it is stored in the case-base with its problem statement.
- Output the solution of the new problem in terms of success or failure.
- Return to the first step, and wait until the next problem comes.

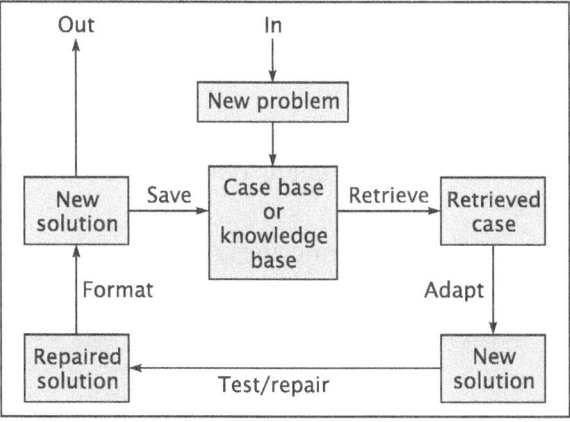

Figure 12.12 The process of case-based reasoning

12.6.5 Genetic Algorithm

A genetic algorithm is a search technique that is generally used in computing true or approximate solutions to optimization and search problems. Genetic algorithms are applied in computer science, engineering, economics, physics, mathematics, and other fields. Genetic algorithms use techniques inspired by evolutionary biology, such as inheritance, mutation, selection, and crossover.

In genetic algorithms, the evolution begins from a population of randomly generated individuals and happens in generations. In each generation, the fitness of every individual in the population is evaluated. Based on the evaluation, multiple individuals are selected from the current population and mutated to form a new population. The next iteration of the algortihm will make use of the newly generated population.

Initialization Initially, multiple solutions are randomly generated to form an initial population. The initial population is selected in such a way that it covers the entire range of possible solutions or the search space. The size of this initial population will depend on the nature of the problem, but it typically contains several hundreds or thousands of possible solutions.

Selection In each generation, a proportion of the existing population is selected to breed a new generation. Individual solutions are selected through a *fitness-based* process that filter solutions as measured by the fitness function.

Reproduction The next step is to produce a second generation population of solutions from the individual solutions selected in the previous step. The new population is formed by the application of genetic operators, such as crossover (recombination) and/or mutation. The child solution that will be formed using genetic operators will share many of the characteristics of its parents.

Generetic operators are applied again to these newly generated solutions to produce child solutions. Thus, the process is continued until a new population of solutions of appropriate size is generated. Genetic algorithms increase the fitness of the population, since only the best individuals are selected for breeding.

Termination The whole process of producing a new population of solutions is repeated until a termination condition has been reached. Common terminating conditions are as follows:

- The desired solution that satisfies the minimum criteria has been found.
- A fixed number of generations have been created.
- Allocated budget in terms of computation time and money has been reached.
- Solutions with maximum fitness have already been generated. This point is reached when successive iterations no longer produce better results.
- Manual inspection.

Refer Fig. 12.13 which shows the pseudo-code and the flow chart of genetic algorithms.

In short, genetic algorithms incorporate ideas of natural evolution. First, an initial population is created randomly using a set of rules where each rule can be represented by a string of bits. For example, assume that samples in a given training set are described by two Boolean attributes, A_1 and A_2, and there are two classes, C_1 and C_2. The rule "if A_2 and not A_1 then C_1" can be enclosed as a string of bits, thus forming a rule "010", where the two leftmost bits represent attributes A_1 and A_2 respectively, and the last bit represents classes, either C_1 or C_2. Genetic operators such as crossover and mutation are applied to create offsprings. While substrings from pairs of rules are swapped to form new pairs of rules in crossover; in mutation, randomly selected bits in a rule's string are inverted.

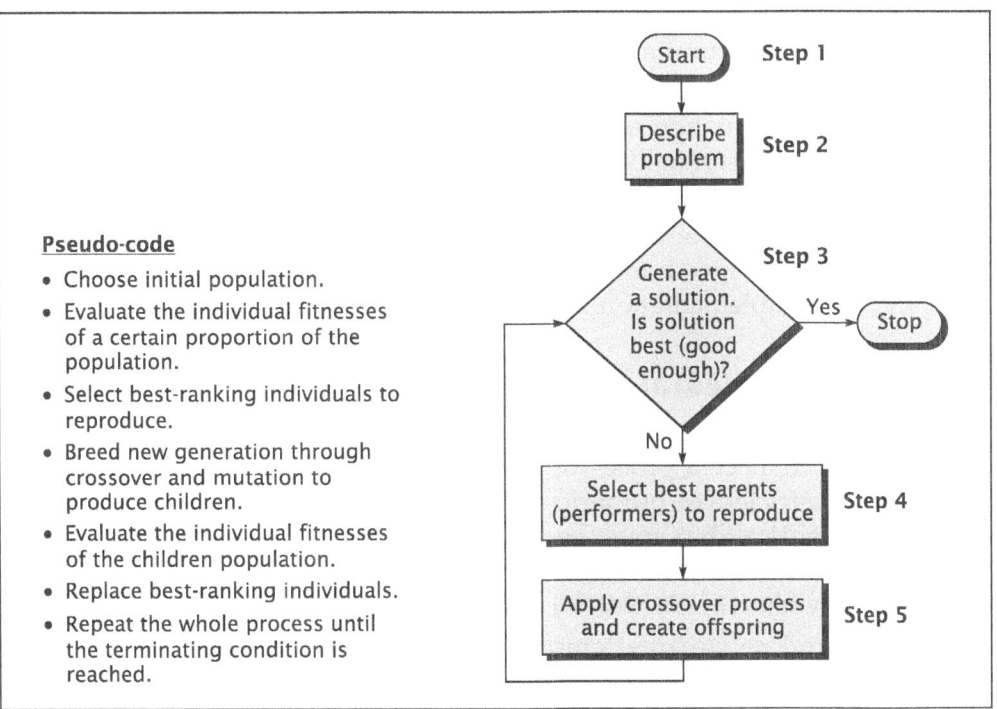

Pseudo-code

- Choose initial population.
- Evaluate the individual fitnesses of a certain proportion of the population.
- Select best-ranking individuals to reproduce.
- Breed new generation through crossover and mutation to produce children.
- Evaluate the individual fitnesses of the children population.
- Replace best-ranking individuals.
- Repeat the whole process until the terminating condition is reached.

Figure 12.13 Pseudo-code and flow chart of genetic algorithm

Limitations of Genetic Algorithms

There are several problems encountered in case of the generation of solutions via a genetic algorithm:

- In many complex problems, genetic algorithms may have a tendency to converge towards local optima rather than the global optimum of the problem. However, this problem can be avoided by any of the following three methods.
  - Using a different fitness function.
  - Increasing the rate of mutation.
  - Using selection techniques that maintain a diverse population of solutions.
- Working with dynamic datasets is difficult, as genomes begin to converge early on, towards solutions which may no longer be valid for later data.
- Selection is an important genetic operator. Some data mining professionals argue on the importance of crossover versus mutation. Some groups say that crossover is most important and mutation is only necessary to ensure that potential solutions are not lost, while others say just the opposite.

- For specific optimization problems and problem instantiations, given the same amount of resources, simpler optimization algorithms may find better solutions than genetic algorithms.
- A mutation rate that is too high may lead to loss of good solutions and unfortunately, there are theoretical but not yet practical upper and lower bounds for these parameters that can help to guide the selection process.
- The speed and efficiency of the algorithm very much depends on the implementation and evaluation of the fitness function.

12.6.6 Neural Networks

A neural network is a parallel computing system of a number of interconnected processor nodes where the input to individual network nodes is restricted to numeric values falling in the closed range [0, 1] and thus, categorical data must be transformed prior to network training.

How Neural Networks Work

Neural networks attempt to mimic a neuron in a human brain. They learn from experience and are useful in detecting unknown relationships that exist between a set of input data and an outcome. Like other data mining approaches, neural networks detect patterns in data, highlight the relationships found in the data, and predict outcomes. Neural networks are widely used because of their ability to predict complex processes.

Neural networks are trained by modifying the strength or *weight* of connections from the inputs to the output. The strength of a connection is either increased or decreased based on its importance for producing a proper outcome. A connection's strength depends on a *weight* that it receives at its input. The process makes use of a mathematical model to adjust the weights, and is called a *learning rule*.

A neural network tries various formulae for predicting the output variable for each example. The process of training a neural network continues until it produces outcome values that fall within a specified accuracy level, or until it satisfies some other stopping criteria.

Figure 12.14 demonstrates a neural network in which each of the processing units takes many inputs and produces an output that is a nonlinear function of the weighted sum of the inputs. The weights assigned to each of the inputs are obtained during a training process that is also called *back-propagation*, in which outputs produced are compared with target outputs and the deviation between them is used as feedback to adjust weights.

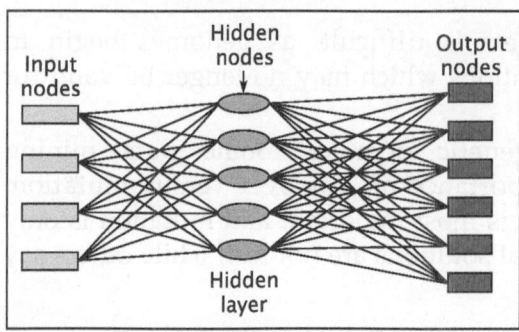

Figure 12.14 A neural network

The process of re-adjusting weights is critical for efficient performance of the neural network model. In Fig. 12.14, there are five *hidden nodes* or middle-layer nodes. The number of hidden nodes can vary. This number can be adjusted by having multiple levels of hidden nodes. However, the number of inputs, hidden nodes, outputs, and the weighting algorithms used to predict the strength of the connections between nodes together determine the complexity of a neural network, its accuracy, and the time it takes to create the neural network model. The criticality of the number of hidden nodes and weights for a neural network calls for the application of different approaches for finding the right number of hidden nodes and re-adjusting the weights.

Analogy with Human Brain

As stated earlier, neural networks mimic human brain, both in structure and the way they operate. Let us draw an analogy between the two.

The human brain is made up of several neurons. Every single neuron can be thought of as a separate processor. The inputs to these neurons are scattered over its dendrites tree. The axons are the white matter in the brain that insulate the neurons and act as an output device for the neuron. The dendrite acts as the input to the neuron as the axon passes the output of one neuron to the dendrite of the next. Each neuron processes the information it receives and passes its results on down the line.

The neural network model reflects the same kind of process. In the neural model, there are nodes that act as processors in a massively parallel processing system or simply processes in a multi-processing system. According to Fig. 12.15, through neurons, the network receives as input the location, age, gender, and the income of customers, and then based on some algorithm, it generates an output. These outputs are then added to get a weighted sum that in turn gives the final result, such as likely to buy or not to buy a particular product.

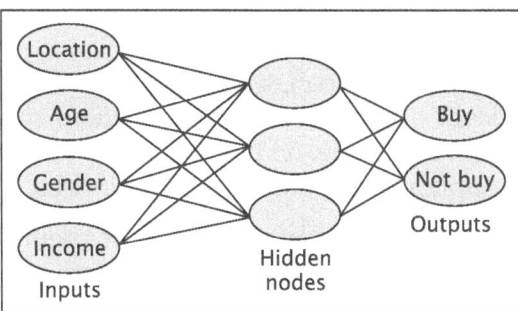

Figure 12.15 Example of a neural network model

Strengths and Weaknesses

The greatest strength of neural networks lies in their ability to accurately predict outcomes of complex problems. This fact is proven by the accuracy tests that are performed against other approaches. However, there are some downfalls to neural networks, such as:

- Neural networks are good for prediction, but not always good for understanding a model. Initial implementations of neural networks were criticized as "black box" prediction engines; but with the new tools on the market today, this criticism is debatable.

- Neural networks are sensitive to the number of training samples. If a network with a large capacity for learning is trained using very few data examples, then the network is said to have memorized its training data. However, neural networks today have effectively eliminated over-training by monitoring test versus training errors.
- Neural networks have very slow training speed, as they require many passes to build. Thus, creation of the most accurate models can be very time-consuming.

Applications of Neural Networks

Neural networks are applicable in almost every situation that involves a relationship between the predictor variables (inputs) and predicted variables (outputs). A few application areas are discussed below:

Detection of medical phenomena A number of health-related indices like a combination of heart beat rate, blood pressure, respiration rate can be monitored. The existence of a particular condition could be associated with a very complex combination of changes in these variables. Neural networks are used to identify the exact problem with the patient so that the appropriate treatment can be prescribed.

Stock market prediction Studying the fluctuations of stock market prices requires complex, multidimensional analysis. Neural networks are applied to make predictions about stock prices depending upon factors, such as past performance and various economic indicators.

Credit assignment When a customer applies for a loan, a lot of information is collected about him/her, e.g. the applicant's age, education, occupation, sex, credit background, etc. After training a neural network on historical data, neural network analysis can be used to classify applicants as good or bad credit risks.

Monitoring the condition of machinery In a manufacturing unit, neural networks can be used for cutting costs by bringing additional expertise to schedule the preventive maintenance of machines. A neural network can be trained to differentiate between the sounds a machine makes when it is running normally as compared to the one that is made in case of a problem. Once the neural network is trained, its expertise can be used to warn a technician of an upcoming breakdown, before it actually occurs and causes downtime.

Engine management Neural networks are used to analyse the input of sensors from an engine. They can be used to control various parameters within which the engine functions, to minimize the consumption of fuel.

12.6.7 Outlier Analysis

Outlier analysis is a primary method for database mining. It can either be used as a standalone tool to get insight into the distribution of a dataset or as a

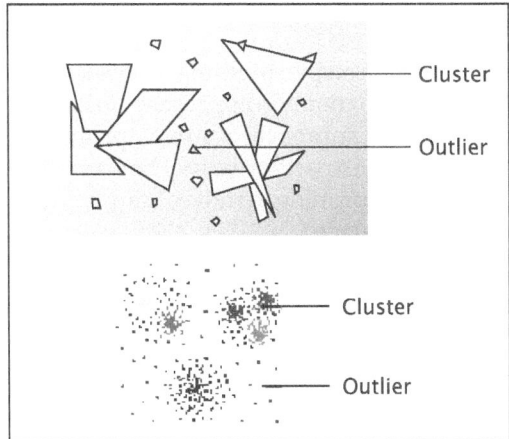

Figure 12.16 Outlier analysis

preprocessing step for other algorithms that operate on the detected clusters. Density-based approaches apply a local cluster criterion in which clusters are treated as regions in the data space in which the objects are dense. These clusters are separated by regions of low object density, also called noise. The noisy regions may have an arbitrary shape and the points inside a region may be arbitrarily distributed. Figure 12.16 segregates the outliers from the cluster objects.

For other KDD applications, finding the outliers, i.e. the rare events is more interesting and useful than finding the common cases. One such example where outlier analysis is applied is in case of detecting criminal activities in e-commerce.

Rare and infrequent events are of interest in data mining in many contexts including fraud detection, marketing, etc. The discovery of such events is classified as *outlier analysis*. According to Hawkins (1980), an outlier is *an observation that deviates so much from other observations as to arouse suspicion that it was generated by a different mechanism.*

One of the approaches applied to detect outliers is to assume a known distribution for the data and to examine the deviation of individuals from the distribution. However, this approach does not scale well for data mining applications. So, the most commonly used approach is to use distance-based methods where the measure outside-ness of an entity is based on its distance to nearby entities. Thus, the two important parameters are: the number of nearby entities and the minimum distance between them.

The third approach is given by Knorr & Ng (1998). They suggest identifying outliers by counting the number of neighbours within a specified radius of a data point. In technical terms, the radius and the threshold number of points are the two important factors of this approach. Although the approach is simple, it is not sufficient for data that is evenly distributed.

Recapitulation

Data mining, the extraction of the hidden predictive information from large databases, is a powerful new technology with a great potential to analyse important information in the data warehouse.

Data mining functionalities include characterization, discrimination, association analysis, classification, prediction, clustering, outlier analysis, and evolution and deviation analysis.

Characterization is summarization of general features of objects in a target class.

Discrimination is the comparison of the general features of objects between two classes referred to as the target class and the contrasting class.

Association analysis studies the frequency of items occurring together in transactional databases and identifies the frequent item sets.

Classification analysis is the organization of data in given classes when class labels are known.

Prediction is used for forecasting in a business context.

Clustering is the organization of data in classes when the class labels are unknown.

Outlier analysis discovers outliers or noise from the database.

Evolution analysis models evolutionary trends in data.

Deviation analysis considers differences between measured values and expected values, and finds the cause of the deviations from the anticipated values.

Knowledge discovery process includes: defining business objectives, preparing data, performing data mining, evaluating results, presenting discoveries and incorporating the usage of discoveries.

From the architectural perspective, there are three different ways in which data mining uses a relational DBMS—they may not use it at all, be loosely coupled, or tightly coupled.

Association discovery algorithms find combinations where the presence of one item suggests the presence of another. Association rules represent affinities among products that are likely to be purchased together. The two parts—support factor and confidence factor—indicate the strength of an association.

Decision trees are based on supervised classification problem where we have a training dataset of records whose class labels are known. Using the training set, the classification process attempts to generate the description of classes, and these descriptions help to classify the unknown records.

The main operations during building a tree are: evaluation of splits for each attribute and the selection of the best split, determination of the splitting condition on the selected splitting attribute, and partitioning the data using the best split.

Tree pruning is a step in building a decision tree. There are two common approaches to it. In the pre-pruning approach, a tree is pruned by halting its construction early. The second approach, post-pruning, removes branches from a fully grown tree.

Clustering is done in such a way that examples that belong to the same group are similar to each other and examples that belong to one cluster are different from that of other clusters.

Partition clustering techniques partition the database into a predefined number (k) of clusters. They are of two types: k-means algorithms, where each cluster is represented by the centre of gravity of the cluster and k-medoid algorithm, where each cluster is represented by one of the objects of the cluster located near the centre.

The hierarchical techniques are of two types: agglomerative hierarchical clustering and divisive hierarchical clustering. Agglomerative hierarchical clustering starts by placing each object in its own cluster and then merges these atomic clusters into larger clusters.

Divisive hierarchical clustering starts with all objects in one cluster and then sub-divides the cluster into smaller pieces.

In case-based reasoning, given a new problem, the technique considers past situations where similar tasks were accomplihsed successfully.

Genetic algorithms are a particular class of evolutionary algorithms that use techniques inspired by evolutionary biology, such as inheritance, mutation, selection, and crossover.

Neural networks learn from experience and are useful in detecting unknown relationships between a set of input data and an outcome. The process of training a network involves modifying the weight of connections from the inputs to the output.

Neural networks use a mathematical model for adjusting the weights which is called a learning rule.

Objective Questions

1. Multiple choice questions

(i) Which database stores geographical information?

    (a) Temporal database

    (b) Spatial database

    (c) Time series database

    (d) Transaction database

    (e) All of these

    (f) None of these

(ii) Which database stores stock market data?

    (a) Temporal database

    (b) Spatial database

    (c) Time series database

    (d) Transaction database

    (e) All of these

    (f) None of these

(iii) Which technique makes clusters by following a bottom-up strategy?

    (a) Agglomerative hierarchical clustering

    (b) Divisive hierarchical clustering

2. Fill in the blanks

(i) Data mining involves the extraction of _____ from large databases.

(ii) _____ discovers association rules from the data.

(iii) _____ is often known as unsupervised classification.

(iv) _____ are data elements that cannot be grouped in any class or cluster.

(v) A transaction database is a set of records representing transactions, each with a _____, _____, and _____.

(vi) Rules with a higher support and confidence factors are considered to be more _____.

(vii) Decision trees are more concerned with _____ classification.

(viii) _____ process is applied to remove some of the lower branches and improve performance of a decision tree.

(ix) For hierarchical clustering algorithms, the termination conditions can be _____ or _____.

(x) _____ is an artificial point in the space of records which represents an average location of the particular cluster.

3. Match the following

1. Data characterization	(a) Data selection, cleaning, and pre-processing; application of data mining algorithm; and interpretation of results
2. Association analysis	(b) Market basket analysis
3. Classification analysis	(c) Uses given class labels to classify other objects in the data whose class labels are not known
4. KDD process	(d) Summarization of general features of objects in a target class

4. State true or false

(i) Data mining needs substantial computing power.

(ii) Data characterization generates rules that are basically the comparison of the general features of objects between two classes.

(iii) Clustering approaches works on the principle of maximizing the inter-cluster similarity.

(iv) Flat files contain text as well as binary data.

(v) Data mining supports model-driven analysis.

(vi) The loosely-coupled approach makes no use of the querying capability provided by the DBMS.

(vii) In unsupervised learning, there is a training set or prior knowledge of the classes.

(viii) Pre-pruning removes branches from a fully grown tree.

(ix) In neural networks, every single neuron can be thought of as a separate processor.

Review Questions

1. Define data mining.

2. Give reasons in favour of why you think data mining is used in today's companies.

3. Why is data mining also known as knowledge discovery?

4. Write a short note on the functionalities of data mining.

5. Describe the characteristics of each type of database that data mining tool can mine.

6. Give a note on the architecture of a data mining system.

7. Explain the steps involved in the KDD process. How is data mining different from KDD?

8. Differentiate between OLAP and data mining. Which tool will you prefer for your company's data warehouse?

9. Compare a DBMS with data mining.

10. Data mining is a multi-disciplinary technique, as it uses knowledge from different subjects. Justify.

11. Data warehouse is a prerequisite for data mining. Justify the statement.

12. Explain the underlying principle of case-based reasoning.

13. What is the significance of market basket analysis? How is it done using data mining?

14. A large retail chain has already deployed a data warehouse. As a data mining consult-

ant of the retail company, you are supposed to find the existing customers who are most likely to respond to a marketing campaign offering new products. Outline the knowledge discovery process, list the phases, and indicate the activities in each phase.

15. Explain the working of decision tree algorithm with the help of an example. Write down the advantages and limitations of this technique.

16. Briefly explain the decision tree construction principle. What is the significance of pruning a decision tree and what approaches are used to accomplish it?

17. Explain clustering analysis in detail. Write some of the applications that clustering finds in the real world.

18. Explain the steps involved in genetic algorithms.

19. Write the genetic algorithm pseudo-code and note some of its shortcomings.

20. Explain the working of neural networks.

21. Give the underlying principle of neural networks. State its advantages and shortcomings. What are the applications of this technique in today's scenario?

22. Why is outlier analysis significant in different industries today? Explain using relevant examples.

13

MOVING INTO
DATA MINING

Learning Objectives

In this chapter, we will see how data mining is widely applied in different applications. We will also introduce terms like spatial mining, text mining, sequence mining, and Web mining.

Case Study

When the data warehouse users of JRTs came to know about data mining, they were very excited about it and decided to have the data mining tool implemented in their warehouse as well. So, they asked David to go about doing this job.

David asked the users why they wanted a data mining tool, but the users could not explain much except that they required a tool to aid them in their business processes. David got confused as which tool to buy, as there are so many specific data mining tools for a particular set of functions. Finally, he decided to buy a tool that provided maximum functions.

This tool helped the users for targeted marketing, customer retention, and demand prediction. It also helped the users to search for a product not only using its product identification number but also by its picture.

If the users entered the image of a red coloured T-shirt of John Players brand, then all the details related to that product were displayed.

The users were very happy with David and due to high satisfaction level of the client, he was given a tremendous hike in his salary.

Before switching to data mining, it is very crucial to know the benefits and applications of data mining, various tools available in the market, and the type of knowledge that they mine.

13.1 INTRODUCTION

Before moving into data mining, we need to ensure that the data warehouse will feed the data mining processes. Irrespective of the data mining technology that will be deployed in the company, the source of data will be the data warehouse. A sound and solid data warehouse will put the data mining operation on a strong foundation.

Data mining techniques produce good results when large volumes of data are available. All the data mining algorithms need data at the lowest level of granularity, so in order to apply data mining algorithms, you must ensure that the data warehouse contains detailed data.

Data mining is all about discovering patterns and relationships from the data. Mining dirty data leads to inaccurate discoveries which can lead to seriously wrong consequences. So, we cannot launch into data mining if the data is not clean enough. Therefore, we must also ensure that the data warehouse contains high-quality data.

After applying the data mining algorithm to discover patterns and relationships from the data, the organization must apply the results and perform suitable actions. Before embarking on a data mining project, you must be clear about the types of problems to solve as well as the types of benefits you expect to obtain. After listing the objectives, you need a way of comparing the data mining algorithms and selecting the most appropriate tool for the specific set of requirements.

When looking for a data mining tool, a tool that supports more than one technique is always preferred. The organization may not presently need a composite tool with many techniques, but a multi-tasking tool opens up more opportunities. Moreover, many data mining users also expect to cross-validate discovered patterns using several techniques. The most available techniques supported by vendor tools in the market today include: (a) cluster detection, (b) decision trees, and (c) link analysis.

Before we get into the details of the criteria for selecting a data mining tool, let us consider the following important observations.

- The tool must enable *integration* with the data warehouse environment by fetching data from the warehouse and being compatible with the underlying metadata architecture.
- The tool must *discover accurate patterns* and relationships. Any erratic patterns discovered will prove to be more dangerous than not discovering the patterns at all.
- At times when the explanation for the working of the model is needed and it is required to know how the results were produced, the tool must be able to *explain the rules* using which the results were discovered.

Paulraj Ponniah in his book *Data Warehousing Fundamentals* (2001) has given a list of criteria for evaluating the data mining tools, as shown in Fig. 13.1.

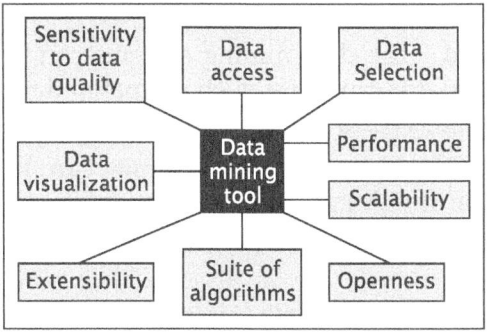

Figure 13.1 Criteria for evaluating data mining tools

Data access The data mining tool must be able to access the data warehouse and bring over the required datasets to its environment.

Data selection While selecting and extracting data from the data warehouse for mining, the tool must be able to perform its operations according to the specified criteria. It must filter out unwanted data and derive new data items from existing ones.

Sensitivity to data quality The data mining tool must be sensitive to the quality of the data it mines. The tools must be able to generate error reports; recognize missing, incomplete, or erroneous data, and compensate for the problem, if possible.

Data visualization Data mining techniques process large volumes of data and produce a wide range of results. Any inability to display results graphically will diminish the value of the tool, so select the tools with good data visualization capabilities.

Extensibility The architecture of the tool must be able to integrate with functions, such as data warehouse administration, data extraction, and metadata management.

Performance The data mining tool must provide consistent performance irrespective of the amount of data to be mined, the algorithm applied, the number of variables, and the level of accuracy.

Scalability The data mining tool must be able to work on massive amounts of data to discover patterns and relationships from them. Therefore, select a tool that scales up easily to handle huge amount of data.

Openness It refers to being able to integrate with the environment and other types of tools to connect to external applications so that the users can access the data mining algorithms from other applications as well. Moreover, the tool must provide sharing of the output with desktop tools, such as graphical charts, spreadsheets, and database utilities.

Suite of algorithms A tool must provide support for different algorithms rather than supporting just one data mining algorithm.

13.2 HOW DO WE CATEGORIZE DATA MINING SYSTEMS?

There are many data mining systems available in the market. Some of these systems are specialized systems that are dedicated to a particular data source or are capable of only limited data mining functionalities, while other systems are more versatile and comprehensive.

Data mining systems can be categorized on the following bases:

According to the type of data source mined The data mining systems can be categorized according to the type of data that it can mine, such as spatial data, multimedia data, time-series data, text data, World Wide Web, etc.

According to the data model drawn The data mining systems can be categorized according to the type of data model involved, such as relational database, object-oriented database, data warehouse, transactional, time-series database, temporal database, etc.

According to the kind of knowledge discovered The data mining systems can be categorized according to the type of knowledge discovered or the data mining functionalities that it is capable to perform, such as characterization, discrimination, association, classification, clustering, etc. Some data mining systems tend to be comprehensive and versatile, as they offer several data mining functionalities together.

According to mining techniques used Data mining systems employ different techniques. The data mining systems can therefore be categorized according to the data analysis approach used, such as machine learning, neural networks, genetic algorithms, statistics, visualization, database-oriented or data warehouse-oriented, etc.

The classification of such systems can also consider the degree of user interaction involved in the data mining process. It includes query-driven systems, interactive exploratory systems, or autonomous systems. A comprehensive data mining system provides a wide range of techniques and offers different degrees of user interaction.

According to the applications Data mining systems can also be classified according to the applications in which they are used. A generic all-purpose data mining system will never fit domain-specific mining tasks, however, data mining systems can be tailored specifically for finance, telecommunications, DNA, stock markets, e-mail, and so on.

13.3 INTERESTING AND USEFUL DATA

The knowledge discovered by applying a data mining technique is very subjective. It is not uncommon for a data mining algorithm to generate or discover a very large number of patterns or rules. In some cases, the number of rules can be in millions. Due to this problem, users often go for a meta-mining phase to mine the oversized data mining results.

In order to cut down the number of patterns or rules discovered that have a high probability of being uninteresting to the users, a measurement on the patterns must be put. Obviously, every user would like to discover all rules or patterns, but only those that are interesting. This measurement, which shows how interesting a discovered pattern is, is often known as *interestingness*. The measure of interestingness of a discovered pattern or rule is based on elements, such as validity of the patterns when tested on new data with some degree of certainty, on the understandability of the patterns, novelty of the patterns, or its usefulness.

However, the discovered patterns are also said to be interesting if they validate a hypothesis sought to be confirmed or unexpectedly contradict a common belief. This issue calls for a meta-rule guided discovery that describes forms of rules before the discovery process.

Generally, the measurements for interestingness are based on thresholds set by the user. Calculating the interestingness of discovered patterns and rules is critical for the success of the mined knowledge and the KDD process as a whole. While there exist some concrete measurements, assessing the interestingness of discovered knowledge is still an important research issue.

13.4 APPLICATIONS OF DATA MINING

There is a wide variety of applications that benefit from data mining, as the technology encompasses a rich collection of techniques that cover a wide range of commercial and non-commercial applications.

Non-commercial use of data mining is more pervasive in the research area. For example, in oil exploration and research, data mining techniques are applied to discover locations that can be suitable for drilling. These locations are identified based on the availability of potential mineral and oil deposits. Similarly, pattern discovery and matching techniques are applied for military operations to assist in identifying the targets.

Medical research is a field where data mining helps the researchers to find correlations between diseases and patient's symptoms. Crime investigation agencies use data mining to connect criminal profiles to crimes. It is also applied in astronomy and cosmology to predict cosmic events.

Apart from this, data mining technology has widespread applications in the commercial arena. Given below is a list of applications of data mining in the business area.

Customer segmentation It is the most widely used application. Businesses use data mining to understand their customers. They form clusters of customers which help in sharing the same information.

Market basket analysis It is widely used in retail stores. Association analysis algorithms uncover affinities between products that are bought together. Data mining also helps business to find customers to whom they can sell higher value items during an auction and notify them of an upcoming auction.

Risk management Data mining techniques are applied in insurance companies and mortgage businesses to uncover the risks associated with potential customers.

Fraud detection Data mining is widely applied by the credit card companies to discover abnormal spending patterns of customers, as these patterns can expose fraudulent use of the cards.

Delinquency tracking Similar to the credit card companies, loan companies also use data mining technology to track customers who are likely to default on repayments.

Demand prediction Data mining is used by retail companies and other businesses to match demand and supply trends to forecast demand for specific products.

13.4.1 Benefits of Data Mining

In the absence of data mining, useful knowledge lying buried under the mountains of data that exist in organizations would have never been discovered, and the benefits of using the discovered patterns and relationships would have never been realized. In order to appreciate the enormous utility of data mining, let us enumerate the types of benefits of data mining that are actually realizable in real-world situations.

- In a manufacturing company, some of the employees of a department can be corrupted and thus, there may be a variation between the purchase orders and the freight bills. Data mining detects such criminal behaviour by uncovering patterns of orders and premature inventory reductions.
- A company can improve the sales of a product by sending direct promotional discounts to its customers through a targeted campaign.
- A retail chain can improve its daily sales by rearranging the shelves based on the discoveries of affinities of products that sell together.
- An airlines company can increase sales by discovering travelling patterns of frequent flyers.
- An insurance company can save large amounts of money by detecting fraudulent claims.
- A manufacturer company can increase sales by forecasting sales of their products based on patterns discovered from the historical data stored in the data warehouse.
- A banking corporation with investment and financial services can prevent losses by detecting early warning signs for attrition in its checking account business.

13.4.2 Data Mining in Retail Industry

Fierce competition and narrow profits have plagued the retail industry. These factors have forced the retail industry to be the one among the first few industries to adopt data warehousing. Over the years, data warehouses have been storing large amounts of data and the data warehouses in the retail industry today are quite mature and ripe. The data warehouse in the retail industry captures detailed point of sale data and includes huge amounts of data on customer shopping history, goods transportation, consumption, and service records.

The quantity of data collected continues to expand rapidly, especially due to increasing ease, availability, and popularity of business conducted on the web. Thus, there is a huge amount of data in the data warehouse and that too at the lowest level of granularity. Such an environment has provided an ideal environment for the application of data mining technology.

All types of businesses in the retail industry including grocery chains and consumer retail stores use data mining, generally for direct marketing and promotion of their products. As we have studied, customer detection and other predictive data mining techniques provide customer segmentation. The retail industry use the knowledge gained by forming clusters of customers, to know better, which products to be promoted within which group of customers.

Retailers also use association analysis algorithms to discover affinities between the products which sell together and to plan their special sale items and also the arrangement of products on the shelves.

Retail data mining also helps to improve the quality of customer service, achieve better customer retention and satisfaction, enhance goods consumption ratios, design effective goods transportation and distribution policies, and reduce the cost of businesses.

Another area of use for data mining in the retail industry relates to sales forecasting. Retail sales depend heavily on the strong seasonal fluctuations, holidays, and weekends. Therefore sales forecasting is a necessity in the retail industry. Predictive data mining is used by the retailers to predict the sales. The applications of data mining algorithms in the retail industry can be shortlisted as below.

- Customer spending patterns.
- Customer purchasing patterns.
- Best promotions.
- Arrangement of products in the store. (market basket analysis)
- Arrangement of promotional displays.
- Planning mailers with coupons.
- Seasonal and regular trends in the sale of products.
- Most profitable customers.
- Multidimensional analysis of customer needs, products, quality, cost, profit, etc.

Apart from this, retail data mining is also used for analysis of effectiveness of sales campaigns. In the retail industry, sales campaigns using advertisements, coupons, and different types of discounts are conducted from time to time to promote products and attract customers. Therefore, a careful analysis of sales campaigns, if done, can help to improve profits on a much larger scale.

13.4.3 Data Mining in Telecommunication Industry

The telecommunication industry has grown tremendously by evolving from offering just local and long-distance telephone services to providing even more comprehensive communication services that comprise of voice, fax, pager, cellular phone, images, e-mail, and the Internet. The industry is rapidly expanding and becoming highly competitive. This calls for the application of data mining to help the company to understand the business involved, identify telecommunication patterns, catch fraudulent activities, make better use of resources, and improve the quality of service.

Customer retention and customer acquisition have become a matter of prime concern for the telecommunication industry. Telecommunication companies compete with one another to attract the customers by offering the best of their services. Fierce competition has driven telecommunication companies to data mining.

In today's competitive market, customers switch to other networks at the slightest problem. Customer retention under such circumstances becomes very crucial and rather difficult. Thus, all the leading companies are already using the data mining technology and reaping its benefits. Given below is a list of data mining applications in the telecommunication industry.

- Retention of customers under the prevailing competitive market.
- Identifying profitable service packages.
- Identification of customers who are most likely to churn.
- Prediction of cellular fraud.
- Factors that enhance the customer's propensity to use the phone.
- Product evaluation compared to the product of the competitors.
- Multidimensional analysis of data, such as calling time, duration of each call, location of the caller, and the type of call, is used to identify and compare the data traffic, system workload, resource usage, user group behaviour, etc.
- Fraudulent activity costs the telecommunication industry a huge amount of money every year. This creates a demand for the application of data mining to identify the fraudulent users and their typical usage patterns, detect attempts to gain fraudulent entry to customer accounts, and discover unusual patterns that may call for special attention.
- The discovery of association and sequential patterns in multidimensional analysis can help the telecommunication industry to promote its services. For example, if you know that a particular group of users makes a lot of long distance calls, then you can promote the sales of specific long-distance and cellular phone combinations and improve the availability of particular services for that customer group.

13.4.4 Data Mining in Banking and Finance

Finance is an area of regular fluctuation and uncertainty. The banking and finance industry generates large volumes of detailed transaction data at the lowest level of detail by capturing every transaction that a customer makes. Therefore, the banking industry provides a fertile ground for the application of data mining algorithms.

The different data mining applications in the banking sector can be listed as follows: (a) fraud detection, (b) delinquency tracking, (c) risk assessment of potential customers, (d) trend analysis, and (e) direct marketing.

In the financial area, requirements for forecasting dominate the industry. For example, forecasting of stock prices with a high level of approximation can bring large profits to the company. Then, it would be far better if the potential financial disaster can be forecasted well in advance. For this purpose, neural network algorithms are widely applied for forecasting, bond trading, portfolio management, and mergers and acquisitions of other companies in the same sector.

Multidimensional data analysis methods are used to analyse the general properties of the financial data, as the manager may like to view the debt and revenue changes by month, region, sector, etc.

Loan payment prediction and customer credit analysis are critical to the business of a bank. Many factors such as loan-to-value ratio, payment-to-income ratio, customer income level, education level, residence region, and credit history can strongly influence loan payment performance and customer credit rating.

Analysis of the customer payment history may reveal the fact that the payment-to-income ratio is an important factor, while education level is not. After going through this fact, the bank may decide to adjust its loan granting policy so that loans can be granted to those whose application was previously denied but whose profile shows relatively low risks.

Classification and clustering methods can be used to identify customer group for *targeted marketing*. For example, customers with similar behaviours regarding banking and loan payments may be grouped together by clustering techniques. When a new customer comes, he can easily be identified and placed in the group which closely represents his profile.

Finally, data mining is also used to detect money laundering and other financial crimes by integrating information from multiple sources like bank transaction database and state crime history databases. Multiple data analysis tools can then be used to detect unusual patterns like large amounts of cash flow at certain periods. Outlier tools can be used to detect unusual amounts of fund transfers or other activities. Similarly, sequential pattern analysis can be used to detect unusual access sequences. These tools are used to identify important relationships and patterns of activities which will in turn help the investigators to focus on suspicious cases for detailed examination.

13.4.5 Data Mining in Biomedical Field

The last few years have seen an explosive growth in biomedical research. The success of this field ranges from the development of new medicines and advancements in cancer therapies to the identification and analysis of the human genome by discovering large-scale sequencing patterns and gene functions. A great deal of biomedical research focuses on DNA analysis which has led to the discovery of genetic causes for many diseases as well as the discovery of new medicines and approaches for disease diagnosis, prevention, and treatment. Data mining has emerged as a powerful tool by substantially contributing to DNA analysis.

The most crucial task in genetic analysis is the similarity search and comparison among DNA sequences. To accomplish this task, gene sequences extracted from diseased and healthy tissues are compared with each other to identify critical differences that exist between the two classes of genes. To compare these two classes of genes, we actually find and compare the frequently occurring patterns of each class. The sequences which occur more frequently in the diseased samples as and when compared with that of the healthy samples indicate the genetic factors of the disease. On the contrary, the sequences occurring more frequently in the healthy samples indicate mechanisms that protect the body from the disease.

Many practitioners have proved that most diseases are not triggered by a single gene but by a combination of genes acting together. Association analysis methods are thus used to determine the kinds of genes that are likely to occur in target samples. Such analysis facilitates the discovery of groups of genes and helps in the study of interactions and relationships that exist between them.

As stated above, a group of genes are responsible for a particular disease, but then, it is not wrong to say that different genes may become active at different stages of the disease. If the sequence of genetic activities can be identified at different stages of a disease, then pharmaceutical research can be targeted to every stage separately, thereby achieving more effective treatment of the disease.

Complex structures and sequencing patterns of genes are presented in the form of graphs, trees, etc. Such visualization tools facilitate pattern understanding, knowledge discovery, and interactive data exploration.

13.4.6 Customer Retention

Customer retention is a critical issue for any business because acquiring a new customer is far more expensive than keeping an existing one. This fact is more applicable if the operating market is getting saturated, as in telecommunication industry. Customer retention is important to almost every company in the competitive market because the cost of acquiring new customers is much greater than the cost of keeping good relationship with current customers.

The most important task in customer retention is to understand the existing customers of the business. This includes getting a clear understanding of the expectations of the customers; their satisfaction; and their demographic, geographic, and psychographic tendencies, etc. When a business understands more about customers and knows more about the customers who are diverting themselves to its competitors, more effective retention strategies can be developed.

The most important customer retention strategy is to identify customers who are likely to leave the organization and move towards its competitors. This is done by performing retention or defection rate analysis. Once such customers are identified, preventive measures can be followed to prevent defections. In order to identify the defection risk, the following data mining techniques can be used:

Defector profiling Profiles of risky customer groups are developed based on their demographic, geographic, and psychographic attributes.

Defection scoring Build neural network predictive model that is capable enough to predict likelihood of defection.

Customer segmentation Perform customer segmentation to group the customers based on similarity in terms of demographic, geographic, and psychographic attributes.

13.4.7 Targeted Marketing

Today, every company invests huge sums of money to execute multiple marketing campaigns each year, thereby offering dozens of products to millions of customers and prospects to support customer acquisition, cross-sell, and retention objectives. Every product manager claims that his promotional campaigns will bring in incremental profit. But for this purpose, these managers need large budgets and unlimited access to customer databases.

Therefore, selecting the appropriate campaign in which the business should invest in, and determining the budget that is needed to acquire new customers versus retaining existing customers are important areas that need to apply data mining. Data mining also helps to determine which customer should get which offers through which communication channel in order to achieve the maximum return on customer acquisition, cross-sell, and retention campaigns.

Data mining considers the interdependencies of financial goals, business constraints, and customer's needs to deliver the offer that is best for the business as well as for the satisfaction of the customers. In order to predict the purchasing behaviours of customers, data mining applications are applied to automate the process of searching the mountains of data. This study would in turn help to offer appropriate promotional campaigns to every individual customer that would result in increasing response rates and campaign effectiveness.

13.4.8 Customer Relationship Management

Several authors have defined customer relationship management (CRM) as a process that manages the interactions between a company and its customers. The database vendors whose main concern lies in automating the process of interacting with customers forms the primary users of the CRM application.

To be successful, database vendors first identify market segments containing customers with high-profit potential and then, formulate and execute campaigns that favourably impact the behaviour of these individuals.

The first task of identifying customers requires significant data about customers and their buying behaviours. Obviously, more the data, the better it is. Data mining can help in this context to find the nuggets of valuable information.

13.4.9 Other Application Areas of Data Mining

Data mining is a technology driven by new applications that require new capabilities which are not currently being supported by today's technology. These new applications are discussed below.

Business and E-commerce Data

This includes a major source of data for data mining applications. Every business has a number of back offices, front-offices, and network applications that produce large amounts of data about the business processes. Data mining technologies have laid the ground for utilizing this enormous amount of data for effective decision-making.

Businesses today interact with millions of customers and thus make billions of transactions. Therefore, to remain competitive businesses require necessary information for their effective functioning. For example, businesses today are keen to know what product the customers are most likely to buy, which customer is likely to switch over to its competitor, etc.

Scientific and Engineering Data

Scientific data which includes genomic data, sensor data, and simulation data is much more complex in structure than business data. Genomic sequencing and mapping, remote satellites, and a variety of other sensors produce large amounts of data.

A fundamental challenge is to understand the relationships among this data. Also, simulation is now accepted as an important mode of science, supplementing theory, and experiment. Today, not only experiments produce large datasets, but so do simulations. Data mining is proving to be a critical link among theory, simulation, and experiment.

Web Data, Multimedia, and Text Documents

The data on the World Wide Web is growing, both in volume and in complexity. Web data includes text, multimedia, and numerical data. Today's technology for retrieving multimedia data from Web is not much satisfactory. Besides, a large number of textual data and other documents as well as the number of users are growing explosively. Hence, it is becoming even more difficult to extract meaningful information from the data archives as the volume grows.

Crime Detection

Let us take an example of bogus official burglaries. In order to apply data mining techniques, let us assume that each case is electronically filed and every case that is stored contains descriptive information about the thieves and their modus operandi.

Once we have this information in hand, any of the clustering techniques can be used to examine a situation where a group of similar physical descriptions coincide with a group of similar modus operandi. If a match is found and the perpetrators are known for the offences, then it simply implies that each of the unsolved cases have been committed by the same people. Alternatively, if the criminal is unknown but a large cluster of cases points to the same offenders, then a strict eye can be kept on these offenders.

Miscellaneous Data

Portfolio management In this field, data mining is used to predict the return on investment, given a particular financial asset, to determine whether to include the asset in a folio or not.

Brand loyalty Data mining is also used to calculate the brand loyalty of a customer. Determining this factor includes prediction of whether a particular customer will switch the brand of the product that he generally uses.

13.4.10 Merits and Demerits of Data Mining

Although data mining facilitates a lot of business operations, it has its flip side as well. Table 13.1 lists the merits and demerits of data mining.

Table 13.1 Merits and demerits of data mining

Merits	Demerits
• Data mining is an automated technique in which the computer does all the work and the user just sits back. The user needs to launch the data mining tool to see what it has found.	• An unguided search through extremely large volumes of data can keep the most powerful computers busy for a long time.
• Data mining is completely independent of the user's preconceived notions of what relationships are likely to exist in the data. This feature enables the tool to find unexpected relationships from the data, some of which could be of great value to the business.	• Although valuable relationships may be found, but a lot more irrelevant relationships also pop up as a result of applying a data mining algorithm. Thus, searching gigabytes and terabytes of data for discovering patterns is one trivial task and then separating the relevant patterns from the irrelevant ones forms another set of difficult tasks.

13.5 WEB MINING

In recent years, we have witnessed an ever-increasing flood of information in the form of digital libraries through the medium of World Wide Web.

Although the Web is rich with information, but gathering useful data is difficult because publication on the Web is largely unorganized. A large number of websites, their dynamism, heterogeneity, high linkage, and diversity turned the World Wide Web into an entanglement that is hard to specify. After having a basic knowledge of different data mining techniques, let us now see whether we can apply data mining to extract implicit, previously unknown information from the massive collection of documents available on the Web. But before starting with Web mining, let us first discuss the reasons for which we use the Web.

Finding relevant information We use the search engines to find specific information on the Web. We specify simple keyword(s) and in response, get a list of pages which are ranked based on their similarity with the given keyword(s). However, finding the relevant information is a big problem even with search engines because it may return some low precision pages, that is, the pages that are not relevant to our query. Secondly, due to the inability to index all the available pages on the Web, we may miss some of the more useful pages.

Discovering new knowledge When we have already collected data from the Web, we may want to extract potentially useful knowledge out of it.

Customizing web pages We may want to customize a web page differently for individual users. Every person who seeks information from the Web has his own preferences regarding the style of the contents and presentations. The information providers like to respond to user queries by aggregating information from several sources in a user-dependent manner.

Learn about individual users Finally, the Web can also be used by organizations to learn more about their customers. They may want to know about what the customers like and what they dislike, the pages that attract them to go further into the website, similarly those web pages which are session killers, those which result in fetching orders from the customers, and so on.

Thus, the Web has to be restructured to cater to the user's needs and expectations for improving Web information searches and navigation. For this purpose, Web analysis tools are widely used. Web mining, which is broadly defined as the automatic discovery and analysis of useful information from the Web, has become the buzzword today.

Web mining is the application of data mining techniques to discover patterns from the Web. It provides a set of techniques that provide a solution to the above problems. Web mining, when talked in terms of data mining, performs three basic operations:

- Clustering that finds a natural grouping of users, pages, etc.
- Association analysis to find URLs that tend to be requested together.
- Predictive analysis for listing the URLs that tend to be accessed.

Web mining can be categorized into three main areas: (a) Web content mining, (b) Web structure mining, and (c) Web usage mining.

13.5.1 Web Content Mining

Web content mining implies the automatic search of information available online and involves mining Web data content. The emphasis here is on the content of the web page.

The Web document usually contains several data types, such as text, image, audio, video, metadata, and hyperlinks where some of this data are semi-structured like HTML documents or structured like the data in the tables or database generated HTML pages. However, most of the data on the Web is unstructured text data. The unstructured characteristic of the Web data forces the Web content mining towards a more complicated approach.

Web content mining widely applies the techniques from other subjects like machine learning, statistical pattern recognition, and data mining for analysing hypertext. Multimedia data mining is a subset of Web content mining that involves mining the high-level information and knowledge from large online multimedia sources. Multimedia data mining on the Web has become the most demanding topic of research, as more and more researchers are working towards a unifying framework for representation and problem solving. Although learning from multimedia is a big challenge, this concept is still under research.

13.5.2 Web Structure Mining

The emphasis of Web structure mining is to generate a structural summary about the website and the web page. Web content mining mainly focuses on the structure of the inner-document, while Web structure mining tries to discover the link structure of the hyperlinks at the inter-document level. Based on the topology of the hyperlinks, Web structure mining categorizes the web pages and generates information about the similarity and relationship between different websites.

Web structure mining also involves discovering the structure of the web document itself and can be used to reveal the structure (schema) of web pages. Web structure mining is useful for navigation purposes and makes it possible to compare/integrate web page schemes. It also facilitates the use of database techniques for accessing information in web pages by providing a reference schema.

Web structure mining reveals structural information that includes the information measuring the following:

- Frequency of the local links in the web tuples in a web table.
- Frequency of web tuples in a web table containing links that are within the same document.
- Frequency of web tuples in a web table that contains links that are global and the links that span different websites.
- Frequency of identical web tuples that appear in the web table or among the web tables.

If a web page is linked to another web page directly, or if certain web pages are considered to be the neighbours of that page, web structure mining will discover the relationships among those web pages. This relationship may exist because of the presence of synonyms, having similar contents both the pages residing on the same web server.

Web structure mining also discovers the nature of the hierarchy or network of hyperlinks in the websites of a particular domain, thereby allowing query processing to be easier and more efficient.

13.5.3 Web Usage Mining

Web usage mining is a relatively new research area, and is gaining more and more attention in recent years. When users visit a website, the only information left behind by them is the path of the web pages that they have accessed. Web usage mining applies data mining techniques to discover user navigation patterns and tries to discover the useful information from the secondary data (the data taken from the web server access logs, proxy server logs, browser logs, user profiles, registration data, user sessions or transactions, cookies, user queries, bookmark data, mouse clicks and scrolls) derived from the user interactions while surfing on the Web.

Web mining lays emphasis on the techniques that could predict the behaviour of every individual user who interacts with the Web, could make a comparison between expected and actual website usage, and make adjustments in the website to the interests of its users. Analysing such data can help the organizations to value its customers by knowing more about them, using accurate cross-marketing strategies across products, and offering them effective promotional campaigns, etc.

Prior web analysis tools simply provided mechanisms to report user activity as recorded in the servers which was later on used to derieve information, such as the number of accesses to the server, the times or time intervals of visits as well as the domain names and the URLs of users of the web server. However, these tools provide little or no support to analyse relationships among the accessed files and directories within the web space. But these days, more sophisticated techniques for discovery and analysis of patterns are emerging. These tools fall into two main categories: *pattern discovery tools* and *pattern analysis tools*.

Generally, the web content and website topology will be used as the information sources for preparing data for web usage mining. But even for effective web usage mining, data cleaning, and data transformation steps are performed before analysis.

The techniques for web usage mining are classified into two approaches. The first approach maps the usage data of the web server into tables before data mining is performed. Data mining techniques such as clustering and classification could then be used to mine the usage data provided this data has been pre-processed. The second approach makes use of the log data directly by utilizing special pre-processing techniques. Web usage mining process involves the following steps: (a) identifying the problem, (b) collecting data, (c) pre-processing of data, and (d) application of pattern discovery and analysis techniques.

13.6 TEXT MINING

Text mining, also known as *text data mining*, refers to the process of deriving high quality information from text. It involves structuring the input text, deriving patterns within the structured data, and finally evaluating and interpretating the output.

Whereas text mining is a new interdisciplinary field, data mining, on the other hand, is a relatively mature technology that is typically applied to the analysis of data stored in structured databases. Text mining applies knowledge discovery and trend analysis to unstructured textual data that data mining applies to structured data. Text mining applies knowledge from various fields such as information extraction, information retrieval, text categorization, probabilistic modelling, linear algebra, machine learning, and computational linguistics to discover structure, patterns, and knowledge.

13.6.1 Applications of Text Mining

Now a days, text mining is widely being applied in many areas, including security, commercial, and academic fields.

Security applications Text mining is widely applied in the classified ECHELON surveillance system.

Software applications Many companies including IBM and Microsoft, are conducting research on text mining techniques and are developing programs to further automate the mining and analysis processes.

Academic applications The text mining technique is of great importance to publishers who hold large databases of information requiring indexing for retrieval. Academic institutions have also taken an initiative to use tools to carry out research with an initial focus on text mining in the biological and biomedical sciences. In the United States of America, the School of Information at the University of California is developing a program called BioText that will assist the bioscience researchers in mining and analysis of textual data.

13.6.2 Implications of Text Mining

Until recently, text-based lexical searches were used to search websites but now, text mining will enable searches which can be directly answered by the semantic web and will also provide support for fighting e-mail spam.

Text mining is different from the web search that we generally make. When the users perform a web search, he actually looks for information which is already known and has been written by someone else. The critical task in this context is to push aside all the material that is not relevant to the user's needs in order to find the relevant information. However, text mining is used to discover unknown information, something that no one yet knows and so could not have yet written down.

The underlying difference between regular data mining and text mining is that in text mining, interesting patterns and knowledge is discovered from natural language text rather than from structured databases of facts. A major problem with text mining is that it is difficult to recognize which of the many relations that are shown are truly interesting.

13.7 TEMPORAL DATA MINING

By considering the time aspect of data in mining techniques, we gain useful insights into the temporal arrangement of events that helps us to understand the concept of cause and effect. Many practitioners and authors have defined temporal data mining as the non-trivial extraction of implicit, potentially useful, and previously unrecorded information with an implicit or explicit temporal content, from large quantities of data. It is considered to be an important extension of data mining.

Temporal data mining succeeds over traditional data mining techniques, as it has the capability to infer casual and temporal relationships, and this is something that non-temporal data mining cannot do. However, data mining from temporal data is not temporal data mining, if the temporal component is either ignored or treated as a simple numerical attribute. Moreover, traditional data mining techniques cannot be applied to mine temporal rules from a database which does not have temporal components stored in it. Thus, the underlying database must be a temporal one.

Let us consider an association rule that states: "Any person who buys a computer also buys a printer." When the temporal aspect is brought into consideration, this rule would be: "Any person who buys a computer also buys a printer after that."

Let us take another example of a temporal rule: "Flooding in the west Indian coast occurs only during the monsoons." The terms during and after are explicitly temporal.

Consider another example: "Data warehousing is being widely used now-a-days." It shows another technique of mining from previously mined rules, to find trends in rule sets.

Consider other examples of temporal knowledge discovery which relates to sequences, such as teaching, internal tests, semester examination, paper correction, grading, result processing which occur every semester. Another example is: "Mr XYZ tends to develop reactions after two weeks with this medicine." Thus, temporal data mining aims at mining new unknown knowledge, which takes into account the temporal aspects of the data.

13.7.1 Types of Temporal Data

Static Static data does not contain any temporal reference. The inferences derived from this data are also free from any temporal aspect.

Sequences In this type of data, although there may be no explicit reference to time, there exists a sort of temporal relationship between data items. The market basket transaction is such an example. The sequence of entry of the transactions implicitly incorporates temporality.

This is to say that if a transaction appears in the database before another transaction, then the former transaction is believed to occur before the other. However, this type of data is often limited to sequence relationships like, before and after, during, overlap, etc. Sequence mining is a major activity performed in temporal data mining.

Time-stamped data This category of data contains explicit temporal information. The relationship between the data elements is quantitative. This means that you cannot only say that one transaction occurred before the other, but also extract temporal distance between them.

Examples of time-stamped data elements include: census data, land-use data, and satellite meteorological data. The inference derived from this data can however be temporal or non-temporal. Another example of time-stamped data is time-series data in which the events are uniformly spaced on the time scale.

Fully-temporal data In this category, the data elements are time-dependent and the inferences taken out from them are also temporal in nature.

13.7.2 Temporal Data Mining Tasks

Temporal association The association rule discovery can be extended to operate on temporal data and can be used to discover associations between temporal as well as non-temporal datasets.

Temporal classification Temporal classification forms cluster of data items along temporal dimensions. For example, clusters of students who attend morning classes and those who prefer studying in evening classes can be formed. Similarly, clusters of students can be formed who opt for higher education.

Temporal characterization For temporal characterization, we extend the concept of decision tree construction based on temporal attributes. For example, a rule could be "The first case of cholera is normally reported after floods that occur during the monsoon rains in the months of July–September."

Trend analysis The analysis of time series data predicts trends in the data. Thus, trend analysis is used to find the relationships of change in one or more static attributes, with respect to changes in the temporal attributes.

Sequence analysis Events that occur at different instants of time may be related to each other by casual relationships. That is to say, an earlier event may appear to cause a later one. In order to discover such relationships, sequences of events may be analysed to discover common patterns. This task discovers frequent events and also predicts certain events that are likely to occur.

13.7.3 Implications of Temporal Data Mining

Many real-world applications deal with huge amounts of temporal data like alarms/events and performance measurements generated by distributed computer systems and by telecommunication networks, the web server logs, online transaction logs, financial data, workflow process logs, and sensor data collected from sensor networks.

Conventionally, temporal data is classified into two groups. One that consists of categorical event streams and another that includes numerical time-series data. Both the types of data have been rigorously studied in data mining. However, several previously less-emphasized aspects of temporal data have proved to be even more important in certain emerging applications, but they still pose several challenges calling for extensive research in the field.

Temporal data mining is being widely used in applications, such as web services, information navigation, system management, adaptive workflow management, program behaviour analysis, security management, and bioinformatics.

It has been found by many practitioners that existing analysis methods are inadequate for their real-world data. To overcome this problem, the practitioners either transform this real-world data so that the existing methods can be applied or reduce the original problems to better studied ones. However, both the methods require more pre-processing effort, more artificial parameters, and less interpretable results. The new aspects of temporal data that deserve theories and algorithms of their own are as follows:

Irregularity Many types of numerical temporal data are not equally paced.

Lack of synchronization In distributed computing environments, data from different sources may not be properly aligned and hence synchronous methods cannot be applied to them. One of the most common examples of such data is the sensor data obtained from networks.

Distributed analysis Temporal data analysis needs to perform data filtering, transformation, and analysis as close as possible to the data sources so that the prohibitive amount of data being transmitted and analysed can be avoided. This requirement calls for a totally new theoretical foundation.

Streaming data Temporal data is stored only temporally and therefore requires near real-time analysis.

Heterogeneous data types These days it is very common to have temporal data partly as categorical events and partly as numerical time series. Thus, it is a big challenge in itself to analyse all possible data in a uniform way.

Huge volume The data stream can be huge for a long, continuous observation period. Apart from this, many types of measurements can be obtained from a large number of data sources. This calls for designing of scalable solutions for analysing a large volume of temporal data, using a large number of data points and a wide variety of measurements.

13.8 SEQUENCE MINING

Sequence mining is applied to find statistically relevant patterns between data examples where the values are delivered in a sequence. These values are often discrete in nature and thus time-series mining is closely related, although it is a different activity altogether. Sequence mining is considered to be a special case of structured data mining.

There are two categories of sequence mining: *string mining* and *itemset mining*. String mining is widely used in biology to examine gene and protein sequences. There are different algorithms to perform alignment of a query sequence with those existing in databases. Itemset mining is widely used in marketing and CRM applications. In addition to this, itemset mining is also a popular approach to text mining. However, this field is not without its limitations. It poses difficulties while:

- Building efficient databases and indexes for sequence information.
- Extracting the frequently occurring patterns.
- Comparing sequences for similarity.
- Recovering missing sequence members.

Mining frequent sequential patterns is widely used in application domains, including market basket data, telecommunication data, and the World Wide Web.

Market basket databases are used to predict future customer behaviour, as each data sequence relates to items bought by an individual customer over time, and frequent patterns can help for such kind of predictions. In telecommunications, frequent sequences of alarm outputs sent by network switches are used to capture relationships between alarm signals so that they can give useful insights for online prediction, analysis, and correction of network faults.

Even in context of the World Wide Web, the server generates huge volumes of daily log data that captures the sequences of page accesses for millions of users. In order to analyse this huge amount of data, sequence mining can be applied.

The most widely used techniques for itemset mining in sequence databases are the influential *apriori algorithm* and the more-recent *FP-Growth* technique. Other fields that apply sequence mining even though there is no explicit temporality in the data are analysing DNA sequence, signal processing, and speech analysis.

13.9 TIME-SERIES ANALYSIS

In statistics and signal processing, the time series data contains a sequence of data points that are collected at successive times and spaced at (often uniform) time intervals. Time-series analysis comprises methods that analyse such time series to understand the underlying theory of the data points (where did they come from? How are they generated?), or to make forecasts or predictions. Time-series analysis is most often used to predict future events based on known past events, that is, to predict future data points before they are measured. The most common example is the opening price of a share of stock based on its past performance.

The result of analysing time-series data is best displayed in a scatter plot where the series value X is plotted on the vertical axis and time t on the horizontal axis. There are two kinds of time-series data:

Continuous time-series data   Here, an observation could be recorded at every instant of time, e.g. lie detectors, electrocardiograms. We denote this using observation X at time t, i.e. $X(t)$.

Discrete time-series data   An observation could be recorded at (usually regularly) spaced intervals. We denote this as X_t. For example, discrete data in economics can relate to weekly share prices, monthly profits; in meteorology it could be related to daily rainfall, wind speed, temperature.

Time-series data, whether it is continuous or discrete, can be described with the help of various components which are explained below.

Trend component   Trend denotes a long-term movement in a time series. Thus, it specifies the underlying direction (an upward or downward tendency) and the rate of change in a time series. Although there are many formal tests to enable detection of trend in time series data, the simplest way is to take averages over a certain period of time.

Cyclical component   Cyclic component refers to the non-seasonal component in the time-series data that varies in a recognizable cycle. For example, in weekly or monthly data, the cyclical component describes any regular fluctuations.

Seasonal component   Seasonal component is that component of variation in a time series data which is dependent on the time of year. It describes any regular fluctuations that occur within a year. The most common examples of seasonal variation include the costs of fruits and vegetables, unemployment figures, and average daily temperature.

It is used to compare the seasonal effects that occur within a year and from year to year. We need to minimize the impact of these seasonal effects so that the time series is easier to cope with.

Irregular component   The irregular component (noise) is that left over, component when the other components of the series (trend, seasonal, and cyclical) have been accounted for.

13.9.1 The Smoothing Technique

Smoothing techniques are used to reduce irregularities or random fluctuations in time-series data so that they may provide a clearer view of the true underlying behaviour of the series.

In some time-series data, the impact of seasonal variation is so strong that it hides the underlying trends or cycles which are crucial to gain useful insights into the process being observed. Thus, smoothing in such cases can help to remove seasonality and make long-term fluctuations in the series stand out more clearly.

The most common type of smoothing technique is moving average smoothing. However, there are other techniques also but as the type of seasonality will vary from series to series, so must the type of smoothing.

Exponential smoothing It is a technique used to smooth the underlying data. This is done be reducing irregularities in time series data, so that a clearer view of the true underlying behaviour of the series can be studied and future values of the time series can be easily predicted.

Moving average smoothing In order to make the long-term trends of a time-series data clearer, we use moving average smoothing. It is a form of average which has been adjusted to allow for seasonal or cyclical components of a time series.

When we plot a variable like the employment rate or the cost of mangoes against the time dimension in a graph, the seasonal or cyclical components present in the data may make it difficult to see the underlying trend. These components can be eliminated by taking a suitable moving average to reduce random fluctuations and to make the long-term trends even more clear.

Running medians smoothing It applies a technique that is analogous to that used for moving averages. The primary goal of this technique is to make a trend clearer by reducing the effects of other fluctuations.

Differencing It is another effective method of removing trends from a time series. It provides a clearer view of the true underlying behaviour of the series.

Autocorrelation It is the correlation or the relationship that exists between the members of a time series of observations. Their examples include weekly share prices and the same values at a fixed time interval later. The autocorrelation technique is used when residual error terms from observations of the same variable at different times are related to each other.

Extrapolation It is a technique in which the value of a variable is estimated at times which have not yet been observed. Although the predicted values of the variable may be reasonably reliable for short times into the future, but in the long run the estimate is liable to become less accurate.

To understand extrapolation, let us consider an example. If Ram was 1.10 m tall on 1 January 2007 and 1.30 m tall on 1 January 2008, then by extrapolation, we can estimate that by 1 January 2009, he would have grown another 0.20 m to be 1.50 m tall. This calculation of height assumes that Ram will continue to grow at the same rate. However, we all know that this assumption is not true, because if Ram continues to grow at the same pace, then by 2012, he would be a giant!

13.10 SPATIAL DATA MINING

The importance of spatial data mining is growing with the increasing significance of large geo-spatial datasets, such as maps, repositories of remote-sensing images, and the decennial census. Spatial data mining is widely applied by the military forces to formulate the Army's strategic, tactical, and operational plans. They use strategic mining to infer enemy tactics (e.g. flank attack), locate lost ammunition dumps and enemy sites.

- The difference between classical and spatial data mining is somewhat similar to the differences between classical and spatial statistics.
- While spatial data is embedded in a continuous space, the classical data is often discrete in nature.
- Spatial patterns are often local, whereas classical data mining techniques lays emphasis on global patterns.
- Classical statistical analysis assumes that data samples are independently generated, whereas in case of spatial data analysis, the assumption about the independence of samples is generally false because spatial data tends to be highly auto-correlated.

For example, generally it is seen that people with similar characteristics, occupation, and background are clustered together in the same neighbourhoods. In spatial statistics, we call this as spatial auto-correlation. If we ignore these spatial auto-correlations while analysing the data that has spatial characteristics, then we may produce inaccurate or inconsistent hypotheses and models.

It has been proved that classical data mining algorithms perform poorly when applied to spatial datasets, thus new methods are needed to analyse spatial data to detect spatial patterns. Spatial data mining is widely applied in the field of spatial statistics, spatial analysis, geographic information systems, machine learning, image analysis, and data mining. The main contributions made to this area include algorithms and data-structures that can scale up to massive (terabytes to peta-bytes) datasets as well as the formalization of newer spatio-temporal patterns.

Location prediction is a technique that discovers a model to infer locations of a spatial phenomenon from the maps of other spatial features. For example, ecologists produce models to protect habitats for endangered species using maps of vegetation, water bodies, climate, and other related species. In such cases, the application of classical data mining techniques will not be fruitful as they might produce weak prediction models, as they do not capture the auto-correlation in spatial datasets.

As we had outliers in classical data mining, here we have spatial outliers (spatial noise) that are significantly different from their neighbourhoods though they may not be significantly different from the entire population. For example, a brand new building in an old area of a growing area is a spatial outlier.

13.10.1 Applications of Spatial Mining

Spatial trend detection in GIS Spatial trends describe a regular change of non-spatial attributes when moving away from certain start objects. Spatial trend analysis is used to study global as well as local trends. Spatial data mining is applied in economics to find spatial trends, e.g. with respect to the economic power, it is an important issue in economic geography.

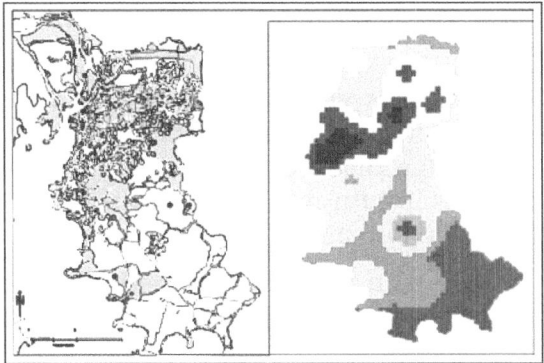

Figure 13.2 Application of spatial mining (distribution of mortality cases in Porto Alegre, Brazil)

Spatial characterization of interesting regions Economic geography is a field that characterizes certain target regions like the areas with a high mortality rate (see Fig. 13.2). Spatial characterization techniques consider the attributes of the target regions as well as of the neighbouring regions.

13.10.2 Techniques in Spatial Mining

Database primitives A set of database primitives for spatial database mining that are sufficient to express most of the spatial data mining algorithms and which can be efficiently supported by a DBMS has already been developed. The use of these database primitives will enable the integration of spatial data mining with existing DBMS and these primitives will catalyze the development of new spatial data mining algorithms. The spatial data mining database primitives are based on the concepts of neighbourhood graphs and neighbourhood paths.

Efficient DBMS support Effective filters allow restricting the search. Neighbourhood indices materialize certain neighbourhood graphs to support efficient processing of the database primitives by a DBMS. These database primitives are implemented on top of the DBMS.

Algorithms for spatial data mining New algorithms for spatial characterization and spatial trend analysis are being developed. For spatial characterization, the underlying principle in determining the class membership of a database object is to consider the non-spatial attributes as well as the attributes of objects in its neighbourhood. However, spatial trend analysis discovers patterns of change of some non-spatial attributes in the neighbourhood of a database object.

13.11 ISSUES AND CHALLENGES IN DATA MINING

We have studied earlier that data mining techniques flourish when used on a data warehouse, but it is not always the case that data mining is used with data warehouses. In that case, data mining systems depend on the underlying databases to supply the data as its input. These source databases present a lot of challenges, mainly because they are often dynamic, incomplete, noisy, and large. Then, there are problems, as these databases may contain incomplete, missing, or irrelevant data.

Limited information Generally, these databases were not designed to be used as a source for data mining systems. So, it is not uncommon that some attributes which are essential for knowledge discovery of the application domain may be absent in the database. This in turn makes it very difficult to discover significant knowledge about a given domain.

Noisy and missing data Attributes that rely on subjective or measurement judgements can lead to errors, which may result in wrong classification of the data. There may be missing data in the database.

However, the issue of missing data can well be handled in many ways like: (a) ignoring the missing values, (b) ignoring the complete record that contains missing value for any attribute, (c) deducing missing values from the known values, and (d) treating missing data as a special value to be included additionally in the attribute domain. Regardless of the way the missing data is treated, the data must be cleaned so that it is free of errors and missing data.

User interaction A data mining user need not be a KDD expert. Rather, anyone should be able to use the data by applying KDD techniques. The KDD process is an interactive and iterative process. It is therefore challenging to provide high performance, rapid-response environment to the users.

The success of the KDD process lies on more of human–computer interaction than on total automation. This enables both novice as well as expert users to use the system. However, this feature may call for the incorporation of the domain knowledge in all steps of the KDD process.

Level of uncertainty The term *uncertainty* is associated with the severity of error and the degree of noise in the underlying data.

Data updates Real-world databases are generally large and keep growing with time. The contents of these databases change as data is added, modified, or deleted. This creates another challenge for data mining, as it becomes difficult to ensure that the rules derived from the underlying dataset are up-to-date and consistent with the most current information.

13.12 CURRENT TRENDS IN DATA MINING

The diversity of data and data mining tasks poses many challenging research issues in data mining. The development of efficient and effective data mining methods and the application of data mining techniques to solve large application problems are important tasks for data mining researchers and application developers. This section describes some of the trends in data mining that reflect these challenges.

Applications exploration The data mining applications available in the market till date helped businesses to gain competitive advantage. But as data mining is becoming popular, it is continuously being used for other applications as well. Besides, the exploration of data mining for businesses is continuously expanding, as e-commerce is becoming the mainstream element of the retail industry.

Since generic data mining systems may pose some limitations in dealing with application-specific problems, a trend towards the development of more application-specific data mining systems is being realized these days.

Scalable data mining methods Data mining systems are expected to be able to handle huge amounts of data efficiently and if possible, interactively. Since a large amount of data is continuously being collected, scalable algorithms for individual and integrated data mining functions has become essential.

Integration with data store systems Database systems, data warehouse systems, and the World Wide Web have become the most widely used information processing systems. Thus, it is necessary that data mining can be smoothly integrated into such an information processing environment.

Standardization of data mining language A data mining system that strictly adheres to a standard language or other standardization efforts will facilitate the systematic development of data mining solutions, improve interoperability among different data mining systems and function, and promote the use of data mining system in industry.

New methods for mining complex types of data Mining complex types of data is an important research issue in data mining. Although a lot has been done for mining geospatial, multimedia, time-series, sequence, and text data, there is still a huge gap between the needs for these applications and the available technology. Thus, a lot of research still needs to be done towards the integration of data mining methods with existing data analysis techniques for the above said data types.

Web mining Today a lot of information is available on the web, and the increasingly important role that the web is playing in the today's businesses, web content mining, web usage mining, and web structure mining is becoming one of the most crucial and flourishing areas in data mining.

Security With the widespread growth of data mining tools, telecommunications and computer networks, the buzzword in the information technology industry is to face the privacy protection and information security issues. In addition to provide data access, the techniques to ensure privacy protection and information security must also be developed.

In addition to this, the five external trends that have a fundamental impact on data mining are discussed here:

Data trends The most crucial trend is the explosion of digital data over last few years. It has been observed that the amount of data has grown between six to ten orders of magnitude. It is always better to use data mining techniques that can automate this data, and extract meaningful knowledge out of it rather than dumping it in archive files without any practical use.

Hardware trends Application of data mining algorithms calls for statistically insensitive computations on large sets of data. The increasing memory and processing speed of computers have enabled the application of such algorithms on large sets of data.

Network trends With the Internet connectivity, it has now become possible to correlate distributed datasets using current algorithms and techniques. Besides this, new protocols and algorithms are being developed that can facilitate distributed data mining using current and next generation networks.

Scientific computing trends Data mining and the KDD process form a crucial part of linking theory, experiment, and simulation that result in large datasets.

Business trends The need of the businesses today is to generate more and more profits by offering higher quality services at a lower cost. In the presence of such high expectations and constraints, data mining is being used to predict opportunities and risks generated by the customer's transactions with a much higher accuracy.

Recapitulation

The criteria for evaluating the data mining tools are: ability to access the data, select the relevant data, sensitivity to the quality of data, good data visualization capabilities, extensible to integrate with data warehouse functions, provide consistent performance, scalable to handle huge amounts of data, open to be able to share the output with other tools and provide support for different algorithms.

Data mining systems can be categorized according to the type of data source mined, the data model involved, the mining techniques used, and their applications.

Data mining generates a very large number of patterns or rules. To reduce the number of patterns or rules discovered that have a high probability to be non-interesting, one has to put a measurement on the patterns explaining how interesting a discovery is, often called interestingness.

In oil exploration and research, data mining techniques discover locations suitable for drilling. In military, it assists to identify targets. Medical research is a field where data mining helps the researchers to find correlations between diseases and patient's symptoms. Crime investigation agencies use data mining to connect criminal profiles to crimes. In astronomy and cosmology, data mining helps to predict cosmic events.

Applications of data mining in the business area include customer segmentation, market basket analysis, risk management, fraud detection, delinquency tracking, demand prediction, direct marketing and promotion of products, and sales forecasting.

Telecommunication industry applies data mining to catch fraudulent activities, make better use of resources, and improve the quality of service for customer retention and customer acquisition.

Banking and financial institutions use data mining for fraud detection, delinquency tracking and risk assessment of potential customers, trend analysis, direct marketing, and forecasting of stock prices.

Web mining is the application of data mining techniques to discover patterns from the Web. Mining techniques in the Web can be categorized into three main areas: Web content mining, Web structure mining, and Web usage mining.

Web content mining describes the automatic search of information resources available online and involves mining web data content.

The goal of Web structure mining is to generate a structural summary about the website and the web page. Based on the topology of the hyperlinks, it will categorize the web pages and generate the information, such as the similarity and relationship between different websites.

Web usage mining is the application of data mining techniques to discover user navigation patterns from the Web.

Text mining is the process of deriving high quality information from text. It applies the same types of analysis, such as knowledge discovery and trend analysis to unstructured textual data that data mining applies to structured data.

Temporal data mining is an extension of data mining and it can be defined as the non-trivial extraction of implicit, potentially useful, and previously unrecorded information with an implicit or explicit temporal content from large quantities of data.

Sequence mining is concerned with finding statistically relevant patterns between data examples where the values are delivered in a sequence. It is a special case of structured data mining. There are two different kinds of sequence mining: *string mining* and *itemset mining*.

Time-series analysis comprises methods that attempt to understand time-series data. Time-series prediction is the use of a model to predict future events based on known past events.

Objective Questions

1. **Multiple choice questions**

    (i) Which type of mining involves mining web data content?

    (a) Web content mining

    (b) Web usage mining

    (c) Web structure mining

    (ii) Which type of mining facilitates the use of database techniques for accessing information in web pages by providing a reference schema?

    (a) Web content mining

    (b) Web usage mining

    (c) Web structure mining

    (iii) Which mining technique discovers the nature of the hierarchy or network of hyperlinks in the web sites of a particular domain?

    (a) Web content mining

    (b) Web usage mining

    (c) Web structure mining

    (iv) Which mining technique discovers user navigation patterns?

    (a) Web content mining

    (b) Web usage mining

    (c) Web structure mining

(v) Missing data in a database can be handled in which of the ways?

   (a) Deducing missing values from known values

   (b) Treating missing data as a special value

   (c) Ignoring the missing values

   (d) All of these

   (e) None of these

2. Fill in the blanks

(i) In astronomy and cosmology, data mining is used to predict _____ events.

(ii) _____ algorithms are applied for bond trading and portfolio management.

(iii) _____ and _____ methods are used to identify customer groups for targeted marketing.

(iv) _____ methods are used to determine the kinds of genes that are likely to occur in target samples.

(v) _____ mining is to generate structural summary about the website.

(vi) _____ refers to the process of deriving high quality information from text.

(vii) Temporal classification forms clusters of data items along _____ dimensions.

(viii) Sequence mining is considered to be a special case of _____ data mining.

(ix) _____ mining is used in biology to examine gene and protein sequences.

(x) Marketing and CRM applications widely makes use of _____ mining.

(xi) _____ denotes a long-term movement in a time series.

(xii) _____ component describes any regular fluctuations that occur within a year.

(xiii) The most common type of smoothing technique is _____.

(xvi) The KDD process is an _____ and _____ process.

(xv) _____ refers to the severity of error and the degree of noise in the data.

3. Match the following

1.	Defector profiling	(a)	String mining and itemset mining
2.	Defection scoring	(b)	Predict the return on investment
3.	Customer segmentation	(c)	Build neural network predictive model that is capable enough to predict likelihood of defection
4.	CRM	(d)	Non-seasonal component in the time series data that varies in a recognizable cycle
5.	Portfolio management	(e)	Value of a variable is estimated at times which have not yet been observed
6.	Sequence mining	(f)	Reduce irregularities or random fluctuations in time series data
7.	Cyclic component	(g)	Group the customers based on similarity in terms of demographic, geographic, and psychographic attribute
8.	Smoothing	(h)	Manages the interactions between a company and its customers
9.	Extrapolation	(i)	Profiles of risky customer groups are developed based on their demographic, geographic and psychographic attributes

4. **State true or false**

(i) Data mining algorithms need data at the lowest level of granularity.

(ii) The measurements for interestingness are based on thresholds set by the user.

(iii) Web data includes text, multimedia, and numerical data.

(iv) Web contains structured data.

(v) Multimedia data mining is a subset of web content mining.

(vi) Text mining is applied to structured data.

(vii) Static data does not contain any temporal reference.

(viii) Time-stamped data contains explicit temporal information.

(ix) The inference derived from time stamp data are always temporal in nature.

(x) Temporal data requires near real-time analysis.

Review Questions

1. How do you categorize a data mining system?

2. Does the application of a data mining functionality always produce interesting patterns or rules? If no, what can be done to limit the discovery of irrelevant patterns or rules?

3. Write an essay on the applications of data mining.

4. What role does data mining play in the retail industry?

5. How is data mining used in the telecommunication industry?

6. Explain the significance of data mining in the banking and financial industry.

7. Why is data mining applied in the biomedical area?

8. How is data mining used for customer retention, target marketing, and CRM?

9. If you are responsible for analysing requirements and selecting a toolset for data mining in your organization, make a list of criteria you will use for the toolset selection.

10. Explain the term web mining in detail. Mention its related areas.

11. What is text mining? How is it different from web content mining? List the areas where text mining is widely being applied these days.

12. Give a brief about temporal data mining.

13. What do you understand by temporal data? Which mining tasks are applied on such data? Explain the challenges in mining the temporal data.

14. Write a short note on sequence mining.

15. What is time-series analysis?

16. Explain time-series data. What are the techniques used to smooth this data so that it could yield accurate results while mining?

17. Explain spatial data mining.

18. List the advantages, disadvantages, and issues in data mining.

19. Write a short note on various trends that affect the data mining technology.

14

TRENDS IN
DATA WAREHOUSING

Learning Objectives

In this chapter, we will learn about different trends in data warehousing technology. We will also see how the data warehousing technology can be integrated with other technology to provide significant benefits.

Last but not the least, we will have a look at the different data warehousing solutions present in the market, so that one can learn about the characteristics of every individual type of data warehouse and then make a decision to buy the data warehouse solution that is best suited for the business.

Case Study

Technology keeps changing at a fast pace. This is especially true of the IT sector, where what we have today is better than the best technology of yesterday. This chapter deals with the current trends that help the project team to develop an up-to-date data warehouse.

The data warehouse which once used to store only alphabetical and numerical data can now even store images, maps, and multimedia files. There are new sophisticated data warehousing tools that have completely replaced the earlier tools.

While building the data warehouse information delivery component, David recollected the previous years when he had to use some other software to draw charts and graphs and then incorporate them in the result set. Now, the data warehousing tool itself does all this and no other software is needed to do it. How simple his life had now become. Thanks to the new technology that minimizes the extra burden of the project team.

There are different types of system solutions for different sets of problems. A single solution cannot fit all the problematic solutions. For example, the functioning of a payroll system is entirely different from that of an accounting system which in turn is strikingly different from that of a stock monitoring system.

To design a data warehouse, the team must know the purpose of creating the data warehouse and then choose a fitting solution. If JRTs want their data warehouse to be used over the Internet, then which data warehouse solution to go for—a data webhouse or a web-enabled data warehouse? This chapter will help you to know more on the different solutions that a data warehouse has to offer.

14.1 INTRODUCTION

Data warehousing is becoming mainstream and is not confined only to high-end businesses. About 90% of the multinational companies have data warehouses or are planning to implement one in the near future. Therefore, it is important to know about the current trends to make sure the warehouse falls in line with the market requirements.

In every industry, data warehousing is revolutionizing the way people do business analysis and make strategic decisions. It is influencing all areas of business ranging from retail stores, financial institutions, manufacturing companies, government undertakings, airlines companies, and utility businesses.

Every company that has implemented data warehouses is realizing the numerous benefits that are showing positive results at the bottom line. Many of these companies are moving towards incorporating web-based technologies to improve the process of delivering information to the end-users. Over the past seven years, vendors have flooded the market with a wide range of products for data warehousing.

14.2 DATA WAREHOUSE SOLUTIONS

Initially, when data warehousing was an absolutely new paradigm, not many vendors were there who could provide data warehouse products and tools. But the last few years have witnessed a drastic change as the market is now attaining a level of maturity to the extent of producing off-the-shelf packages and becoming increasingly stable.

These days, the data warehousing vendors are merging to form stronger and more viable companies or are extending the range of their solutions by acquiring other companies. Some data warehousing vendors are also offering suites of products, either of their own or from groups of other vendors, piecing them together and offering them as integrated data warehousing solutions to the organizations who have implemented the data warehousing technology.

With an increasing demand for data warehousing solutions, even the traditional database companies are also in the data warehousing market. For this, they have begun to offer data warehousing solutions built around their database products and are packaging data extraction and transformation tools with their

DBMS. Besides, query and reporting tools are enhanced for data warehousing and some database vendors are even trying to enhance their data base product by offering sophisticated products such as data mining tools.

Fundamentally, one single solution of a data warehouse will not fit all the warehouse scenarios. The type of data warehouse depends on a number of business factors such as

Business objectives Many organizations that tend to build a data warehouse are generally not certain about priorities or options. These priorities impact the warehouse in terms of its size, location, frequency of use, and maintenance.

Location of current data One of the major challenges in delivering data to the user is understanding where the data is, in what format, and the characteristics of this data so that appropriate tools can be selected.

Need to move the data When the data warehouse project is started, it is assumed that the data from the source systems will be moved to a separate location, however keeping the data in the same location where it originally resides seems a simpler option. The decision to move the data to a separate location or not will depend on a number of factors like quality of the data, size of data, performance impact on the operational system, etc.

Location to which the data needs to be moved This is a significant issue in the design of a data warehouse. Before designing for any data movement you must first decide that whether the data store is host-based or LAN based.

Decision-support requirements The most important data warehouse implementation decision is to determine what query tools are needed, deployable and available, and whether there exists the need to feed the data into other applications like EIS or not. For a poorly built data warehouse, a range of tools will need to be deployed to address different needs of decision makers.

14.2.1 Implementation Alternatives

Depending upon the criteria specified above, users can exercise a lot of flexibility in choosing the type of warehouse to implement. There a number of alternatives for a LAN-based local warehouse that supports a specific data mart. Two of the fundamental types of data warehouse are:

- Host-based warehouses that are usually controlled by IT and run on traditional systems.
- LAN-based warehouses that are usually managed either centrally or from the workgroup environment.

These can be further defined based on the location of the source data as follows: (a) Host-based data warehouses, (b) LAN-based workgroup data warehouses, (c) Multistage data warehouses, and (d) Stationary data warehouses.

14.2.2 Host-based Data Warehouses

There are two types of host based data warehousing solutions that can be implemented.

- Host-based mainframe data warehouses that are generally supported by robust and reliable high-capacity systems and mainly resides on high volume databases.
- Host-based LAN data warehouses that manage delivery of data either centrally or from a workgroup environment.

Single Host-based Data Warehouses

Those data warehouses that reside on high-volume databases are the host based type of data warehouses. Generally, the DBMS selected is DB2 with a variety of disparate sources like VSAM, DB2, flat files, and Information Management System. Before designing, building, and implementing a single host-based data warehouse, some additional considerations must be made because:

- These databases have a large capacity to store enormous amounts of data.
- These warehouses usually have complex source systems.
- They require continuous maintenance as they are used for mission critical applications.

In order to successfully build such a data warehouse, the following phases have to be completed.

- Unload phase that involves selecting and scrubbing the source data.
- Transform phase that involves activities for translating the data into appropriate formats and defining the rules for accessing and storing it.
- Load phase for moving the data directly into the warehouse.

An integrated metadata repository is the nerve centre of any data warehouse environment. It is usually required for documenting the data sources, data translation rules, and user access to the warehouse. The metadata should be able to provide its users all the information related to what data exists in both the operational system and data warehouse, where that data is located, the mapping of the operational data to warehouse fields, and how the end-user can access the desired data.

Host-based Single Stage (LAN) Data Warehouses

With a LAN-based warehouse, the data can be delivered either centrally or from the workgroup (data mart) environment. This helps the business departments to meet and manage their own information needs without burdening centralized IT resources. The advantage here is that the users can enjoy the autonomy of their own data mart without compromising the overall data integrity and security in the enterprise. Even though LAN-based data warehouses are commonly used due to the ease of access and cost benefits, they have to cater to certain challenges as given below.

- They are normally limited by both DBMS and hardware scalability factors.
- Many organizations who have implemented LAN-based data warehouses could not implement adequate job scheduling, recovery management, organized maintenance, and performance monitoring procedures to support the warehousing solutions.
- The data warehouses depend on other platforms for their source data feed. Creating an environment that has features like data integrity, recoverability, and security calls for a very diligent design, careful planning, and implementation. Otherwise, synchronization of changes and loads from the source systems to the data warehouse server could cause a series of problems.

A LAN-based warehouse supports data from multiple sources that often require minimal amount of initial investment and technical know-how. The warehouse usually has a robust amount of historical data and data aggregated at different levels. A LAN-based warehouse driven by a metadata repository supports the DSS applications by enabling its users to understand the data which is a crucial ingredient of the data warehouse.

14.2.3 LAN-based Workgroup Data Warehouses

A LAN-based workgroup data warehouse is an integrated architecture for building and maintaining a data warehouse in a LAN environment. It extracts data from multiple sources and provides a number of LAN-based warehouses. The database chosen for such warehouses includes DB2, Oracle, SYBASE, and Informix.

A LAN-based data warehouse is specially designed for the workgroup environment and is considered to be an ideal solution for organizations that wish to deploy a number of data marts as well apart from the enterprise wide data warehouse. LAN-based workgroup data warehouse calls for minimal initial investment and technical know how. The advantages of this data warehouse include low startup cost and ease of use that thereby allows a workgroup to quickly build and easily manage its own custom data mart. With the escalating needs of the workgroup, a LAN-based workgroup can easily expand to integrate with a larger, more centralized warehouse.

In a LAN-based workgroup warehouse, the delivery of data can be managed either centrally or from the workgroup environment. This is another advantage as it enables the business departments to manage their own information needs without burdening the IT. This, in turn, gives them full autonomy of their data mart without compromising on the overall data integrity and security in the enterprise.

In case of a LAN-based workgroup warehouse, users need minimal technical knowledge to build and maintain a data store that is customized for use at the department, business unit, or workgroup level. A LAN-based workgroup warehouse delivers data providing transparent access to the data in the warehouse.

A carefully selected toolset for the data warehouse allows the users to control the way the data is transformed into meaningful business information and enables them to automate the extraction, transfer, and refreshment process in the data warehouse. Some other common issues associated with a LAN-based workgroup warehouses includes:

- Lack of understanding regarding how to distribute data and support data redundancy for performance reasons.
- Many organizations are not able to have adequate job scheduling, recovery management, and performance monitoring to support robust warehousing solutions.
- Even though LAN-based warehousing solutions provide cost benefits but their use can be limited by both hardware and DBMS limitations.
- In large organizations, similar skills needed for database design, maintenance, and recovery are not present in every individual data mart or workgroup environment.

14.2.4 Multistage Data Warehouses

A multistage data warehouse is best suited for environments in which the end-users require access to both, current data for up-to-the-minute decisions as well as summarized/aggregated data for making long-term strategic decisions. In this configuration, the operation data store and the data warehouse may reside on host-based or LAN based databases, depending on the volume and the usage requirements.

In a multistage data warehouse, the operation data store (ODS) serves as the source for the data warehouse. Here, the ODS will store only the most up-to-date records whereas the data warehouse will store both the historical data records as well as the current data records. Initially, the records in both ODS and the data warehouse databases will be the same but as the data grows their contents would have a striking contrast. Tactical decisions can be made from the data in the ODS whereas the long-term strategic decisions require the historical trend analysis that is only available from the data warehouse. Figure 14.1 shows a multistage data warehouse. However, multistage warehouses need to resolve many problems before the enterprise can implement them. Some of these are listed here.

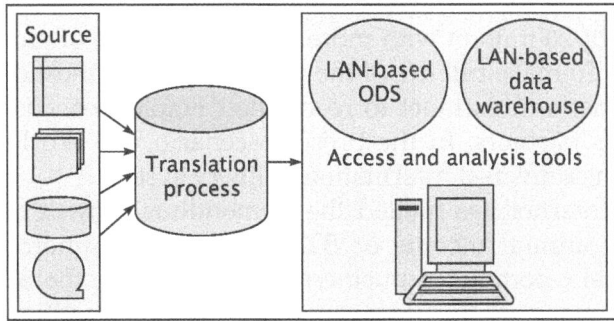

Figure 14.1 Multistage data warehouse

- Maintenance of data.
- Frequent updates to the ODS.
- Handling of highly complex source systems.
- Need to offer more rapid response time.
- Need for synchronization of changes and loads from sources to server.
- Need for highly skilled people who are well versed in many technologies.
- Limitations of hardware scalability.

14.2.5 Stationary Data Warehouses

In stationary data warehouses, as the name suggests, the data is not moved from the sources as shown in Fig. 14.2. Rather in such a warehouse the users are given direct access to the data. Factors like infrequent access, data volumes, and the corporate necessities dictate such an approach.

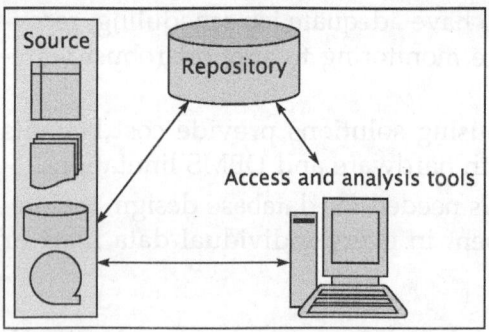

Figure 14.2 Stationary data warehouse

Implementation of a stationary data warehouse requires highly specialized and sophisticated middleware technology with a single interface to the user. However even this solution is not problem free. The issues that must be resolved before an organization decides to go for a stationary data warehouse includes:

- Identifying the source location of the data.
- To enable the users to query different DBMS as if they were all a single DBMS with a single API.
- Effect on the performance of the system.

14.3 WEB-ENABLED DATA WAREHOUSE

The most remarkable phenomenon that has impacted computing and communication over the past several years is the *Internet*. With just four computer systems in 1969, the Internet has now grown to a gigantic size by linking at least 100 million hosts and is still growing exponentially. The number of websites has reached the magnificent figure of 26 million with more than 150 million of global users accessing the Internet. To make full use of the web technology, most of the companies have built intranet and extranet to reach their employees, customers, suppliers, and business partners. In the present scenario, the World Wide Web is considered to be the universal information delivery system.

In the past few years, the Internet has fuelled the tremendous growth of electronic commerce with the annual income of B2B electronic commerce exceeding $300 billion. The total e-commerce business will soon cross the $1 trillion mark. In today's marketplace, no business can survive the competition without the web. The number of companies conducting business over the Net is now above 400,000.

14.3.1 Bringing the Warehouse to the Web

The World Wide Web has become the primary resource of information today. The concept of making the desired information available freely across 24×7 is extremely appealing. The Internet provides a huge, diverse, and dynamic medium that is experiencing an explosive growth of information. This has in turn opened new horizons in terms of knowledge acquisition and appliance. We all know that the web has diminished the cost of delivering information. The data warehouse is primarily designed to deliver information and the Internet makes it cost-effective to do so. A web-enabled data warehouse or a *data webhouse* is a new concept in which the web forces us to rethink data warehouse design and deployment.

According to Kohavi (2001), the web is an amazing experimental laboratory. This is very true because compared with the traditional businesses, it is much easier to change a site's contents according to users' response analysis. Thus, a web-enabled data warehouse uses the web for delivering the information and collaborating among its users. With the passage of time, the number of data warehouse opting for a webhouse is constantly increasing. With web-enabled warehouse, more users can be connected with a proportionate increase in communication costs. The exponential growth of the web, along with its networks, servers, users, and web pages, has forced the organizations to adopt the Internet, intranet, and extranet as information transmission media.

A data warehouse professional is expected to tap into the enormous potential of the Internet and web technology for enhancing the value of the data warehouse. For this, the developer needs to enhance the data warehouse to support and expand the company's business over the Net.

The organization's traditional data warehouse needs to be converted into a web-enabled data warehouse. For this, the data warehouse should be brought to the web and the web should be taken to the data warehouse.

Need for Bringing the Warehouse to the Web

In the early implementations of the data warehouse, it was only intended to be used by managers, executives, business analysts, and a few other high-level employees as a tool for strategic analysis and decision-making. Information from the data warehouse was delivered using a client-server model.

But today's data warehouses are no longer restricted to a selected group of users, as companies today want to increase the productivity of all the members in their value chain. For this, useful information from the enterprise-wide data warehouse must be provided to the internal employees as well as the external people like the customers, suppliers, and all other business partners.

The trend these days is to open your data warehouse to every community of users in the value chain, and perhaps also to the general public. In order to accomplish the requirement to serve the information to the users 24×7 without incurring extra costs for information delivery, the Internet is considered to be the most viable option.

Using Web for Delivering Information

The users view the web as a tremendous source of information. The data warehouse users, customers, and the business partners already use the web, so they all can be easily connected with it. These days, the companies prefer using the underlying web technology to connect their users, customers, and business partners. Let us take a look at the information delivery mechanisms that companies prefer to adopt. It is important to note that in each case, users access information with web browsers.

Internet The Internet, as an information transmission medium, is the most cost-effective mechanism. You can exchange the information with anyone, whether it is internal users, external customers, or business partners. But utmost care needs to be taken to safeguard the critical data, as the data will be transferred over a public network.

Intranet It can be linked with a private computer network. Although an intranet is a private network but it makes use of the data communication standards of the public Internet. However, the data and information transferred is very secure, as the applications posting information over the intranet reside within the firewall. This way, you can avail all the benefits of the web technology and have your data safe and protected from unauthorized users.

Extranet It is a new web technology which is neither completely open like the Internet nor restricted just for internal users as in case of intranet. An extranet is similar to the intranet with a difference that it is open for selective access by outside parties like customers, suppliers, and business partners.

Figure 14.3 shows how the information from the data warehouse can be transferred using the web technology. Whatever technology you may choose for the data warehouse, the transmission protocols remain the same.

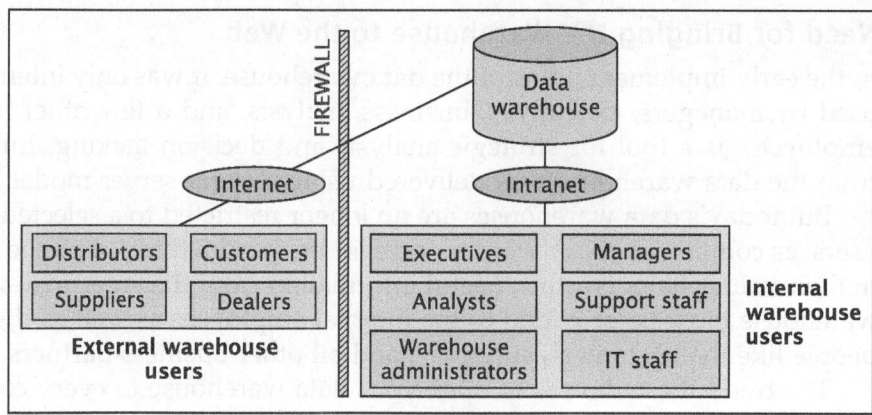

Figure 14.3 Data warehouse and the Web

Merits

The following list summarizes the merits of bringing the data warehouse to the web.

- With a web browser, users can access all the information.
- Minimal training is required to learn how to access the available information.
- Web browsers can run on any type of system.
- Through the existing web technology, data in any form (text, graphics, images, charts, multimedia) can be easily accessed.
- Having direct contact with business partners and customers strengthens the relationship.
- Web-enabled data warehouses require low deployment and maintenance costs.
- Faster response time increases users' interest in finding information.
- Web browsers make the information access extremely easy and intuitive.
- The data can be accessed 24×7.
- Users can customize the presentation display.

The Roadblocks

Till now, we have read only the plus points of using a data webhouse, but the organization has to do a lot of tedious work to adapt the web to act as the underlying mechanism of delivering information to its users. Table 14.1 gives the features of the traditional method of delivering information and states how these features have to be adopted for using web as the information delivering mechanism.

Table 14.1 Traditional method and the Web

Attribute	Traditional Method	Web
- Information technique	- Information is pulled by the users using queries and reports.	- Information should be pushed to the users.
- User friendly	- At times retrieving the desired data can be complicated.	- Should be more user friendly and information must be pushed automatically.
- Response time	- Can take several hours.	- Has to provide quick response.
- Downtime	- There are downtimes.	- Has to provide information 24×7. Downtimes cannot be tolerated.
- Multimedia data	- May contain only textual data.	- Has to support for audio, video, textual, numeric, and graphical data.
- Scalability	- Data warehouse systems are scalable	- Needs even more scalability as more access means more users and more data.

Hence, after web-enabling the data warehouse using the same web browser used for accessing the Internet, the yardstick of the users differs. The end-users want to work with the same interface that they use in an Internet session.

The Super-growth Problem

The data warehouses have started adopting the web as the information delivery mechanism because it is a new outlook on information delivery and revolutionizes the entire process of providing information. The end-users can use the same old web browser to execute their queries easily and at anytime during the day.

The usage of the data warehouse is not only limited to the internal users but extends far beyond that as even the parties from outside the organization can now be granted access to the data warehouse content.

As the number of users expands, scalability is no more a problem before the data warehouse team. The data warehouse also requires minimal training costs as the usage of the web browser is already known to the end users.

There are two factors which foster the growth of the data warehouse and results in the expansion of its usage. First, the data warehouse provides a totally open window that never shuts down. Second, it provides an easy, intuitive, and user friendly information access using the web browser.

With the increase in the user population, especially because of opening the data warehouse to the customers and business partners through extranet, you get a steep expansion curve. Figure 14.4 explains the super-growth in a web data warehouse environment.

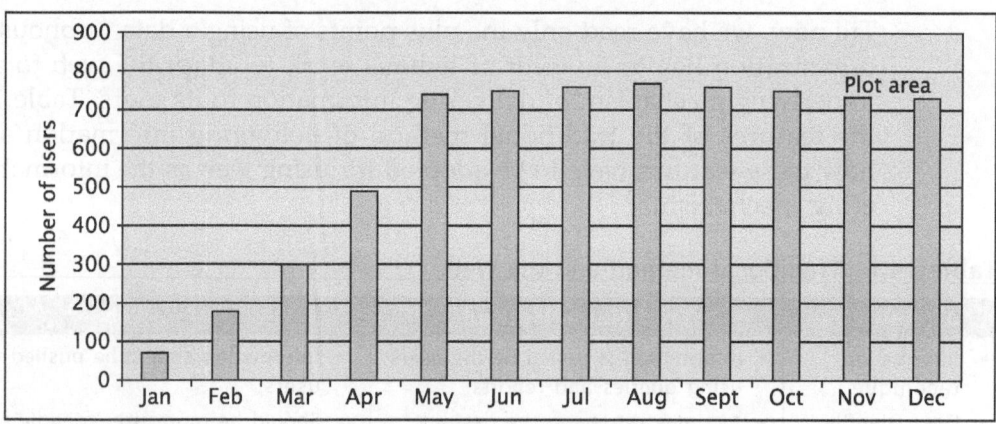

Figure 14.4 Super-growth chart of a data warehouse

In a web-enabled data warehouse, the number of users will grow faster than your ability to scale up the warehouse to meet the expanding usage requirements. Adding of processors, disk drives, or fast memory is not enough to meet the escalating demand, so how will you handle this super-growth is not a trivial question to answer.

When the data warehouse is web-enabled, you should not become overenthusiastic and open the warehouse instantly to the public. It would simply be like opening the floodgates without warning, so you have to open the data warehouse in well defined stages. This is very much necessary if the usage pattern of the warehouse is not very clear.

To handle the super-growth problem, first let a few of the internal users have access and then add some more users to the access group. More and more users can be included in staged increments, so that growth managing becomes easy.

It has been seen that the super-growth problems occur only in the initial stages of deployment of the web data warehouse. From Fig. 14.4, it is clear that after the initial stages, the usage curve level offs, or at least the rate of increase becomes manageable for the data warehouse team.

Features of a Data Webhouse

In this section, we will discuss the nature of the web-enabled data warehouse or the data webhouse. Figure 14.5 shows how the web makes the data warehouse available for all users.

- It is a fully distributed system. A number of different independent nodes form a distributed system.
- A web-enabled system goes beyond the client/server system as the distribution of tasks as well as the arrangement of the components is drastically different.
- The system delivers the information using the web browsers.
- Security is a major concern because of the openness of the system.
- Like the web, the data webhouse supports many forms of data like textual, numeric, graphical, audio, and video.
- The system displays the requested information within reasonable response time.
- For ease of use and effective publication on the web, user interface is an important factor. The analysis of the clickstream data provides the data regarding how good the interface actually is.
- The data webhouse necessitates a well distributed architecture comprising small scale data marts.
- The data webhouse architecture comprises of linked data marts that necessitates having fully conformed dimensions and standardized facts.
- The data webhouse should provide information at all times.
- The data webhouse is meant to be opened for internal as well as external users like the employees, customers, suppliers, and business partners.
- Supports the storage of atomic-level data for analysing the clickstream data. This calls for crawling through the lowest level of data.

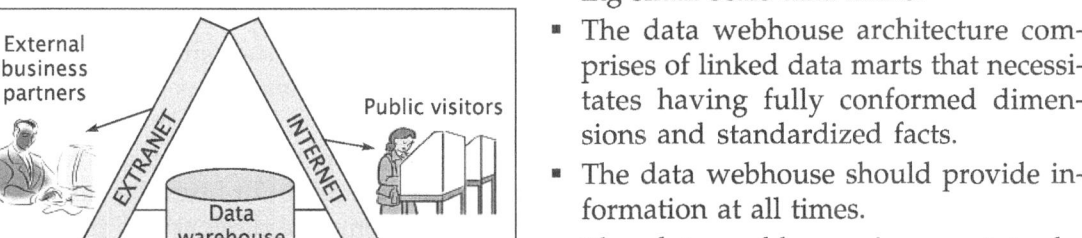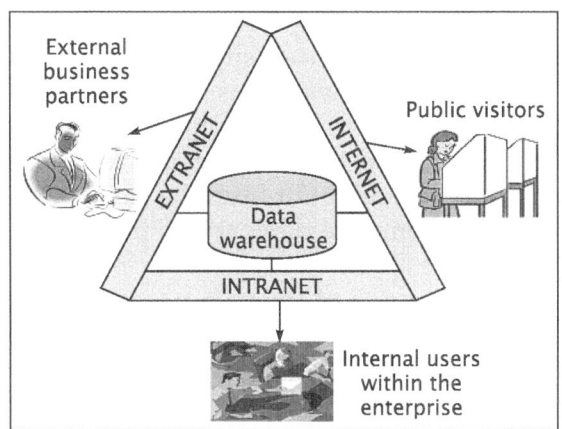

Figure 14.5 Data Warehouse is meant for all users.

14.3.2 Bringing the Web to the Warehouse

The end-user applications are increasingly being developed using web pages. The web revolution has increased everybody's expectations to such great heights that all sorts of information will be seamlessly published through web browser interface. The users for data warehouse data have grown from internal management to encompass everybody including customers, partners, and much larger pool of internal employees.

The web's focus on the customer experience has inspired many organizations to be aware of learning about the customer and giving them information that they want. Today, the data warehouse has enabled the analysis of the customer clickstream data; this rebirth of data warehousing architecture is called the data webhouse.

The data webhouse helps the marketing manager or the analyst to record every customer interaction that will be used by them to understand customer behaviour, interests, and needs in greater depth than ever before. This understanding in turn offers growth, profit, customer satisfaction, in fact everything that any organization could want.

The Internet stores the clickstream data that records every mouse click or keystroke of every customer who visits the web site thereby generating a more complete customer record than ever before.

The data webhouse is a web instantiation of the data warehouse and plays a central and a crucial role in the operations of the web-enabled business. It has the following features:

- Stores and publishes click stream data and other behavioural data from the web that helps in understanding of customer behaviour.
- Acts as a medium that publishes data to the customers, business partners, and employees while simultaneously protecting the enterprise's data against unattended use.

Bringing the web to the data warehouse involves capturing the clickstream data of all the people who visit the organization's web site. The data thus captured is used to perform all the traditional data warehousing functions. In the data warehouse environment, this process has to be accomplished in near real-time. You need to extract, transform and load the clickstream data to the webhouse repository. The dimensional schemas are built from the clickstream data and finally the information delivery systems are deployed to present the information from the webhouse.

Clickstream data is used to track the sequence of the web pages that are visited by the people who visits the company's website. This data helps to understand what sequence of pages triggers purchases, what attracts people, and what makes them come back. Clickstream data enables the analyst to understand the following:

- Customer demand and buying patterns.
- The effect of marketing promotions on the products sales.
- Collection of customer demographic data.
- Feedback on the design of the website.

A clickstream webhouse is considered to be the most important tool for identifying, prioritizing and retaining e-commerce customers. The webhouse can generate the following useful information:

- Statistics of the entire website.
- Ad metrics.
- The sequence of pages that resulted in fetching orders.
- The sequence of pages that could not fetch orders.
- Pages that turned out to be the session killers.
- Relationships between customer profiles and page activities.
- The pages of the web site get the most visitors?
- The pages of the website that are considered to be superfluous or visited infrequently?
- The click profiles of a variety of customers, viz. new, existing, profitable, complaining, unregistered, etc.

From Fig. 14.6, we conclude that while bringing the web to the warehouse, data from various operational systems, external sources, and also from the web is included in the data warehouse. But bringing content from the web is not that easy, as the content on the web is disparate and fragmented. So you need to build a special search and extract system to fetch useful data from mounds of information to be stored into the data warehouse. Before extraction, you must also verify the accuracy of the source data.

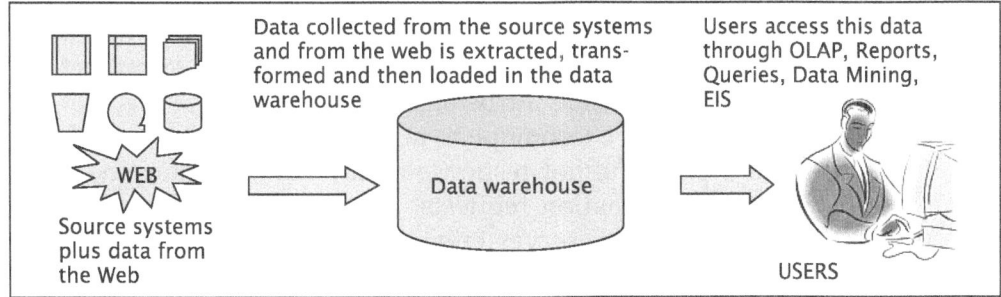

Figure 14.6 Bringing the web to the warehouse

Data Webhouse Architecture

The need for strategic decision-making requires a comprehensive snapshot of the business in real time and in turn provides information related to broad questions about customer behaviour. These days, data warehouse has become an active player in the web revolution. It however, requires restating and adjusting the data warehouse thinking. Even though a data web house is just a simple variation of the traditional data warehouse, the architecture of a data webhouse is entirely different from that of a traditional data warehouse.

Before considering the structure of the data webhouse, let us first go over the components that need to be pulled together to make up the web-enabled data warehouse. Look at the list below.

- The data webhouse configuration is distributed component architecture that goes far beyond client-server computing. For a data webhouse, the usual two-tier or three-tier technology is simply not sufficient. With more number of users accessing the data webhouse, new servers must be added without any difficulty thereby forming a distributed architecture.
- With the user nodes spread out, there is a need to strive for minimum administration on the client side.
- Appropriate database must be chosen to support the distributed environment.
- The project team must pay special attention to the administration and maintenance of the data webhouse. It should accurately list out the business dimensions, hierarchies within the dimensions and the facts or measures, aggregations and level of summarizations.
- The web interface consists of a browser, search engine, push technologies, home pages and hypertext links, Java, and ActiveX applets.
- Since HTML is universally deployed, so use it as much as possible. It is always better to use Java or plug ins for complex ad hoc analysis.

Figure 14.7 shows the web architecture configuration with the overall arrangement of its components. The complexity of the data webhouse architecture is much more than the two-tier or three-tier architecture as it calls for additional tiers to accommodate the requirements of web computing. To implement the architecture, the organization must have a web server between the browser clients and the database and the firewall to protect the corporate applications from outside intrusions.

The most effective technique to take pressure off the main database engine is to build a powerful hot response cache that can anticipate the predictable and repeated information requests. The multiple jobs running in the main webhouse application server creates the cache's data. Once this data gets stored in the hot response cache, the data objects can be fetched from it on demand. The cache can be used to store not only simple types of data but can also store complex file objects.

The hot response cache is therefore a file server and not a database. Its primary goal is to support the application server's needs. All applications must be aware of the existence of the hot response cache and should therefore be able to probe it to see if the information they want is present in it or not.

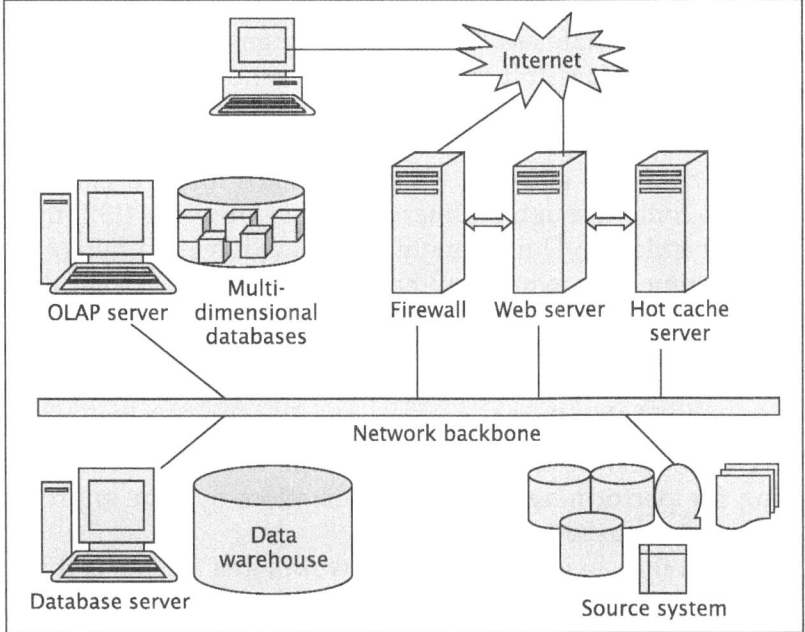

Figure 14.7 Web architecture configuration

Finally, the strategy of seeking a precomputed result and defaulting if necessary to the base data is exactly the way conventional aggregates works in the data warehouse. The data warehouse aggregate navigator search for aggregates to answer portions of an overall report query. If the navigator finds the aggregate, it uses the same; otherwise it gracefully defaults to computing the answer slowly from the base data. A data webhosue is simply a refinement of the traditional data warehouse and not a distinct deviation from it.

14.3.3 Building a Clickstream Data Webhouse

To build a clickstream data webhouse, a simple four-step methodology is used to form the dimensional model. The steps of this strategy include:

- First define the source of data.
- Determine the granularity of fact table.
- Determine the dimensions that are appropriate for the chosen level of grain.
- Determine the facts according to the data granularity level.

Data Source for the Clickstream Data Webhouse

We need to put the most granular or detailed data possible describing the clicks on the web server. With data at the lowest level of detail, each web server will potentially obtain a record for every page hit with information like precise date and time of page click; remote client's IP address; page requested;

and cookie information, if available. However, the primary issue is that the page hits are often stateless. Therefore, a page hit may just be a random isolated event that is difficult to interpret as part of a user session.

The second serious problem is whether recording the remote client's IP address will help in analysis of user behaviour or not. If the only client identification is the IP address, we cannot learn much because most of the Internet users come through an Internet service provider (ISP) that assigns IP addresses dynamically. Thus, remote users will have a different address at a later point of time than what they have now. So even though the individual session by the customer can be tracked but we can't be sure when the user returns to the site in a different session.

Dimensions and the Facts

A sound data webhouse schema can boost the web analysis. It enhances data processing for performing web personalization, system improvement, site modification, and business intelligence.

Every event that an individual user invokes in a session is the grain of the clickstream data mart fact table. Each event becomes an individual record, and each record is an event on a web page. Take an example, if an organization has 10,000 user sessions per day on its web site, and if on an average each session involves seven events, then 70,000 new records will be added in the fact table every day. See the below diagram for the clickstream data mart's dimensional model. The dimensions are date, time, user, page, product, event, and session.

The above dimensional model is quite simple and very intuitive. The targeting event implies when the event occurred and therefore, a calendar date and a time of day are in order. The specific point of time when the event took place can be captured by the Time dimension.

The Page dimension stores records related to an individual page type and describe the context for a web page event. The page dimension is important as it contains all the information that tells the analyst the user's web site location. Every web page must contain certain descriptors identifying the location and type of page. For this purpose, a complete path name is not as interesting as such basic attributes as "Product Details," Company Profile, Frequently Asked Questions, and Place an Order Form. A well designed web site must contain a hierarchical description associated with each page that gives more detail about that page. For each page event, the facts that are stored includes: the page_seconds, which specifies the number of seconds elapsed before the next page event; the units_ordered and the order_amt.

The Event dimension describes what happened on a certain page at a particular point in time. For example, what did the user do on the page: Open Page, Refresh Page, Click Link, or Enter Data.

The context within which the events occurred is also important. For instance, the local context of a particular user session may be Requesting

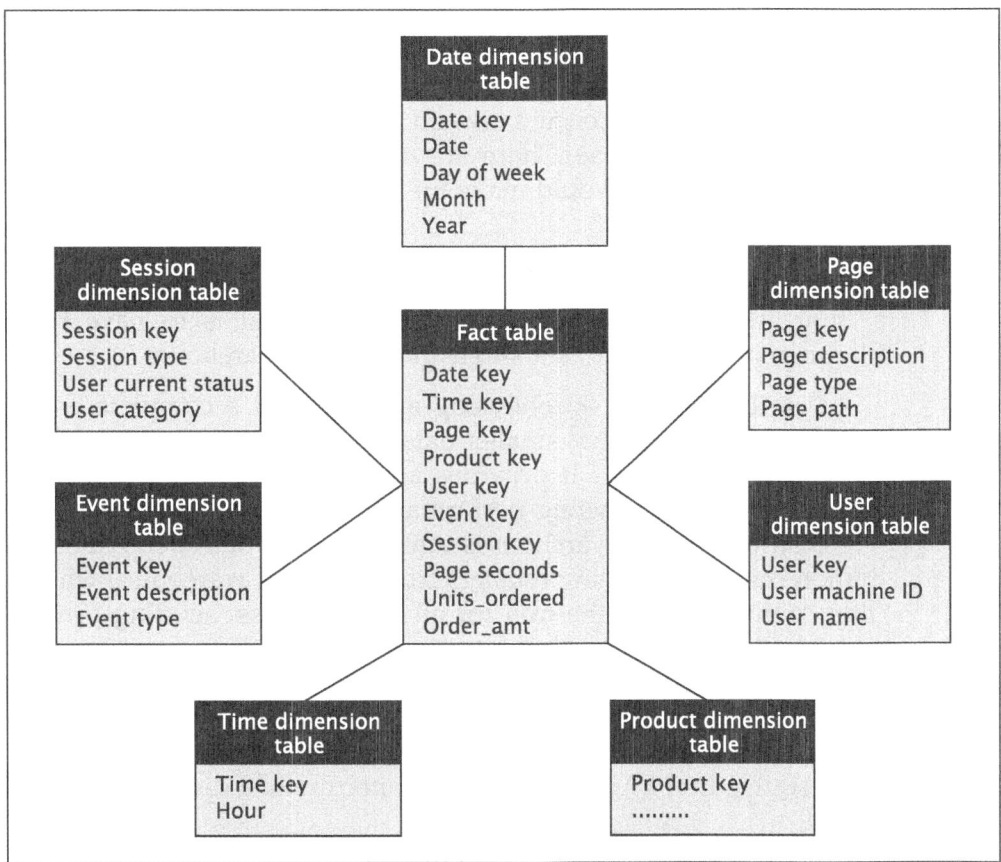

Figure 14.8 Clickstream data mart's dimensional model

Product Information, but the overall session context might be Ordering a Product. Therefore, both the contexts along with the related success status must be recorded in a Session dimension. This dimension is very important, as it throws light on issues like the number of customers who wanted the product information page before ordering or canceling the order or began an ordering process, but never completed it.

Thus, we see that the session dimension does much more than simply grouping together all the page events that constitute a single user's session. Using this dimension, the individual user sessions may be categorized as searching for information, random browsing, price and feature shopping, or placing an order. All these activities can be tagged with simple criteria regarding what the user does during the session.

14.4 DISTRIBUTED DATA WAREHOUSE

Before understanding what a distributed data warehouse is, let us first look at some basic definitions.

"If you believe a data warehouse is a single physical database, then a distributed data warehouse would be where there are different physical databases that work together as a single physical database. In other words, there is no difference between a distributed data warehouse and a distributed database. There are others who will say that the data marts unioned together would make up a distributed data warehouse. It depends on your definition."   —*Chuck Kelley*

"A distributed data warehouse is a conglomeration of separate components that are connected via a network. The goal is to have these separate components appear as a single global data warehouse."   — *Joe Oates*

Distributed data warehousing encompasses a complete enterprise-wide data warehouse that has smaller data stores built separately and joined physically over a network. It provides access to the end-users through relevant reports without impacting performance.

Distributed data warehouses can be thought of as being identical to distribution centres supplying retailers from a central warehouse where a distribution centre acts like the hub for all merchandise, sending products to individual retail stores for customer consumption.

Similarly, a distributed data warehouse which acts as the nucleus of all enterprise data, sends relevant data to individual data marts from which users can access information for query processing, report formulating and for strategic analysis. Figure 14.9 illustrates the architecture of a distributed data warehouse.

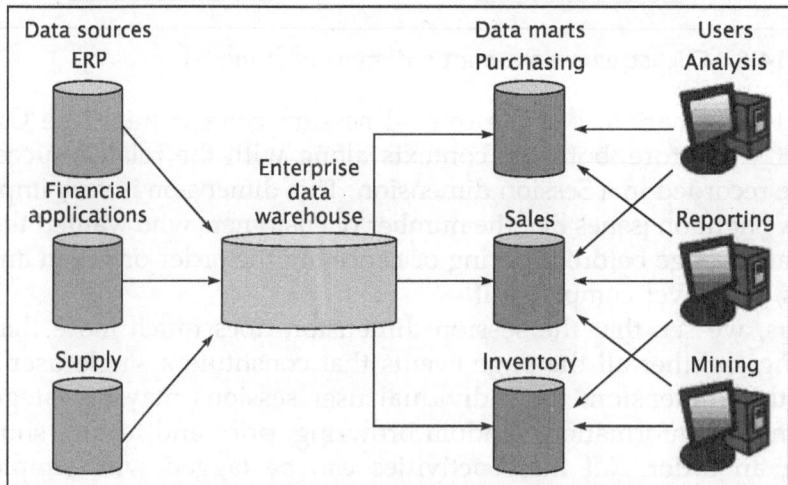

Figure 14.9 Architecture of a distributed data warehouse

14.4.1 Advantages of Distributed Data Warehousing

Distributed data warehousing offers several advantages over the traditional data warehouses. First, a distributed data warehouse is designed to support integrated data flows between a centralized data warehouse and individual data marts. This enables the end-users to gain rapid access to enterprise-wide information irrespective of where data marts are actually located. It acts as an advantage as communication between geographically-dispersed data marts in a non-distributed environment is often restricted or even non-existent.

A distributed model improves system performance by allowing data to be spread across several data marts so that reports can be run over smaller datasets, which will in turn offer rapid response times as well as broad access to data without compromising the integrity or performance of production applications on the centralized data warehouse. Table 14.2 lists the benefits and the risks of a distributed data warehouse.

Table 14.2 Benefits and risks of distributed data warehouse

Benefits	Risks
• Provides support to multiple, geographically distributed business departments.	• Majority of the ETL tools do not support a geographically distributed ETL environment with a global metadata repository and in case they do support, the ETL process is very complex.
• Allows every business division to have multiple data marts.	• It is expensive.
• The enterprise-wide data warehouse stores the data for the entire organization.	• Central coordination and management is required that is purely based on access to a global metadata repository.
• The components of the distributed data warehouse environment are synchronized. using a global metadata repository.	• Complex environment which thereby leads to higher development costs and risks.

14.4.2 Distributed vs. Centralized Warehouse

With its massive growth, the Internet has now become the backbone to distribute the data warehouse. As stated before, a distributed data warehouse is an integrated set of individual data stores that are physically distributed across a company's communication infrastructure. In a distributed data warehouse environment, independent data marts are dispersed throughout the organization and as the users query the data from the distributed data warehouse, the data is combined from these systems by either the client-tier or middle-tier applications.

Supporters of the distributed data warehouse state that distribution of the data solves several problems encountered by one large system. Apart from this the, size of data warehouses being in terabytes creates administrative and maintenance challenges.

The data warehouse project team always faces an issue as to whether to distribute or centralize the data warehouse. In the first place, it may seem attractive to distribute but then they cannot ignore a few painful realities before making the final decision. Distributing the data warehouse may even be a patently bad idea. Initially, the statements made above may have been true and the decision to distribute in some environments might not have been all that devastating but with the current technology, it is not only possible to create a single enterprise-wide data warehouse, but it may be preferable also.

How metrics are calculated will vary from one system to another in a distributed environment. Even if the calculations are done in the same manner throughout all the systems, the source data may vary due to differing refresh rates. Apart from this, multiple systems may disagree with one another and yet be correct within their own context. In a distributed data warehouse, when two systems disagree, there is no single version of the truth. However, this is not the case in a centralized system where there is a single arbitrator of the truth: the data warehouse.

There are other drawbacks also for a distributed data warehouse environment as compared with a centralized environment. In the centralized system, data can be pre-aggregated for faster retrieval but in a distributed environment, every time we wish to sum the data across systems, we have to extract the data first and then perform our calculations. The distributed environment solution to this problem could be to pre-aggregate the data in an independent system within the middle tier, thereby creating the centralized data warehouse and further complicating a complex problem.

Hardware and software advances today have eliminated many problems that made the option to distribute the data warehouse attractive. For example, data warehouses up to 50 or 60 terabytes are no longer a problem. With the advancements in parallel database systems and storage arrays the size issue has been easily resolved. Besides pre-aggregated data reduces the need for full table scans, and bitmapped indexing is used to enhance the performance when full table scans are needed.

14.5 VIRTUAL DATA WAREHOUSE

Some businesses today are moving towards a simple data warehousing tool that provides end users with direct access to operational data on legacy databases, also known as a virtual data warehouse. In contrast to the traditional data warehouses, in the 'virtual' scenario, data is not moved from source databases to a target data warehouse. Moreover, a target database and data warehouse is not even actually present within a virtual environment. Instead, end users are provided with intuitive end-user tools to access data directly from operational systems, using common business terms for strategic analysis rather than accessing the enterprise wide data warehouse.

Some businesses think virtual data warehouse to be a good option because it enables businesses to access and analyse data from operational systems, such as Oracle Financials or SAP R/3, without having to rely on IT personnel to extract and process the data. Virtual data warehouses make use of the existing legacy systems as database servers. This reduces the investment needed for buying additional hardware and software.

The virtual data warehousing technology is extremely simple as it nullifies the need for complex data extraction and transformation tools, metadata repositories, or separate data warehouse databases. Accessing the data directly from legacy systems with intuitive front-end data warehousing tools saves huge investment in mainframe hardware, software, databases, and skill sets. Apart from this, data warehousing is not an easy task as building a data warehouse calls for a huge investment and once built, data warehouse systems are complex to manage and maintain.

14.5.1 Why to Go for a Virtual Data Warehouse?

Before answering this question, first we need to think how appropriate is a full-fledged data warehouse for businesses ranging from the typical small industries to the large multi-national, or from simple single-point access to corporate data through to complex analysis of a huge multidimensional corporate data store? It should be noted that each data warehousing solution is as different from the next as each business is from that of its competitor.

There are many organizations today that need the power and sophistication of large-scale data warehousing solutions, and that can spend huge amounts of money to achieve the benefits that such systems offer. But there are other small and medium scale businesses whose requirements are far simpler than this and thus they do not need the power of such a complex data warehouse.

The needs of these businesses can be typically summarized as:

- Providing simple access to information from across the company, using different delivery methods.
- Avoiding the same information to be entered into different systems.
- Providing consolidated reporting from across the organization, along with roll-up and drill-down analysis to enable the users to have access to applications like EIS and data mining.

The requirements of data warehousing solution can be placed under the above categories and to meet these needs, virtual data warehousing is an alternative approach to the traditional data warehouse. The other benefits include the following.

Minimal investment   A virtual warehouse calls for minimal investment in additional hardware and software as it tends to utilize existing legacy systems as database servers and the only real investment need to be done to implement middleware technology. Thus, this solution is relatively quick to implement and thereby quick to carry out the task of analysis.

Less time, risk, and complexity involved   Virtual data warehouses allow users to extract important information from disparate legacy applications, without the time, expense, and risk to data required by traditional data warehousing.

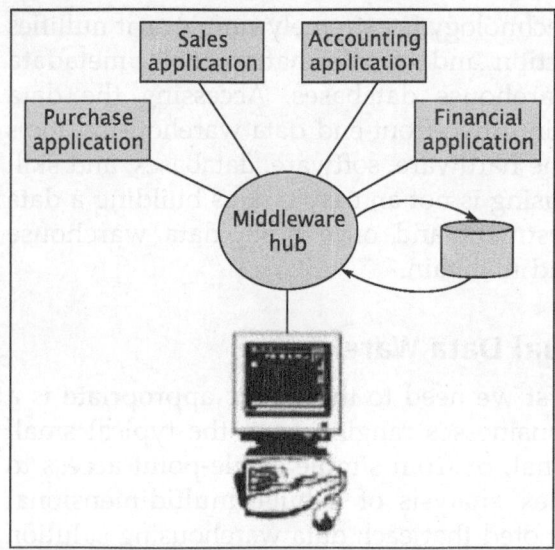

Figure 14.10 Middleware architecture

Vendors that offer virtual warehouse solutions, include nQuire Software, Inc.'s nQuire Suite 3.0 and Cohera Corporation's Cohera Content Integration System software. However, building a virtual data warehouse is not considered to be a viable long-term solution to building a data warehouse infrastructure.

Practical implementation Virtual data warehousing give its users an appearance of a real, 'physical' data warehouse, but without a central, large database being needed to support this view.

A virtual data warehouse is implemented using middleware technology (see Fig. 14.10) which combines both hardware and software that handles the acquisition, transformation and delivery of information from the various systems to the user.

The basic difference between a virtual data warehouse and a physical data warehouse is the absence of an intermediate permanent data store. The middleware technology provides the illusion of a single system with which the user transacts.

As seen in the figure above, the middleware architecture usually chosen for a virtual data warehouse application uses a 'hub-and-spoke' scheme, where the middleware links to all central systems and to all front-end users, with information being routed, transformed and consolidated through the central hub.

Thus, the middleware technology of virtual data warehouses succeeds in providing users with a single point of access to all corporate information via whatever delivery mechanism is most convenient to each user.

14.5.2 Limitations

Till now we have only been talking about the benefits of virtual data warehousing. However, the limitations of a virtual data warehouse are not less. Let us go through serious limitations posed by a virtual data warehouse.

Not a true solution A virtual data warehouse is not a true data warehousing solution, as it does not include the following features:

- A data warehouse database.
- A historical data.
- A ccess to summarization or aggregation of data.
- A central metadata repository.
- The ability to cleanse and reorganize data.
- A centralized ETL functionality to clean and standardize data.

Effects business transactions While using virtual data warehouses, online operations gets disrupted since query functions access data directly from the source files. For example, a query like "Display the sales of every product in a store and also list the turnover for top ten highest and lowest selling items" can result in a massive number of query functions that can severely impact the performance of the operational systems that are actually responsible to run the business.

Not a long-term promising solution Although, virtual data warehouses may help the business to save money initially but a true data warehousing solution will have to be re-implemented on a dedicated separate server at some time in the future. Moreover, switching from a virtual data warehouse to a dedicated warehouse may be extremely disruptive if it occurs at a time when the data warehouse is widely used by a large number of users to support decision making.

Performance overhead For a virtual data warehouse you need to performance tune the database of each source application to optimize it for the countless queries it will have input to.

Data standardization problem The tools have difficulty differentiating between meanings of the data elements. For example, different source applications for the virtual data warehouse might store the gender of customers as F or M, or 1 or 2. So, you need to spend a lot of time writing a rule for each application to sort out this difference, and these rules will have to be enforced at each extraction point from each source system.

This situation of extracting data from a virtual data warehouse would be like searching for a needle in a haystack, trying to ferret all of the inconsistencies that need to be resolved. With a centralized data warehouse, the data is validated and transformed at a single point.

Another related problem that exists in case of a virtual data warehouse is the challenge for middleware applications to handle semantic differences in data of various source systems. For example: customer_id and product_id or CUST_ID and PROD_ID.

Heterogeneous data sources According to analysts, T. Friedman and K. Strange, "The increased fragmentation of data subject areas across multiple sources leads to numerous discrepancies in the syntax and semantics of the data." They say that the problem is magnified because the average enterprise has between five and seven DBMS technologies, and approximately 50 sources of data.

Dirty data With a virtual data warehouse in place, data cleansing is also a problem. Except for the capabilities native to the source applications, most data cleansing functionality is absent in a virtual data warehouse environment which may result in gibberish result sets for user queries.

Limited analysis Virtual data warehouses considerably limit analysis capabilities, especially in context of analysing historical data. Generally, the organizations axe the historical data from their operational systems and put it in offline storage. This avoids any slowdown in the processing performance of the systems. Therefore, practically it is not feasible to use a virtual data warehouse that draws on such operational systems to analyse the historical data.

A virtual data warehouse also limits analysis, as there is no repository that consolidates data from different subject areas or from multiple source applications in one area, viz. customer, billing, operations management, etc.

Conclusion In case an organization decides to go for a virtual data warehouse to support direct access to operational data, it should only be to provide temporary facilities, and will eventually need to be replaced with a true data warehouse.

Thus, using middleware layers to look at the total enterprise wide data as a virtual data warehouse does not eliminate the necessity for classic data warehousing as in many large organizations, data volumes are so enormous that isolating information in a dedicated warehouse is the only viable option. Table 14.3 summarizes the issues and risks involved in case of virtual data warehousing.

Table 14.3 Virtual data warehousing—issues and risks

Virtual Data Warehouse	Issues	Risks
Data warehouse is a collection of information, available or accessible, on some terms, to some community of users.	A data warehouse is a very large component offering a range of data services, through a number of well-defined interfaces.	Not a data warehouse
A warehouse may be centralized, physically distributed, or virtual.	A virtual data warehouse is implemented through complex mechanisms and may even be distributed across multiple platforms and locations, but this complexity can be hidden from data users.	No historical data
A virtual data warehouse is implemented using middleware technology to provide a single point access to information available.	The virtual data warehouse approach separates following aspects of data warehousing: • Users are given direct access to source databases. • Data is not moved from source databases. • No target database means no data warehouse. • Provides single, unified front end to multiple hosts. • Hides the complexity of host systems.	Queries may disrupt the performance of operational systems

14.6 OPERATIONAL DATA STORE

We have seen that a data warehouse can never deliver the data in a millisecond. Data is delivered in milliseconds in operational systems. Due to the sheer volume of data, accessing data in a few sub-seconds is far beyond imagination.

However, there are some applications that need data to be delivered within a few seconds. Does this mean that such operations cannot be executed in the data warehouse environment? No, certainly not. The data warehouse technology supports an additional concept of operational data store (ODS).

ODS is the database that is accessed when a high performance processing must be done. Having an ODS in place is optional and its need depends on the nature of the business.

The ODS shares some similarity with the data warehouse. Like a data warehouse, as ODS

- Resides outside the operational environment.
- Supports DSS processing.
- Uses integrated data.

Data flows from the ODS to the data warehouse at some occasions while at other occasions it flows from the data warehouse to the ODS, as shown in Fig. 14.11. Although the data flow between an ODS and a data warehouse is bi-directional, in no situation does an ODS reside inside a data warehouse.

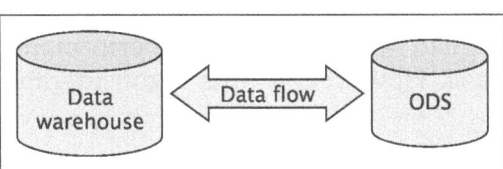

Figure 14.11 Data flow between ODS and data warehouse

These two are entirely different structures. Unlike data warehouse, an ODS is designed to provide high performance, real time processing. An ODS is said to have a 2–3 second response time.

Carefully look at Fig. 14.11. The ODS is much smaller than the data warehouse. Why? Following are the reasons:

- While the data warehouse contains historical as well as current data, the ODS is designed to contain only current data.
- The data warehouse contains large quantities of data as it is deployed to serve all types of end-users. But the ODS is designed to serve only one type of processing and thus, the ODS contains much less diversified data than the data warehouse.
- While the data warehouse contains detailed data, the ODS is designed to store summarized data.

Nature of Data

In striking contrast with the data warehouse, an ODS contains a very limited amount of historical data. While the data warehouse stores 5–10 years of historical data, the ODS stores only a month's old data. Due to this basic difference, applications that need historical data are run against the data warehouse database, and the applications that need current data for analysis are run against the ODS.

Underlying Technology

The ODS is designed using a hybrid approach since a part of it is designed using relational technology and the rest is designed using multidimensional technology. As discussed before, relational technology is used where flexibility of data analysis is more important and multidimensional technology is used where high performance is required.

Updates in ODS

We know that a data warehouse is not updated. Once a record is written into it, it is never deleted or changed. If there are some changes in the real world, then they are applied by adding additional rows in the database. This is not the case when it comes to an ODS. Since an ODS contains current data, it is updated the way we update operational systems.

Transaction Integrity

We all know that a data warehouse is rarely updated and it does not support high performance transaction processing, so there is not much need of having transaction integrity in the underlying DBMS. This results in much lower overhead on the data warehouse DBMS. However, this is not the case in the ODS environment. The ODS DBMS requires transaction integrity that calls for backup and recovery procedures. These procedures are mandatory to be implemented in an ODS as it is designed to support high performance processing and updates into its database. However, it puts a considerable overhead on the underlying DBMS.

Profile Records

The ODS supports profile records. A profile record is one that is formed from many observations about an entity. A profile record creates a synopsis from multiple occurrences of data. A sample profile record is shown in Fig. 14.12.

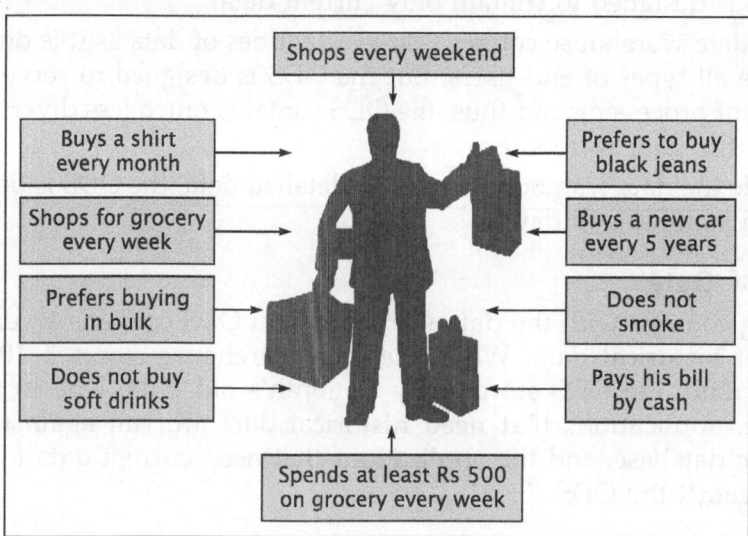

Figure 14.12 A sample profile record

The profile record in an ODS is created by scanning the detailed historical data that exist in the data warehouse. The advantages of a profile record are:

- It can be accessed very quickly.

- It nullifies the need to study the detailed historical data to extract useful information.
- It contains information about every aspect like the profile record stores data about buying habits, paying habits, and preferences.

Figure 14.13 shows a sample profile record, but in general the profile record stores information like the customer name, his address, gender, income level, his telephone number, number of children, birth date, automobiles owned, paying habits, borrowing habits, reading habits, purchasing habits, etc. Therefore, a profile record captures massive amounts of data very concisely. Once the information is captured in a profile record, it can be easily and quickly accessed as when the need arises. Figure 14.13 shows the manner in which a profile record is created from a data warehouse.

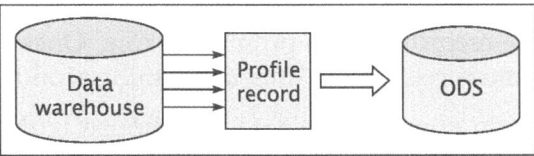

Figure 14.13 Creation of profile record

Classes of ODS   An ODS is categorized into four classes depending upon how fast the data arrives into it. This done by calculating the time elapsed between the occurrence of a transaction and the arrival of that transaction in the ODS. Table 14.4 lists these classes.

Table 14.4 ODS classes

Class	Features	Application
Class I	- It takes a few milliseconds for the data to arrive in the ODS, once a transaction takes place. - The time elapsed is transparent to the users. - Expensive as it needs challenging technology. - Emphasizes on speed of update and synchronization data. - No time for data integration.	- Rarely used. - Applied in airline reservation system.
Class II	- It takes several hours for the data to arrive in the ODS, once a transaction takes place. - The end-user can visualize that there is a time gap between the arrival and occurrence of the transaction. - Built using simple technology. - Ample time for data integration. - Inexpensive.	- Used commonly. - Applied to update name and address change of a customer.
Class III	- There is an overnight gap or longer between the occurrence of transaction and arrival of data in the ODS. - Inexpensive. - Can be built with conventional technology	- Used for applying sales transactions.
Class IV	- The time gap between occurrence of transaction and its arrival into the ODS is much longer, often in some months or years. - The source of data can be a data warehouse or some other. - May be created from output of special reports or projects. - Creation of a Class IV data may be a one time event.	- A survey of customer buying habits.

ODS and the Web When a customer visits the website, it needs to fetch details of that customer. This means at this point of time, the Web needs data. In the absence of any profile record, the website would have to get the required data from the data warehouse. This would consume a lot of time, as it would call for fetching and analysing several records. It will not be surprising if the response time is in several minutes or even hours. Obviously, the Internet user will get bogged and leave the website if the website takes so long to do its task.

Therefore, the Web environment fetches data from the ODS and not the data warehouse. This is where profile records play a prominent role. Once a profile record is in place, the access time is reduced to only a few milliseconds.

ODS example In a telecommunication company, a data warehouse is deployed to store data of every single telephone call made by its customers. This data warehouse contains millions of records. In this situation, an ODS is also deployed that organizes the data by every customer and then creates a profile record for every customer. These profile records store a summary about the customers, e.g. how many phone calls are made by the customer, where does he/she makes maximum calls, how many long distance calls are made, etc.

The operators of the telephone company are then given access to the ODS. When a customer calls the operator, he can get all the information about the calling customer on his screen. This would in turn help to provide better and quick service to the customer.

14.7 INTEGRATION WITH OTHER TECHNOLOGIES

In this section, we will see how data warehousing is widely being integrated with other mature technologies. We will also learn how data warehousing, when integrated with these technologies, can help the organizations to reap fruitful seeds.

14.7.1 Data Warehousing and ERP

Enterprise Resource Planning (ERP) software is a recent addition to the manufacturing and information systems that organizes the flow of data from the first process to the last. For any business, the information flow begins when the first manufacturer traded with the first merchants. In the absence of ERP software all this information was not captured. According to Anne Marie Smith, in her paper *Data Warehousing & ERP—A Combination of Forces* (2002), the ERP software attempts to link all the internal company processes into a common set of applications that share a common database. Therefore, the common database enables an ERP system to serve as a source for a robust data warehouse to support sophisticated decision support and analysis.

The ERP software is divided into functional areas of operation where each functional area is composed of numerous business processes. The common functional areas of operation include: marketing and sales, production and operations (materials management, inventory, etc.), accounting and finance, and human resources. Initially, businesses had clear divisions among the different functional areas and IS development was totally delineated so that systems did not share data or processes. This scenario made cross-functional analysis of information almost impossible. The independence among functional areas created artificial barriers that needed to be overcome.

The ERP software was designed to eliminate the barriers that exist in sharing data and processes when companies implement information systems. ERP software coordinates the entire business process and stores all the captured data in a common database, so that it can be accessed by all the applications that are part of the ERP suite. This allows the companies to achieve many cost savings and related benefits for transaction processing and management reporting.

Integrating ERP with Data Warehousing

With the introduction of data warehousing technology in the 1990s, companies started exploring the ways they can capture, store, and manipulate data for analysis and decision support.

But before data warehousing was widely used, these companies had instituted the ERP software to coordinate the common functions of an enterprise. ERP software is characterized by a central database as its hub that allows different applications to share and reuse data more efficiently than ever before. The existence of a central ERP database has laid the grounds for developing a corporate-wide data warehouse that can be used for strategic analysis.

Data warehouses today are the cornerstone of the decision-support systems. William Inmon, in his book *Building a Data Warehouse*, has defined it as a collection of integrated, subject-oriented databases where each unit of data is specific to some period of time. Data warehouses can contain detailed data, lightly summarized data, and highly summarized data, all formatted for analysis and decision support. However, Ralph Kimball in his book *Data Warehouse Toolkit*, has given a more succinct definition: "a copy of transaction data specifically structured for query and analysis." Both these definitions emphasize on the analytic features of the warehouse and highlight the historical nature of the data stored in it.

In today's scenario, the ERP market is huge and crossing a $45 billion mark. The organizations are adopting ERP application packages offered by big vendors like SAP, Baan, JD Edwards, and PeopleSoft. The main reason behind its popularity is that most companies are running different disparate applications that cannot present a single unified view of the corporate information. These organizations have outdated legacy systems. Hence, reconciliation of data extracted from the source systems to produce the desired information is extremely difficult and in some cases next to impossible. ERP vendors seemingly came to the rescue of such companies.

The most demanding feature of an ERP package is that it supports practically every phase of the business right from inventory control, customer billing, human resources to production management, product costing, and budgetary control. This feature makes the ERP package even more complex.

When the ERP was introduced in the early 1990s, it promised to provide its customers an integrated corporate-wide data repository that the companies were looking for. It contained cleansed, transformed, and integrated data stored in one place to support decision-making. But soon companies that went for the ERP technology realized that the relational databases designed for running business transactions were not at all suitable for providing strategic information. Moreover, in ERP data repositories, there was no provision for data from external sources and from other operational systems in the company. As a result, the companies which are already using some ERP package or those companies which are planning to get some ERP package are now finding the integration of data warehousing with ERP as a better alternative.

Issues in Integrating ERP

An ERP solution satisfies the user's quest for information via queries and reports, but the main drawback is the inability to merge ERP data with outside data sources (e.g., market reference, legacy, or specialized system). To merge this type of data is often beyond the scope of most ERP solutions. Therefore, using a data warehouse for analysis purpose off-loads the ERP solution and improves system performance.

With the use of the ERP's common database and the implementation of data warehouse support products, companies are now able to design a decision data warehouse database that allows cross-functional area analysis and comparisons for better decision-making.

In a data warehouse environment, the data flows from the source system into the data warehouse database. For a successful data warehouse, identification of the correct source system is very essential. It is even more critical in a data warehouse that includes an ERP along with more traditional transaction systems. Integration of data from multiple sources (ERP database and others) demands a lot of attention to the metadata and business logic that populated the source data elements, so that the right data and the right source systems are chosen.

Another issue with ERP data is the need for storing historical data in the enterprise's data warehouse. Traditionally, the enterprise data warehouse is designed to store historical data, and ERP technology does not store historical data. When a large amount of historical data gets collected in the ERP environment, the ERP environment is either purged or the data is archived to a remote storage facility. For example, suppose an enterprise data warehouse needs five years of historical data to be stored in it, while the ERP holds six-months-old data at the most. If the enterprise is satisfied with collecting a historical set of data, then there is no problem with ERP as a source for data warehouse data.

The other important issue in building a data warehouse in the ERP environment is that of metadata. As the data moves from the ERP to the data warehouse environment, the metadata must also be moved and transformed into the format required by the data warehouse. There is a significant difference between operational system metadata and a data warehouse metadata. Operational metadata is primarily for the developer and programmer, whereas data warehouse metadata is primarily for the end-user. As stated earlier, the metadata of the ERP application's database must be converted according to the structure and format of the data warehouse. But this conversion is not easy and requires experienced data administrators and users to collaborate in the effort.

Willian Inmon suggests some guidelines for using the ERP database as a source for a data warehouse. According to Inmon, there should be a solid interface that will pull the data from the ERP environment to the data warehouse environment. This interface must have the following features:

- Ease of use.
- Ability to access the ERP data.
- Capability to capture the meaning of the data that has to be moved into the warehouse.
- Aware of referential integrity constraints.
- Aware of hierarchical relationships that exist in the data.
- Aware of the business rules.
- Aware of data structures supported by the ERP.
- Efficient in accessing ERP data, supporting direct data movement and change data capture.
- Support timely access of ERP data.
- Ability to understand the format of data.

Thus, the development of data warehouses with ERP as factors in the information systems explosion must be addressed and resolved by experienced IT professionals with a clear understanding of the challenges that each environment poses. Integrating ERP data into a data warehouse can lead to an excellent source of data for analysis and decision-making. As a final note, ignoring the wealth of data and information available from an ERP is equivalent to ignoring a valuable corporate resource, one that can serve as a foundation for a superior data warehouse.

Common Misconceptions

These days, many companies are taking competitive advantage by analysing business metrics. For this, they are investing millions in implementing ERP solutions that often include reporting and analytical tools. Now the question is, whether these companies really need a data warehouse tool set? The answer is yes—despite some common misconceptions that are given below.

- ERP systems are enterprise-wide, thus it is easy and straightforward to merge the data with other sources.
- An ERP solution can satisfy all the reporting needs of the end-users. This is not true because there are drawbacks such as the inability to merge ERP data with outside data sources (e.g., market reference, legacy, or specialized system). Capturing and analysing this data is beyond the scope of most ERP solutions. Therefore, a data warehouse is used for reporting to off-load the ERP solution and improve the performance of the system.
- The ERP stores data of high quality. This is a misconception as many users assume ERP data is accurate because it is entered via an ERP interface. But in fact a quality management or data cleansing tool must be used to ensure the accuracy of the data.
- ERP data is accessed quickly and easily. ERP systems have complex data storage. For example, product description may be stored in one table while product stock data in another table. The analysts want all of this information together and thus rely on the data warehouse developer to identify all the appropriate tables to get the required pieces.
- ERP system gives great performance. With the increase in the operational store of the ERP solution, the changed data will have to be updated in the data warehouse. But for this, the update mechanism will have to go through the entire ERP system, update existing records, and insert new ones. This is an inefficient process. Therefore, to ensure high performance, the update mechanism should only extract changed or new records.

Conclusion

ERP data warehousing is a framework of information objects that becomes the foundation of business intelligence, knowledge support systems, and other business applications across the enterprise, leveraging the infrastructure of ERP applications.

ERP data warehousing is not just about extracting data from an ERP application package, it is about supporting services needed to construct a data warehouse and collection of integrated applications, to enable the end-users to formulate reports, analyse, and control business events across the enterprise.

14.7.2 Data Warehousing and Knowledge Management

The year 1999 marked the genesis of knowledge management (KM) systems in many corporations and since then, it is catching on very rapidly. While operational systems deal with data, the data warehouse systems are designed to empower the users by capturing, integrating, storing, and transforming the data into useful information for strategic analysis. KM takes this empowerment to a higher level by providing knowledge to use the right information, at the right time, and the right place.

Knowledge is actionable information and KM is a systematic process for capturing, integrating, organizing, and communicating the knowledge. It is a vehicle to share corporate knowledge in order to make its employees more effective and productive in their work. In an organization, knowledge exists in the form of procedures, documents, reports analysing exception conditions, objects, what-if cases, text streams, video clips, etc.

A knowledge management system stores all such knowledge in a knowledge repository, better known as a *knowledge warehouse*. Thus, as stated before, the primary difference between a knowledge warehouse and a data warehouse is that a data warehouse contains structured information and a knowledge warehouse holds unstructured information. For this purpose, it is crucial for a KM framework to have tools for searching and retrieving unstructured information. Figure 14.14 shows the integration of KM and data warehouse.

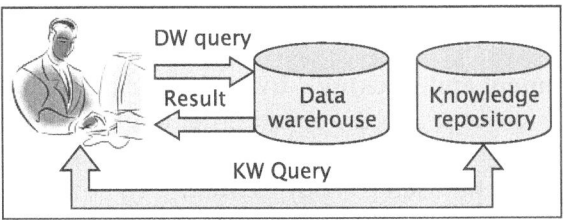

Figure 14.14 Integration of knowledge repository and data warehouse

14.7.3 Data Warehousing and EIS

Prior to data warehousing, there were executive information systems (EIS), which supported the notion that computations should be available to everyone in the organization and not just the clerical community who perform the day-to-day transactions. In spite of it being a good idea to deliver the computations to everyone and displaying beautiful GUI screens with data displayed in a very elegant and a presentable manner, EIS had no concept of infrastructure needed to get those numbers to the executives.

Before the data warehouses first appeared in the market, EIS was a big failure, as the executives had better things to do than worry about issues such as sources of data, quality of data, currency of data, etc. Thus, we can conclude that EIS died due to lack of a proper infrastructure in place. Presentation of data in an elegant fashion was hardly of any use when the data itself was unbelievable and inaccurate.

Thus, EIS disappeared. But the promises and notions of EIS are still valuable and real. Consequently, EIS has appeared again in the market in the form of OLAP and other DSS applications like CRM. All these applications are related to data warehousing, unlike the earlier form of EIS.

Integrating EIS with Data Warehousing

EIS is one of the most potent forms of computing. With the help of EIS, the executives can pinpoint problems and detect trends that are of vital importance to the business. Therefore, it will not be wrong to say that EIS represents one of the most sophisticated applications of computer technology.

EIS processing is designed to help the business executives and managers to make decisions, thereby providing a window into the organization. Some typical applications of EIS as given by W.H. Inmon are listed below.

Trend analysis EIS helps the analysts to learn about the prevailing trends in the market. The executives are interested in both negative and positive trends. For example, if the business is getting worse, then they must be able to find out why the business is showing a downturn, at what rate, and what can be the remedial actions that can be taken. On the other hand, if the business is growing, then the executives must be aware of the factors that are responsible for the upturn, what can be done to accelerate these success factors and can these success factors be applied to other parts of the business as well.

Key performance indicator measurement and tracking Every organization has several performance indicators which in a single measurement reveal some aspect of the working of the business. These key performance indicators when collected over a period of time can also be used to spot trends.

Drill-down analysis Drilling down refers to the activity of analysing the data at a summary number and then continuing analyses by breaking that summary into a successively finer levels of detail. By looking at the details hidden behind the summary, the executives can get a picture of how the business is actually doing.

Problem monitoring It helps in discovering potential problems in the working of the business and taking remedial steps as soon as possible.

Competitive analysis The executives compare the data of their organization with that of their competitors to see where they stand in the market. It helps them to analyse the areas where they lack behind. On the other hand, if the organization is in a better position, then the executives need to know their strong points and work in order to maintain their position even in the future.

Data Warehouse as a basis for EIS

A data warehouse operates most effectively way in an EIS environment. The data warehouse is tailor-made for the needs of the EIS analyst. Once a data warehouse is in place, it becomes much easier for the analysts to work. The foundation of a data warehouse in an EIS environment helps the analyst to concentrate on their analysis rather than worrying about the following issues:

- Searching for sources of data.
- Creating special extract programs from the source systems.
- Dealing with non-integrated data.
- Creating and linking detailed and summary data.
- Finding the best possible time basis for keeping the historical data.

Thus, the data warehouse provides the basis or the infrastructure that the EIS analyst needs to support EIS processing. With a sound data warehouse in place, the EIS analyst's job changes from a data engineer to that of doing true analysis. The data warehouse also lays the way for flexible and responsive sessions, as the data in the data warehouse stores data at the detailed level which can be easily shaped in a manner to cater for future needs of the data analysts.

Data warehouses today not only store detailed data, but store the data at different levels of aggregations/summarizations. This feature of a data warehouse helps the analysts to perform drill-down and roll-up operations.

14.7.4 Data Warehousing and CRM

Fierce competition has forced many companies to pay greater attention to retain customers and winning new ones. With such prevailing conditions in the market, customer loyalty programs have become the norm. For the same purpose, companies are now moving away from mass marketing to one-on-one marketing. In the present scenario, customer focus has become the keyword. For this, the companies are concentrating more and more on customer experience and customer intimacy to provide better customer service. This drives the organization towards embracing CRM systems and thus, multiple vendors are offering turnkey CRM solutions that promise to enable one-on-one service to customers.

When the company is gearing up to be more attuned to high levels of customer service, you will have to make the data warehouse more focused on the customer by making it CRM-ready which is not an easy task by any means. Despite all these problems, the payoff from a CRM data warehouse is substantial.

The data warehouse must hold details of every transaction made with the customer. For this purpose, not only detailed sales data is needed but also the details of every other type of encounter with each customer are required. As already explained, data stored at the most granular level provides maximum flexibility for the CRM-ready data warehouse. No doubt making a data warehouse CRM-ready will tremendously increase the data volumes, but this is not a big problem, as today's technology facilitates large volumes of atomic data to be placed across multiple storage management devices that can be accessed through the end-users tools.

To make the data warehouse CRM-ready, some other functions also need to be enhanced. For example, to store customer-related data, complex cleansing and transformation functions have to be performed. Before inserting this data into the warehouse, duplicate values have to be eliminated, then combined to form distinct households, and enriched with the addition of external demographic data. For this purpose, traditional data warehousing tools are not suited for specialized requirements of customer-focused applications.

Active Data Warehousing

With the emergence of active data warehouse architectures, a new generation of analytic applications in the business intelligence arena have come up. Traditional data warehouse implementations focused on reporting and strategic decision-making applications, whereas active data warehouse deployments augment strategic decision-support to tactical decision-making applications. The active data warehouse architecture is centred on acquiring data in near real-time to deliver information that will be used to support strategic decisions in seconds and provide round-the-clock availability.

Analytic CRM applications are one of the most benefited applications by the emergence of active data warehouse implementations. The evolution of these applications involves five distinct stages that are closely tied to the underlying capability of the data warehouse foundation. These stages include: mass marketing, segment marketing, target-marketing, event-based-marketing, and interactive marketing.

Mass marketing The data warehouse repository is used to store customer names, addresses, product ownership, preferences, and other personal details about the customers. The data warehouse is refreshed on a periodic basis, usually once in a week or month, and the data extracts are used to deliver name and address information to mail house operations, call centres, e-mail servers, and other channels.

Product ownership information helps the marketing team to exclude customers who should not receive offers for products that they already own. In this initial stage of analytic CRM, the data warehouse is accessed in a batch-oriented fashion, as data loading is performed on a batch basis.

Automated mass marketing implies contacting anyone and everyone for whom a name and contact information can be obtained. However, getting the right offer to the right customer calls for a bit more sophisticated approach than the mass marketing approach. The main drawback of mass marketing approach is that most individuals are completely over-saturated with direct marketing offers and thus, reasonable response rates cannot be expected from this approach.

Segment marketing The segment marketing approach differs from mass marketing, as it focuses on delivering product offerings differentiated by customer segment. The data warehouse is more than just a big database of customer's detail. Understanding various customer segments and thus designing of product offerings is done by rigorous analysis.

Marketing campaigns are then targeted accordingly and to accomplish it, a packaged tool for facilitating segment definitions, product analysis, and campaign management becomes essential. Besides this, a richer set of data about customer demographics is required to accurately describe the segment definitions. To capture this data, either external sources can be used or internal processes can be re-designed. However, a combination of these two approaches is typically the best strategy.

Target marketing The fundamental innovation here is to treat each customer as an individual. Use of data mining technology into the analytic CRM environment plays a crucial role in target marketing deployment. Predictive models that apply data mining technique are constructed to understand individual customer behaviours and to initiate developing one-to-one customer relationships. In target marketing, every customer and prospect is scored based on their propensity to buy a particular product even before a marketing communication actually takes place. This approach is used to determine whether it makes economic sense to initiate the communication with that individual.

In addition to this, data mining techniques are applied to predict the lifetime value of customers so that questions regarding the risk of attrition of the customers or cross-sell opportunities can be answered. Using data mining to do this, an organization will reduce its direct marketing costs by 50% or more.

Event-based marketing Event-based marketing lays emphasis on personalized marketing communication driven by individual behaviour patterns. A key architectural component required for the realization of event-based marketing is a framework for enabling *software event detectives* which allow capturing of business rules for identifying events relevant to a customer relationship and then initiate personalized communications in response to such events.

Event detection is quite complex and involves detecting changes in customer behaviours, such as a difference in banking activities or calling patterns. An important dimension of relevance is the timeliness with which events are detected and actions are taken. The second aspect where time is an important factor is that data warehouse content must be incrementally refreshed on a daily basis to make customer activities visible to the software event detectives.

Interactive marketing The interactive marketing stage of the analytic CRM tends to integrate the analytic and operational CRM. Operational CRM is concerned on managing the workflow of a customer interaction. The data warehouse environment calls for extreme service levels to support interactive marketing. Thus, a high query performance for analytic CRM is desirable, often in the range of a few sub-seconds to allow immediate response, especially when cooperating with the operational CRM environment.

14.8 TRENDS IN DATA WAREHOUSING

In the early phases, the most significant factors which drove many companies to move into data warehousing were fierce competition and the need for customized marketing. The telecommunications and banking industries are the dominant users of data warehouses spending as much as 15% of technology budgets on this technology. The organizations in these industries collect large volumes of transaction data which is transformed to make strategic decisions.

In the early stages of data warehousing, it was used exclusively for global corporations, as it was expensive to build a data warehouse and the tools needed were also not adequate in the market. So, only big organizations could afford to spend on the data warehousing technology which was rather a new paradigm. But today, data warehousing is implemented even in the medium-sized and smaller companies, as they are now able to afford the cost of building a data warehouse. With such popularity of the data warehousing technology, the database vendors have now added features that assist in building data warehouses using the DBMS. Apart from this, to support this technology to the maximum, packaged solutions have also become inexpensive and the operating systems are made even more robust.

These days, in the retail and telecommunications industries, data warehouses storing several terabytes of data are not uncommon. Every telecommunication company generates millions of call-detail transactions in a year. In order to promote its products and services, the executives analyse these transactions at a detailed level, thereby requiring the data to be stored at the lowest level of detail. Same is the case with a retail chain with hundreds of stores. Everyday, each store generates thousands of point-of-sale transactions and every such transactions needs to be stored. Thus, data warehouses in these industries are very large in size.

Some experts feel that technology has been driving data warehousing, as there has been a tremendous progress in software. Very soon, data warehousing will find better solutions for optimizing queries, indexing very large tables, enhancing SQL, improving data compression, and expanding dimensional modelling. The main question to answer in today's scenario is—what must the organization do to take advantage of the trend in the data warehouse?

14.8.1 Multiple Data Types

The first iteration of the data warehouse may just include numeric data. But including structured numeric data alone is not enough because users need to consider other data types as well to make strategic decisions. Traditionally, companies included numeric data in their data warehouses. But, now these companies need unstructured data as well to carry out their analysis.

Consequently, decision-support systems were divided into two groups—data warehousing and KM. While data warehousing dealt with structured data, KM involved unstructured data. But these days, working with just numerical data is not enough for analysing data through every angle. For example, these days, marketing data contains not only structured numeric data but also unstructured data in the form of images. The marketing analyst may just want to analyse sales numbers in a particular region or may want to see the images to conclude whether the new packaging style has lead to any greater sales number or not.

Now the organizations are integrating both structured and unstructured data in their data warehouses. Figure 14.15 shows the different types of data that must be included in the data warehouse to support decision-making more effectively.

The vendors these days are addressing the need for handling unstructured data which is often multimedia data, by treating it just as another data type. But

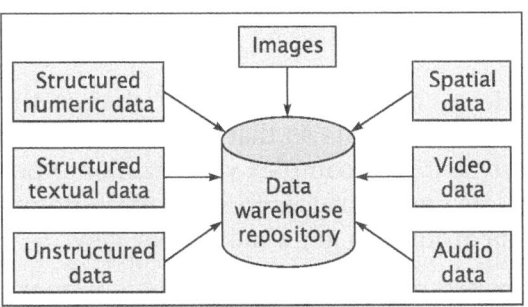

without the ability to search through the unstructured data, integration of this data is of no use to the end-users. Therefore, the vendors are now providing powerful search engines that can search even the unstructured data to respond to the users' needs. Query by image content is such an example. When multiple images fit the search argument, all the selected images are displayed one after the other. The vendors are also providing support to unstructured data by making their product to pre-index images based on shapes, colours, and textures.

Figure 14.15 Multiple data types in a data warehouse

While searching the free form textual data, the search engines pre-index the textual documents so that they can be located using keywords, character strings, phrases, wild cards, proximity operators, and Boolean operators. But the task of searching audio and video data directly is still in the research stage. To help the user to search audio and video data, they are described using free-form text, and then searched using textual search methods that are currently available.

14.8.2 Data Visualization

If the data warehouse provides results of querying the data using only output lists or spreadsheets, then it will not be wrong to say that the warehouse is outdated. These days, users expect to see the results in the form of graphics and charts, as visualization of the result sets in the form of charts boosts the process of analysis by helping the user to understand the data quickly and easily. The major trends that have shaped the direction of data visualization software in the last decade include the following.

More chart types These days, users prefer to visualize data in the form of graphical charts. For this purpose the numeric results are converted into a pie chart, a scatter plot, or another chart type for better visualization. Today, the list of these other chart types has expanded rapidly to help the users visualize the results more easily and interactively.

Interactive visualization Visualization techniques are no longer static. Thus, dynamic chart types have now become the trend. With these dynamic charts, the data warehouse users can review a result chart, manipulate it, and then see newer views online.

Data visualization software now supports a wide range of chart types. Simple graphs have just become outdated. The current needs of users are entirely different from what it used to be. Different users need different graphs to carry out their work. For example, the technical and scientific users need scatter plots and constellation graphs, and business analysts who are responsible for analysing spatial data need maps and other three-dimensional representations. In the last few years, the following trends have shaped the direction of data visualization software.

Chart manipulation A user can rotate a chart or dynamically change the chart type to get a better interpretation of the results so that it becomes easier for him to understand the data and analyse it. The complex visualization types like that of constellation and scatter plots enable a user to select data points with a mouse and then move the points around to get a more clear view.

Drill-down Initially the visualization presents the results at the summary level but if the users are interested in seeing detailed data, they can drill-down the visualization to display further visualizations at subsequent levels of detail.

Advanced interaction The advanced interaction techniques offer a minimally invasive user interface. The most advanced user interaction technique is the visual query which enables the user to see the outlying data points in a scatter plot, select a few of them with the mouse, and ask for a new visualization of just those selected points. The data visualization software performs three functions:

- Generates the appropriate query from the selection.
- Submits the query thus formed to the database.
- Displays the results to the users in another representation.

14.8.3 Agent Technology

A software agent works on the principle of assisting the process, learning from past experiences and thus, evolving knowledge about abnormal situations. It is viewed as an add-on component of a regular data warehousing system. The tasks usually performed by data warehouses are preserved and includes extra tasks related to the treatment of abnormal situations.

The software agents have two main parts—the data extraction agents and the error analysis and treatment agents. The data extraction agents are programs that extract data according to predefined user directives and execute error detection and classification procedures. The error analysis agent goes one step further by taking care of the abnormal situations notified by the extraction agents.

In case of abnormal situations, they propose possible solutions and print reports about the situation. For example, when the extracted data is not found to be in compliance with the established quality standards, the process is deployed. In case the agent is able to recover the affected data, data will then be moved to the next process, otherwise the problem will be reported to the analysis agents that will keep the treatment process going. Only if the problem gets solved, the data will be inserted into the data warehouse or else, it will be discarded.

All the events that occur are registered in an abnormal situation reports' database which is periodically mined to enhance the whole process. It is necessary to collect information about the different kinds of errors for which a solution has to be provided. Finally, all the information collected is integrated into the knowledge bases of the analysis and solvers agents.

No doubt, the agent programs must know other programs with which they can communicate, what they can communicate, and finally how they can communicate. This calls for a robust communication medium and an adequate communication language that can sustain all inter-agent communication acts. For this, the Foundation for Intelligent Physical Agents (FIPA) is the most widely used standard and protocol. It enables the agents to be spread across multiple platforms which is essential for this kind of application area.

Applications

A software agent is defined as a program that performs a predefined programmable task on behalf of the user. For example, software agents can be used to sort and filter e-mail according to user-specified rules. The same principle is applied in a data warehouse where software agents are used to alert the users of predefined business conditions.

With the growth in size of a data warehouse, the agent technology is getting widely applied. For example, the business analyst may want to identify threat and opportunity conditions that can offer advantages to the business enterprise. The analyst has to execute multiple queries and perform complex analysis to discover such conditions, as these are exception conditions. These threat conditions and opportunities are discovered only after the analyst goes through intense interactive analysis which generally consumes a lot of time, perhaps on a daily basis.

But with the agent technology implemented in the data warehouse, whenever a threat or opportunity condition is discovered through elaborate analysis, the event is described in detail to a software agent program. In future, whenever this condition is encountered, the program will automatically signal to the analyst. Here the agent technology plays a vital role.

Software agents are also used for routine monitoring of business performance. For example, the business executive may want to be notified every time the corporate-wide sales drop below monthly targets, thrice in a row. Thus, a software agent program may be implemented to alert him every time this condition happens. Similarly, the agent may be deployed to know every time the monthly sales promotion in all the stores is successful.

The diversity of data sources and large volumes of data has lead to an urge for automation. In spite of all the key benefits realized by a sound decision-support system and database management systems, very little can be accomplished without quality enforcement. Agent technology is used to perform error monitoring and control automatically.

14.9 DATA WAREHOUSE FUTURES

The last decade has witnessed a tremendous increase in the data warehouse database sizes. Large-scale organizations have started using 10 + TB systems. By another few years, the trend will move towards petabyte systems (1PB = 1024 TB). As the size of the database grows, the estimate of what constitutes a very large database (VLDB) continues to grow. The acronym VLDB has become so stretched that it is now being replaced by another acronym ELDB or extensively large database which are approximately above 100 TB.

Limitations in the currently available hardware and software force organizations to restrict the amount of data that can be kept online. For example, a telecommunication company may require its data warehouse to store at least 1 TB of data for just one month. In such a scenario, it becomes hard to envision the requirement to store a year or more of data online.

Data warehouse databases will now not only store numeric and textual data but will also store large amount of multimedia data and perform operations on them as well. The software that allows integration and manipulation of non-textual and textual data are easily available in the market, and it is this non-textual data that will bring about the business requirements for PB databases.

However, size is not the only factor that affects the complexity of the tasks involved in planning, building, and running data warehouse systems. With more and more number of users accessing the data warehouse, the ELDB requires radically different architectures and designs. With the increase in Internet and the Web applications usage, the requirement of customers to access data online is also going up, which in turn, adds to the user base of the ELDB systems.

When compared with the current scenario, the future shape of data warehouses will be entirely different. The need to handle large quantities of data and satisfy a huge user base will drive solutions towards distributed databases and three-tier architecture. The large volumes of the data in an ELDB will necessitate the spreading of the data over multiple databases for ease of management.

Distributed data warehouses that exist today suffer from severe performance problems as database boundaries are crossed. Therefore, problems such as query optimization across database boundaries will need to be solved. Most of the data warehouses built today are two-tier client-server architectures. But the increasing popularity of the Web and intranet that allows users to access integrated data automatically introduces multi-tiers into the organization's architecture.

However, it will take a few years from now before 1+PB open-systems data warehouse becomes a reality. The challenge that prevails in the market today is data warehouses of the order of 10+ TB (two orders of magnitude short of a petabyte). The hardware and software technologies will actually influence how the market will develop in future. Thus, it is impossible to predict anything in the IT marketplace today, but it is definite that the data warehouse will continue to be the leading edge technology.

Recapitulation

Real-time data which is used by operational applications contains all the individual, detailed data records where each update overwrites the previous entry.

Reconciled data contains detailed records from the real-time level that has been cleansed, adjusted, or enhanced so that the data can be used for informational applications.

Derived data is summarized, averaged, or aggregated from multiple sources of the real time or reconciled data for improved processing capability.

A changed data store contains a record of all the changes: additions, updations, and deletions to the selected real-time data. This data typically reflects the history of changes and is necessary for business users to spot trends and predict the future market.

Metadata stores data about data. It maintains system information such as how the data was derived, from which legacy systems, and what transformation rules were applied to it.

Single host-based data warehouses reside on high-volume databases running DBMS like DB2 with a variety of disparate sources like VSAM, DB2, flat files, and IMS.

With a LAN-based warehouse, data delivery can be managed either centrally or from the workgroup environment so that business groups can manage their information needs without burdening centralized IT resources, thereby enjoying the autonomy of their own data mart.

A LAN-based workgroup warehouse is an integrated architecture for building and maintaining a data warehouse in a LAN environment. In this warehouse, you extract data from a variety of sources and provide multiple LAN-based warehouses.

Multistage data warehouses are well suited to environments where the end-users require access to both detailed data for up-to-the-minute decisions as well as summarized and aggregated data for long-term strategic decisions.

In a stationary data warehouse, the data is not moved from the sources, but the users are given direct access to the data.

To handle the super-growth problem, let a few of your internal users have access to the data webhouse, and then add some more users to the access group in staged increments, so that managing the growth becomes easy.

Data webhouse is a web instantiation of the data warehouse that helps the marketing analyst to record every customer interaction, which they will use to understand customer behaviour, interests, and needs in greater depth than ever before.

A distributed data warehouse is a conglomeration of separate components that are connected via a network. The goal is to have these separate components appear as a single global data warehouse image.

In a distributed data warehouse model, the integrated data flows between a centralized data warehouse and individual data marts, allowing users to gain rapid access to enterprise-wide information.

Virtual data warehouses provide the end-users with direct access to operational data on legacy databases. The data is not moved from source databases to a target data warehouse as in a traditional data warehouse.

A virtual data warehouse does not include a data warehouse database, contains no historical data, has little summarization or aggregation of data, does not have central metadata, and does not have the ability to cleanse and reorganize data.

Decision support systems are divided into two categories: *data warehousing* which deals with structured data and *knowledge management* which involves the unstructured data.

A software agent is a program that is capable of performing a predefined programmable task on behalf of the user. Within the data warehouse, it is being used to alert the users of predefined business conditions.

Knowledge management is a systematic process for capturing, integrating, organizing, and communicating accumulated knowledge. It is a vehicle to share corporate knowledge so that the employees may be more effective and productive in their work.

The evolution of analytic CRM applications involves five distinct stages: mass marketing, segment marketing, target-marketing, event-based-marketing, and interactive marketing.

Automated mass marketing allows for efficient contact with anyone and everyone. The segment marketing approach is focused on delivering product offerings differentiated by the customer segment.

Target marketing treats each customer as an individual and develops one-to-one customer relationships.

Event-based marketing focuses on enabling personalized marketing communication driven by individual behaviour patterns.

The interactive marketing stage involves integration between analytic and operational CRM.

With the help of EIS, the executives can pinpoint problems and detect trends. A data warehouse is tailor-made for the needs of the EIS analyst, so that the EIS analyst's job changes from a data engineer to that of doing true analysis.

Objective Questions

1. **Multiple choice questions**

    (i) Which network provides selective access by outside parties?
    - (a) Internet
    - (b) Intranet
    - (c) Extranet
    - (d) All of these

    (ii) Which dimension stores information about the contexts and its related success status?
    - (a) Page
    - (b) Event
    - (c) Session
    - (d) All of these

    (iii) From the features given below, select the characteristics of Class 1.
    - (a) It takes a few milliseconds for the data to arrive in the ODS once a transaction takes place.
    - (b) Built using simple technology.
    - (c) May be created from output of special reports or projects.
    - (d) Emphasizes on speed of update and synchronization data.
    - (e) No time for data integration.

    (iv) From the features given below, select the characteristics of Class 2.
    - (a) The time elapsed is thus transparent to the users.
    - (b) Ample time for data integration.
    - (c) Inexpensive.
    - (d) Can be built with conventional technology.
    - (e) The source of data can be a data warehouse or some other.

    (v) Which marketing technique implies contacting everyone for whom contact information can be obtained?
    - (a) Automated mass marketing
    - (b) segment marketing approach
    - (c) Targeted marketing
    - (d) event-based marketing

2. **Fill in the blanks**

    (i) In multistage data warehouses, _____ serves as the source for the data warehouse.

    (ii) Bringing the Web to the data warehouse involves capturing the _____ data.

(iii) Clickstream data is extracted, transformed, and loaded in the _____ repository.

(iv) Intranet uses the data communication standards of the _____.

(v) Page hits are often _____.

(vi) A _____ data warehouse does not have a central metadata repository.

(vii) ODS supports _____ processing.

(viii) The data flow between ODS and data warehouse is _____ directional.

(ix) _____ is used to determine whether it makes economic sense to initiate the communication with that individual.

(x) _____ is a program that performs a predefined programmable task on behalf of the user.

3. **Match the following**

1. Host-based warehouses
(a) Track the sequence of the web pages that are visited by the people.

2. LAN-based warehouses
(b) Provides knowledge to use the right information, at the right time and the right place.

3. Clickstream data
(c) Removes extraneous data and summarize/aggregate the clickstream data.

4. Hot response cache
(d) Anticipate the predictable and repeated information requests.

5. Virtual data warehouse
(e) Synopsis from multiple occurrences of data.

6. Granularity manager
(f) Contains current data.

7. ODS
(g) Performs error monitoring and control automatically.

8. Profile record
(h) End-users with direct access to operational data on legacy databases.

9. Knowledge management
(i) Managed either centrally or from the workgroup environment.

10. Agent technology
(j) By IT and run on traditional systems.

4. **State true or false**

(i) ODS stores the current records.

(ii) Intranet is a private computer network.

(iii) The data webhouse is meant to be opened for internal as well as external users.

(iv) The hot response cache is a database and not a file server.

(v) The data warehouse is designed using the information push technique.

(vi) Virtual data warehouse contains a lot of historical data.

(vii) Middleware technology is a combination of both hardware and software components.

(viii) ODS is accessed when a high-performance processing must be done.

(ix) The ODS DBMS requires transaction integrity that calls for backup and recovery procedures.

(x) A data warehouse contains unstructured information and a knowledge warehouse holds structured information.

(xi) A CRM-ready data warehouse needs summarized data.

Review Questions

1. Describe the different configurations of data that can be defined to satisfy the requirements of a particular data warehouse implementation.

2. List and explain the different factors on which the choice of a data warehouse depends.

3. Write an essay on the different types of data warehouses based on the location of the source data.

4. What is a data webhouse? What are the added advantages of linking the Web to the already existing data warehouse?

5. As a database administrator of a data warehouse, list the activities that you would have to perform to adapt your data warehouse for the Web. Make a list of different technologies that you would like to use for your data webhouse.

6. Explain the term 'super-growth' in a data webhouse. How do you handle it?

7. Make a comparison between the traditional data warehouse and a web-enabled data warehouse.

8. Write a short note on the architecture of a data webhouse. Why is it called a multi-tier architecture?

9. What is a clickstream data webhouse? Explain its significance. Draw the star schema explaining how you would collect information for such a warehouse.

10. What do you understand by a distributed data warehouse? Is it correct to compare it with a distributed database? How is the distributed data warehouse different from that of a traditional warehouse? Explain the merits, demerits, issues, and the risks involved in making such a warehouse.

11. Compare a traditional data warehouse with the virtual data warehouse.

12. What is a virtual data warehouse? Explain the meaning of the term 'virtual'. Write down its merits, demerits, issues, and risks involved. Also suggest some cases in which you will prefer building a virtual data warehouse rather than a physical data warehouse.

13. State some of the factors that indicate the continued growth in data warehousing.

14. Why are data warehouses continuing to grow in size? Justify your answer.

15. Why is it important to store structured as well as unstructured information a data warehouse? Give examples of structured and unstructured data elements that you would like to store when building a data warehouse for a large group of hospitals in the country.

16. What is the significance of agent technology in a data warehouse environment?

17. What do you understand by CRM? How can you make your data warehouse CRM-ready?

18. List the techniques that you think would improve the data visualization of the output results.

19. What are the differences between a data warehouse and a knowledge repository?

20. Why is parallel processing necessary in a data warehouse environment?

21. List the advancements that have taken place in query tools and browser tools.

22. Write a short note on the integration of data warehouse and ERP.

23. Explain the significance of active data warehousing.

24. Highlight the difference between bringing the Web to the warehouse and bringing the warehouse to the Web.

25. What are the significant roles that a data warehouse plays in the EIS?

GLOSSARY

Access path The path chosen by a database management system to access or retrieve the data from the data warehouse.

Ad hoc query An information request that is normally fabricated and run a single time. It is difficult to anticipate such queries in advance.

Aggregation A technique that speeds up query performance. Facts are summed up for selected dimensions from the original fact table to form a aggregate table that has fewer rows.

Aggregate data Data in summarized form which is often stored in aggregate tables to speed up query execution.

Alerts A notification from an event that has exceeded a predefined threshold limit.

Architect A person who defines how the environment for the data warehouse, analytical applications, or operational system is built.

Architecture A framework for organizing the planning and implementation of data resources. It includes the set of data, processes, and technologies that will be used for the creation and operation of data warehouse systems.

Atomic data Data at the lowest level of detail.

Attributes Attribute of an entity refers to the properties of that entity. Each property will have one or more values associated with it. When the physical model of a system is built, entities become tables, and attributes become columns.

Base tables These tables contain detailed data.

Best-of-breed Best-of-breed tools are the ones which are most effective, powerful, functional and optimal. While selecting tools, an organization may either choose a suite of products from the same vendor (where some of the tools in the suite are not appropriate) or choose the best product in each category, i.e., best-of-breed, and integrate those tools themselves.

Bitmapped indexes Bitmapped index involves building streams of bits where each bit is related to the column value for a single row of data in a table. The use of bitmapped indexes on low-cardinality fields is used to improve query performance.

Business analyst One who analyses the operation and data of the business to develop a business solution.

Bulk data transfer A software-based mechanism which moves large data files. This technique supports compression, blocking and buffering to optimize transfer times.

Business data Information about people, places, things, business rules, and events, which is used to operate the business. It is different from metadata, as metadata is used define and describe the business data.

Business metadata The information that describes and defines business data.

Business rules Policies that are used to run a business. The business rules contain constraints on the behaviour of the business.

Business transaction A unit of work acted upon by a data capture system to create, modify, or delete business data. Each business transaction describes a single valued fact along a single business event.

Central warehouse A database created by extracting data from several operational systems. The central warehouse adheres to a single, consistent, enterprise data model to ensure consistency of decision-support data across the corporation.

Change management The complete set of processes that ensure that changes are implemented in a visible, controlled and orderly fashion.

Clickstream The series of page visits and associated clicks executed by a website visitor when navigating through the site. Clickstream data is analysed by a company to understand which products, website content, or screens were of most interest to a given customer.

Conformed dimension A dimension having exactly the same meaning and content when being referred from different fact tables.

Cross selling Selling an additional category of products as a result of the customer's original purchase.

Cube A fundamental structure for information in an OLAP system that stores multidimensional information, having one cell for each possible combination of dimensions.

Data Items that are represented by facts, text, graphics, bit-mapped images, sound, analog or digital live-video segments.

Data access tool An end-user tool that allows users to retrieve the desired data by building SQL queries by pointing and clicking on a list of tables and fields in the data warehouse.

Data acquisition The process of extracting, transforming, and moving data from source systems and external data sources to the data warehouse database objects.

Data analysis and presentation tools A software program that provides a logical view of data in a warehouse.

Data dictionary A database that stores data about data. It is a catalog of all data elements, containing their names, structures, and information about their usage.

DBA A person who is responsible for the physical aspect of the data warehouse. His primary task is to include physical design, performance, and maintenance activities including backup and recovery.

DBMS Software that structures and manipulates data, thereby ensuring data security, recovery, and integrity.

Data cleansing The process of transforming data in its current state to a predefined, standardized format using packaged software or program modules.

Data extraction software A software program that reads one or more sources of data and creates a new image of the data.

Database index A mechanism to locate and access data within a database. An index may be built on one or more columns and be a means of enforcing uniqueness on their values.

Data loading The process of populating a data warehouse with data. It may either be done using utility programs, user-written programs, or specialized software from independent vendors.

Data mapping A process that assigns a source data element to a target data element.

Data mart An implementation of an analytical application that serves a single department, subject area, or limited part of the organization. Usually a data mart is designed to store summarized data that will be used for decision support.

Data mining It is also referred to as the discovery mode of data analysis, or analysing detail data to unearth unsuspected or unknown relationships, patterns and associations that might be of value to the organization.

Data model The model shows data elements that are grouped into records, as well as the association around those records.

Data modeling A technique that defines and analyses data requirements needed to support the business functions of an enterprise.

Data partitioning The process of logically and/or physically partitioning data into segments that can be easily maintained or accessed. It helps in improving query performance.

Data pivot A process of rotating the view of data for analysis purpose.

Data scrubbing The process of filtering, merging, decoding, and translating source data to clean the data for the data warehouse.

Data staging area It is a system that stands between the legacy systems and the data warehouse. The data staging area is where the ETL process takes place. Users cannot access this area.

Data transformation Creating valuable information from raw data. This includes decoding production data and merging of records from multiple DBMS formats.

Data warehouse A collection of transformed and integrated data, stored for the purpose of providing strategic information to the entire enterprise.

Data warehouse architecture An integrated set of products that enables the extraction and transformation of operational data to be loaded into the data warehouse database for end-user analysis.

Data warehouse management tools Softwares that extract data from operational systems; transforms this data and load it into the data warehouse.

Database A large collection of data organized for rapid search and retrieval.

Database schema The logical and physical definition of a database structure.

Decentralized database A centralized database that is partitioned according to a business or a subject area. The ownership is also moved to the owners of the subject area.

Decentralized warehouse A remote data source that users can access via a central gateway. The gateway provides a logical view of corporate data in terms that users can understand.

DSS A decision-support system is specifically designed to allow business end-users to perform data analyses on their own.

De-duplication Also known as record linkage, it is the task of finding the same (duplicate) entry in multiple files. De-duplication is used when two or more datasets are merged.

Degenerate dimension It key in the fact table but does not join a corresponding dimension table because all its interesting attributes are already included in other analytic dimensions.

Denormalization It is a process of combining similar data into a single entity (table or file). Denormalization is done to provide rapid access for specific user needs but the drawback is its degree of data redundancy in a data record.

Dependent data mart Also called an architected data mart. Shares common business rules, semantics, and definitions. A dependent data mart uses from a central metadata repository to define local metadata so that all the components of the architecture are linked via a common metadata.

Derived data Data that is obtained by applying a computational step. Derived data may be produced by getting the result of relating two or more elements of a single transaction.

Desktop applications Query and analysis tools that access the source database or data warehouse across a network using an appropriate database interface.

Dimension A structural attribute of a list of members, all of which are of a similar type in the user's perception of the data. For example, all months, quarters, years, etc. make up a time dimension; likewise all cities, regions, countries, etc. make up a geography dimension.

Dimensional model A technique of data modeling suited for data warehousing. In a dimensional model, two types of tables are formed: dimensional tables and fact tables.

Dimensional table It stores records related to a particular dimension. It does not store any fact or measure.

Dirty data Data that is inconsistent, missing, incomplete, or erroneous. Source data often contains a high percentage of dirty data.

Downtime A general condition wherein users cannot use or access computing systems, applications, data or information for a number of reasons.

Drill-across Analysing the data across dimensions.

Drill-down Exploring detailed data that was used to create aggregations. Drill-down levels depend on the granularity of the data in the data warehouse.

Drill-through Analysing the data by going from an OLAP cube into the relational database.

Drill-up Analysing the data to a parent attribute.

Dynamic queries Queries that are dynamically generated by desktop-resident query tools. These queries are executed at run-time.

End-user data Data that is formatted for end-user query processing.

End-user tool Data delivery that allows the knowledge workers to access information in a data warehouse using *ad hoc* queries.

Enterprise A complete business consisting of functions, divisions, or other components that work together to accomplish specific objectives and defined goals.

Enterprise data Data that is defined to be used across a corporate environment.

Enterprise data warehouse A centralized warehouse that is designed to serve the entire enterprise.

Enterprise modeling The development of a common and consistent view that would help to understand data elements and their relationships across the enterprise.

Enterprise resource planning ERP systems comprise of software programs which tie together all the function of an enterprise like finance, manufacturing, sales and human resource.

ER diagramming A process that depicts the data elements and the relationships that exist between these data elements.

Environment The word environment encompasses the conditions surrounding data, such as databases, data formats, servers, network and any other components that impact the data.

Event analysis A process of analysing notifications and taking appropriate action depending on the notification event.

Executive information systems (EIS) Tools programmed to provide canned reports to the top-level executives. They offer strong reporting and drill-down capabilities.

Extendibility The ability to add a new functionality to existing services without major software rewrites or without redefining the basic architecture.

Extract frequency The latency of data extracts or the frequency at which data extracts are needed in the data warehouse, such as daily versus weekly, monthly, quarterly, etc.

Extranet Organization's network which is opened for internal users and selected business partners. Extranet allows the suppliers, distributors and other authorized users to connect to a company's network.

Fact table A central table in a data warehouse schema that contains facts or measures along with keys of dimension tables that relate to the facts.

Factless fact table A fact table that does not store any fact or measure.

Filters Criteria to choose a specific subset of information in a data warehouse.

Firewall A combination of specialized hardware and software setup that monitors traffic between an internal network and an external network. It is deployed for security purposes to keep unauthorized outsiders from tampering with or accessing information on a networked computer system.

Foreign key It is the primary key of one table that is placed into another related table. Foreign keys represent a relationship among different tables and supports navigation among tables.

Front-end The component of the data warehouse architecture that helps to access and analyse data.

Granularity Level of data summarization.

Helpdesk A support system designed to assist end-users with technical and functional issues.

Hierarchy It defines the path of navigation for rolling up and drilling down. All attributes in a hierarchy belong to the same dimension.

Historical data Data from previous time periods which is analysed for trend analysis and for comparisons to previous periods.

Historical database A database that is specifically designed to provide an historical perspective on the data.

Hybrid OLAP A product that can simultaneously provide multidimensional analysis of data stored in MDDBS as well as RDBMS.

Horizontal partitioning It divides a single logical table into multiple physical tables. The large table is split horizontally, that is, based on the rows. Horizontal partitioning is employed when the users need to access or to isolate a readily identifiable subset of the parent table's rows.

Hub and spoke configuration A configuration of interconnected systems in which a single central system (the hub) acts as the central point for exchanging data with the other systems (spokes).

HTML A standard for defining and creating Web documents.

Hypercube An OLAP product that stores multidimensional data.

Information Data that has been processed to provide some knowledge to the person who receives it. Information is the output of information systems.

Infrastructure The architectural elements that are used to build the data warehouse environment.

Integration The process of combining data from multiple sources of data to provide a single collection of data to the warehouse.

Interoperability The ability of heterogeneous types of hardware and software to work together.

Intranet A subset of the Internet used internally by an organization. Unlike the Internet, Intranets are private networks that are accessible only from within the organization.

Java A cross-platform source programming language that enables programmers to distribute the applications over networks and the Internet.

Joins An operation performed on tables in such a way that the data from two tables is combined in a larger, more detailed joined table.

Joint application development (JAD) A process developed for designing a computer-based system. It brings together end-users and IT professionals in a highly focused workshop. JAD reduces the likelihood of errors that are expensive to correct in time.

Key performance indicator (KPI) A business calculation that provides macro-level insights into the business process to manage profitability.

Latency The delay between the moment something is initiated and the moment its first effect begins. For example, RAM latency is the amount of time a computer needs to wait to get data from random access memory. Similarly, data latency is the delay time for data to be updated in a system.

Legacy system Any existing operational system that acts as a source of data for the warehouse.

Logical data model Actual implementation of a conceptual module in a database. A conceptual module may be built upon multiple logical data models.

Market basket It refers to a specific type of basket or a list of items that are usually purchased together. The list is used for analysing the items the customer prefers to purchase in conjugation.

Market segmentation The process of partitioning markets into groups of potential customers who have similar purchase behaviour.

Market share A company's sales expressed in terms of the entire industry' sales. It is given as a percentage of the sales for the total industry.

Metadata synchronization The process of consolidating, relating and synchronizing data elements with the same or similar meaning from different systems to allow easier access.

Metrics A framework to gather measurements of success/failure on a regulated, timed basis that can be audited and verified.

Middleware A communication layer that enables the applications to interact across different hardware and network environments.

MIPS Acronym for millions of instructions per second.

Multidimensional OLAP (MOLAP) An analytical processing technique in which multidimensional data cubes are created and stored in separate proprietary databases.

Multidimensional array A group of data cells arranged by the dimensions of the data. A three-dimensional array can be visualized as a cube with each dimension forming a side of the cube.

Multidimensional database (MDBMS) A powerful database that enables the end-users to analyse large amounts of multidimensional data.

Niche marketing A marketing segmentation strategy in which the focus is on serving one segment of the market. It is similar to segmented marketing, but the only difference is

that a niche is a small distinguishable segment that can be uniquely served.

Normalization The process of reducing a complex table into its simplest, most stable structure. Normalization process removes redundant attributes, keys, and relationships from a conceptual data model.

Null value It signifies that either the value for that row is missing, unknown, not yet known, or inapplicable. Placing a zero in the row would not reflect the accurate state of the row, because zero is a value.

Object A person, place, thing, or concept that has characteristics of interest to an environment. In an object-oriented system, an object is an entity that includes descriptions of data.

Online analytical processing (OLAP) It enables the end-users to view the same data from different perspectives in order to facilitate decision-making.

OLAP client End-user applications that request slices from OLAP servers and provide two-dimensional or multidimensional displays, user modifications, selections, ranking, calculations, etc., for data visualization, navigation and analysis purposes.

One-to-one marketing A prime principle of CRM that treats each customer as an individual.

Online transaction processing (OLTP) Processing that is designed to support daily business operations.

Operational data Data that supports the production systems which are designed to run the business.

Operational data store (ODS) An ODS is an integrated database of operational data that contains current or near-term data. For example, an ODS may contain 30 to 60 days of information.

Operational database It is the source of data for the data warehouse. It is designed to store detailed data for running the day-to-day operations of the business. The data stored in an operational database continually changes as updates are made, and reflect the current value of the last transaction.

Operational systems Also known as OLTP systems, they include applications that run the business on a day-to-day basis using real-time data.

Parallelism The ability to perform parallel execution of the functions.

Partitioning The process of dividing a table into pieces (partitions). The table can be partitioned either horizontally or vertically.

Periodicity The frequency of data loading or data updates or data refresh of the data warehouse, e.g. daily, weekly, monthly.

Performance alert It is a notification via email, portal or wireless device of a key trend or business event that is associated with a goal.

Persistent data Data that outlasts the execution of a particular program. Persistent data is used to store the records of the enterprise and is available for reuse.

Physical data model In a physical data model, data and their relationships are represented in the form of a diagram. A physical data model is process dependent, which means that it is denormalized to provide maximum performance efficiency.

Planned downtime Scheduled time for loss of computing-system usage due to operations such as database backups, maintenance and periodic events.

Platform Technology that forms a base on which other technologies or processes are built and operated to provide interoperability, simplify implementation, streamline deployment and promote maintenance of solutions.

Portal A website that is the first place where users visit when using the Web. A portal site consists of a catalog of sites, a search engine or both and may also offer email and other services to entice people to use that site as the main point of entry or portal to the Web.

Power users Knowledge workers who are capable of formulating complex business queries

and writing sophisticated reports with little need of help.

Predictive analytics Techniques of directed and undirected knowledge discovery that apply knowledge of statistical algorithms, neural networks and optimization research to predict the behaviour of customers, products, services, market dynamics and other critical business transactions.

Primary key Every record in the table is uniquely identified by a column or a combination of columns. This column or a combination of columns which is used to uniquely identify a row in the table is called the primary key of the table.

Process management A combination of all the functions that supports the definition of inter-related process steps and the management of their execution across multiple hardware and software platforms.

Production data Source data which is obtained from different systems or applications running within the organization.

Project plan The project plan includes tasks, deliverables and resources. It must also say who will perform these tasks.

Protocol A set of rules or conventions that lays the ground for the communication between processes. Protocol specifies the format and content of messages to be exchanged.

Quality assurance The process of ensuring an accurate result which satisfies quality parameters as specified by the end-user.

Query An SQL statement to retrieve data from the warehouse so that the data can be analysed and used for decision support.

Query response times The time taken by the warehouse engine to process a complex query across large volumes of data and return the results to the user.

Query tools Softwares that enables the users to create and direct specific questions to a database. These tools facilitate the retrieval of desired data from the database.

RDBMS A database management system in which the data is stored, viewed and manipulated in tabular form. Data is stored in rows and columns and the related information of different tables are joined to each other.

Redundancy Storing multiple copies of the same data.

Redundancy control The process of managing a distributed data environment to limit excessive copying, update, and transmission costs associated with redundant data.

Reference data Data that is used solely to categorize other data elements found in the database.

Referential integrity Enforcement of the relationships that exist between tables based on the definition of a primary key and foreign key.

Refresh The process of updating the data warehouse database objects with new data at scheduled times. Data warehouse refresh occurs after the initial load and is monitored via warehouse management procedures.

Relational database A collection of data stored in the form of related tables.

Replicated data Data that is copied from a data source to one or more target environments based on replication rules. We can have the entire table replicated or have rectangular extracts.

Reporting An automated business process or related functionality that facilitates its users with a detailed, formal account of relevant or requested information.

Risk The potential of an adverse condition occurring on a project which will prohibit the project to meet its expectations. Thus, every organization needs to perform management of risk assessment and a strategy for its mitigation.

Relational OLAP (ROLAP) A product that enables the users to perform multidimensional analysis of data and perform aggregations on the stored data.

Roll-up queries Queries that summarize data at a higher level than that of the previous level of detail.

Scalable Ability to increase the number of users, the size of the databases and the complexity of the queries and reports without any sort of changes being made to the existing platform or architecture.

Scope It is referred to as an itemized accounting and definition of the agreed-upon project deliverable in terms of functionality as well as data. In the field of data warehousing, the data scope, is more critical than the functional scope as it is needed for correctly estimating the development effort.

Scope creep The addition of new requirements, source data or users to the initial agreement of the project.

Schema A diagrammatic representation of the structure or framework of something. It specifies the logical and physical definition of data elements, their physical characteristics and the relationship that exists between them.

SELECT An SQL statement (command) that specifies data retrieval operations in a relational database.

Server A computer that performs standard functions for clients in response to standard messages received from them.

Slice and dice Retrieving data from a hypercube to perform complex data analysis function provided by MDBMS tools. While slice operations make selection of data based on one dimension, the dice operation specifies multiple dimensions to set the criteria for data selection.

Slowly changing dimensions these are categorized as Type I, Type II, Type III changes. These changes involve maintaining a history by adding related rows or new columns, or simply ignoring the problem by retaining only the current data.

Symmetrical multi-processing (SMP) It is basically a shared approach of parallel computing.

Snowflake schema It consists of a set of tables wherein a single, central fact table is surrounded by normalized dimension tables. Snowflake schema implements dimensional tables that are partially or fully normalized.

Source data   The data from the operational systems that will populate the data warehouse.

SQL   It is a language that supports accessing relational, or non-relational compliant database systems.

SQL query tool   An end-user tool which accepts SQL statements to be executed against one or more relational databases.

Star schema   It is a relational database schema for representing multidimensional data. It is a collection of tables wherein a single, central fact table is surrounded by a number of de-normalized dimension tables.

Static query   A stored, parameterized procedure which is purposely optimized to access data from the warehouse.

Summarization tables   Tables that are created along frequently accessed dimensions to speed up query performance. However, redundancies increase the amount of data in the warehouse.

Supply chain   The optimal flow of a product from the site of its production through intermediate locations to the site where it will be finally used.

Surrogate key   It is a system generated sequence number established for uniquely identifying the rows of the dimension tables.

Terabyte   A unit of measurement which equals 1000 gigabytes.

Time variant system   It has explicit dependence on time. A data warehouse is a time-variant database that stores historical as well as current data to analyse the past, monitor the present and predict the future.

Top-down methodology   Approach in which a data warehouse is built first and then the data marts are built.

Transaction data   It stores data related to the transactions that operational systems are designed to automate.

Transactional system   An information system designed to store and record day-to-day business information that are centered on applications. These systems are optimized for storing large volumes of data, but are not appropriate for analysing that data.

Triggering data   Data that is responsible for selecting and loading data on a scheduled basis.

Unplanned downtime   It refers to the unanticipated, duration-variable loss of computing-system usage as a result of natural disasters, power outages, hardware or software failures, and human intervention.

Unstructured data   Data stored in any document, file, image, report, form, etc. that has no defined or standard structure. Unstructured data cannot be defined in terms of rows and columns or records, and the data cannot be examined with standard access.

Vertical partitioning   Vertical partitioning is a technique of dividing a single logical table into multiple physical tables based on the columns.

Virtual enterprise data warehouse   An enterprise data warehouse constructed of multiple data marts and a request broker computer application. In a virtual data warehouse environment, the data warehouse does not exist physically.

Visualization   The presentation of results in a format that makes the results easily understandable by the users. It focuses beyond displaying results in just numbers with a display, and includes graphs and charts making copious use of colours and figures.

Web services   These are platform-neutral and vendor-independent protocols that facilitate distributed processing to be performed using XML and other web-based technologies.

Workload   The quantity of processing that needs to be done in terms of machine cycles and the disk I/Os.

SELECT BIBLIOGRAPHY

Agrawal, R., A. Gupta, S. Sarawagi (1997). Modeling multidimensional databases. In: 13th Int. Conf. on Data Engineering, pp 232–243.

Anahory, S., D. Murray (2005). *Data Warehousing in the Real World—A Practical Guide for Building Decision Support Systems*, Pearson Education.

Baralis, E., S. Paraboschi, E. Teniente (1997). Materialized View Selection in a Multidimensional Database. Proc. 23rd VLDB Conf., Athens, Morgan Kaufmann.

Baralis, E., S. Paraboschi, E. Teniente (1997). Materialized view selection in multidimensional database. Proc. 23rd Int. Conf. on VLDB, Athens, Greece, pp 156–165.

Barquin, R., S. Edelstein (1996). *Planning and Designing the Data Warehouse*, Prentice Hall.

Batini, C., S. Ceri, S. Navathe (1992). *Conceptual Database Design*, Benjamin/Cummings.

Bertino, E., E. Ferrari, G. Guerrini (1997). T_Chimera: A Temporal Object-Oriented Data Model. TAPOS 3(2), pp 103–125.

Cabibbo, L., R. Torlone (1997). "Querying multidimensional databases," In: 6th Int. workshop on database programming languages (DBPL'97).

Cabibbo, L., R. Torlone (1997). Querying multidimensional databases. In: 6th Int. Workshop on Database Programming Languages.

Cabibbo, L., R. Torlone (1998). A procedural to a visual query language for OLAP. In: 10th Int. Conference on Scientific and Statistical Database Management, IEEE Computer Society Press, pp 74–83.

Cabibbo, L., R. Torlone (1998). A logical approach to multidimensional databases, eds. H.J. Schek, F. Saltor, I. Ramos, G. Alonso, *Advances in DB technology*, Springer, pp 183–197.

Castellanos, M., F. Saltor, M. García (1994). A Canonical Model for the Interoperability among Object Oriented and Relational Models. In: Ozsu, T. *et al.* (eds.), *Distributed Object Management* (Edmonton, 1992), Morgan Kaufmann, pp 309–314.

Chaudhuri, S., K. Shim (1994). Including group-by in query optimization. Proc. 20th Int. Conf. on VLDB, pp 354–366.

Chaudhuri, S., U. Dayal An overview of data warehousing and OLAP technology. SIGMOD Record, 26 (1), pp 65–74.

Chen, M. S., J. Han, P. S. Yu (1996). *Data mining: An overview from a database perspective*. IEEE Trans. Knowledge and Data Engineering, 8:866–883.

Colliat, G. (1996). OLAP, relational and multidimensional database systems, SIGMOD 25 (3), pp 64–69.

Davenport, T., J. Harris (2007). *Competing on Analytics: The New Science of Winning*. Harvard Business School Press.

Dekeyser, S., B. Kuijpers, J. Paredaens, J. Wijsen (1998). Nested data cubes for OLAP. In Int. Workshop on Data Warehousing & Data Mining, Singapore, Springer Verlag, pp 129–140.

Ericsson, R. (2004). *Building Business Intelligence Applications with .NET*, 1st ed., Charles River Media. pp. 28–29.

Fahrner, C., G. Vossen (1995). A survey of database transformations based on the Entity-Relationship model. *Data & Knowledge Engineering*, 15 (3), pp 213–250.

Fauvet, M., J. Canavaggio, P. Scholl (1997). Modeling Histories in Object DBMS. Proc. 8th Int. Conf. DEXA, Toulouse, Springer-Verlag, pp 112–121.

Fayyad, U. M., G. Piatetsky-Shapiro, P. Smyth, R. Uthurusamy (1996). Advances in *Knowledge Discovery and Data Mining*, AAAI/MIT Press.

Firestone, J. M. (1998). Architectural evolution in datawarehousing and distributed knowledge management architecture. White Paper, Executive Information Systems, Inc.

Frawley, W. J., G. Piatetsky-Shapiro, C. J. Matheus (1991). *Knowledge Discovery* in *Databases: An Overview*. In: G. Piatetsky-Shapiro *et al.* (eds.), Knowledge Discovery in Databases, AAAI/MIT Press.

Furtado, P., P. Baumann (1999). Storage of multi-dimensional arrays based on arbitrary tiling. In 15th Int. Conf. on Data Engineering, pp 480–489.

Garcia-Molina, H. *et al.* (1997). The TSIMMIS approach to mediation: data models and languages. Journal of Intellingent Information Systems, 8:117–132.

Gebhardt, M., M. Jarke, S. Jacobs (1997). A toolkit for negotiation support interfaces to multi-dimensional data. In: ACM SIGMOD Int. Conf. on Manag. of Data, pp 348–356.

Golfarelli, M., D. Maio, S. Rizzi (1998). Conceptual design of data warehouses from ER schemes. Proc. Hawaii International Conference on System Sciences, Kona, Hawaii, pp 334–343.

Golfarelli, M., D. Maio, S. Rizzi (1998). The Dimensional Fact Model: a conceptual model for data warehouses. Int. Journal of Cooperative Information Systems, 7(2-3):215–247.

Gray, J., A. Bosworth, A. Lyman, H. Pirahesh (1995). Data-Cube: a relational aggregation operator generalizing group-by, cross-tab and sub-totals, *Technical Report* MSR-TR-95-22, Microsoft Research.

Gupta, A., V. Harinarayan, D. Quass (1995). Aggregate-query processing in data-warehousing environments. Proc. 21th Int. Conf. on Very Large Data Bases, Zurich, Switzerland.

Gupta, H., V. Harinarayan, A. Rajaraman (1997). Index selection for OLAP. Proc. Int. Conf. Data Engineering, Binghamton, UK.

Gyssens, M., L.V.S. Lakshmanan (1997). A foundation for multi-dimensional databases. In 33rd Int. Conf. on Very Large Data Bases, pp 106–115.

Hammer, J., H. García-Molina, J. Widom, W. Labio, Y. Zhuge (1995). "The Stanford Data Warehousing Project," *IEEE Data Engineering Bulletin*.

Han, J., M. Kamber (2001). *Data Mining Concepts and Techniques*, Morgan Kauffman Publishers.

Harinarayan, V., A. Rajaraman, J. Ullman (1996). Implementing Data Cubes Efficiently. Proc. ACM SIGMOD Conf., Montreal.

Harinarayan, V., A. Rajaraman, J. Ullman (1996). Implementing Data Cubes Efficiently. Proc. of ACM Sigmod Conf., Montreal, Canada.

Hugh, P.G., J. Watson (1998). *Decision Support in the Data Warehouse*, Prentice Hall PTR.

Hurtado, C., A. Mendelzon, A. Vaisman (1999). Maintaining data cubes under dimension updates. In 15th Int. Conf. on Data Engineering, pp 346–355.

Imhoff, C. (1999). *The Corporate Information Factory*. DMReview Magazine.

Imielinski, T., H. Mannila (1996). A database perspective on knowledge discovery. Communications of ACM, 39:58–64.

Inmon, B., C. Batini, S. Ceri, S. Navathe (1992). *Conceptual Database Design*, Benjamin/Cummings.

Inmon, W. (1992). What is a Data Warehouse? *PRISM Tech Topic*, Vol.1, No.1.

Inmon, W. (1993). Information Architecture for the 90s: Legacy Systems, Operational Data Store. Data Warehouse. *PRISM Tech Topic*, Vol.1, No.13.

Inmon, W. (1993). The Operational Data Store. *PRISM Tech Topic*, Vol.1, No.17.

Inmon, W. H. (1996). *Building the Data Warehouse*, 2nd ed., John Wiley & Sons.

Jarke, M. *et. al.* (2000). Concept Based Design of Data Warehouses: The DWQ Demonstrators. ACM SIGMOD Int. Conf. on Manag. of Data, p 591.

Jarke, M., M. Lenzerini, Y. Vassiliou, P. Vassiliadis (eds.) (2000). Fundamentals of data warehousing. Springer-Verlag.

Johnson, T., D. Shasha (1997). Hierarchically split cube forests for decision support: description and tuned design. *Bulletin of Technical Committee on Data Engineering*, 20 (1).

Kimball, R. (1996). *The data warehouse toolkit*, John Wiley & Sons.

Kimball, R., M. Ross (2002). The Data Warehouse Toolkit: The Complete Guide to Dimensional Modeling. 2nd ed., p 310. Wiley.

Labio, W., D. Quass, B. Adelberg (1997). Physical Database Design for Data Warehouses. Proc. Int'l. Conf. on Data Engineering, IEEE, pp 277–288, Birmingham.

Lehner, W. (1998). Modeling Large Scale OLAP Scenarios. In: 6th Int. Conference on Extending Database Technology, Springer-Verlag, pp 153–167.

Lomet, D., B. Salzberg (1990). The Hb-Tree: a multidimensional indexing method with good guaranteed performance. *ACM Trans. On Database Systems* **15**, 44, pp 625–658.

Lomet, D., B. Salzberg (1990). The Hb-Tree: a multidimensional indexing method with good guaranteed performance. *ACM Trans. On Database Systems*, 15(44), pp 625–658.

O'Neil, P., G. Graefe (1995). Multi-table joins through bitmapped join indices. ACM SIGMOD Record, 24(3), pp 8–11.

Ozsoyoglu, G., M. Ozsoyoglu, V. Matos (1987). Extending Relational Algebra and Relational Calculus with Set-valued Attributes and Aggregation Functions. ACM TODS 12(4).

Piatetsky-Shapiro, G., W. J. Frawley (1991). *Knowledge Discovery in Databases*, AAAI/MIT Press.

Pissinou, N., K. Makki, Y. Yesha (1993). On Temporal Modeling in the Context of Object Databases. ACM SIGMOD Record, 22 (3), pp 8–15.

Pooniah, P. (2001). *Data Warehousing Fundamentals*, John Wiley & Sons.

Rafanelli, M., F.L. Ricci (1991). A functional model for macro-databases. SIGMOD 20(1).

Ross, K., D. Srivastava, D. Chatziantoniou (1998). Complex aggregation at multiple granularities. Proc. Int. Conf. on Extending Database Technology, pp. 263–277.

Saltor, F., B. Campderrich, E. Rodríguez, L. Rodríguez (1996). On Schema Levels for Federated DB Systems. In: Yetongnon & Hariri (eds.), Proc. ISCA Int'l. Conf. on Parallel and Distributed Computing Systems, ISCA, Dijon, pp 766–771.

Samos, J. (1995). Definition of External Schemas in Object Oriented Databases. In: Murphy, J., Stone, B. (eds.), Proc. Int'l Conf. on Object Oriented Information Systems, Springer-Verlag, Dublin, pp 154–166.

Samos, J., F. Saltor (1996). External Schema Generation Algorithms for Object Oriented Databases. In: Patel, D. *et al.* (eds.), Proc. Int'l Conf. on Object Oriented Information Systems, Springer-Verlag, pp 317–332, London.

Samos, J., F. Saltor (1998). Integration of Derived Classes in Object Schemas. In: Int'l. workshop on Issues and Applications of Database Technology, Berlin.

Samos, J., F. Saltor, J. Sistac, A. Bardes (1998). Database architecture for dataware—An Architecture for Data Warehousing supporting Data Independence and Interoperability housing: an evolutionary approach. In: Database and Expert Systems Applications, pp 746–756.

Sarawagi, S (1997). Indexing OLAP Data. Data Engineering Bulletin 20(1): 36-43.

Sarawagi, S. (1997). Indexing OLAP data. *Bulletin of Technical Committee on Data Engineering*, 20 (1).

Schlegel, K. (2007). Emerging Technologies Could Prove Disruptive to the Business Intelligence Market. Gartner Group.

Sheth, A., J. Larson (1990). Federated Database Systems for Managing Distributed, Heterogeneous and Autonomous Databases. ACM Computing Surveys, 22 (3).

Shoshani, A (1997). OLAP and Statistical Databases: Similarities and Differences. Tutorials of PODS.

Singh, H. (1999). *Interactive Data Warehousing*, Prentice-Hall, p 444.

Snodgrass, R. (1995). Temporal Object-Oriented Databases: A Critical Comparison. In: Kim, W. (ed.): Modern Database Systems, ACM Press, pp 386–408.

Thornthwaite, W. (1998). From Bauhaus to warehouse: Understanding data warehouse architecture requirements. DCI's Data Warehouse Summit, Phoenix, AZ.

Tsichritzis, D., A. Klug (eds.) (1978). The ANSI/ X3/SPARC Framework, AFIPS Press, Montvale, NJ.

Vassiliadis, P. (1998). Modeling multidimensional databases, cubes and cube operations. In: 10th Int. Conference on Scientific and Statistical Database Management, IEEE Computer Society Press, pp 53–62.

Vassiliadis, P., T. Sellis (1999). A survey of logical models for OLAP databases. ACM SIGMOD Record, 28(4):64–69.

Watson, H. J., P. Gray (2001). *Decision Support in the Data Warehouse*, Prentice Hall Professional Technical Reference.

Widom, J. (1995). Research Problems in Data Warehousing. Proc. of the Int'l. Conf. on Information and Knowlege Management, Baltimore.

Wiederhold, G. (1992). Mediators in the architecture of future information systems. IEEE Computer, 25:38–49.

Wuu, G., U. Dayal (1992). A Uniform Model for Temporal Object-Oriented Databases. Proc. IEEE Data Engineering Conference.

Y. Zhuge, H. Garcia-Molina J. L. Wiener, The Strobe Algorithms for Multi-Source Warehouse Consistency. Proc. Conference on Parallel and Distributed Information Systems, Miami Beach, FL (1996).

Yang, J. (1998). *Warehouse Information Prototype at Stanford (WHIPS)*, [1], Stanford University.

Yang, J., J. Widom (1997). *Maintaining Temporal Views over Non-Historical Information Sources for Data Warehousing*, Technical note, Stanford University.

INDEX